GREAT BRITAIN & II

*TOURIST and MOTORING ATLAS / ATLAS ROUTIER et TOURISTIQUE / STRASSEN~~
TOERISTISCHE WEGENATLAS / ATLANTE STRADALE e TURISTICO / ATLAS DE CARRETERAS y TURISTIU~~*

Contents
Sommaire / Inhaltsübersicht / Inhoud / Sommario / Sumario

Inside front cover: key to map pages
Intérieur de couverture : tableau d'assemblage / Umschlaginnenseite: Übersicht / Binnenzijde van het omslag: overzichtskaart
-Copertina interna: quadro d'insieme / Portada interior: mapa índice

II - III

Channel Tunnel - Tunnel sous la Manche
Folkestone Terminal - Terminal de Calais (F)
Shipping Services
Liaisons maritimes / Schiffsverbindungen / Scheepvaartverbindingen / Collegamenti marittimi / Líneas marítimas

IV - XXI

Main road map
Grands axes routiers / Durchgangsstraßen / Grote verbindingswegen / Grandi arterie stradali / Carreteras principales
1 inch = 15.8 miles - 1:1 000 000 - 1 cm = 10 km

1 - 119

Key | **1**
Légende / Zeichenerklärung / Verklaring van de tekens / Legenda / Signos convencionales

Great Britain & Ireland | **2 - 119**
Grande-Bretagne & Irlande / Großbritannien & Irland / Groot-Brittannië & Ierland
Gran Bretagna & Irlanda / Gran Bretaña & Irlanda
1 inch = 4.75 miles - 1: 300 000 - 1 cm = 3 km

120 - 147

Index Great Britain | **120 - 138**
Index Grande-Bretagne / Register Großbritannien / Register Groot-Brittannië / Indice Gran Bretagna / Índice Gran Bretaña

Index Ireland | **139 - 147**
Index Irlande / Register Irland / Register Ierland / Indice Irlanda / Índice Irlanda

148 - 192

Key | **148**
Légende / Zeichenerklärung / Verklaring van de tekens / Legenda / Signos convencionales

Town plans Great Britain | **149 - 185**
Plans de ville Grande-Bretagne / Stadtpläne Großbritannien / Stadsplattegronden Groot-Brittannië
Piante di città Gran Bretagna / Planos de ciudades Gran Bretaña

Town plans Ireland | **186 - 191**
Plans de ville Irlande / Stadtpläne Irland / Stadsplattegronden Ierland / Piante di città Irlanda / Planos de ciudades Irlanda

Eochair / Allwedd / Comnarthai ar phleanna bailte / Symbolau ar gynlluniau'r trefi | **192**

Back of the guide: distances
En fin de volume : distances / Am Ende des Buches: Entfernungen / Achter in het boek: afstanden
Alla fine del volume: distanze / Al final del volumen: distancias

Channel Tunnel
Tunnel sous la Manche

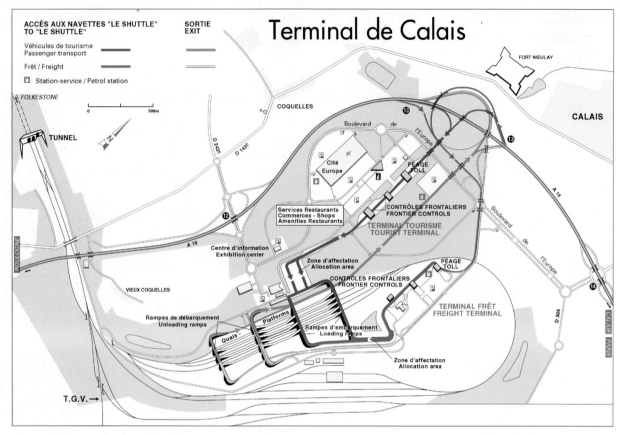

Terminal de Calais

ACCÈS AUX NAVETTES "LE SHUTTLE"
TO "LE SHUTTLE"

SORTIE
EXIT

Véhicules de tourisme
Passenger transport

Frêt / Freight

Station-service / Petrol station

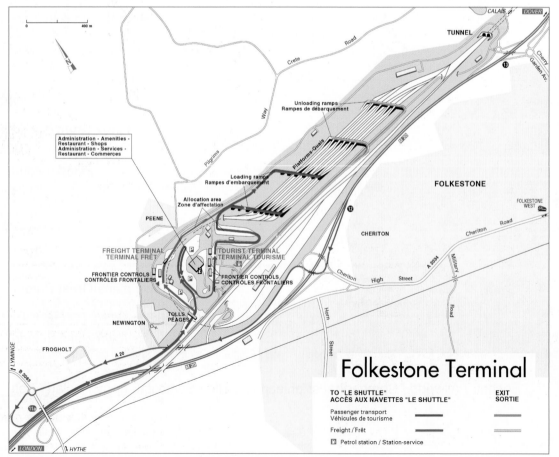

Folkestone Terminal

TO "LE SHUTTLE"
ACCÈS AUX NAVETTES "LE SHUTTLE"

EXIT
SORTIE

Passenger transport
Véhicules de tourisme

Freight / Frêt

Petrol station / Station-service

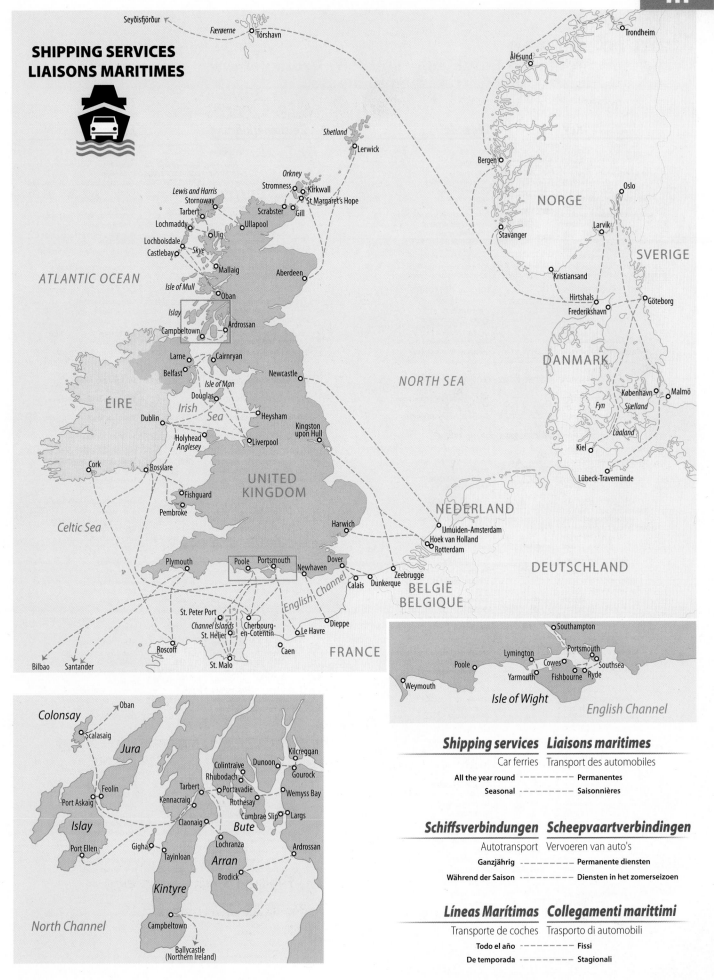

SHIPPING SERVICES
LIAISONS MARITIMES

Shipping services — *Liaisons maritimes*
Car ferries — Transport des automobiles

All the year round	Permanentes
Seasonal	Saisonnières

Schiffsverbindungen — *Scheepvaartverbindingen*
Autotransport — Vervoeren van auto's

Ganzjährig	Permanente diensten
Während der Saison	Diensten in het zomerseizoen

Líneas Marítimas — *Collegamenti marittimi*
Transporte de coches — Trasporto di automobili

Todo el año	Fissi
De temporada	Stagionali

Seyðisfjörður, Færøerne, Tórshavn, Trondheim, Ålesund, Shetland, Lerwick, Bergen, NORGE, Oslo, Orkney, Stromness, Kirkwall, St Margaret's Hope, Scrabster, Gill, Ullapool, Lewis and Harris, Stornoway, Tarbert, Lochmaddy, Uig, Larvik, SVERIGE, Stavanger, Lochboisdale, Skye, Castlebay, Mallaig, Aberdeen, Kristiansand, Göteborg, ATLANTIC OCEAN, Isle of Mull, Oban, Islay, Ardrossan, Hirtshals, Frederikshavn, Campbeltown, NORTH SEA, DANMARK, Larne, Cairnryan, Belfast, Newcastle, København, Malmö, ÉIRE, Isle of Man, Fyn, Sjælland, Douglas, Heysham, Irish Sea, Dublin, Kingston upon Hull, Laaland, Holyhead Anglesey, Liverpool, Kiel, Cork, Rosslare, UNITED KINGDOM, Lübeck-Travemünde, Fishguard, Pembroke, Celtic Sea, NEDERLAND, IJmuiden-Amsterdam, Harwich, Hoek van Holland, Rotterdam, Plymouth, Poole, Portsmouth, Dover, DEUTSCHLAND, Newhaven, Zeebrugge, English Channel, Calais, Dunkerque, BELGIË BELGIQUE, St. Peter Port, Channel Islands, St. Hélier, Cherbourg-en-Cotentin, Le Havre, Dieppe, Roscoff, Caen, FRANCE, Bilbao, Santander, St. Malo

Southampton, Lymington, Portsmouth, Poole, Cowes, Southsea, Weymouth, Yarmouth, Fishbourne, Ryde, Isle of Wight, English Channel

Colonsay, Oban, Scalasaig, Jura, Kilcreggan, Colintraive, Dunoon, Rhubodach, Gourock, Tarbert, Portavadie, Wemyss Bay, Feolin, Kennacraig, Rothesay, Port Askaig, Claonaig, Cumbrae Slip, Largs, Bute, Islay, Lochranza, Port Ellen, Gigha, Tayinloan, Arran, Ardrossan, Brodick, Kintyre, Campbeltown, North Channel, Ballycastle (Northern Ireland)

IV

Main road map
Grands axes routiers / Durchgangsstraßen / Grote verbindingswegen
Grandi arterie stradali / Carreteras principales

Key	Légende	Zeichenerklärung	Legenda
Roads	**Routes**	**Straßen**	**Strade**
Motorway	Autoroute	Autobahn	Autostrada
Motorway: single carriageway	Route-auto	Autostraße	Strada-auto
Motorway (unclassified)	Autoroute et assimilée	Autobahn oder Schnellstraße	Autostrada, strada di tipo autostradale
Dual carriageway with motorway characteristics	Double chaussée de type autoroutier	Schnellstraße mit getrennten Fahrbahnen	Doppia carreggiata di tipo autostradale
Interchanges: complete, limited, not specified	Échangeurs : complet, partiels, sans précision	Anschlussstellen: Voll- bzw. Teilanschluss, ohne Angabe	Svincoli: completo, parziale, imprecisato
Interchange numbers	Numéros d'échangeurs	Anschlussstellennummern	Svincoli numerati
Recommended MICHELIN main itinerary	Itinéraire principal recommandé par MICHELIN	Von MICHELIN empfohlene Hauptverkehrsstraße	Itinerario principale raccomandato da MICHELIN
Recommended MICHELIN regional itinerary	Itinéraire régional ou de dégagement recommandé par MICHELIN	Von MICHELIN empfohlene Regionalstraße	Itinerario regionale raccomandato da MICHELIN
Road surfaced - unsurfaced	Route revêtue - non revêtue	Straße mit Belag - ohne Belag	Strada rivestita - non rivestita
Motorway/Road under construction	Autoroute - Route en construction	Autobahn/Straße im Bau	Autostrada - Strada in costruzione
Road widths	**Largeur des routes**	**Straßenbreiten**	**Larghezza delle strade**
Dual carriageway	Chaussées séparées	Getrennte Fahrbahnen	Carreggiate separate
2 wide lanes	2 voies larges	2 breite Fahrspuren	2 corsie larghe
2 lanes - 2 narrow lanes	2 voies - 2 voies étroites	2 Fahrspuren - 2 schmale Fahrspuren	2 corsie - 2 corsie strette
Distances (total and intermediate)	**Distances** (totalisées et partielles)	**Straßenentfernungen** (Gesamt- und Teilentfernungen)	**Distanze** (totali e parziali)
On motorway in kilometers	Sur autoroute en kilomètres	Auf der Autobahn in Kilometern	Su autostrada in chilometri
Toll roads - Toll-free section	Section à péage - Section libre	Mautstrecke - Mautfreie Strecke	Tratto a pedaggio - Tratto esente da pedaggio
On road in kilometers	Sur route en kilomètres	Auf der Straße in Kilometern	Su strada in chilometri
On motorway (Great Britain) in miles - in kilometers	Sur autoroute (Grande Bretagne) en miles - en kilomètres	Auf der Autobahn (Großbritannien) in Meilen - in Kilometern	Su autostrada (Gran Bretagna) in miglia - in chilometri
Toll roads - Toll-free section	Section à péage - Section libre	Mautstrecke - Mautfreie Strecke	Tratto a pedaggio - Tratto esente da pedaggio
On road in miles	Sur route en miles	Auf der Straße in Meilen	Su strada in miglia
Numbering - Signs	**Numérotation - Signalisation**	**Nummerierung - Wegweisung**	**Numerazione - Segnaletica**
European route - Motorway	Route européenne - Autoroute	Europastraße - Autobahn	Strada europea - Autostrada
Other roads	Autres routes	Sonstige Straßen	Altre strade
Destination on primary route network	Localités jalonnant les itinéraires principaux	Richtungshinweis auf der empfohlenen Fernverkehrsstraße	Località delimitante gli itinerari principali
Safety Warnings	**Alertes Sécurité**	**Sicherheitsalerts**	**Segnalazioni stradali**
Snowbound, impassable road during the period shown	Enneigement : période probable de fermeture	Eingeschneite Straße: voraussichtl. Wintersperre	Innevamento: probabile periodo di chiusura
Pass and its height above sea level	Col et sa cote d'altitude	Pass mit Höhenangabe	Passo ed altitudine
Steep hill - Toll barrier	Forte déclivité - Barrière de péage	Starke Steigung - Mautstelle	Forte pendenza - Casello
Ford	Gué	Furt	Guado
Transportation	**Transports**	**Verkehrsmittel**	**Trasporti**
Airport	Aéroport	Flughafen	Aeroporto
Transportation of vehicles: year-round - seasonal	Transport des autos : permanent - saisonnier	Autotransport: ganzjährig - saisonbedingte Verbindung	Trasporto auto: tutto l'anno - stagionale
by boat	par bateau	per Schiff	su traghetto
by ferry	par bac	per Fähre	su chiatta
Ferry (passengers and cycles only)	Bac pour piétons et cycles	Fähre für Personen und Fahrräder	Traghetto per pedoni e biciclette
Motorail	Auto/Train	Autoreisezug	Auto/treno
Administration	**Administration**	**Verwaltung**	**Amministrazione**
Administrative district seat	Capitale de division administrative	Verwaltungshauptstadt	Capoluogo amministrativo
Parador / Pousada	Parador / Pousada	Parador / Pousada	Parador / Pousada
Administrative boundaries	Limites administratives	Verwaltungsgrenzen	Confini amministrativi
National boundary	Frontière	Staatsgrenze	Frontiera
Principal customs post	Douane principale	Hauptzollamt	Dogana principale
Secondary customs post	Douane avec restriction	Zollstation mit Einschränkungen	Dogana con limitazioni
Restricted area for foreigners / Military property	Zone interdite aux étrangers / Zone militaire	Sperrgebiet für Ausländer / Militärgebiet	Zona vietata agli stranieri / Zona militare
Sights	**Lieux touristiques**	**Sehenswürdigkeiten**	**Mete e luoghi d'interesse**
2- and 3-star MICHELIN Green Guide sites	Sites classés 2 et 3 étoiles par le Guide Vert MICHELIN	Sehenswürdigkeiten mit 2 und 3 Sternen im Grünen Reiseführer MICHELIN	Siti segnalati con 2 e 3 stelle dalla Guida Verde MICHELIN
Religious building	Édifice religieux	Sakral-Bau	Edificio religioso
Historic house, castle	Château	Schloss, Burg	Castello
Monastery	Monastère	Kloster	Monastero
Stave church	Église en bois debout	Stabkirche	Chiesa in legno di testa
Wooden church	Église en bois	Holzkirche	Chiesa in legno
Open air museum	Musée de plein air	Freilichtmuseum	Museo all'aperto
Antiquities	Site antique	Antike Fundstätte	Sito antico
Rock carving	Gravure rupestre	Felsbilder	Incisione rupestre
Prehistoric monument	Monument mégalithique	Vorgeschichtliches Steindenkmal	Monumento megalitico
Rune stone - Ruins	Pierre runique - Ruines	Runenstein - Ruine	Pietra runica - Rovine
Cave - Windmill	Grotte - Moulin à vent	Höhle - Windmühle	Grotta - Mulino a vento
Other places of interest	Autres curiosités	Sonstige Sehenswürdigkeit	Altri luoghi d'interesse
Scenic route	Parcours pittoresque	Landschaftlich schöne Strecke	Percorso pittoresco
Other signs	**Signes divers**	**Sonstige Zeichen**	**Simboli vari**
Recreation ground	Parc de loisirs	Erholungspark	Parco divertimenti
Dam - Waterfall	Barrage - Cascade	Staudamm - Wasserfall	Diga - Cascata
National park - Nature park	Parc national - Parc naturel	Nationalpark - Naturpark	Parco nazionale - Parco naturale

Signos Convencionales

Carreteras
Autopista
Carretera
Autopista, Autovía
Autovía
(otra vía similar a las autopistas)
Accesos:
completo, parcial, sin precisar
Números de los accesos
Itinerario principal
recomendado por MICHELIN
Itinerario regional
recomendado por MICHELIN
Carretera asfaltada - sin asfaltar
Autopista - Carretera en construcción

Ancho de las carreteras
Calzadas separadas
Dos carriles anchos
Dos carriles - Dos carriles estrechos

Distancias
(totales y parciales)
En autopista en kilómetros
Tramo de peaje - Tramo libre

En carretera en kilómetros

En autopista (Gran Bretaña)
en millas - en kilómetros
Tramo de peaje - Tramo libre

En carretera en millas

Numeración - Señalización
Carretera europea - Autopista
Otras carreteras
Localidades situadas en
los principales itinerarios

Alertas Seguridad
Nevada:
Período probable de cierre
Puerto y su altitud
Pendiente Pronunciada - Barrera de peaje
Vado

Transportes
Aeropuerto
Transporte de coches:
todo el año - de temporada
por barco
por barcaza
Barcaza para el paso de peatones y vehículos dos ruedas
Auto-tren

Administración
Capital de división administrativa
Parador / Pousada
Límites administrativos
Frontera
Aduana principal
Aduana con restricciones
Zona prohibida a los extranjeros /
Propiedad militar

Curiosidades
Lugares clasificados con 2 y 3 estrellas
por la Guía Verde MICHELIN
Edificio religioso
Castillo
Monasterio
Iglesia de madera
Iglesia de madera
Museo al aire libre
Zona de vestigios antiguos
Grabado rupestre
Monumento megalítico
Piedra rúnica - Ruinas
Cueva - Molino de viento
Otras curiosidades
Recorrido pintoresco

Signos diversos
Zona recreativa
Presa - Cascada
Parque nacional - Parque natural

Verklaring van de tekens

Wegen
Autosnelweg
Autoweg
Autosnelweg of gelijksoortige weg
Gescheiden rijbanen
van het type autosnelweg
Aansluitingen:
volledig, gedeeltelijk, zonder aanduiding
Afritnummers
Michelin
Hoofdweg
Michelin
Regionale weg
Verharde weg - onverharde weg
Autosnelweg - Weg in aanleg

Breedte van de wegen
Gescheiden rijbanen
2 brede rijstroken
2 rijstroken - 2 smalle rijstroken

Afstanden
(totaal en gedeeltelijk)
Op autosnelwegen in kilometers
Gedeelte met tol - Tolvrij gedeelte

Op andere wegen in kilometers

Op autosnelwegen (Groot Brittannië)
in mijlen - in kilometers
Gedeelte met tol - Tolvrij gedeelte

Op andere wegen in mijlen

Wegnummers - Bewegwijzering
Europaweg - Autosnelweg
Andere wegen
Plaatsen langs een hoofdweg
met bewegwijzering

Veiligheidswaarschuwingen
Sneeuw:
vermoedelijke sluitingsperiode
Bergpas en hoogte boven de zeespiegel
Steile helling - Tol
Wad

Vervoer
Luchthaven
Vervoer van auto's:
het hele jaar - tijdens het seizoen
per boot
per veerpont
Veerpont voor voetgangers en fietsers
Autotrein

Administratie
Hoofdplaats van administratief gebied
Parador / Pousada
Administratieve grenzen
Staatsgrens
Hoofddouanekantoor
Douanekantoor met beperkte bevoegdheden
Terrein verboden voor buitenlanders /
Militair gebied

Bezienswaardigheden
Locaties met 2 en 3 sterren volgens
de Groene Gids van MICHELIN
Kerkelijk gebouw
Kasteel
Klooster
Stavkirke (houten kerk)
Houten kerk
Openluchtmuseum
Overblijfsel uit de Oudheid
Rotstekening
Megaliet
Runensteen - Ruïne
Grot - Molen
Andere bezienswaardigheden
Schilderachtig traject

Diverse tekens
Recreatiepark
Stuwdam - Waterval
Nationaal park - Natuurpark

E 50   A3
25   28   103
Lancaster
11-4
650
STRASBOURG

0   10   20   30   40 miles
0   10   20   30   40   50   60 km

Republic of Ireland: All distances
and speed limits are signed in kilometres.

République d'Irlande: Les distances
et les limitations de vitesse sont exprimées en
kilomètres.

Irland: Alle Entfernungsangaben und
Geschwindigkeitsbegrenzungen in km.

Ierland: Alle afstanden en
maximumsnelheden zijn uitsluitend
in kilometers aangegeven.

Repubblica d'Irlanda: Distanze e limiti
di velocità sono espressi soltanto in chilometri.

República de Irlanda: Distancias y límites de
velocidad están expresados sólo en kilómetros.

Key to 1:1 000 000 map pages
Légende des cartes au 1/1 000 000
Zeichenerklärung der Karten 1:1 000 000
Verklaring van de tekens voor kaarten met schaal 1:1 000 000
Legenda carte scala 1:1 000 000
Signos convencionales de los mapas a escala 1:1 000 000

ENGLAND

UNITARY AUTHORITIES

1	Bath and North East Somerset
	Bedford
	Blackburn with Darwen
	Blackpool
	Bracknell Forest
	Brighton and Hove
7	Buckinghamshire
8	Cambridgeshire
9	Central Bedfordshire
10	Cheshire East
11	Cheshire West and Chester
	City of Bristol
13	Cornwall
14	Cumbria
	Derby
16	Derbyshire
17	Devon
18	Dorset
19	Durham
20	East Riding of Yorkshire
21	East Sussex
22	Essex
23	Gloucestershire
	Greater London
	Greater Manchester
26	Halton
27	Hampshire
	Hartlepool
29	Herefordshire
30	Hertfordshire
31	Kent
	Kingston-upon-Hull
33	Lancashire
	Leicester
35	Leicestershire
36	Lincolnshire
	Luton
38	Medway
39	Merseyside
	Middlesbrough
41	Milton Keynes
42	Norfolk

43	North East Lincolnshire
44	North Lincolnshire
45	North Somerset
46	North Yorkshire
47	Northamptonshire
48	Northumberland
49	Nottinghamshire
	Nottingham
51	Oxfordshire
	Peterborough
	Plymouth
	Portsmouth
	Reading
56	Redcar and Cleveland
57	Rutland
58	Shropshire
59	Somerset
60	South Gloucestershire
61	South Yorkshire
	Southend-on-Sea
63	Staffordshire
	Stockton-on-Tees
	Stoke-on-Trent
66	Suffolk
67	Surrey
	Swindon
69	Telford and Wrekin
70	Thurrock
	Torbay
72	Tyne and Wear
	Warrington
74	Warwickshire
75	West Berkshire
76	West Midlands
77	West Sussex
78	West Yorkshire
79	Wiltshire
	Windsor and Maidenhead
	Wokingham
82	Worcestershire
	York

SCOTLAND

UNITARY AUTHORITIES

1	Aberdeen City
2	Aberdeenshire
3	Angus
4	Argyll and Bute
5	Clackmannanshire
	City of Edinburgh
	City of Glasgow
8	Dumfries and Galloway
9	Dundee City
10	East Ayrshire
11	East Dunbartonshire
12	East Lothian
13	East Renfrewshire
14	Falkirk
15	Fife
16	Highland

17	Inverclyde
18	Midlothian
19	Moray
20	North Ayrshire
21	North Lanarkshire
22	Orkney Islands
23	Perth and Kinross
24	Renfrewshire
25	Scottish Borders
26	Shetland Islands
27	South Ayrshire
28	South Lanarkshire
29	Stirling
30	West Dunbartonshire
31	West Lothian
32	Na H-Eileanan Siar (Western Isles)

NORTHERN IRELAND

DISTRICT COUNCILS

1	Antrim and Newtownabbey
2	Ards and North Down
3	Armagh, Banbridge and Craigavon
4	Belfast
5	Causeway Coast and Glens
6	Derry and Strabane

7	Fermanagh and Omagh
8	Lisburn and Castlereagh
9	Mid and East Antrim
10	Mid Ulster
11	Newry, Mourne and Down

WALES

UNITARY AUTHORITIES

1	Anglesey/Sir Fôn
2	Blaenau Gwent
3	Bridgend/Pen-y-bont ar Ogwr
4	Caerphilly/Caerffili
5	Cardiff/Caerdydd
6	Carmarthenshire/Sir Gaerfyrddin
7	Ceredigion
8	Conwy
9	Denbighshire/Sir Ddinbych
10	Flintshire/Sir y Fflint
11	Gwynedd

12	Merthyr Tydfil/Merthyr Tudful
13	Monmouthshire/Sir Fynwy
14	Neath Port Talbot/Castell-nedd Phort Talbot
15	Newport/Casnewydd
16	Pembrokeshire/Sir Benfro
17	Powys
18	Rhondda Cynon Taff/Rhondda Cynon Taf
19	Swansea/Abertawe
20	Torfaen/Tor-faen
21	Vale of Glamorgan/Bro Morgannwg
22	Wrexham/Wrecsam

32

32 = UNITARY AUTHORITIES

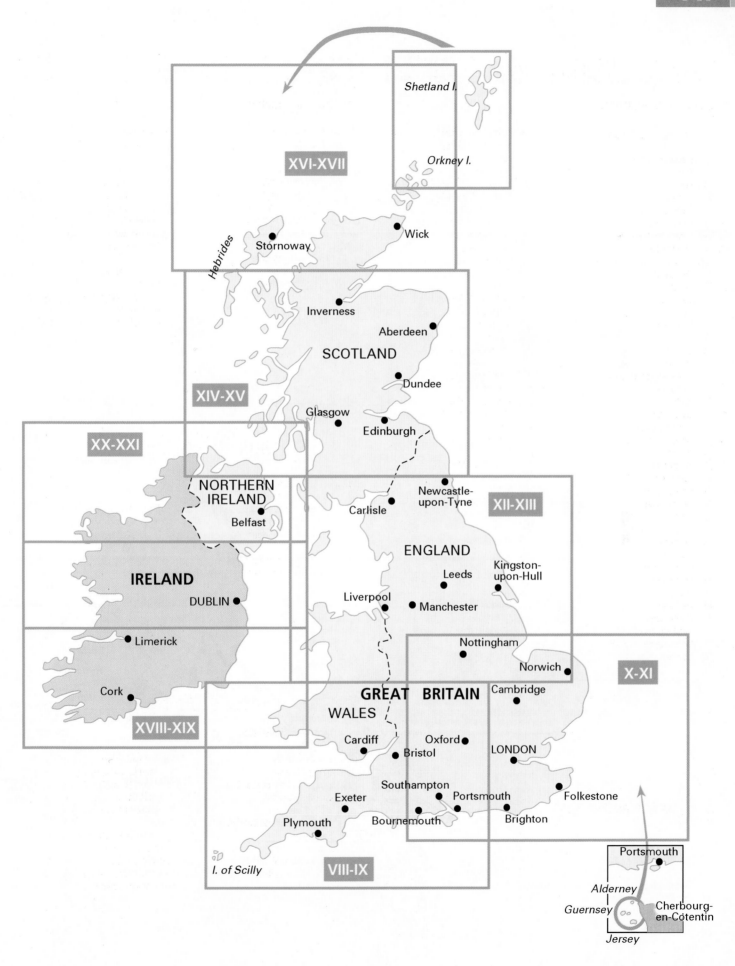

St. George's Channel

Saltee Islands
...e Harbour/
Ros Láir
...Point

ST. GEORGE'S CHANNEL

Strumble Head
Pembrokeshire Coast
National Park
St. David's Head
St. David's
Haverfordwest/Hwlffordd
St. Bride's Bay
Milford Haven/
Aberdaugleddau
Neyland
Pembroke Dock
Pembroke
St. Govan's Head

Fishguard/
Abergwaun
Newport
Narberth
Whitland
Saundersfoot
Tenby/
Dinbych-y-pysgod
Pendine
Carmarthen Bay

Cardigan
Newcastle
Emlyn
Crymmych
Carmarthen/
Caerfyrddin
St. Clears
Kidwelly
Burry
Port
Llanelli
Rhossili
Worms Head
Port-
Eynon
The Mumbles

Aberaeron
New Quay
Aberporth
Synod
Inn
58
93
Tregaron
Lampeter
Llandysul
23
31
16
27
74
46
30
48
132
52
Cross
Hands
Pontarddulais
SWANSEA/
ABERTAWE
Port
Talbot
Porthcawl

Llanrhystud
Elan Valley
Llanwrtyd
Wells
Llandovery
85 Llandeilo
53
Llangadog
Brecon
National
Ammanford
19
Pontardawe
Neath/
Castell · Nedd
Maesteg
68
42
Aberdare/
Aberdâr
Merthyr
53
33
Bridgend/
Pen-y-bont

BRISTOL CHANNEL

Lundy

Lynton Lynmouth Porlock
Combe
Ilfracombe Martin
Croyde
Braunton
Northam
Barnstaple
Exmoor
National
Simonsbath
Tarr
steps
South
Molton
35
56
Tiverton

Hartland Point
Clovelly
Bideford
Cliffs of
Morwenstow
Kilkhampton
Stratton
Bude
Great
Torrington
Holsworthy
Hatherleigh
Winkleigh
Crediton
EXETE
High
Willhays
Moretonhampstead
Tintagel
Launceston
Camelford
Lydford
Gorge
Dartmoor
National
Bovey
Tracey
177
109
Padstow
Wadebridge
113
182
Callington
Tavistock
Princetown
Park
Ashburton
Newton
Abbot
Buckfastleigh
Bodmin
Liskeard
Buckland Abbey
78
126
Lostwithiel
West
Looe
Saltash
Plympton
41
66
Totnes
Newquay
Fraddon
Fowey
Polperro
PLYMOUTH
Plymstock
Torpoint
Modbury
Dartmouth
St. Austell
Truro
Trewithen
Tregony
Mevagissey
Trelissick Garden
Kingsbridge
Camborne
St. Ives
Redruth
Penryn
St. Mawes
Salcombe
Start Poi
Hayle
Falmouth
St. Just
Penzance
Helston
Glendurgan
Garden
Land's End
St. Michael's
Mount
Sennen
Mount's Bay
St. Keverne
Subtropical
Gardens
Tresco
St. Martin's
Isles of Scilly
St. Mary's
Lizard
Lizard Point

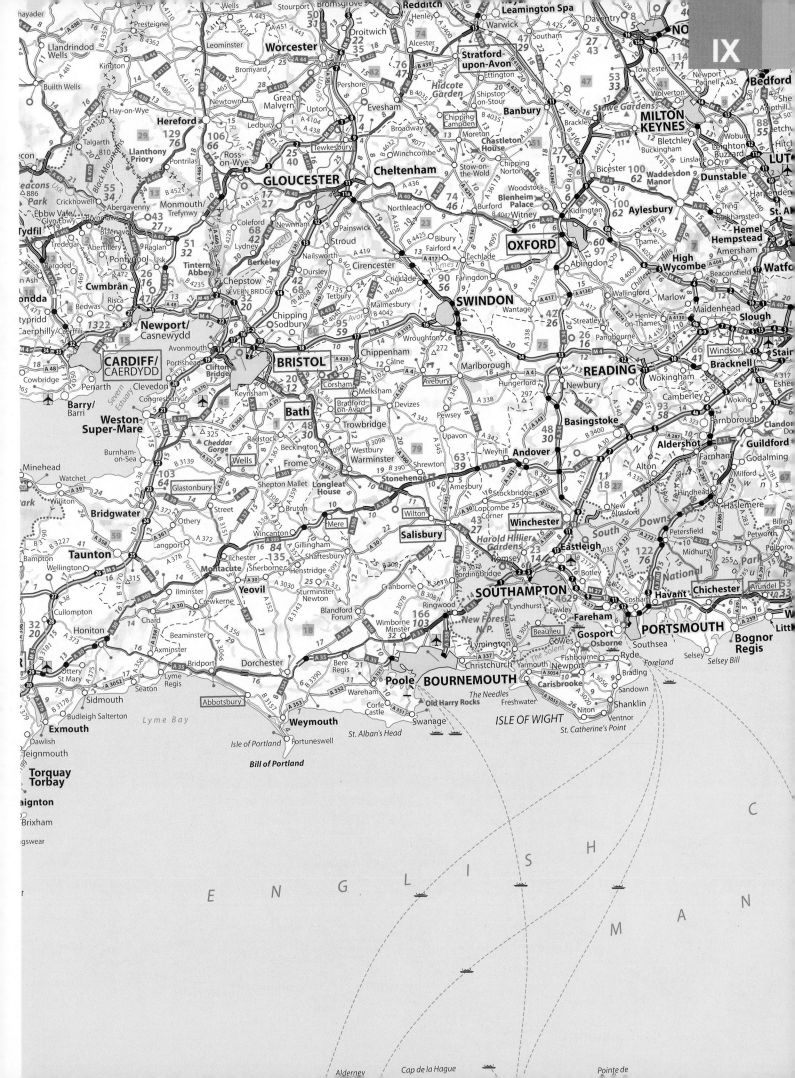

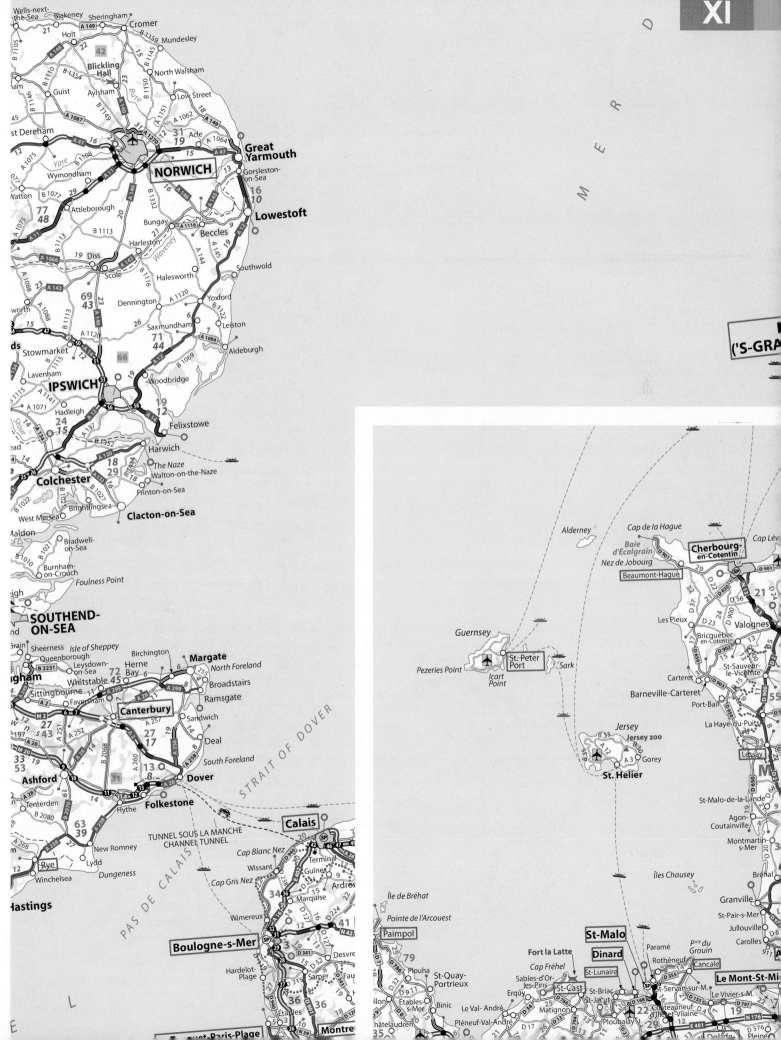

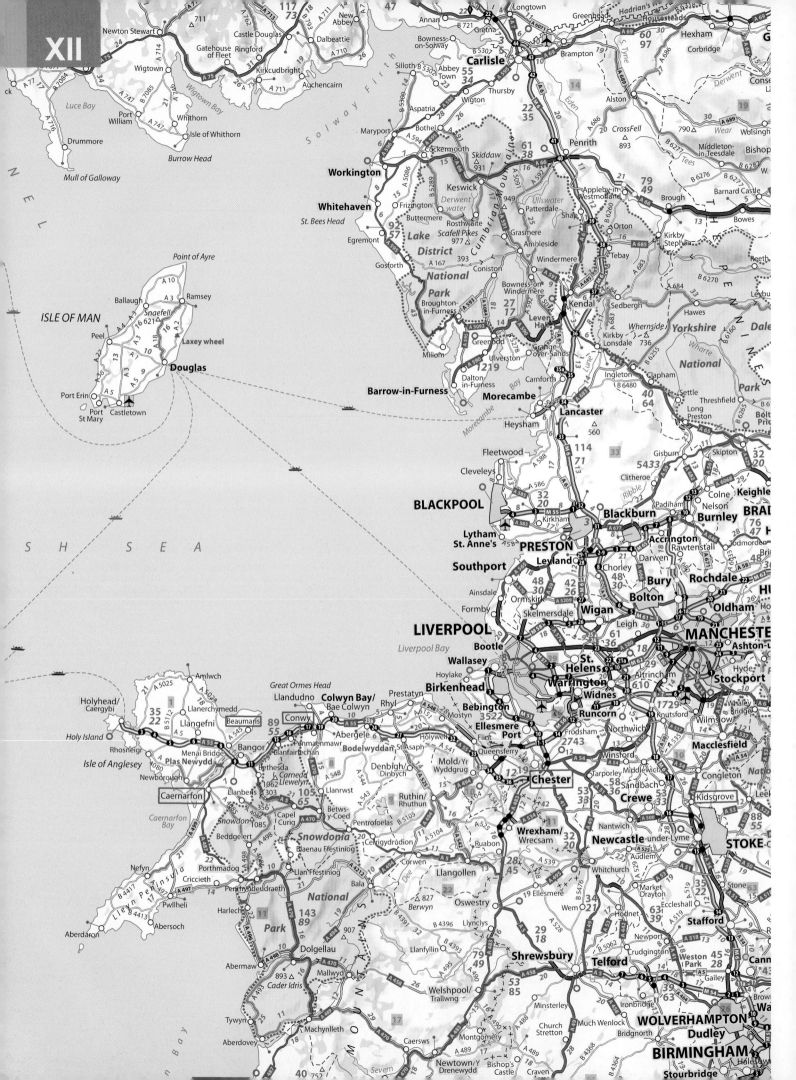

South Shields
SUNDERLAND
Washington
Seaham
Houghton-le-Spring
Horden
Durham
Hartlepool
Redcar
Marske-by-the-Sea
Saltburn-by-the-Sea
Brotton
Billingham
Guisborough
Loftus
Whitby
Stockton-on-Tees
Darlington
MIDDLESBROUGH
Eaglescliffe
Richmond
North York Moors National Park
Cleveland Hills
Scalby
Scarborough
Northallerton
Rievaulx Abbey
Helmsley
Pickering
Filey
Bedale
Thirsk
Flamborough Head
Ripon
Easingwold
Malton
Norton
Bridlington
Pateley Bridge
Boroughbridge
Knaresborough
YORK
Wetwang
Driffield
Beeford
Hornsea
Harrogate
Wetherby
Tadcaster
Market Weighton
Leven
Otley
Harewood
Beverley
LEEDS
Selby
Barlby
KINGSTON UPON HULL
Withernsea
Bradford
Garforth
Castleford
Howden
Goole
Hedon
Patrington
Kilnsea
Halifax
Snaith
Barton-upon-Humber
Immingham Dock
Spurn Head
Dewsbury
Wakefield
Pontefract
Thorne
Crowle
Scunthorpe
Immingham
Grimsby
Cleethorpes
Huddersfield
Barnsley
Bentley
Doncaster
Brigg
Caistor
Conisbrough
Epworth
Market Rasen
Rotherham
Bawtry
Louth
Mablethorpe
Sutton-on-Sea
SHEFFIELD
Maltby
Gainsborough
Wragby
Castleton
Worksop
Retford
Alford
Chapel-en-le-Frith
Dronfield
Staveley
Tuxford
Lincoln
Horncastle
Partney
Spilsby
Skegness
Baslow
Chesterfield
Ollerton
Woodhall Spa
Bakewell
Hardwick Hall
Chatsworth House
Clay Cross
Mansfield
Haddon Hall
Matlock
Alfreton
Sutton-in-Ashfield
Southwell
Leadenham
Boston
Holkham
Wells-next-the-Sea
Blakeney
Sheringham
Dovedale
Belper
Ripley
Heanor
Hucknall
Newark-on-Trent
Sleaford
Hunstanton
Holt
Ashbourne
Ilkeston
NOTTINGHAM
Donington
Sutterton
Houghton Hall
Blickling Hall
Uttoxeter
DERBY
West Bridgford
Bingham
Grantham
Holbeach
Long Sutton
King's Lynn
Fakenham
Guist
Aylsham
Sudbury
Long Eaton
Belvoir Castle
Rempstone
Spalding
Wisbech
East Dereham
Burton-upon-Trent
Loughborough
Melton Mowbray
Bourne
Crowland
Outwell
Swaffham
Wymondham
Swadlincote
Shepshed
Stamford
Guyhirn
Downham Market
Oxburgh Hall
Attleborough
Ashby de la Zouch
Coalville
Oakham
Eye
Whittlesey
March
Watton
Lichfield
Tamworth
Oadby
Uppingham
Corby
Weldon
Oundle
PETERBOROUGH
Ramsey
Littleport
Brandon
Thetford
Sutton Coldfield
Hinckley
LEICESTER
Market Harborough
Boughton House
Chatteris
Ely
Diss
Nuneaton
Bedworth
Lutterworth
Husbands Bosworth
Kettering

Kinnairds Head
Fraserburgh
Lossiemouth
Buckie   Macduff
Banff   Cullen
Elgin   Loch of Strathbeg
Nairn   Fochabers
Forres   Keith
Rattray Head
Peterhead
Inverness
Buchan Ness
Alness   Invergordon
Cromarty
Fortrose
Tore
Black Isle
Turriff
New Deer
Mintlaw
Huntly
Dufftown
Rothes
Craigellachie
Dava
Grantown-on-Spey
Carrbridge
Dulnain Bridge
Glenmore Forest Park
Aviemore
Cairn Gorm
Kingussie
Newtonmore
Cairngorm Mountains
Ben Macdui
Cairngorms National Park
Cairn Ban
Laggan
Dalwhinnie
Pass of Drumochter
Rhynie
Mossat
Alford
Oldmeldrum
Inverurie
Kintore
Pitmedden Garden
Ellon
Cruden Bay
Newburgh

ABERDEEN

Craigievar Castle
Crathes Castle
Banchory
Stonehaven
Inverbervie
Laurencekirk
Marykirk
Montrose

Blair Castle
Blair Atholl
Kinloch Rannoch
Pitlochry
Schiehallion
Ben Lawers
Aberfeldy
Dunkeld
Killin
Lochearnhead
Crieff
Ben Vorlich
Callander
Auchterarder
Doune
Dunblane
Bridge of Allan
Dollar

Perth

Blairgowrie
Coupar Angus
Meigle
Glamis Castle
Glamis
Forfar
Kirriemuir
Brechin

DUNDEE

Arbroath
Carnoustie
Monifieth
Tayport
Newport-on-Tay
Buddon Ness
Leuchars
St. Andrews
Cupar
Auchtermuchty
Newburgh
Falkland
Fife Ness
Crail
Anstruther
Pittenweem
Glenrothes
Leven
Saint Monans
Elie
Methil
Buckhaven

Stirling
Alloa
Kincardine
Dunfermline
Kinross
Lochgelly
Kirkcaldy
Cowdenbeath
Burntisland
Kilsyth
Falkirk
Grangemouth
Bo'Ness
Rosyth
Inverkeithing
S. Queensferry
Firth of Forth
North Berwick
Dunbar
Cockburnspath
Siccar Point & Huttons Unconformity
St Abb's Head National Nature Reserve
Eyemouth

Cumbernauld
Linlithgow
Hopetoun House
Leith
Musselburgh
Prestonpans
Aberlady
East Linton
Haddington
Tranent

EDINBURGH

Bathgate
Armadale
Whitburn
Livingston
Loanhead
Dalkeith
Lammermuir Hills
Duns
Berwick-upon-Tweed
Clydebank
Airdrie
Coatbridge
Motherwell
Wishaw
East Kilbride
Hamilton
Strathaven
Kilmarnock
Penicuik
Rosslyn Chapel
Pentland Hills
West Linton
Carluke
Lanark
Carnwath
Biggar
Peebles
Innerleithen
Moorfoot Hills
Lauder
Greenlaw
Coldstream
Holy Island
Galston
Mauchline
Douglas
Abington
Broad Law
Galashiels
Melrose
Abbey Dryburgh
Kelso
Mellerstain
Belford
Bamburgh Castle
Cumnock
New Cumnock
Sanquhar
Elvanfoot
Moffat
Beattock
Selkirk
Newtown St Boswells
Jedburgh
Hawick
Wooler
The Cheviot
Alnwick
Warkworth
Amble
Drumlanrig castle
Thornhill
Langholm
Lochmaben
Lockerbie
Carter Bar
Northumberland
The Cheviot Hills
National Park
Otterburn
Rothbury
Felton
Kielder Res.
Morpeth
Ashington
Newbiggin-by-the-Sea
Blyth

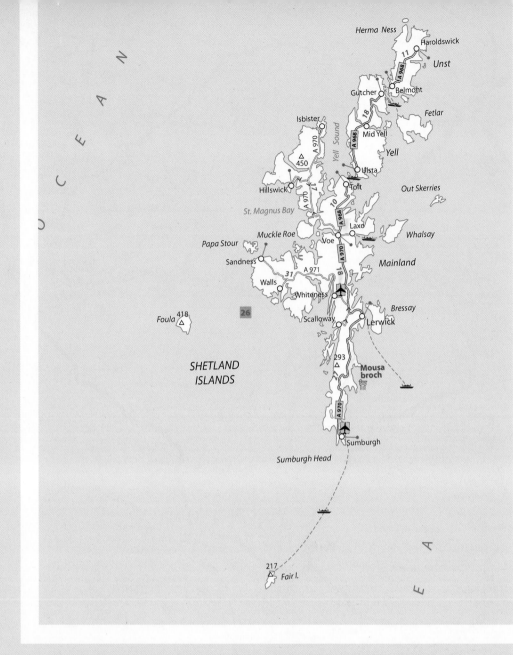

Herma Ness
Haroldswick
11
A 968
Unst
Gutcher
Belmont
18
Isbister
A 970
Mid Yell
Fetlar
A 968
Yell
Yell Sound
450
Ulsta
Out Skerries
Hillswick
Toft
A 970
St. Magnus Bay
A 968
Whalsay
Muckle Roe
Laxo
Papa Stour
Voe
A 970
Sandness
A 971
Mainland
31
Walls
Whiteness
Bressay
Foula 418
26
Scalloway
Lerwick

SHETLAND
ISLANDS
293
Mousa
broch
A 970
Sumburgh
Sumburgh Head

217
Fair I.

Butt of Lewis
Port of Ness
A 857
Kinlo
16
LEWIS
Barvas
A 857
THE MINCH
A 858
Scourie
Flannan I.
Carloway
292
12
Broad
Bay
Portnaguran
Eddrachillis
Bay
Callanish
Standing
Stones
A 858
Stornoway
Tiumpan Head
Garynahine
34
A 866
Eye Peninsula
574
Rubha Còigeach
Loch
36
Kebock Head
A 859
Hushinish
572
Coigach
B 887
743
Clisham
799
NA H-EILEANAN
West Loch Tarbert
Tarbert
SIAR
Loch Broom
St. Kilda
A 859 24
Toe Head
Rubha Réidh
Gruinard
Bay
Laide
29

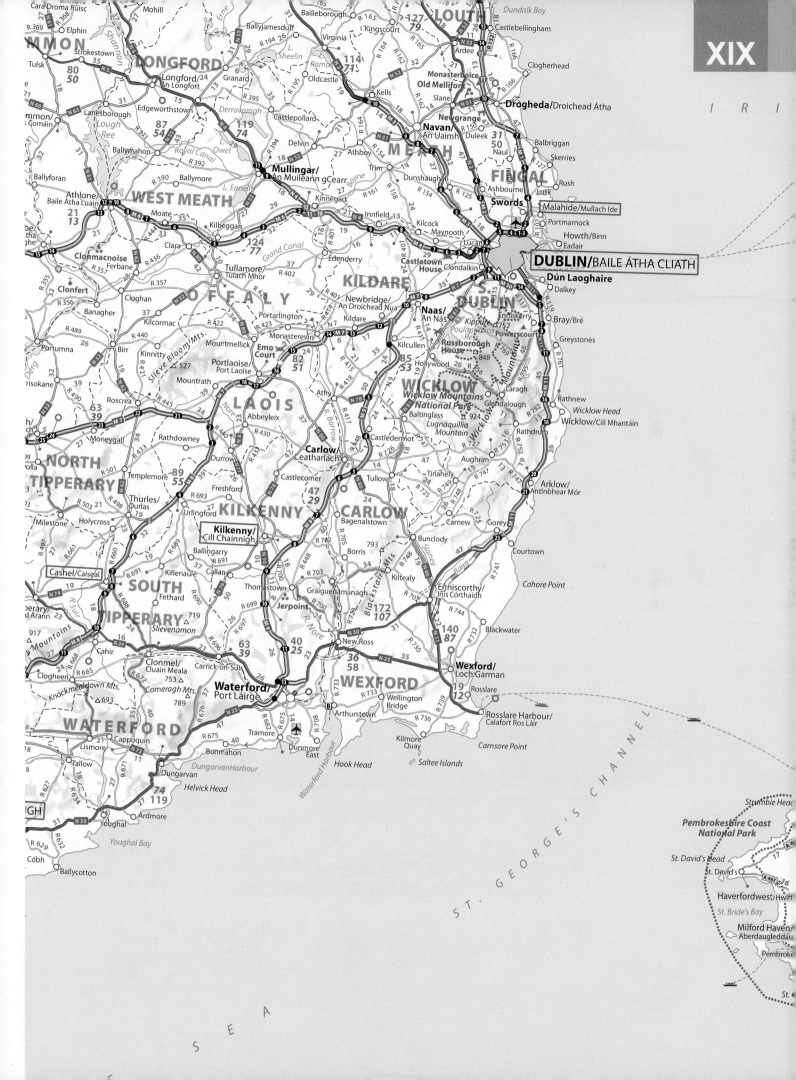

Blc

Aran Island

Gweebarra

Rossan Point   Glencolumbkille

R 263   Killybeg

Bunglass Cliffs

Donegal

Bun
Bun

Inishmurray

65
40
Rosses
Point

Erris Head

Broad
Haven   Ballycastle   Killala   Easky   Slygo Bay

Belmullet   Glenamoy   379 △   Bay   R 297   Strandhill

R 314   50   19   R 314   27   N 59   Inishcrone   Mountains   53   Ballysadare

19   R 315   543

Inishkea   R 313   M A Y O   Ballina/   Mountains   SLIGO 29

Bangor   N 59   32   Crossmolina   Béal an Átha   The   Ballym

Oweniny   11   R 294   32   Tubbercurry   47   N 17

BlacksodBay   R 316   Corrib   R 310   47   R 294

670   Ballycroy   32   △ 720   31   R 312   16   Nephin   Moy   29   R 293   Gorteen   34

Keel   △   R 312 98   698   804   Charlestown   Loga

Achill Island   R 319   27   Mulrany   18   R 317   Pontoon   39   Foxford   N 26   40   45

Corraun △   N 59   R 312   24   Swinford   R 320   Ballaghaderreen   C

521   Newport   Castlebar/   39   N 5   ROSC

Clare Island   Clew Bay   18   Caisleán an   24   Kiltimagh   R 322

Westport/   R 311   Bharraigh   N 5   Manulla   R 324   Frenchpark

Cathair na Mart   18   N 5   29   29   R 323

11   23   R 330   Ballintubber   R 331   Ballyhaunis   N 60   Castler

Louisburgh   Croagh   764   23   19   Suck   Ro

Inishturk   Patrick   66   31   Robe   Claremorris

Mweelrea   Murrisk   41   63   N 17   35   R 360

Inishbofin   Mts   32   681   Lough   39   Clare   Dunmore   R 328

Inishshark   817   Leenane   Mask   Ballinrobe   31   Glennamaddy

Killary Harbour   R 336   Kilmaine   R 332

RinvylePt.   Letterfrack   35   Maumturk Mts   Clonbur   31   Cong   R 334   50   Tuam/Tuaim

The   728   R 345   Lough   27   Mount

Twelve Pins   701 △   Connemara   Corrib   Headford   Bellew

Clifden   N 59   35   79   Maam   N 59   34   27   R 63

49   Cross   Oughterard   44   21   19

Slyne Head   R 341   21   18   Athenry   45

Roundstone   R 340   Gortmore   G A L W A Y   11   13   28   R 348   M 6

Carna   Galway/   17   14   16   31

R 314   Gaillimh   19   13

Lettermullan   Kilkieran   R 336   Spiddal   Barna   Oranmore   104   14   R 350

Gorumna   Bay   39   Galway Bay   65   27

Island   BlackHead   Craughwell

Inishmore   Kilronan   Loughrea

Dun   Inishmaan   40   Ardrahan

Aonghasa   R 477   Kinvarra   R 65   25

Inisheer   R 480   16   R 353

Aran Islands   Lisdoonvarna   N 67   29   R 476   Gort   45

Key	Légende	Zeichenerklärung
Roads	**Routes**	**Straßen**
Motorway - Service areas	Autoroute - Aires de service	Autobahn - Tankstelle mit Raststätte
Dual carriageway with motorway characteristics	Double chaussée de type autoroutier	Schnellstraße mit getrennten Fahrbahnen
Interchanges: complete, limited	Échangeurs : complet, partiels	Anschlussstellen: Voll - bzw. Teilanschlussstellen
Interchange numbers	Numéros d'échangeurs	Anschlussstellennummern
International and national road network	Route de liaison internationale ou nationale	Internationale bzw.nationale Hauptverkehrsstraße
Interregional and less congested road	Route de liaison interrégionale ou de dégagement	Überregionale Verbindungsstraße oder Umleitungsstrecke
Road surfaced - unsurfaced	Route revêtue - non revêtue	Straße mit Belag - ohne Belag
Footpath - Waymarked footpath / Bridle path	Sentier - Sentier balisé/Allée cavalière	Pfad - Ausgeschilderter Weg / Reitpfad
Motorway / Road under construction (when available: with scheduled opening date)	Autoroute - Route en construction (le cas échéant : date de mise en service prévue)	Autobahn - Straße im Bau (ggf. voraussichtliches Datum der Verkehrsfreigabe)
Road widths	**Largeur des routes**	**Straßenbreiten**
Dual carriageway	Chaussées séparées	Getrennte Fahrbahnen
4 lanes - 2 wide lanes	4 voies - 2 voies larges	4 Fahrspuren - 2 breite Fahrspuren
2 lanes - 2 narrow lanes	2 voies - 2 voies étroites	2 Fahrspuren - 1 Fahrspur
Distances (total and intermediate)	**Distances** (totalisées et partielles)	**Entfernungen** (Gesamt- und Teilentfernungen)
Toll roads on motorway	Section à péage sur autoroute	Mautstrecke auf der Autobahn
Toll-free section on motorway	Section libre sur autoroute	Mautfreie Strecke auf der Autobahn
in miles - in kilometers	en miles - en kilomètres	in Meilen - in Kilometern
on road	sur route	Auf der Straße
Numbering - Signs	**Numérotation - Signalisation**	**Nummerierung - Wegweisung**
Motorway - GB: Primary route	Autoroute - GB : itinéraire principal (Primary route)	Autobahn - GB: Empfohlene Fernverkehrsstraße (Primary route)
IRL : National primary and secondary route	IRL : itinéraire principal (National primary et secondary route)	IRL: Empfohlene Fernverkehrsstraße (National primary und secondary route)
Other roads	Autres routes	Sonstige Straßen
Destination on primary route network	Localités jalonnant les itinéraires principaux	Richtungshinweis auf der empfohlenen Fernverkehrsstraße
Obstacles	**Obstacles**	**Verkehrshindernisse**
Roundabout - Pass and its height above sea level (meters)	Rond-point - Col et sa cote d'altitude (en mètres)	Verkehrsinsel - Pass mit Höhenangabe (in Meter)
Steep hill (ascent in direction of the arrow)	Forte déclivité (flèches dans le sens de la montée)	Starke Steigung (Steigung in Pfeilrichtung)
IRL: Difficult or dangerous section of road	IRL : Parcours difficile ou dangereux	IRL: Schwierige oder gefährliche Strecke
In Scotland: narrow road with passing places	En Écosse : route très étroite avec emplacements pour croisement	In Schottland: sehr schmale Straße mit Ausweichstellen (passing places)
Level crossing: railway passing, under road, over road	Passages de la route : à niveau, supérieur, inférieur	Bahnübergänge: schienengleich, Unterführung, Überführung
Prohibited road - Road subject to restrictions	Route interdite - Route réglementée	Gesperrte Straße - Straße mit Verkehrsbeschränkungen
Toll barrier - One way road	Barrière de péage - Route à sens unique	Mautstelle - Einbahnstraße
Height limit under 15'6" IRL, 16'6" GB	Hauteur limitée au dessous de 15'6" IRL, 16'6" GB	Beschränkung der Durchfahrtshöhe bis 15'6" IRL, 16'6' GB
Load limit (under 16 t.)	Limites de charge (au-dessous de 16 t.)	Höchstbelastung (angegeben, wenn unter 16 t)
Transportation	**Transports**	**Verkehrsmittel**
Railway - Passenger station	Voie ferrée - Gare	Bahnlinie - Bahnhof
Airport - Airfield	Aéroport - Aérodrome	Flughafen - Flugplatz
Transportation of vehicles: (seasonal services in red)	Transport des autos: (liaison saisonnière en rouge)	Autotransport: (rotes Zeichen: saisonbedingte Verbindung)
by boat	par bateau	per Schiff
by ferry (load limit in tons)	par bac (charge maximum en tonnes)	per Fähre (Höchstbelastung in t)
Ferry (passengers and cycles only)	Bac pour piétons et cycles	Fähre für Personen und Fahrräder
Accommodation - Administration	**Hébergement - Administration**	**Unterkunft - Verwaltung**
Administrative boundaries	Limites administratives	Verwaltungshauptstadt
Scottish and Welsh borders	Limite de l'Écosse et du Pays de Galles	Grenze von Schottland und Wales
National boundary - Customs post	Frontière - Douane	Staatsgrenze - Zoll
Sport & Recreation Facilities	**Sports - Loisirs**	**Sport - Freizeit**
Golf course - Horse racetrack	Golf - Hippodrome	Golfplatz - Pferderennbahn
Racing circuit - Pleasure boat harbour	Circuit automobile - Port de plaisance	Rennstrecke - Yachthafen
Caravan and camping sites	Camping, caravaning	Campingplatz
Waymarked footpath - Country park	Sentier balisé - Base ou parc de loisirs	Ausgeschilderter Weg - Freizeitanlage
Safari park, zoo - Bird sanctuary, refuge	Parc animalier, zoo - Réserve d'oiseaux	Tierpark, Zoo - Vogelschutzgebiet
IRL: Fishing - Greyhound track	IRL : Pêche - Cynodrome	IRL: Angeln - Windhundrennen
Tourist train	Train touristique	Museumseisenbahn
Funicular, cable car, chairlift	Funiculaire, téléphérique, télésiège	Standseilbahn, Seilbahn, Sessellift
Sights	**Curiosités**	**Sehenswürdigkeiten**
Principal sights: see THE GREEN GUIDE	Principales curiosités : voir LE GUIDE VERT	Hauptsehenswürdigkeiten: siehe GRÜNER REISEFÜHRER
Towns or places of interest, Places to stay	Localités ou sites intéressants, lieux de séjour	Sehenswerte Orte, Ferienorte
Religious building - Historic house, castle	Édifice religieux - Château	Sakral-Bau - Schloss, Burg
Ruins - Prehistoric monument - Cave	Ruines - Monument mégalithique - Grotte	Ruine - Vorgeschichtliches Steindenkmal - Höhle
Garden, park - Other places of interest	Jardin, parc - Autres curiosités	Garten, Park - Sonstige Sehenswürdigkeit
IRL: Fort - Celtic cross - Round Tower	IRL : Fort - Croix celte - Tour ronde	IRL: Fort, Festung - Keltisches Kreuz - Rundturm
Panoramic view - Viewpoint	Panorama - Point de vue	Rundblick - Aussichtspunkt
Scenic route	Parcours pittoresque	Landschaftlich schöne Strecke
Other signs	**Signes divers**	**Sonstige Zeichen**
Industrial cable way	Transporteur industriel aérien	Industrieschwebebahn
Telecommunications tower or mast - Lighthouse	Tour ou pylône de télécommunications - Phare	Funk-, Sendeturm - Leuchtturm
Power station - Quarry	Centrale électrique - Carrière	Kraftwerk - Steinbruch
Mine - Industrial activity	Mine - Industries	Bergwerk - Industrieanlagen
Refinery - Cliff	Raffinerie - Falaise	Raffinerie - Klippen
National forest park - National park	Parc forestier national - Parc national	Waldschutzgebiet - Nationalpark

Verklaring van de tekens

Wegen

Autosnelweg - Serviceplaatsen
Gescheiden rijbanen van het type autosnelweg
Aansluitingen: volledig, gedeeltelijk
Afritnummers
Internationale of nationale verbindingsweg
Interregionale verbindingsweg

Verharde weg - Onverharde weg
Pad - Bewegwijzerd wandelpad / Ruiterpad
Autosnelweg in aanleg - weg in aanleg
(indien bekend: datum openstelling)

Breedte van de wegen

Gescheiden rijbanen
4 rijstroken - 2 brede rijstroken
2 rijstroken - 2 smalle rijstroken

Afstanden (totaal en gedeeltelijk)

Gedeelte met tol op autosnelwegen
Tolvrij gedeelte op autosnelwegen
in mijlen - in kilometers
op andere wegen

Wegnummers - Bewegwijzering

Autosnelweg - GB: Hoofdweg
(Primary route)
IRL: Hoofdweg
(National primary en secondary route)
Andere wegen
Plaatsen langs een autosnelweg van Primary route met bewegwijzering

Hindernissen

Rotonde - Bergpas en hoogte boven de zeespiegel (in meters)
Steile helling (pijlen in de richting van de helling)
IRL: Moeilijk of gevaarlijk traject
In Schotland: smalle weg met uitwijkplaatsen

Wegovergangen:
gelijkvloers, overheen, onderheen
Verboden weg - Beperkt opengestelde weg
Tol - Weg met eenrichtingverkeer
Vrije hoogte indien lager dan
15'6" IRL, 15'6" GB
Maximum draagvermogen (indien minder dan 16 t)

Vervoer

Spoorweg - Reizigersstation
Luchthaven - Vliegveld
Vervoer van auto's: (tijdens het seizoen: rood teken)
per boot
per veerpont (maximum draagvermogen in t.)
Veerpont voor voetgangers en fietsers

Verblijf - Administratie

Administratieve grenzen
Grens van Schotland en Wales

Staatsgrens - Douanekantoor

Sport - Recreatie

Golfterrein - Renbaan
Autocircuit - Jachthaven
Kampeerterrein (tent, caravan)
Sentiero segnalato - Recreatiepark
Safaripark, dierentuin - Vogelreservaat
IRL: Vissen - Hondenrenbaan
Toeristentreintje
Kabelspoor, kabelbaan, stoeltjeslift

Bezienswaardigheden

Belangrijkste bezienswaardigheden: zie DE GROENE GIDS
Interessante steden of plaatsen, vakantieoorden
Kerkelijk gebouw - Kasteel
Ruïne - Megaliet - Grot
Tuin, park - Andere bezienswaardigheden
IRL: Fort - Keltisch kruis - Ronde toren
Panorama - Uitzichtpunt
Schilderachtig traject

Diverse tekens

Kabelvrachtvervoer
Telecommunicatietoren of -mast - Vuurtoren
Elektriciteitscentrale - Steengroeve
Mijn - Industrie
Raffinaderij - Klif
Staatsbos - Nationaal park

Legenda

Strade

Autostrada - Aree di servizio
Doppia carreggiata di tipo autostradale
Svincoli: completo, parziale
Svincoli numerati
Strada di collegamento internazionale o nazionale
Strada di collegamento interregionale o di disimpegno

Strada rivestita - non rivestita
Sentiero - Sentiero segnalato / Pista per cavalli
Autostrada, strada in costruzione
(data di apertura prevista)

Larghezza delle strade

Carreggiate separate
4 corsie - 2 corsie larghe
2 corsie - 2 corsie strette

Distanze (totali e parziali)

Tratto a pedaggio su autostrada
Tratto esente da pedaggio su autostrada
in miglia - in chilometri
su strada

Numerazione - Segnaletica

Autostrada - GB: itinerario principale
(Strada «Primary»)
IRL: itinerario principale
(Strada «National primary» e «Secondary»)
Altre Strade
Località delimitante gli itinerari principali

Ostacoli

Rotonda - Passo ed altitudine (in metri)
Forte pendenza (salita nel senso della freccia)
IRL: Percorso difficile o pericoloso
In Scozia: Strada molto stretta con incrocio

Passaggi della strada:
a livello, cavalcavia, sottopassaggio
Strada vietata - Strada a circolazione regolamentata
Casello - Strada a senso unico
Limite di altezza inferiore a
15'6" IRL, 16'6" GB
Limite di portata (inferiore a 16 t.)

Trasporti

Ferrovia - Stazione viaggiatori
Aeroporto - Aerodromo
Trasporto auto: (stagionale in rosso)
su traghetto
su chiatta (carico massimo in t.)
Traghetto per pedoni e biciclette

Risorse alberghiere - Amministrazione

Confini amministrativi
Confine di Scozia e Galles

Frontiera - Dogana

Sport - Divertimento

Golf - Ippodromo
Circuito Automobilistico - Porto turistico
Campeggi, caravaning
Sentiero segnalato - Area o parco per attività ricreative
Parco con animali, zoo - Riserva ornitologica
IRL: Pesca - Cinodromo
Trenino turistico
Funicolare, funivia, seggiovia

Mete e luoghi d'interesse

Principali luoghi d'interesse, vedere LA GUIDA VERDE
Località o siti interessanti, luoghi di soggiorno
Edificio religioso - Castello
Rovine - Monumento megalitico - Grotta
Giardino, parco - Altri luoghi d'interesse
IRL: Forte - Croce celtica - Torre rotonda
Panorama - Vista
Percorso pittoresco

Simboli vari

Teleferica industriale
Torre o pilone per telecomunicazioni - Faro
Centrale elettrica - Cava
Miniera - Industrie
Raffineria - Falesia
Parco forestale nazionale - Parco nazionale

Signos convencionales

Carreteras

Autopista - Áreas de servicio
Autovía
Enlaces: completo, parciales
Números de los accesos
Carretera de comunicación internacional o nacional
Carretera de comunicación interregional o alternativo

Carretera asfaltada - sin asfaltar
Sendero - Sendero señalizado / Camino de caballos
Autopista, carretera en construcción
(en su caso: fecha prevista de entrada en servicio)

Ancho de las carreteras

Calzadas separadas
Cuatro carriles - Dos carriles anchos
Dos carriles - Dos carriles estrechos

Distancias (totales y parciales)

Tramo de peaje en autopista
Tramo libre en autopista
en millas - en kilómetros
en carretera

Numeración - Señalización

Autopista - GB: Vía principal
(Primary route)
IRL: Vía principal
(National primary et secondary route)
Otras carreteras
Localidad en itinerario principal

Obstáculos

Rotonda - Puerto y su altitud (en métros)
Pendiente Pronunciada (las flechas indican el sentido del ascenso)
IRL: Recorrido difícil o peligroso
En escocia: carretera muy estrecha con ensanchamientos para poder cruzarse

Pasos de la carretera:
a nivel, superior, inferior
Tramo prohibido - Carretera restringida
Barrera de peaje - Carretera de sentido único
Altura limitada
(15'6" IRL, 16'6"GB)
Limite de carga (inferior a 16 t)

Transportes

Línea férrea - Estación de viajeros
Aeropuerto - Aeródromo
Transporte de coches: (Enlace de temporada: signo rojo)
por barco
por barcaza (carga máxima en toneladas)
Barcaza para el paso de peatones y vehículos dos ruedas

Alojamiento - Administración

Límites administrativos
Límites de Escocia y del País de Gales

Frontera - Puesto de aduanas

Deportes - Ocio

Golf - Hipódromo
Circuito de velocidad - Puerto deportivo
Camping, caravaning
Sendero señalizado - Parque de ocio
Reserva de animales, zoo - Reserva de pájaros
IRL: Pêche - Cynodrome
Tren turístico
Funicular, Teleférico, telesilla

Curiosidades

Principales curiosidades: ver LA GUÍA VERDE
Localidad o lugar interesante, lugar para quedarse
Edificio religioso - Castillo
Ruinas - Monumento megalítico - Cueva
Jardín, parque - Curiosidades diversas
IRL: Fortaleza - Cruz celta - Torre redonda
Vista panorámica - Vista parcial
Recorrido pintoresco

Signos diversos

Transportador industrial aéreo
Emisor de Radiodifusión - Faro
Central eléctrica - Cantera
Mina - Industrias
Refinería - Acantilado
Parque forestal nacional - Parque nacional

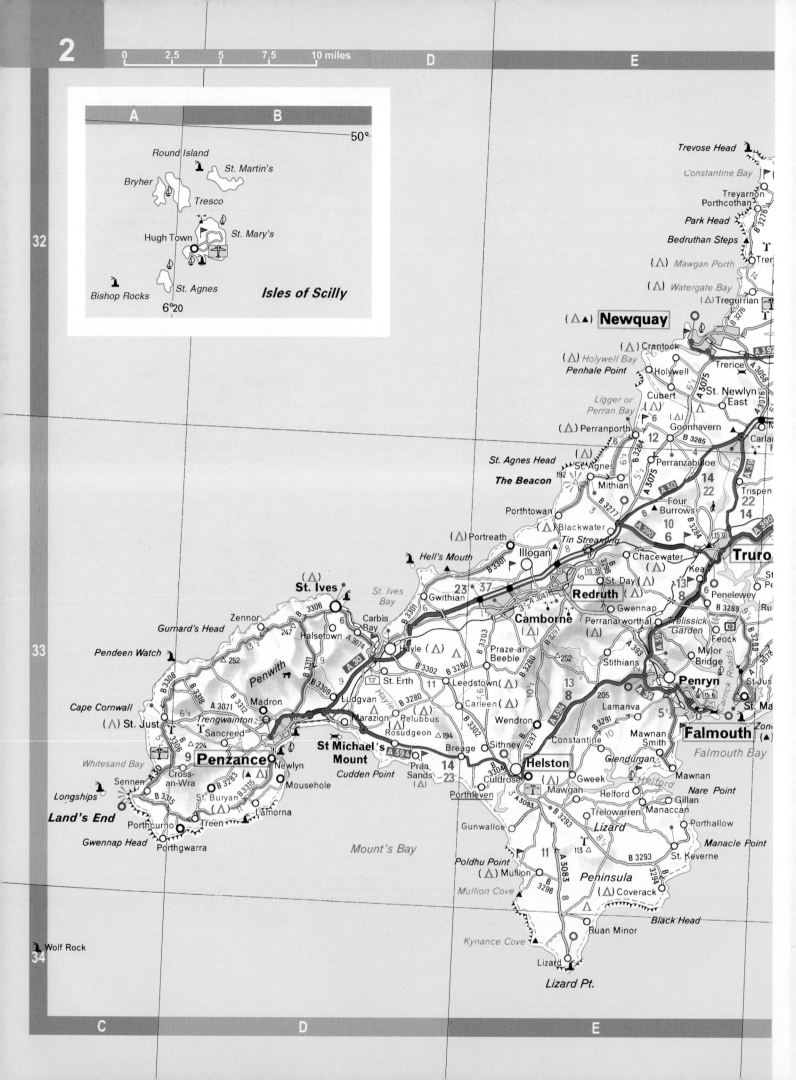

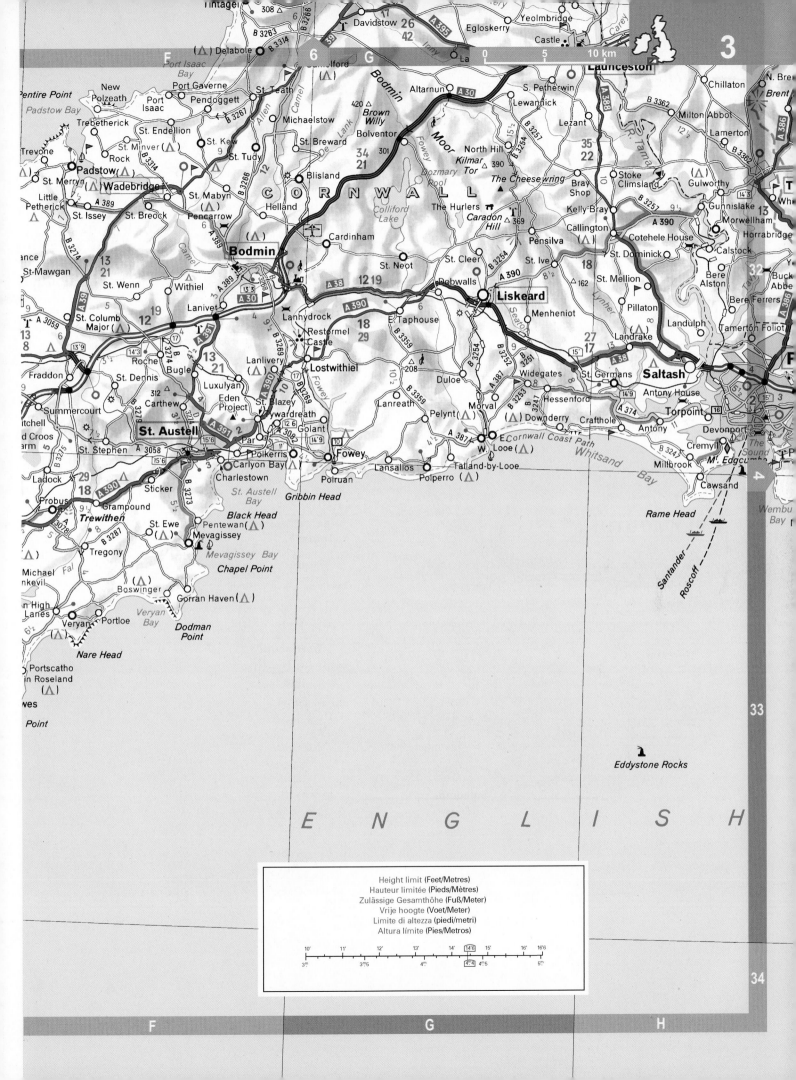

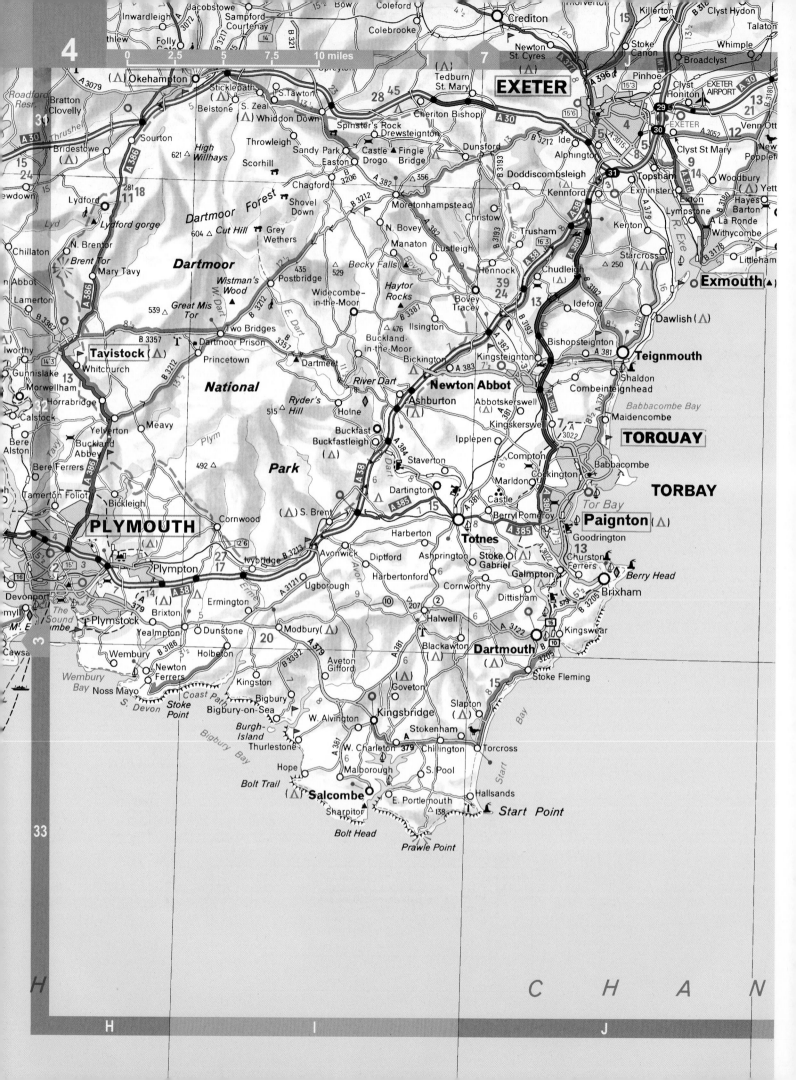

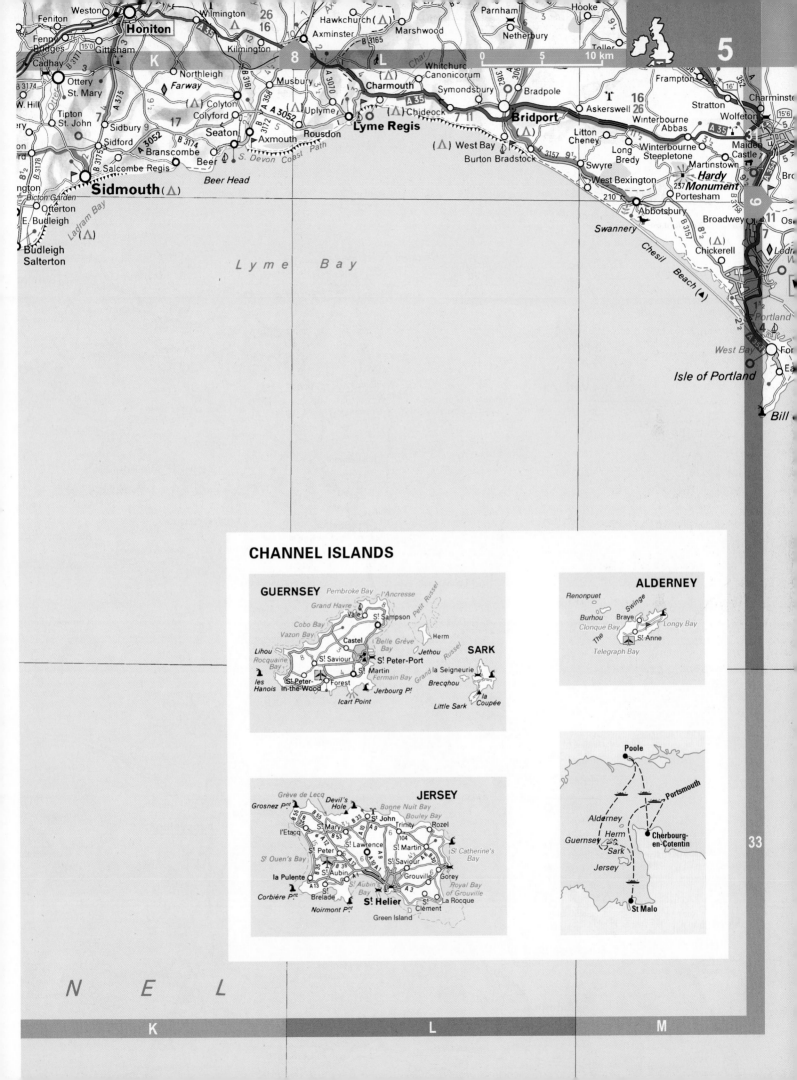

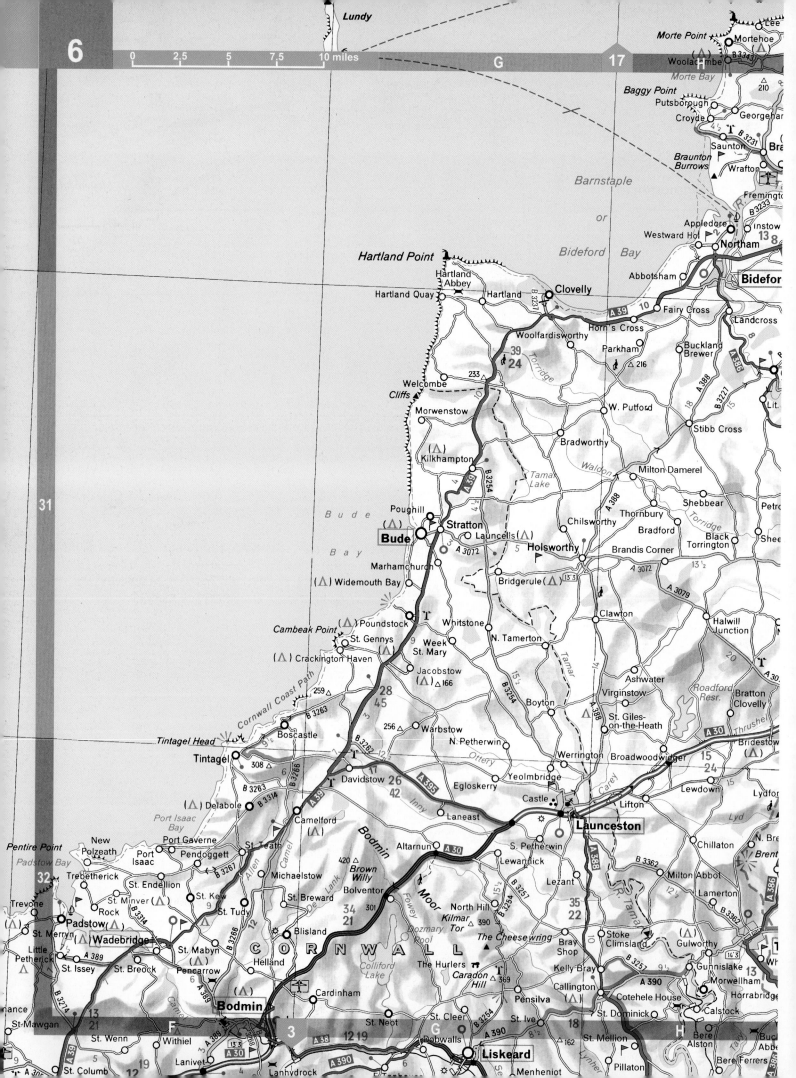

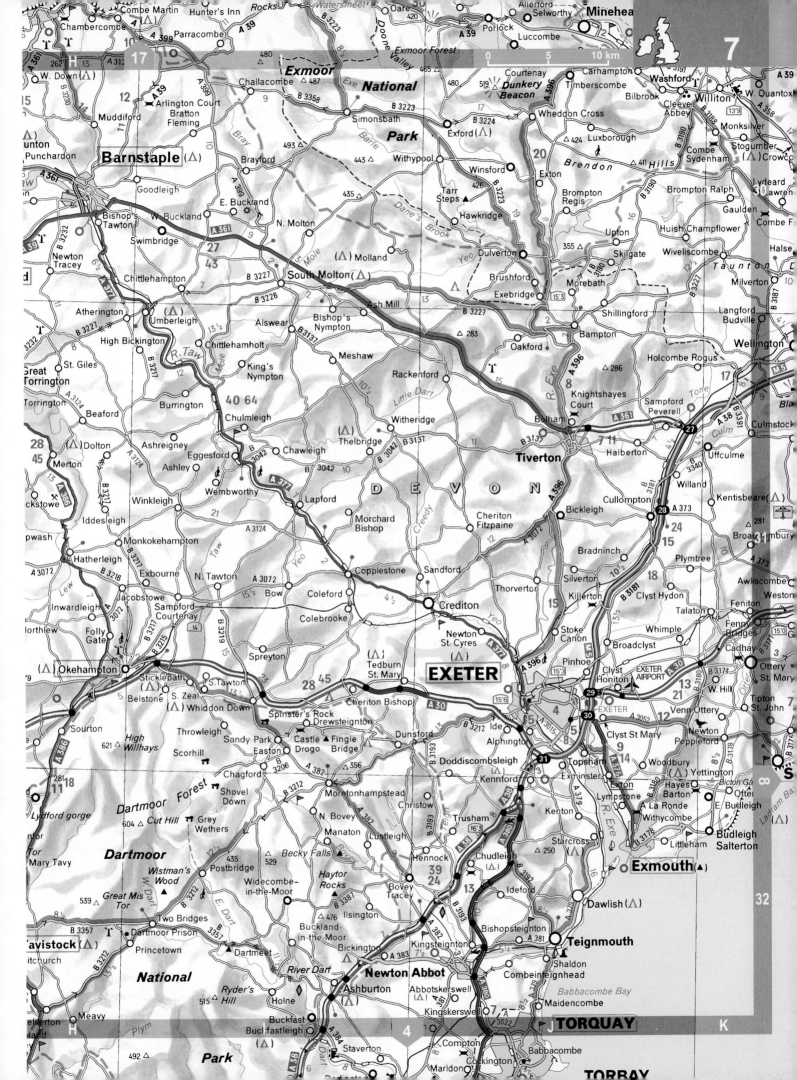

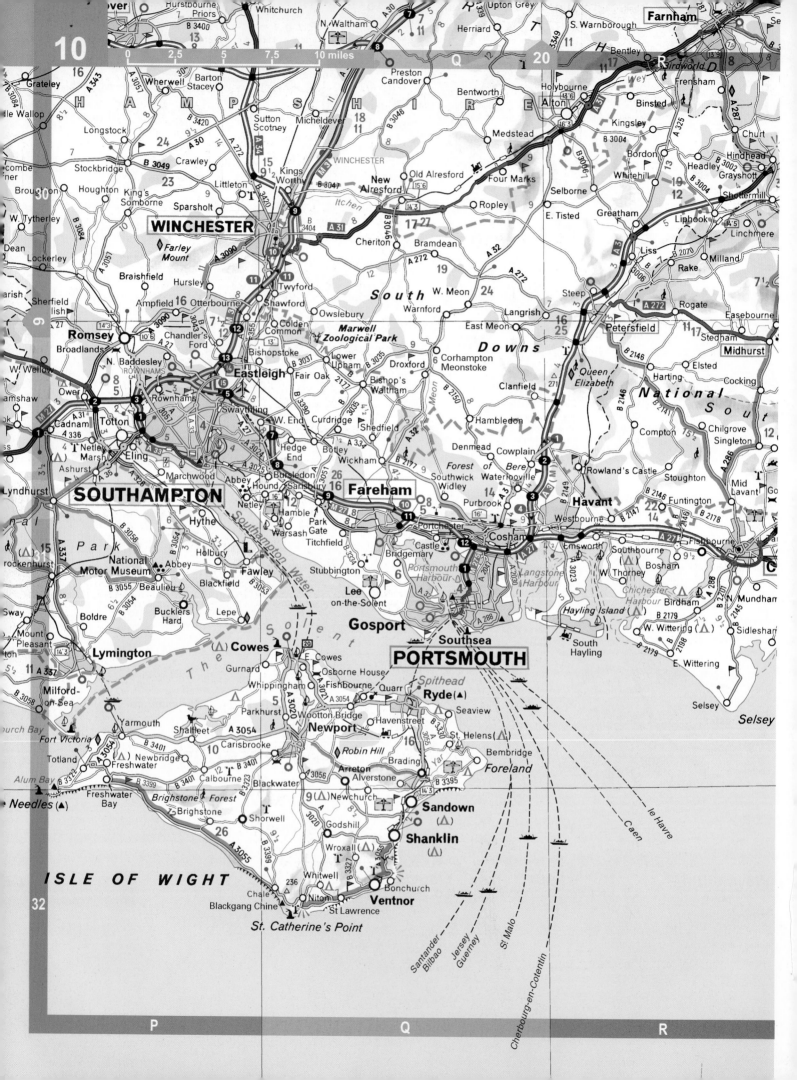

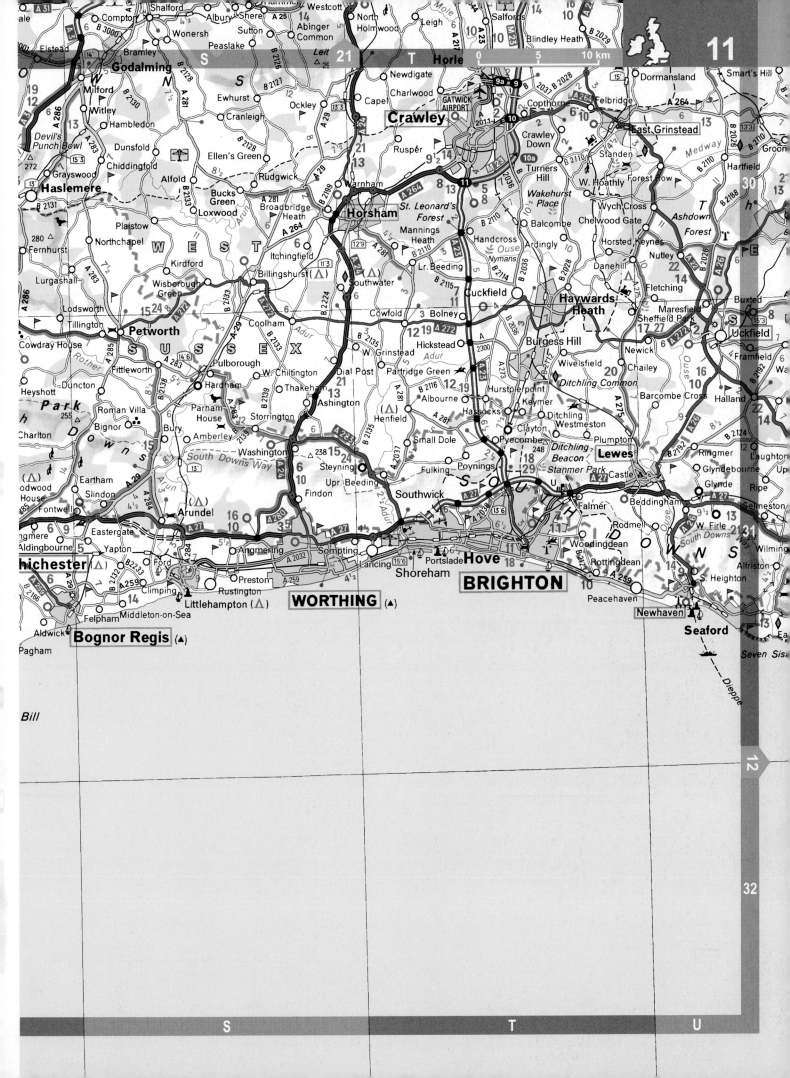

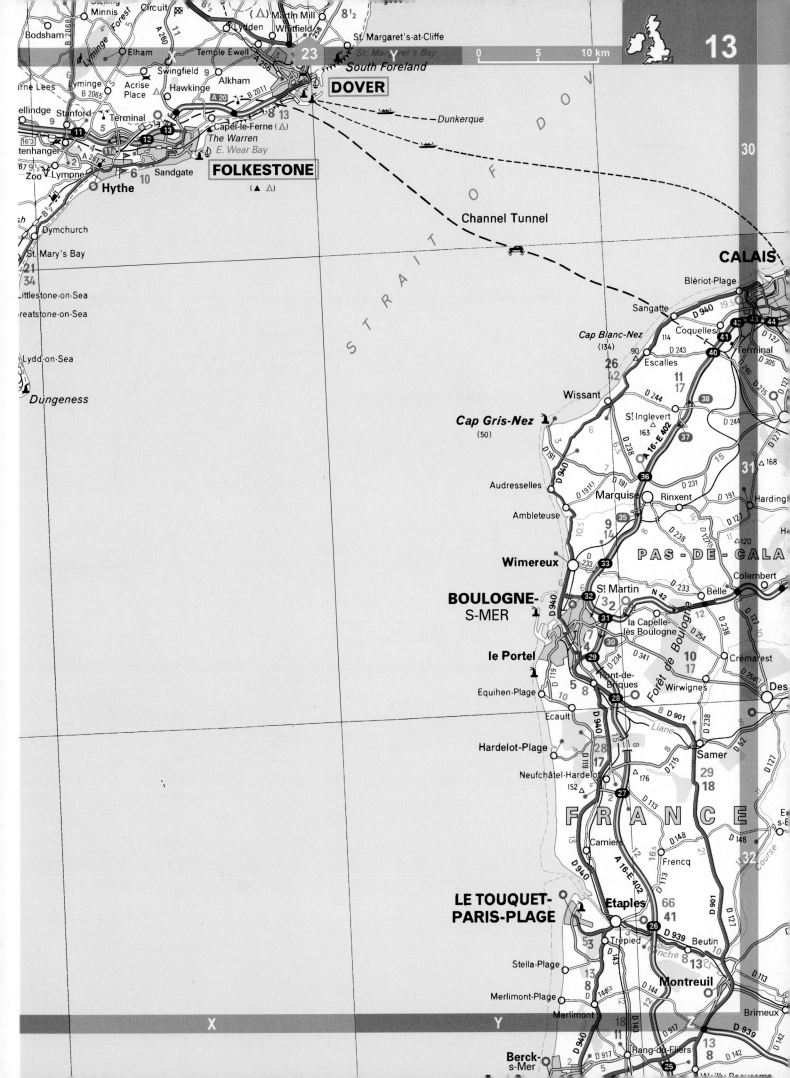

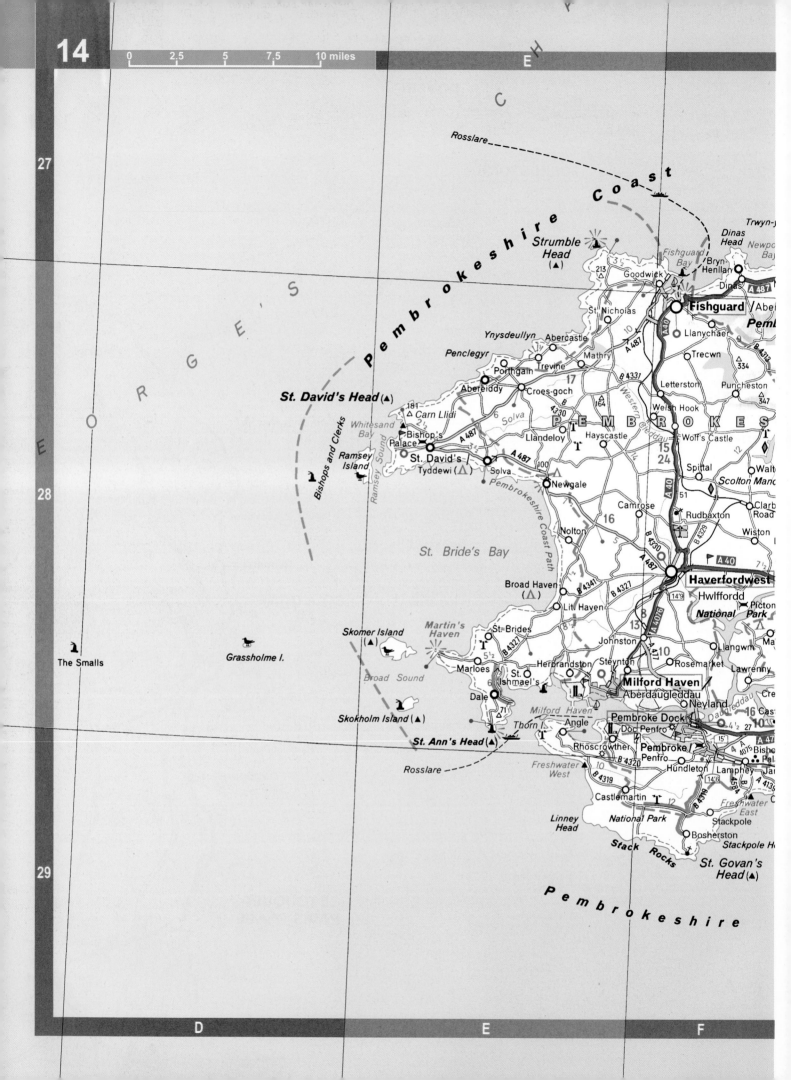

0 2.5 5 7.5 10 miles

E

C

Rosslare

Pembrokeshire Coast

Trwyn-y

27

Strumble
Head
(▲)

213

Dinas
Head

Newpo

Fishguard
Bay

Bryn-
Henllan

Goodwick

Dinas

A 487

Fishguard / Aber

Pemb

St. Nicholas

Llanychaer

Ynysdeullyn

Abercastle

A 487

Trecwn

Penclegyr

Trevine

Mathry

10

334

Porthgain

17

Letterston

Puncheston

St. David's Head (▲)

Abereiddy

Croes-goch

B 4331

Welsh Hook

347

181

B
4330

164

PEMBROKES

Carn Llidi

Solva

6

Wolf's Castle

12

Whitesand
Bay

Bishop's
Palace

A 487

Llandeloy

Hayscastle

15
24

Spittal

Walt

Bishops and Clerks

Ramsey
Island

St. David's

A 487

100

Scolton Man

Tyddewi (△)

Solva

Newgale

Camrose

51

Rudbaxton

Clarb
Road

28

Ramsey Sound

A 40

B 4330

Wiston

St. Bride's Bay

16

Nolton

5

B 4329

A 40

2½

Haverfordwest

Broad Haven
(△)

B 4341

B 4327

14'9

Hwlffordd

Picton

The Smalls

Grassholme I.

Skomer Island
(▲)

Martin's
Haven

St. Brides

Lit. Haven

8½

National Park

Johnston

13

Llangwm

Ma

Marloes

5½

B 4327

Herbrandston

Steynton

A 477

10

Rosemarket

Lawrenny

Broad Sound

St.
Ishmael's

6

Milford Haven

Neyland

16

Cas

Dale

71

Aberdaugleddau

Skokholm Island (▲)

Thorn I.

Angle

Pembroke Dock
Doc Penfro

4½

27

10

St. Ann's Head (▲)

Rhoscrowther

Pembroke /
Pentro

15'

A 47

Rosslare

Freshwater
West

10

B 4320

Hundleton

Lamphey

Ja

14'6

B 4319

Freshwater
East

Castlemartin

12

29

Linney
Head

National Park

Stackpole

Bosherston

Stack Rocks

Stackpole H

St. Govan's
Head (▲)

Pembroke

Pembrokeshire

D

E

F

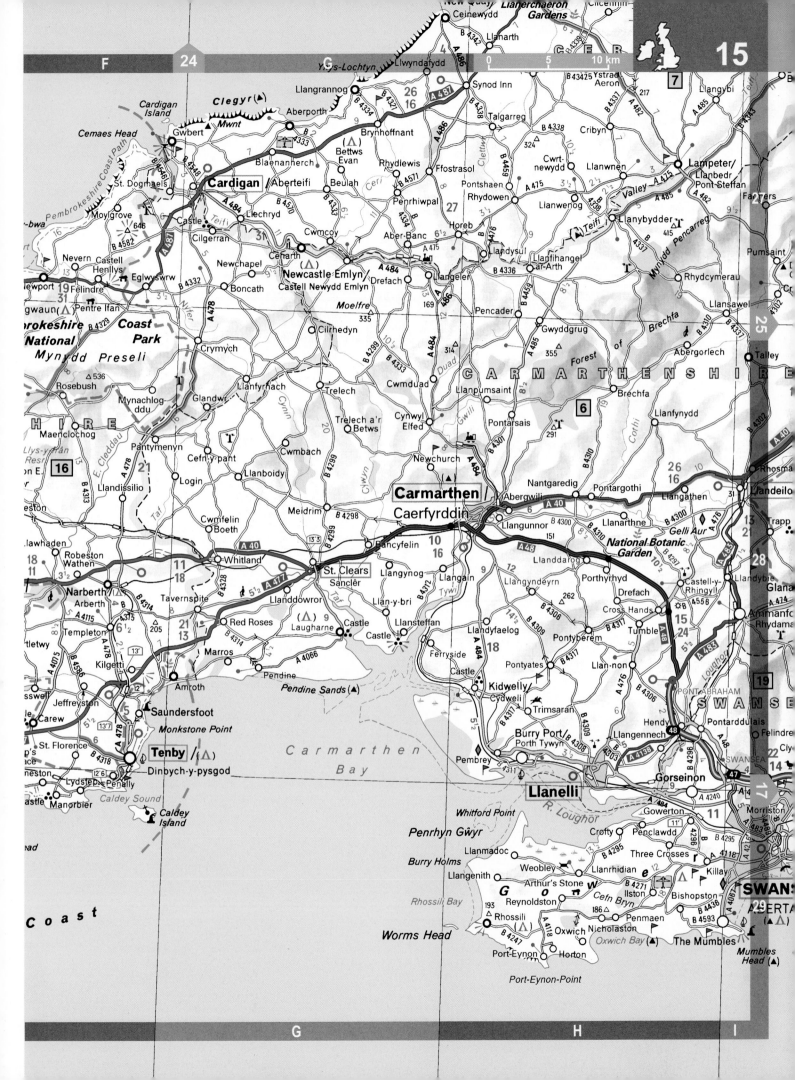

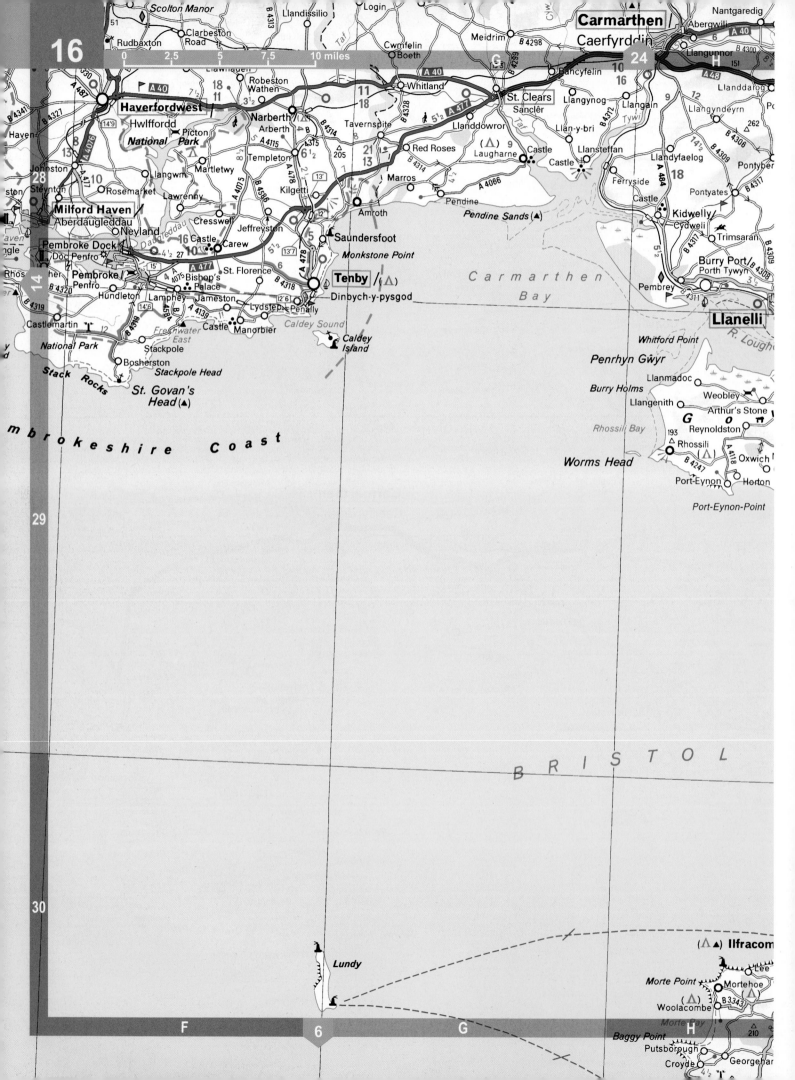

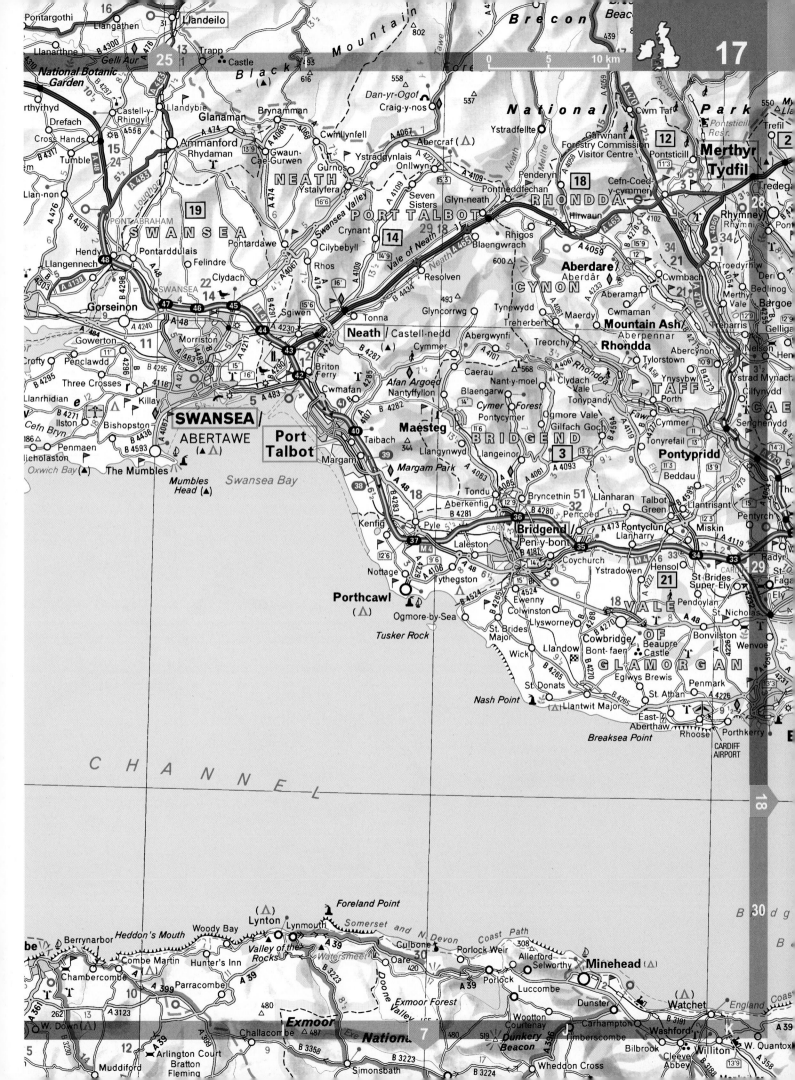

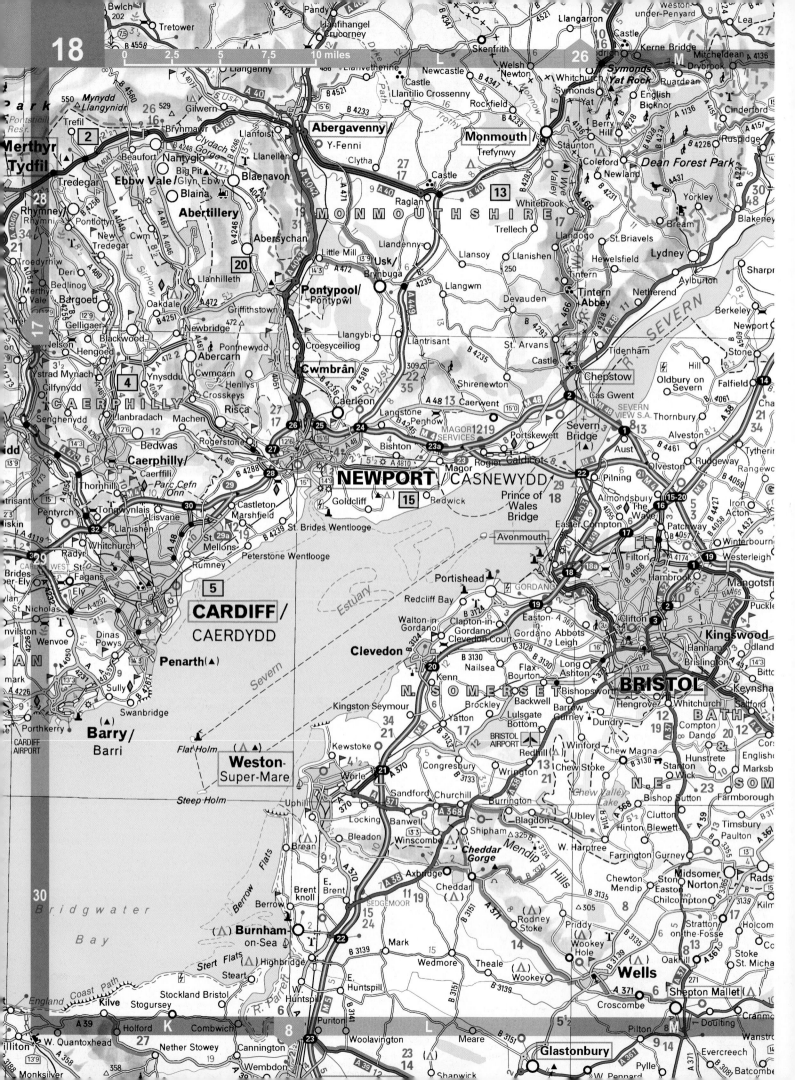

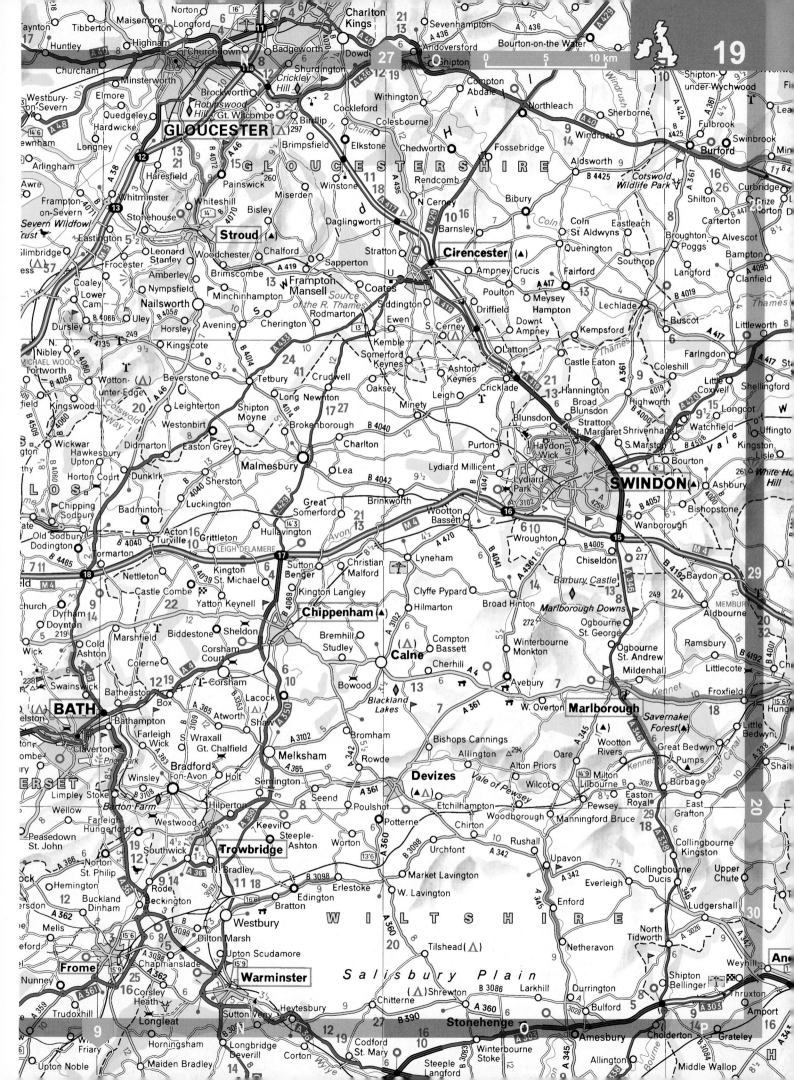

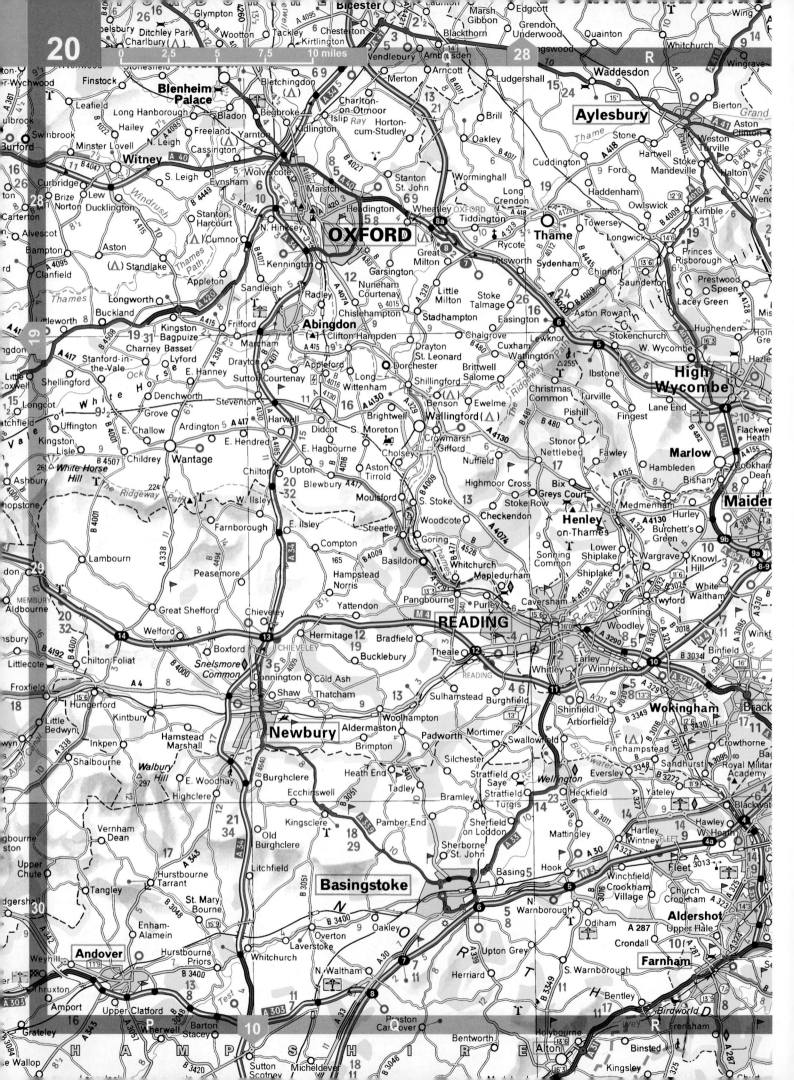

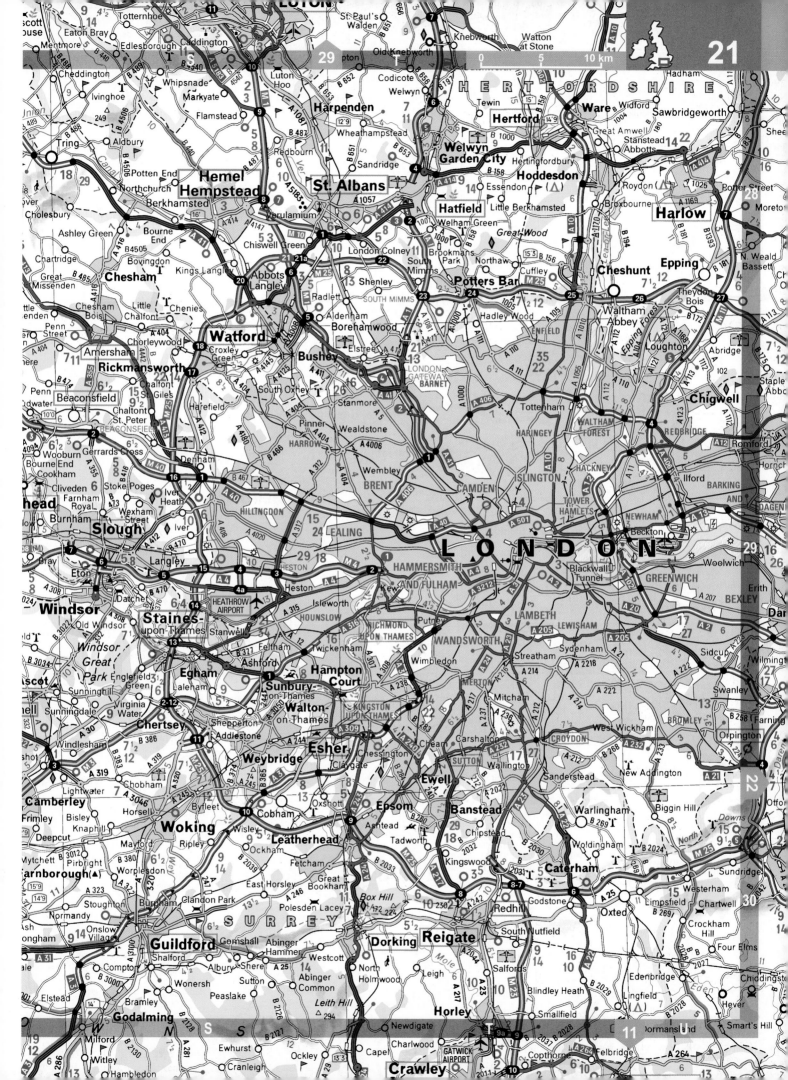

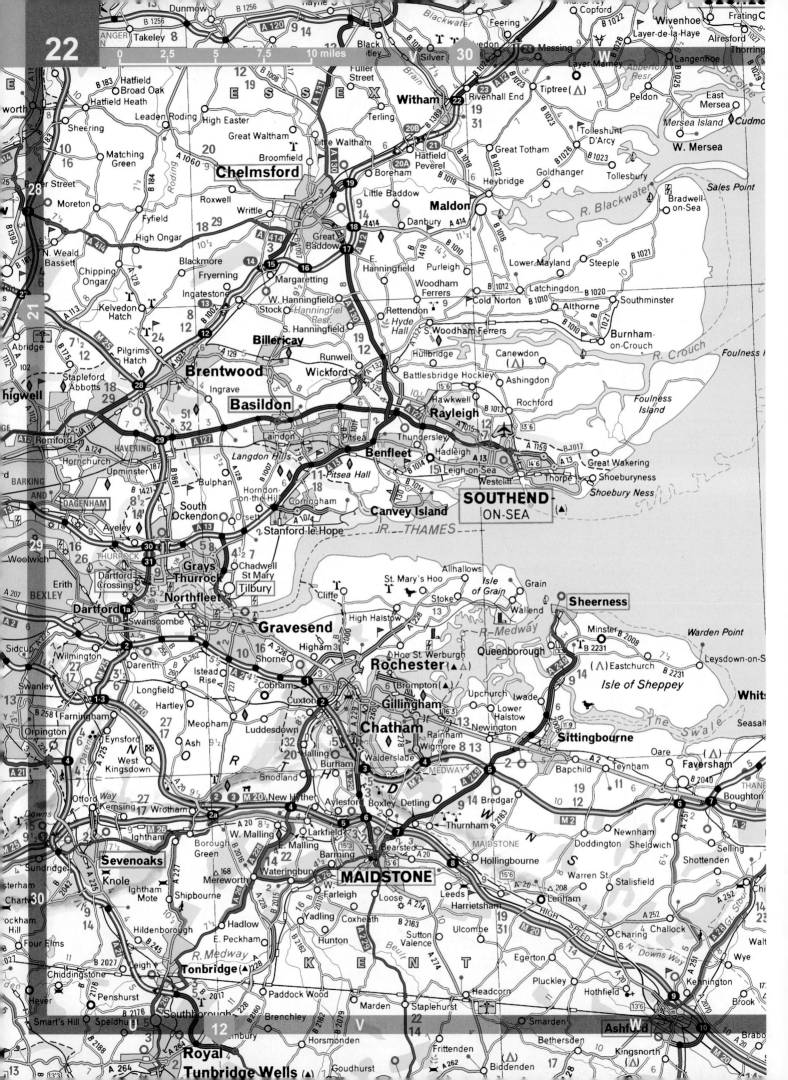

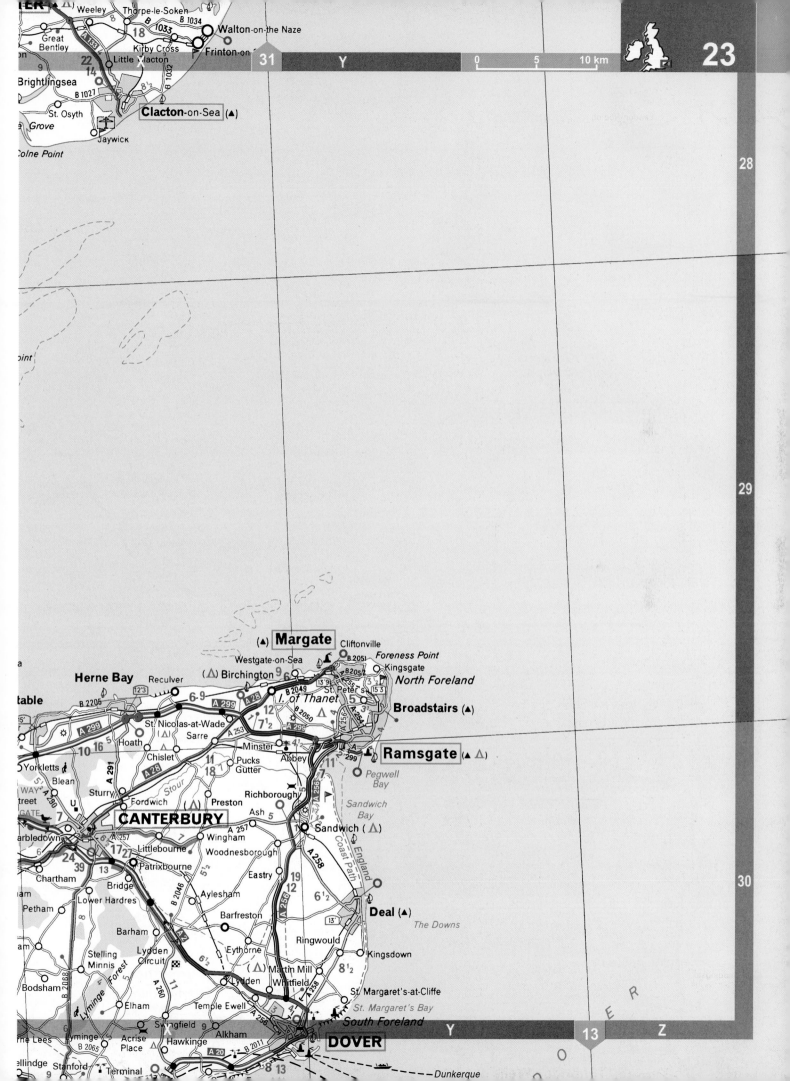

0   5   10 km

Weeley   Thorpe-le-Soken
Great
Bentley   Walton-on-the Naze
18   Kirby Cross   Frinton-on-
Little Clacton   31   Y
22   14
B 1027
Brightlingsea
St. Osyth   Clacton-on-Sea (▲)
Grove   Jaywick
Colne Point

28

29

30

(▲) **Margate**   Cliftonville
Westgate-on-Sea   Foreness Point
(△) Birchington   9 6   B 2051   Kingsgate
Herne Bay   Reculver   13 9   B 2052   North Foreland
12 3   6 9   A 299   St. Peter's   3   15 3
A 28   I. of Thanet   5
table   B 2205   12   B 2049   **Broadstairs** (▲)
St. Nicolas-at-Wade   7 ½   B 2050   A 256
15   A 299   (△)   Sarre   A 253   Minster   4 ½
10 16 5   Hoath   Abbey   **Ramsgate** (▲ △)
Yorkletts   Chislet   11   Pucks   11   A 299
Blean   A 291   18   Gutter   7   Pegwell
WAY   Sturry   Stour   Bay   Sandwich
street   Fordwich   (∆)   Preston   Richborough   Bay
GATE   7   Ash   5   England   Sandwich (△)
arbledown   **CANTERBURY**   A 257   Wingham   A 258   Coast Path
24   17 27   Littlebourne   Woodnesborough   Path
39   13   Patrixbourne   5 ½   Eastry   19   6 ½
Chartham   Bridge   Aylesham   12
Petham   Lower Hardres   B 2046   Barfreston   A 256   13   **Deal** (▲)
Barham   Ringwould   The Downs
Stelling   Lydden   6 ½   Kingsdown
Bodsham   Minnis   Circuit   (△) Martin Mill   8 ½
A 260   Lydden   Whitfield   St. Margaret's-at-Cliffe
Elham   Temple Ewell   3   A 258   St. Margaret's Bay
ne Lees   Swingfield   9   4   South Foreland
Lyminge   Acrise   Alkham   E   R
llindge   Stanford   Place   Hawkinge   A 20   B 2011   **DOVER**   13   Z
9   Terminal   8 13   Dunkerque

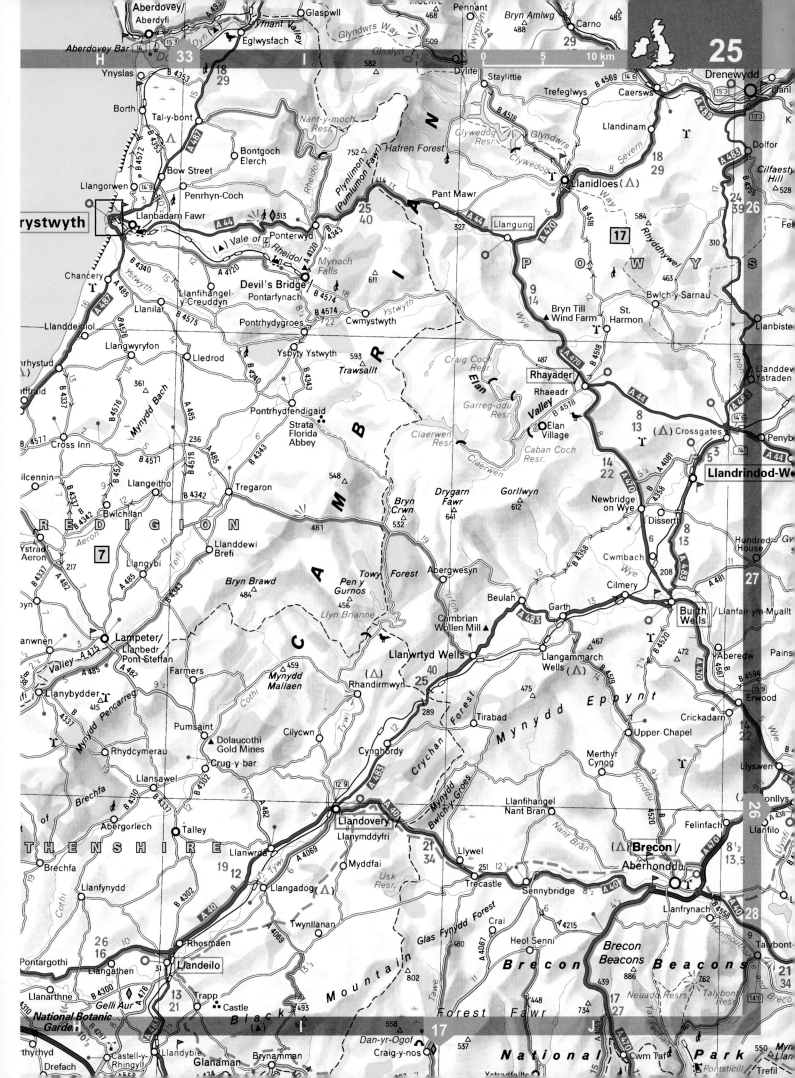

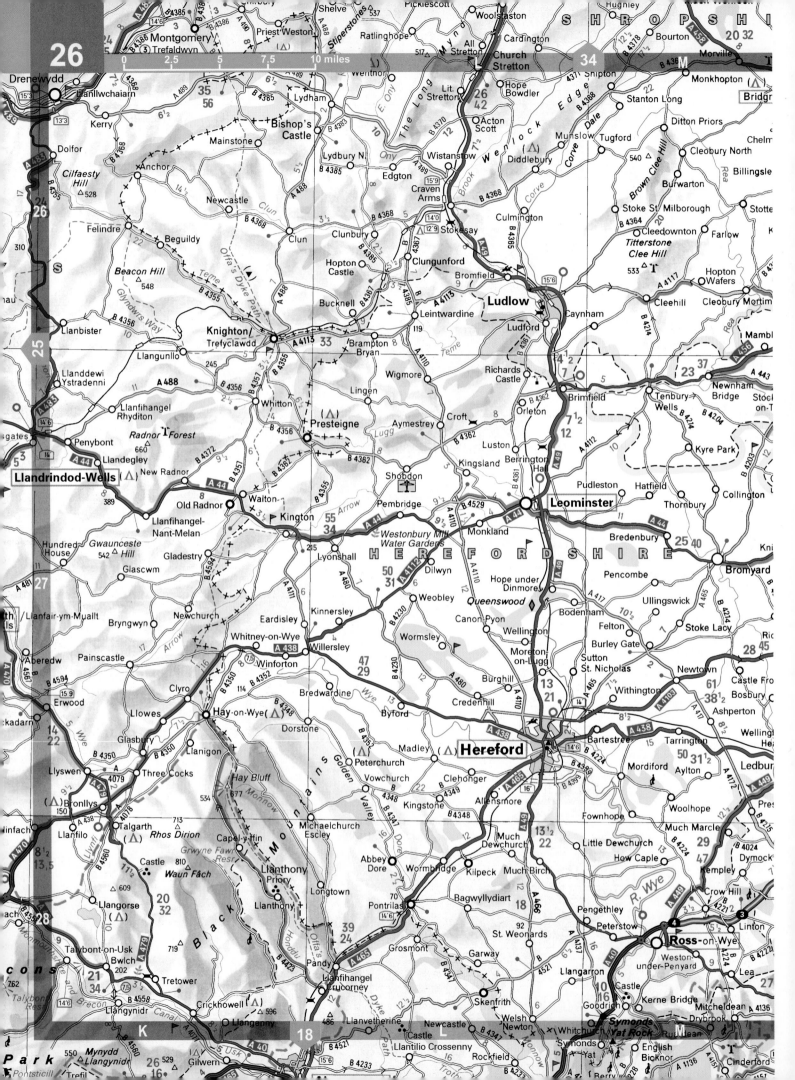

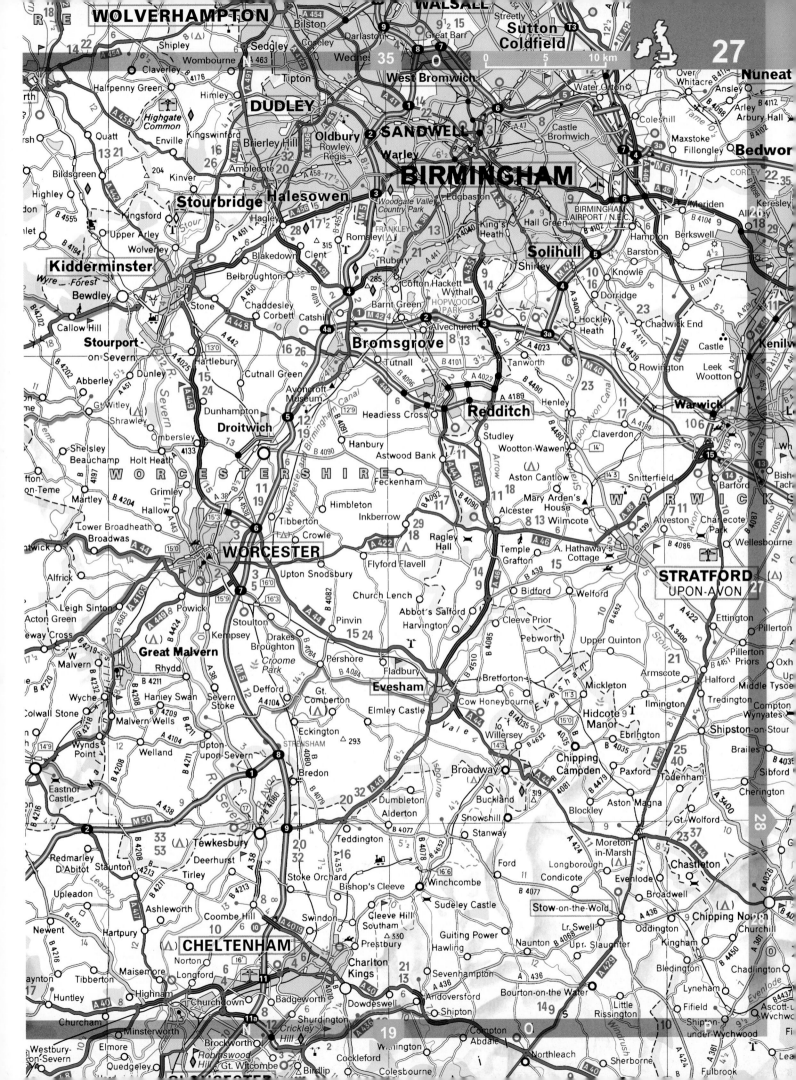

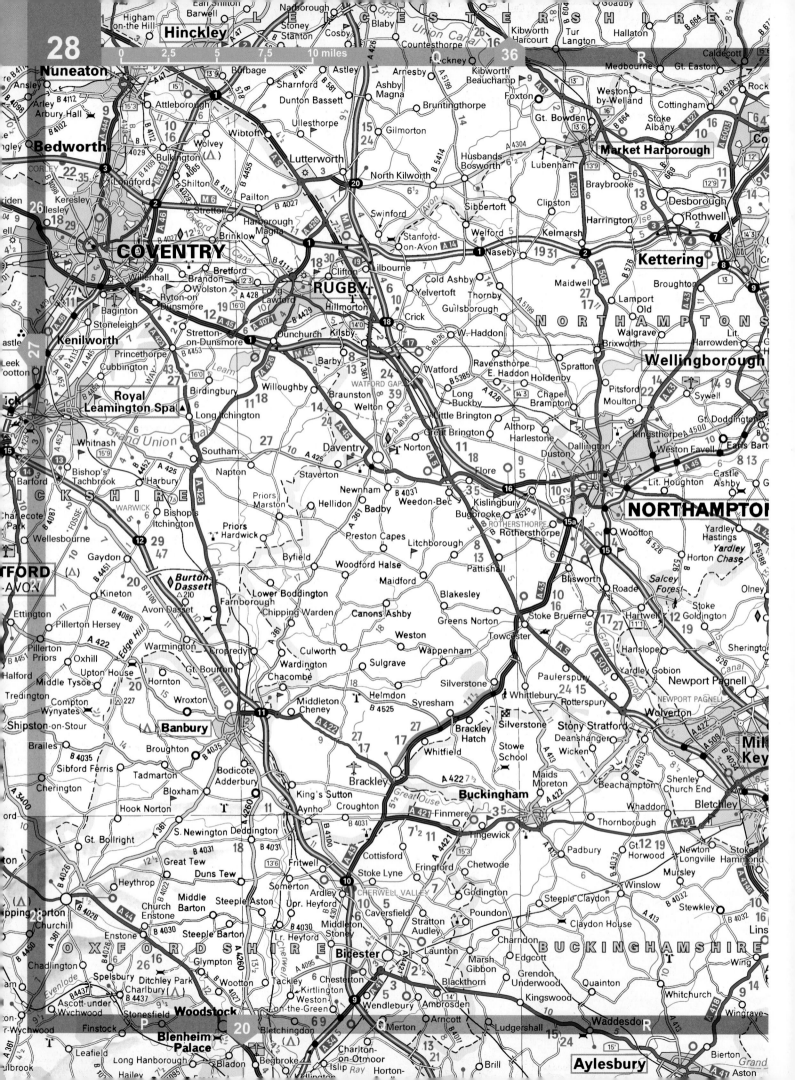

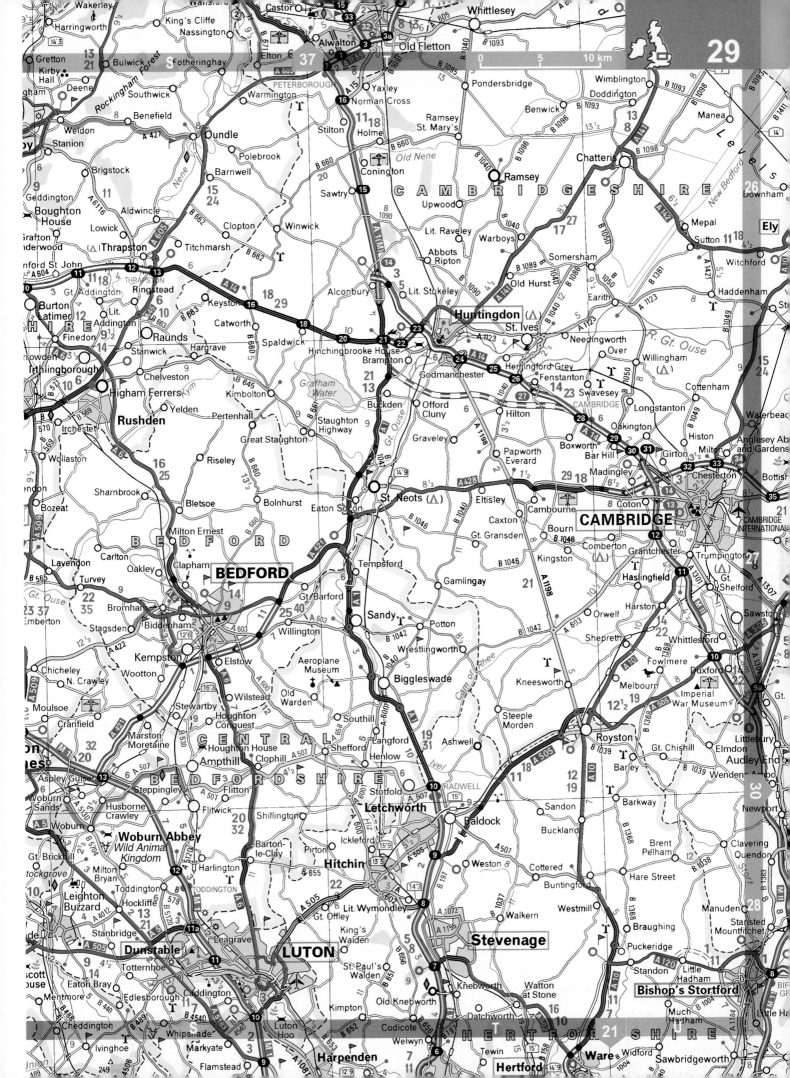

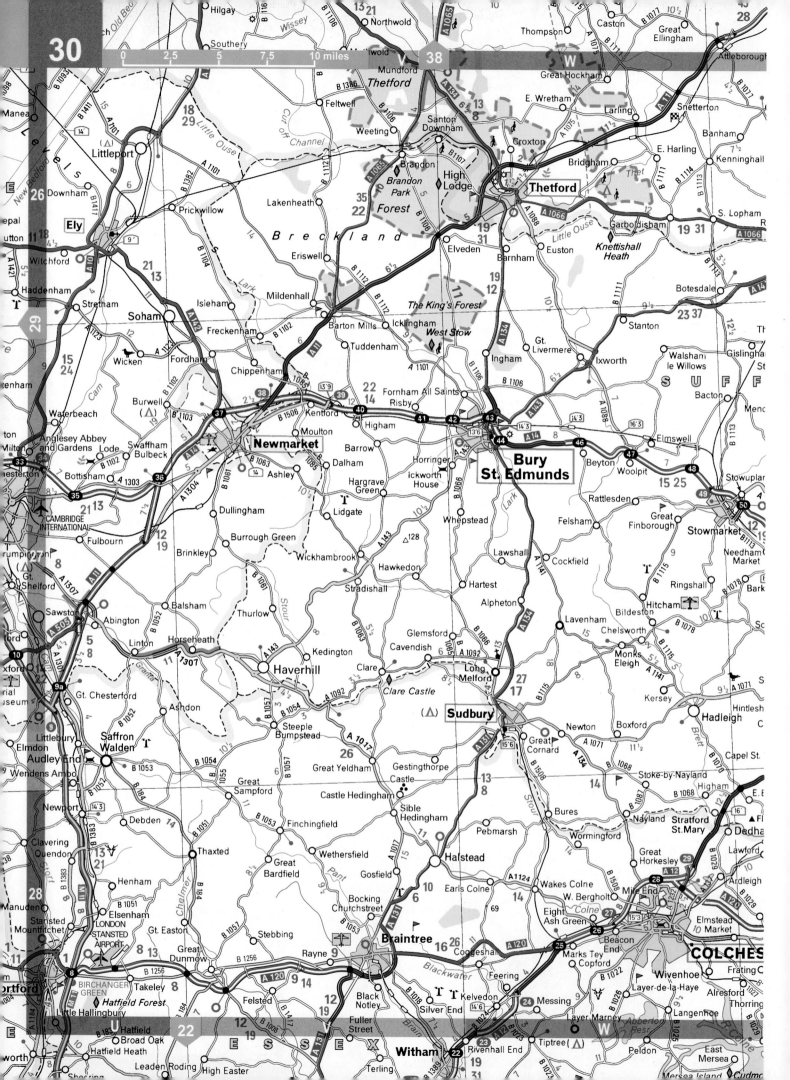

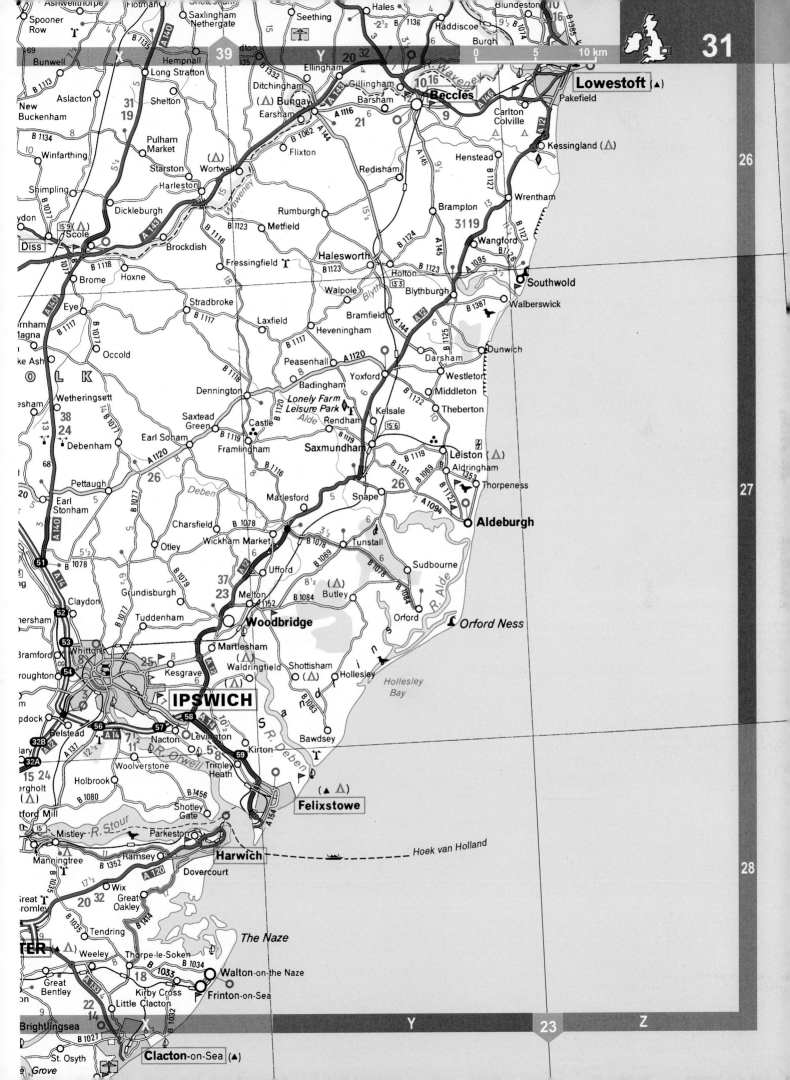

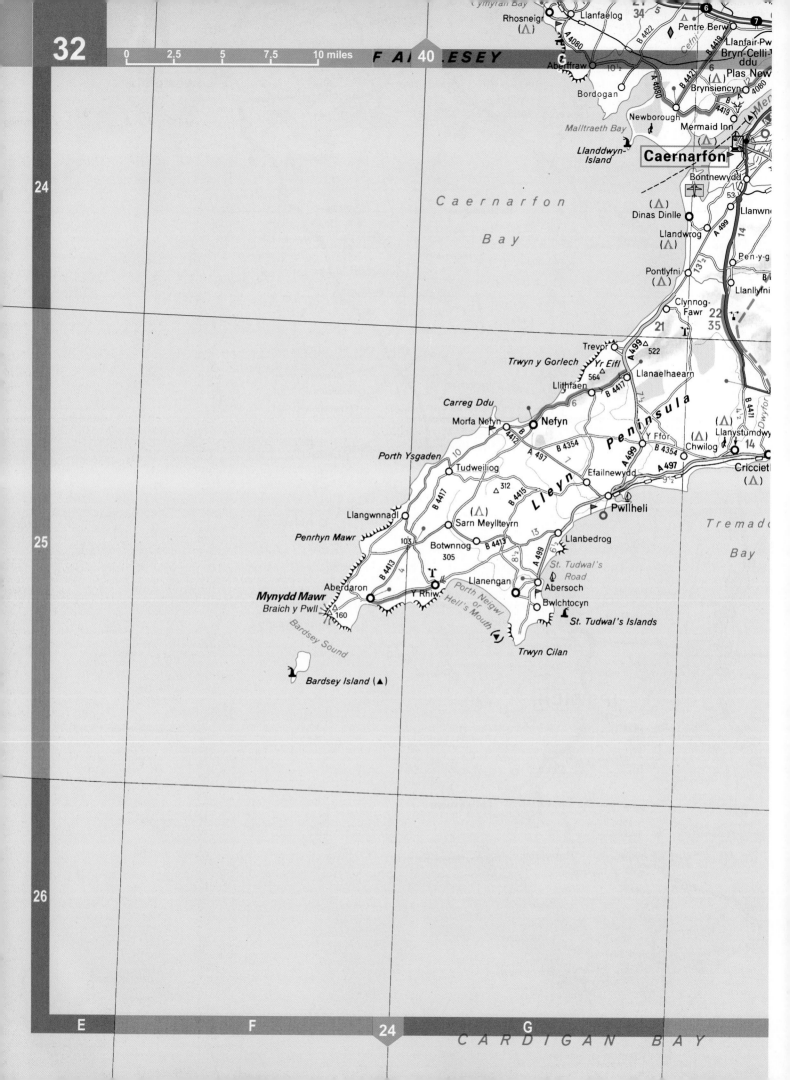

(Ymyran Bay)

Rhosneigr
(Δ)

Llanfaelog

Pentre Berw

Cefni

Llanfair-Pw
Bryn-Celli-
ddu

Plas New

F A N 40 ESEY

Aberffraw

Bordogan

Newborough

Malltraeth Bay

Llanddwyn-
Island

Brynsiencyn

(Δ)

Mermaid Inn

Caernarfon

Bontnewydd

C a e r n a r f o n

B a y

Dinas Dinlle
(Δ)

Llandwrog
(Δ)

Pontllyfni
(Δ)

Llanwn

Pen-y-g

Llanllyfni

Clynnog-
Fawr

Trevor

A 499   522

Trwyn y Gorlech

Yr Eifl

Llanaelhaearn

Llithfaen

564

B 4417

Carreg Ddu

Morfa Nefyn

Nefyn

Y Ffor

Chwilog

Llanystumdwy

Porth Ysgaden

B 4354

A 497

Efailnewydd

A 497

Cricciet
(Δ)

Tudweiliog

312

B 4415

Pwllheli

Llangwnnadl

Sarn Meyllteyrn

(Δ)

Penrhyn Mawr

103

Botwnnog
305

B 4413

13

Llanbedrog

A 499

Tremado

B a y

Aberdaron

Mynydd Mawr

Braich y Pwll   160

Y Rhiw

Llanengan

Abersoch

Bwlchtocyn

St. Tudwal's
Road

St. Tudwal's Islands

Porth Neigwl
or
Hell's Mouth

Trwyn Cilan

Bardsey Sound

Bardsey Island (▲)

E   F   24   G

C A R D I G A N   B A Y

L l e y n   P e n i n s u l a

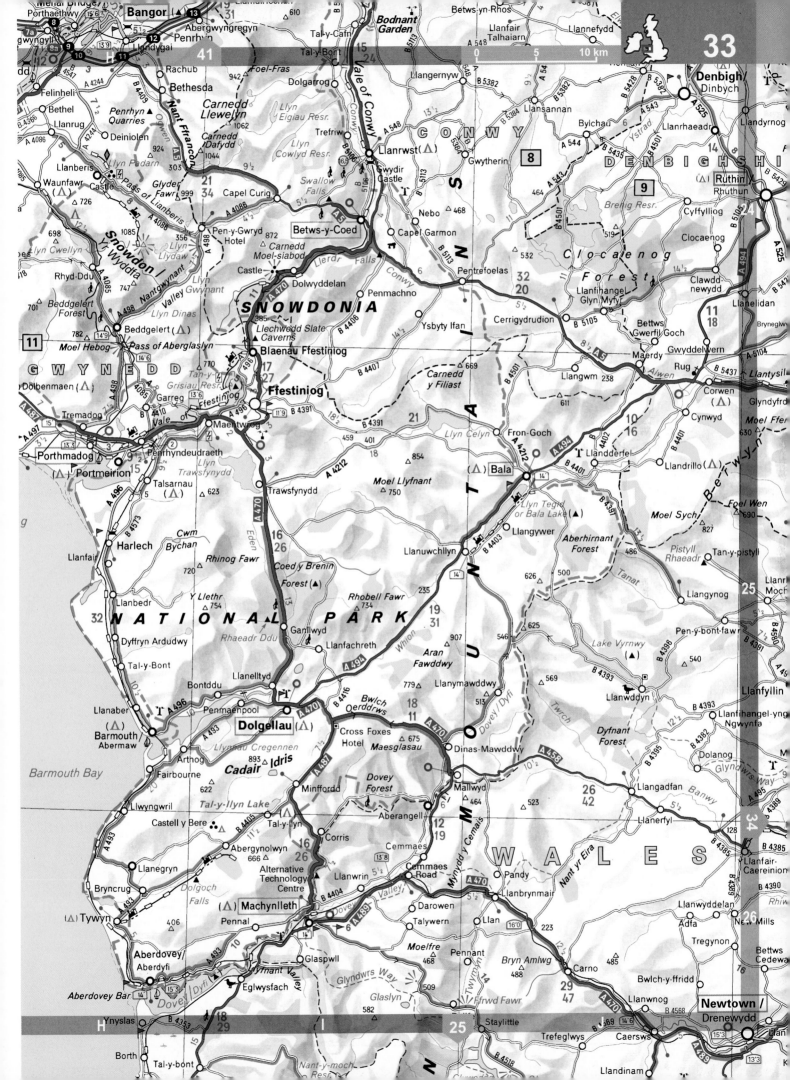

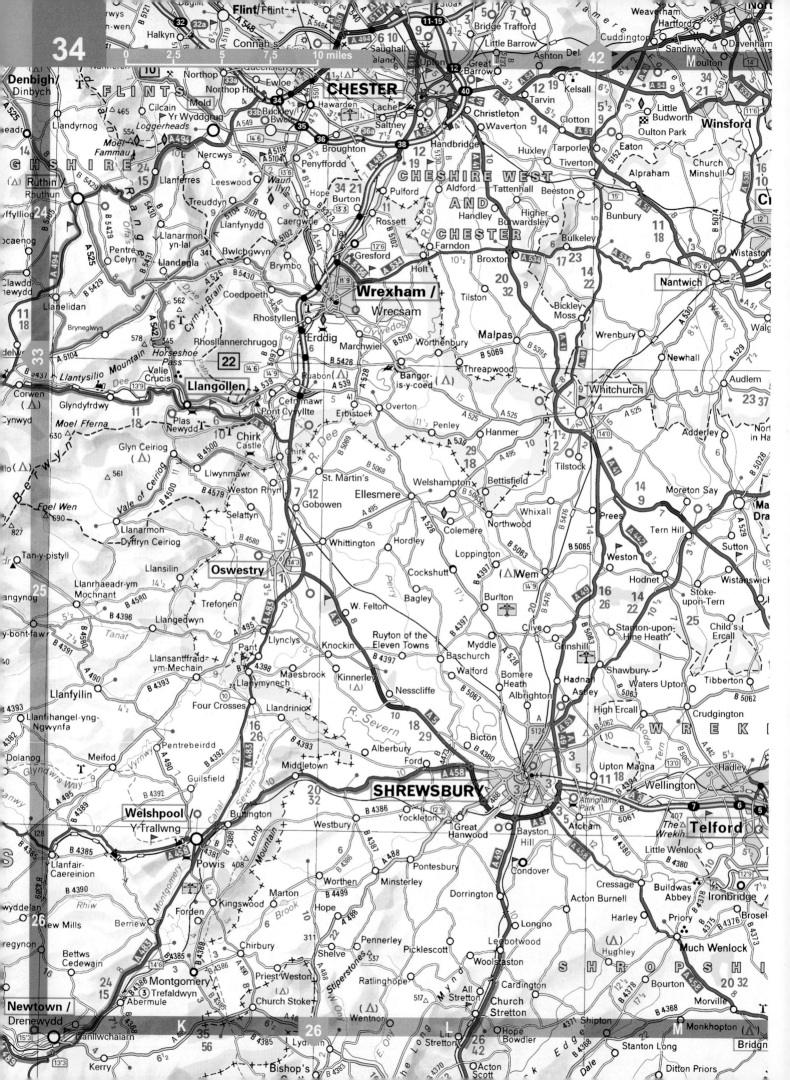

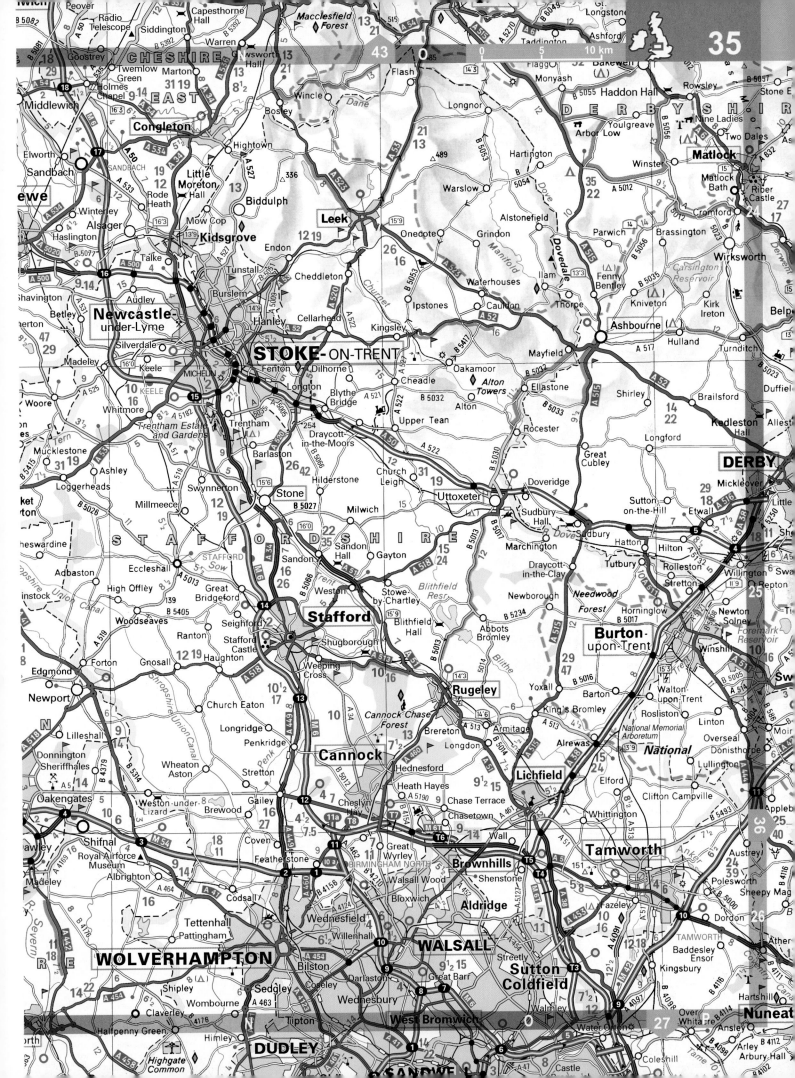

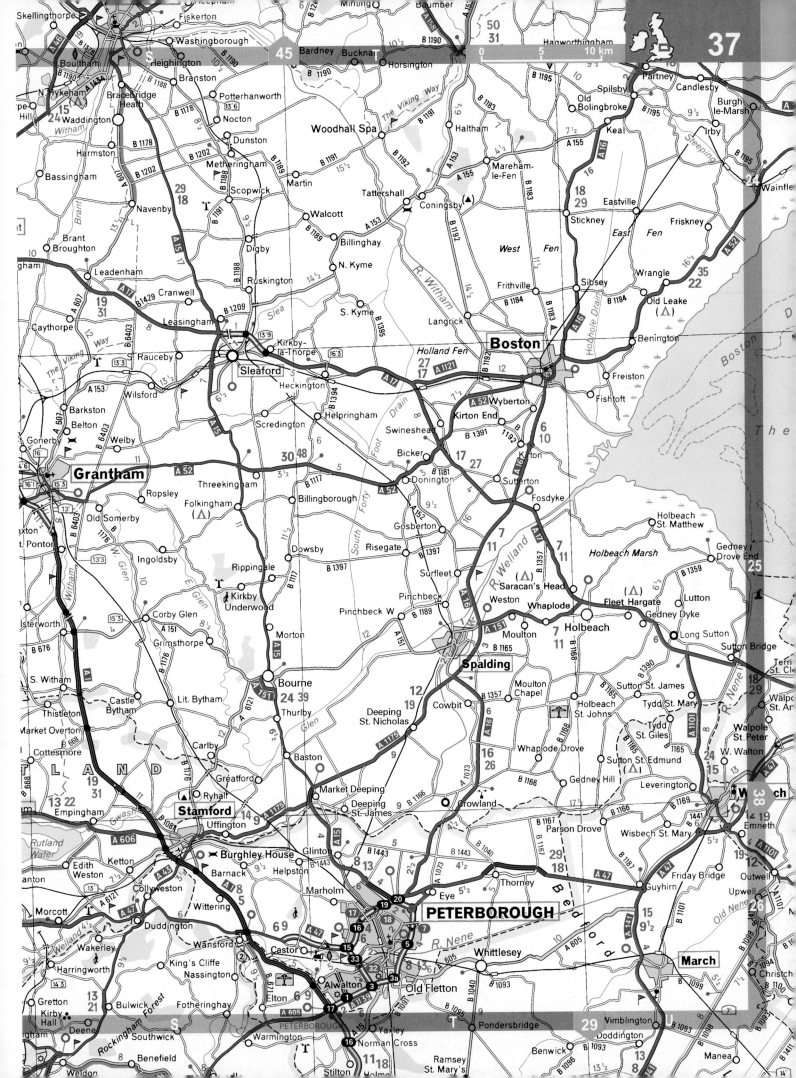

0   2.5   5   7.5   10 miles

W

Chapel St.Leonards

A 52

Burgh-le-Marsh
A 158
Irby
B 1195

Skegness

5½

24

B 1195

Wainfleet All Saints

35

B 52

37

Boston

Deeps

Long Sand

Lynn Deeps

Brancaster Bay

Holkham Bay

Holme-next-the-Sea   Titchwell   17   6   Holkham   Wells-next-the-Sea   Cley-next-the-Sea   Salth

A 149   Brancaster   7   A 149   8   Stiffkey   Blakeney   21   Kelling

The Wash

Hunstanton   Thornham   Burnham Market   B 1155   Holkham Hall   Wighton   Binham   Letheringsett   Bod

(△)   Ringstead   A 149   B 1153   6   B 1355   N. Creake   9   B 1105   Hindringham   12   22   B 1110

B 1161   Heacham   B 1454   Docking   Stanhoe   Creake South   10   Little Walsingham   Great Snoring   Thursford Green   A 148   35   Briston

Sedgeford   10   Great Bircham   Syderstone   B 1355   Sculthorpe   Lit. Snoring   (△)   Barney   Briston

Snettisham (△)   16   Shernborne   9½   B 1454   Tattersett   (△) Fakenham   Hindolveston

Dersingham   Houghton Hall   Harpley   Hempton   A 1067   Wood Dalling

(△) Sandringham House   Castle Rising   B 1439   B 1153   East Rudham   Colkirk   Great Ryburgh   Guist   Foulsham

Babingley   A 149   A 148   Hillington   14   22   35   S. Raynham   9   Whissonsett   B 1110   3½   Reeph

N. Wootton   Grimston   Great Massingham   Weasenham St. Peter   Wellingham   Brisley   N. Elmham   Bawdeswell

S. Wootton   A 148   8   B 1145   Litcham   NORFOLK   Lyng   Wensu

King's Lynn   Gaywood   4½   Gayton   Longham   Swanton Morley   Elsing

Terrington St. Clement   Clenchwarton   12   A 149   7   Castle Acre   Gt. Dunham   **East Dereham**   Hocke

18   Walpole St. Andrew   B 1145   Priory   26   16   Little   A 47   B 1147

29   E. Winch   Narborough   7   Wendling   Necton   12 19   Yaxham   Mattishal

24   Wiggenhall St. Mary Magdalen   W. Winch   22 14   14   Nar   W. Bradenham   A 1075   Shipdham   Garvestone   Barnham Broom

15   **Wisbech**   14   9   Marham   Swaffham   B 1077   Ashill   Cranworth   Kimberley

2 19   Emneth   11   Shouldham   11   Gooderstone   Saham Toney   Hingham   **Wymond**

19 12   A 1101   Stow Bridge   18   Stradsett   18   Yare   45

Outwell   46   A 1122   11   Hilborough   11   Watton   28

Upwell   Downham Market   Crimplesham   Oxburgh Hall   B 1108   Caston   Great Ellingham

26   Nordelph   Denver   W. Dereham   Stoke Ferry   Whittington   Northwold   10   Thompson   Caston   Attleborough

Christchurch   Hilgay   B 1160   13   21   Methwold   B 1108   A 1075

Welney   Southery   B 1386   Mundford   **Thetford**   E. Wretham   Larling   Snetterton

U   30   V   B 1386   Feltwell   Santon Downham   W

Gedney Drove End   25   Sutton   Sutton Bridge   R. Nene   A 17

Walpole St. Peter   Tilney St. Lawrence   W. Walton

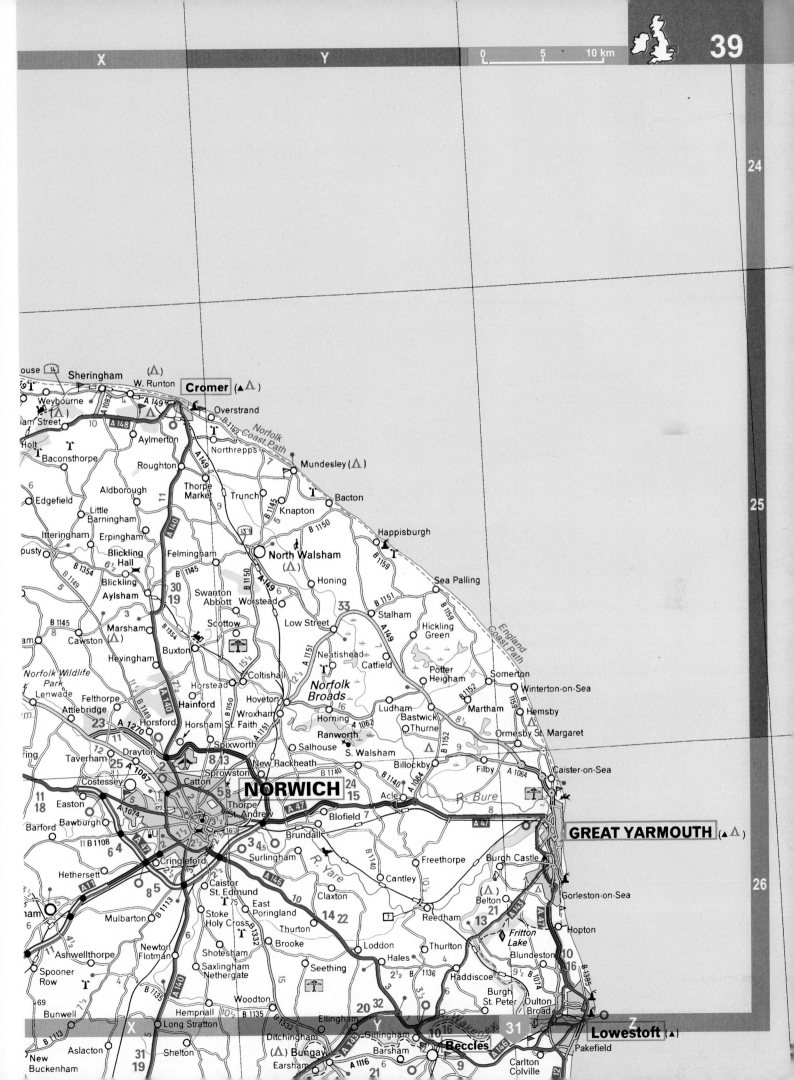

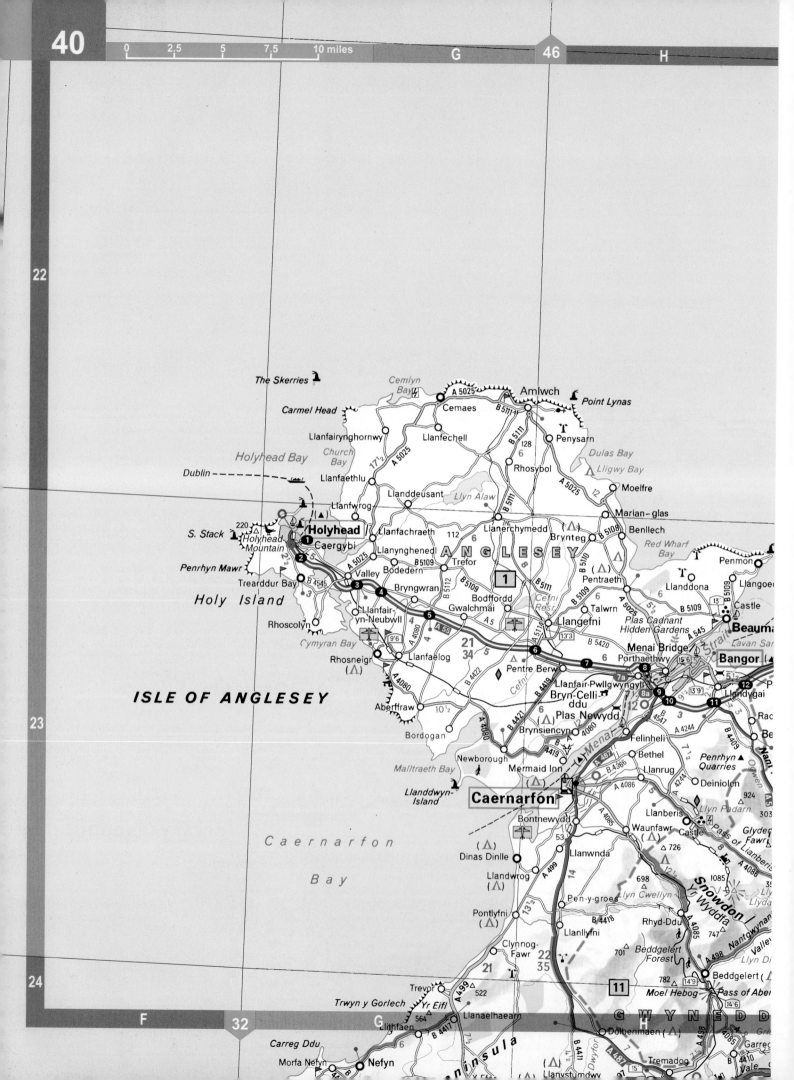

0   2.5   5   7.5   10 miles

22

The Skerries

Cemlyn Bay

A 5025   Amlwch

Carmel Head   Point Lynas

Cemaes

Llanfairynghornwy   Llanfechell   B 5111

Church Bay   128   Penysarn

Holyhead Bay   17²   A 5025   Rhosybol   6

Dublin - - - -   Llanfaethlu   *Dulas Bay*

Llanfwrog   Llanddeusant   *Llygwy Bay*

A 5025   Moelfre

Llyn Alaw

S. Stack   220   Holyhead   Llanfachraeth   112   Marian - glas

Holyhead Mountain   Caergybi   Llanynghenedl   Llanerchymedd   B 5108   Benllech

A N G L E S E Y   Brynteg   B 5110   *Red Wharf Bay*

Penrhyn Mawr   B 5109   Trefor   Penmon

Valley   Bodedern   Pentraeth   Llanddona   B 5109   Llangoed

Trearddur Bay   B 4545   Bryngwran   B 5112   B 5109   Plas Cadnant   Castle

Holy Island   Bodffordd   Talwrn   A 5025   Hidden Gardens   **Beauma**

Rhoscolyn   Llanfair-   Gwalchmai   A 5   *Cefni Res.*   A 545   *Lavan Sar*

yn-Neubwll   A 4080   A 5   Llangefni   B 5420

9'6   A 55   Menai Bridge   **Bangor**

Cymyran Bay   4   13'3   A 5111

Rhosneigr   21   A 5114   6   Porthaethwy   15'6   12

(Δ)   Llanfaelog   34   Pentre Berw   Llanfair-Pwllgwyngyll   7a   8a   9   13'9   Llandygai

ISLE OF ANGLESEY   A 4080   B 4419   Bryn-Celli-   8   10   11

ddu   *Cefni*   Plas Newydd   12

Aberffraw   10½   A 4421   Brynsiencyn   A 4080   4547   A 4244   B 4409

Bordogan   A 4080   Plas Newydd   A 487

Malltraeth Bay   Newborough   Mermaid Inn   Bethel   B 4366   Llanrug   Penrhyn   Quarries

Caernarfon   Bontnewydd   Felinheli   7½   Deiniolen   924

Bay   *Llanddwyn Island*   **Caernarfon**   53   A 4086   Llanberis   Castle   303

Dinas Dinlle   Waunfawr   *Llyn Padarn*   Glyder   Fawr

Llandwrog   A 499   Δ 726   *Pass of Llanberis*   A 4086

(Δ)   14   1085

Pontllyfni   13½   Pen-y-groes   698   *Llyn Cwellyn*   **Snowdon**   Yr Wyddfa   *Llydaw*

(Δ)   Llanllyfni   B 4418   Rhyd-Ddu   A 4085   747

Clynnog-   701   *Beddgelert Forest*   *Nantgwynant*

Fawr   22   *Moel Hebog*   *Llyn Di*

21   35   782   14'6   **Beddgelert**

Trevor   **11**   Pass of Aber

Trwyn y Gorlech   522   Moel Hebog   14'6

Yr Eifl   564   Llanaelhaearn

Llithfaen   B 4417   6   **G W Y N E D D**

Carreg Ddu   Dolbenmaen   A 498

Morfa Nefyn   Nefyn   B 4411   Tremadog   A 4410   Garreg

Llanystumdwy   15

22

23

24

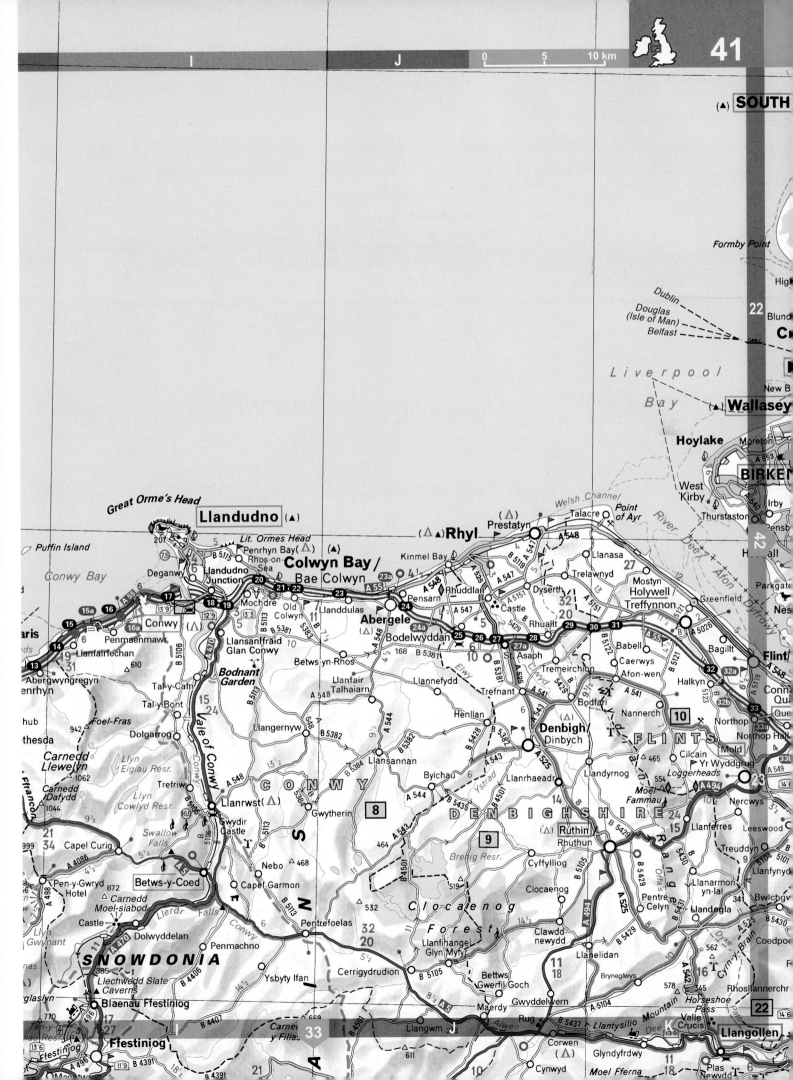

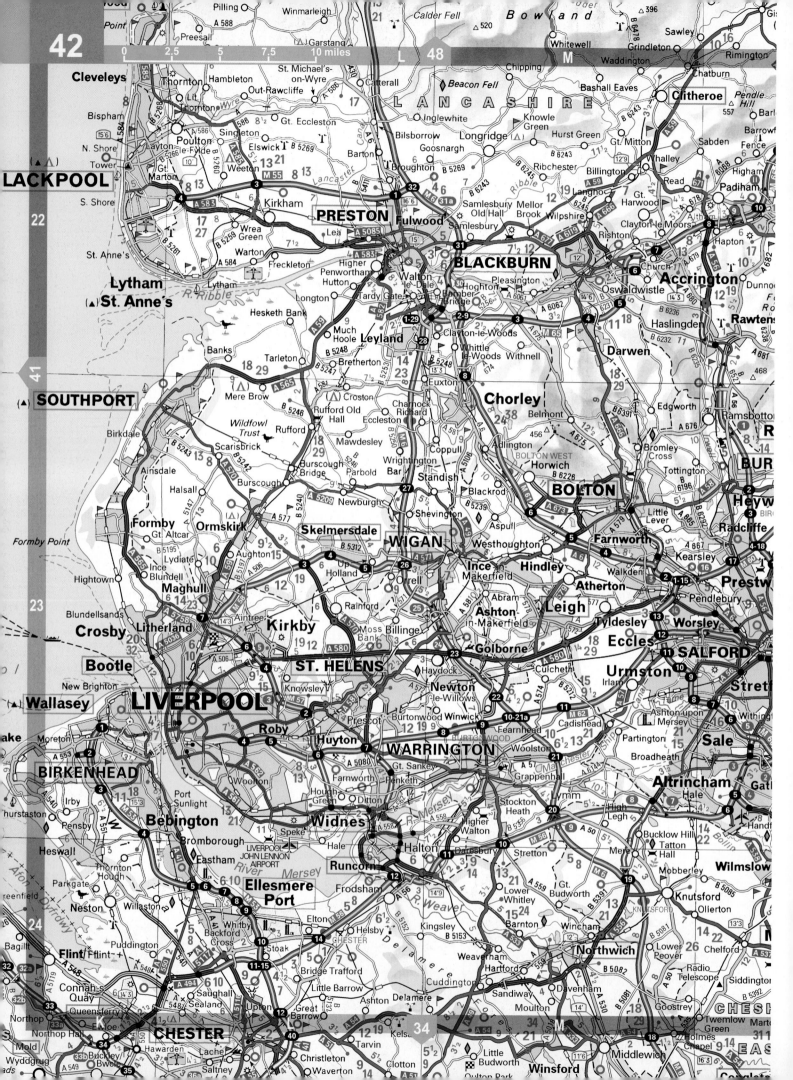

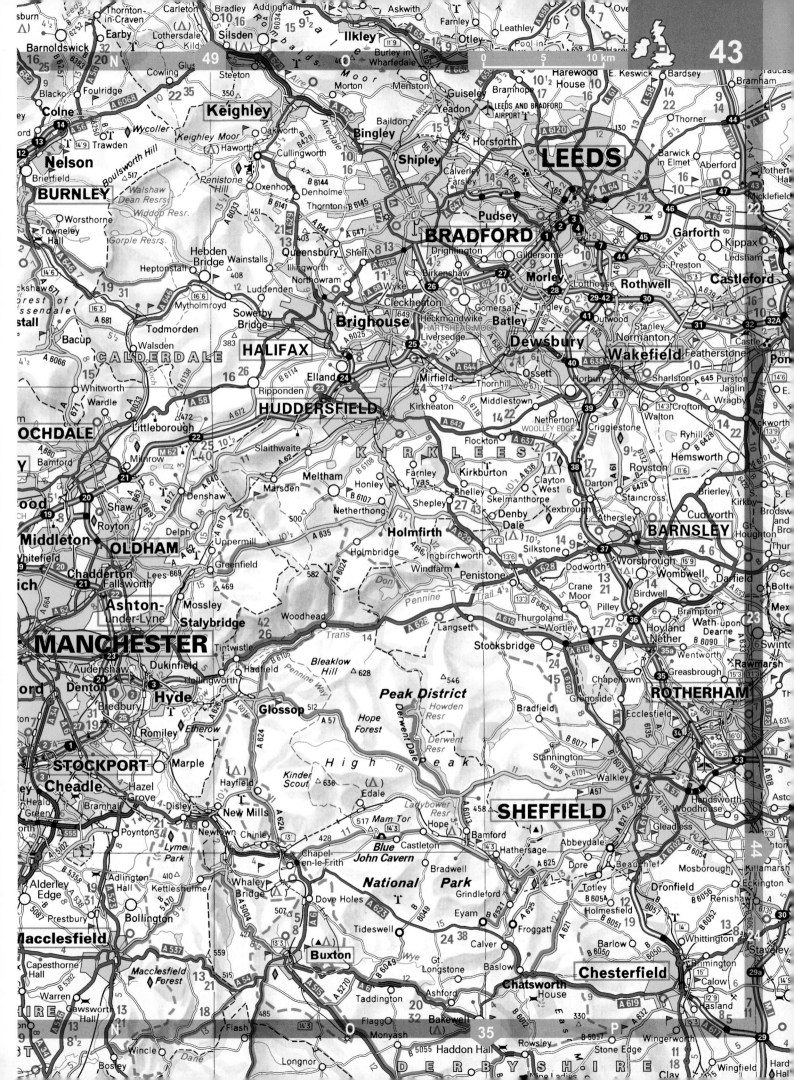

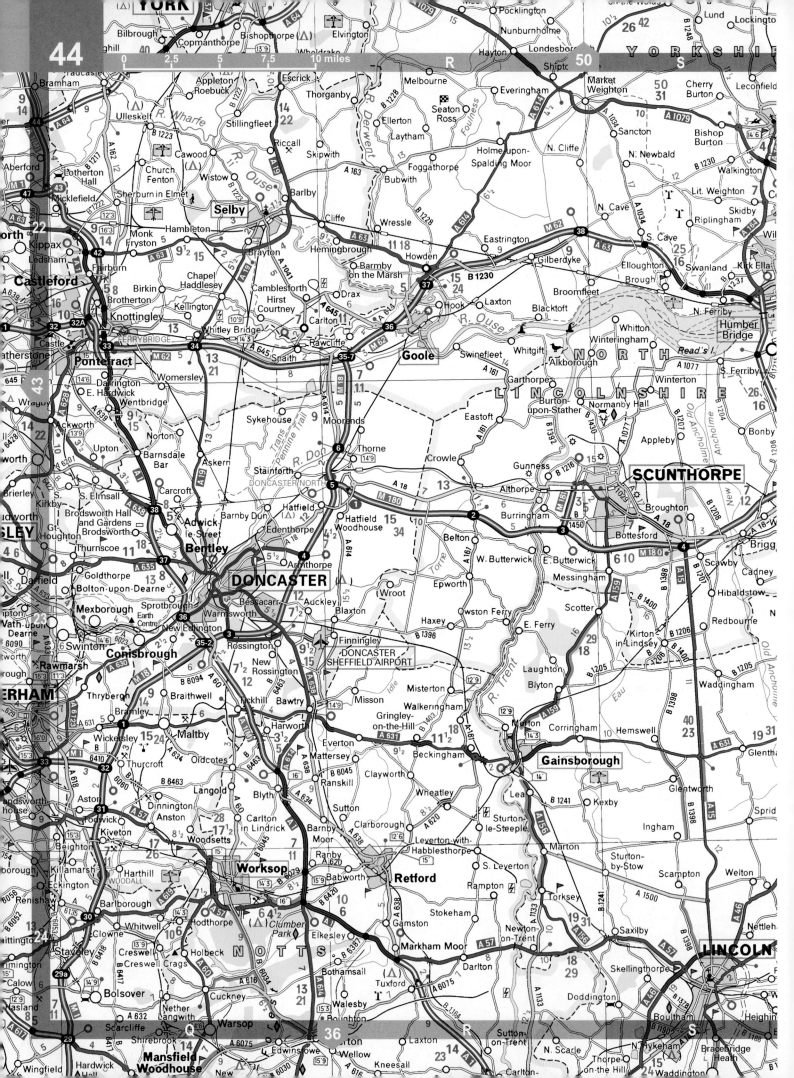

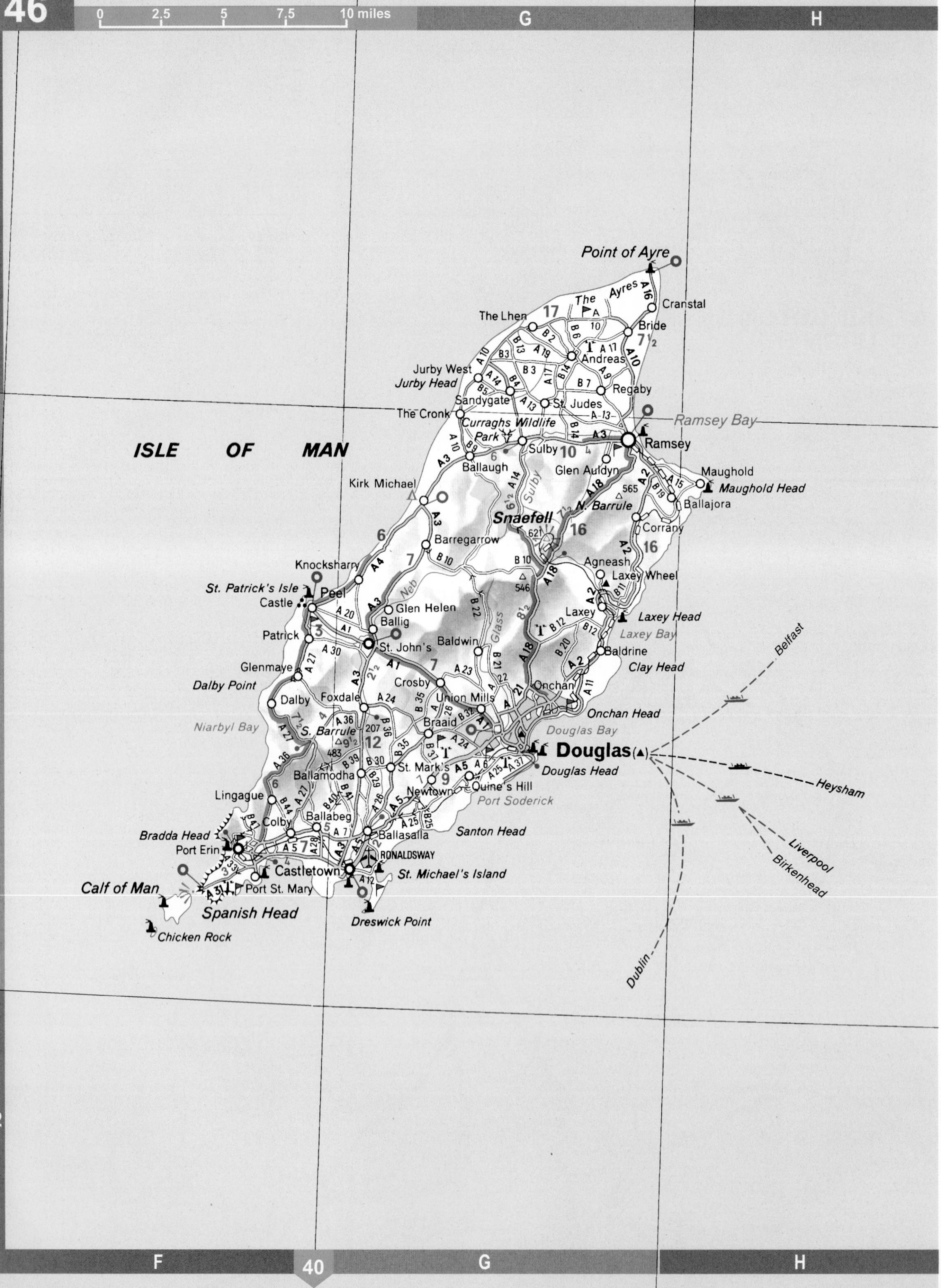

0   2.5   5   7.5   10 miles

20

21

22

Point of Ayre

The Ayres A 16   Cranstal

The Lhen   **17**   A   Bride   7½

B 2   B 6   10   A 10

A 10   B 3   B 13   A 19   A 17   A 10

Jurby West   B 14   Andreas

Jurby Head   B 5   B 4   A 17   A 9   A 10

A 14   A 13   St. Judes   B 7   Regaby

Sandygate   A 13   A 13

The Cronk   *Curraghs Wildlife*   *Ramsey Bay*

A 10   *Park*   B 14   A 3   Ramsey

ISLE   OF   MAN   B 9   Sulby   **10**   4

A 10   6   Ballaugh   Glen Auldyn   Maughold

Kirk Michael   A 14   A 18   565   *Maughold Head*

A 3   *Sulby*   N. Barrule   B 19   A 15   Ballajora

6   *Snaefell*   **16**   Corrany

Barregarrow   621   A 2   **16**

7   B 10   B 10   A 18   Agneash   A 2

Knocksharry   A 4   546   Laxey Wheel   B 11

St. Patrick's Isle   *Neb*   A 2   Laxey   *Laxey Head*

Castle   Peel   Glen Helen   8½   B 12   B 12   *Laxey Bay*

A 20   Ballig   A 18   B 20   Baldrine

Patrick   **3**   A 1   St. John's   Baldwin   *Glass*   A 2   *Clay Head*

A 30   **7**   B 21   22   Onchan

Glenmaye   A 27   A 3   Crosby   A 23   A 21   A 11

Dalby Point   2½   A 24   B 35   Union Mills   *Onchan Head*

Niarbyl Bay   Dalby   Foxdale   B 31   *Douglas Bay*

4   A 36   207   B 36   Braaid   A 1

7½ S. Barrule   9½   B 35   A 24   **Douglas** (▲)

A 27   483   B 39   B 30   St. Mark's   A 5   A 6   *Douglas Head*

12   1   **9**   Quine's Hill

Ballamodha   B 29   Newtown   A 25   A 37

6   Lingague   B 29   A 5   A 25   *Port Soderick*

B 41   Colby   Ballabeg   A 7   Ballasalla   *Santon Head*

Bradda Head   B 41   **5**   A 3

Port Erin   A 5   **7**   RONALDSWAY

3¾   A 31   Castletown   A 12   *St. Michael's Island*

Calf of Man   Port St. Mary   A 12

Spanish Head   *Dreswick Point*

Chicken Rock

Belfast

Heysham

Liverpool

Birkenhead

Dublin

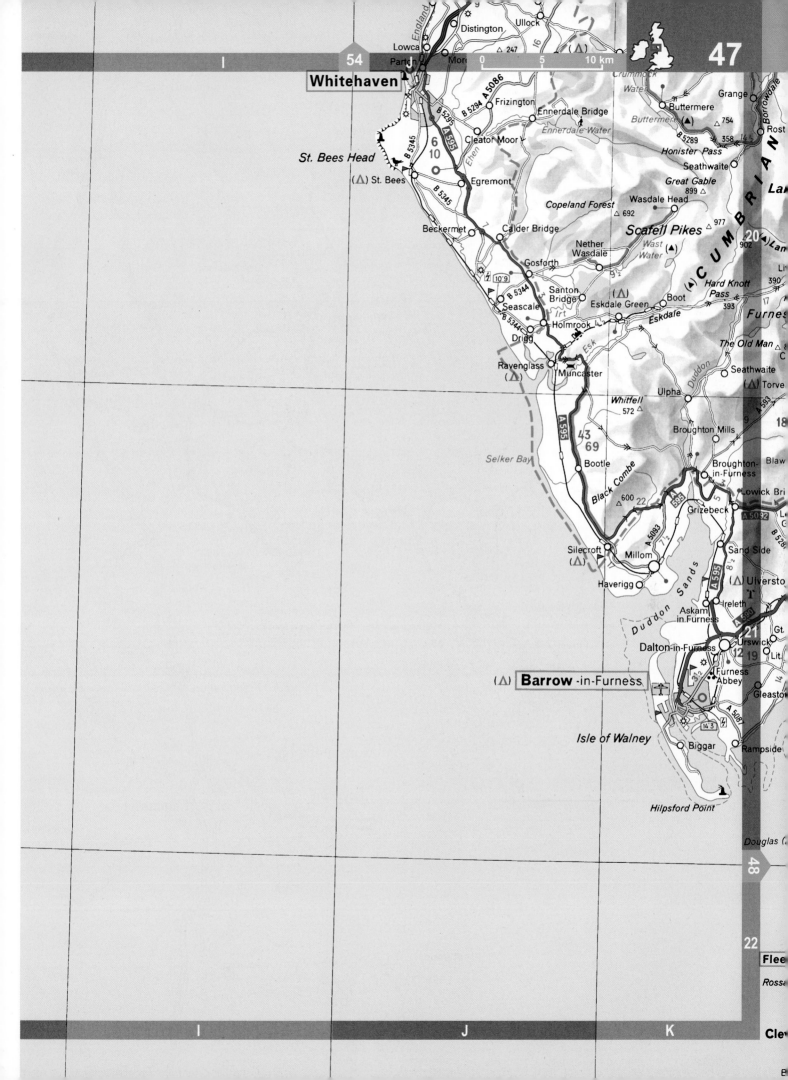

Whitehaven

St. Bees Head

(△) St. Bees

Beckermet

Seascale

Drigg

Ravenglass
(△)

Selker Bay

Silecroft
(△)

Haverigg

(△) Barrow -in-Furness

Isle of Walney

Hilpsford Point

Distington
Ullock
Lowca
Parton
Mor

Frizington
Ennerdale Bridge
Cleator Moor
Egremont
Calder Bridge
Gosforth
Santon
Bridge
Holmrook
Muncaster
Bootle

Millom
Sand Side

Askam
in Furness
Ireleth
Dalton-in-Furness
Urswick
Furness
Abbey
Biggar
Rampside
Gleasto

Distington
△ 247
16
(△)

Crummock
Water
Grange
Buttermere
Buttermere (△)
△ 754
B 5289 △ 358
Honister Pass
Seathwaite

Ennerdale Water

Great Gable
899 △
Copeland Forest
Wasdale Head
△ 692
△ 977
Scafell Pikes

Nether
Wasdale
Wast
Water
(△)
Eskdale Green
Boot
Eskdale
393

Hard Knott
Pass

Furnes
The Old Man
Seathwaite
(△) Torve
Ulpha
Whitfell
572 △
Broughton Mills
Broughton-
in-Furness
Blaw
Lowick Bri
Grizebeck
Black Combe
△ 600
22

Gt.
12 19
Lit.

CUMBRIAN La

20
902
Lan
Lit
390
17

18

B 5295 A 5086

B 5294
B 5595
A 595
6
10
B 5345

B 5345
7

B 5344
10'9

B 5344

A 595

43
69

A 5093

A 595
A 5092

A 590
21

A 5087
14 3

England

0   5   10 km

I

I

J

J

K

48

22

Douglas (

Flee
Rossa
Clev

Ehen

Irt

Esk

Esk

Duddon

Duddon Sands

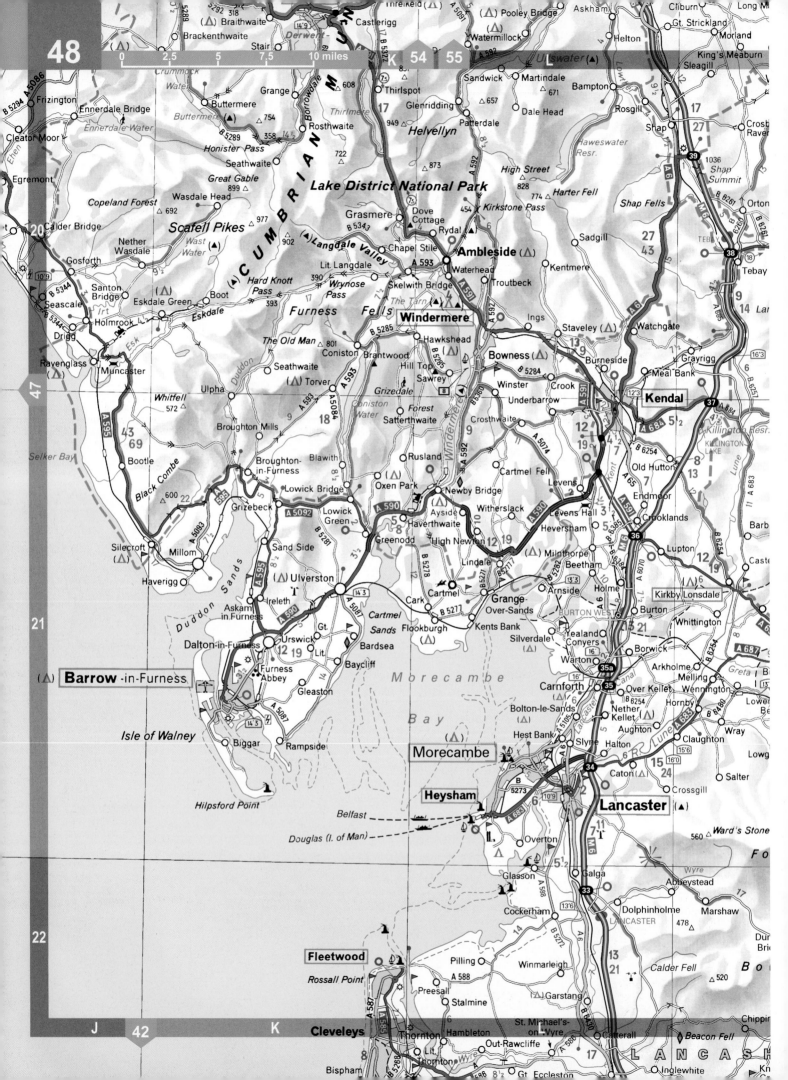

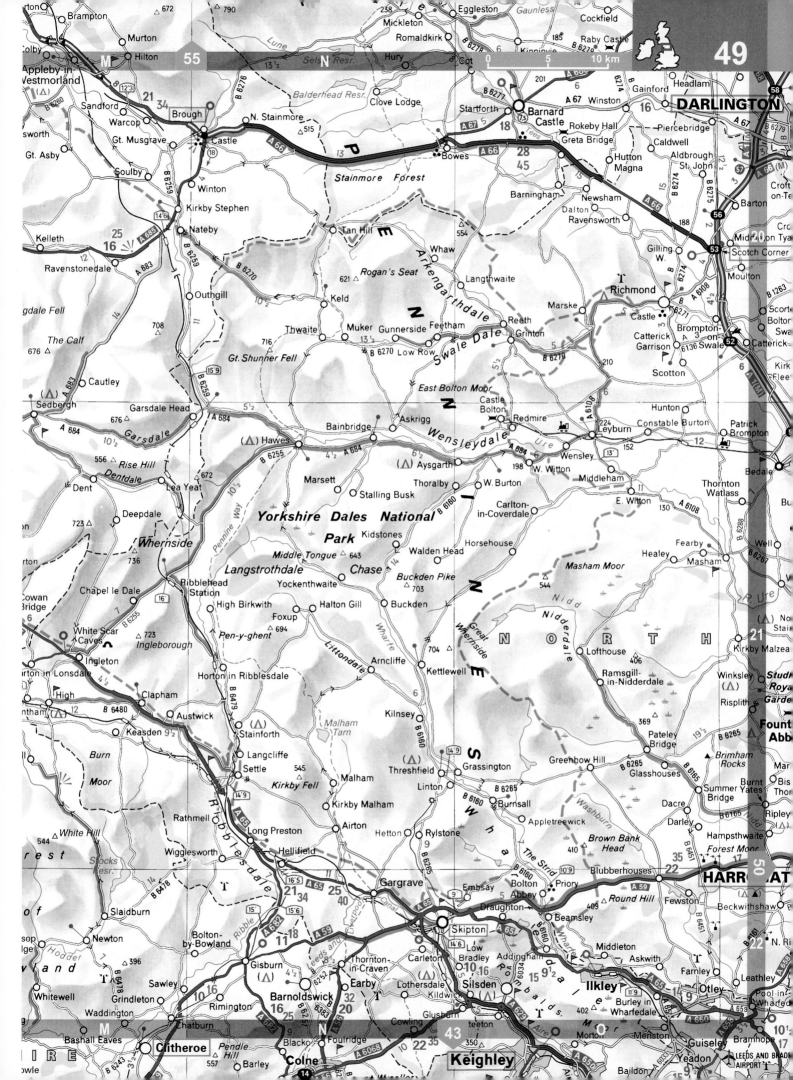

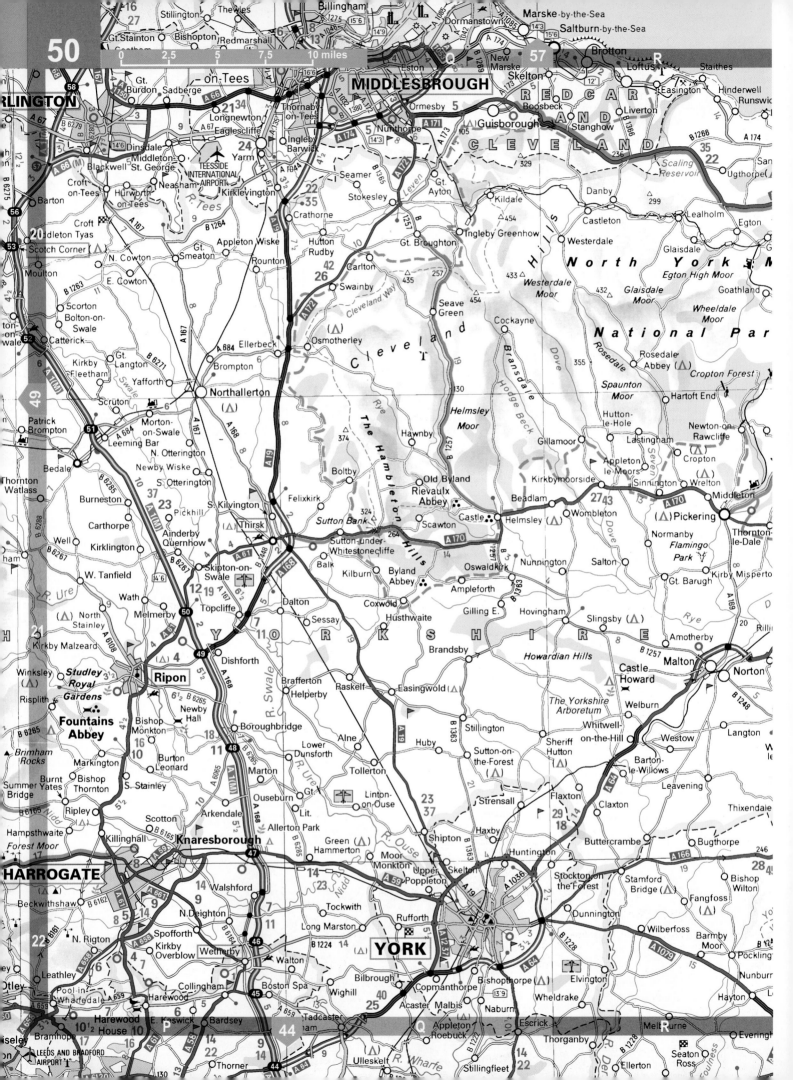

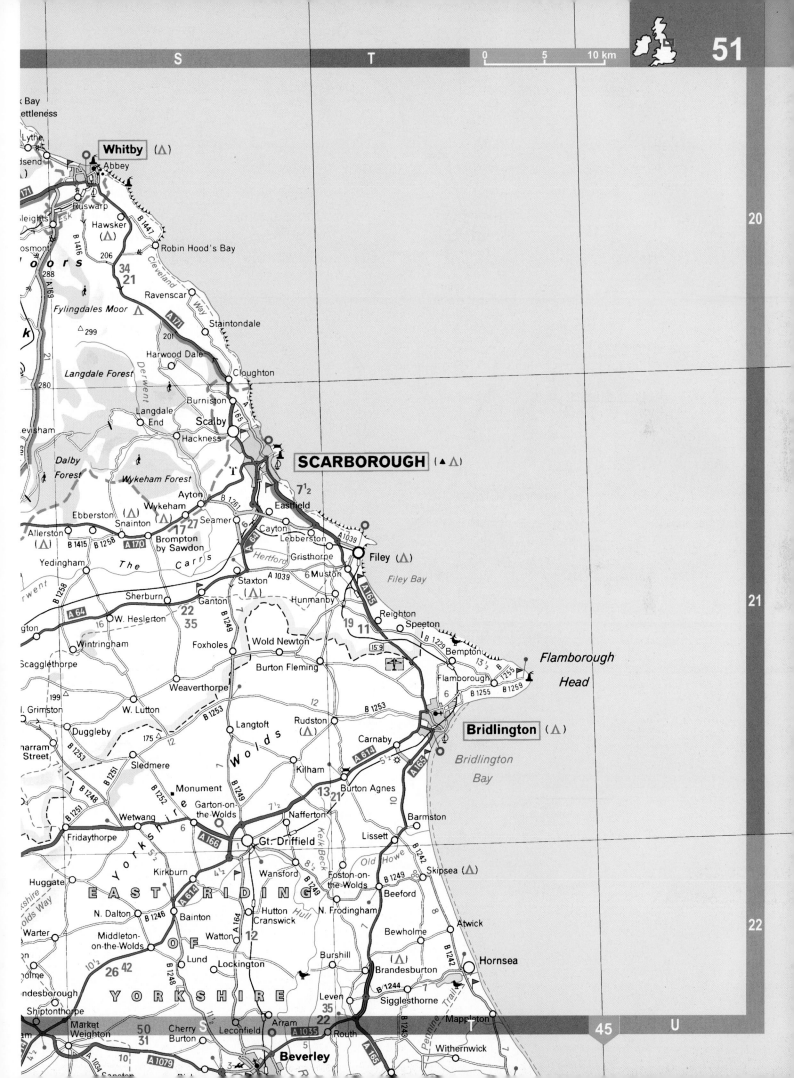

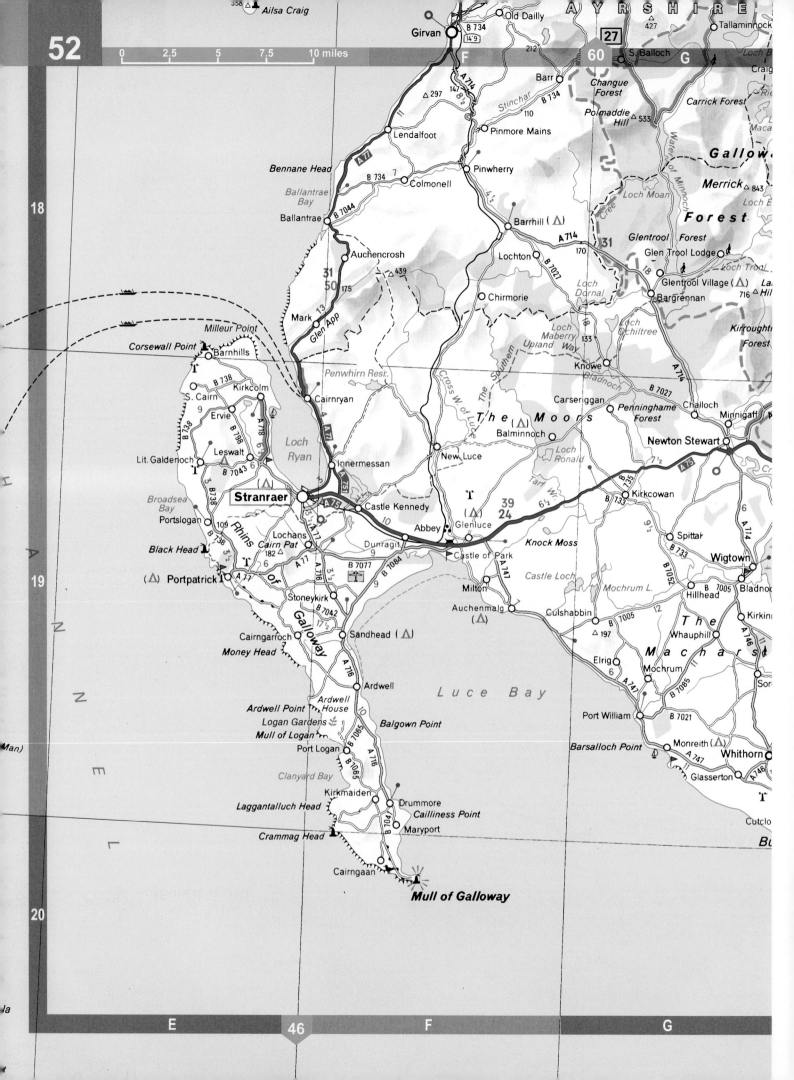

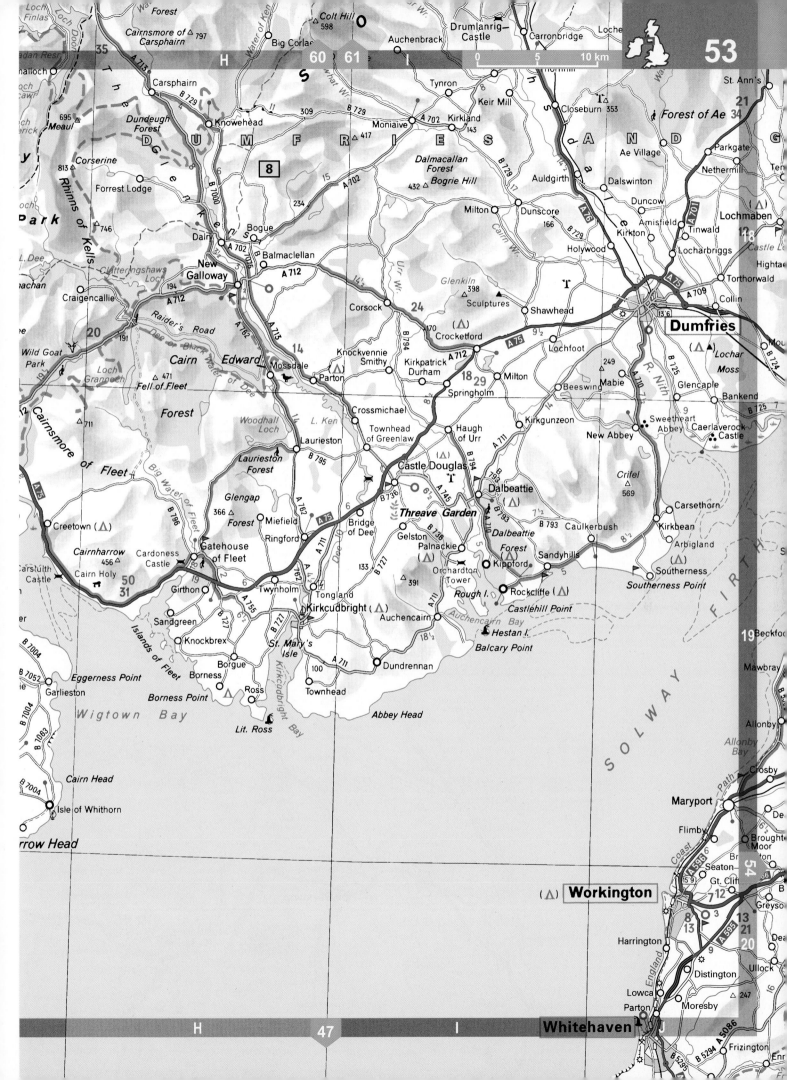

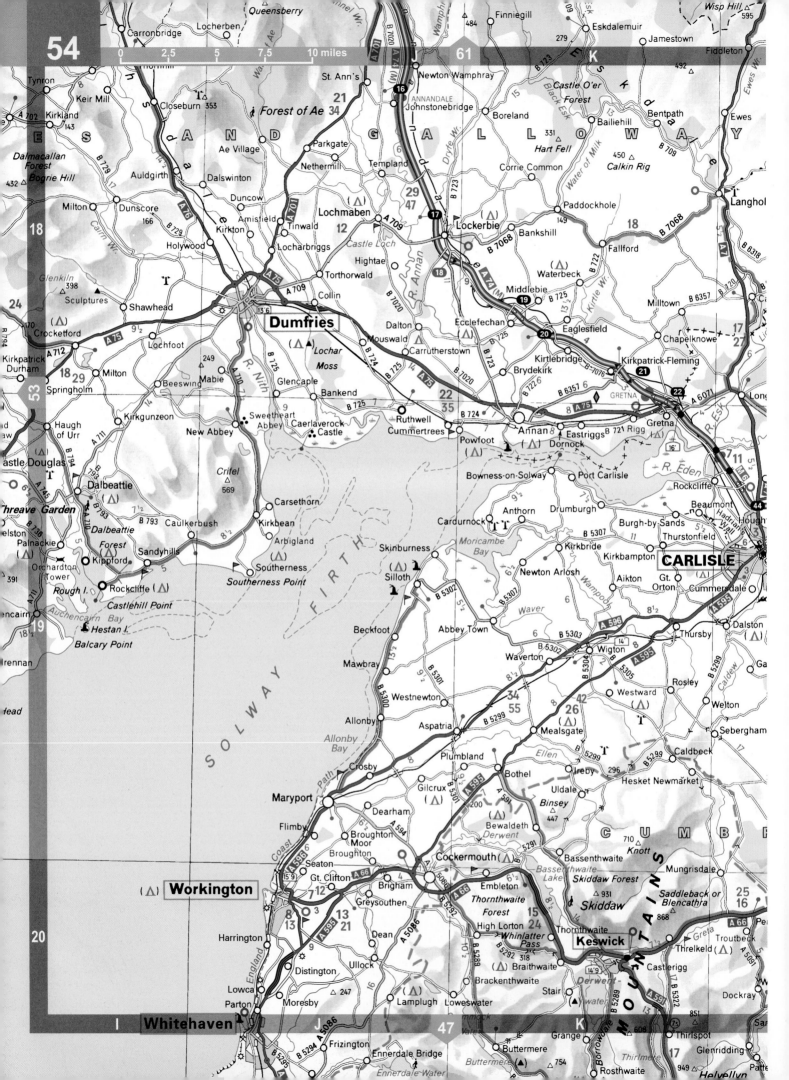

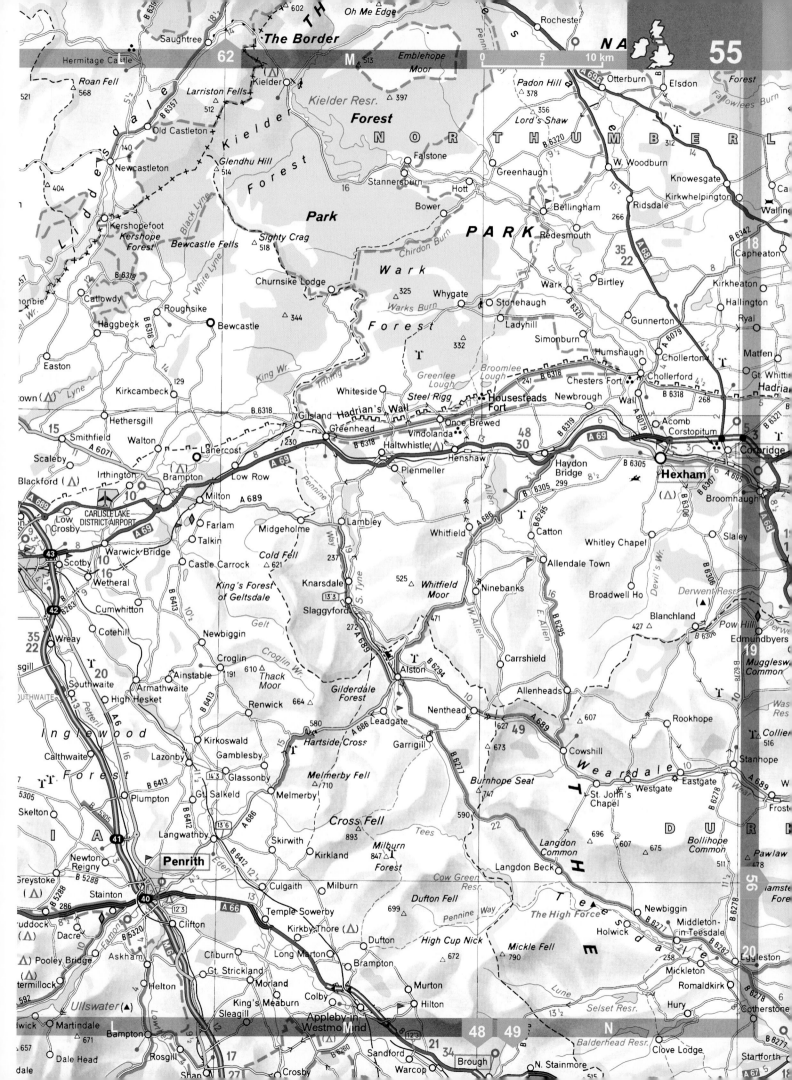

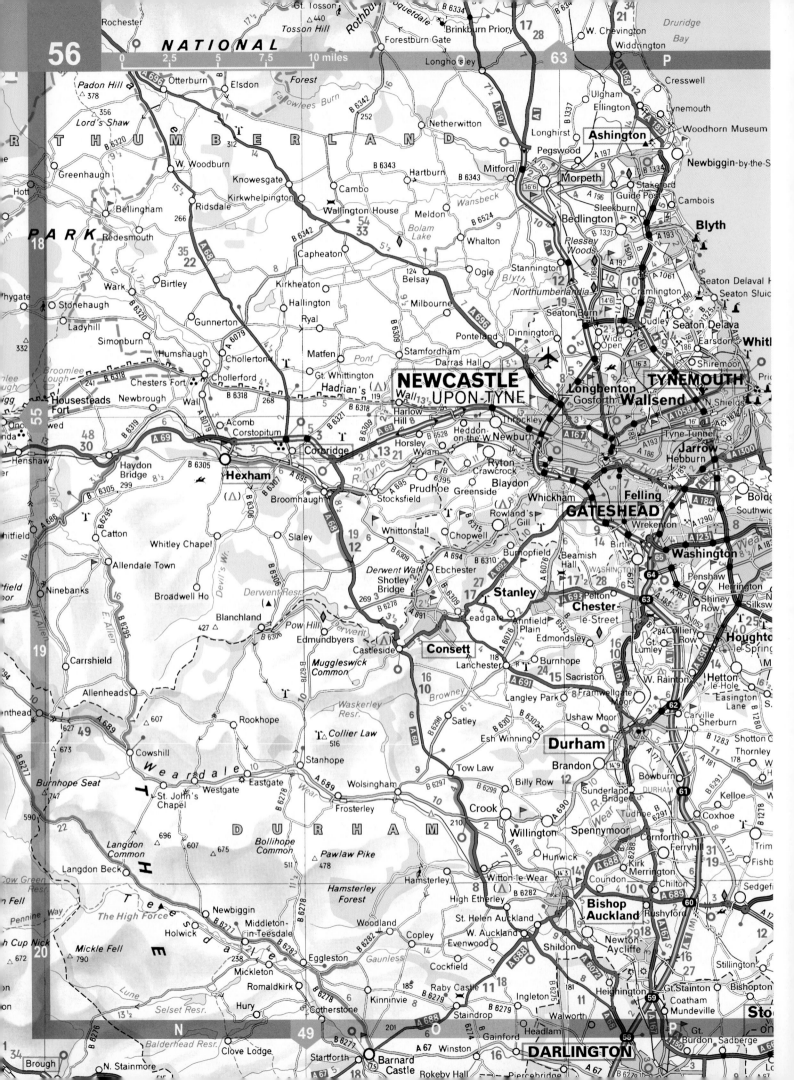

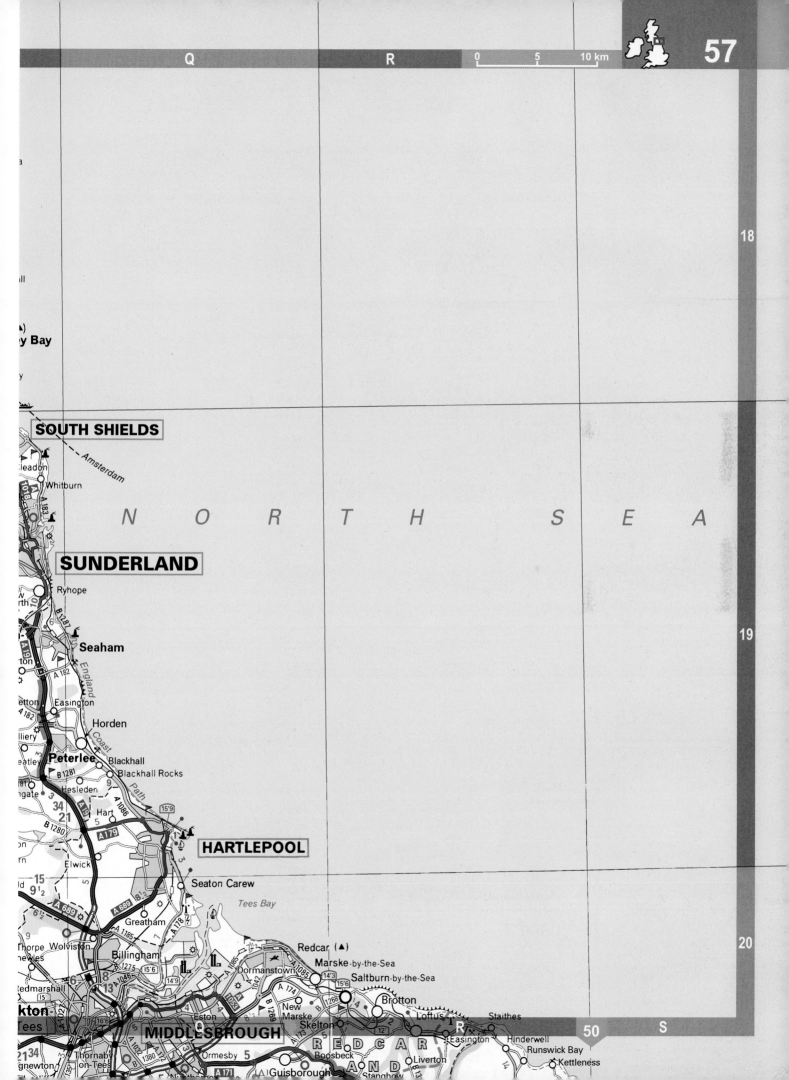

0 5 10 km

18

SOUTH SHIELDS

Amsterdam

Cleadon

Whitburn

N O R T H   S E A

SUNDERLAND

Ryhope

19

Seaham

England

Easington

Horden

Coast

Peterlee

Blackhall

Blackhall Rocks

Hesleden

Path

Hart

15'9

A 1086

Elwick

HARTLEPOOL

15

9½

Seaton Carew

Tees Bay

Greatham

20

Thorpe Wolviston

Billingham

Redcar (▲)

Marske-by-the-Sea

Dormanstown

Saltburn-by-the-Sea

14'3

15'6

13

New Marske

Brotton

Eston

Skelton

Loftus

Staithes

50

MIDDLESBROUGH

Thornaby-on-Tees

Ormesby

R E D C A R

Boosbeck

Easington

Hinderwell

Runswick Bay

Liverton

Kettleness

A N D

Guisborough

Stanghow

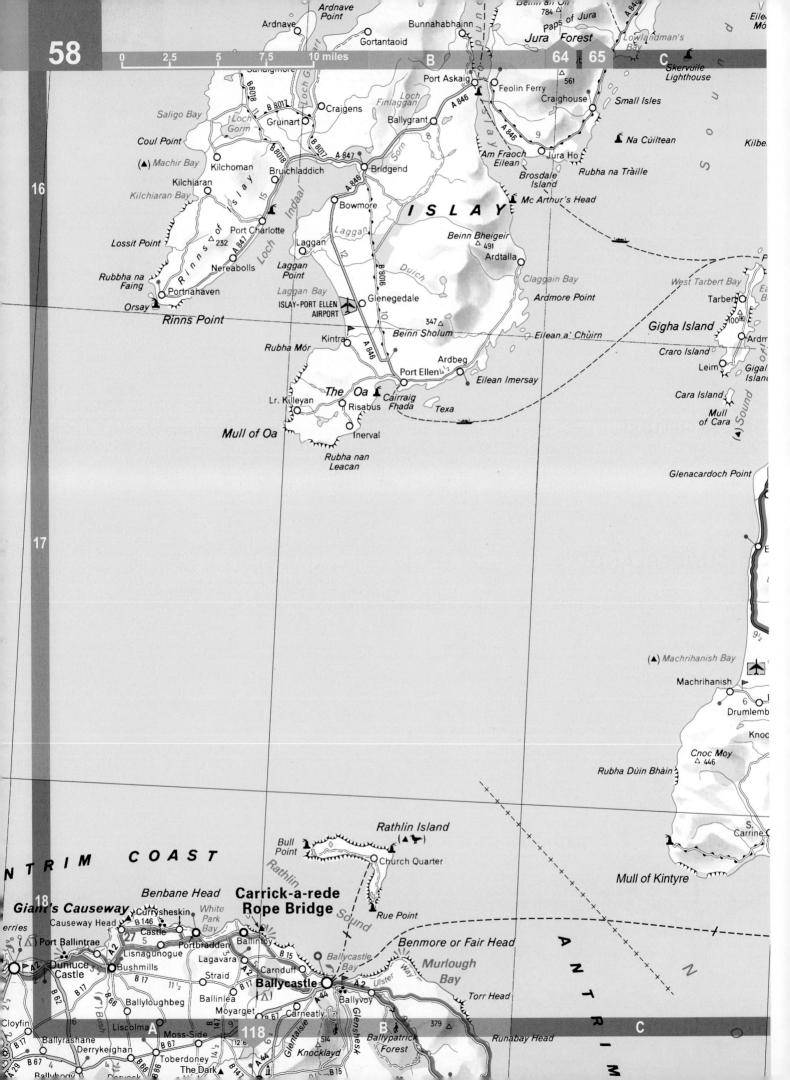

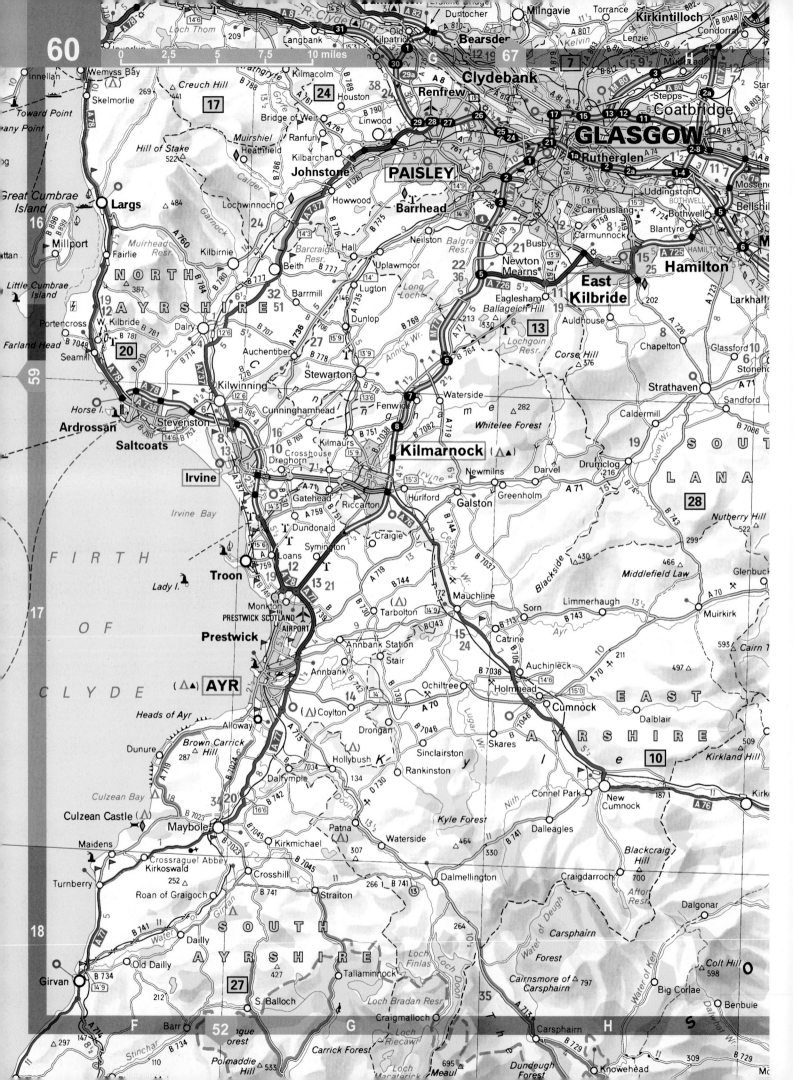

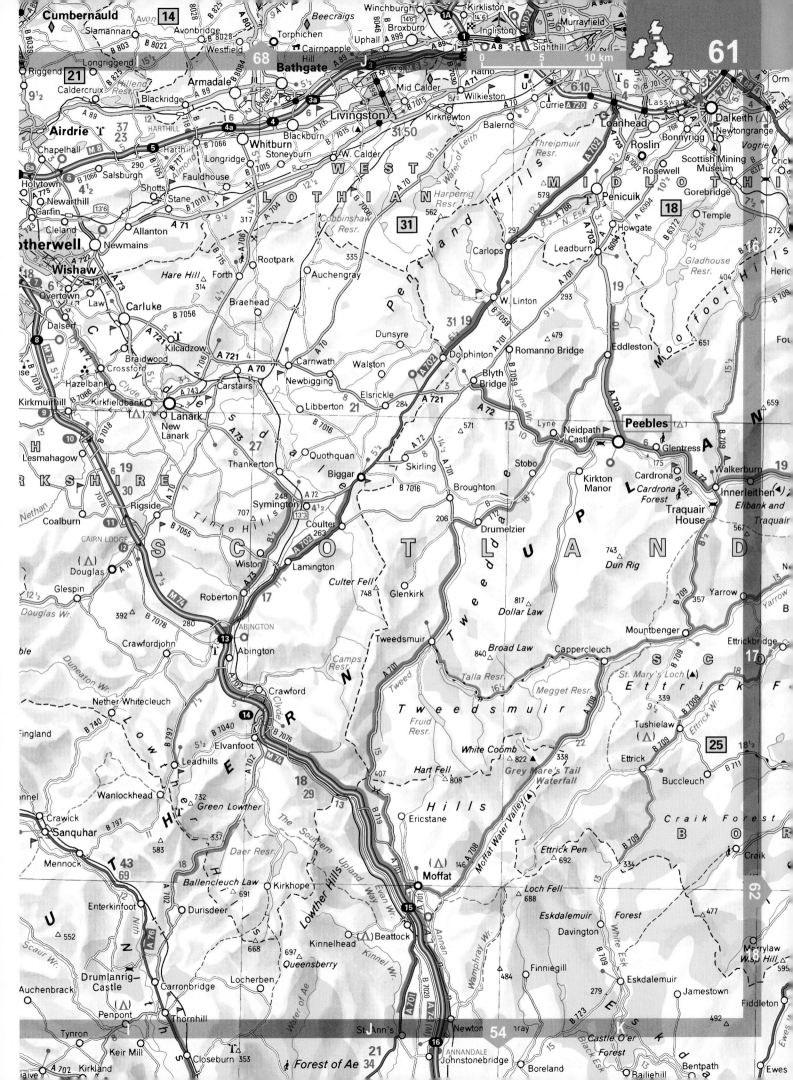

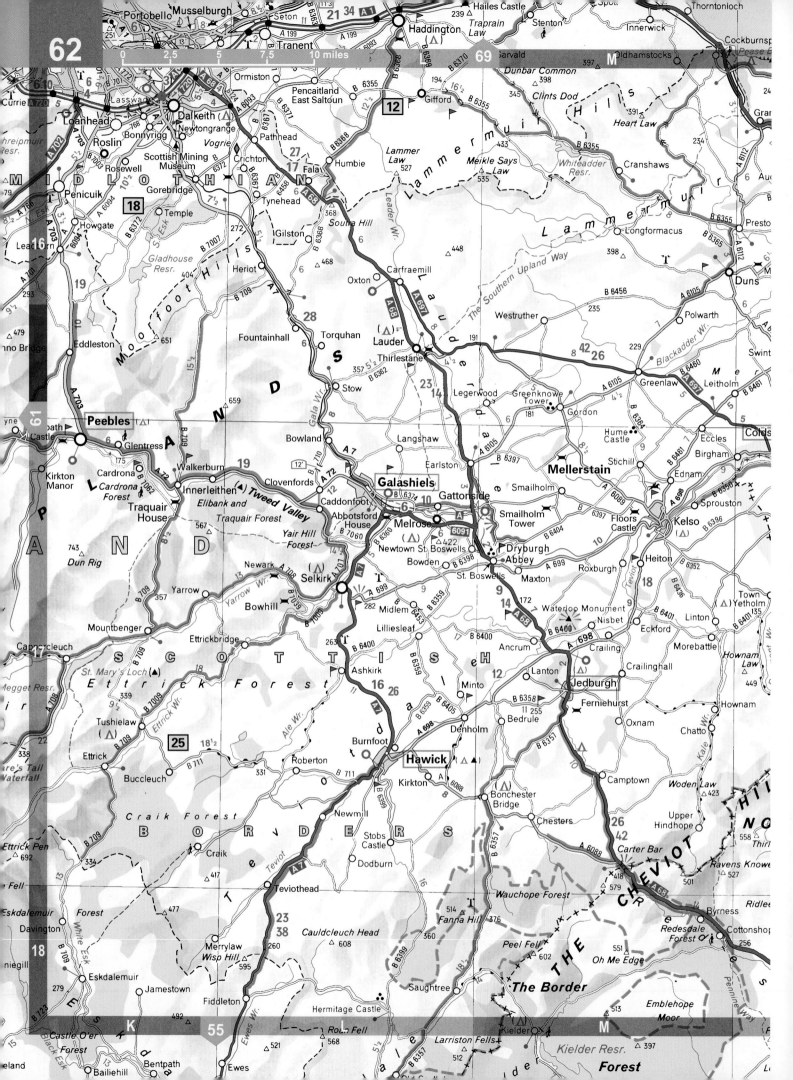

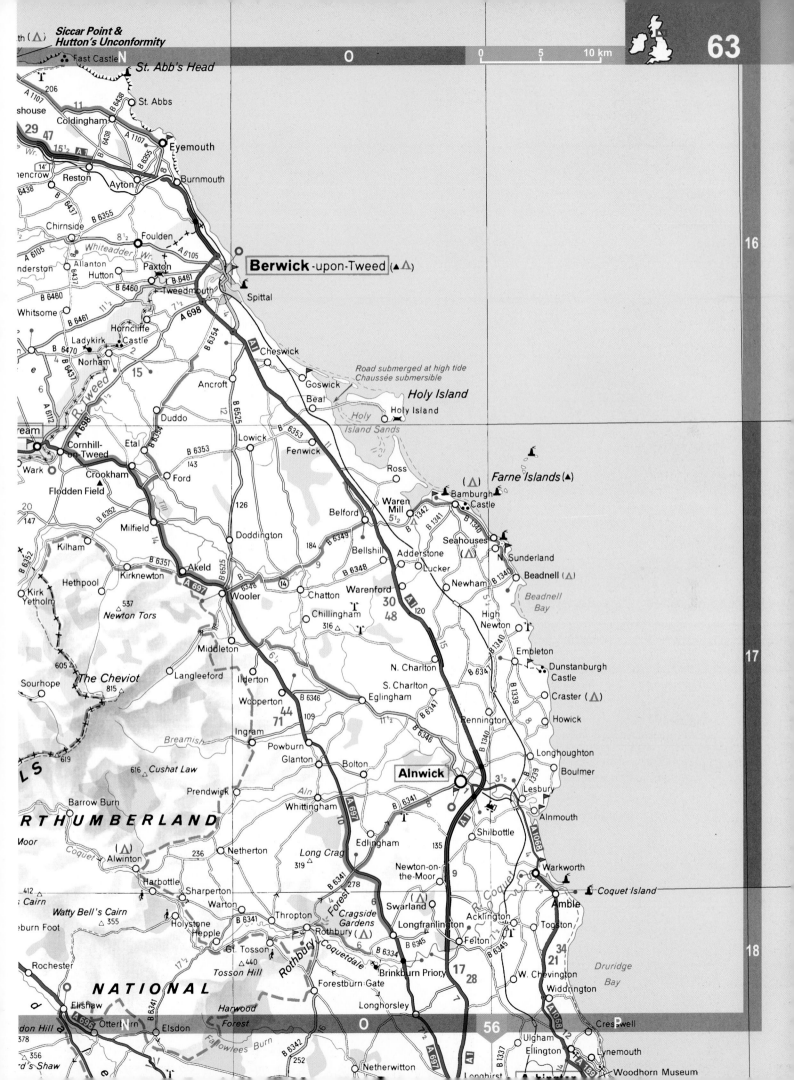

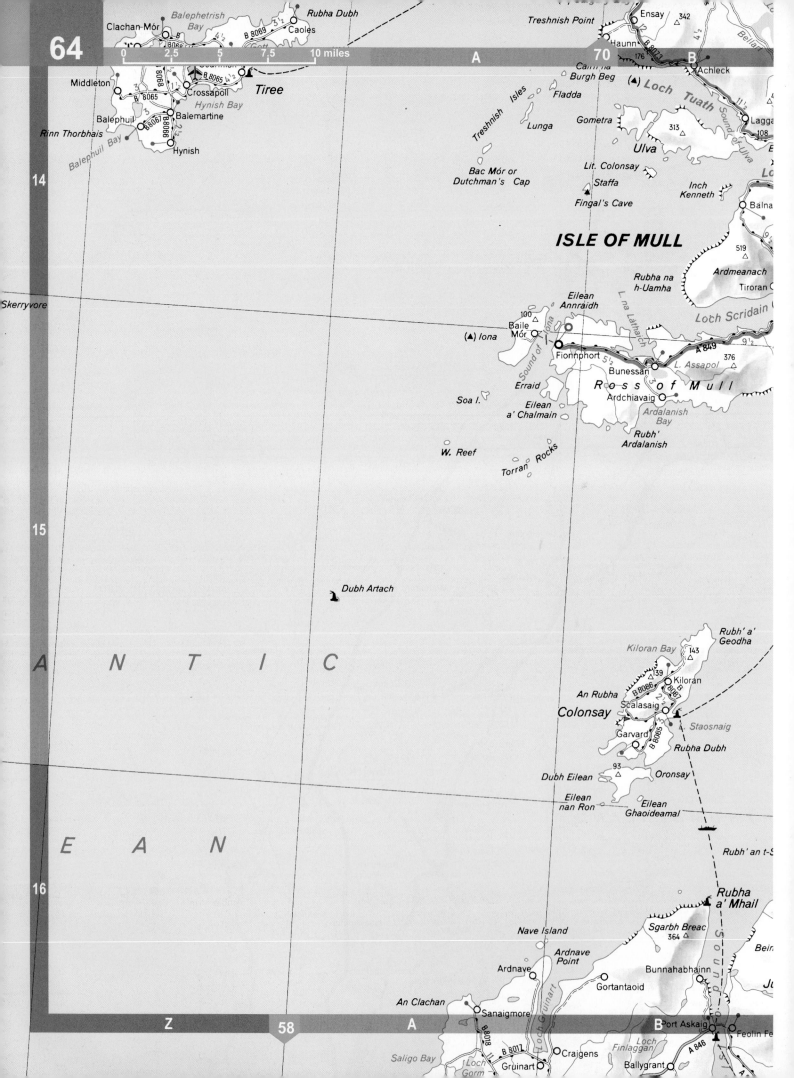

Balephetrish Bay

Rubha Dubh

Clachan-Mór

B 8069

Caoles

B 8069

Gott

0   2.5   5   7.5   10 miles

Middleton

B 8068

B 8065

Tiree

Crossapoll

Hynish Bay

Balephuil

B 8067 B 8066

Balemartine

Rinn Thorbhais

Hynish

Balephuil Bay

Treshnish Point

Ensay   342

Haunn   176

B 8073

Achleck

Carn na Burgh Beg

(▲)

Loch Tuath

Fladda

Lagga   108

Sound of Ulva

Treshnish Isles

Lunga

Gometra   313

Ulva

Lit. Colonsay

Inch Kenneth

Bac Mór or Dutchman's Cap

Staffa

▲

Fingal's Cave

Balna

ISLE OF MULL

Rubha na h-Uamha

Ardmeanach

Tiroran

Skerryvore

519

L. na Làthaich

Loch Scridain

Eilean Annraidh

100

△

Baile Mór

(▲) Iona

Fionnphort

5½

Bunessan

Erraid

Soa I.

Eilean a' Chalmain

A 849   9½

L. Assapol   376

3½

Ross of Mull

Ardchiavaig

Ardalanish Bay

Rubh' Ardalanish

W. Reef

Torran Rocks

Dubh Artach

Rubh' a' Geodha

Kiloran Bay   143   △

△ 139

Kiloran

An Rubha

B 8086

B 8087

2½

Colonsay

Scalasaig

Garvard

B 8085

3

Staosnaig

Rubha Dubh

Dubh Eilean

93   △

Oronsay

Eilean nan Ron

Eilean Ghaoideamal

Rubh' an t-S

Rubha a' Mhail

Nave Island

Sgarbh Breac   364   △

Ardnave Point

Ardnave

Bunnahabhainn

An Clachan

Sanaigmore

Gortantaoid

B 8018

Port Askaig

Feolin Fe

Saligo Bay

Loch Gorm

B 8017

Craigens

Loch Finlaggan

Ballygrant

A 846

Loch Gruinart

Gruinart

A N T I C

E A N

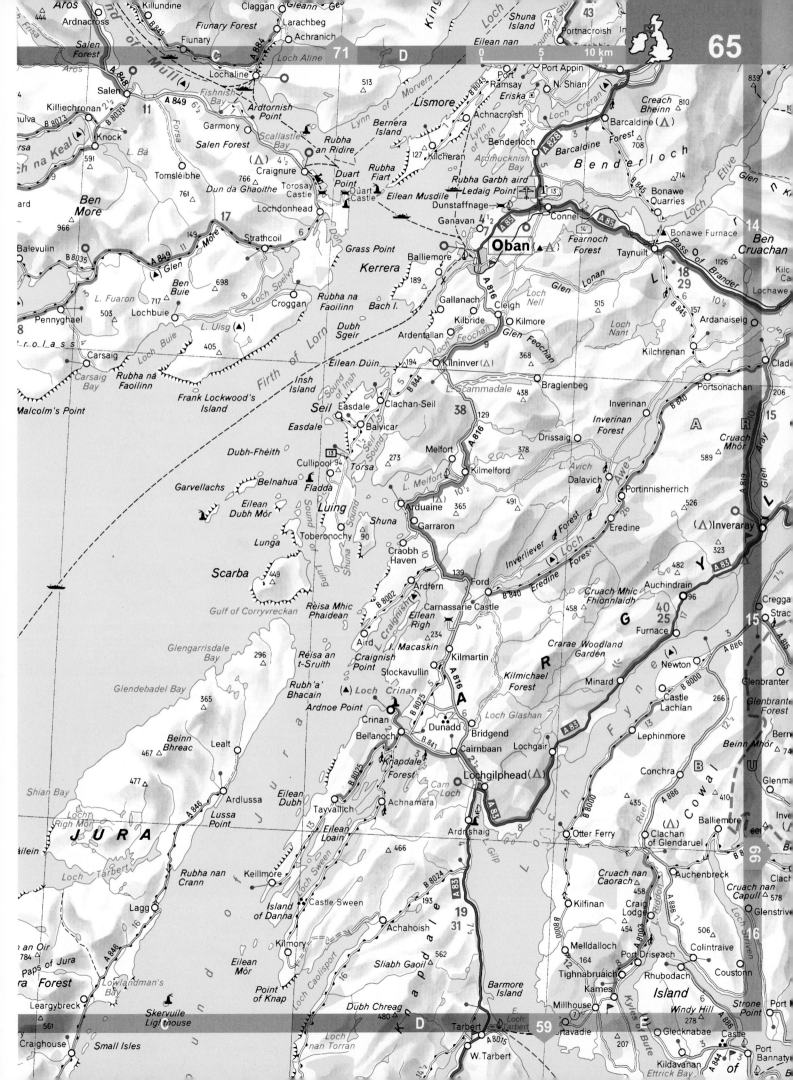

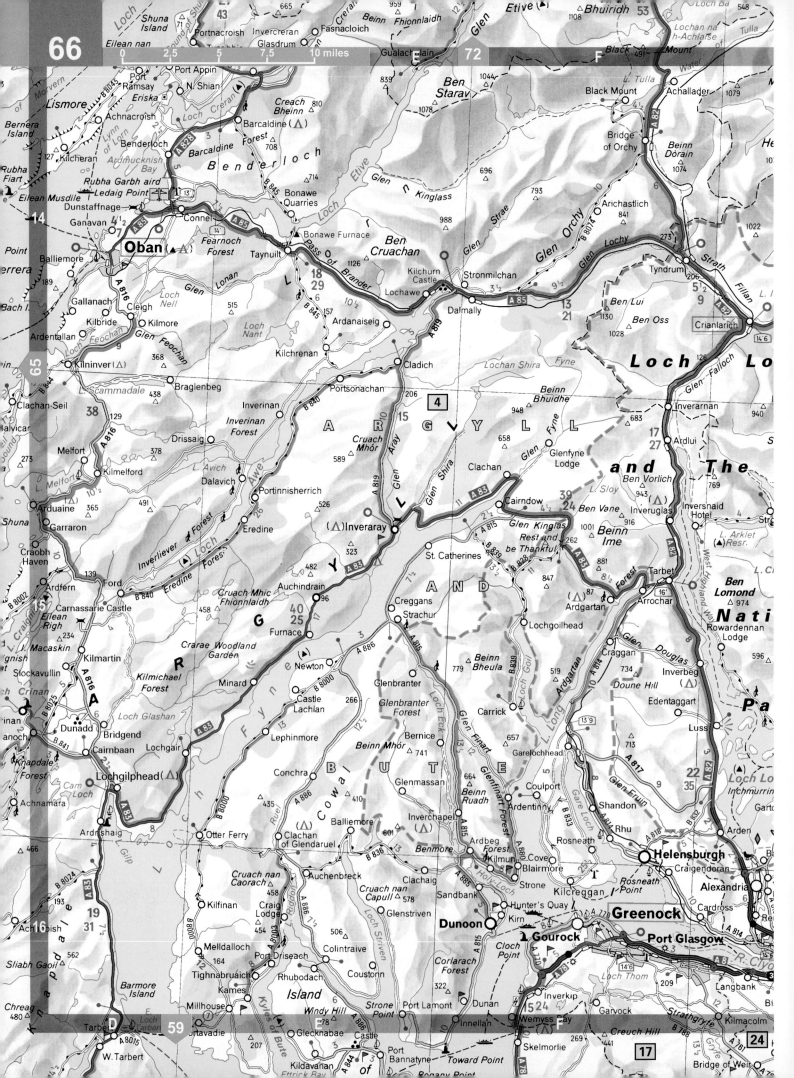

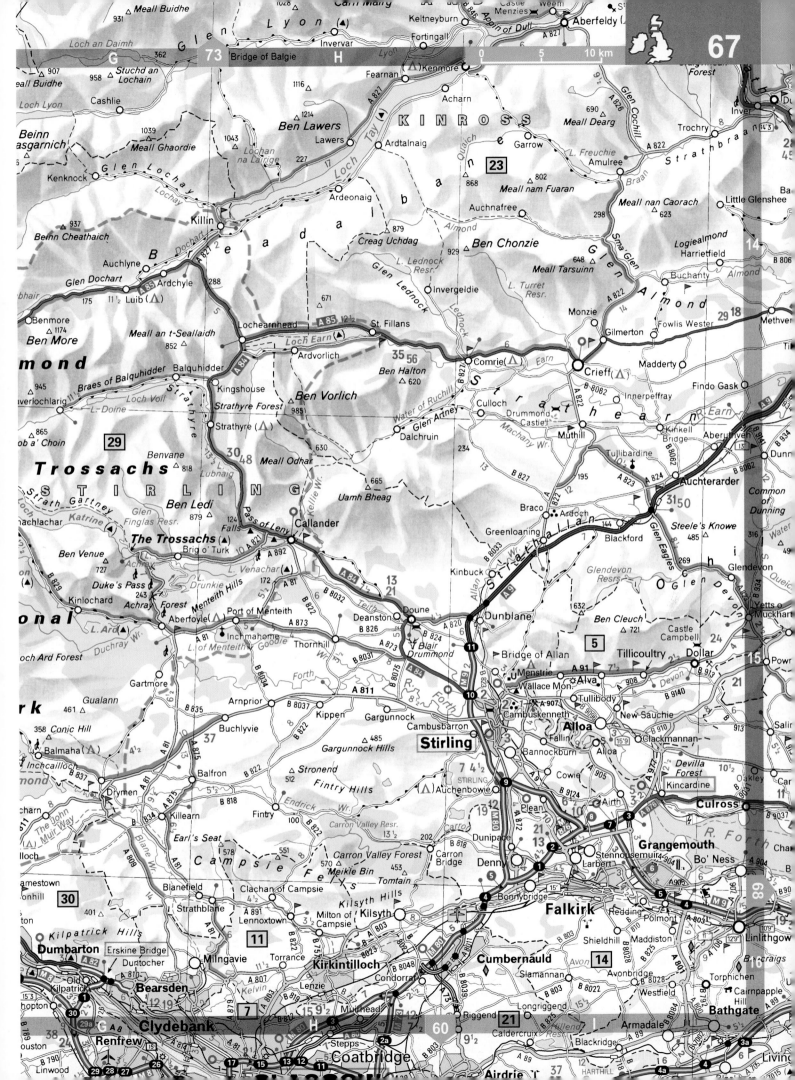

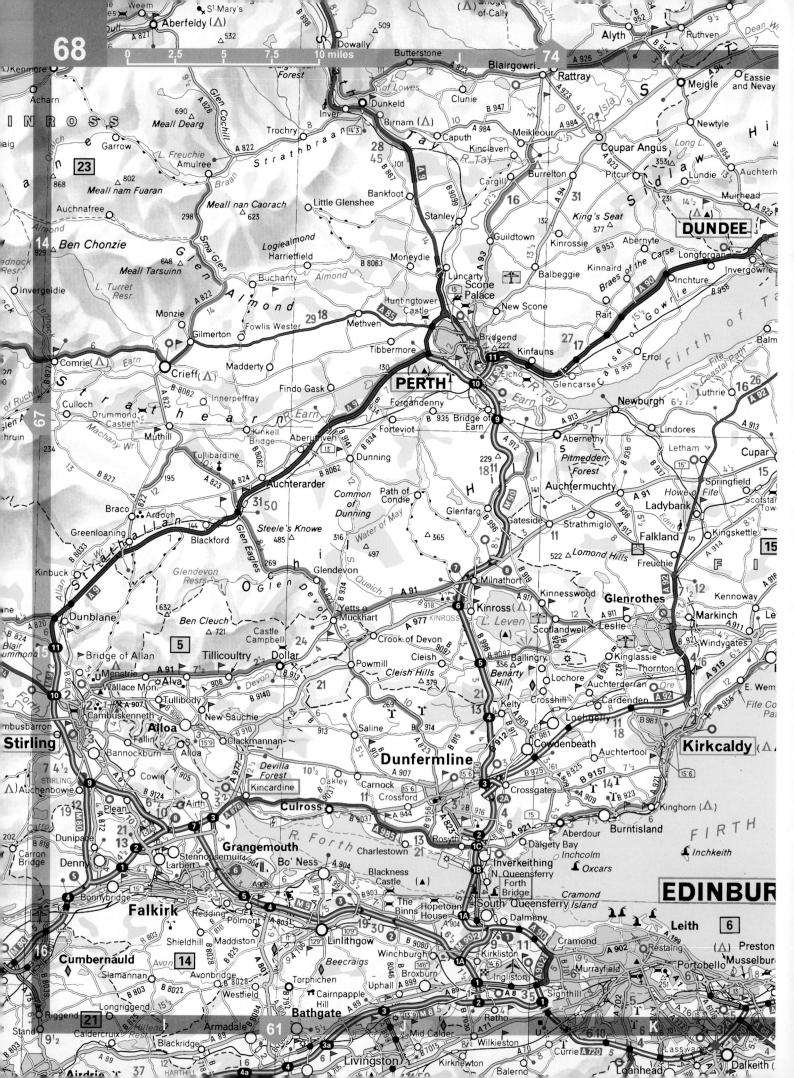

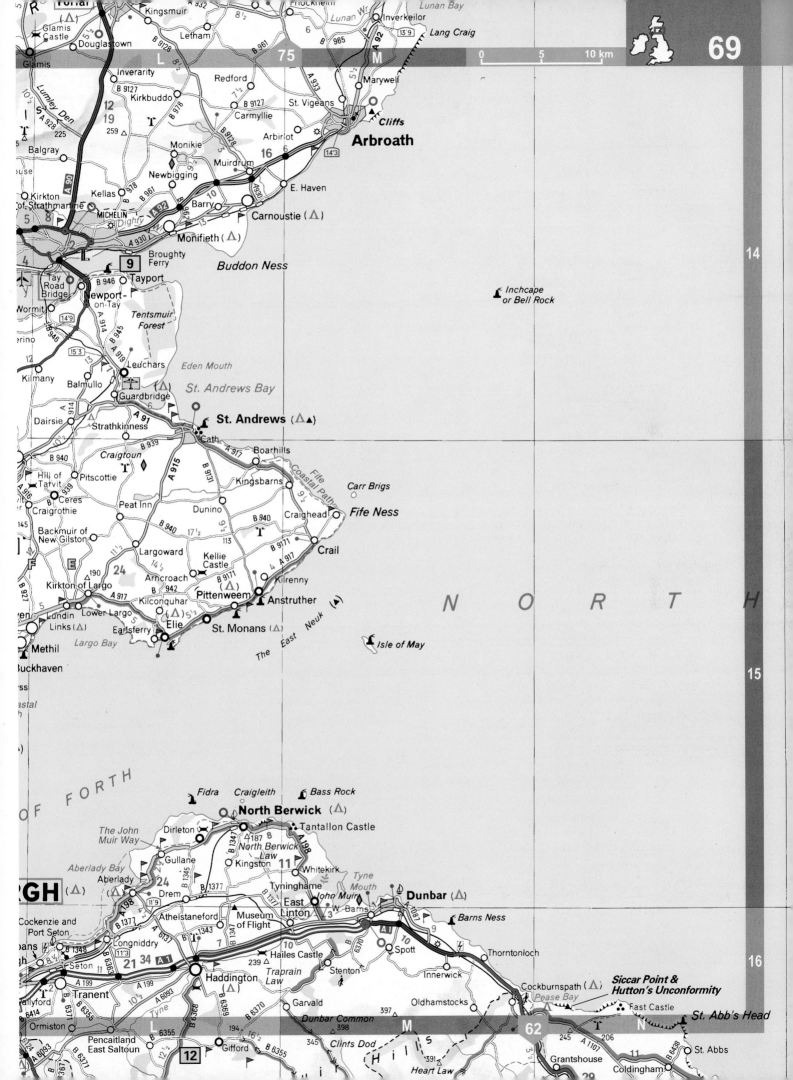

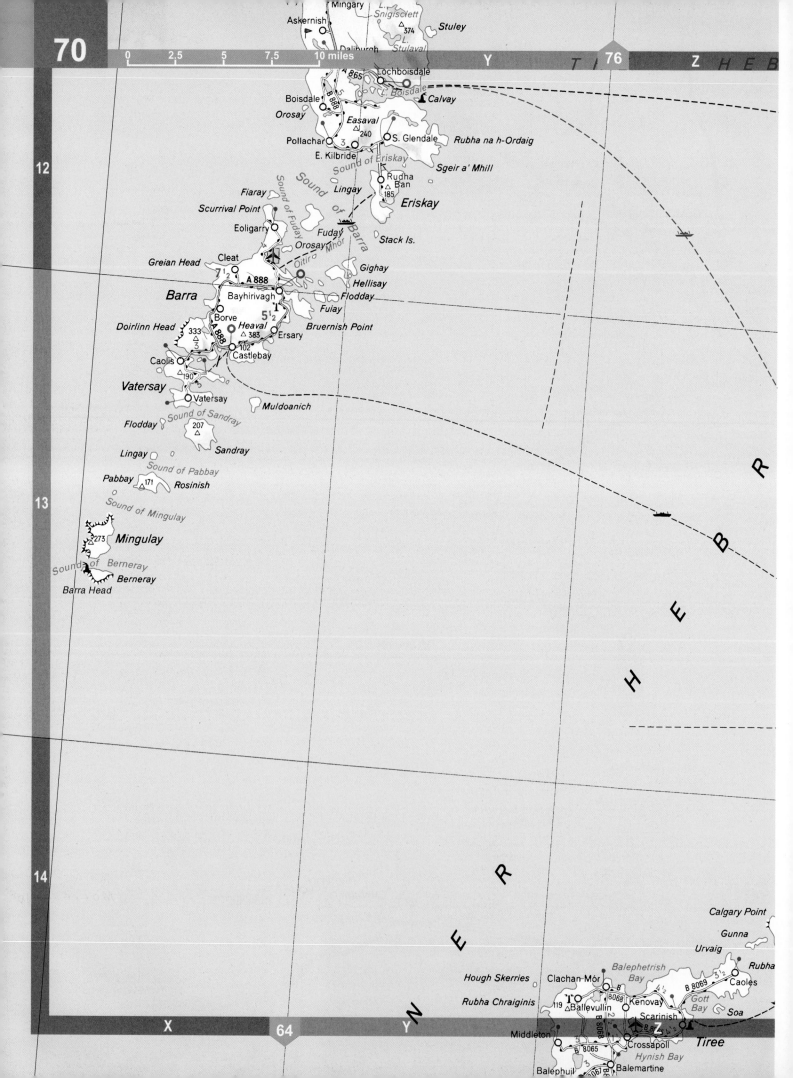

Mingary
Askernish
△ 374   *Stuley*
L.
Snigisclett
L.
Stulaval
Daliburgh
Y   T I R E   Z   H E B

0   2.5   5   7.5   10 miles

Lochboisdale
A 865
12

Boisdale
B 888
L. Boisdale   *Calvay*
Orosay
Easaval   S. Glendale   *Rubha na h-Ordaig*
△ 240
Pollachar   3
E. Kilbride   *Sgeir a' Mhill*
Sound of Eriskay   Rudha
Ban   **Eriskay**
Fiaray   *Sound of Fuday*   *Lingay*   △ 185
Scurrival Point   *Sound*
Eoligarry   *Fuday*   *of Barra*
Orosay   Stack Is.
Cleat   *Mhór*   *Gighay*
Greian Head   *Oitir*   *Hellisay*
7 1/2   A 888   *Floday*
Barra   Bayhirivagh   *Fuiay*
1 1/2
Borve   5 1/2   *Bruernish Point*
Doirlinn Head   333   *Heaval*   Ersary
A 888   △ 383
△   3   102
Caolis   Castlebay
△ 190
13   **Vatersay**
Floday   Vatersay
Sound of Sandray   *Muldoanich*
207
△
Lingay   o   *Sandray*
Sound of Pabbay
Pabbay △ 171   *Rosinish*
Sound of Mingulay

273
△   **Mingulay**
Sounds of Berneray
Berneray
Barra Head

R
E
B
14   B

E

Calgary Point
Gunna
R   *Urvaig*
E   *Rubha*
Balephetrish
Bay
N   Hough Skerries   Clachan-Mór   B 8069   Caoles
Rubha Chraiginis   119   Ballevullin   Kenovay   Gott
Y   △   Bay   Soa
X   Z   Scarinish
Middleton   Crossapoll   *Tiree*
B 8065   *Hynish Bay*
Balephuil   Balemartine

M i n g i n i s h

L. Eynort

Sgurr a'
Ghreadaidh 973
965

Sgurr Alasdair 993
The Cuillin

27 570

Red Hill
Br

732

14

Strathaird

301

Heast

610

0   5   10 km

77   **B**

Glenbrittle

L. Brittle

Rubh'an
Dùnain

Soay Sound

Loch Scavaig

Creitheach

L. Slapin

B 8083

9

Kilmarie

134

Rubha Suisnish

L. Eishort

Ord

299

Drumfearn

17

Isleornsay

Ornsay

Sanda

Mol-Chlach

141

Elgol

Soay

Rubha na
h-Easgainne

Tokavaig

10

Rubh' Ard
Slisneach

Tarskavaig Point

Tarskavaig

Teangue

Knock
Bay

12

Kilmore

S

**Clan Donald
Centre**

Armadale
Bay

Airor

A 851

Canna

A'Chill
210

Rubha Shamhnan
Insir

Ardvasar

280

4

Garrisdale Point

Sanday

Sound of Canna

Kilmory

Aird of Sleat

Rubh'
Point of Sleat

Mallaig

Rubha Raonuill

Inv

Humla

A' Bhrideanach

Orval

Oigh-sgeir

3

2

571

4 2

Kinloch

Harris

Loch Scresort

548

Bracora

Stoul

RHUM

Askival
812

Morar

Rubha nam
Meirleach

Bay of
Laig

Cleadale

Eilean Ighe

Luinga Bheag

Sound of Rhum

Rubha an
Fhasaidh

3 ½

Eigg

Arisaig

19

599

Luinga Mhór

L. nan Ceall

An Sgurr
393

Galmisdale

Rubh' Arisaig

Druimindarroch

L. nan Uamh

Eilean nan Each

Eilean
Chathastail

Eilean
an t- Snidhe

Eilean
an t- Snidhe

Sound of Arisaig

Ardnish

Port Mór

137

Muck

Sound of Eigg

Eilean nan Gobhar

L. Ailort

Rubha na
Faing Móire

Roshven

13

Glenuig

19

Rubha Aird
Druimnich

Eilean Shona

Farquhar's
Point

L. Moidart

Moi

Kinlochm

Sanna

Kilmory

Ockle

357

Ardtoe

Doirlinn

103

Portuairk

Achosnich

Meall
nan Con

437

Ardnamurchan

Acharacle

Dalnabreck

A 861

Kilchoan

L. Mudle

133

B 8007

Kentra
Bay

3

Ardshealach

Resipole

Sròn Bheag

528

Ben
Hiant

490

Glenmore

Salen

B 8007

7

Loch

Sunart

Cairns of Coll

Point of
Ardnamurchan

Súil Ghorm

Eilan Mór

Ardslignish

Ardmore Point

Glenborrodale

Oronsay

Carna

72

Rubha Mór

Sorisdale

B 8012

Arnabost

B 8071

Coll

Auliston
Point

Rubha
nan Gall

169

Loch Teacuis

571

Ballyhaugh

104

B 8071

Arinagour

Loch Eatharna

Glengorm

Quinish Point

Tobermory

Calve
Island

Drimnin

Mor v e r n

19

Arileod

B 8070

Eilean
Ornsay

Caliach Point

Croig

Mishnish

5

A 848

451

550

Loch Arienas

Claggan

14

Crossapol
Bay

Dubh

Mornish

Calgary

Dervaig

6 ½

B 8073

134

Aros

10

Killundine

B 849

Fiunary Forest

Larachbeg

Achranich

(▲) *Calgary Bay*

Ensay

342

4 ½

Loch Frisa

444

Ardnacross

Sound

Salen
Forest

Fiunary

L. Aline

Treshnish Point

Haunn

176

B 8073

2

Bellart

Salen

of

Mull

Lochaline

nish Isles

Cairn na
Burgh Beg

(▲) Loch Tuath

A   **B**

Achleck

65

A 848

424

Killiechronan

B 8035

11

A 849

Ardtornish
Point

Fladda

Gometra

Lagganulva

B 8073

Salen

Garmony

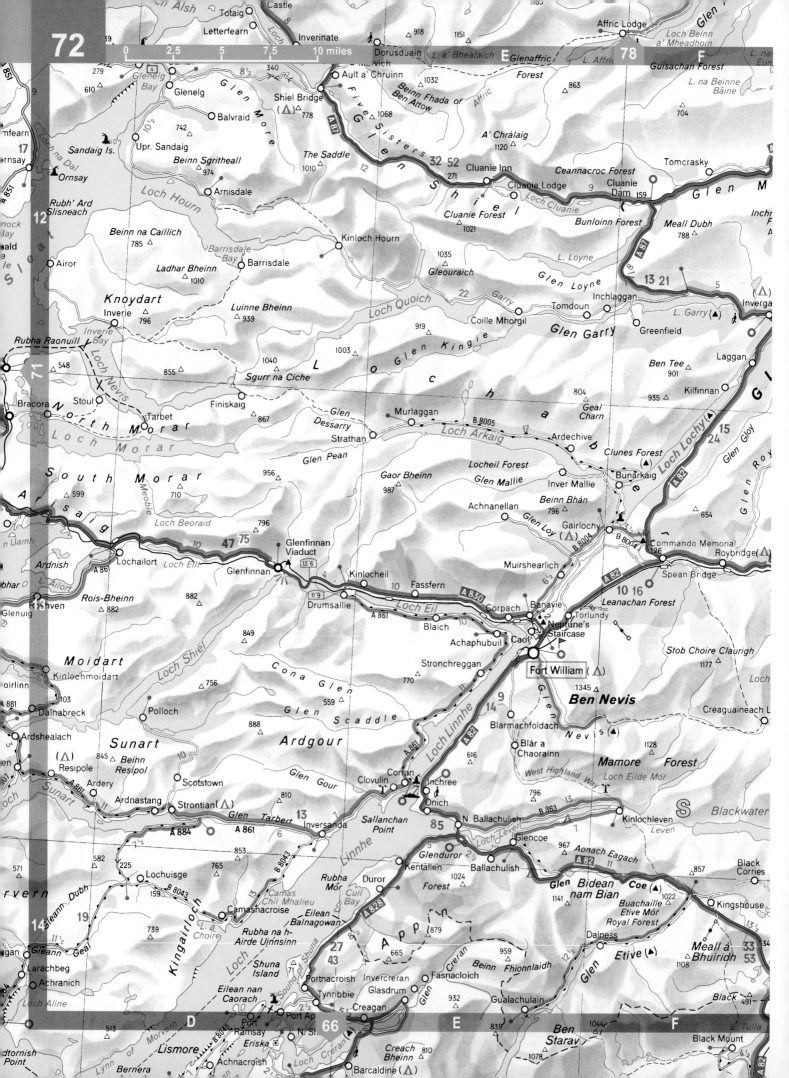

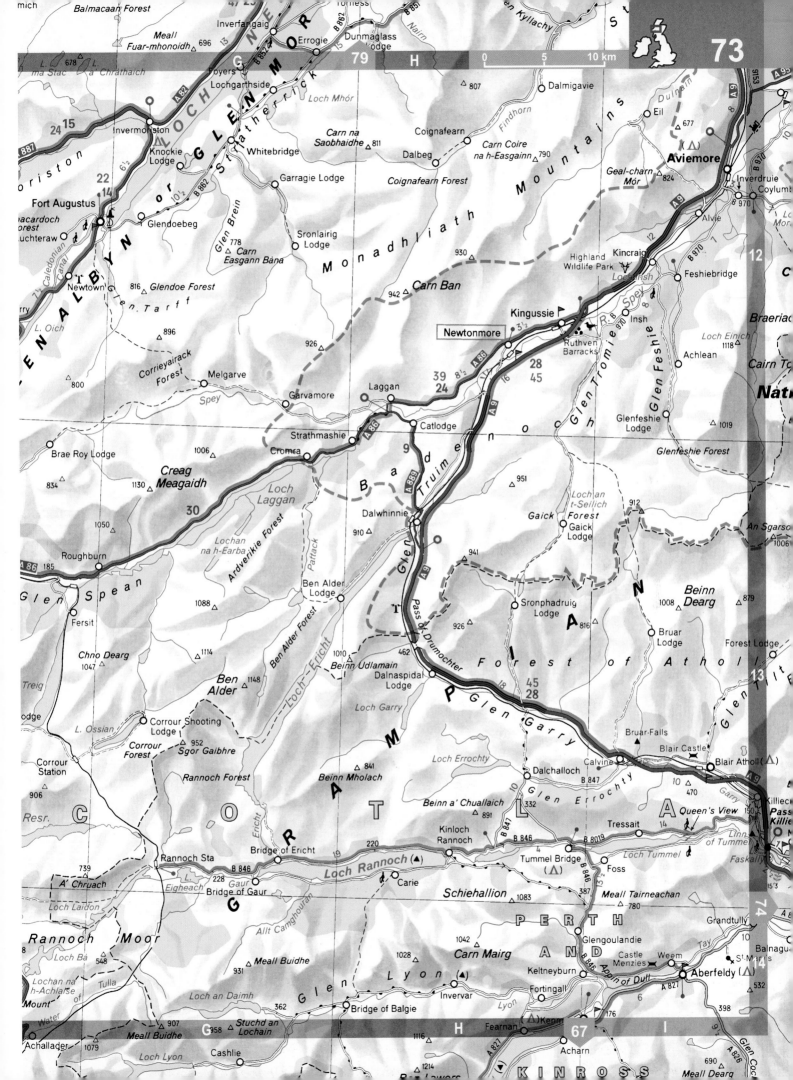

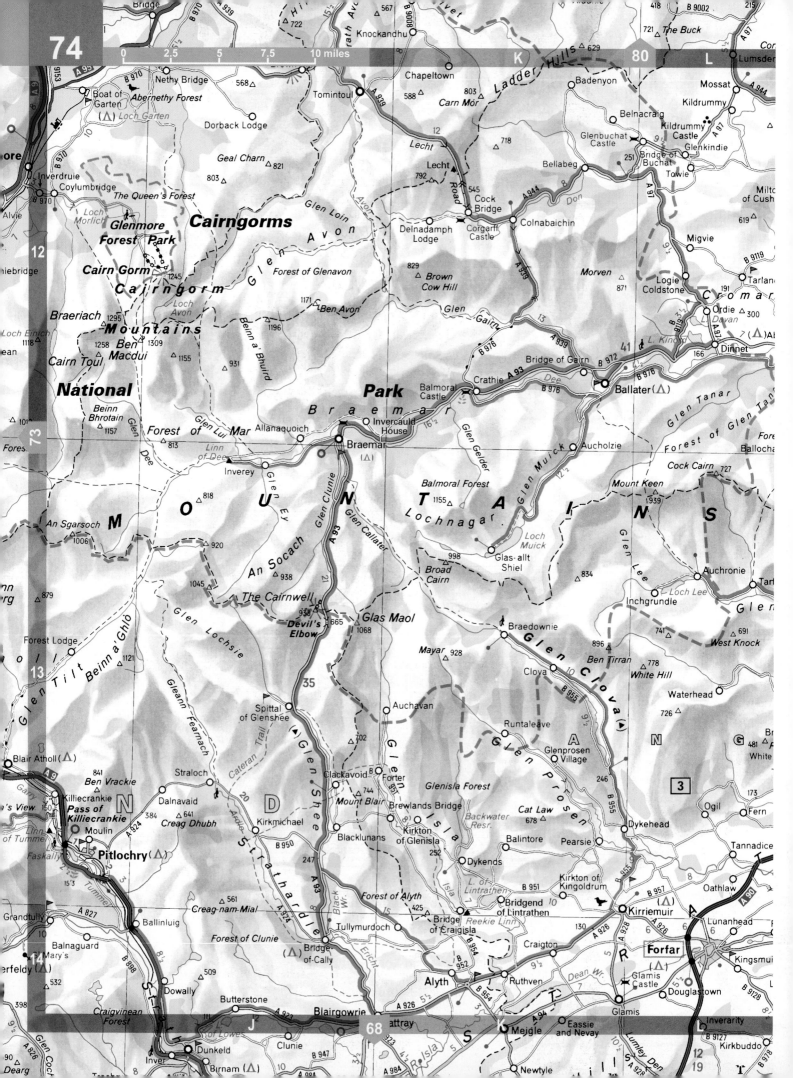

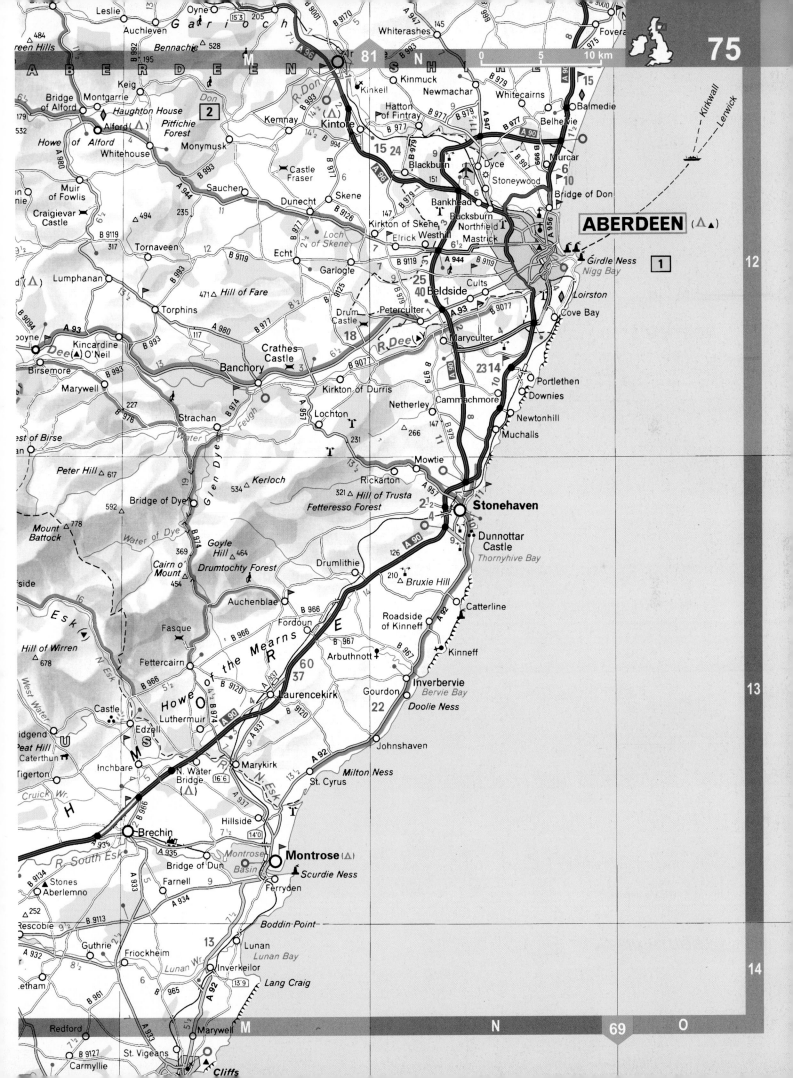

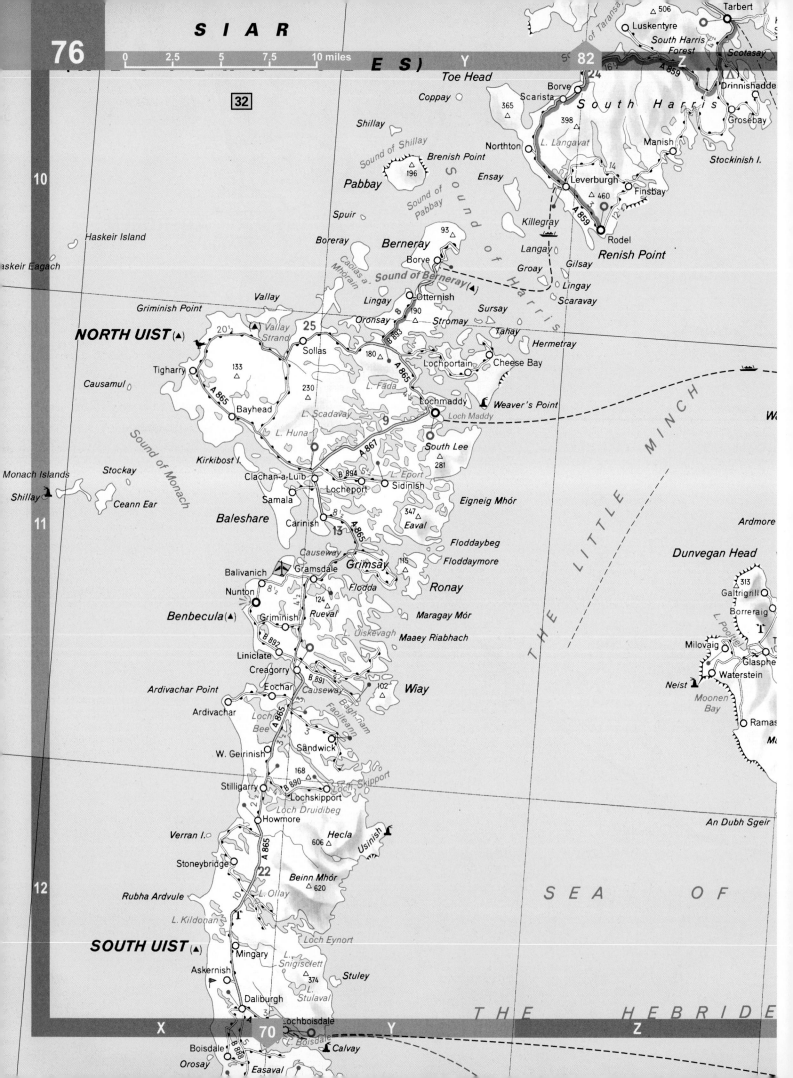

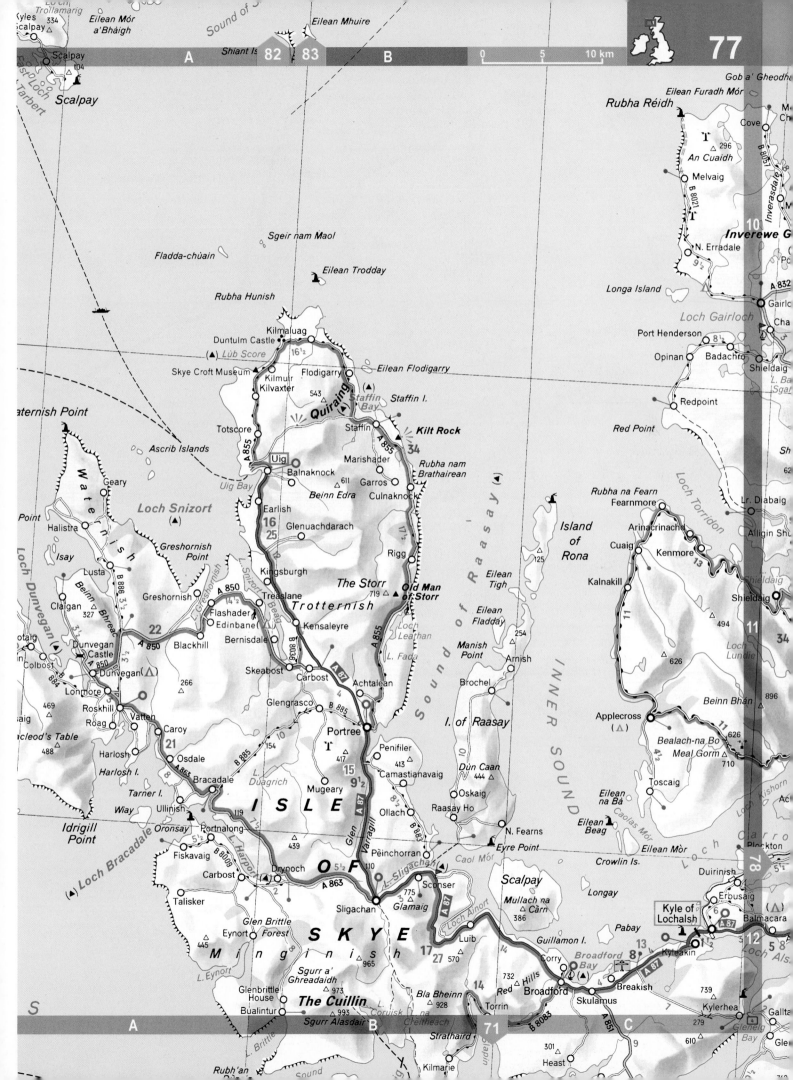

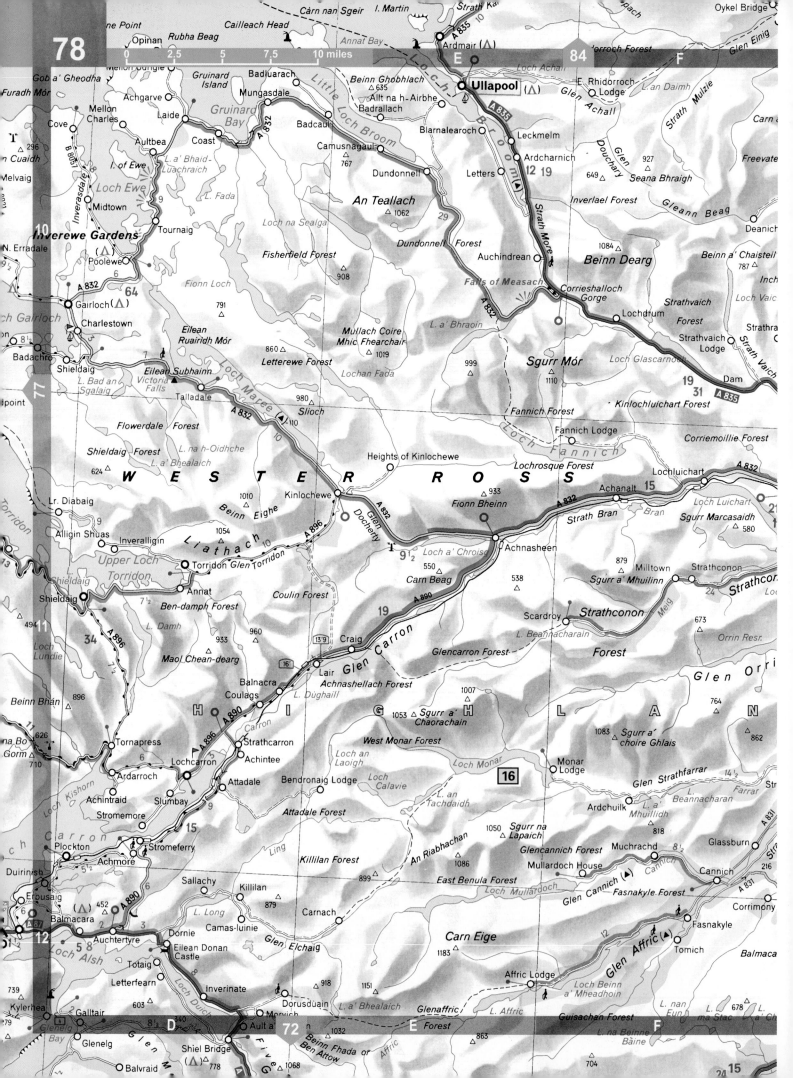

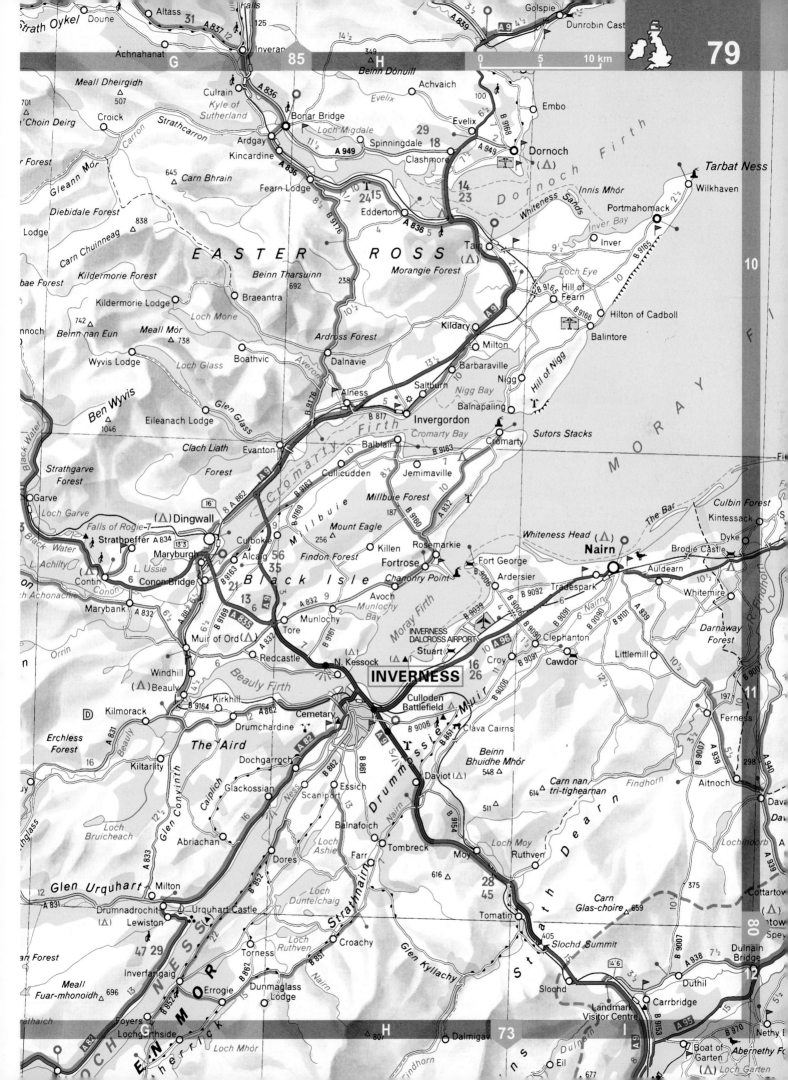

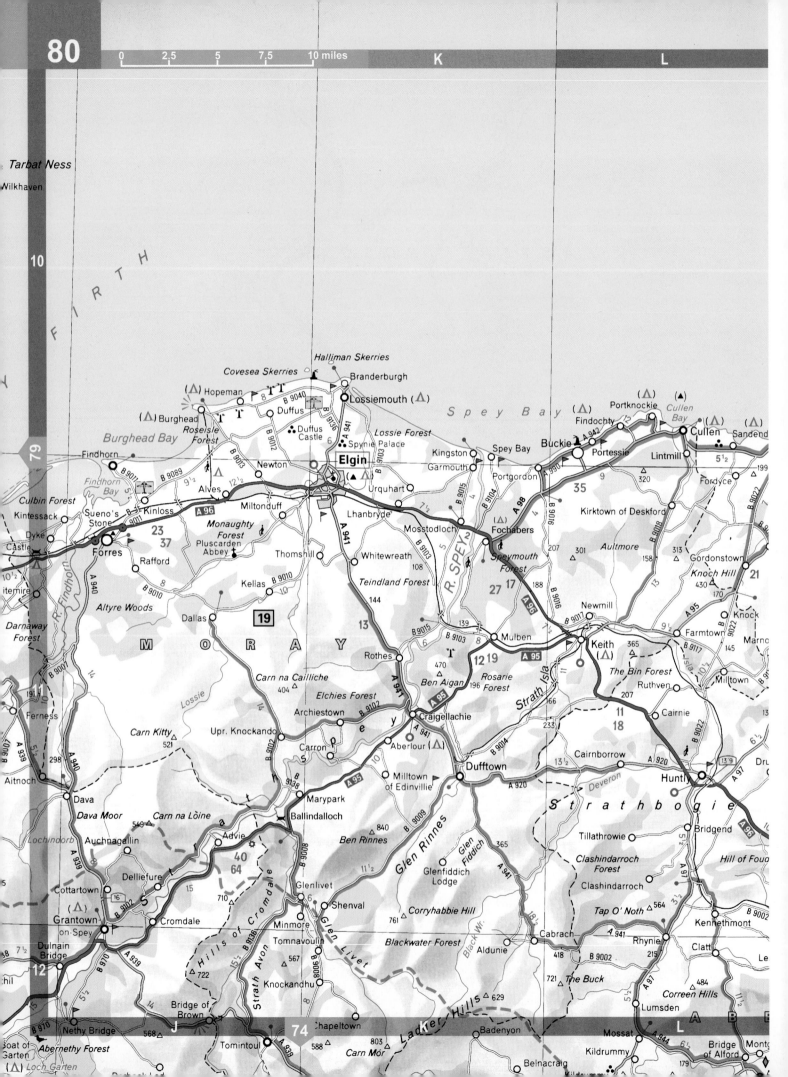

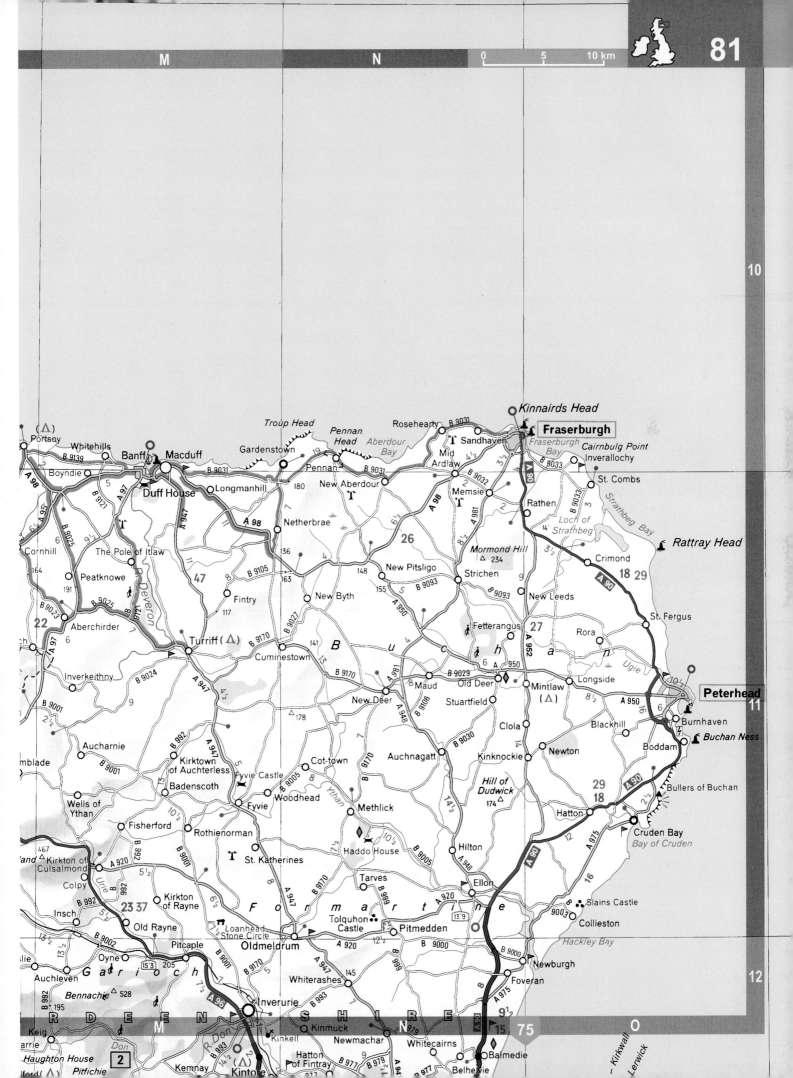

0   5   10 km

Butt of Lewis

Eoropie
Habost   Port of Ness
Skigersta
Cross
Dell
Ness
B 8015

Loch Langavat

Cellar Head

248
Muirneag

Tolsta
Tolsta Head
B 895

Gress

Back

12 ½

Portnaguran
Tiumpan Head

Broad Bay
(▲)

Melbost   12   Garrabost
A 866
Knock   Bayble
Eye Peninsula
Chicken Head

T H E   M I N C H

8

Har

Eddrachillis Bay

Point of Stoer

Culkein
Eilean Chrona
Clashnessie

Stoer

Clachtoll
B 869
Achmelvich

9

Baddidarach

Soyea Island

A' Chleit   Kirkaig Point
Inver

Rubha Còigeach
Eilean Mór

Rubha Mór
Reiff   Brae of Achnahaird
6
Eilean Mullagrach   Altandhu
Badnagyle
Osgaig   Sta
Isle Ristol   Polbain
L. Bad a' Ghaill
Glas-leac Mór
Achiltibuie
Tanera Mór   Badenscallie
Tanera Beg
Loch
Summer Is.   Horse I.   Cumhacraig
Achduart
C
Eilean Dubh
Priest Island
Bottle I.
Càrn nan Sgeir   10   Martin

ck Head

òraidh

84

Mhuire

Greenstone Point   *Rubha Beag*
Opinan
Stattic Point   Scoraig
Mellon Udrigle
Annat Bay

Gob a' Ghe
Eilean Furadh Mór
Rubha Réidh
Achgarve   Gruinard Island   Badluarach
Mungasdale
Mellon Charles
Laide
Gruinard Bay
Little Loch
Beinn Ghobhla
△ 635
Allt na h-A
Badralla

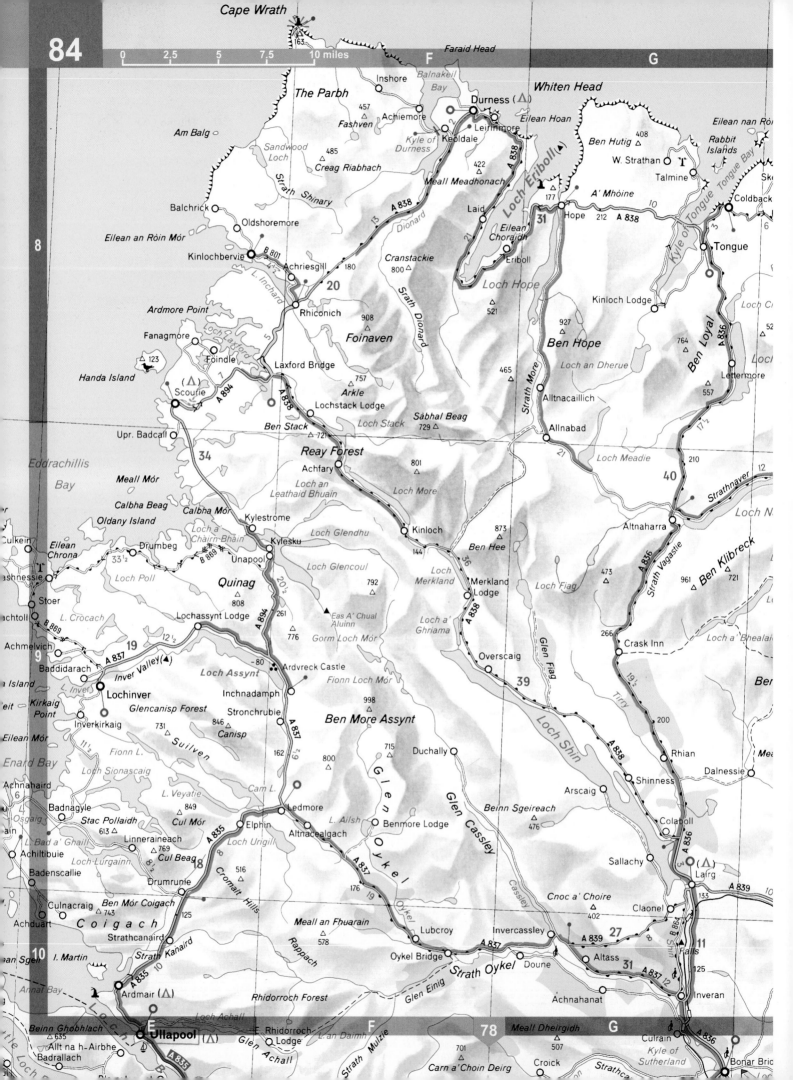

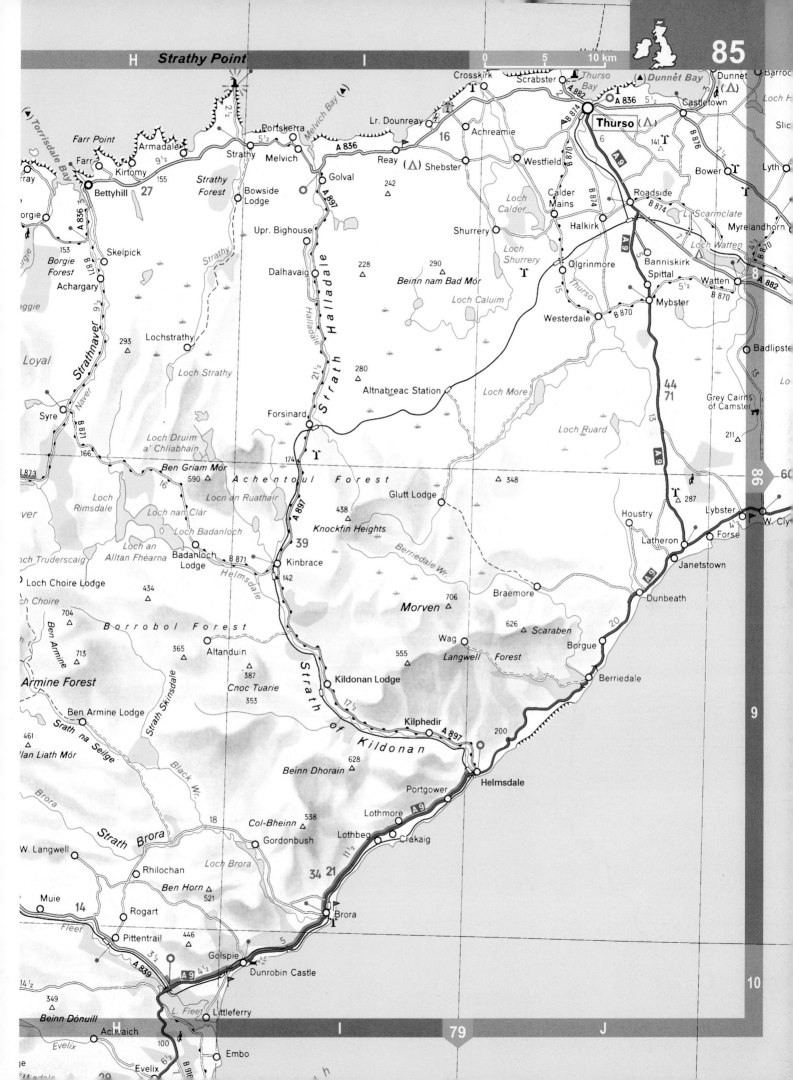

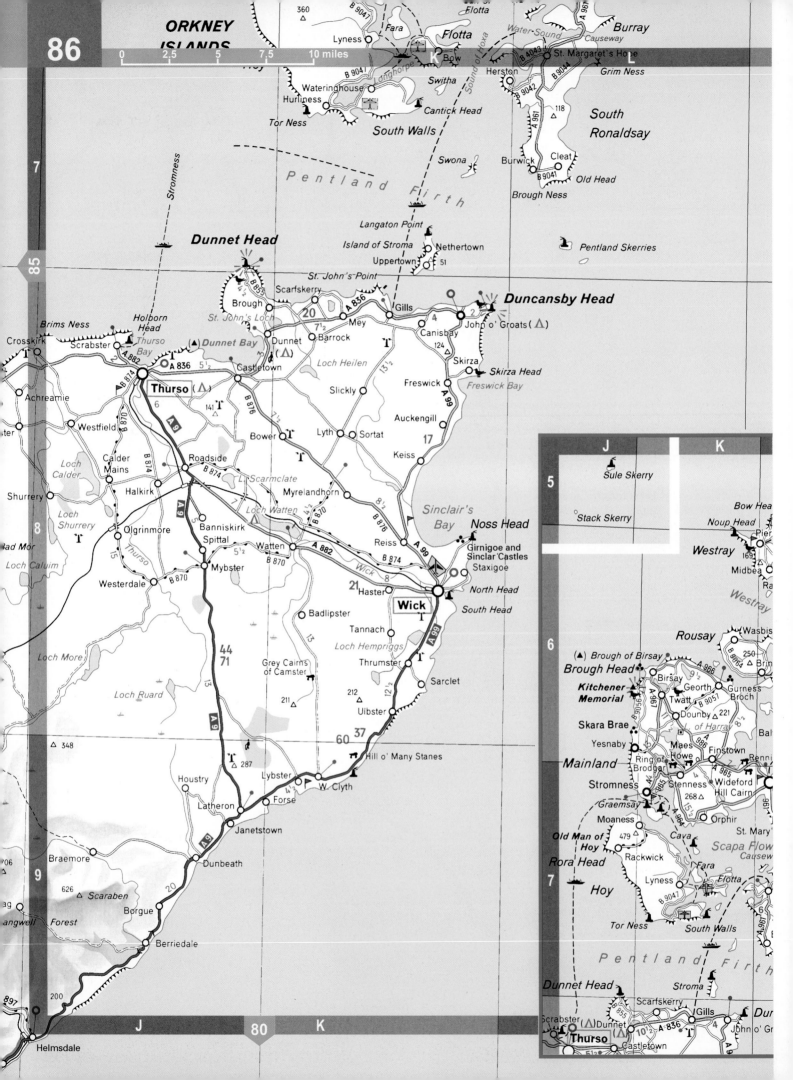

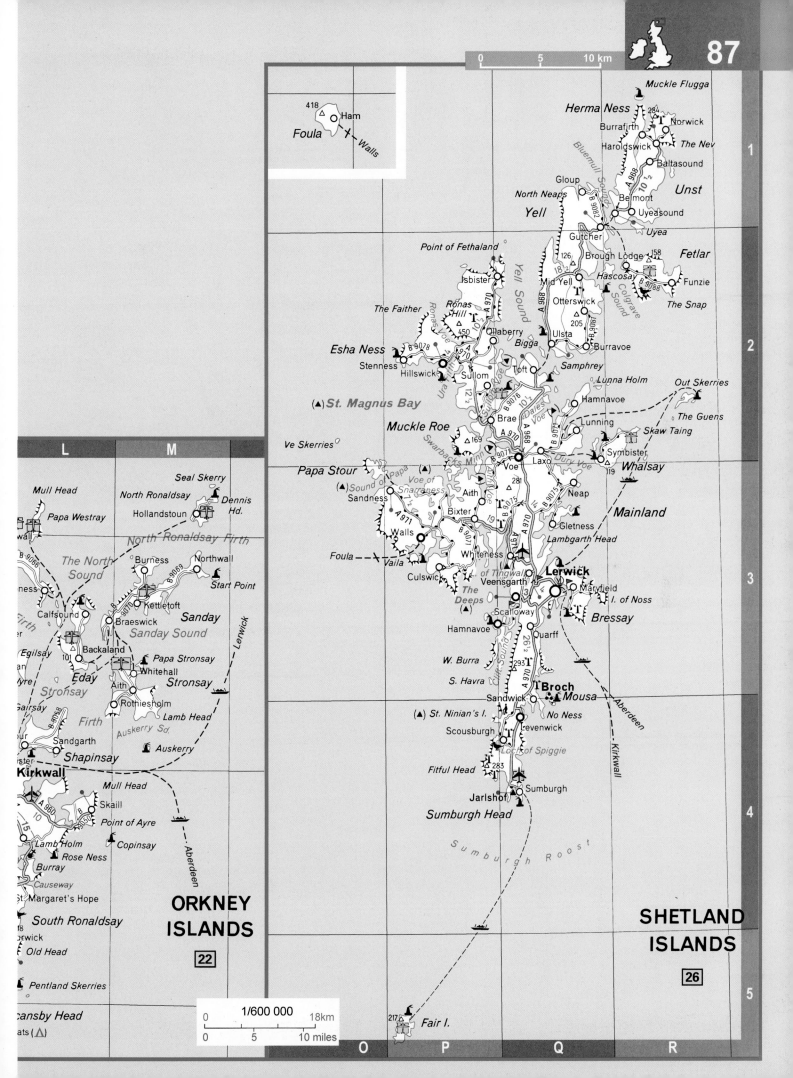

0   5   10 km

Foula
418 △ ● Ham
✝ Walls

Muckle Flugga
Herma Ness
Burrafirth   284 △ ✝ Norwick
Haroldswick   The Nev
Baltasound

Gloup
North Neaps   Unst
                 Be mont
Yell   Uyeasound
         Gutcher   Uyea

Point of Fethaland   126   Brough Lodge   Fetlar
Isbister   Hascosay
                    Mid Yell
The Faither   Ronas   18¼   Otterswick
         Hill   205   Funzie
Esha Ness   450 △ Ollaberry   Bigga   The Snap
Stenness   Sullom   Ulsta   Burravoe
Hillswick   Samphrey
         Toft   Lunna Holm   Out Skerries
(▲)St. Magnus Bay   Hamnavoe   The Guens
              Brae   Lunning   Skaw Taing
Muckle Roe   Symbister
Ve Skerries   Voe Laxo   Whalsay
Papa Stour   (▲)Sound of Papa   Aith   Mainland
    Sandness   281   Neap
         Bixter   Gletness
Walls   19   Lambgarth Head
Foula   Vaila   Whiteness   Lerwick
    Culswick   L. of Tingwall   Maryfield   I. of Noss
         Veensgarth   Bressay
         The   Scalloway
         Deeps   Quarff
Hamnavoe   Broch
W. Burra   26½   Mousa
S. Havra   293   Aberdeen
Sandwick   No Ness   Kirkwall
(▲) St. Ninian's I.   Trevenwick
Scousburgh
    Loch of Spiggie
Fitful Head   283 △
         Sumburgh
Jarlshof
Sumburgh Head   Sumburgh Roost

SHETLAND
ISLANDS

26

ORKNEY section:

L   M
Seal Skerry
Mull Head   North Ronaldsay   Dennis
Papa Westray   Hd.
    Hollandstoun
North Ronaldsay Firth
The North   Burness   Northwall
Sound   Start Point
    Kettletoft   Sanday
Calfsound   Braeswick   Sanday Sound
Eday   Backaland   Papa Stronsay
    Aith   Whitehall   Stronsay
    Rothiesholm   Lamb Head
Stronsay
Firth   Sandgarth   Auskerry Sd.   Auskerry
Shapinsay
Kirkwall   Mull Head
    Skaill
    Point of Ayre
Lamb Holm   Copinsay
Rose Ness
Burray
Causeway
Margaret's Hope
South Ronaldsay
Old Head
Pentland Skerries
cansby Head
oats (△)

ORKNEY
ISLANDS

22

1/600 000   18km
0   5   10 miles

217 ✝ Fair I.

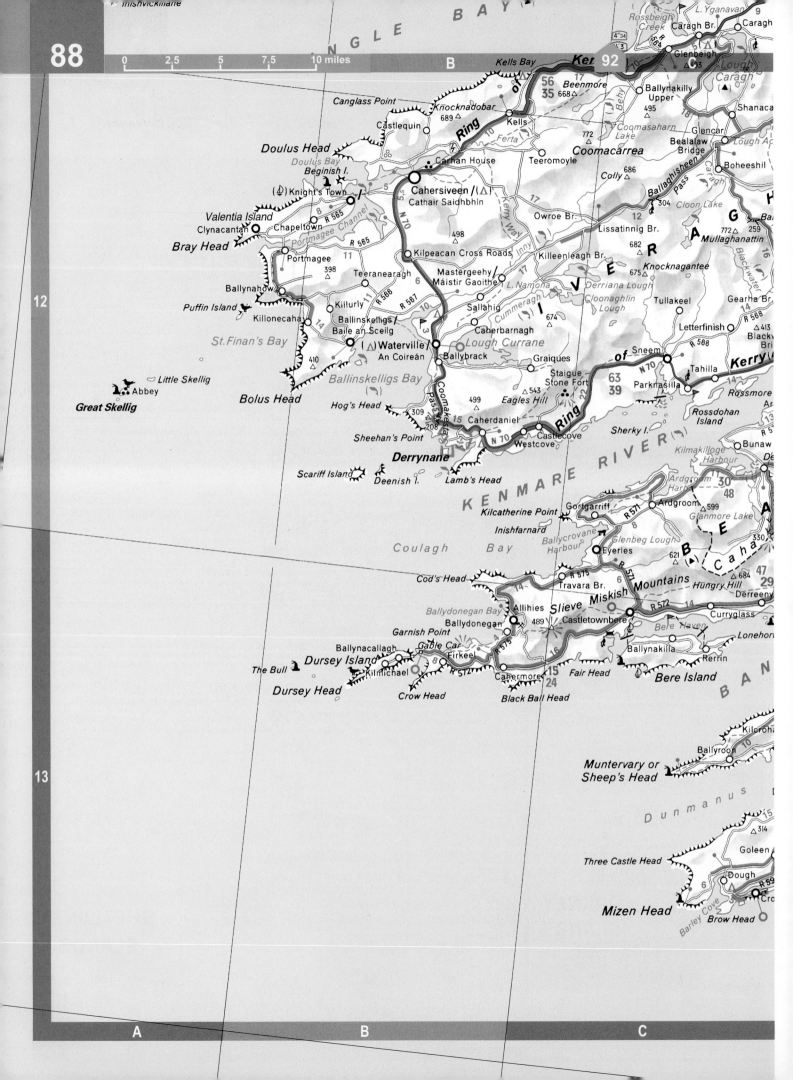

DINGLE BAY

INISHVICKILLANE

0 2.5 5 7.5 10 miles

B Kells Bay Ker 92

Canglass Point Knocknadobar 689△ Kells 56 35 17 668△ Beenmore Ballynakilly Upper 495

Castlequin Carhan House Teeromoyle Coomacarrea Glencar Coomasaharn Lake 772△ Bealalaw Bridge Lough Ac Shanaca

Doulus Head Doulus Bay Beginish I. Cahersiveen / (△) Cathair Saidhbhín Owroe Br. Colly△ 686 Ballaghisheen Pass 304 Cloon Lake Boheeshil

Knight's Town R 565 N 70 498△ Kerry Way 12 682△ 772△ 259 Ba

Valentia Island Chapeltown Clynacantan Bray Head Portmagee 11 R 565 Kilpeacan Cross Roads Killeenleagh Br. 17 675△ Knocknagantee Mullaghanattin Blackwater 16

Ballynahow 398△ R 566 Teeranearagh 6 Mastergeehy / Máistir Gaoithe L. Namona Derriana Lough Gearha Br. R 568

Puffin Island Killurly 11 R 567 10 Sallahig Cummeragh 674△ Cloonaghlin Lough Tullakeel Letterfinish R 568 Blackw Bri

Killonecaha Ballinskelligs / Baile an Sceilg 3 Caherbarnagh △413 Kerry

St. Finan's Bay 14 Waterville / An Coireán Lough Currane Sneem N 70 R 568

Little Skellig 410△ Ballybrack Graigues Staigue Stone Fort 63 39 Tahilla Rossmore Ar

Abbey Bolus Head Hog's Head 309 △543 Eagles Hill Parknasilla R 5

Great Skellig 208 15 Caherdaniel 499△ Sherky I. Rossdohan Island Bunaw

Sheehan's Point N 70 Castlecove Westcove KENMARE RIVER Kilmakilloge Harbour De

Derrynane Ring

Scariff Island Deenish I. Lamb's Head Kilcatherine Point Gortgarriff R 571 Ardgroom 599△ 30 48

Coulagh Bay Inishfarnard Ballycrovane Harbour Glenbeg Lough Glanmore Lake 684△ 47

Cod's Head Eyeries 832△ B Caha 29

Ballydonegan Bay Travara Br. R 575 6 Slieve Miskish Mountains Hungry Hill Derreeny

Garnish Point Allihies R 572 14 Curryglass

Ballynacallagh Ballydonegan 489△ Castletownbere Bere Haven Lonehor

The Bull Dursey Island Cable Car Firkeel R 575 16 Ballynakilla Rerrin BAN

Kilmichael R 512 8 15 Fair Head Bere Island

Dursey Head Crow Head Cahermore 24 Black Ball Head

Kilcroha

Muntervary or Sheep's Head Ballyroon 10

DUNMANUS

△314

Three Castle Head Goleen R 59

Dough

Mizen Head Barley Cove Brow Head Cro

A B C

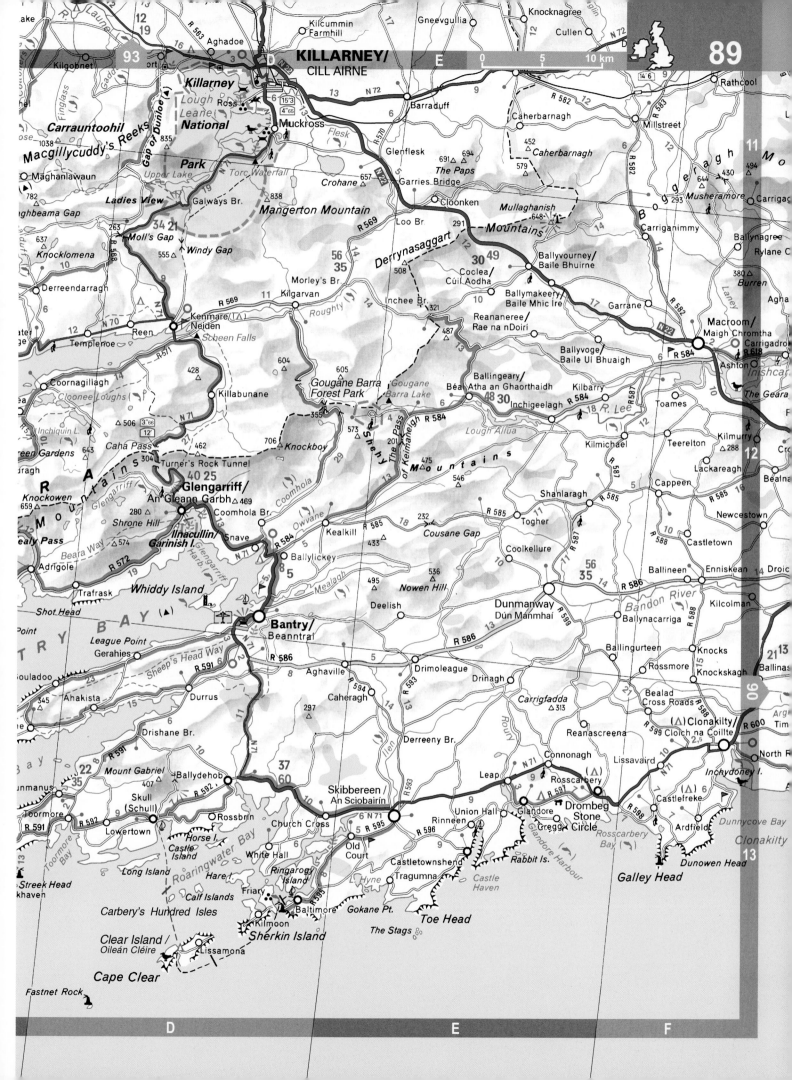

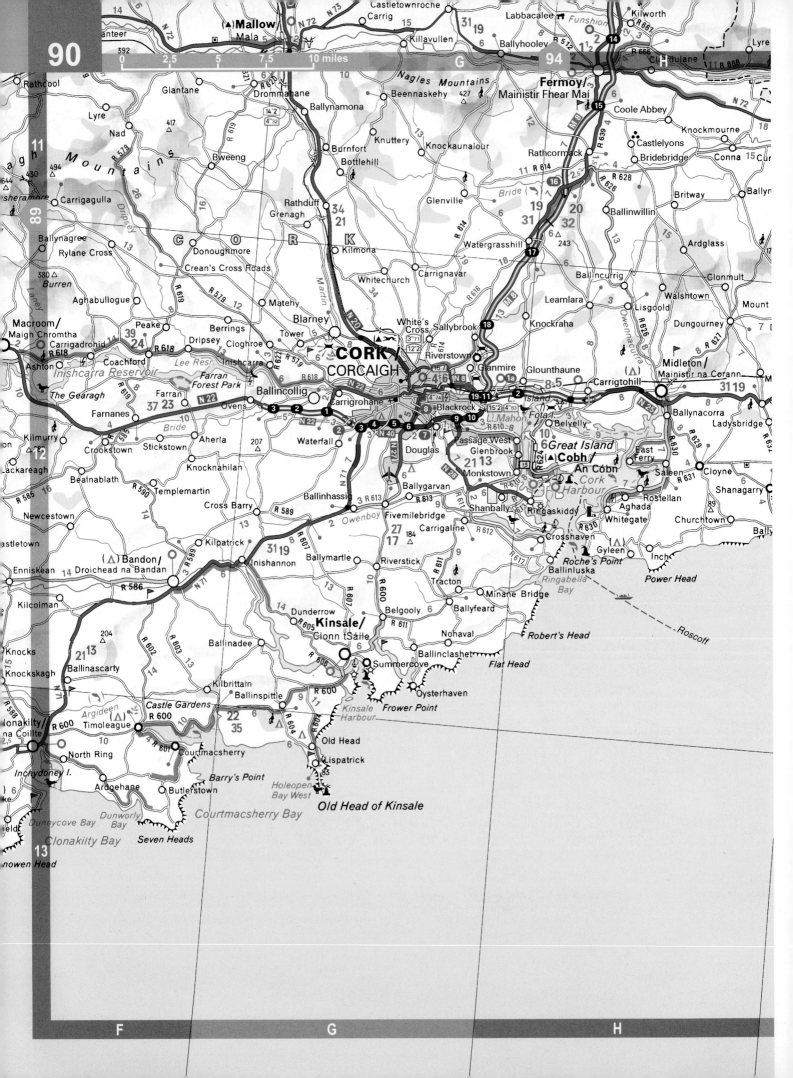

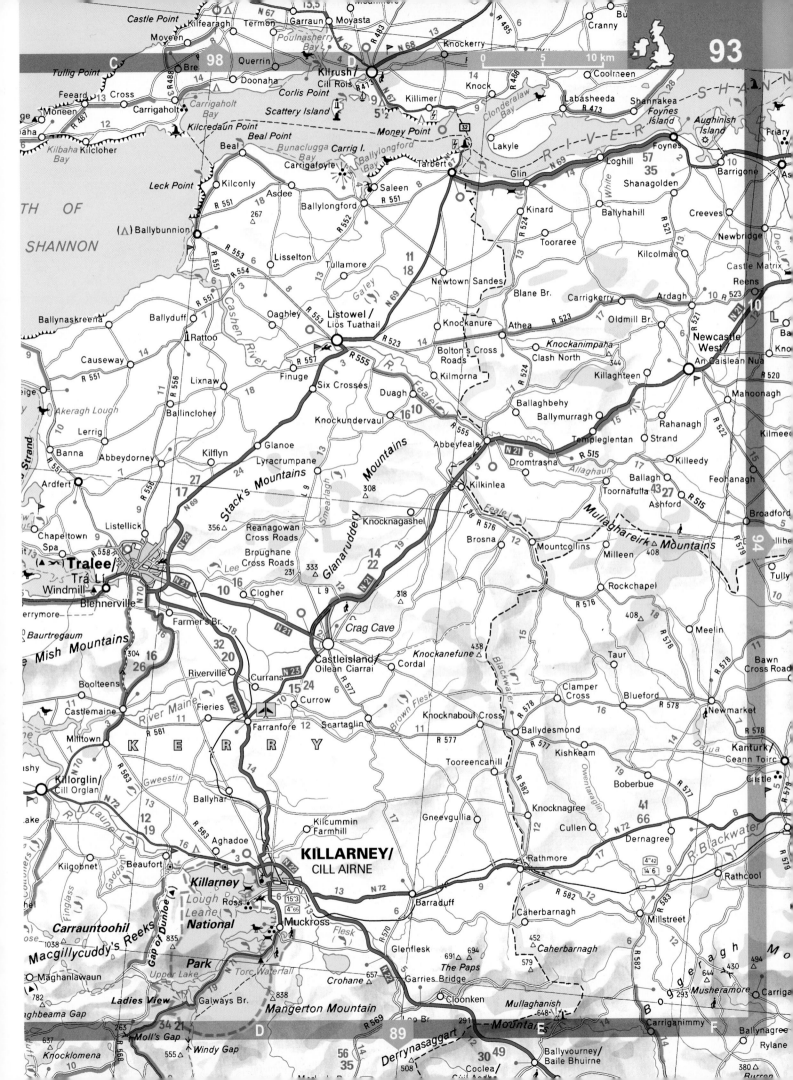

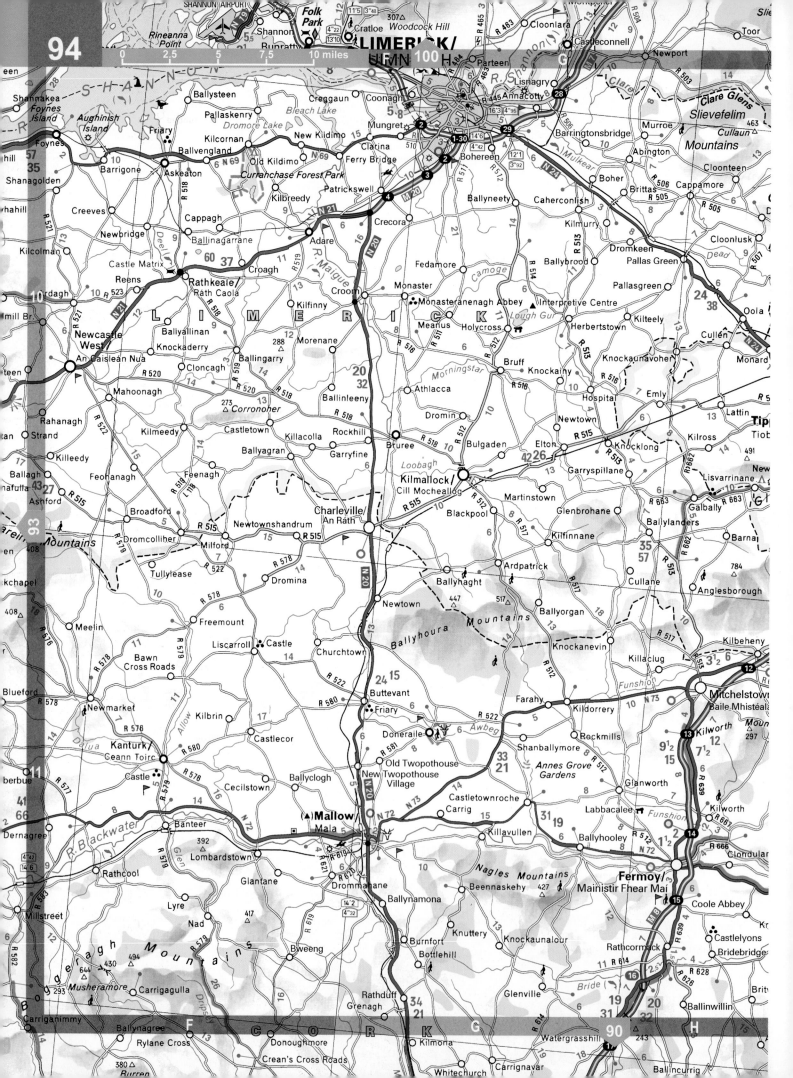

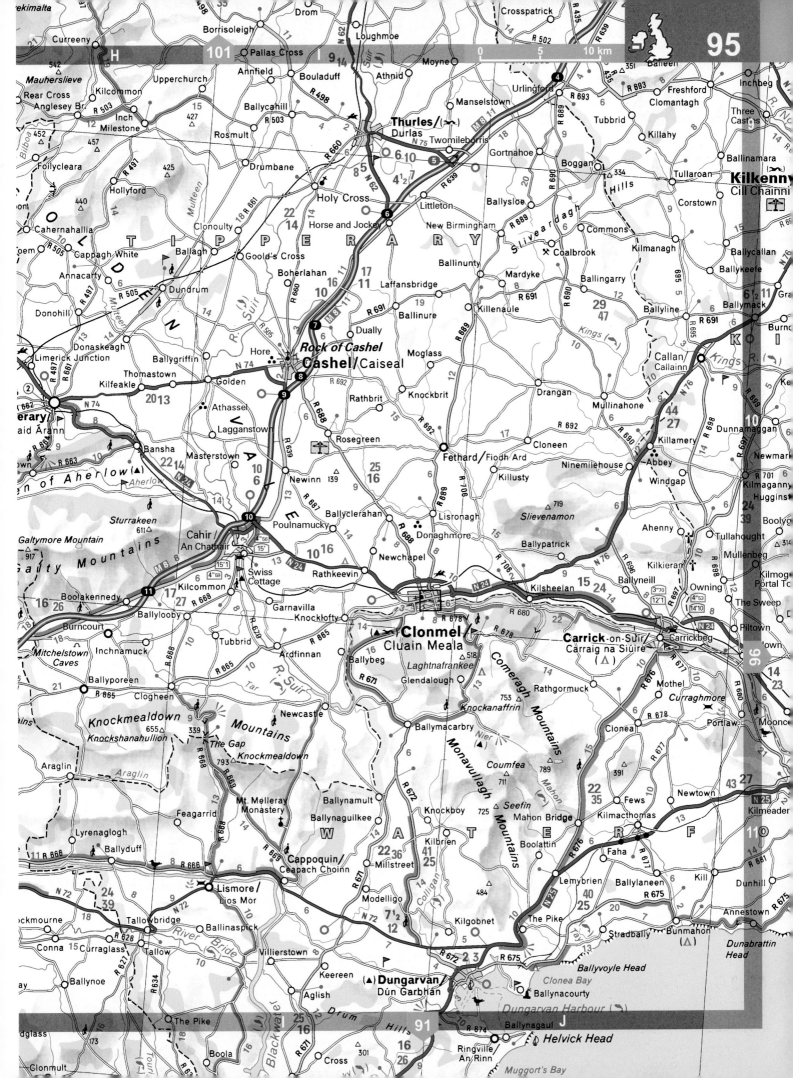

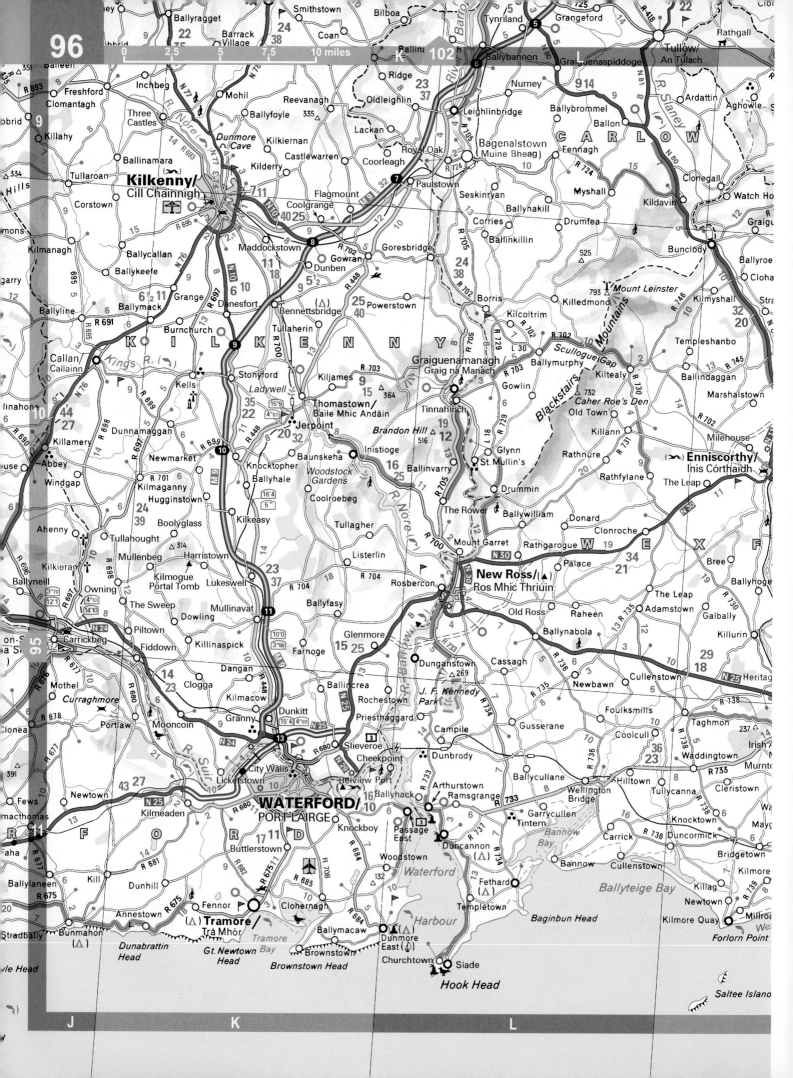

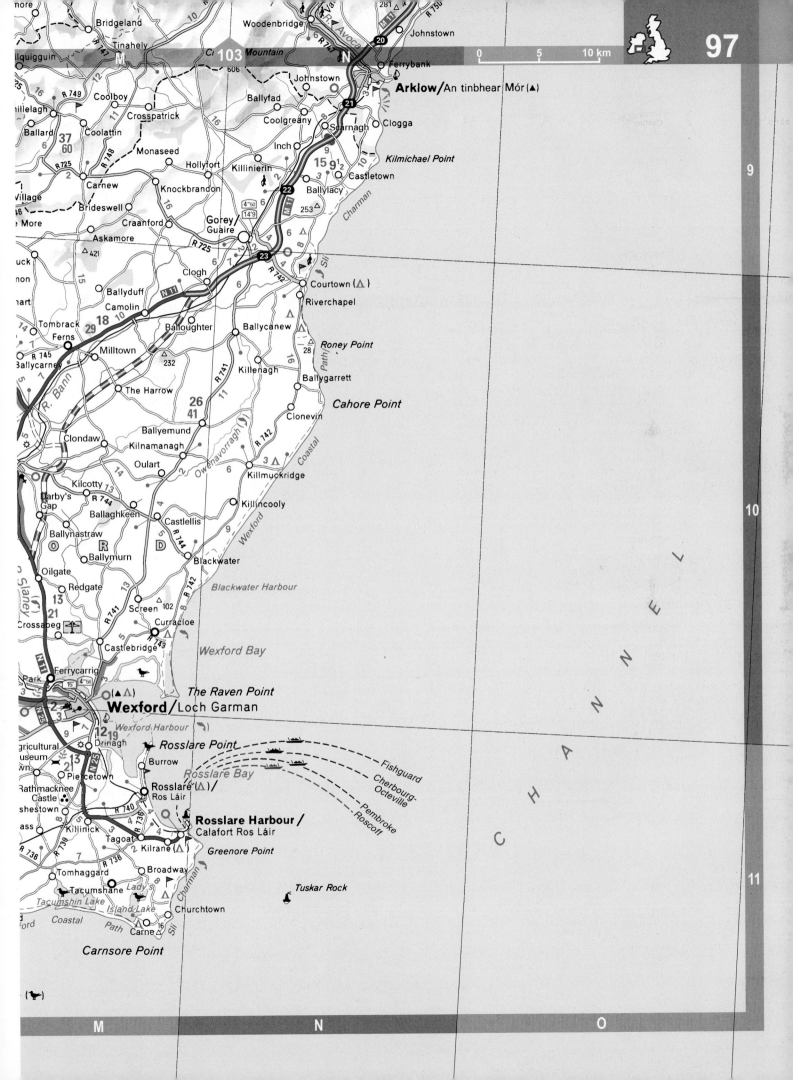

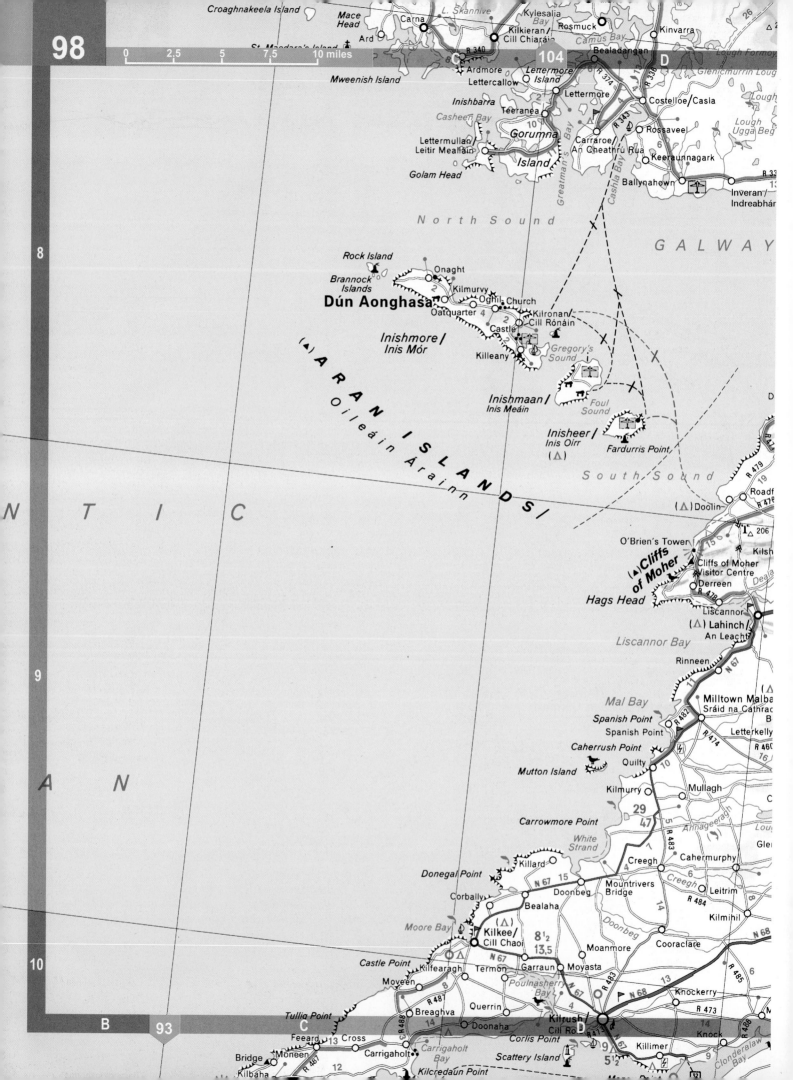

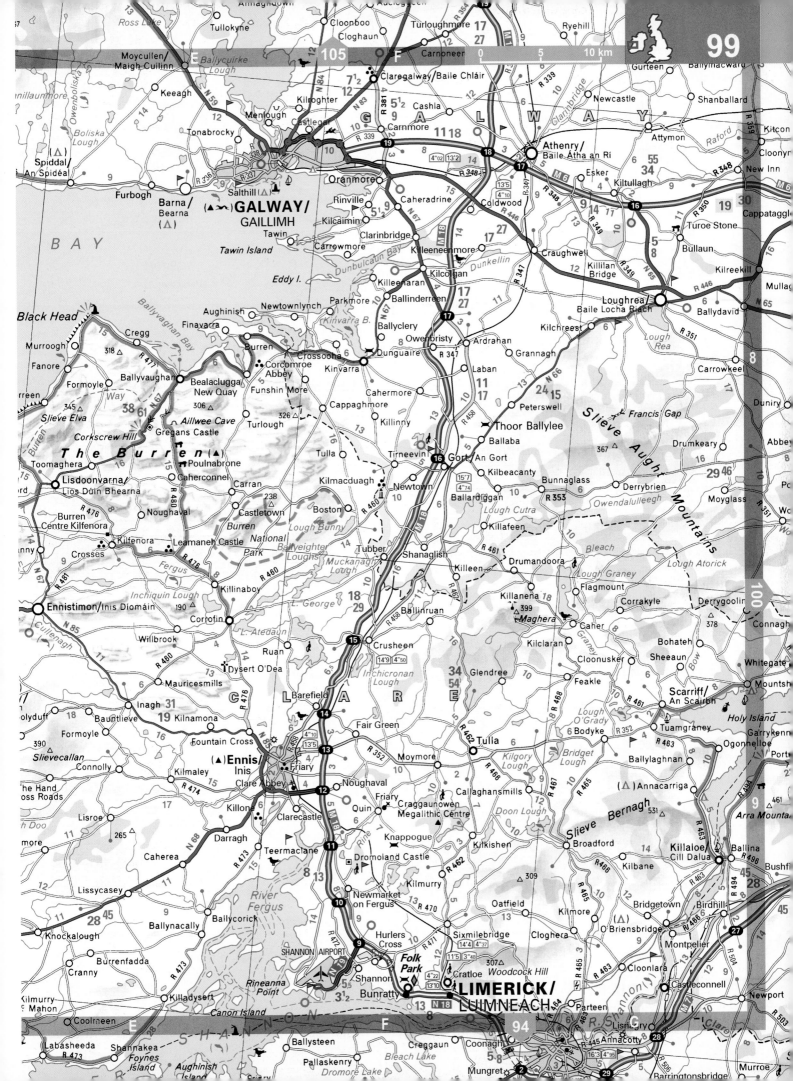

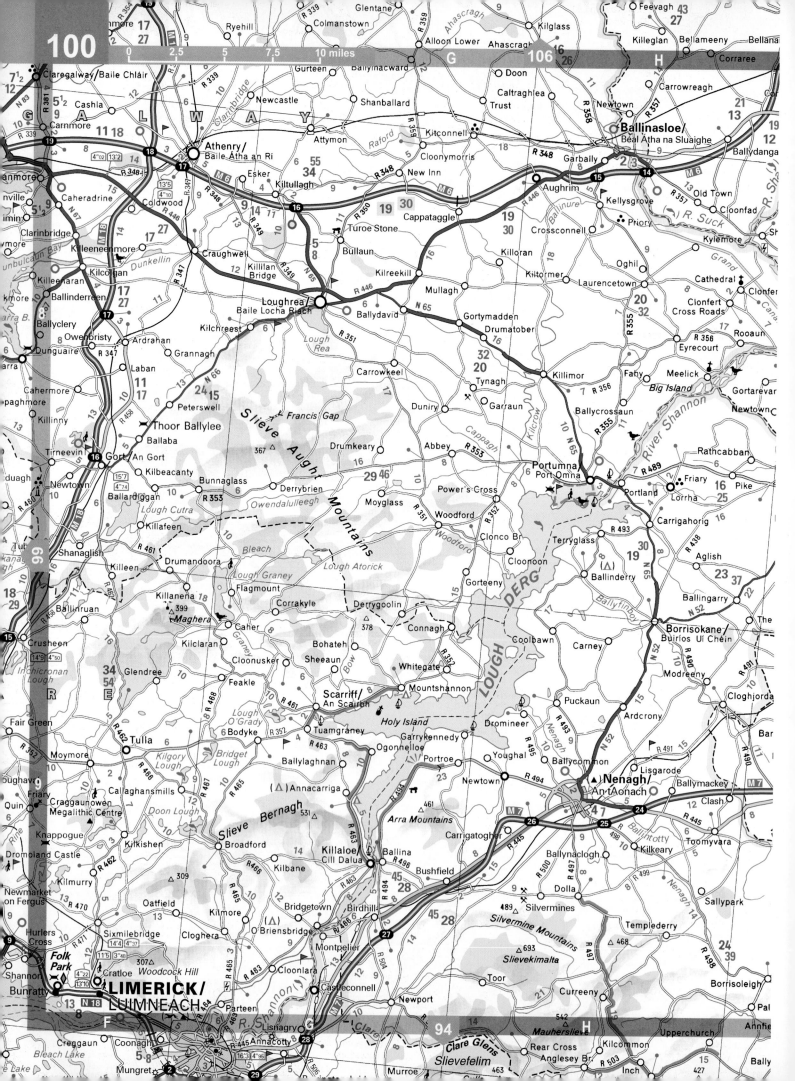

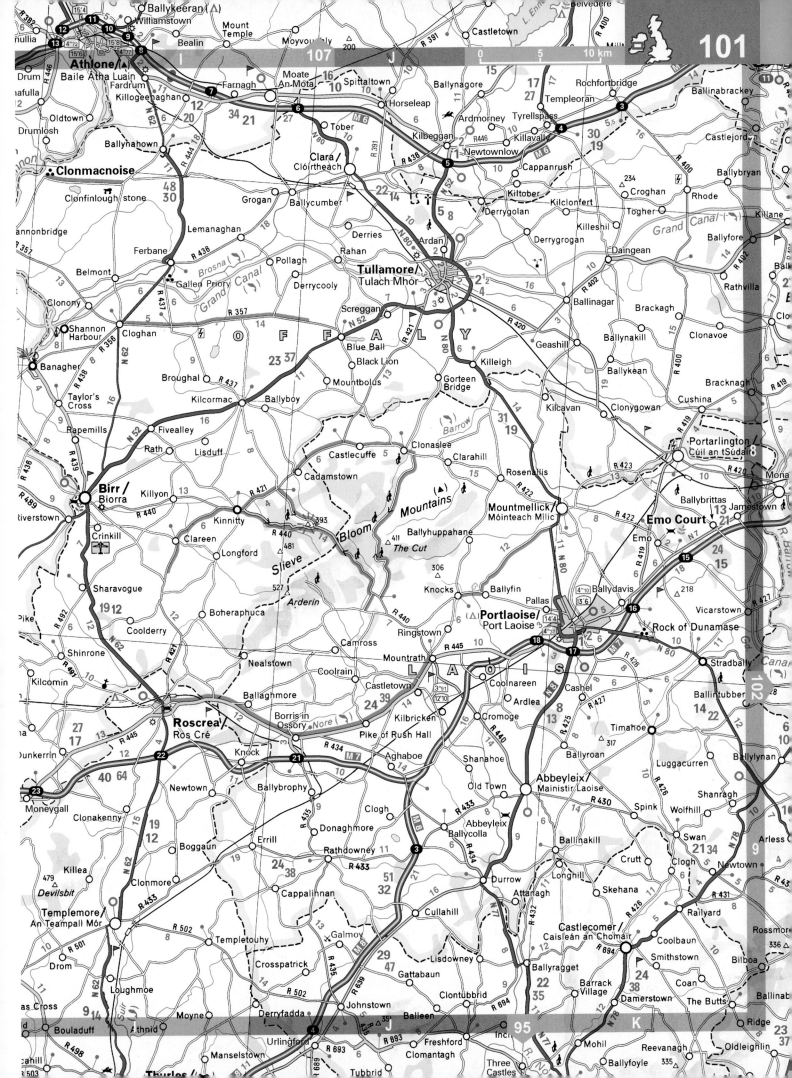

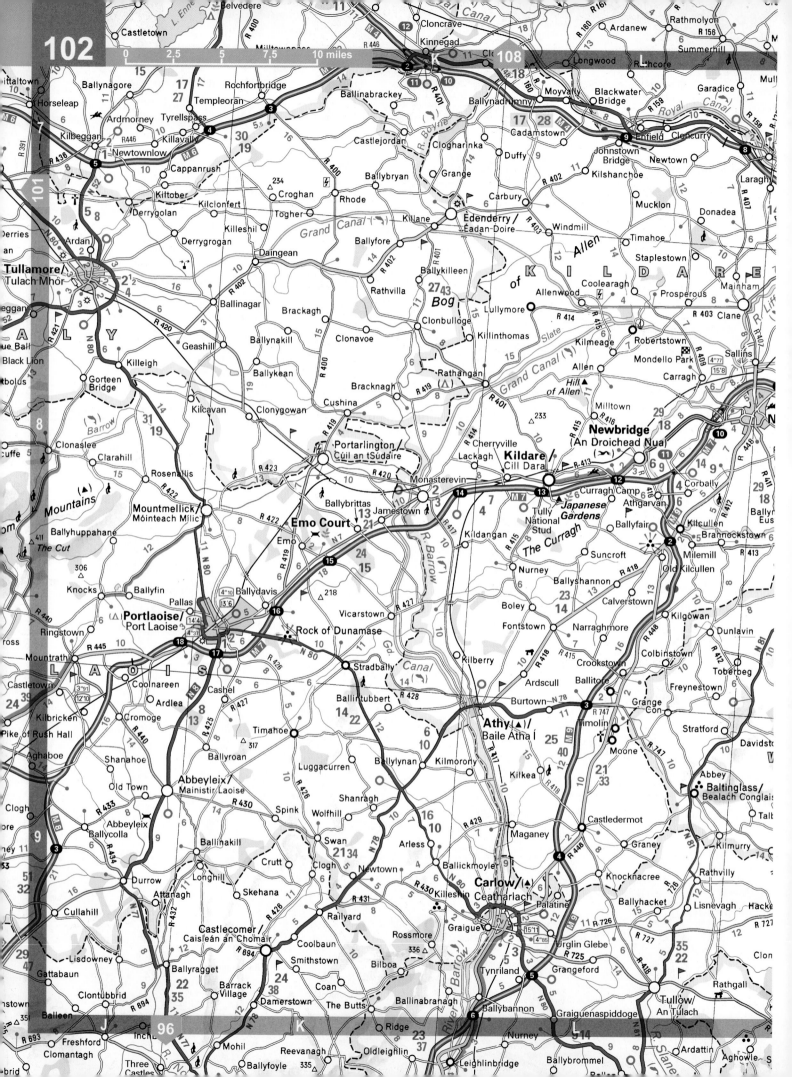

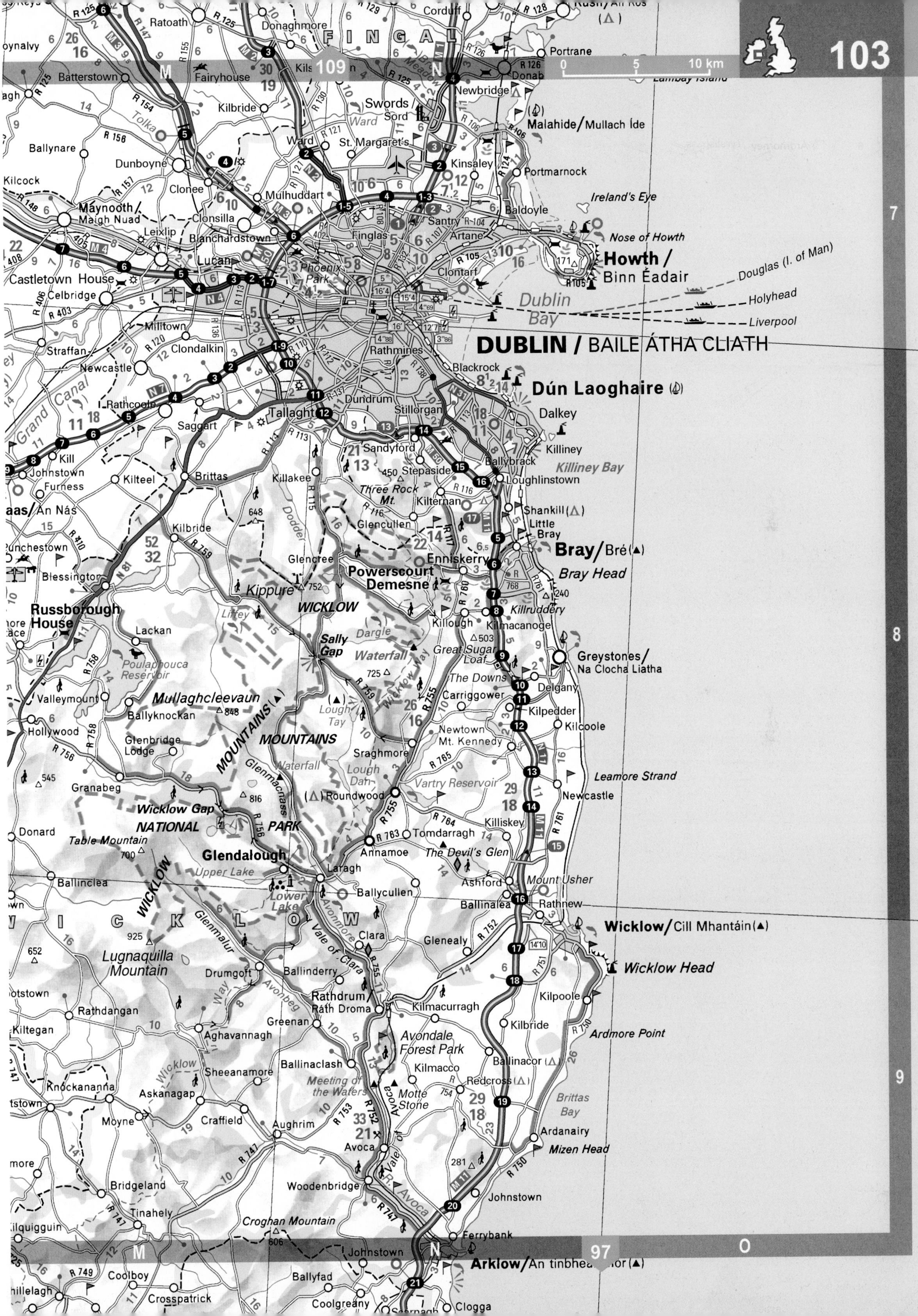

FINGAL

0   5   10 km

Portrane
Donab
Newbridge
Malahide/Mullach Íde
Portmarnock
Ireland's Eye
Nose of Howth
Howth / Binn Éadair
Douglas (I. of Man)
Holyhead
Liverpool
Dublin Bay

DUBLIN / BAILE ÁTHA CLIATH

Swords / Sord
St. Margaret's
Kinsaley
Baldoyle
Santry
Artane
Clontarf
Finglas
Phoenix Park
Rathmines
Blackrock
Dún Laoghaire
Dalkey
Killiney
Ballybrack
Loughlinstown
Shankill
Little Bray
Killiney Bay
Bray / Bré
Bray Head

Ratoath
Donaghmore
Fairyhouse
Kilbride
Battlestown
Ballynare
Dunboyne
Clonee
Kilcock
Máynooth / Maigh Nuad
Mulhuddart
Ward
Clonsilla
Blanchardstown
Leixlip
Lucan
Castletown House
Celbridge
Milltown
Clondalkin
Straffan
Newcastle
Rathcoole
Saggart
Tallaght
Dundrum
Stillorgan
Sandyford
Stepaside
Three Rock Mt.
Kilternan
Glencullen
Enniskerry
Powerscourt Demesne
Killough
Kilmacanoge
Killruddery
Great Sugar Loaf
Greystones / Na Clocha Liatha
Delgany
Kilpedder
Kilcoole
Newtown Mt. Kennedy

Kill
Johnstown
Furness
aas / An Nás
Kilteel
Kilbride
Brittas
Killakee
Punchestown
Blessington
Russborough House
Lackan
Kippure
WICKLOW
Sally Gap
Waterfall
Dargle
The Downs
Carriggower
Leamore Strand
Newcastle

Valleymount
Hollywood
Ballyknockan
Glenbridge Lodge
Mullaghcleevaun
MOUNTAINS
Lough Tay
Sraghmore
Vartry Reservoir
Killiskey
Granabeg
Glenmacnass
Wicklow Gap
Lough Dan
Roundwood
NATIONAL PARK
Donard
Table Mountain
Glendalough
Annamoe
The Devil's Glen
Ashford
Mount Usher
Laragh
Ballycullen
Ballinaclea
Upper Lake
Lower Lake
Ballinalea
Rathnew
Wicklow / Cill Mhantáin
Wicklow Head

Ballinclea
Clara
Glenealy
Lugnaquilla Mountain
Drumgoff
Ballinderry
Kilteg an
Rathdangan
Rathdrum / Ráth Droma
Kilmacurragh
Kilpoole
Greenan
Kilbride
Aghavannagh
Ardmore Point
Knockananna
Sheeanamore
Avondale Forest Park
Kilmacco
Ballinacor
Redcross
Moyne
Craffield
Aughrim
Avoca
Motte Stone
Ardanairy
Mizen Head

Bridgeland
Tinahely
Woodenbridge
Johnstown
Brittas Bay
Ferrybank
Arklow / An tInbhear Mór
Coolboy
Ballyfad
Coolgreany
Clogga
Crosspatrick
Croghan Mountain

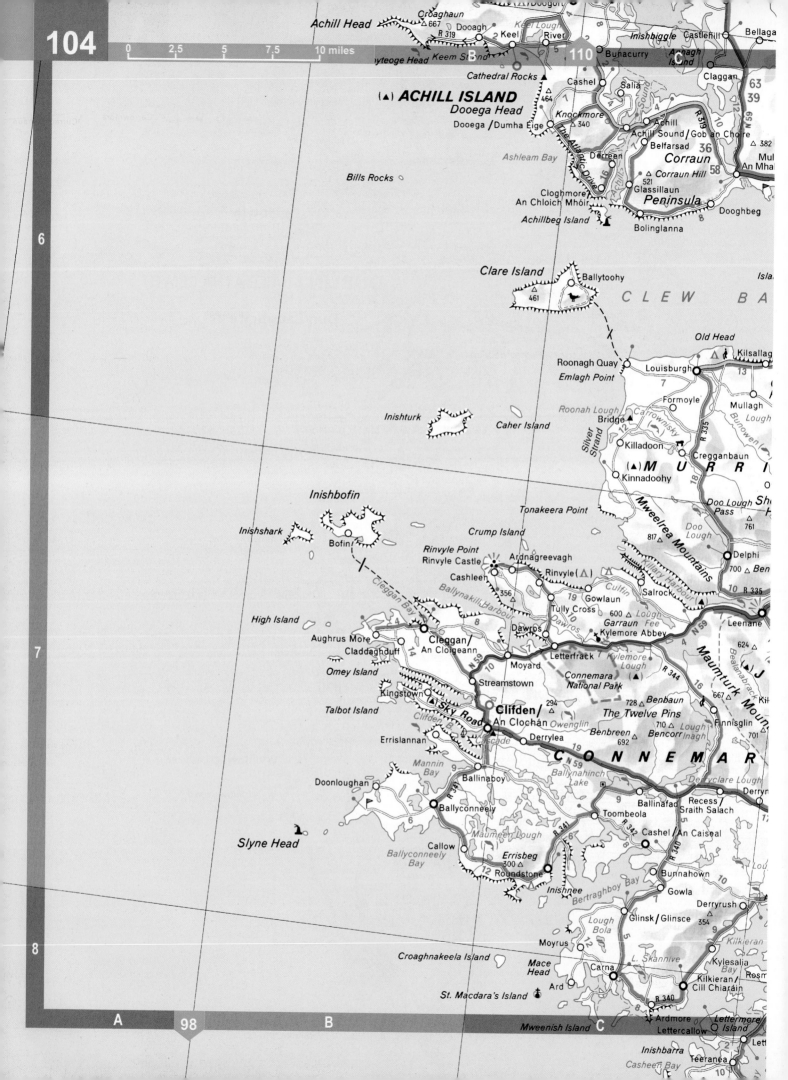

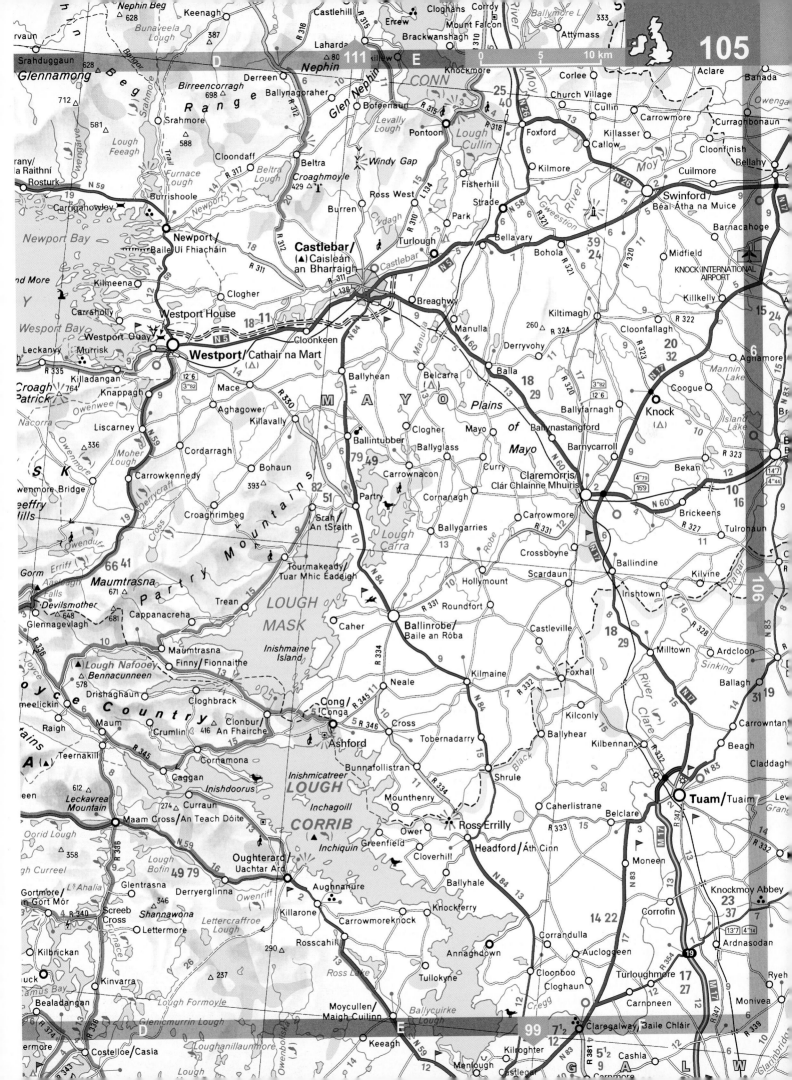

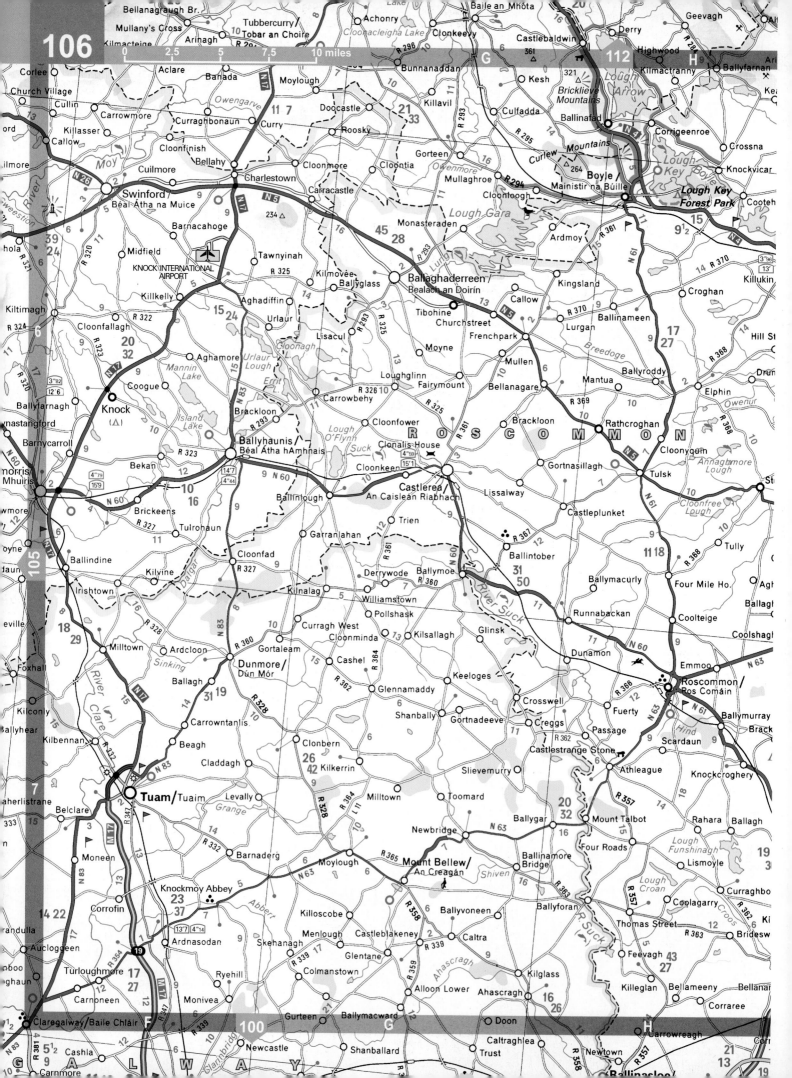

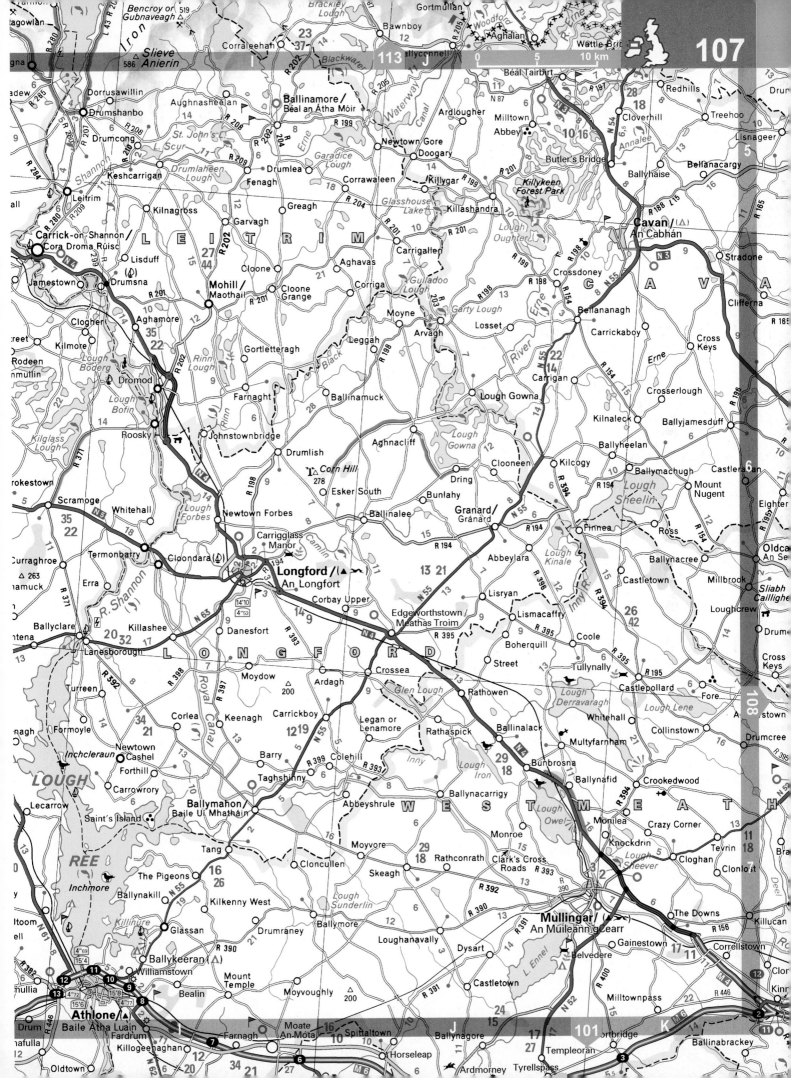

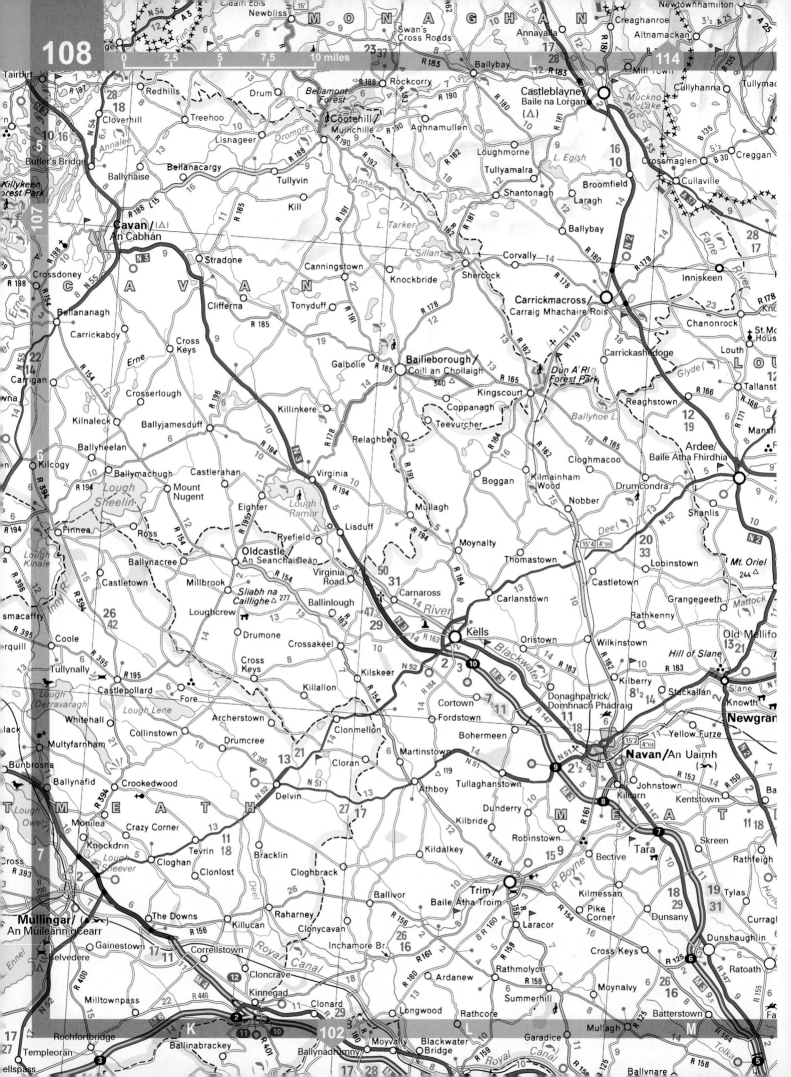

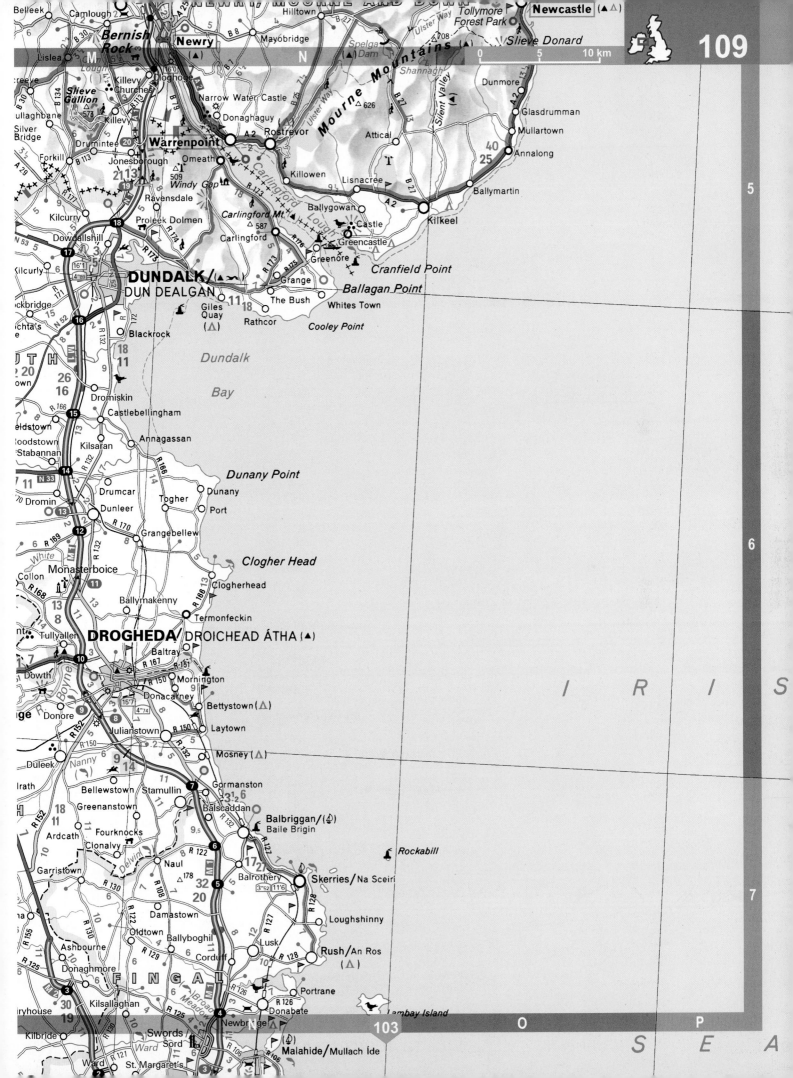

0 2.5 5 7.5 10 miles

A T L A N T

B

Benwee Head

Erris Head   Kid Island

Broad Haven

Eagle Island   Rinroe Point

Aghadoon

Annagh Head   Corclogh   6   138   Knocknalina   11   266

Inver

Belmullet /
Beal an Mhuirthead

Inishglora   R 313

Corraun Point   An Geata Mór   R 314   Barnata

Bart na

Drumreagh   Trawmore   Bunnahowen /
Mullet Peninsula   Bay   Bun na hAbhna   240

Elly Bay   12
                              19

Inishkea North   Doolough Point   Srahmore

Tristia

Inishkea South   Aghleam   Dooyork   Geesala /

105   Gaoth Saile

Fallmore   Blacksod   10   6
          Point

Black Rock   Duvillaun More   Duvillaun Beg   Blacksod   Shranamani
                                   Bay
          Tullaghan
          Bay

Doohooma

Owenduff

Saddle Head   Ridge Point   Doona

Slievemore   Fahy Lough

671   Valley   Ballycroy

Achill Head   Croaghaun   (Δ) Doogort
          667   Dooagh   Keel   River   Inishbiggle   Castlehill   Bellaga

R 319   Keel   2   Bunacurry   Annagh

Moyteoge Head   Keem Strand   Island

A   104   B   Cathedral Rocks   Cashel   Salia   C   63

(Δ) **ACHILL ISLAND**   464   Knockmore   39
Dooega Head   Achill
Dooega / Dumha Eige   340   R 319

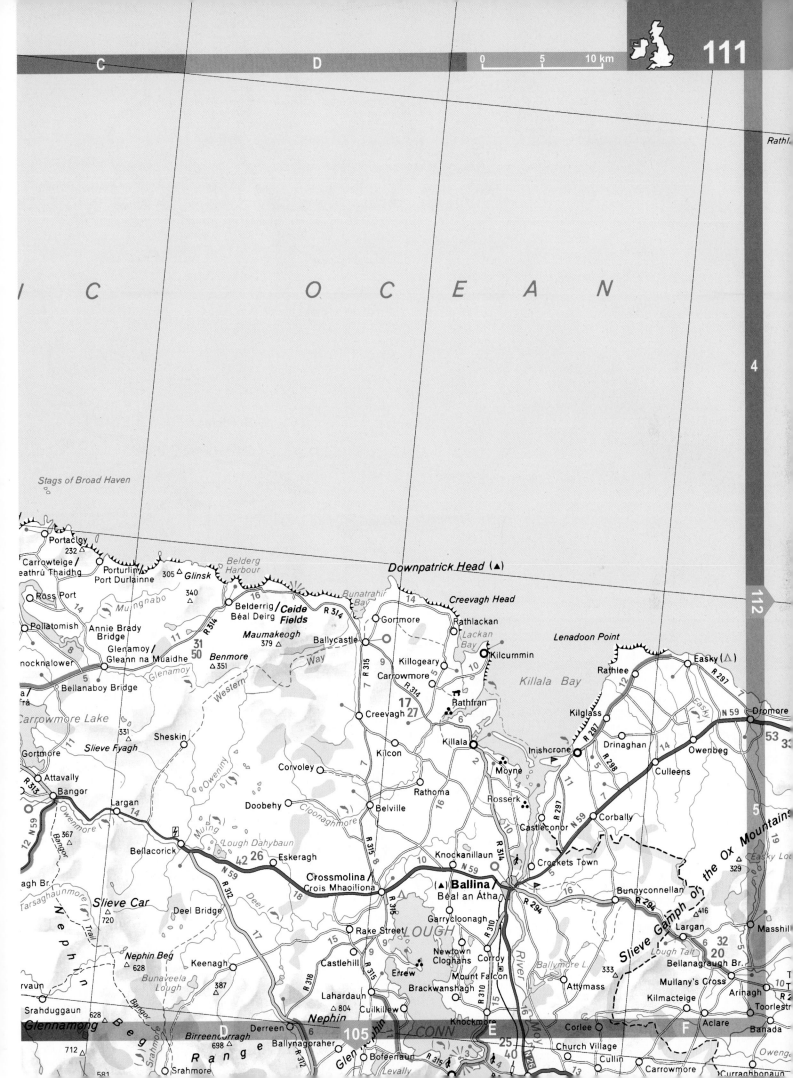

ATLANTIC OCEAN

Stags of Broad Haven

Portacloy
232
Carrowteige /
Ceathrú Thaidhg
Porturlin /
Port Durlainne
305 Glinsk
Belderg
Harbour
Downpatrick Head (▲)
Creevagh Head
Ross Port
340
16
14
Bunatrahir
Bay
Muingnabo
Belderrig / Ceide
Béal Deirg Fields
R 314
Gortmore
Rathlackan
Pollatomish
R 314
Maumakeogh
379
Ballycastle
Lenadoon Point
Killogeary
Lackan
Bay
Kilcummin
Easky (△)
Annie Brady
Bridge
11
Benmore
351
Western
9
Carrowmore
R 314
7
Rathlee
Rathfran
nocknalower
Glenamoy /
Gleann na Muaidhe
31
50
Way
R 315
Killala Bay
Kilglass
R 297
N 59
Dromore
Glenamoy
5
Bellanaboy Bridge
Creevagh
17
27
6
Rathfran
Inishcrone
Drinaghan
14
Owenbeg
53 33
Carrowmore Lake
331
Sheskin
Kilcon
Killala
2
Moyne
11
R 298
5
Culleens
5
Gortmore
Attavally
Corvoley
Rathoma
Rosserk
R 297
N 59
Corbally
Bangor
Largan
14
Doobehy
Belville
16
Castleconor
Owenmore
N 59
R 313
12 N 59
367
Bellacorick
42 26
Eskeragh
Knockanillaun
N 59
Crockets Town
5
16
Bunnyconnellan
Easky Lo
329
Muing
Lough Dahybaun
Crossmolina /
Crois Mhaoilíona
10
(▲) Ballina
Béal an Átha
R 294
R 294
Largan
32
20
416
Slieve Car
Deel Bridge
720
18
Garrycloonagh
LOUGH
R 310
Lough Talt
333
Bellanagraugh Br.
Nephin Beg
628
Keenagh
387
Rake Street
15
9
Newtown
Cloghans
Corroy
Mount Falcon
Mullany's Cross
Castlehill
Errew
Brackwanshagh
Attymass
Kilmacteige
Arinagh
Toorlestr
Srahduggaun
628
Glennamong
712
Beg
Birreencorragh
698
Ballynagoraher
Derreen
6
105
Nephin
804
Cuilkillew
Lahardaun
Knockmore
CONN
Corlee
Aclare
Banada
Srahmore
581
Bofeenaun
Levally
Cullin
Curraghbonaun

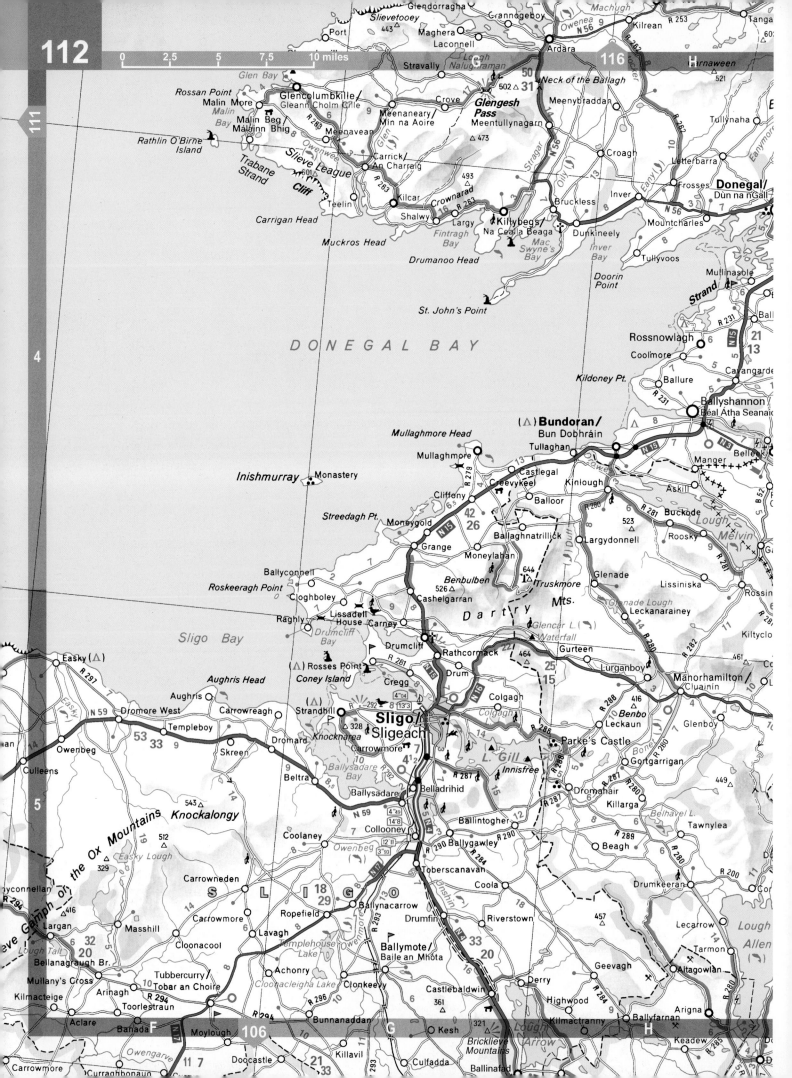

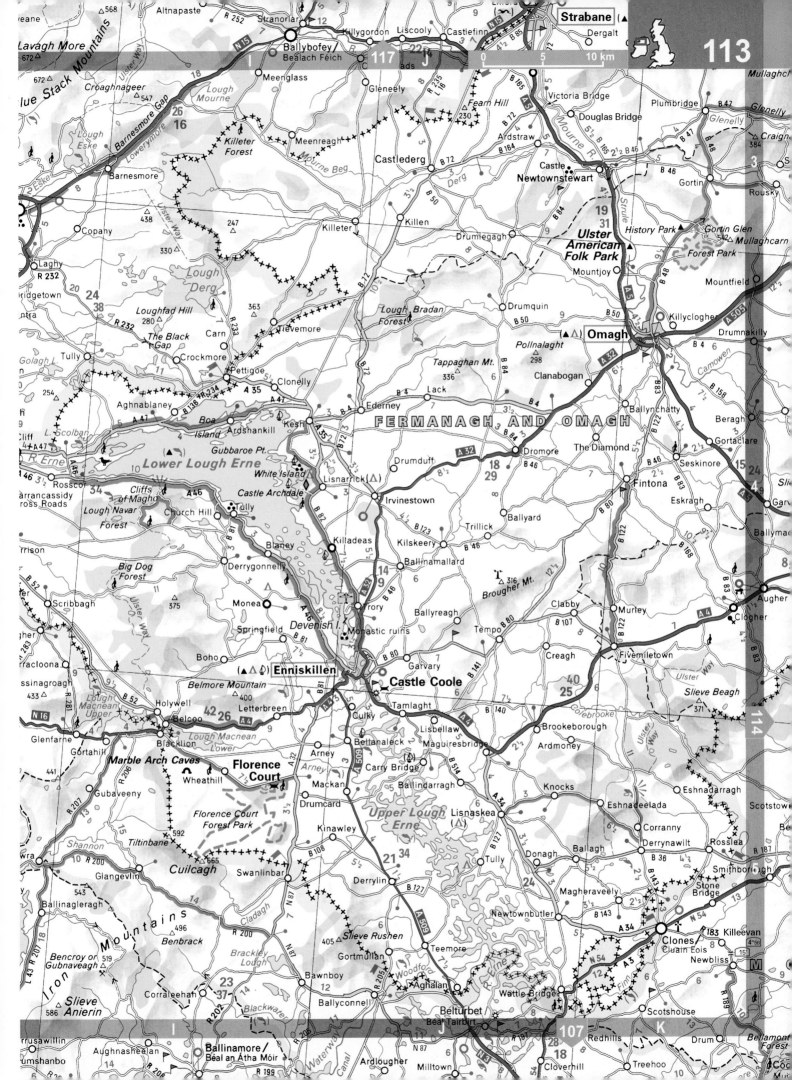

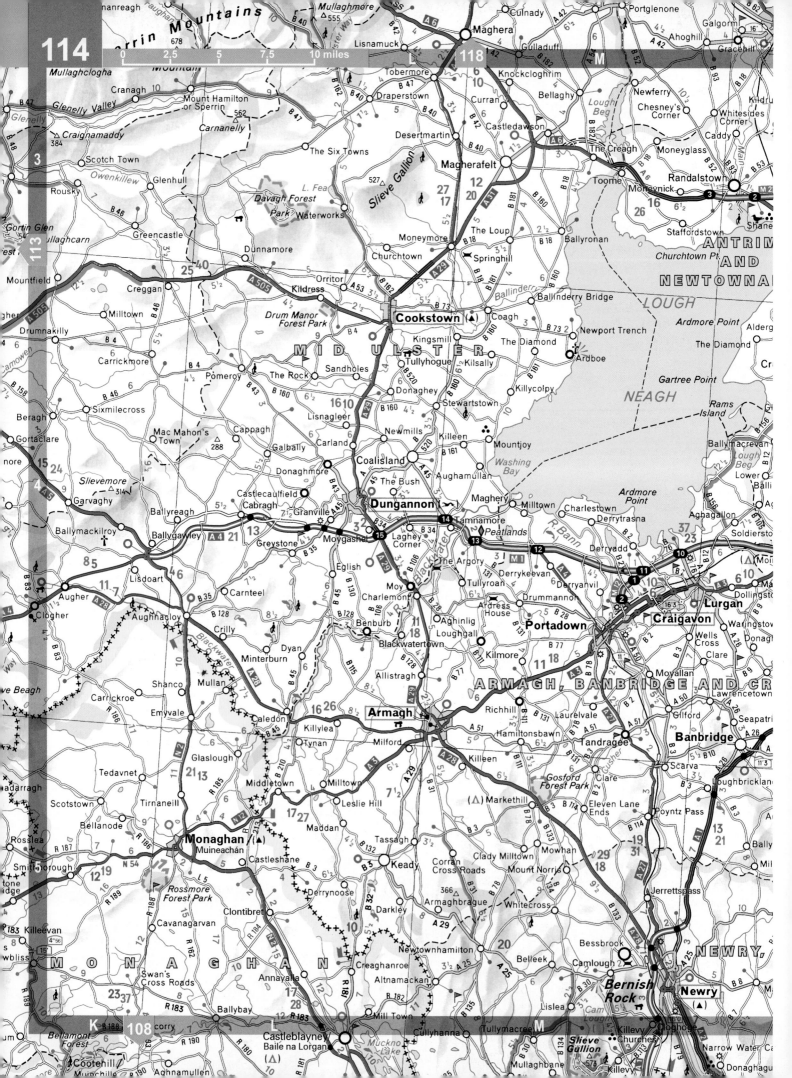

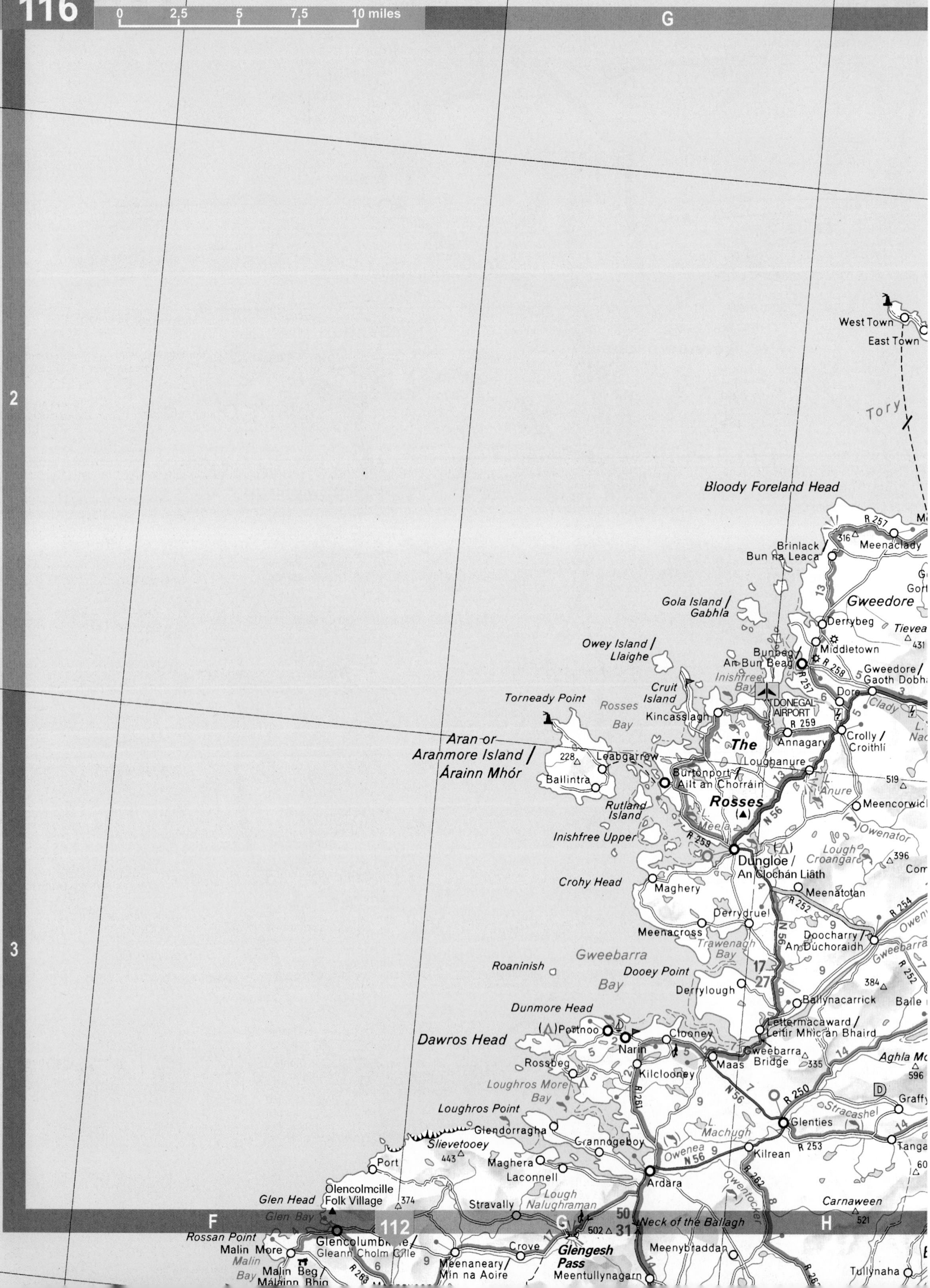

0   2.5   5   7.5   10 miles

2

West Town
East Town

Tory

Bloody Foreland Head

R 257   M

Brinlack /   316   Meenaclady
Bun na Leaca

13   *Gweedore*   Go
Gort

Gola Island /   Derrybeg   *Tievea*
Gabhla   431

Middletown
Owey Island /   Bunbeg /   R 258   Gweedore /
Llaighe   An Bun Beag   Gaoth Dobha

Inishfree   R 257   Dore   Clady   L.
Bay   DONEGAL   R 259   5   Nac
Cruit   AIRPORT
Torneady Point   *Island*   Kincasslagh   Crolly /
   Annagary   Croithlí
Aran or   *Rosses*   The   519
Aranmore Island /   228   Leabgarrow   *Bay*   Loughanure
Árainn Mhór   Burtonport /   Anure   Meencorwic
   Ballintra   Ailt an Chorráin   13
   Rutland   **Rosses**   N 56
   Island   (▲)   *Meela*   Owenator
   Inishfree Upper   R 259   *Lough*
   Dungloe /   (▲)   *Croangar*   396
   An Clochán Liath   Com

Crohy Head   Maghery   Meenatotan   R 254
   R 252   Owen
   Derrydruel   N 56   Doocharry /   R 252
   Meenacross   *Trawenagh*   An Dúchoraidh   *Gweebarra*
   Gweebarra   *Bay*   384   Baile
Roaninish   *Bay*   Dooey Point   17   9
   Derrylough   27   Ballynacarrick
Dunmore Head   Lettermacaward /
   (▲) Portnoo   Clooney   Leitir Mhic an Bhaird
Dawros Head   2   Narin   5   Gweebarra   14   *Aghla Mo*
   Rossbeg   5   Maas   Bridge   335   596
   Kilclooney   D
   Loughros More   R 261   N 56   R 250   Graffy
   Bay   Glendorragha   L.   *Stracashel*
Loughros Point   Machugh   Glenties   14
   Crannogeboy   Owenea   R 253   Tanga
Slievetooey   Maghera   Kilrean   60
   443   Laconnell   N 56   *Owentocher*   *Carnaweth*
Port   Ardara   521
Glencolmcille   374   Stravally   *Lough*
Folk Village   *Nalughraman*   50
Glen Head   Olencolmcille   502 △ 31   *Neck of the Ballagh*
Glen Bay   112   **Glengesh**
Rossan Point   Glencolumbkille   **Pass**   Meenybraddan
Malin More   Gleann Cholm Cille   Crove   Meentullynagarn
Malin   Meenaneary /   Tullynaha
Bay   Malin Beg /   Mín na Aoire
   Málainn Bhig   R 263   9

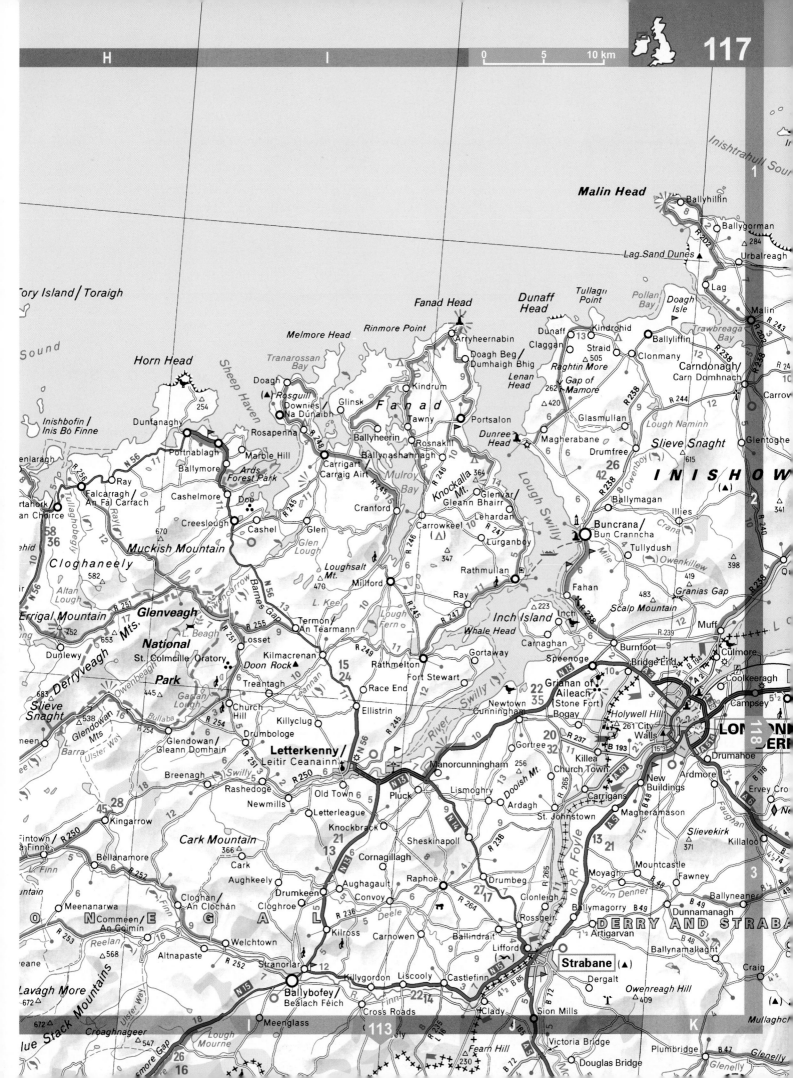

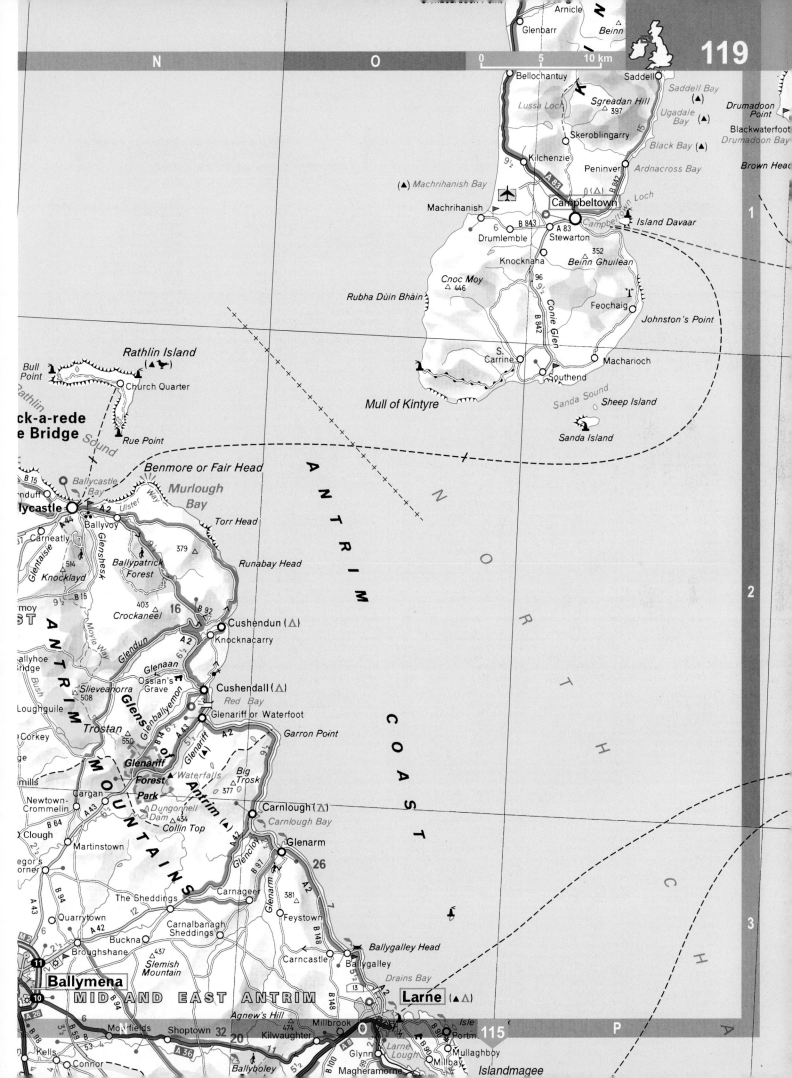

Page number / Numéro de page / Seitenzahl
Paginanummer / Numero di pagina / Número de Página

Grid coordinates / Coordonnées de carroyage
Koordinatenangabe / Verwijstekens ruitsysteem

Place / Localité / Ort ⟶ Achmelvich .... 84 E 9 ⟵ Coordinate riferite alla quadrettatura
Plaatsen / Località / Localidad

Coordenadas en los mapas

A

A Chill .... 71 A 12
A La Ronde .... 4 J 32
Abbas Combe .... 9 M 30
Abberley .... 27 M 27
Abbey .... 23 X 30
Abbey Dore .... 26 L 28
Abbey Town .... 54 K 19
Abbeydale .... 43 P 23
Abbeystead .... 48 L 22
Abbots Bromley .... 35 O 25
Abbots Langley .... 21 S 28
Abbots Leigh .... 18 M 29
Abbots Ripton .... 29 T 26
Abbotsbury .... 5 M 32
Abbotsford House .... 62 L 17
Abbotskerswell .... 4 J 32
Aber Banc .... 15 G 27
Aberaeron .... 24 H 27
Aberaman .... 17 J 28
Aberangell .... 33 I 25
Abercarn .... 18 K 29
Abercastle .... 14 E 28
Aberchirder .... 81 M 11
Abercynon .... 17 J 29
Aberdâr / Aberdare .... 17 J 28
Aberdare / Aberdâr .... 17 J 28
Aberdaron .... 32 F 25
Aberdaugleddau /
    Milford Haven .... 14 E 28
Aberdeen .... 75 N 12
Aberdour .... 68 K 15
Aberdour Bay .... 81 N 10
Aberdovey / Aberdyfi .... 33 H 26
Aberdyfi / Aberdovey .... 33 H 26
Aberedw .... 25 J 27
Abereiddy .... 14 E 28
Aberfeldy .... 73 I 14
Aberffraw .... 32 G 24
Aberford .... 43 P 22
Aberfoyle .... 67 G 15
Abergavenny / Y-Fenni .... 18 K 28
Abergele .... 41 J 23
Abergolech .... 15 H 28
Abergwaun / Fishguard .... 24 F 28
Abergwesyn .... 25 I 27
Abergwili .... 15 H 28
Abergwynfi .... 17 J 29
Abergwyngregyn .... 41 H 23
Abergynolwyn .... 33 I 26
Aberhonddu / Brecon .... 25 J 28
Aberkenfig .... 17 J 29
Aberlady .... 69 L 15
Aberlemno .... 75 L 13
Aberlour .... 80 K 11
Abermaw / Barmouth .... 33 H 25
Abermule .... 34 K 26
Abernethy .... 68 K 15
Abernyte .... 68 K 14
Aberpennar / Mountain Ash 17 J 28
Aberporth .... 15 G 27
Abersoch .... 32 G 25
Abersychan .... 18 K 28
Abertawe / Swansea .... 17 I 29
Aberteifi / Cardigan .... 15 G 27
Abertillery .... 18 K 28
Aberuthven .... 67 J 15
Aberystwyth .... 25 H 26
Abingdon .... 20 Q 28
Abinger Common .... 21 S 30
Abinger Hammer .... 21 S 30
Abingto Cambs. .... 30 U 27
Abington South Lanarkshire 61 I 17
Aboyne .... 75 L 12
Abriachan .... 79 G 11
Abridge .... 21 U 29
Accrington .... 42 M 22
Achahoish .... 65 D 16
Achallader .... 66 F 14
Achanalt .... 78 F 11
Achaphubuil .... 72 E 13
Acharacle .... 71 C 13
Achargary .... 85 H 8
Acharn .... 67 H 14

Achduart .... 83 E 10
Achgarve .... 78 D 10
Achiemore .... 84 F 8
Achiltibuie .... 83 D 9
Achintee .... 78 D 11
Achintraid .... 78 D 11
Achlean .... 73 I 12
Achleck .... 64 B 14
Achmelvich .... 84 E 9
Achmore .... 78 D 11
Achnahanat .... 84 G 10
Achnamara .... 65 D 15
Achnanellan .... 72 E 13
Achnasheen .... 78 E 11
Achnashellach Forest .... 78 E 11
Achosnich .... 71 B 13
Achranich .... 71 C 14
Achray (Loch) .... 67 G 15
Achreamie .... 85 I 8
Achriesgill .... 84 F 8
Achtalean .... 77 B 11
Achvaich .... 79 H 10
Acklington .... 63 P 18
Ackworth .... 44 P 23
Acle .... 39 Y 26
Acomb .... 55 N 19
Acrise Place .... 13 X 30
Acton Burnell .... 34 L 26
Acton Scott .... 26 L 26
Acton Turville .... 19 N 29
Adbaston .... 35 M 25
Adderbury .... 28 Q 27
Adderley .... 34 M 25
Adderstone .... 63 O 17
Addingham .... 49 O 22
Addlestone .... 21 S 29
Adfa .... 33 J 26
Adlington .... 42 M 23
Adlington Hall .... 43 N 24
Advie .... 80 J 11
Adwick-le-Street .... 44 Q 23
Ae (Forest of) .... 53 J 18
Ae Village .... 53 J 18
Afan Argoed .... 17 J 29
Affric (Glen) .... 78 F 12
Affric Lodge .... 78 E 12
Afon Dyfrdwy / Dee (River) .34 K 24
Afon Dyfrdwy (River) /
    Dee Wales .... 41 K 23
Afon-wen .... 41 K 23
Agneash .... 46 G 21
Aikton .... 54 K 19
Ailort (Loch) .... 72 C 13
Ailsa Craig .... 59 E 18
Ainderby Quernhow .... 50 P 21
Ainort (Loch) .... 77 B 12
Ainsdale .... 42 K 23
Air Uig .... 82 Y 9
Aird .... 65 D 15
Aird (The) .... 79 G 11
Aird of Sleat .... 71 C 12
Airdrie .... 61 I 16
Airigh na h-Airde (Loch) .... 82 Z 9
Airor .... 72 C 12
Airth .... 67 I 15
Airton .... 49 N 21
Aith Orkney Is. .... 87 M 6
Aith Shetland Is. .... 87 P 3
Aitnoch .... 80 I 11
Akeld .... 63 N 17
Albourne .... 11 T 31
Albrighton .... 35 N 26
Albyn or Mor (Glen) .... 73 F 12
Alcaig .... 79 G 11
Alcester .... 27 O 27
Alconbury .... 29 T 26
Aldborough .... 39 X 25
Aldbourne .... 19 P 29
Aldbrough .... 45 T 22
Aldbrough St. John .... 49 O 20
Aldbury .... 21 S 28
Alde (River) .... 31 Y 27
Aldeburgh .... 31 Y 27
Aldenham .... 21 S 28
Alderbury .... 9 O 30

Alderholt .... 9 O 31
Alderley Edge .... 43 N 24
Alderney Channel I. 5
Aldershot .... 20 R 30
Alderton .... 27 N 28
Aldford .... 34 L 24
Aldingbourne .... 11 R 31
Aldingham .... 31 Y 27
Aldsworth .... 19 O 28
Aldunie .... 80 K 12
Aldwick .... 11 R 31
Alexandria .... 66 G 16
Alfold Crossways .... 11 S 30
Alford Aberdeenshire .... 75 L 12
Alford Lincs. .... 45 U 24
Alfreton .... 36 P 24
Alfrick .... 27 M 27
Alfriston .... 12 U 31
Aline (Loch) .... 65 C 14
Alkborough .... 44 S 22
Alkham .... 13 X 30
All Stretton .... 34 L 26
Allanaquoich .... 74 J 12
Allanton
    North Lanarkshire .... 61 I 16
Allanton Scottish Borders .... 63 N 16
Allendale Town .... 55 N 19
Allenheads .... 55 N 19
Allensmore .... 26 L 27
Allerford .... 17 J 30
Allerston .... 51 S 21
Allestree .... 36 P 25
Allhallows .... 22 V 29
Alligin Shuas .... 78 D 11
Allington Kennet .... 19 O 29
Allington Salisbury .... 9 O 30
Allnabad .... 84 G 8
Alloa .... 67 I 15
Allonby .... 54 J 19
Alloway .... 60 G 17
Allt na h-Airbhe .... 78 E 10
Alltan Fhèarna (Loch an) .... 85 H 9
Alltnacaillich .... 84 G 8
Almond (Glen) .... 67 I 14
Almondbank .... 68 J 14
Almondsbury .... 18 M 29
Alness .... 79 H 10
Alnmouth .... 63 P 17
Alnwick .... 63 O 17
Alpheton .... 30 W 27
Alphington .... 4 J 31
Alpraham .... 34 M 24
Alresford .... 30 X 28
Alrewas .... 35 O 25
Alsager .... 35 N 24
Alsh (Loch) .... 78 D 12
Alston .... 55 M 19
Alstonefield .... 35 O 24
Alswear .... 7 I 31
Altadnduin .... 85 H 9
Altandhu .... 83 D 9
Altarnun .... 3 G 32
Altass .... 84 G 10
Alternative Technology
    Centre .... 33 I 26
Altham .... 42 M 22
Althorne .... 22 W 29
Althorpe .... 44 R 23
Altnabreac Station .... 85 I 8
Altnacealgach .... 84 F 9
Altnaharra .... 84 G 9
Alton Hants. .... 10 R 30
Alton Staffs. .... 35 O 25
Alton Pancras .... 9 M 31
Alton Priors .... 19 O 29
Alton Towers .... 35 O 25
Altrincham .... 42 M 23
Alum Bay .... 10 P 31
Alva .... 67 I 15
Alvaston .... 36 P 25
Alvechurch .... 27 O 26
Alvediston .... 9 N 30
Alves .... 80 J 11
Alvescot .... 19 P 28

Alvie .... 73 I 12
Alvingham .... 45 U 23
Alwinton .... 63 N 17
Alyth .... 74 K 14
Amberley .... 11 S 31
Amble .... 63 P 18
Amblecote .... 27 N 26
Ambleside .... 48 L 20
Ambrosden .... 28 Q 28
Amersham .... 21 S 29
Amesbury .... 9 O 30
Amhuinnsuidhe .... 82 Y 10
Amisfield .... 53 J 18
Amlwch .... 40 G 22
Ammanford / Rhydaman .... 15 I 28
Amotherby .... 50 R 21
Ampleforth .... 50 Q 21
Amport .... 20 P 30
Ampthill .... 29 S 27
Amroth .... 15 G 28
Amulree .... 67 I 14
An Riabhachan .... 78 E 11
An Socach .... 74 J 13
An Teallach .... 78 E 10
Anchor .... 26 K 26
Ancroft .... 63 O 16
Ancrum .... 62 M 17
Andover .... 20 P 30
Andoversford .... 27 O 28
Andreas .... 46 G 20
Angle .... 14 E 28
Anglesey (Isle of) 40
Anglesey Abbey .... 30 U 27
Angmering .... 11 S 31
Annan .... 54 K 19
Annan (River) .... 61 J 18
Annat .... 78 D 11
Annat Bay .... 83 E 10
Annbank .... 60 G 17
Annbank Station .... 60 G 17
Anne Hathaway's Cottage .. 27 O 27
Annesley-Woodhouse .... 36 Q 24
Annfield Plain .... 56 O 19
Ansley .... 28 P 26
Anstey .... 36 Q 25
Anston .... 44 Q 23
Anstruther .... 69 L 15
Anthorn .... 54 K 19
Antony House .... 3 H 32
Appin .... 72 E 14
Appleby
    North Lincolnshire .... 44 S 23
Appleby-in-Westmorland .... 55 M 20
Appleby Magna .... 36 P 25
Applecross .... 77 C 11
Appledore Devon .... 6 H 30
Appledore Kent .... 12 W 30
Appleford .... 20 Q 29
Appleton .... 20 P 28
Appleton Roebuck .... 44 Q 22
Appleton Wiske .... 50 P 20
Appletreewick .... 49 O 21
Arberth / Narberth .... 15 F 28
Arbigland .... 53 J 19
Arbirlot .... 69 M 14
Arbor Low .... 35 O 24
Arborfield .... 20 R 29
Arbroath .... 69 M 14
Arbury Hall .... 28 P 26
Arbuthnott .... 75 N 13
Archiestown .... 80 K 11
Ard (Loch) .... 67 G 15
Ardanaiseig .... 66 E 14
Ardarroch .... 78 D 11
Ardcharnich .... 78 E 10
Ardchiavaig .... 64 B 15
Ardchuilk .... 78 F 11
Ardchyle .... 67 H 14
Ardechive .... 72 E 13
Arden .... 66 G 15
Ardentallan .... 65 D 14
Ardeonaig .... 67 H 14
Ardersier .... 79 H 11
Ardery .... 72 C 13

Ardfern .... 65 D 15
Ardgartan .... 66 F 15
Ardgay .... 79 G 10
Ardgour .... 72 D 13
Ardhasaig .... 82 Z 10
Ardingly .... 11 T 30
Ardington .... 20 P 29
Ardivachar .... 76 X 11
Ardleigh .... 30 W 28
Ardley .... 28 Q 28
Ardlui .... 66 F 15
Ardlussa .... 65 C 15
Ardmair .... 84 E 10
Ardminish .... 58 C 16
Ardmolich .... 71 C 13
Ardmore Point Isle of Skye .77 A 11
Ardnacross .... 71 C 14
Ardnamurchan .... 71 B 13
Ardnastang .... 72 D 13
Ardnave .... 64 A 16
Ardnave Point .... 64 B 16
Ardpatrick .... 59 D 16
Ardradour .... 65 D 15
Ardrishaig .... 71 C 13
Ardrossan .... 59 F 17
Ardshealach .... 71 C 13
Ardslignish .... 71 C 13
Ardtalla .... 58 B 16
Ardtalnaig .... 67 H 14
Ardtoe .... 71 C 13
Ardvasar .... 71 C 12
Ardverikie Forest .... 73 G 13
Ardvorlich .... 67 H 14
Ardwell .... 52 F 19
Argyll .... 65 D 15
Argyll Forest Park .... 66 F 15
Arichastlich .... 66 F 14
Arienas (Loch) .... 71 C 14
Arinagour .... 71 A 14
Arisaig .... 71 C 13
Arivruaich .... 82 Z 9
Arkaig (Loch) .... 72 E 13
Arkendale .... 50 P 21
Arkengarthdale .... 49 N 20
Arkholme .... 48 M 21
Arklet (Loch) .... 66 G 15
Arley .... 27 P 26
Arlingham .... 19 M 28
Arlington Court .... 7 I 30
Armadale Highland .... 85 H 8
Armadale West Lothian .... 61 I 16
Armadale Bay .... 71 C 12
Armitage .... 35 O 25
Armthorpe .... 44 Q 23
Arnabost .... 71 A 14
Arncliffe .... 49 N 21
Arncott .... 20 Q 28
Arncroach .... 69 L 15
Arne .... 9 N 31
Arnesby .... 28 Q 26
Arnicle .... 59 D 17
Arnisdale .... 72 D 12
Arnish .... 77 B 11
Arnol .... 82 A 8
Arnold .... 36 Q 25
Arnprior .... 67 H 15
Arnside .... 48 L 21
Aros .... 65 B 14
Arreton .... 10 Q 31
Arrochar .... 66 F 15
Arscaig .... 84 G 9
Arundel .... 11 S 31
Ascog .... 59 E 16
Ascot .... 21 R 29
Ascott House .... 29 R 28
Ascott-under-Wychwood .. 28 P 28
Ascrib Islands .... 77 A 11
Asfordby .... 36 R 25
Ash Kent .... 23 X 30
Ash Surrey .... 20 R 30
Ash Mill .... 7 I 31
Ashbourne .... 35 O 24
Ashburton .... 4 I 32

Ashbury .... 19 P 29
Ashby de la Zouch .... 36 P 25
Ashby Magna .... 28 Q 26
Ashcott .... 8 L 30
Ashdon .... 30 U 27
Ashford Kent .... 12 W 30
Ashford Surrey .... 21 S 29
Ashford-in-the-Water
    Derbs. .... 43 O 24
Ashie (Loch) .... 79 H 11
Ashill Breckland .... 38 W 26
Ashill South Somerset .... 8 L 31
Ashingdon .... 22 W 29
Ashington Northumb .... 56 P 18
Ashington West Sussex .... 11 S 31
Ashkirk .... 62 L 17
Ashleworth .... 27 N 28
Ashley
    East Cambridgeshire .... 30 V 27
Ashley
    Newcastle-under-Lyme ...35 M 25
Ashley Torridge .... 7 I 31
Ashley Green .... 21 S 28
Ashmore .... 9 N 31
Ashover .... 36 P 24
Ashperton .... 26 M 27
Ashreigney .... 7 I 31
Ashtead .... 21 T 30
Ashton .... 34 L 24
Ashton-in-Makerfield .... 42 M 23
Ashton Keynes .... 19 O 29
Ashton-under-Lyne .... 43 N 23
Ashton-upon-Mersey .... 42 M 23
Ashurst .... 10 P 31
Ashwell North Hertfordshire 29 T 27
Ashwell Rutland .... 36 R 25
Ashwellthorpe .... 39 X 26
Askam in Furness .... 47 K 21
Askern .... 44 Q 23
Askernish .... 76 X 12
Askerswell .... 5 L 31
Askham .... 55 L 20
Askrigg .... 49 N 21
Askwith .... 49 O 22
Aslacton .... 31 X 26
Aslockton .... 36 R 25
Aspatria .... 54 K 19
Aspley Guise .... 29 S 27
Assynt (Loch) .... 84 E 9
Astley .... 34 L 25
Aston Vale Royal .... 44 Q 23
Aston West Oxfordshire .... 20 P 28
Aston Clinton .... 20 R 28
Aston Magna .... 27 O 27
Aston Rowant .... 20 R 28
Aston Tirrold .... 20 Q 29
Astwood Bank .... 27 O 27
Atcham .... 34 L 25
Athelhampton Hall .... 9 N 31
Athelney .... 8 L 30
Athelstaneford .... 69 L 16
Atherington .... 7 H 31
Atherstone .... 36 P 26
Atherton .... 42 M 23
Atlow (Forest of) .... 73 H 13
Attadale .... 78 D 11
Attleborough Breckland .... 38 X 26
Attleborough
    Nuneaton and Bedworth ..28 P 26
Attlebridge .... 39 X 25
Atwick .... 51 T 22
Atworth .... 19 N 29
Aucharnie .... 81 M 11
Auchavan .... 74 K 13
Auchenblae .... 75 M 13
Auchenbowie .... 67 I 15
Auchenbrack .... 61 I 18
Auchenbreck .... 65 E 16
Auchencairn .... 53 I 19
Auchencrosh .... 52 F 18
Auchencrow .... 63 N 16
Auchengray .... 61 J 16
Auchenmalg .... 52 F 19
Auchentiber .... 60 G 16

A

Auchindrean .... 78 E 10
Auchinleck .... 60 H 17
Auchleven .... 81 M 12
Auchlyne .... 67 G 14
Auchnafree .... 67 I 14
Auchnagallin .... 80 J 11
Auchnagatt .... 81 N 11
Aucholzie .... 74 K 12
Auchronie .... 74 L 13
Auchterarder .... 67 I 15
Auchteraw .... 73 F 12
Auchterderran .... 68 K 15
Auchterhouse .... 68 K 14
Auchtermuchty .... 68 K 15
Auchtertyre .... 78 D 12
Auckengill .... 86 K 8
Auckley .... 44 Q 23
Audenshaw .... 43 N 23
Audlem .... 34 M 25
Audley .... 35 N 24
Audley End .... 30 U 27
Aughton near Lancaster .. 48 L 21
Aughton near Ormskirk ... 42 L 23
Auldearn .... 79 I 11
Auldgirth .... 53 I 18
Auldhouse .... 60 H 16
Ault a' Chruinn .... 72 D 12
Aultbea .... 78 D 10
Aust .... 18 M 29
Austrey .... 35 P 26
Austwick .... 49 M 21
Avebury .... 19 O 29
Aveley .... 22 U 29
Avening .... 19 N 28
Aveton Gifford .... 4 I 33
Aviemore .... 73 I 12
Avoch .... 79 H 11
Avon (Glen) .... 74 J 12
Avon (River) R. Severn .. 28 Q 26
Avon (River) Wilts. .... 9 O 31
Avonbridge .... 67 I 16
Avonmouth .... 18 L 29
Avonwick .... 4 I 32
Awe (Loch) .... 65 E 15
Awliscombe .... 8 K 31
Awre .... 19 M 28
Axbridge .... 18 L 30
Axminster .... 8 L 31
Axmouth .... 5 K 31
Aylburton .... 18 M 28
Aylesbury .... 20 R 28
Aylesford .... 22 V 30
Aylesham .... 23 X 30
Aylsham .... 39 X 25
Aylton .... 26 M 27
Aymestrey .... 26 L 27
Aynho .... 28 Q 28
Ayr .... 60 G 17
Aysgarth .... 49 O 21
Ayside .... 48 L 21
Ayton Scarborough .... 51 S 21
Ayton Scottish Borders .. 63 N 16

B

Bà (Loch) .... 65 C 14
Babbacombe Bay .... 4 J 32
Babcary .... 8 M 30
Babell .... 41 K 23
Babworth .... 44 R 24
Back .... 83 B 9
Backaland .... 87 L 6
Backmuir of New Gilston .. 69 L 15
Backwater Reservoir .... 74 K 13
Backwell West Town .... 18 L 29
Baconsthorpe .... 39 X 25
Bacton Mid Suffolk .... 30 X 27
Bacton North Norfolk .... 39 Y 25
Bacup .... 43 N 22
Bad a' Ghaill (Loch) .... 84 E 9
Bad an Sgalaig (Loch) .... 78 D 10
Badachro .... 77 C 10
Badanloch (Loch) .... 85 H 9
Badanloch Lodge .... 85 H 9
Badcaul .... 78 D 10
Baddesley Ensor .... 35 P 26
Baddidarach .... 84 E 9
Badenoch .... 73 H 13
Badenscallie .... 83 E 9
Badenyon .... 74 K 12
Badlipster .... 86 K 8
Badluarach .... 78 D 10
Badminton .... 19 N 29
Badrallach .... 78 E 10
Bae Colwyn / Colwyn Bay ..41 I 23
Bagh nam Faoileann .... 76 Y 11
Bagillt .... 41 K 23
Bagley .... 34 L 25

Bagshot .... 21 R 29
Bagworth .... 36 P 25
Bagwyllydiart .... 26 L 28
Baile Mòr .... 64 A 15
Bailiehill .... 54 K 18
Bainbridge .... 49 N 21
Bainton .... 51 S 22
Bakewell .... 35 O 24
Bala .... 33 J 25
Balallan .... 82 A 9
Balbeggie .... 68 J 14
Balblair .... 79 H 10
Balcary Point .... 53 I 19
Balchrick .... 84 E 8
Balcombe .... 11 T 30
Balderton .... 36 R 24
Baldock .... 29 T 28
Baldrine .... 46 G 21
Baldwin .... 46 G 21
Balemartine .... 64 Z 14
Balephetrish Bay .... 70 Z 14
Balephuil .... 64 Z 14
Balephuil Bay .... 64 Z 14
Balerno .... 61 J 16
Baleshare .... 76 X 11
Balevulin .... 65 B 14
Balfour .... 87 L 6
Balfron .... 67 H 15
Balgray .... 69 L 14
Balintore Angus .... 74 K 13
Balintore Highland .... 79 I 10
Balivanich .... 76 X 11
Balk .... 50 Q 21
Ballabeg .... 46 F 21
Ballachulish .... 72 E 13
Ballajora .... 46 G 21
Ballamodha .... 46 G 21
Ballantrae .... 52 E 18
Ballasalla .... 46 G 21
Ballater .... 74 K 12
Ballaugh .... 46 G 21
Balliemore near Dunoon ... 65 E 15
Balliemore near Oban ..... 65 D 14
Ballig .... 46 G 21
Ballingry .... 68 K 15
Ballinluig .... 74 J 14
Ballochan .... 75 L 12
Ballochroy .... 59 D 16
Ballyhaugh .... 71 A 14
Balmacellan .... 53 H 18
Balmaha .... 67 G 15
Balmedie .... 75 N 12
Balminnoch .... 52 F 19
Balmoral Castle .... 74 K 12
Balmullo .... 69 L 14
Balnacra .... 78 D 11
Balnafoich .... 79 H 11
Balnaguard .... 74 I 14
Balnahard .... 64 B 14
Balnakeil Bay .... 84 F 8
Balnaknock .... 77 B 11
Balnapaling .... 79 H 10
Baltonsborough .... 8 M 30
Balvicar .... 65 D 15
Balvraid .... 72 D 12
Bamburgh Castle .... 63 O 17
Bamford .... 43 O 23
Bampton Cumbria .... 48 L 20
Bampton Devon .... 7 J 31
Bampton Oxon. .... 20 P 28
Banavie .... 72 E 13
Banbury .... 28 P 27
Banchory .... 75 M 12
Bancyfelin .... 15 G 28
Bandenscoth .... 81 M 11
Banff .... 81 M 10
Bangor .... 40 H 23
Bankend .... 53 J 18
Bankfoot .... 68 J 14
Bankhead .... 75 N 12
Banks .... 42 L 22
Bankshill .... 54 K 18
Banniskirk .... 85 J 8
Bannockburn .... 67 I 15
Banstead .... 21 T 30
Banwell .... 18 L 30
Bapchild .... 22 W 30
Bar Hill .... 29 U 27
Barbaraville .... 79 H 10
Barbon .... 48 M 21
Barcaldine .... 65 E 14
Bardney .... 45 T 24
Bardsea .... 48 K 21
Bardsey .... 43 P 22
Bardsey Island .... 32 F 25

Barford .... 39 X 26
Barford-St. Martin .... 9 O 30
Barfreston .... 23 X 30
Bargoed .... 18 K 28
Bargrennan .... 52 G 18
Barham .... 23 X 30
Barking .... 30 X 27
Barking and Dagenham
  London Borough .... 21 U 29
Barkston .... 37 S 25
Barkway .... 29 U 28
Barlaston .... 35 N 25
Barlborough .... 44 Q 24
Barlestone .... 36 P 26
Barley North Hertfordshire .. 29 U 27
Barley Pendle .... 42 N 22
Barlow .... 43 P 24
Barmby on the Marsh ..... 44 R 22
Barming .... 22 V 30
Barmouth / Abermaw ...... 33 H 25
Barmouth Bay .... 33 H 25
Barmston .... 51 T 21
Barnack .... 37 S 26
Barnard Castle .... 49 O 20
Barnby Dun .... 44 Q 23
Barnby Moor
  East Riding of Yorks. ... 50 R 22
Barnby Moor Notts. ...... 44 Q 23
Barnet London Borough ... 21 T 29
Barnetby-le-Wold .... 45 S 23
Barney .... 38 W 25
Barnham .... 30 W 26
Barnham Broom .... 38 X 26
Barnhill .... 80 J 11
Barnhills .... 52 E 18
Barningham .... 49 O 20
Barnoldswick .... 49 N 22
Barnsley .... 43 P 23
Barnstaple .... 7 H 30
Barnston .... 42 M 24
Barnwell .... 29 S 26
Barr .... 52 F 18
Barra .... 70 X 13
Barra (Sound of) .... 70 X 12
Barra Head .... 70 X 13
Barregarrow .... 46 G 21
Barrhead .... 60 G 16
Barrhill .... 52 F 18
Barri / Barry .... 18 K 29
Barrington .... 8 L 31
Barrisdale .... 72 D 12
Barrisdale Bay .... 72 D 12
Barrmill .... 60 G 16
Barrock .... 86 K 8
Barrow .... 30 V 27
Barrow Burn .... 63 N 17
Barrow Gurney .... 18 L 29
Barrow-in-Furness .... 47 K 21
Barrow-upon-Humber ..... 45 S 22
Barrow-upon-Soar .... 36 Q 25
Barrowby .... 36 R 25
Barrowford .... 43 N 22
Barry Angus .... 69 L 14
Barsham .... 31 Y 26
Barston .... 27 O 26
Bartestree .... 26 M 27
Barton Eden .... 49 P 20
Barton Lancs. .... 42 L 22
Barton-le-Clay .... 29 S 28
Barton le Willows .... 50 R 21
Barton Mills .... 30 V 26
Barton-on-Sea .... 9 P 31
Barton-under-Needwood ... 35 O 25
Barton-upon-Humber ..... 44 S 22
Barvas .... 82 A 8
Barwell .... 36 P 26
Barwick-in-Elmet .... 43 P 22
Baschurch .... 34 L 25
Bashall Eaves .... 42 M 22
Basildon Berks. .... 20 Q 29
Basildon Essex. .... 22 V 29
Basing .... 20 Q 30
Basingstoke .... 20 Q 30
Baslow .... 43 P 24
Bass Rock .... 69 M 15
Bassenthwaite .... 54 K 19
Bassingham .... 37 S 24
Baston .... 37 S 25
Bastwick .... 39 Y 25
Batcombe .... 8 M 31
Bath .... 19 M 29
Bathampton .... 19 N 29
Batheaston .... 19 N 29
Bathgate .... 61 J 16
Batley .... 43 P 22

Battle .... 12 V 31
Baumber .... 45 T 24
Bawburgh .... 39 X 26
Bawdeswell .... 38 X 25
Bawdsey .... 31 Y 27
Bawtry .... 44 Q 23
Bayble .... 83 B 9
Baycliff .... 48 K 21
Baydon .... 19 P 29
Bayhead .... 76 X 11
Bayston Hill .... 34 L 25
Beachamption .... 28 R 27
Beachy Head .... 12 U 31
Beacon (The) .... 2 E 33
Beacon End .... 30 W 28
Beaconsfield .... 21 S 29
Beadlam .... 50 R 21
Beadnell Bay .... 63 P 17
Beaford .... 7 H 31
Beal .... 63 O 16
Beaminster .... 8 L 31
Beamish Hall .... 56 P 19
Beamsley .... 49 O 22
Bearsden .... 67 G 16
Bearsted .... 22 V 30
Beattock .... 61 J 18
Beauchief .... 43 P 24
Beaufort .... 18 K 28
Beaulieu .... 10 P 31
Beauly .... 79 G 11
Beauly Firth .... 79 G 11
Beaumaris .... 40 H 23
Beaumont .... 54 K 19
Beaupré Castle .... 17 J 29
Bebington .... 42 L 23
Beccles .... 31 Y 26
Beckfoot .... 54 J 19
Beckingham .... 44 R 23
Beckington .... 19 N 30
Beckley .... 12 V 31
Beckton .... 21 U 29
Bedale .... 50 P 21
Beddau .... 17 J 29
Beddgelert .... 33 H 24
Beddingham .... 11 U 31
Bedford .... 29 S 27
Bedgebury Pinetum .... 12 V 30
Bedlington .... 56 P 18
Bedlinog .... 17 K 28
Bedrule .... 62 M 17
Bedwas .... 18 K 29
Bedworth .... 28 P 26
Bee (Loch) .... 76 X 11
Beer .... 5 K 31
Beeston .... 36 Q 25
Beeswing .... 53 I 18
Begdbroke .... 20 Q 28
Beguildy .... 26 K 26
Beighton .... 44 P 23
Beinn a' Ghlò .... 74 I 13
Beinn a' Mheadhoin (Loch) .78 F 12
Beinn Dearg Highland ..... 78 F 10
Beinn Dearg
  Perthshire and Kinross ... 73 I 13
Beinn Heasgarnich .... 67 G 14
Beinn Ime .... 66 F 15
Beith .... 60 G 16
Belbroughton .... 27 N 26
Belchford .... 45 T 24
Belford .... 63 O 17
Belhelvie .... 75 N 12
Bellabeg .... 74 K 12
Bellingham .... 55 N 18
Bellshill
  Berwick-upon-Tweed ... 63 O 17
Bellshill North Lanarkshire .. 60 H 16
Belmont .... 87 R 1
Belnacraig .... 74 K 12
Belnahua .... 65 C 15
Belper .... 36 P 24
Belsay .... 56 O 18
Belstead .... 31 X 27
Belstone .... 4 I 31
Belton Lincs. .... 37 S 25
Belton Norfolk .... 39 Y 26
Belton North Lincs. .... 44 R 23
Belton Rutland .... 36 R 26
Belvoir .... 36 R 25
Bembridge .... 10 Q 31
Bempton .... 51 T 21
Ben Alder .... 73 G 13
Ben Alder Lodge .... 73 G 13
Ben Armine Forest .... 85 H 9
Ben Armine Lodge .... 85 H 9
Ben Chonzie .... 67 I 14
Ben Cruachan .... 65 E 14
Ben-damph Forest .... 78 D 11

Ben Hope .... 84 G 8
Ben Klibreck .... 84 G 9
Ben Lawers .... 67 H 14
Ben Ledi .... 67 H 15
Ben Lomond .... 66 G 15
Ben Loyal .... 84 G 8
Ben Macdui .... 74 I 12
Ben More Argyll and Bute . 65 B 14
Ben More Stirling .... 67 G 14
Ben More Assynt .... 84 F 9
Ben Starav .... 66 E 14
Ben Vorlich .... 67 H 14
Ben Wyvis .... 79 G 10
Benbecula .... 76 X 11
Benbuie .... 60 H 18
Benderloch Argyll and Bute .. 65 D 14
Benderloch Mountain ..... 65 E 14
Bendronaig Lodge .... 78 E 11
Benenden .... 12 V 30
Benfleet .... 22 V 29
Benigton .... 37 U 25
Benllech .... 40 H 23
Benmore .... 67 G 14
Benmore Lodge .... 84 F 9
Benson .... 20 Q 29
Bentley Doncaster .... 44 Q 23
Bentley East Hampshire ... 20 R 30
Bentpath .... 54 K 18
Bentworth .... 10 Q 30
Benwick .... 29 T 26
Beoraid (Loch) .... 72 D 13
Bere Alston .... 3 H 32
Bere Ferrers .... 3 H 32
Bere Regis .... 9 N 31
Berkeley .... 18 M 28
Berkhamsted .... 21 S 28
Berneray near Barra .... 70 X 13
Berneray near North Uist .. 76 Y 10
Bernice .... 66 E 15
Bernisdale .... 77 B 11
Berriew .... 34 K 26
Berrington Hall .... 26 L 27
Berrow .... 18 K 30
Berry Head .... 4 J 32
Berry Hill .... 18 M 28
Berry Pomeroy .... 4 J 32
Berrynarbor .... 17 H 30
Bervie Bay .... 75 N 13
Berwick-St. John .... 9 N 31
Berwick-upon-Tweed ..... 63 O 16
Berwyn .... 33 J 25
Bessacarr .... 44 Q 23
Bethel .... 33 H 24
Bethersden .... 12 W 30
Bethesda .... 33 H 24
Betley .... 35 M 24
Bettisfield .... 34 L 25
Bettws Cedewain .... 34 K 26
Bettws Evan .... 15 G 27
Bettws Gwerfil Goch ..... 33 J 24
Bettyhill .... 85 H 8
Betws-y-Coed .... 33 I 24
Betws yn Rhos .... 41 J 23
Beulah near Cardigan ..... 15 G 27
Beulah
  near Llandrindod-Wells .. 25 J 27
Beverley .... 45 S 22
Beverstone .... 19 N 29
Bewaldeth .... 54 K 19
Bewcastle .... 55 L 18
Bewdley .... 27 N 26
Bewholme .... 51 T 22
Bexhill .... 12 V 31
Bexley London Borough ... 21 U 29
Beyton .... 30 W 27
Bhaid-Luachraich (Loch) .. 78 D 10
Bhealaich (Loch a') .... 84 G 9
Bhraoin (Loch a') .... 78 E 10
Bhrollum (Loch) .... 82 A 10
Bibury .... 19 O 28
Bicester .... 28 Q 28
Bicker .... 37 T 25
Bickerton .... 4 I 32
Bickleigh Mid Devon .... 7 J 31
Bickleigh South Hams .....4 H 32
Bicton .... 34 L 25
Bicton gardens .... 5 K 31
Biddenden .... 12 V 30
Biddenham .... 29 S 27
Biddestone .... 19 N 29
Biddulph .... 35 N 24
Bidean nam Bian .... 72 E 14
Bideford .... 6 H 30
Bidford .... 27 O 27
Bieldside .... 75 N 12
Bierton .... 20 R 28

Big Corlae .... 60 H 18
Bigbury .... 4 I 33
Bigbury-on-Sea .... 4 I 33
Biggar Barrow-in-Furness .. 47 K 21
Biggar South Lanarkshire .. 61 J 17
Biggin Hill .... 21 U 30
Biggleswade .... 29 T 27
Bignor .... 11 S 31
Bildeston .... 30 W 27
Bildsgreen .... 27 M 26
Bill of Portland .... 8 M 32
Billericay .... 22 V 29
Billesdon .... 36 R 26
Billingborough .... 37 S 25
Billinge .... 42 L 23
Billingham .... 57 Q 20
Billinghay .... 37 T 24
Billingshurst .... 11 S 30
Billingsley .... 27 M 26
Billington .... 42 M 22
Billockby .... 39 Y 26
Billy Row .... 56 O 19
Bilsington .... 12 W 30
Bilsthorpe .... 36 Q 24
Bilston .... 35 N 26
Bilton .... 45 T 22
Binbrook .... 45 T 23
Binfield .... 20 R 29
Bingham .... 36 R 25
Bingley .... 43 O 22
Binham .... 38 W 25
Binns (The) .... 68 J 16
Binsted .... 10 R 30
Birchington .... 23 X 29
Birdham .... 10 R 31
Birdingbury .... 28 P 27
Birdwell .... 43 P 23
Birdworld .... 10 R 30
Birgham .... 62 N 17
Birkdale .... 42 K 23
Birkenhead .... 42 K 23
Birkin .... 44 Q 22
Birling Gap .... 12 U 31
Birmingham .... 27 O 26
Birnam .... 68 J 14
Birsay .... 86 K 6
Birsemore .... 75 L 12
Birstall .... 36 Q 25
Birtley Gateshead .... 56 P 19
Birtley Tynedale .... 55 N 18
Birtsmorton Court .... 27 N 27
Bisham .... 20 R 29
Bishop Auckland .... 56 P 20
Bishop Burton .... 44 S 22
Bishop Monkton .... 50 P 21
Bishop Sutton .... 18 M 29
Bishop Thornton .... 50 P 21
Bishop Wilton .... 50 R 22
Bishops Cannings .... 19 O 29
Bishop's Castle .... 26 L 26
Bishop's Caundle .... 9 M 31
Bishop's Cleeve .... 27 N 28
Bishop's Itchington .... 28 P 27
Bishops Lydeard .... 8 K 30
Bishop's Nympton .... 7 I 31
Bishop's Palace
  near St. David's .... 14 E 28
Bishop's Palace near Tenby 16 F 28
Bishop's Stortford .... 30 U 28
Bishop's Tachbrook .... 28 P 27
Bishop's Tawton .... 7 H 30
Bishop's Waltham .... 10 Q 31
Bishopsteignton .... 4 J 32
Bishopstocke .... 10 Q 31
Bishopston .... 15 H 29
Bishopstone Salisbury ....9 O 30
Bishopstone Swindon ..... 19 P 29
Bishopsthorpe .... 50 Q 22
Bishopton Darlington ..... 56 P 20
Bishopton Renfrewshire .. 67 G 16
Bishton .... 18 L 29
Bisley .... 19 N 28
Bispham .... 42 K 22
Bix .... 20 R 29
Blaby .... 36 Q 26
Black Bay .... 59 D 17
Black Corries .... 72 F 13
Black Isle .... 79 G 11
Black Mount .... 66 F 14
Black Mountain .... 25 I 28
Black Mountains .... 26 K 28
Black Notley .... 30 V 28
Black Torrington .... 6 H 31
Black Water Valley .... 78 F 10
Blackawton .... 4 I 32

A
B
C
D
E
F
G
H
I
J
K
L
M
N
O
P
Q
R
S
T
U
V
W
X
Y
Z

Blackburn *Aberdeenshire* ...75 N 12
Blackburn *Lancs.* ......42 M 22
Blackburn *West Lothian* ......61 J 16
Blackfield ......10 P 31
Blackford *Cumbria* ......54 L 19
Blackford
  Perthshire and Kinross ...67 I 15
Blackhall ......57 Q 19
Blackhall Rocks ......57 Q 19
Blackhill *Aberdeenshire* ...81 O 11
Blackhill *Highland* ......77 A 11
Blacklunans ......74 J 13
Blackmoor Gate ......17 I 30
Blackmore ......22 U 28
Blackness Castle ......68 J 15
Blacko ......43 N 22
Blackpool ......42 K 22
Blackridge ......61 I 16
Blackthorn ......28 Q 28
Blacktoft ......44 R 22
Blackwater *Hart* ......20 R 30
Blackwater *Isle of Wight* ...10 Q 31
Blackwater (River) ......22 W 28
Blackwater Reservoir ......72 F 13
Blackwaterfoot ......59 D 17
Blackwell ......50 P 20
Blackwood ......18 K 29
Bladnoch ......52 G 19
Bladon ......20 P 28
Blaenannherch ......15 G 27
Blaenau Ffestiniog ......33 I 25
Blaenavon ......18 K 28
Blaengarw ......17 J 29
Blaengrwrach ......17 J 28
Blagdon ......18 L 30
Blaich ......72 E 13
Blaina ......18 K 28
Blair Atholl ......73 I 13
Blair Castle ......73 I 13
Blairgowrie ......68 J 14
Blairmore ......66 F 16
Blakeney *Glos.* ......18 M 28
Blakeney *Norfolk* ......38 X 25
Blakesley ......28 Q 27
Blamerino ......68 K 14
Blandford Forum ......9 N 31
Blanefield ......67 H 16
Blàr a Chaorainn ......72 E 13
Blarmachfoldach ......72 E 13
Blarnalearoch ......78 E 10
Blawith ......48 K 21
Blaxton ......44 R 23
Blaydon ......56 O 19
Bleadon ......18 L 30
Bleaklow Hill ......43 O 23
Blean ......23 X 30
Bleasby ......36 R 24
Blenheim Palace ......20 P 28
Bletchingdon ......20 Q 28
Bletchley ......28 R 27
Bletsoe ......29 S 27
Blewbury ......20 Q 29
Blickling ......39 X 25
Blickling Hall ......39 X 25
Blidworth ......36 Q 24
Blindley Heath ......21 T 30
Blisland ......3 F 32
Blisworth ......28 R 27
Blithe ......35 O 25
Blithfield Hall ......35 O 25
Blithfield Reservoir ......35 O 25
Blockley ......27 O 27
Blofield ......39 Y 26
Bloxham ......28 P 27
Blubberhouses ......49 O 22
Blue John Cavern ......43 O 23
Bluemull Sound ......87 Q 1
Blundellsands ......42 K 23
Blundeston ......39 Z 26
Blyth *Northumb.* ......56 P 18
Blyth *Notts.* ......44 Q 23
Blythburgh ......31 Y 27
Blythe Bridge ......35 N 25
Blyton ......44 R 23
Bo' Ness ......68 J 15
Boarhills ......69 L 15
Boat of Garten ......74 I 12
Boathvic ......79 G 10
Bocking Churchstreet ......30 V 28
Boddam ......81 O 11
Bodedern ......40 G 23
Bodelwyddan ......41 J 23
Bodenham ......26 L 27
Bodfari ......41 J 24
Bodfordd ......40 G 23
Bodham Street ......39 X 25
Bodiam Castle ......12 V 30

Bodicote ......28 Q 27
Bodmin ......3 F 32
Bodmin Moor ......3 G 32
Bodnant Garden ......41 I 23
Bognor Regis ......11 R 31
Bogue ......53 H 18
Boisdale ......70 X 12
Boisdale (Loch) ......70 Y 12
Boldon ......56 P 19
Bolham ......7 J 31
Bollin (River) ......42 N 23
Bollington ......43 N 24
Bolney ......11 T 31
Bolnhurst ......29 S 27
Bolsover ......44 Q 24
Boltby ......50 Q 21
Bolton *Alnwick* ......63 O 17
Bolton *Bolton* ......42 M 23
Bolton Abbey ......49 O 22
Bolton-by-Bowland ......49 N 22
Bolton-le-Sands ......48 L 21
Bolton on Swale ......50 P 20
Bolton-upon-Dearne ......44 Q 23
Bomere Heath ......34 L 25
Bonar Bridge ......79 G 10
Bonawe Quarries ......65 E 14
Bonby ......44 S 23
Boncath ......15 G 27
Bonchester Bridge ......62 M 17
Bonhill ......66 G 16
Bonnybridge ......67 I 16
Bonnyrigg ......61 K 16
Bont-faen / Cowbridge ......17 J 29
Bontgoch Elerch ......25 I 26
Bontnewydd ......32 H 24
Boosbeck ......50 R 20
Boot ......47 K 20
Bootle *Cumbria* ......47 J 21
Bootle *Merseyside* ......42 K 23
Border Forest Park (The) ...55 M 18
Bordogan ......32 G 24
Boreham ......22 V 28
Boreham Street ......12 V 31
Borehamwood ......21 T 29
Boreland ......54 K 18
Borgue
  Dumfries and Galloway ....53 H 19
Borgue *Highland* ......85 J 9
Borness ......53 H 19
Borough Green ......22 U 30
Boroughbridge ......50 P 21
Borreraig ......77 Z 11
Borrobol Forest ......85 H 9
Borrowash ......36 P 25
Borth ......25 H 26
Borve *Barra Isle* ......70 X 13
Borve *Eilean Siar* ......70 X 13
Borve *Isle of Lewis* ......82 A 8
Borve *South Harris* ......76 Y 10
Borwick ......48 L 21
Bosbury ......26 M 27
Boscastle ......6 F 31
Boscombe ......9 O 31
Bosham ......10 R 31
Bosherston ......16 F 29
Bosley ......35 N 24
Boston ......37 T 25
Boston Spa ......50 P 22
Boswinger ......3 F 33
Botesdale ......30 W 26
Bothamsall ......44 R 24
Bothel ......54 K 19
Bothwell ......60 H 16
Botley ......10 Q 31
Bottesford *Melton* ......36 R 25
Bottesford
  North Lincolnshire ......44 S 23
Bottisham ......30 U 27
Botwnnog ......32 G 25
Boughton ......36 Q 24
Boughton House ......29 R 26
Boughton Street ......22 W 30
Boulmer ......63 P 17
Boultham ......44 S 24
Bourn ......29 T 27
Bourne ......37 S 25
Bournemouth ......9 O 31
Bourton *North Dorset* ......9 N 30
Bourton
  Vale of White Horse ...19 P 29
Bourton-on-the-Water ...27 O 28
Bovey Tracey ......4 I 32
Bovingdon ......21 S 28
Bow ......7 I 31
Bow Street ......25 H 26
Bowden ......62 L 17
Bower *Highland* ......85 K 8

Bower *Tynedale* ......55 M 18
Bowerchalke ......9 O 30
Bowes ......49 N 20
Bowhill ......62 L 17
Bowland ......62 L 17
Bowland (Forest of) ......49 M 22
Bowmore ......58 B 16
Bowness ......48 L 20
Bowness-on-Solway ......54 K 19
Bowood House ......19 N 29
Box ......19 N 29
Box Hill ......21 T 30
Boxford *Babergh* ......30 W 27
Boxford *West Berkshire* ...20 P 29
Boxley ......22 V 30
Boxworth ......29 T 27
Boyton ......6 G 31
Bozeat ......29 R 27
Braaid ......46 G 21
Brabourne Lees ......12 W 30
Bracadale (Loch) ......77 A 12
Bracebridge Heath ......37 S 24
Brackley ......28 Q 27
Brackley Hatch ......28 Q 27
Bracknell ......20 R 29
Braco ......67 I 15
Bracora ......72 C 13
Bradan Resr (Loch) ......60 G 18
Bradfield *Sheffield* ......43 P 23
Bradfield *West Berkshire* ...20 Q 29
Bradford *Bradford* ......43 O 22
Bradford *Taunton Deane* ...8 K 31
Bradford Abbas ......8 M 31
Bradford-on-Avon ......19 N 29
Brading ......10 Q 31
Bradninch ......7 J 31
Bradpole ......5 L 31
Bradwell ......43 O 24
Bradwell-on-Sea ......22 W 28
Bradworthy ......6 G 31
Brae ......87 P 2
Brae of Achnahaird ......83 D 9
Brae Roy Lodge ......73 F 13
Braeantra ......79 G 10
Braedownie ......74 K 13
Braehead ......61 J 16
Braemar ......74 J 12
Braemore ......85 J 9
Braeriach ......74 I 12
Braeswick ......87 L 6
Brafferton Helperby ......50 Q 21
Bragar ......82 A 8
Braglenbeg ......65 D 15
Braich y Pwll ......32 F 25
Braidwood ......61 I 16
Bràigh Mòr ......82 Y 9
Brailes ......28 P 27
Brailsford ......35 P 25
Braintree ......30 V 28
Braishfield ......10 P 30
Braithwaite ......44 Q 23
Bramcote ......36 Q 25
Bramfield ......31 Y 27
Bramford ......31 X 27
Bramhall ......43 N 23
Bramham ......43 P 22
Bramhope ......43 P 22
Bramley
  Basingstoke and Deane ...20 Q 30
Bramley
  South Yorks. ......44 Q 23
Bramley *Surrey* ......21 S 30
Brampton *Cambs.* ......29 T 27
Brampton *Cumbria* ......55 L 19
Brampton *Eden* ......55 M 20
Brampton *Rotherham.* ......43 P 23
Brampton *Suffolk* ......31 Y 26
Brampton Bryan ......26 L 26
Brancaster ......38 V 25
Branderburgh ......80 K 10
Brandesburton ......51 T 22
Brandon *Durham* ......56 P 19
Brandon *Suffolk* ......30 V 26
Brandsby ......50 Q 21
Branscombe ......5 K 31
Bransgore ......9 O 31
Branston ......37 S 24
Brant Broughton ......37 S 24
Brassington ......35 P 24
Bratton ......19 N 30
Bratton Clovelly ......6 H 31
Bratton Fleming ......7 I 30
Braughing ......29 U 28
Braunston *Daventry* ......28 Q 27
Braunston *Rutland* ......36 R 26
Braunton ......6 H 30
Bray-on-Thames ......21 R 29

Bray Shop ......3 G 32
Braybrooke ......28 R 26
Brayford ......7 I 30
Brayton ......44 Q 22
Breaclete ......82 Z 9
Breadalbane ......67 G 14
Breage ......2 D 33
Breamore House ......9 O 31
Brean ......18 K 30
Breasclete ......82 Z 9
Breaston ......36 Q 25
Brechin ......75 M 13
Breckland ......30 V 26
Brecon / Aberhonddu ......25 J 28
Brecon Beacons
  National Park ......25 J 28
Bredbury ......43 N 23
Bredgar ......22 W 30
Bredon ......27 N 27
Bredwardine ......26 L 27
Bremhill ......19 N 29
Brenchley ......12 V 30
Brendon Hills ......7 J 30
Brenig Reservoir ......33 J 24
Brenish ......82 Y 9
Brent *London Borough* ...21 T 29
Brent Knoll ......18 L 30
Brent Pelham ......29 U 28
Brentwood ......22 U 29
Brenzett ......12 W 30
Brereton ......35 O 25
Bressay ......87 Q 3
Bretford ......28 P 26
Bretherton ......42 L 22
Brewham ......9 M 30
Brewlands Bridge ......74 K 13
Brewood ......35 N 25
Bride ......46 G 20
Bridestowe ......4 H 31
Bridge ......23 X 30
Bridge of Alford ......75 L 12
Bridge of Allan ......67 I 15
Bridge of Avon ......80 J 11
Bridge of Balgie ......73 H 14
Bridge of Brown ......74 J 12
Bridge of Buchat ......74 L 12
Bridge of Craigisla ......74 K 13
Bridge of Dee ......53 I 19
Bridge of Don ......75 N 12
Bridge of Dun ......75 M 13
Bridge of Dye ......75 M 13
Bridge of Earn ......68 J 14
Bridge of Ericht ......73 G 13
Bridge of Gairn ......74 K 12
Bridge of Gaur ......73 G 13
Bridge of Orchy ......66 F 14
Bridge of Weir ......60 G 16
Bridge Trafford ......42 L 24
Bridgemary ......10 Q 31
Bridgend *Aberdeenshire* ...80 L 11
Bridgend *Angus* ......75 L 13
Bridgend *Argyll and Bute* ...65 D 15
Bridgend *Islay* ......58 B 16
Bridgend
  Perthshire and Kinross ...68 J 14
Bridgend / Pen-y-bont ...17 J 29
Bridgend of Lintrathen ...74 K 13
Bridgerule ......6 G 31
Bridgham ......30 W 26
Bridgnorth ......27 M 26
Bridgwater ......8 L 30
Bridlington ......51 T 21
Bridport ......5 L 31
Brierfield ......43 N 22
Brierley ......43 P 23
Brierley Hill ......27 N 26
Brigg ......44 S 23
Brigham ......54 J 20
Brighouse ......43 O 22
Brighstone ......10 P 32
Brighstone Forest ......10 P 32
Brightling ......12 V 31
Brightlingsea ......22 X 28
Brighton ......11 T 31
Brightwell ......20 Q 29
Brigstock ......29 S 26
Brill ......20 Q 28
Brimfield ......26 L 27
Brimham Rocks ......49 O 21
Brimington ......43 P 24
Brimpsfield ......19 N 28
Brimpton ......20 Q 29
Brinkburn Priory ......63 O 18
Brinkley ......30 V 27

Brinklow ......28 P 26
Brinkworth ......19 O 29
Brinyan ......86 L 6
Brisley ......38 W 25
Brislington ......18 M 29
Bristol ......18 M 29
Briston ......38 X 25
Briton Ferry ......17 I 29
Brittle (Loch) ......71 B 12
Brixham ......4 J 32
Brixton ......4 H 32
Brixworth ......28 R 27
Brize Norton ......20 P 28
Broad Bay ......83 B 9
Broad Blunsdon ......19 O 29
Broad Chalke ......9 O 30
Broad Haven ......14 E 28
Broad Hinton ......19 O 29
Broad Law ......61 J 17
Broad Oak ......12 V 31
Broadbridge Heath ......11 S 30
Broadclyst ......7 J 31
Broadford ......77 C 12
Broadlands ......10 P 31
Broadmayne ......9 M 31
Broadstairs ......23 Y 29
Broadstone ......9 O 31
Broadwas ......27 M 27
Broadway ......27 O 27
Broadwell Ho ......55 N 19
Broadwey ......8 M 32
Broadwindsor ......8 L 31
Broadwoodwidger ......6 H 31
Brochel ......77 B 11
Brockdish ......31 X 26
Brockenhurst ......10 P 31
Brockley ......18 L 29
Brockworth ......19 N 28
Brodick ......59 E 17
Brodick Bay ......59 E 17
Brodick Castle ......59 E 17
Brodie Castle ......79 I 11
Brodsworth ......44 Q 23
Brodsworth Hall ......44 Q 23
Brokenborough ......19 N 29
Brolass ......65 B 14
Bromborough ......42 L 24
Brome ......31 X 26
Bromfield ......26 L 26
Bromham *Bedford* ......29 S 27
Bromham *Kennet* ......19 N 29
Bromley *London Borough* ...21 U 29
Brompton *Kent* ......22 V 29
Brompton *near Northallerton* 50 P 20
Brompton-by-Sawdon ......51 S 21
Brompton on Swale ......49 O 20
Brompton Ralph ......7 K 30
Brompton Regis ......7 J 30
Bromsgrove ......27 N 26
Bromyard ......26 M 27
Bronllys ......26 K 27
Brook ......22 W 30
Brooke ......39 Y 26
Brookmans Park ......21 T 28
Broom (Loch) ......78 E 10
Broomfield *Chelmsford* ...22 V 28
Broomfield *Sedgemoor* ...8 K 30
Broomfleet ......44 S 22
Broomhaugh ......56 O 19
Brora ......85 I 9
Brosna ......34 M 26
Brotherton ......44 Q 22
Brotton ......57 R 20
Brough
  East Riding of Yorkshire ...44 S 22
Brough *Eden* ......49 N 20
Brough *Highland* ......86 J 8
Brough Head ......86 J 6
Brough Lodge ......87 R 2
Brough of Birsay ......86 J 6
Broughton *Cumbria* ......54 J 19
Broughton
  Flintshire / Sir y Fflint ...34 L 24
Broughton *Hants.* ......10 P 30
Broughton *Lancs.* ......42 L 22
Broughton *North Lincs.* ...44 S 23
Broughton *Northants.* ......28 R 26
Broughton *Oxon.* ......28 P 27
Broughton *Scottish Borders* .61 J 17
Broughton-in-Furness ......47 K 21
Broughton Mills ......47 K 21
Broughton Moor ......54 J 19
Broughton Poggs ......19 P 28
Broughty Ferry ......69 L 14
Brownhills ......35 O 26
Brownsea Island ......9 O 31

Broxbourne ......21 T 28
Broxburn ......68 J 16
Bruar Lodge ......73 I 13
Bruichladdich ......58 A 16
Brundall ......39 Y 26
Brushford ......7 J 30
Bruton ......8 M 30
Brydekirk ......54 K 18
Brymbo ......34 K 24
Brympton ......8 M 31
Bryn-Henllan ......24 F 27
Brynamman ......17 I 28
Brynbuga / Usk ......18 L 28
Bryncethin ......17 J 29
Bryneglwys ......34 K 24
Bryngwran ......40 G 23
Bryngwyn ......26 K 27
Brynhoffnant ......15 G 27
Brynmawr ......18 K 28
Brynsiencyn ......32 H 24
Brynteg ......40 H 23
Bualintur ......71 B 12
Bubwith ......44 R 22
Buccleuch ......61 K 17
Buchanty ......67 I 14
Buckingham ......28 R 27
Buckland *Herts.* ......29 T 28
Buckland *Oxon.* ......20 P 28
Buckland Abbey ......4 H 32
Buckland Brewer ......6 H 31
Buckland Dinham ......19 M 30
Buckland in-the-Moor ......4 I 32
Buckland Newton ......8 M 31
Buckland St. Mary ......8 K 31
Bucklers Hard ......10 P 31
Buckley / Bwcle ......34 K 24
Buckminster ......36 R 25
Bucknall ......37 T 24
Bucknell ......26 L 26
Bucks green ......11 S 30
Bucksburn ......75 N 12
Bude ......6 G 31
Budleigh Salterton ......5 K 32
Bugbrooke ......28 Q 27
Bugle ......3 F 32
Bugthorpe ......50 R 21
Buildwas Abbey ......34 M 26
Builth Wells /
  Llanfair-ym-Muallt ......25 J 27
Bulford ......19 O 30
Bulkéley ......34 L 24
Bulkington ......28 P 26
Bulwell ......36 Q 24
Bulwick ......37 S 26
Bunarkaig ......72 F 13
Bunessan ......64 B 15
Bungay ......31 Y 26
Bunnahabhainn ......64 B 16
Bunny ......36 Q 25
Buntingford ......29 T 28
Burbage *Leics.* ......28 P 26
Burbage *Wilts.* ......19 O 29
Burchett's Green ......20 R 29
Bures ......30 W 28
Burford ......19 P 28
Burgess Hill ......11 T 31
Burgh-by-Sands ......54 K 19
Burgh Castle ......39 Y 26
Burgh-le-Marsh ......38 U 24
Burgh-St. Peter ......39 Y 26
Burghead ......80 J 10
Burghfield ......20 Q 29
Burghill ......26 L 27
Burghley House ......37 S 26
Burham ......22 V 30
Burley ......9 O 31
Burley-in-Wharfedale ......49 O 22
Burlton ......34 L 25
Burneside ......48 L 20
Burneston ......50 P 21
Burnfoot ......62 L 17
Burnham ......21 S 29
Burnham Market ......38 W 25
Burnham-on-Crouch ......22 W 29
Burnham-on-Sea ......18 L 30
Burnhaven ......81 O 11
Burnhope ......56 O 19
Burniston ......51 S 21

Burnley .....43 N 22
Burntisland .....68 K 15
Burrafirth .....87 R 1
Burravoe .....87 Q 2
Burray .....87 L 7
Burrelton .....68 K 14
Burringham .....44 R 23
Burrington North Devon .....7 I 31
Burrington North Somerset ..18 L 30
Burrow Head .....53 G 19
Burry Port /Porth Tywyn .....15 H 28
Burscough .....42 L 23
Burscough Bridge .....42 L 23
Burshill .....51 S 22
Bursledon .....10 Q 31
Burslem .....35 N 24
Burstwick .....45 T 22
Burton Christchurch .....9 O 31
Burton Ellesmere
  Port and Neston .....48 L 21
Burton South Lakeland .....48 L 21
Burton Wrecsam / Wrexham 34 L 24
Burton Agnes .....51 T 21
Burton Bradstock .....5 L 31
Burton Constable Hall .....45 T 22
Burton Fleming .....51 S 21
Burton in Lonsdale .....49 M 21
Burton Joyce .....36 Q 25
Burton Latimer .....29 R 26
Burton Leonard .....50 P 21
Burton Pidsea .....45 T 22
Burton-upon-Stather .....44 R 23
Burton-upon-Trent .....35 O 25
Burwarton .....26 M 26
Burwash .....12 V 31
Burwell Cambs. .....30 U 27
Burwell Lincs. .....45 U 24
Bury Bury .....42 N 23
Bury Chichester .....11 S 31
Bury St. Edmunds .....30 W 27
Busby .....60 H 16
Buscot .....19 P 28
Bushey .....21 S 29
Bute (Island of) .....59 E 16
Bute (Kyles of) .....59 E 16
Bute (Sound of) .....59 E 16
Butleigh .....8 L 30
Butley .....31 Y 27
Butt of Lewis .....83 B 8
Buttercrambe .....50 R 21
Buttermere .....47 K 20
Butterstone .....68 J 14
Buttington .....34 K 25
Buxted .....12 U 31
Buxton Derbs. .....43 O 24
Buxton Norfolk .....39 X 25
Bwcle / Buckley .....34 K 24
Bwlch .....26 K 28
Bwlch Oerddrws .....33 I 25
Bwlch y Ffridd .....33 J 26
Bwlch-y-Groes .....25 I 28
Bwlch-y-Sarnau .....25 J 26
Bwlchgwyn .....34 K 24
Bwlchllan .....25 H 27
Byfield .....28 Q 27
Byfleet .....21 S 30
Byland Abbey .....50 Q 21
Byrness .....62 M 18

C

Cabrach .....80 K 12
Cadair Idris .....33 I 25
Caddington .....29 S 28
Caddonfoot .....62 L 17
Cadhay .....5 K 31
Cadishead .....42 M 23
Cadnam .....10 P 31
Cadney .....44 S 23
Cadwell Park .....45 T 24
Caerau .....17 J 29
Caerdydd / Cardiff .....18 K 29
Caerffili / Caerphilly .....18 K 29
Caerfyrddin / Carmarthen ..15 H 28
Caergwrle .....34 K 24
Caergybi / Holyhead .....40 G 23
Caerlaverock Castle .....53 J 19
Caerleon .....18 L 29
Caernarfon .....32 H 24
Caernarfon Bay .....32 G 24
Caerphilly / Caerffili .....18 K 29
Caersws .....25 J 26
Caerwent .....18 L 29
Caerwys .....41 K 23
Caillness Point .....52 F 19
Cairn Edward Forest .....53 H 18
Cairn Gorm .....74 J 12

Cairn Table .....60 H 17
Cairn Toul .....74 I 12
Cairnborrow .....80 L 11
Cairndow .....66 F 15
Cairngaan .....52 F 20
Cairngarroch .....52 E 19
Cairnie .....80 L 11
Cairnpapple Hill .....67 J 16
Cairnryan .....52 E 19
Cairnsmore of Carsphairn ..60 H 18
Cairnsmore of Fleet .....53 G 19
Cairraig Fhada .....58 B 17
Caister-on-Sea .....39 Z 26
Caistor .....45 T 23
Calbourne .....10 P 31
Caldbeck .....54 K 19
Caldecott .....36 R 26
Calder (Loch) .....85 J 8
Calder Bridge .....47 J 20
Calder Mains .....85 J 8
Caldercruix .....61 I 16
Calderdale .....43 N 22
Caldermill .....60 H 17
Caldey Island .....15 F 29
Caldicot .....18 L 29
Caldwell .....49 O 20
Calf of Man .....46 F 21
Calfsound .....87 L 6
Calgary .....71 B 14
Calgary Bay .....71 B 14
Caliach Point .....71 B 14
Calke Abbey .....36 P 25
Callander .....67 H 15
Callater (Glen) .....74 J 13
Callington .....3 H 32
Calne .....19 N 29
Calow .....43 P 24
Calstock .....3 H 32
Calthwaite .....55 L 19
Calvay .....70 Y 12
Calver .....43 P 24
Calverton .....36 Q 24
Calvine .....73 I 13
Cam .....29 U 27
Cam Loch .....84 E 9
Camas Chil Mhalieu .....72 D 14
Camas-luinie .....78 D 12
Camasnacroise .....72 D 14
Camastianavaig .....77 B 11
Camber .....12 W 31
Camberley .....20 R 30
Camblesforth .....44 Q 22
Cambo .....56 O 18
Cambois .....56 P 18
Camborne .....2 E 33
Cambrian Mountains .....25 I 27
Cambridge .....29 U 27
Cambusbarron .....67 I 15
Cambuskenneth .....67 I 15
Camden London Borough ....21 T 29
Camelford .....6 F 32
Cammachmore .....75 N 12
Campbeltown .....59 D 17
Campsie Fells .....67 H 15
Camptown .....62 M 17
Campville .....35 P 25
Camrose .....24 E 28
Camusnagaul .....78 E 10
Candlesby .....37 U 24
Canewdon .....22 W 29
Canisbay .....86 K 8
Canna .....71 A 12
Cannich .....78 F 11
Cannich (Glen) .....78 F 11
Cannington .....8 K 30
Cannock .....35 N 25
Canonbie .....54 L 18
Canons Ashby .....28 Q 27
Canterbury .....23 X 30
Cantley .....39 Y 26
Canvey Island .....22 V 29
Caol .....72 E 13
Caolas a' Mhòrain .....76 Y 10
Caoles .....70 Z 14
Caolis .....70 X 13
Caolisport (Loch) .....65 D 16
Cape Cornwall .....2 C 33
Cape Wrath .....84 E 8
Capel .....11 T 30
Capel Curig .....33 I 24
Capel Garmon .....33 I 24
Capel Le Ferne .....13 X 30
Capel St. Mary .....31 X 27
Capel-y-Ffin .....26 K 28
Capesthorne Hall .....43 N 24
Capheaton .....56 O 18
Cappercleuch .....61 K 17

Caputh .....68 J 14
Cara Island .....58 C 17
Carbis Bay .....2 D 33
Carbost Minginish .....77 A 12
Carbost Trotternish .....77 B 11
Cardenden .....68 K 15
Cardiff / Caerdydd .....18 K 29
Cardigan / Aberteifi .....15 G 27
Cardigan Bay .....24 G 26
Cardington .....34 L 26
Cardinham .....3 G 32
Cardrona .....61 K 17
Cardross .....66 G 16
Cardurnock .....54 K 19
Carew .....15 F 28
Carfraemill .....62 L 16
Cargill .....68 J 14
Carhampton .....7 J 30
Carie .....73 H 13
Carinish .....76 Y 11
Carisbrooke .....10 Q 31
Cark .....48 L 21
Carlbt .....37 S 25
Carleen .....2 D 33
Carleton .....49 N 22
Carlisle .....55 L 19
Carlops .....61 J 16
Carloway .....82 Z 9
Carlton Bedford .....29 S 27
Carlton Hambleton .....50 Q 20
Carlton
  Hinckley and Bosworth ..36 P 26
Carlton North Yorks. .....44 Q 22
Carlton Notts. .....36 Q 25
Carlton Colville .....31 Z 26
Carlton in Lindrick .....44 Q 23
Carlton-on-Trent .....36 R 24
Carluke .....61 I 16
Carmarthen / Caerfyrddin ..15 H 28
Carmel Head .....40 G 22
Carmunnock .....60 H 16
Carmyllie .....69 L 14
Carn Ban .....73 H 12
Carn Coire na h-Easgainn ..73 H 12
Carn Eige .....78 E 12
Carn Glas-choire .....79 I 11
Carn Mairg .....73 H 14
Carnaby .....51 T 21
Carnach .....78 E 12
Carnassarie Castle .....65 D 15
Carnedd Llewelyn .....33 I 24
Carnforth .....48 L 21
Carno .....33 J 26
Carnock .....68 J 15
Carnoustie .....69 L 14
Carnwath .....61 J 16
Carradale .....59 D 17
Carradale Bay .....59 D 17
Carrbridge .....79 I 12
Carrick .....66 F 15
Carrick Roads .....2 E 33
Carron .....80 K 11
Carron (Loch) .....77 C 11
Carron Bridge .....67 H 15
Carrshield .....55 N 19
Carrutherstown .....54 J 18
Carsaig .....65 C 15
Carse of Gowrie .....68 K 14
Carseriggan .....52 G 19
Carsethorn .....53 J 19
Carsluith .....53 G 19
Carsphairn .....53 H 18
Carstairs .....61 I 16
Carterton .....19 P 28
Carterway Heads .....56 O 19
Carthew .....3 F 32
Carthorpe .....50 P 21
Cartmel .....48 L 21
Carville .....56 P 19
Cas-Gwent / Chepstow .....18 M 29
Casnewydd / Newport .....18 K 29
Cassington .....20 P 28
Cassley (Glen) .....84 F 9
Castell-Nedd / Neath .....17 I 29
Castell Newydd Emlyn /
  Newcastle Emlyn .....15 G 27
Castell-y-Rhingyll .....15 H 28
Castle Acre .....38 W 25
Castle Ashby .....28 R 27
Castle Bytham .....37 S 25
Castle Campbell .....67 I 15
Castle Cary .....8 M 30
Castle Combe .....19 N 29
Castle Donington .....36 P 25
Castle Douglas .....53 I 19

Castle Drogo .....4 I 31
Castle Eaton .....19 O 29
Castle Fraser .....75 M 12
Castle frome .....26 M 27
Castle Hedingham .....30 V 28
Castle Howard .....50 R 21
Castle Kennedy .....52 F 19
Castle Lachlan .....65 E 15
Castle Loch .....52 F 19
Castle Rising .....38 V 25
Castlebay .....70 X 13
Castleford .....43 P 22
Castlemartin .....16 E 29
Castlerigg .....54 K 20
Castleton
  Casnewydd / Newport .....18 K 29
Castleton Derbs. .....43 O 23
Castleton North Yorks. .....50 R 20
Castletown Highland .....85 J 8
Castletown Isle of Man .....46 G 21
Catacol .....59 E 16
Catacol Bay .....59 D 16
Caterham .....21 T 30
Catfield .....39 Y 25
Catlodge .....73 H 12
Caton .....48 L 21
Catrine .....60 H 17
Catsgore .....8 L 30
Catterick .....50 P 20
Catterick Garrison .....49 O 20
Catterline .....75 N 13
Cattistock .....8 M 31
Catton Broadland .....39 X 26
Catton Tynedale .....55 N 19
Catworth .....29 S 26
Cauldcleuch Head .....62 L 18
Cauldon .....35 O 24
Caulkerbush .....53 I 19
Cautley .....49 M 20
Cava .....86 K 7
Cavendish .....30 V 27
Caversfield .....28 Q 28
Caversham .....20 R 29
Cawdor .....79 I 11
Cawood .....44 Q 22
Caxton .....29 T 27
Caynham .....26 M 26
Caythorpe .....37 S 24
Cayton .....51 S 21
Ceall (Loch nan) .....71 C 13
Cefn Bryn .....15 H 29
Cefn-Coed-y-cymmer .....17 J 28
Cefn-mawr .....34 K 25
Cefn-y-Pant .....15 G 28
Ceinewydd / New Quay .....24 G 27
Ceiriog (Vale of) .....34 K 25
Cemaes .....40 G 22
Cemaes Head .....15 F 27
Cemmaes .....33 I 26
Cemmaes road .....33 I 26
Cenarth .....15 G 27
Ceres .....69 L 15
Cerne Abbas .....8 M 31
Cerrigydrudion .....33 J 24
Chacewater .....2 E 33
Chacombe .....28 Q 27
Chaddesden .....36 P 25
Chadlington .....28 P 28
Chadwell St. Mary .....22 V 29
Chagford .....4 I 31
Chailey .....11 T 31
Chàirn Bhain (Loch a') .....84 E 9
Chalfont St. Giles .....21 S 29
Chalfont St. Peter .....21 S 29
Chalford .....19 N 28
Chalgrove .....20 Q 29
Challaborough .....7 I 30
Challacombe .....7 I 30
Challoch .....52 G 19
Challock .....22 W 30
Chambercombe Manor .....17 H 30
Chandler's Ford .....10 P 31
Channel Islands 5
Chapel Brampton .....28 R 27
Chapel-en-le-Frith .....43 O 24
Chapel Haddlesey .....44 Q 22
Chapel le Dale .....49 M 21
Chapel St. Leonards .....45 V 24
Chapel Stile .....48 K 20
Chapelhall .....61 I 16
Chapelknowe .....54 K 18
Chapelton .....60 H 16
Chapeltown Moray .....74 K 12
Chapeltown Sheffield .....43 P 23
Chapmanslade .....19 N 30
Chard .....8 L 31

Chardstock .....8 L 31
Charfield .....19 M 29
Charing .....22 W 30
Charlbury .....28 P 28
Charlecote Park .....27 P 27
Charleston Manor .....12 U 31
Charlestown Highland .....78 C 10
Charlestown Restormel .....3 F 33
Charlton .....19 N 29
Charlton Horethorne .....8 M 30
Charlton Kings .....27 N 28
Charlton Marshall .....9 N 31
Charlton Musgrove .....9 M 30
Charlton on Otmoor .....20 Q 28
Charlwood .....11 T 30
Charminster .....8 M 31
Charmouth .....5 L 31
Charney Basset .....20 P 29
Charsfield .....31 X 27
Chartham .....23 X 30
Chartridge .....21 S 28
Chartwell .....21 U 30
Chastleton .....27 P 28
Chatburn .....42 M 22
Chatham .....22 V 29
Chatsworth House .....43 P 24
Chatteris .....29 U 26
Chatto .....62 M 17
Chatton .....63 O 17
Chawleigh .....7 I 31
Cheadle Gtr. Mches. .....43 N 23
Cheadle Staffs. .....35 O 25
Checkendon .....20 Q 29
Cheddar .....18 L 30
Cheddar Gorge .....18 L 30
Cheddington .....21 S 28
Cheddleton .....35 N 24
Chedington .....8 L 31
Chedworth .....19 O 28
Cheese Bay .....76 Y 11
Chellaston .....36 P 25
Chelmarsh .....27 M 26
Chelmsford .....22 V 28
Cheltenham .....27 N 28
Chepstow / Cas-Gwent .....18 L 29
Cherhill .....19 O 29
Cherington Cotswold .....19 N 28
Cherington
  Stratford-on-Avon .....27 P 27
Cheriton .....10 Q 30
Cheriton Bishop .....4 I 31
Cheriton Fitzpaine .....7 I 31
Cherry Burton .....44 S 22
Chertsey .....21 S 29
Cherwell (River) .....28 Q 28
Cheselbourne .....9 M 31
Cheshunt .....21 T 28
Chesil Beach .....8 M 32
Cheslyn Hay .....35 N 26
Chester .....34 L 24
Chester-le-Street .....56 P 19
Chesterfield .....43 P 24
Chesters Fort .....55 N 18
Chesterton Cambridge .....29 U 27
Chesterton Cherwell .....28 Q 28
Cheswardine .....35 M 25
Cheswick .....63 O 16
Cheviot (The) .....63 N 17
Cheviot Hills (The) .....62 M 17
Chew Magna .....18 M 29
Chew Stoke .....18 M 30
Chewton Mendip .....18 M 30
Chicheley .....29 R 27
Chichester .....10 R 31
Chickerell .....5 M 32
Chicklade .....9 N 30
Chiddingfold .....11 S 30
Chiddingly .....12 U 31
Chiddingstone .....22 U 30
Chideock .....5 L 31
Chidham .....10 R 31
Chieveley .....20 Q 29
Chigwell .....21 U 29
Chilcompton .....18 M 30
Child Okeford .....9 N 31
Childrey .....20 P 29
Child's Ercall .....34 M 25
Chilham .....22 W 30
Chillingham .....63 O 17
Chilmark .....9 N 30
Chiltern Hills .....20 R 29
Chilton Sedgefield .....56 P 20

Chilton
  Vale of White Horse .....20 Q 29
Chilton Folia .....20 P 29
Chippenham
  East Cambridgeshire .....30 V 27
Chippenham
  North Wiltshire .....19 N 29
Chipping .....42 M 22
Chipping Campden .....27 O 27
Chipping Norton .....28 P 28
Chipping Ongar .....22 U 28
Chipping Sodbury .....19 M 29
Chipping Warden .....28 Q 27
Chirbury .....34 K 26
Chirk .....34 K 25
Chirk Castle .....34 K 25
Chirmorie .....52 F 18
Chirnside .....63 N 16
Chirton .....19 O 30
Chiseldon .....19 O 29
Chislet .....23 X 30
Chiswell Green .....21 S 28
Chitterne .....19 N 30
Chittlehamholt .....7 I 31
Chittlehampton .....7 I 30
Chobham .....21 S 29
Cholderton .....9 O 30
Cholesbury .....21 S 28
Chollerton .....55 N 18
Cholsey .....20 Q 29
Chon (Loch) .....67 G 15
Chopwell .....56 O 19
Chorley .....42 M 23
Chorleywood .....21 S 29
Christchurch Christchurch .....9 O 31
Christchurch Fenland .....38 U 26
Christian Malford .....19 N 29
Christleton .....34 L 24
Christmas Common .....20 R 29
Christow .....4 J 32
Chroisg (Loch a') .....78 E 11
Chudleigh .....4 J 32
Chulmleigh .....7 I 31
Church .....42 M 22
Church Crookham .....20 R 30
Church Eaton .....35 N 25
Church Enstone .....28 P 28
Church Fenton .....44 Q 22
Church Knowle .....9 N 32
Church Leigh .....35 O 25
Church Lench .....27 O 27
Church Minshull .....34 M 24
Church Stoke .....34 K 26
Church Stretton .....34 L 26
Churcham .....19 M 28
Churchdown .....27 N 28
Churchill North Somerset ..18 L 29
Churchill Oxon. .....27 P 28
Churchingford .....8 K 31
Churnet .....35 N 24
Churnsike Lodge .....55 M 18
Churston Ferrers .....4 J 32
Churt .....10 R 30
Chwilog .....32 H 25
Cifynydd .....17 K 29
Cilcain .....34 K 24
Cilcennin .....25 H 27
Cilgerran .....15 G 27
Cilmery .....25 J 27
Cilrhedyn .....15 G 28
Cilybebyll .....17 I 28
Cilycwm .....25 I 27
Cinderford .....18 M 28
Cirencester .....19 O 28
City of London
  London Borough .....21 T 29
Clachaig .....66 F 15
Clachan Argyl .....66 F 15
Clachan Kintyre .....59 D 16
Clachan Mòr .....70 Z 14
Clachan of Campsie .....67 H 16
Clachan of Glendaruel .....65 E 15
Clackavoid .....74 J 13
Clackmannan .....67 I 15
Clacton-on-Sea .....23 X 28
Claggain Bay .....58 B 16
Claggan .....71 C 14
Claidh (Loch) .....82 A 10
Claigan .....77 A 11
Clandon Park .....21 S 30
Clanfield .....10 Q 31
Claonel .....84 G 9
Clapham Beds. .....29 S 27
Clapham North Yorks. .....49 M 21
Clapton-in-Gordano .....18 L 29

A B C D E F G H I J K L M N O P Q R S T U V W X Y Z

Clàr (Loch nan) ....85 H 9
Clarbeston Road ....24 F 28
Clare ....30 V 27
Clashindarroch ....80 L 11
Clashmore ....79 H 10
Clashnessie ....84 E 9
Clatt ....80 L 12
Clatteringshaws (Loch) ......53 H 18
Clauchlands Point ....59 E 17
Clavering ....29 U 28
Claverley ....27 N 26
Claverton Manor ....19 N 29
Clawdd-newydd ....33 J 24
Clawton ....6 G 31
Claxton *Ryedale* ....50 R 21
Claxton *South Norfolk* ......39 Y 26
Clay Cross ....36 P 24
Claydon ....31 X 27
Claydon House ....28 R 28
Claypole ....36 R 24
Clayton ....11 T 31
Clayton-le-Moors ....42 M 22
Clayton West ....43 P 23
Cleadale ....71 B 13
Cleadon ....57 P 19
Cleat ....70 X 12
Cleator Moor ....47 J 20
Cleckheaton ....43 O 22
Cleedownton ....26 M 26
Cleehill ....26 M 26
Cleethorpes ....45 T 23
Cleeve Abbey ....7 J 30
Cleeve Prior ....27 O 27
Clehonger ....26 L 27
Cleigh ....65 D 14
Clenchwarton ....38 V 25
Clent ....27 N 26
Cleobury Mortimer ....26 M 26
Cleobury North ....26 M 26
Clephanton ....79 I 11
Clevedon ....18 L 29
Clevedon-Court ....18 L 29
Cleveland Hills ....50 Q 20
Cleveleys ....42 K 22
Cley Next the Sea ....38 X 25
Cliburn ....55 M 20
Cliffe *Edway* ....22 V 29
Cliffe *Selby* ....44 R 22
Clifton
  City of Nottingham ......36 Q 25
Clifton *Eden* ....55 L 20
Clifton *Rugby*
  North Warwickshire ......27 O 26
Clifton Hampden ....20 Q 29
Clifton-upon-Teme ....27 M 27
Clipston ....28 R 26
Clisham ....82 Z 10
Clitheroe ....42 M 22
Clive ....34 L 25
Cliveden House ....21 R 29
Clocaenog ....33 J 24
Clocaenog Forest ....33 J 24
Clola ....81 O 11
Clophill ....29 S 27
Clopton ....29 S 26
Closeburn ....53 I 18
Clotton ....34 L 24
Clouds Hill ....9 N 31
Cloughton ....51 S 20
Clova ....74 K 13
Clova (Glen) ....74 K 13
Clove Lodge ....49 N 20
Clovelly ....6 G 31
Clovenfords ....62 L 17
Clovulin ....72 E 13
Clowne ....44 Q 24
Cluanie Loch ....72 E 12
Cluanie Lodge ....72 E 12
Clumber Park ....44 Q 24
Clun ....26 K 26
Clunbury ....26 L 26
Clunes Forest ....72 F 13
Clungunford ....26 L 26
Clunie ....68 J 14
Clutton ....18 M 30
Clwydian Range ....34 K 24
Clydach ....17 I 28
Clyde (Firth of) ....59 F 17
Clyde (River) ....61 J 17
Clydebank ....60 G 16
Clydesdale ....61 I 16
Clyffe Pypard ....19 O 29
Clynnog-Fawr ....32 G 24
Clyro ....26 K 27
Clyst Honiton ....4 J 31
Clyst Hydon ....7 J 31
Clytha ....18 L 28
Clywedog Resr. ....25 J 26

Coalburn ....61 I 17
Coaley ....19 N 28
Coalville ....36 P 25
Coast ....78 D 10
Coatbridge ....60 H 16
Coates ....19 N 28
Cobham ....21 S 30
Cock Bridge ....74 K 12
Cockayne ....50 Q 20
Cockburnspath ....69 M 16
Cockenzie and Port Seton ..69 L 16
Cockerham ....48 L 22
Cockermouth ....54 J 20
Cockfield *Babergh* ....30 W 27
Cockfield *Teesdale* ....56 O 20
Cocking ....10 R 31
Cockleford ....19 N 28
Cockshutt ....34 L 25
Coddington ....36 R 24
Codford St. Mary ....9 N 30
Codicote ....21 T 28
Codnor ....36 P 24
Codsall ....35 N 26
Coe (Glen) ....72 F 14
Coed y Brenin Forest ....33 I 25
Coedpoeth ....34 K 24
Coggeshall ....30 W 28
Coigach ....84 E 10
Coignafearn ....73 H 12
Coignafearn Forest ....73 H 12
Coille Mhorgil ....72 E 12
Colaboll ....84 G 9
Colbost ....77 A 11
Colby *Eden* ....55 M 20
Colby *Isle of Man* ....46 F 21
Colchester ....30 W 28
Cold Ash ....20 Q 29
Cold Ashby ....28 Q 26
Cold Ashton ....19 M 29
Cold Fell ....55 M 19
Cold Norton ....22 W 28
Coldbackie ....84 G 8
Colden Common ....10 Q 31
Coldingham ....63 N 16
Coldstream ....63 N 17
Colebrooke ....7 I 31
Coleford *Glos.* ....18 M 28
Coleford *Somerset* ....18 M 30
Colemere ....34 L 25
Coleorton ....36 P 25
Coleshill
  North Warwickshire ..27 O 26
Coleshill
  Vale of White Horse ......19 P 29
Colgrave Sound ....87 R 2
Colkirk ....38 W 25
Coll *Argyll and Bute* ....71 A 14
Coll *Eilean Siar* ....83 B 9
Colliery Row ....56 P 19
Collieston ....81 O 11
Collin ....53 J 18
Collingbourne Ducis ....19 P 30
Collingbourne Kingston ......19 P 30
Collingham *Notts.* ....36 R 24
Collingham *West Yorks.* ....50 P 22
Collington ....26 M 27
Collyweston ....37 S 26
Colmonell ....52 F 18
Coln (River) ....19 O 28
Colnabaichin ....74 K 12
Colne ....43 N 22
Colne (River) ....22 X 28
Colonsay ....64 B 15
Colpy ....81 M 11
Colsterworth ....37 S 25
Coltishall ....39 Y 25
Colwall Stone ....27 M 27
Colwinston ....17 J 29
Colwyn Bay / Bae Colwyn ..41 I 23
Colyton ....5 K 31
Combe Florey ....8 K 30
Combe Martin ....17 H 30
Combe-St. Nicholas ....8 L 31
Combeinteignhead ....4 J 32
Comberton ....29 U 27
Combwich ....8 K 30
Come-to-Good ....2 E 33
Compton *Berks.* ....20 Q 29
Compton *Guildford* ....21 S 30
Compton *West Sussex* ......10 R 31
Compton Abdale ....19 O 28
Compton Basset ....19 O 29
Compton Castle ....4 J 32
Compton Dando ....18 M 29
Compton Wynyates ....28 P 27
Comrie ....67 I 14
Cona Glen ....72 D 13

Conchra ....65 E 15
Condicote ....27 O 28
Condover ....34 L 26
Congleton ....35 N 24
Congresbury ....18 L 29
Coningsby ....37 T 24
Conington ....29 T 26
Conisbrough ....44 Q 23
Coniston ....48 K 20
Connah's Quay ....42 K 24
Connel ....65 D 14
Connel Park ....60 H 17
Conon Bridge ....79 G 11
Consett ....56 O 19
Constantine Bay ....2 E 32
Contin ....79 G 11
Convinth (Glen) ....79 G 11
Conway Falls ....33 I 24
Conwy ....41 I 23
Conwy (River) ....33 I 24
Conwy (Vale of) ....33 I 24
Cooden Beach ....12 V 31
Cookham ....21 R 29
Coolham ....11 S 31
Coombe Bissett ....9 O 30
Copdock ....31 X 27
Copford ....30 W 28
Copley ....56 O 20
Copmanthorpe ....50 Q 22
Copplestone ....7 I 31
Coppull ....42 M 23
Copthorne ....11 T 30
Coquet (River) ....63 N 17
Corbridge ....55 N 19
Corby ....28 R 26
Corby Glen ....37 S 25
Corfe Castle ....9 N 32
Corfe Mullen ....9 N 31
Corgarff Castle ....74 K 12
Corhampton ....10 Q 31
Cornforth ....56 P 19
Cornhill ....81 L 11
Cornhill-on-Tweed ....63 N 17
Cornwood ....4 I 32
Cornworthy ....4 J 32
Corpach ....72 E 13
Corpusty ....39 X 25
Corran ....72 E 13
Corrany ....46 G 21
Corrie ....59 E 17
Corrie Common ....54 K 18
Corrimony ....78 F 11
Corringham *Thurrock* ......22 V 29
Corringham *West Lindsey* ..44 R 23
Corris ....33 I 26
Corry ....77 C 12
Corryvreckan (Gulf of) ......65 C 15
Corscombe ....8 L 31
Corsham ....19 N 29
Corsham Court ....19 N 29
Corsley Heath ....19 N 30
Corsock ....53 I 18
Corstorpitum ....55 N 19
Corton ....9 N 30
Corwen ....33 J 25
Cosby ....36 Q 26
Cosham ....10 Q 31
Costessey ....39 X 26
Cot-town ....81 N 11
Cotehill ....55 L 19
Cotgrave ....36 Q 25
Cotham ....36 R 24
Cotherstone ....49 O 20
Cothi *River* ....25 H 28
Coton ....29 U 27
Cotswold Wildlife Park ......19 O 28
Cottenham ....29 U 27
Cottered ....29 T 28
Cottesmore ....37 S 25
Cottingham
  East Riding of Yorks. ....45 S 22
Cottingham *Northants.* ....28 R 26
Cottisford ....28 Q 28
Cottonshopeburn Foot ......62 M 18
Coulags ....78 D 11
Coulport ....66 F 15
Coulter ....61 J 17
Coundon ....56 P 20
Countesthorpe ....36 Q 26
Coupar Angus ....68 K 14
Coustonn ....66 E 16
Cove *Argyll and Bute* ......66 F 15
Cove *Highland* ....78 C 10
Cove Bay ....75 N 12
Coventry ....28 P 26
Coverack ....2 E 33
Cow Honeybourne ....27 O 27

Cowal ....65 E 15
Cowan Bridge ....48 M 21
Cowbit ....37 T 25
Cowbridge / Bont-faen ......17 J 29
Cowdenbeath ....68 J 15
Cowdray House ....10 R 31
Cowes *Isle of Wight* ......10 Q 31
Cowfold ....11 T 31
Cowie ....67 I 15
Cowling ....43 N 22
Cowplain ....10 Q 31
Coxheath ....22 V 30
Coxhoe ....56 P 19
Coxwold ....50 Q 21
Coylton ....60 G 17
Coylumbridge ....74 I 12
Crackington Haven ....6 G 31
Crafthole ....3 H 32
Craggan ....66 F 15
Cragside Gardens ....63 O 18
Crai ....25 J 28
Craig ....78 E 11
Craig Lodge ....65 E 16
Craig-y-nos ....17 I 28
Craigdarroch ....60 H 18
Craigellachie ....80 K 11
Craigencallie ....53 G 18
Craigendoran ....66 F 16
Craigens ....58 B 16
Craighead ....69 M 15
Craighouse ....58 C 16
Craigie ....60 G 17
Craigievar Castle ....75 L 12
Craigmalloch ....53 G 18
Craignish (Loch) ....65 D 15
Craignure ....65 C 14
Craigrothie ....69 L 15
Craigton ....74 K 14
Craik ....62 K 17
Crail ....69 M 15
Crailing ....62 M 17
Crailinghall ....62 M 17
Crakaig ....85 I 9
Cramlington ....56 P 18
Cramond ....68 K 16
Cranborne ....9 O 31
Cranbrook ....12 V 30
Crane Moor ....43 P 23
Cranford St. John ....29 S 26
Cranleigh ....11 S 30
Cranmore ....18 M 30
Cranshaws ....62 M 16
Cranstal ....46 G 20
Cranwell ....37 S 24
Cranworth ....38 W 26
Crask Inn ....84 G 9
Craster ....63 P 17
Crathes Castle ....75 M 12
Crathie ....74 K 12
Crathorne ....50 Q 20
Craven Arms ....26 L 26
Crawcrook ....56 O 19
Crawford ....61 J 17
Crawfordjohn ....61 I 17
Crawick ....61 I 17
Crawley *Hants.* ....10 P 30
Crawley *West Sussex* ......11 T 30
Crawley Down ....11 T 30
Creag Meagaidh ....73 G 13
Creagan ....65 E 14
Creagorry ....76 Y 11
Creake South ....38 W 25
Credenhill ....26 L 27
Crediton ....7 J 31
Creech St. Michael ....8 K 30
Creetown ....53 G 19
Creggans ....66 E 15
Cregrina (Loch) ....65 D 14
Cressage ....34 M 26
Cresswell *Castle Morpeth* ..56 P 18
Cresswell *Pembrokeshire /
  Sir Benfro* ....15 F 28
Creswell ....44 Q 24
Cruden Bay ....81 O 11
Crewe ....35 M 24
Crewkerne ....8 L 31
Crianlarich ....66 G 14
Cribyn ....15 H 27
Criccieth ....33 H 25
Crich ....36 P 24
Crichton ....62 L 16
Crick ....28 Q 26
Crickadarn ....25 K 27
Cricket St. Thomas ....8 L 31
Crickhowell ....26 K 28
Cricklade ....19 O 29
Crickley Hill ....19 N 28

Crimond ....81 O 11
Crimplesham ....38 V 26
Crinan ....65 D 15
Crinan (Loch) ....65 D 15
Cringleford ....39 X 26
Croachy ....79 H 12
Crocketford ....53 I 18
Crockham Hill ....21 U 30
Croes-goch ....14 E 28
Croft *Herefordshire* ......26 L 27
Croft *Richmondshire* ......50 P 20
Croft-on-Tees ....50 P 20
Crofty ....15 H 29
Croggan ....65 C 14
Croglin ....55 M 19
Croick ....79 G 10
Croig ....71 B 14
Cromalt Hills ....84 E 9
Cromar ....74 L 12
Cromarty ....79 H 10
Cromarty Bay ....79 H 10
Cromarty Firth ....79 H 11
Cromdale ....80 J 11
Cromdale (Hills of) ....80 J 12
Cromer ....39 X 25
Cromford ....35 P 24
Cromore ....82 A 9
Cromra ....73 G 13
Crondall ....20 R 30
Cronk (The) ....46 G 21
Crook *South Lakeland* ....48 L 20
Crook *Wear Valley* ......56 O 19
Crook of Devon ....68 J 15
Crookham ....63 N 17
Crookham Village ....20 R 30
Crooklands ....48 L 21
Cropredy ....28 Q 27
Cropston ....36 Q 25
Cropwell Bishop ....36 R 25
Crosby *Allerdale* ....54 J 19
Crosby *Isle of Man* ......46 G 21
Crosby *Sefton* ....42 K 23
Crosby Ravensworth ......48 M 20
Croscombe ....18 M 30
Cross ....83 B 8
Cross Fell ....55 M 19
Cross Hands ....15 H 28
Cross Inn ....25 H 27
Crossaig ....59 D 16
Crossapoll ....64 Z 14
Crossbost ....82 A 9
Crossford ....61 I 16
Crossgates ....68 J 15
Crossgill ....48 L 21
Crosshill *Fife* ....68 K 15
Crosshill *South Ayrshire* ..60 G 18
Crosshouse ....60 G 17
Crosskeys ....18 K 29
Crosskirk ....85 J 8
Crossmichael ....53 I 19
Crossraguel Abbey ....60 F 18
Crossways ....9 N 31
Croston ....42 L 23
Crouch (River) ....22 W 29
Croughton ....28 Q 28
Crow Hill ....26 M 28
Crowborough ....12 U 30
Crowcombe ....8 K 30
Crowhurst ....12 V 31
Crowland ....37 T 25
Crowle *Doncaster* ....44 R 23
Crowle *Wychavon* ....27 N 27
Crowlin Island ....77 C 11
Crowmarsh Gifford ....20 Q 29
Crowthorne ....20 R 29
Croxley Green ....21 S 29
Croxton ....30 W 26
Croxton Kerrial ....36 R 25
Croy ....79 H 11
Croyde ....6 H 30
Croydon *London Borough* ..21 T 29
Cruckton ....34 L 26

Cudworth ....43 P 23
Cuffley ....21 T 28
Cuhxham ....20 Q 29
Cuilicudden ....79 H 11
Cuillin Sound ....71 B 12
Cuillin (The) ....77 B 12
Culbokie ....79 G 11
Culdrose ....2 E 33
Culgaith ....55 M 20
Culkein ....83 D 9
Cullen ....80 L 10
Cullen Bay ....80 L 10
Cullingworth ....43 O 22
Cullipool ....65 D 15
Culloch ....67 I 14
Cullompton ....7 J 31
Culmington ....26 L 26
Culmstock ....8 K 31
Culnacraig ....84 E 10
Culrain ....79 G 10
Culross ....68 J 15
Culshabbin ....52 G 19
Culswic ....87 P 3
Culter Fell ....61 J 17
Cults ....75 N 12
Culzean Castle ....59 F 17
Cumbernauld ....67 I 16
Cumbrian Moutains ....48 K 20
Cuminestown ....81 N 11
Cummersdale ....54 L 19
Cummertrees ....54 J 19
Cumnock ....60 H 17
Cumnor ....20 P 28
Cumwhitton ....55 L 19
Cunninghamhead ....60 G 17
Cupar ....69 K 15
Curbridge ....20 P 28
Curdridge ....10 Q 31
Currie ....61 K 16
Curry Rivel ....8 L 30
Cutcloy ....53 G 19
Cutnall green ....27 N 27
Cuxton ....22 V 29
Cwm ....18 K 28
Cwm Bychan ....33 H 25
Cwm Taf ....17 J 28
Cwmafan ....17 I 29
Cwmaman ....17 J 28
Cwmbach *Carmarthenshire /
  Sir Gaerfyrddin* ....15 G 28
Cwmbach *Powys / Powys* ..25 J 27
Cwmbach *Rhondda, Cynon, Taf /
  Rhondda, Cynon, Taff* ..17 J 28
Cwmbrân ....18 L 29
Cwmcarn ....18 K 29
Cwmcoy ....15 G 27
Cwmllynfell ....17 I 28
Cwmystwyth ....25 I 26
Cwnduad ....15 G 28
Cwnfelin Boeth ....15 G 28
Cwrt-Newydd ....15 H 27
Cydweli / Kidwelly ....15 H 28
Cyffylliog ....33 J 24
Cymmer ....17 J 29
Cymyran Bay ....40 G 23
Cynwyl Elfed ....15 G 28

D

Dacre *Eden* ....55 L 20
Dacre *Harrogate* ....49 O 21
Daglingworth ....19 N 28
Dailly ....60 F 18
Daimh (Loch an) ....73 G 14
Dairsie or Osnaburgh ......69 L 14
Dalavich ....65 E 15
Dalbeattie ....53 I 19
Dalbeg ....73 H 12
Dalblair ....60 H 17
Dalby ....46 F 21
Dalchalloch ....73 H 13
Dalchruin ....67 H 15
Dale ....14 E 28
Dale Head ....48 L 20
Dalgonar ....60 H 18
Dalham ....30 V 27
Dalhavaig ....85 I 8
Daliburgh ....76 X 12
Dalkeith ....61 K 16
Dallas ....80 J 11
Dalleagles ....60 H 17
Dallington *Northampton* ..28 R 27
Dallington *Rother* ....12 V 31
Dalmally ....66 F 14
Dalmellington ....60 G 18
Dalmeny ....68 J 16
Dalmigavie ....73 H 12
Dalnabreck ....71 C 13

Dalnaspidal Lodge .....73 H 13
Dalnavaid .....74 J 13
Dalnavie .....79 H 10
Dalness .....72 F 14
Dalry
  Dumfries and Galloway ....53 H 18
Dalry North Ayrshire .....60 F 16
Dalrymple .....60 G 17
Dalston .....54 L 19
Dalswinton .....53 I 18
Dalton
  Dumfries and Galloway ....54 J 18
Dalton North Yorks. .....50 P 21
Dalton in Furness .....47 K 21
Damerham .....9 O 31
Damh (Loch) .....78 D 11
Dan-yr-Ogof .....17 I 28
Danbury .....22 V 28
Danby .....50 R 20
Dane .....35 N 24
Danehill .....11 U 30
Darenth .....22 U 29
Darfield .....43 P 23
Darlington .....50 P 20
Darowen .....33 I 26
Darras Hall .....56 O 18
Darrington .....44 Q 22
Darsham .....31 Y 27
Dartford .....22 U 29
Dartford Tunnel .....22 U 29
Dartington .....4 I 32
Dartmeet .....4 I 32
Dartmoor National Park .....4 I 32
Dartmouth .....4 J 32
Darton .....43 P 23
Darvel .....60 H 17
Darwen .....42 M 22
Datchet .....21 S 29
Datchworth .....29 T 28
Dava .....80 J 11
Daventry .....28 Q 27
Davidstow .....6 G 32
Davington .....61 K 18
Daviot .....79 H 11
Dawley .....34 M 26
Dawlish .....4 J 32
Deal .....23 Y 30
Dean .....54 J 20
Dean Forest Park .....18 M 28
Deanich Lodge .....78 F 10
Deanston .....67 H 15
Dearham .....54 J 19
Debden .....30 U 28
Deben (River) .....31 X 27
Debenham .....31 X 27
Deddington .....28 Q 28
Dedham .....30 W 28
Dee / Afon Dyfrdwy (River)
  Wales .....41 K 23
Dee (River) Scotland .....75 N 12
Dee (River) / Afon Dyfrdwy .34 K 24
Deene .....29 S 26
Deepcut .....21 R 30
Deepdale .....49 M 21
Deeping-St. James .....37 T 25
Deeping St. Nicholas .....37 T 25
Deeps (The) .....87 P 3
Defford .....27 N 27
Deiniolen .....33 H 24
Delabole .....6 F 32
Delamere .....34 M 24
Delamere Forest .....42 L 24
Dell .....83 B 8
Dellifure .....80 J 11
Delnadamph Lodge .....74 K 12
Delph .....43 N 23
Denbigh / Dinbych .....33 J 24
Denby Dale .....43 P 23
Denchworth .....20 P 29
Denham .....21 S 29
Denholm .....62 L 17
Denmead .....10 Q 31
Dennington .....31 Y 27
Denny .....67 I 15
Dent .....49 M 21
Denton South Kesteven .....36 R 25
Denton Stockport .....43 N 23
Denver .....38 V 26
Derby .....36 P 25
Deri .....18 K 28
Dersingham .....38 V 25
Dervaig .....71 B 14
Derwent (River) R. Ouse ....44 R 22
Derwent (River) R. Trent ..36 P 24
Derwent (River) R. Tyne ..56 O 19
Derwent Dale .....43 O 23
Derwent Reservoir Derbs. ..43 O 23

Derwent Reservoir
  Northumb. .....56 N 19
Derwent Water .....54 K 20
Desborough .....28 R 26
Desford .....36 Q 26
Detling .....22 V 30
Devauden .....18 L 28
Deveron (River) .....81 M 11
Devil's Beef Tub .....61 J 17
Devil's Bridge / Pontarfynach 25 I 26
Devil's Elbow .....74 J 13
Devil's Punch Bowl .....10 R 30
Devizes .....19 O 29
Devonport .....3 H 32
Dewsbury .....43 P 22
Dherue (Loch an) .....84 G 8
Dial Post .....11 S 31
Dickleburgh .....31 X 26
Didcot .....20 Q 29
Diddlebury .....26 L 26
Digby .....37 S 24
Dilhorne .....35 N 25
Dilton Marsh .....19 N 30
Dilwyn .....26 L 27
Dinas .....24 F 27
Dinas Dinlle .....32 G 24
Dinas Head .....24 F 27
Dinas-Mawddwy .....33 I 25
Dinas Powys .....18 K 29
Dinbych / Denbigh .....33 J 24
Dinbych-y-pysgod / Tenby ..15 F 28
Dingwall .....79 G 11
Dinnet .....74 L 12
Dinnington
  Newcastle upon Tyne ..56 O 18
Dinnington Rotherham ..44 Q 23
Dinsdale .....50 P 20
Dinton .....9 O 30
Diptford .....4 I 32
Dirleton .....69 L 15
Dishforth .....50 P 21
Diss .....31 X 26
Disserth .....25 J 27
Distington .....53 J 20
Ditcheat .....8 M 30
Ditchingham .....31 Y 26
Ditchley Park .....28 P 28
Ditchling .....11 T 31
Ditton Priors .....26 M 26
Doc Penfro /
  Pembroke Dock .....16 F 28
Docherty (Glen) .....78 E 11
Dochgarroch .....79 H 11
Docking .....38 V 25
Dockray .....54 L 20
Dodburn .....62 L 17
Doddington Cambs. .....29 U 26
Doddington Kent .....22 W 30
Doddington Lincs. .....44 S 24
Doddington Northumb. ....63 O 17
Dodington .....19 M 29
Dodman Point .....3 F 33
Dodworth .....43 P 23
Doirlinn .....71 C 13
Dolanog .....33 J 25
Dolbenmaen .....33 H 25
Dolfor .....26 K 26
Dolgarrog .....33 I 24
Dolgellau .....33 I 25
Dolgoch Falls .....33 I 26
Dollar .....67 I 15
Dolphinholme .....48 L 22
Dolton .....7 H 31
Don (River) R. Ouse ....44 Q 23
Don (River) R. Spey ....74 K 12
Doncaster .....44 Q 23
Donhead-St. Andrew ....9 N 30
Donhead-St. Mary .....9 N 30
Donington .....37 T 25
Donington Park Circuit ..36 P 25
Donisthorpe .....36 P 25
Donnington Berks. .....20 Q 29
Donnington Salop .....35 M 25
Donyatt .....8 L 31
Doon (Loch) .....60 G 18
Dorback Lodge .....74 J 12
Dorchester Dorset .....8 M 31
Dorchester Oxon. .....20 Q 29
Dordon .....35 P 26
Dore .....43 P 24
Dores .....79 H 11
Dorking .....21 T 30
Dormansland .....11 U 30
Dormanstown .....57 Q 20
Dornie .....78 D 12
Dornoch .....79 H 10

Dornoch Firth .....79 H 10
Dornock .....54 K 19
Dorrington .....34 L 26
Dorstone .....26 K 27
Dorusduain .....78 D 12
Douchary (Glen) .....78 F 10
Dougarie .....59 D 17
Douglas Isle of Man .....46 G 21
Douglas
  South Lanarkshire .....61 I 17
Douglastown .....74 L 14
Dounby .....86 K 6
Doune Highland .....84 G 10
Doune Stirling .....67 H 15
Dove (River) .....35 O 24
Dove Cottage .....48 K 20
Dove Holes .....43 O 24
Dovedale .....35 O 24
Dover .....13 X 30
Dovercourt .....31 X 28
Doveridge .....35 O 25
Dovey / Dyfi (River) .....33 I 26
Dowally .....74 J 14
Dowdeswell .....27 N 28
Dowlish Wake .....8 L 31
Down Ampney .....19 O 28
Downderry .....3 G 32
Downham .....30 U 26
Downham Market .....38 V 26
Downies .....75 N 12
Downton .....9 O 31
Dowsby .....37 S 25
Doynton .....19 M 29
Drakes Broughton .....27 N 27
Draughton .....49 O 22
Drax .....44 R 22
Draycott .....36 P 25
Draycott-in-the-Clay .....35 O 25
Draycott-in-the-Moors .....35 N 25
Drayton Norfolk .....39 X 25
Drayton Oxon. .....20 Q 29
Drayton-St. Leonard .....20 Q 29
Drefach near Carmarthen ..15 H 28
Drefach
  near Newcastle-Emlyn ..15 G 27
Dreghorn .....60 G 17
Drem .....69 L 15
Drenewydd / Newtown ....26 K 26
Dreswick Point .....46 G 21
Driffield .....19 O 28
Drigg .....47 J 20
Drighlington .....43 P 22
Drimnin .....71 C 14
Drinnishadder .....76 Z 10
Drissaig .....65 E 15
Droitwich .....27 N 27
Dronfield .....43 P 24
Drongan .....60 G 17
Droxford .....10 Q 31
Druidibeg (Loch) .....76 Y 12
Druim a' Chliabhain (Loch) .85 H 8
Druimindarroch .....71 C 13
Drum Castle .....75 M 12
Drumbeg .....84 E 9
Drumblade .....81 L 11
Drumburgh .....54 K 19
Drumchardine .....79 G 11
Drumclog .....60 H 17
Drumelzier .....61 J 17
Drumfearn .....71 C 12
Drumlanrig Castle .....61 I 18
Drumlemble .....58 C 17
Drumlithie .....75 M 13
Drummond Castle .....67 I 14
Drummore .....52 F 19
Drummossie Muir .....79 H 11
Drumnadrochit .....79 G 11
Drumrunie .....84 E 9
Drumsallie .....72 D 13
Drumtochty Forest .....75 M 13
Druridge Bay .....63 P 18
Drybrook .....18 M 28
Dryburgh Abbey .....62 M 17
Drygarn Fawr .....25 J 27
Drymen .....67 G 15
Drynoch .....77 B 12
Duchally .....84 F 9
Ducklington .....20 P 28
Duddington .....37 S 26
Duddo .....63 N 16
Dudley Dudley .....35 N 26
Dudley North Tyneside ....56 P 18
Duff House .....81 M 11
Dufftown .....80 K 11
Duffield .....36 P 25
Duffus .....80 J 10
Dufton .....55 M 20

Duggleby .....51 S 21
Duich (Loch) .....78 D 12
Duirinish .....77 C 12
Duke's Pass .....67 G 15
Dukinfield .....43 N 23
Dullingham .....30 V 27
Dulnain Bridge .....80 J 12
Duloe .....3 G 32
Dulverton .....7 J 30
Dumbarton .....67 G 16
Dumbleton .....27 O 27
Dumfries .....53 J 18
Dun Carloway Broch .....82 Z 9
Dunan .....66 F 16
Dunbar .....69 M 15
Dunbeath .....85 J 9
Dunblane .....67 I 15
Duncansby Head .....86 K 8
Dunchurch .....28 Q 26
Duncow .....53 J 18
Duncton .....11 S 31
Dundee .....69 K 14
Dundonald .....60 G 17
Dundrennan .....53 I 19
Dundry .....18 M 29
Dunecht .....75 M 12
Dunfermline .....68 J 15
Dungeness .....13 W 31
Dunholme .....44 S 24
Dunino .....69 L 15
Dunipace .....67 I 15
Dunkeld .....68 J 14
Dunkery Beacon .....7 J 30
Dunkeswell .....8 K 31
Dunkirk .....19 N 29
Dunley .....27 N 27
Dunlop .....60 G 16
Dunmaglass Lodge .....79 H 12
Dunnet .....85 J 8
Dunnet Bay .....85 J 8
Dunnet Head .....86 J 7
Dunning .....68 J 15
Dunnington .....50 R 22
Dunnockshaw .....42 N 22
Dunnottar Castle .....75 N 13
Dunoon .....66 F 16
Dunragit .....52 F 19
Dunrobin Castle .....85 I 10
Duns .....62 M 16
Duns Tew .....28 P 28
Dunscore .....53 I 18
Dunsfold .....11 S 30
Dunsford .....4 I 31
Dunsop Bridge .....49 M 22
Dunstable .....29 S 28
Dunstaffnage Castel .....65 D 14
Dunstanburgh Castle .....63 P 17
Dunster .....17 J 30
Dunston .....37 S 24
Dunstone .....4 I 32
Dunsyre .....61 J 16
Duntelchaig (Loch) .....79 H 11
Dunton bassett .....28 Q 26
Dunure .....59 F 17
Dunvegan .....77 A 11
Dunvegan (Loch) .....77 A 11
Dunvegan Castle .....77 A 11
Dunvegan Head .....76 Z 11
Durdle Door .....9 N 32
Durham .....56 P 19
Durisdeer .....61 I 18
Durleigh .....8 L 30
Durlston Head .....9 O 32
Durness .....84 F 8
Durrington .....19 O 30
Dursley .....19 M 28
Dury Voe .....87 Q 2
Duston .....28 R 27
Duthil .....79 I 12
Duxford .....29 U 27
Dyce .....75 N 12
Dyfi / Dovey (River) .....33 I 26
Dyke .....80 I 11
Dykehead .....74 K 13
Dykends .....74 K 13
Dymchurch .....13 W 30
Dymock .....27 M 28
Dyserth .....41 J 23

E
Eaglescliffe .....50 P 20
Eaglesfield .....54 K 18
Eaglesham .....60 H 16
Eakring .....36 R 24
Earba (Lochan na h-) ....73 G 13

Earby .....49 N 22
Eardisley .....26 K 27
Earl Shilton .....36 Q 26
Earl Soham .....31 X 27
Earl Stonham .....31 X 27
Earley Winnersh .....20 R 29
Earlish .....77 A 11
Earls Barton .....28 R 27
Earls Colne .....30 W 28
Earlsferry .....69 L 15
Earlston .....62 L 17
Earn (Loch) .....67 H 14
Earn (River) .....67 J 14
Earsdon .....56 P 18
Earsham .....31 Y 26
Eartham .....11 S 31
Easdale .....65 D 15
Easebourne .....10 R 31
Easington Easington .....57 P 19
Easington
  East Riding of Yorkshire ...45 U 23
Easington
  Redcar and Cleveland .....50 R 20
Easington
  South Oxfordshire .....20 Q 28
Easington Lane .....56 P 19
Easingwold .....50 Q 21
Eassie and Nevay .....68 K 14
East Aberthaw .....17 J 29
East Barkwith .....45 T 24
East Bergholt .....30 X 28
East Brent .....18 L 30
East Budleigh .....5 K 32
East Butterwick .....44 R 23
East-Challow .....20 P 29
East Chinnock .....8 L 31
East-Coker .....8 M 31
East Cowes .....10 Q 31
East Cowton .....50 P 20
East Dereham .....38 W 25
East Ferry .....44 R 23
East Glen (River) .....37 S 25
East Grafton .....19 P 29
East Grinstead .....11 T 30
East Hagbourne .....20 Q 29
East-Halton .....45 T 23
East Hanney .....20 P 29
East Hardwick .....44 Q 23
East Harling .....30 W 26
East Haven .....69 L 14
East Hendred .....20 P 29
East Hoathly .....12 U 31
East Horsley .....21 S 30
East Huntspill .....18 L 30
East Ilsley .....20 Q 29
East Keswick .....50 P 22
East Kilbride Eilean Siar ..70 X 12
East Kilbride
  South Lanarkshire .....60 H 16
East-Knoyle .....9 N 30
East Knoyle .....9 N 30
East Lambrook .....8 L 31
East Leake .....36 Q 25
East Linton .....69 M 16
East Loch Roag .....82 Z 9
East Loch Tarbet .....77 Z 10
East Looe .....3 G 32
East Lulworth .....9 N 32
East Markham .....44 R 24
East Meon .....10 Q 31
East Mersea .....22 W 28
East Midlands Airport ..36 Q 25
East Moor .....35 P 24
East Norton .....36 R 26
East-Poringland .....39 Y 26
East Portlemouth .....4 I 33
East Rhidorroch Lodge ..78 F 10
East-Rudham .....38 W 25
East-Saltourn .....62 L 16
East Tisted .....10 R 30
East Wemyss .....68 K 15
East-Winch .....38 V 25
East Wittering .....10 R 31
East-Woodhay .....20 P 29
East-Wretham .....30 W 26
Eastbourne .....12 U 31
Eastchurch .....22 W 29
Eastdean .....12 U 31
Easter-Compton .....18 M 29
Easter Ross .....79 G 10
Eastergate .....11 S 31
Eastfield .....51 S 21
Eastgate .....55 N 19
Eastham .....42 L 24
Eastington .....19 N 28

Eastleach .....19 O 28
Eastleigh .....10 P 31
Eastoft .....44 R 23
Easton Carlisle .....55 L 18
Easton Dorset .....8 M 32
Easton Norfolk .....39 X 26
Easton-Grey .....19 N 29
Easton-in-Gordano .....18 L 29
Easton-Royal .....19 O 29
Eastriggs .....54 K 19
Eastrington .....44 R 22
Eastry .....23 X 30
Eastville .....37 U 24
Eastwood .....36 Q 24
Eaton .....34 M 24
Eaton Bray .....29 S 28
Eaton Socon .....29 T 27
Ebbw Vale / Glyn Ebwy ....18 K 28
Ebchester .....56 O 19
Ebrington .....27 O 27
Eccles .....62 M 17
Ecchinswell .....20 Q 29
Ecclefechan .....54 K 18
Eccles .....42 M 23
Eccleshall .....35 N 25
Echt .....75 M 12
Eckford .....62 M 17
Eckington Derbs. .....43 P 24
Eckington Worc. .....27 N 27
Edale .....43 O 23
Edburton .....11 T 31
Eday .....87 L 6
Eddleston .....61 K 16
Edderton .....79 H 10
Eddrachillis Bay .....84 E 9
Eden (River) .....55 M 19
Eden Project .....3 F 32
Edenbridge .....21 U 30
Edentaggart .....66 F 15
Edenthorpe .....44 Q 23
Edgefield .....39 X 25
Edgmond .....35 M 25
Edgton .....26 L 26
Edinbane .....77 A 11
Edinburgh .....68 K 16
Edington .....19 N 30
Edith Weston .....37 S 26
Edlesborough .....29 S 28
Edlingham .....63 O 17
Edmondsley .....56 P 19
Edmundbyers .....56 O 19
Edwalton .....36 Q 25
Edwinstowe .....36 Q 24
Edzell .....75 M 13
Efailnewydd .....32 G 25
Egerton .....22 W 30
Eggerness Point .....53 G 19
Eggleston .....56 N 20
Egham .....21 S 29
Egilsay .....87 L 6
Eglingham .....63 O 17
Egloskerry .....6 G 32
Eglwys Brewis .....17 J 29
Eglwysfach .....33 I 26
Eglwyswrw .....15 F 27
Egremont .....47 J 20
Egton .....50 R 20
Eigg .....71 B 13
Eigheach (Loch) .....73 G 13
Eight Ash Green .....30 W 28
Eil .....73 I 12
Eil (Loch) .....72 E 13
Eilde Mór (Loch) .....72 F 13
Eilean a' Chalmain .....64 A 15
Eilean Beag .....77 C 11
Eilean Chathastail .....71 B 13
Eilean Donan Castle .....78 D 12
Eilean Flodigarry .....77 B 10
Eilean Mhuire .....82 A 10
Eilean Mòr .....77 C 11
Eilean na Bà .....83 D 9
Eilean nan Each .....71 B 13
Eilean Trodday .....77 B 10
Eileanach Lodge .....79 G 10
Eilt (Loch) .....72 D 13
Eishken .....82 A 9
Eishort (Loch) .....71 C 12
Elan Valley .....25 J 27
Elan Village .....25 J 27
Elcho .....68 J 14
Elgin .....80 K 11
Elgol .....71 B 12
Elham .....23 X 30
Elie .....69 L 15
Eling .....10 P 31
Elkesley .....44 R 24
Elkstone .....19 N 28

A B C D E F G H I J K L M N O P Q R S T U V W X Y Z

Elland ....43 O 22
Ellastone ....35 O 25
Ellen's Green ....11 S 30
Ellerbeck ....50 P 20
Ellerton ....44 R 22
Ellesmere ....34 L 25
Ellesmere Port ....42 L 24
Ellingham ....31 Y 26
Ellington ....56 P 18
Ellon ....81 N 11
Elloughton ....44 S 22
Elmdon ....29 U 27
Elmley Castle ....27 N 27
Elmore ....19 N 28
Elmstead Market ....30 W 28
Elmswell ....30 W 27
Elphin ....84 E 9
Elrick ....75 N 12
Elrig ....52 G 19
Elsdon ....55 N 18
Elsenham ....30 U 28
Elsham ....45 S 23
Elsrickle ....61 J 16
Elstead ....21 R 30
Elstree ....21 T 29
Elswick ....42 L 22
Eltisley ....29 T 27
Elton ....37 S 26
Elveden ....30 W 26
Elvington ....50 R 22
Elwick ....57 Q 19
Elworth ....35 M 24
Ely ....30 U 26
Emberton ....28 R 27
Embleton Allerdale ......54 K 20
Embleton Alnwick ....63 P 17
Embo ....79 I 10
Embsay ....49 O 22
Emneth ....37 U 26
Empingham ....37 S 25
Emsworth ....10 R 31
Enaclete ....82 Z 9
Enard Bay ....83 D 9
Enderby ....36 Q 26
Endmoor ....48 L 21
Endon ....35 N 24
Enfield London Borough ..21 T 29
Enford ....19 O 30
Englefield Green ....21 S 29
English Bicknor ....18 M 28
Englishcombe ....19 M 29
Enham Alamein ....20 P 30
Enmore ....8 K 30
Ensay ....71 B 14
Enstone ....28 P 28
Enterkinfoot ....61 I 18
Enville ....27 N 26
Eochar ....76 X 11
Eoligarry ....70 X 12
Eoropie ....83 B 8
Eorsa ....65 B 14
Eport (Loch) ....76 Y 11
Epping ....21 U 28
Epping Forest ....21 U 29
Epsom ....21 T 30
Epworth ....44 R 23
Erddig ....34 K 24
Eredine ....65 E 15
Eredine Forest ....65 D 15
Eriboll ....84 F 8
Eriboll (Loch) ....84 F 8
Ericht (Loch) ....73 G 13
Ericstane ....61 J 17
Eridge Green ....12 U 30
Eriska ....65 D 14
Eriskay ....70 Y 12
Erisort (Loch) ....82 A 9
Eriswell ....30 V 26
Erlestoke ....19 N 30
Ermington ....4 I 32
Erpingham ....39 X 25
Erraid ....64 A 15
Errochty (Loch) ....73 H 13
Errogie ....79 G 12
Errol ....68 K 14
Ersary ....70 X 13
Erskine Bridge ....67 G 16
Ervie ....52 E 19
Erwood ....25 K 27
Esh Winning ....56 O 19
Esha Ness ....87 P 2
Esher ....21 S 29
Esk (Glen) ....75 L 13
Esk (River) ....54 K 19
Eskdale ....54 K 18
Eskdalemuir ....61 K 18
Essendon ....21 T 28

F

Essich ....79 H 11
Eston ....57 Q 20
Etal ....63 N 17
Etchilhampton ....19 O 29
Etchingham ....12 V 30
Etherow (River) ....43 N 23
Etherow Park ....43 N 23
Etive (Glen) ....72 F 14
Etive (Loch) ....65 E 14
Eton ....21 S 29
Ettington ....27 P 27
Ettrick ....61 K 17
Ettrick Forest ....62 K 17
Ettrick Pen ....61 K 17
Etwall ....35 P 25
Euston ....30 W 26
Euxton ....42 L 22
Evanton ....79 G 11
Evelix ....79 H 10
Evenlode ....27 O 28
Evenwood ....56 O 20
Evercreech ....8 M 30
Everingham ....44 R 22
Everleigh ....19 O 30
Everleigh ....19 O 30
Evershot ....8 M 31
Eversley ....20 R 29
Everton ....44 R 23
Evesham ....27 O 27
Evesham (Vale of) ....27 O 27
Ewe (Isle of) ....78 D 10
Ewell ....21 T 29
Ewelme ....20 Q 29
Ewenny ....17 J 29
Ewes ....54 L 18
Ewhurst ....11 S 30
Exbourne ....7 I 31
Exe (River) ....7 J 31
Exebridge ....7 J 30
Exeter ....4 J 31
Exford ....7 J 30
Exminster ....4 J 31
Exmoor National Park ..7 I 30
Exmouth ....4 J 32
Exton ....7 J 30
Eyam ....43 O 24
Eye Cambs. ....37 T 26
Eye Suffolk ....31 X 27
Eye Peninsula ....83 B 9
Eyemouth ....63 N 16
Eynort ....77 A 12
Eynort (Loch) Highland ..77 A 12
Eynort (Loch) Western Isles ..76 Y 12
Eynsford ....22 U 29
Eynsham ....20 P 28
Eyre Point ....77 B 12
Eythorne ....23 X 30

F

Fada (Loch) ....76 Y 11
Failsworth ....43 N 23
Fair Isle ....87 P 5
Fair Oak ....10 Q 31
Fairbourne ....33 H 25
Fairburn ....44 Q 22
Fairford ....19 O 28
Fairlie ....59 F 16
Fairlight ....12 V 31
Fakenham ....38 W 25
Fala ....62 L 16
Faldingworth ....45 S 23
Falfield ....18 M 29
Falkirk ....67 I 16
Falkland ....68 K 15
Fallford ....54 K 18
Fallin ....67 I 15
Falmer ....11 T 31
Falmouth ....2 E 33
Falstone ....55 M 18
Fanagmore ....84 E 8
Fangfoss ....50 R 22
Fannich (Loch) ....78 E 11
Fannich Lodge ....78 F 11
Fara ....86 K 7
Fareham ....10 Q 31
Faringdon ....19 P 29
Farlam ....55 L 19
Farleigh-Hungerford ....19 N 30
Farley Mount ....10 P 30
Farlow ....26 M 26
Farmborough ....18 M 29
Farmers ....25 I 27
Farmtown ....80 L 11
Farnborough Hants. ....20 R 30
Farnborough Warw. ....28 P 27
Farnborough
    West Berkshire ......20 P 29

Farndon Chester ....34 L 24
Farndon
    Newark and Sherwood ..36 R 24
Farne Islands ....63 P 17
Farnell ....75 M 13
Farnham Dorset ....9 N 31
Farnham Surrey ....20 R 30
Farnham Royal ....21 S 29
Farningham ....22 U 29
Farnley ....49 O 22
Farnsfield ....36 Q 24
Farnworth ....42 M 23
Farr ....85 H 8
Farrington Gurney ......18 M 30
Farway ....5 K 31
Fasnakyle ....78 F 12
Fasnakyle Forest ....78 F 11
Fasque ....75 M 13
Fassfern ....72 E 13
Fauldhouse ....61 I 16
Faversham ....22 W 30
Fawley ....10 P 31
Fazeley ....35 O 26
Fearby ....49 O 21
Fearn Lodge ....79 H 10
Fearnan ....67 H 14
Fearnmore ....77 C 11
Featherstone Staffs. ....35 N 26
Featherstone West Yorks. ..43 P 22
Feelindre ....15 F 27
Feering ....30 W 28
Feetham ....49 N 20
Felbridge ....11 T 30
Felindre Carmarthenshire /
    Sir Gaerfyrddin ......25 I 28
Felindre Powys ....26 K 26
Felinfach ....25 K 28
Felinheli ....33 H 24
Felixkirk ....50 Q 21
Felixstowe ....31 Y 28
Felling ....56 P 19
Felmingham ....39 Y 25
Felpham ....11 S 31
Felsham ....30 W 27
Felsted ....30 V 28
Feltham ....21 S 29
Felthorpe ....39 X 25
Felton ....63 O 18
Feltwell ....30 V 26
Fence ....42 N 22
Feniton ....8 K 31
Fenny Bentley ....35 O 24
Fenstanton ....29 T 27
Fenton Stoke-on-Trent ..35 N 25
Fenton West Lindsey ..44 R 24
Fenwick
    Berwick-upon-Tweed ..63 O 17
Fenwick East Ayrshire ..60 G 17
Feochaig ....59 D 17
Feochan (Loch) ....65 D 14
Feock ....2 E 33
Feolin Ferry ....58 B 16
Fern ....74 L 13
Ferndown ....9 O 31
Ferness ....79 I 11
Fernhurst ....11 R 30
Ferryden ....75 M 13
Ferryhill ....56 P 19
Ferryside ....15 G 28
Fersit ....73 F 13
Feshie (Glen) ....73 I 12
Feshiebridge ....73 I 12
Fetcham ....21 S 30
Fetlar ....87 R 2
Fetterangus ....81 N 11
Fettercairn ....75 M 13
Fewston ....49 O 22
Ffestiniog ....33 I 25
Ffestiniog (Vale of) ....33 H 25
Fflint / Flint ....42 K 24
Fforest Fawr ....17 J 28
Ffostrasol ....15 G 27
Fiaray ....70 X 12
Fiddleton ....62 L 18
Fifield ....27 P 28
Filby ....39 Y 26
Filey ....51 T 21
Fillongley ....27 P 26
Filton ....18 M 29
Finchampstead ....20 R 29
Finchingfield ....30 V 28
Findhorn ....80 J 11
Findhorn (River) ....73 H 12
Findhorn Bay ....80 J 11
Findo Gask ....68 J 14
Findochty ....80 L 10
Findon ....11 S 31

Finedon ....29 S 26
Fingest ....20 R 29
Fingland ....60 I 17
Finiskaig ....72 D 13
Finmere ....28 Q 28
Finniegill ....61 K 18
Finningley ....44 R 23
Finsbay ....76 Z 10
Finstock ....20 P 28
Finstown ....86 K 6
Fintry Aberdeenshire ..81 M 11
Fintry Stirling ....67 H 15
Fionn Loch ....78 D 10
Fionn Loch Mór ....84 F 9
Fionnphort ....64 A 15
Fishbourne Chichester ..10 R 31
Fishbourne Isle of Wight ..10 Q 31
Fisherfield Forest ....78 D 10
Fisherford ....81 M 11
Fishguard / Abergwaun ..24 F 28
Fishnish Bay ....65 B 14
Fishtoft ....37 U 25
Fiskavaig ....77 A 12
Fiskerton ....44 S 24
Fittleworth ....11 S 31
Fittleton ....19 O 30
Fiunary ....71 C 14
Fivehead ....8 L 30
Flackwell Heath ....21 R 29
Fladbury ....27 N 27
Fladda-Chùain ....77 A 10
Flagg ....35 O 24
Flamborough ....51 T 21
Flamborough Head ......51 T 21
Flamingo Park ....50 R 21
Flamstead ....21 S 28
Flash ....35 O 24
Flashader ....77 A 11
Flatford Mill ....30 X 28
Flax Bourton ....18 L 29
Flaxton ....50 R 21
Fleckney ....36 Q 26
Fleet ....20 R 30
Fleet (Islands of) ....53 H 19
Fleet (Loch) ....79 H 10
Fleet Hargate ....37 U 25
Fleetwood ....48 K 22
Flimby ....53 J 19
Flint / Fflint ....42 K 24
Flintham ....36 R 24
Flitton ....29 S 27
Flitwick ....29 S 27
Flixton ....50 R 21
Flodday near Hellisay ..70 X 13
Flodday near Sandray ..70 X 13
Flodden Field ....63 N 17
Flodigarry ....77 B 11
Flookburgh ....48 L 21
Floors Castle ....62 M 17
Flotta ....86 K 7
Flowerdale Forest ....78 D 11
Flyford Flavell ....27 N 27
Fochabers ....80 K 11
Foggathorpe ....44 R 22
Foinaven ....84 F 8
Foindle ....84 E 8
Folkestone ....13 X 30
Folkingham ....37 S 25
Folly Gate ....7 H 31
Fontmell Magna ....9 N 31
Ford Argyll and Bute ..65 D 15
Ford Arun ....11 S 31
Ford
    Berwick-upon-Tweed ..63 N 17
Ford
    Buckinghamshire ....20 R 28
Ford Cotswold ....27 O 28
Ford
    Shrewsbury and Atcham ..34 L 25
Forde Abbey ....8 L 31
Forden ....34 K 26
Fordham ....30 V 27
Fordingbridge ....9 O 31
Fordoun ....75 M 13
Fordwich ....23 X 30
Fordyce ....80 L 11
Foreland ....10 Q 31
Foreland Point ....17 I 30
Foremark Reservoir ....36 P 25
Forest Lodge ....74 I 13
Forest Row ....11 U 30
Forestburn Gate ....63 O 18
Forfar ....74 L 14
Forgandenny ....68 J 14
Formby ....42 K 23
Formby Point ....42 K 23
Fornham All Saints ....30 W 27

Forres ....80 J 11
Forrest Lodge ....53 H 18
Forse ....85 K 9
Forsinard ....85 I 8
Fort Augustus ....73 F 12
Fort George ....79 H 11
Fort Victoria ....10 P 31
Fort William ....72 E 13
Forter ....74 K 13
Forteviot ....68 J 14
Forth ....61 I 16
Forth (Firth of) ....68 K 15
Forth (River) ....67 G 15
Forth Bridges ....68 J 15
Fortingall ....73 H 14
Forton ....35 M 25
Fortrose ....79 H 11
Fortuneswell ....8 M 32
Fosdyke ....37 T 25
Foss ....73 I 13
Foston ....36 R 25
Foston on the Wolds ..51 T 22
Fotherby ....45 T 23
Fotheringhay ....29 S 26
Foulden ....63 N 16
Foulness Point ....22 W 29
Foulridge ....43 N 22
Foulsham ....38 X 25
Fountainhall ....62 L 16
Fountains Abbey ....50 P 21
Four Crosses ....34 K 25
Four Elms ....21 U 30
Four Marks ....10 Q 30
Fovant ....9 O 30
Foveran ....81 N 12
Fowey ....3 G 32
Fowlmere ....29 U 27
Fownhope ....26 M 27
Foxdale ....46 G 21
Foxholes ....51 S 21
Foxton ....28 R 26
Foxup ....49 N 21
Foyers ....73 G 12
Fraddon ....3 F 32
Framfield ....12 U 31
Framlingham ....31 Y 27
Frampton-on-Severn ..19 M 28
Framwellgate Moor ....56 P 19
Frant ....12 U 30
Fraserburgh ....81 O 10
Fraserburgh Bay ....81 O 10
Freckenham ....30 V 27
Freckleton ....42 L 22
Freeland ....20 P 28
Freethorpe ....39 Y 26
Freevater Forest ....79 F 10
Freiston ....37 U 25
Fremington ....7 H 30
Frensham ....10 R 30
Freshwater ....10 P 31
Freshwater Bay ....10 P 31
Freshwater East ....16 F 29
Freshwater West ....14 E 29
Fressingfield ....31 X 26
Freswick ....86 K 8
Freuchie ....68 K 15
Freuchie (Loch) ....67 I 14
Friday Bridge ....37 U 26
Fridaythorpe ....51 S 21
Frimley ....21 R 30
Fringford ....28 Q 28
Frinton-on-Sea ....31 X 28
Friockheim ....75 M 14
Frisa (Loch) ....71 B 14
Friskney ....37 U 24
Frithville ....37 T 24
Frittenden ....12 V 30
Fritton ....28 Q 28
Fritwell ....28 Q 28
Frizington ....47 J 20
Frocester ....19 N 28
Frodsham ....42 L 24
Froggatt ....43 P 24
Frome ....19 N 30
Frosterley ....56 O 19
Froxfield ....20 P 29
Fuday ....70 X 12
Fuiay ....70 X 13
Fulbourn ....30 U 27
Fulford ....37 U 24
Fulking ....11 T 31
Fuller Street ....22 V 28
Fulwood ....42 M 22
Funtington ....10 R 31
Funzie ....87 R 2
Furness Abbey ....47 K 21
Furness Fells ....48 K 20
Fyfield ....22 U 28
Fyvie ....81 M 11

G

Gaddesby ....36 R 25
Gaick Lodge ....73 H 13
Gainford ....49 O 20
Gainsborough ....44 R 23
Gairloch ....78 C 10
Gairlochy ....72 F 13
Gairsay ....87 L 6
Gaitsgill ....54 L 19
Galashiels ....62 L 17
Galgate ....48 L 22
Gallan Head ....82 Y 9
Gallanach ....65 D 14
Galloway Forest Park ..52 G 18
Galltair ....72 D 12
Galmisdale ....71 B 13
Galmpton ....4 J 32
Galson ....82 A 8
Galston ....60 G 17
Galtrigill ....76 Z 11
Gamblesby ....55 M 19
Gamlingay ....29 T 27
Ganavan ....65 D 14
Ganton ....51 S 21
Garboldisham ....30 W 26
Gardenstown ....81 N 10
Garelochhead ....66 F 15
Garenin ....82 Z 9
Garforth ....43 P 22
Gargrave ....49 N 22
Gargunnock ....67 H 15
Garioch ....81 M 12
Garlieston ....53 G 19
Garlogie ....75 M 12
Garmony ....65 C 14
Garmouth ....80 K 11
Garrabost ....83 B 9
Garragie Lodge ....73 G 12
Garraron ....65 D 15
Garreg ....33 H 25
Garrigill ....55 M 19
Garrisdale Point ....71 A 12
Garros ....77 B 11
Garrow ....67 I 14
Garry (Glen) Highland ..72 E 12
Garry (Glen)
    Perthshire and Kinross ..73 H 13
Garry (Loch) ....72 F 12
Garsington ....20 Q 28
Garten (Loch) ....74 I 12
Garth ....25 J 27
Garthorpe ....44 R 23
Gartmore ....67 G 15
Gartocharn ....67 G 15
Garton-on-The-Wolds ..51 S 21
Garvald ....69 M 16
Garvamore ....73 G 12
Garve ....79 F 11
Garvellachs ....65 C 15
Garvestone ....38 W 26
Garvock ....66 F 16
Garway ....26 L 28
Garynahine ....82 Z 9
Gatehouse of Fleet ....53 H 19
Gateshead ....56 P 19
Gateside ....68 K 15
Gatley ....42 N 23
Gatwick Airport ....11 T 30
Gaulden Manor ....8 K 30
Gavard ....64 B 15
Gaydon ....28 P 27
Gayton King's Lynn
    and West Norfolk ....38 V 25
Gayton Stafford ....35 N 25
Gaywood ....38 V 25
Geary ....77 A 11
Geddington ....29 R 26
Gedney Drove End ......37 U 25
Gedney Hill ....37 T 25
Gelligaer ....18 K 28
Gelston ....53 I 19
Georgeham ....6 H 30
Georth ....86 K 6
Gerrards Cross ....21 S 29
Gestingthorpe ....30 V 27
Gifford ....62 L 16
Gigha (Sound of) ....58 C 17
Gigha Island ....58 C 16
Gighay ....70 Y 12
Gilberdyke ....44 R 22
Gilcrux ....54 J 19
Gildersome ....43 P 22
Gilfach Goch ....17 J 29
Gillamour ....50 R 21
Gilling East ....50 Q 21

Gilling West 49 O 20
Gillingham *Dorset* 9 N 30
Gillingham *Kent* 22 V 29
Gillingham *South Norfolk* 31 Y 26
Gills 86 K 8
Gilmerton 67 I 14
Gilmorton 28 Q 26
Gilston 62 L 16
Gilwern 18 K 28
Girthon 53 H 19
Girton 29 U 27
Girvan 59 F 18
Gisburn 49 N 22
Gisland 55 M 19
Gittisham 8 K 31
Gladestry 26 K 27
Glaisdale 50 R 20
Glamis 74 K 14
Glamis Castle 74 L 14
Glanaman 17 I 28
Glandwr 15 G 28
Glanton 63 O 17
Glas-allt-Shiel 74 K 13
Glas-leac Mór 83 D 9
Glas Maol 74 J 13
Glasbury 26 K 27
Glascarnoch (Loch) 78 F 10
Glascwm 26 K 27
Glasdrum 72 E 14
Glasgow 60 H 16
Glasphein 76 Z 11
Glaspwll 33 I 26
Glass (Loch) 79 G 10
Glassburn 78 F 11
Glasserton 52 G 19
Glassford 60 H 16
Glasshouses 49 O 21
Glasson 48 L 22
Glassonby 55 M 19
Glastonbury 8 L 30
Gleadless 43 P 23
Gleann Beag 78 F 10
Gleann Mór 79 G 10
Gleaston 48 K 21
Glecknabae 59 E 16
Glemsford 30 V 27
Glen auldyn 46 G 21
Glen Brittle Forest 77 B 12
Glen Finglas Reservoir 67 G 15
Glen More Forest Park 74 I 12
Glen Shee 74 J 13
Glen Trool Lodge 52 G 18
Glenbarr 59 C 17
Glenborrodale 71 C 13
Glenbranter 66 E 15
Glenbrittle House 77 B 12
Glenbuchat Castle 74 K 12
Glenbuck 60 I 17
Glencaple 53 J 18
Glencarse 68 K 14
Glencoe 72 E 13
Glencoul (Loch) 84 F 9
Glendoebeg 73 G 12
Glendurgan Garden 2 E 33
Glenegedale 58 B 16
Glenelg 72 D 12
Glenelg Bay 72 D 12
Glenfarg 68 J 15
Glenfeshie Lodge 73 I 12
Glenfiddich Lodge 80 K 11
Glenfield 36 Q 26
Glenfinnan 72 D 13
Glenforsa Airport 65 C 14
Glenfyne Lodge 66 F 15
Glengorm 71 B 14
Glengoulandie 73 H 14
Glengrasco 77 B 11
Glenkens (The) 53 H 18
Glenkin die 74 L 12
Glenkirk 61 J 17
Glenlivet 80 J 11
Glenluce 52 F 19
Glenmassan 66 E 15
Glenmaye 46 F 21
Glenmore 71 C 13
Glenprosen Village 74 K 13
Glenridding 48 L 20
Glenrothes 68 K 15
Glenside 82 A 9
Glenstriven 66 E 16
Glentham 44 S 23
Glentress 61 K 17
Glentrool Village 52 G 18
Glentworth 44 S 23
Glenuachdarach 77 B 11
Glenuig 71 C 13
Glespin 61 I 17
Gletness 87 Q 3
Glinton 37 T 26
Glossop 43 O 23
Gloucester 27 N 28
Gloup 87 Q 1
Glusburn 49 O 22
Glutt Lodge 85 I 9
Glympton 28 P 28
Glyn Ceiriog 34 K 25
Glyn-Ebwy / Ebbw Vale 18 K 28
Glyn-neath 17 J 28
Glyncorrwg 17 J 28
Glynde 11 U 31
Glyndebourne 11 U 31
Glyndyfrdwy 34 K 25
Gnosall 35 N 25
Goadby 36 R 26
Goat Fell 59 E 17
Goathland 50 R 20
Gobowen 34 K 25
Godalming 21 S 30
Godmanchester 29 T 27
Godmanstone 8 M 31
Godshill 10 Q 32
Godstone 21 T 30
Goil (Loch) 66 F 15
Golborne 42 M 23
Goldcliff 18 L 29
Goldhanger 22 W 28
Goldthorpe 44 Q 23
Golspie 85 I 10
Gomersal 43 O 22
Gometra 64 B 14
Gomshall 21 S 30
Gooderstone 38 V 26
Goodleigh 7 I 30
Goodrich 26 M 28
Goodrington 4 J 32
Goodwick 24 F 27
Goodwood House 10 R 31
Goole 44 R 22
Goonhavern 2 E 32
Goostrey 42 M 24
Gordon 62 M 16
Gordonbush 85 I 9
Gordonstown 80 L 11
Gorebridge 61 K 16
Goring 20 Q 29
Gorm Loch Mór 84 F 9
Gorran Haven 3 F 33
Gorseinon 15 H 29
Gorsleston-on-Sea 39 Z 26
Gortantaoid 64 B 16
Gosberton 37 T 25
Gosfield 30 V 28
Gosforth *Cumbria* 47 J 20
Gosforth
Newcastle upon Tyne 56 P 18
Gosport 10 Q 31
Goswick 63 O 16
Gotham 36 Q 25
Gott Bay 70 Z 14
Goudhurst 12 V 30
Gourdon 75 N 13
Gourock 66 F 16
Gowerton 15 H 29
Goxhill 45 T 22
Graemsay 86 K 7
Grafton Underwood 29 S 26
Grain 22 W 29
Grainthorpe 45 U 23
Granby 36 R 25
Grandtully 74 I 14
Grange-over-Sands 48 L 21
Grangemouth 67 I 15
Grantchester 29 U 27
Grantham 37 S 25
Grantown-on-Spey 80 J 12
Grantshouse 62 N 16
Grasby 45 S 23
Grasmere 48 K 20
Grassington 49 O 21
Grateley 9 P 30
Graveley 29 T 27
Gravesend 22 V 29
Gravir 82 A 9
Grayrigg 48 M 20
Grays Thurrock 22 V 29
Grayshott 10 R 30
Grayswood 11 R 30
Greasbrough 43 P 23
Great Addington 29 S 26
Great Altcar 42 K 23
Great Amwell 21 T 28
Great Asby 49 M 20
Great Ayton 50 Q 20
Great Baddow 22 V 28
Great Bardfield 30 V 28
Great Barford 29 S 27
Great Barr 35 O 26
Great Barrow 34 L 24
Great Barugh 50 R 21
Great Bedwyn 19 P 29
Great Bentley 31 X 28
Great Bernera 82 Z 9
Great Bircham 38 V 25
Great-Bollright 28 P 28
Great Bookham 21 S 30
Great Bourton 28 Q 27
Great Bowden 28 R 26
Great Brickhill 29 R 28
Great Bridgeford 35 N 25
Great Bromley 30 X 28
Great Broughton 50 Q 20
Great-Budworth 42 M 24
Great Burdon 50 P 20
Great Chalfield 19 N 29
Great Chesterford 30 U 27
Great Chishill 29 U 27
Great Clifton 53 J 20
Great Coates 45 T 23
Great-Comberton 27 N 27
Great Cornard 30 W 27
Great Cubley 35 O 25
Great Cumbrae Island 59 F 16
Great-Dalby 36 R 25
Great Doddington 28 R 27
Great Driffield 51 S 21
Great-Dunham 38 W 25
Great Dunmow 30 V 28
Great Easton *Essex* 30 U 28
Great Easton *Leics.* 28 R 26
Great Eccleston 42 L 22
Great Ellingham 38 W 26
Great Finborough 30 W 27
Great Glen 36 Q 26
Great Gonerby 37 S 25
Great Gransden 29 T 27
Great Harrowden 28 R 27
Great Harwood 42 M 22
Great Hockham 30 W 26
Great Horkesley 30 W 28
Great Horwood 28 R 28
Great Houghton 43 P 23
Great Langton 50 P 20
Great-Limber 45 T 23
Great Livermere 30 W 27
Great Lumley 56 P 19
Great Malvern 27 N 27
Great Marton 42 K 22
Great Massingham 38 W 25
Great Milton 20 Q 28
Great Missenden 21 R 28
Great Mitton 42 M 22
Great Musgrave 49 M 20
Great Oakley 31 X 28
Great Ormes Head 41 I 22
Great Orton 54 K 19
Great Ouse (River) 38 V 25
Great Ouseburn 50 Q 21
Great Ponton 37 S 25
Great Ryburgh 38 W 25
Great Salkeld 55 L 19
Great Sampford 30 V 28
Great Shefford 20 P 29
Great Shelford 29 U 27
Great Smeaton 50 P 20
Great Somerford 19 N 29
Great Stainton 56 P 20
Great Strickland 55 L 20
Great Torrington 6 H 31
Great Tosson 63 O 18
Great Totham 22 W 28
Great Urswick 48 K 21
Great Wakering 22 W 29
Great Waltham 22 V 28
Great Whernside 49 O 21
Great Whittington 56 O 18
Great Witley 27 M 27
Great Wolford 27 P 27
Great Wyrley 35 N 26
Great Yarmouth 39 Z 26
Great Yeldham 30 V 27
Greatford 37 S 25
Greatham *Cleveland* 57 Q 20
Greatham *Hants.* 10 R 30
Greatstone-on-Sea 12 W 31
Green Hammerton 50 Q 21
Greenfield
Flintshire / Sir y Fflint 41 K 23
Greenfield *Highland* 72 F 12
Greenhaugh 55 N 18
Greenhead 55 M 19
Greenholm 60 H 17
Greenhow Hill 49 O 21
Greenlaw 62 M 16
Greenloaning 67 I 15
Greenock 66 F 16
Greenodd 48 K 21
Greens Norton 28 Q 27
Greenside 56 O 19
Greenwich
London Borough 21 U 29
Grendon 28 R 27
Grendon Underwood 28 Q 28
Gresford 34 L 24
Greshornish 77 A 11
Greshornish (Loch) 77 A 11
Gress 83 B 9
Gretna 54 K 19
Gretton 37 R 26
Greys Court 20 R 29
Greysouthen 54 J 20
Greystoke 55 L 19
Griffithstown 18 K 28
Griminish 76 X 11
Grimley 27 N 27
Grimoldby 45 U 23
Grimsay 76 Y 11
Grimsby 45 T 23
Gringley on the Hill 44 R 23
Grinshill 34 L 25
Grinton 49 O 20
Gristhorpe 51 T 21
Grittleton 19 N 29
Groby 36 Q 26
Grogport 59 D 17
Groombridge 12 U 30
Grosebay 76 Z 10
Grosmont *Monmouthshire / Sir Fynwy* 26 L 28
Grosmont *Scarborough* 50 R 20
Grove 20 P 29
Gruinard Bay 78 D 10
Gruinard Island 78 D 10
Gruinart 58 B 16
Gruinart (Loch) 64 B 16
Grunavat (Loch) 82 Z 9
Grundisburgh 31 X 27
Gualachulain 66 E 14
Guardbridge 69 L 14
Guernsey *Channel I.* 5
Guesting 12 V 31
Guildford 21 S 30
Guildtown 68 J 14
Guilsborough 28 Q 26
Guisborough 50 Q 20
Guiseley 43 O 22
Guist 38 W 25
Gullane 69 L 15
Gunna 70 Z 14
Gunnerside 49 N 20
Gunnerton 55 N 18
Gunness 44 R 23
Gunnislake 3 H 32
Gunthorpe 36 R 25
Gurnard 10 Q 31
Gurness Broch 86 K 6
Gurnos 17 I 28
Gussage All Saints 9 O 31
Gutcher 87 Q 1
Guthrie 75 L 14
Guyhirn 37 U 26
Gwalchmai 40 G 23
Gwaun-Cae-Gurwen 17 I 28
Gwbert-on-Sea 15 F 27
Gweek 2 E 33
Gwennap 2 E 33
Gwithian 2 D 33
Gwyddelwern 33 J 24
Gwyddgrug 15 H 28
Gwydir Castle 33 I 24
Gwytherin 33 I 24

H

Habost 83 B 8
Hackney *London Borough* 21 T 29
Haddenham *Bucks.* 20 R 28
Haddenham *Cambs.* 29 U 26
Haddington 69 L 16
Haddiscoe 39 Y 26
Haddo House 81 N 11
Haddon Hall 35 P 24
Hadfield 43 O 23
Hadleigh *Essex* 22 V 29
Hadleigh *Suffolk* 30 W 27
Hadley 34 M 25
Hadlow 22 V 30
Hadnall 34 L 25
Hadrian's Wall 55 M 18
Haggbeck 55 L 18
Hagley 27 N 26
Hagworthingham 45 U 24
Hailsham 12 U 31
Hainford 39 X 25
Hainton 45 T 23
Halam 36 R 24
Halberton 7 J 31
Hale 42 M 23
Hales 39 Y 26
Halesowen 27 N 26
Halesworth 31 Y 26
Halford 27 P 27
Halifax 43 O 22
Halistra 77 A 11
Halkirk 85 J 8
Hall 60 G 16
Halland 12 U 31
Hallaton 36 R 26
Halling 22 V 29
Hallington 55 N 18
Halloughton 36 R 24
Hallow 27 N 27
Hallsands 4 J 33
Halsall 42 L 23
Halse 8 K 30
Halsetown 2 D 33
Halstead 30 V 28
Halstock 8 M 31
Haltham 37 T 24
Halton *Aylesbury Vale* 20 R 28
Halton *Lancaster* 48 L 21
Halton Gill 49 N 21
Haltwhistle 55 M 19
Halwell 4 I 32
Halwill Junction 6 H 31
Hamble 10 Q 31
Hambleden 20 R 29
Hambledon *Hants.* 10 Q 31
Hambledon *Surrey* 11 S 30
Hambleton *Lancs.* 42 L 22
Hambleton *North Yorks.* 44 Q 22
Hambleton Hills (The) 50 Q 21
Hambridge 8 L 31
Hamilton 60 H 16
Hammersmith and Fulham
London Borough 21 T 29
Hamnavoe *near Brae* 87 Q 2
Hamnavoe *near Scallway* 87 P 3
Hampreston 9 O 31
Hampstead Norris 20 Q 29
Hampsthwaite 50 P 21
Hampton Court 21 S 29
Hampton in Arden 27 O 26
Hamstead Marshall 20 P 29
Hamsterley 56 O 19
Hamstreet 12 W 30
Hamworthy 9 N 31
Handa Island 84 E 8
Handbridge 34 L 24
Handbury 27 N 27
Handcross 11 T 30
Handforth 43 N 23
Handley 34 L 24
Handsworth 43 P 23
Hanham 18 M 29
Hanley 35 N 24
Hanley Swan 27 N 27
Hanningfield 22 V 28
Hannington 19 O 29
Hanslope 28 R 27
Happisburgh 39 Y 25
Hapton 42 N 22
Harberton 4 I 32
Harbertonford 4 I 32
Harbledown 23 X 30
Harborough Magna 28 Q 26
Harbottle 63 N 17
Harbury 28 P 27
Harby 36 R 25
Hardham 11 S 31
Hardwick 44 Q 24
Hardwick Hall 36 Q 24
Hardwicke 19 N 28
Hardy Monument 5 M 31
Hardy's Cottage 9 M 31
Hare Street 29 U 28
Haresfield 19 N 28
Harewood House 50 P 22
Hargrave 29 S 27
Hargrave Green 30 V 27
Haringey *London Borough* 21 T 29
Harlaxton 36 R 25
Harlech 33 H 25
Harleston 31 X 26
Harlestone 28 R 27
Harley 34 M 26
Harlington 29 S 28
Harlosh 77 A 11
Harlow 21 U 28
Harlow Hill 56 O 18
Harmston 37 S 24
Haroldswick 87 R 1
Harpenden 21 S 28
Harpley 38 V 25
Harport (Loch) 77 A 12
Harray (Loch of) 86 K 6
Harrietfield 67 J 14
Harrington *Allerdale* 53 J 20
Harrington *Kettering* 28 R 26
Harringworth 37 S 26
Harris *Highland* 71 A 13
Harris *Western Isles* 82 Y 10
Harris (Sound of) 76 Y 10
Harrogate 50 P 22
Harrow *London Borough* 21 S 29
Harston 29 U 27
Hartburn 56 O 18
Hartest 30 W 27
Hartfield 11 U 30
Harthill *North Lanarkshire* 61 I 16
Harthill *Rotherham* 44 Q 24
Harting 10 R 31
Hartington 35 O 24
Hartland 6 G 31
Hartland Quay 6 G 31
Hartlebury 27 N 26
Hartlepool 57 Q 19
Hartley 22 U 29
Hartley Wintney 20 R 30
Hartpury 27 N 28
Hartshill 36 P 26
Hartwell 20 R 28
Hartwell 28 R 27
Harvington 27 O 27
Harwell 20 Q 29
Harwich 31 X 28
Harwood Dale 51 S 20
Harworth 44 Q 23
Hascosay 87 R 2
Haselbury Plucknett 8 L 31
Hasland 43 P 24
Haslemere 11 R 30
Haslingden 42 N 22
Haslingfield 29 U 27
Haslington 35 M 24
Hassocks 11 T 31
Haster 86 K 8
Hastings 12 V 31
Hatch Court 8 L 31
Hatfield
County of Herefordshire 26 M 27
Hatfield *Herts.* 21 T 28
Hatfield *South Yorks.* 44 Q 23
Hatfield Broad Oak 22 U 28
Hatfield Heath 22 U 28
Hatfield Peverel 22 V 28
Hatfield Woodhouse 44 R 23
Hatherleigh 7 H 31
Hathern 36 Q 25
Hathersage 43 P 24
Hatton *Aberdeenshire* 81 O 11
Hatton *Derbs.* 35 O 25
Hatton of Fintray 75 N 12
Haugh of Urr 53 I 19
Haughton 35 N 25
Haunn 71 B 14
Havant 10 R 31
Havenstreet 10 Q 31
Haverfordwest / Hwlffordd 16 F 28
Haverhill 30 V 27
Haverigg 47 K 21
Havering *London Borough* 22 U 29
Haverthwaite 48 K 21
Hawarden 34 K 24
Hawes 49 N 21
Hawick 62 L 17
Hawkchurch 8 L 31
Hawkedon 30 V 27
Hawkesbury Upton 19 M 29
Hawkhurst 12 V 30
Hawkridge 7 J 30
Hawkshead 48 L 20
Hawkwell 22 V 29
Hawley 20 R 30
Hawling 27 O 28
Haworth 43 O 22
Hawsker 51 S 20
Haxby 50 Q 21
Haxey 44 R 23
Hay-on-Wye 26 K 27
Haydock 42 M 23
Haydon Bridge 55 N 19
Haydon Wick 19 O 29
Hayfield 43 O 23

Hayle — 2 D 33
Hayling Island — 10 R 31
Hayscastle — 14 E 28
Hayton — 50 R 22
Haywards Heath — 11 T 31
Hazel Grove — 43 N 23
Hazelbank — 61 I 16
Hazelbury Bryan — 9 M 31
Hazlemere — 21 R 29
Heacham — 38 V 25
Headcorn — 22 V 30
Headington — 20 Q 28
Headless Cross — 27 O 27
Headley — 10 R 30
Heads of Ayr — 60 F 17
Healey — 49 O 21
Healing — 45 T 23
Heanor — 36 P 24
Heast — 71 C 12
Heath End — 20 Q 29
Heath Hayes — 35 O 25
Heather — 36 P 25
Heathfield *Renfrewshire* — 60 F 16
Heathfield *Wealden* — 12 U 31
Heathrow Airport — 21 S 29
Hebburn — 56 P 19
Hebden Bridge — 43 N 22
Hebrides (Sea of the) — 76 Z 12
Heckfield — 20 R 29
Heckington — 37 T 25
Heddon on the Wall — 56 O 19
Hedge End — 10 Q 31
Hednesford — 35 O 25
Hedon — 45 T 22
Heighington *Durham* — 56 P 20
Heighington *Lincs.* — 44 S 24
Heights of Kinlochewe — 78 E 11
Helensburgh — 66 F 15
Helford — 2 E 33
Hellifield — 49 N 22
Hellingly — 12 U 31
Hellisay — 70 X 12
Hell's Mouth or Porth Neigwl — 32 G 25
Helmdon — 28 Q 27
Helmsdale — 85 J 9
Helmsley — 50 Q 21
Helpringham — 37 T 25
Helpston — 37 S 26
Helsby — 42 L 24
Helston — 2 E 33
Helton — 55 L 20
Helvellyn — 48 K 20
Hemel Hempstead — 21 S 28
Hemingbrough — 44 R 22
Hemingford Grey — 29 T 27
Hemington — 19 M 30
Hempnall — 39 X 26
Hempton — 38 W 25
Hemsby — 39 Z 25
Hemswell — 44 S 23
Hemsworth — 43 P 23
Hemyock — 8 K 31
Hendy — 15 H 28
Henfield — 11 T 31
Hengoed — 18 K 29
Henham — 30 U 28
Henley — 27 O 27
Henley-on-Thames — 20 R 29
Henllan — 33 J 24
Henllys — 18 K 29
Henlow — 29 T 27
Hennock — 4 J 32
Henshaw — 55 M 19
Henstead — 31 Y 26
Henstridge — 9 M 31
Heol Senni — 25 J 28
Hepple — 63 N 18
Heptonstall — 43 N 22
Herbrandston — 14 E 28
Hereford — 26 L 27
Heriot — 62 L 16
Herm *Channel I.* — 5
Herma Ness — 87 R 1
Hermitage — 20 Q 29
Hermitage Castle — 62 L 18
Herne Bay — 23 X 29
Herriard — 20 Q 30
Herrington — 56 P 19
Herstmonceux — 12 U 31
Hertford — 21 T 28
Hesket Newmarket — 54 K 19
Hesketh Bank — 42 L 22
Hesleden — 57 Q 19
Hessenford — 3 G 32
Hessle — 45 S 22
Hest Bank — 48 L 21

Heswall — 42 K 24
Hethersgill — 55 L 19
Hethpool — 63 N 17
Hetton-le-Hole — 56 P 19
Heveningham — 31 Y 27
Hever — 21 U 30
Heversham — 48 L 21
Hevingham — 39 X 25
Hewelsfield — 18 M 28
Hexham — 55 N 19
Heybridge — 22 W 28
Heysham — 48 L 21
Heyshott — 11 R 31
Heytesbury — 9 N 30
Heythrop — 28 P 28
Heywood — 43 N 23
Hibaldstow — 44 S 23
Hickling — 36 R 25
Hickling Green — 39 Y 25
Hidcote Manor Garden — 27 O 27
High Bentham — 49 M 21
High Bickington — 7 I 31
High Birkwith — 49 N 21
High Easter — 22 V 28
High Ercall — 34 M 25
High Etherley — 56 O 20
High Force (The) — 55 N 20
High Halden — 12 W 30
High Halstow — 22 V 29
High Ham — 8 L 30
High Hesket — 55 L 19
High Newton *Alnwick* — 63 P 17
High Newton *South Lakeland* — 48 L 21
High Offley — 35 N 25
High Ongar — 22 U 28
High Peak — 43 O 23
High Willhays — 4 I 31
High Wycombe — 20 R 29
Higham *Kent* — 22 V 29
Higham *Lancs.* — 42 N 22
Higham *North East Derbyshire* — 36 P 24
Higham *Suffolk* — 30 V 27
Higham Ferrers — 29 S 27
Higham on the Hill — 36 P 26
Highbridge — 18 L 30
Highclere — 20 P 29
Highcliffe — 9 O 31
Higher Penwortham — 42 L 22
Highland Wildlife Park — 73 I 12
Highley — 27 M 26
Highmoor Cross — 20 R 29
Hightae — 54 J 18
Hightown *Congleton* — 35 N 24
Hightown *Sefton* — 42 K 23
Highworth — 19 O 29
Hilborough — 38 W 26
Hildenborough — 22 U 30
Hilderstone — 35 N 25
Hilgay — 38 V 26
Hill — 18 M 29
Hill of Fearn — 79 I 10
Hill of Tarvit — 69 L 15
Hillhead — 52 G 19
Hillingdon *London Borough* — 21 S 29
Hillington — 38 V 25
Hillside — 75 M 13
Hillswick — 87 P 2
Hilmarton — 19 O 29
Hilperton — 19 N 30
Hilpsford Point — 47 K 21
Hilton *Aberdeenshire* — 81 N 11
Hilton *Eden* — 55 M 20
Hilton *Huntingdonshire* — 29 T 27
Hilton *North Dorset* — 9 N 31
Hilton *South Derbyshire* — 35 P 25
Hilton of Cadboll — 79 I 10
Himbleton — 27 N 27
Hinchingbrooke House — 29 T 27
Hinckley — 36 P 26
Hinderwell — 50 R 20
Hindhead — 10 R 30
Hindley — 42 M 23
Hindolveston — 38 X 25
Hindon — 9 N 30
Hingham — 38 W 26
Hinstock — 34 M 25
Hintlesham — 31 X 27
Hinton-Blewett — 18 M 30
Hirst Courtney — 44 Q 22
Hirwaun — 17 J 28
Histon — 29 U 27
Hitcham — 30 W 27
Hitchin — 29 T 28

Hockering — 38 X 25
Hockerton — 36 R 24
Hockley — 22 V 29
Hockley Heath — 27 O 26
Hockliffe — 29 S 28
Hoddesdon — 21 T 28
Hodnet — 34 M 25
Hodthorpe — 44 Q 24
Hogsthorpe — 45 U 24
Holbeach — 37 T 25
Holbeach-St. Johns — 37 T 25
Holbeach-St. Matthew — 37 U 25
Holbeck — 44 Q 24
Holbrook — 31 X 28
Holbury — 10 P 31
Holcombe — 18 M 30
Holcombe Rogus — 7 J 31
Holdenby — 28 R 27
Holford — 8 K 30
Holkam Hall — 38 W 25
Hollandstoun — 87 M 5
Hollesley — 31 Y 27
Hollesley Bay — 31 Y 27
Hollingbourne — 22 V 30
Hollingworth — 43 O 23
Hollybush — 60 G 17
Hollym — 45 U 22
Holmbridge — 43 O 23
Holme *Huntingdonshire* — 29 T 26
Holme *South Lakeland* — 48 L 21
Holme-next-the-Sea — 38 V 25
Holme upon Spalding-Moor — 44 R 22
Holmer Green — 21 R 29
Holmes Chapel — 35 M 24
Holmesfield — 43 P 24
Holmfirth — 43 O 23
Holmhead — 60 H 17
Holmpton — 45 U 22
Holnest — 8 M 31
Holsworthy — 6 G 31
Holt *Dorset* — 9 O 31
Holt *Norfolk* — 38 X 25
Holt *Wilts.* — 19 N 29
Holt *Wrexham* — 34 L 24
Holt Heath — 27 N 27
Holton *Lincs.* — 45 T 24
Holton *Norfolk* — 31 Y 26
Holton *South Somerset* — 8 M 30
Holton Heath — 9 N 31
Holton-le-Clay — 45 T 23
Holwick — 55 N 20
Holy Island *Anglesey* — 40 F 23
Holy Island *North Ayrshire* — 59 E 17
Holy Island *Northumb.* — 63 O 16
Holybourne — 10 R 30
Holyhead / Caergybi — 40 G 23
Holystone — 63 N 18
Holywell — 2 E 32
Holywell / Treffynnon — 41 K 23
Holywell Bay — 2 E 32
Holywood — 53 J 18
Honing — 39 Y 25
Honington — 8 K 31
Honiton — 8 K 31
Hoo St. Werburgh — 22 V 29
Hook *Basingstoke and Deane* — 20 R 30
Hook *East Riding of Yorkshire* — 44 R 22
Hook Norton — 28 P 28
Hooke — 8 M 31
Hope *Derbs.* — 43 O 23
Hope *Flintshire* — 34 K 24
Hope *Highland* — 84 G 8
Hope *South Shropshire* — 34 L 26
Hope (Loch) — 84 G 8
Hope Bowdler — 26 L 26
Hope under Dinmore — 26 L 27
Hopeman — 80 J 10
Hopetoun House — 68 J 16
Hopton — 39 Z 26
Horam — 12 U 31
Horbling — 37 S 25
Horbury — 43 P 23
Horden — 57 Q 19
Hordley — 34 L 25
Horeb — 15 G 27
Horley — 21 T 30
Hornby — 48 M 21
Horncastle — 45 T 24
Hornchurch — 22 U 29
Horncliffe — 63 N 16
Horning — 39 Y 25
Horninglow — 35 P 25
Horn's Cross — 6 H 31
Hornsea — 51 T 22
Hornton — 28 P 27
Horrabridge — 4 H 32

Horseheath — 30 V 27
Horsehouse — 49 O 21
Horsell — 21 S 30
Horsford — 39 X 25
Horsforth — 43 P 22
Horsham — 11 T 30
Horsham St. Faith — 39 X 25
Horsington *East Lindsey* — 37 T 24
Horsington *South Somerset* — 9 M 30
Horsley *Stroud* — 19 N 28
Horsley *Tynedale* — 56 O 19
Horsmonden — 12 V 30
Horstead — 39 Y 25
Horsted Keynes — 11 T 30
Horton *Abertawe / Swansea* — 15 H 29
Horton *East Dorset* — 9 O 31
Horton *South Somerset* — 8 L 31
Horton Court — 19 M 29
Horton-in-Ribblesdale — 49 N 21
Horwich — 42 M 23
Hoton — 36 Q 25
Hott — 55 M 18
Houghton — 10 P 30
Houghton Hall — 38 V 25
Houghton House — 29 S 27
Houghton-le-Spring — 56 P 19
Houghton-on-the-Hill — 36 R 26
Houghton — 55 L 19
Hounslow *London Borough* — 21 S 29
Hourn (Loch) — 72 D 12
Housesteads Fort — 55 N 18
Houston — 60 G 16
Houstry — 85 J 9
Hove — 11 T 31
Hoveton — 39 Y 25
Hovingham — 50 R 21
How Caple — 26 M 28
Howden — 44 R 22
Howe of the Mearns — 75 M 13
Howick — 63 P 17
Howmore — 76 X 12
Hownam — 62 M 17
Howwood — 60 G 16
Hoxa (Sound of) — 86 K 7
Hoxne — 31 X 26
Hoy — 86 J 7
Hoylake — 41 K 22
Hoyland Nether — 43 P 23
Huby — 50 Q 21
Hucknall — 36 Q 24
Huddersfield — 43 O 23
Huggate — 51 S 22
Hugh Champflower — 7 J 30
Huish Episcopi — 8 L 30
Hull (River) — 45 S 22
Hulland — 35 P 24
Hullavington — 19 N 29
Hullbridge — 22 V 29
Humber (River) — 45 T 23
Humber Bridge — 44 S 22
Humberston — 45 T 23
Humbleton — 45 T 22
Hume Castle — 62 M 17
Humshaugh — 55 N 18
Hundleton — 16 F 28
Hundred House — 26 K 27
Hungerford — 20 P 29
Hunmanby — 51 T 21
Hunstanton — 38 V 25
Hunter's Inn — 17 I 30
Hunter's Quay — 66 F 16
Huntingdon — 29 T 26
Huntington — 50 Q 22
Huntingtower Castle — 68 J 14
Huntly — 80 L 11
Hunton — 49 O 21
Huntspill — 18 L 30
Hunwick — 56 O 19
Hurlford — 60 G 17
Hurn — 9 O 31
Hursley — 10 P 30
Hurst Green — 12 V 30
Hurstbourne Priors — 20 P 30
Hurstbourne Tarrant — 20 P 30
Hurstpierpoint — 11 T 31
Hurworth-on-Tees — 50 P 20
Hury — 55 N 20
Husbands Bosworth — 28 Q 26
Huthwaite — 36 Q 24
Huttoft — 45 U 24
Hutton *Scottish Borders* — 63 N 16

Hutton *South Ribble* — 42 L 22
Hutton Cranswick — 51 S 22
Hutton Rudby — 50 Q 20
Huxley — 34 L 24
Huyton — 42 L 23
Hwlffordd / Haverfordwest — 16 F 28
Hyde — 43 N 23
Hynish — 64 Z 14
Hynish Bay — 64 Z 14
Hythe *Hants.* — 10 P 31
Hythe *Kent* — 13 X 30

I
Ibsley — 9 O 31
Ibstock — 36 P 25
Ickleford — 29 T 28
Icklingham — 30 V 27
Ickworth House — 30 V 27
Iddesleigh — 7 H 31
Ideford — 4 J 32
Iden — 12 W 31
Iden Green — 12 V 30
Idmiston — 9 O 30
Idrigill Point — 77 A 12
Ightham — 22 U 30
Ightham Mote — 22 U 30
Ilchester — 8 L 30
Ilderton — 63 O 17
Ilfracombe — 17 H 30
Ilkeston — 36 Q 25
Ilkley — 49 O 22
Illogan — 2 E 33
Ilmington — 27 O 27
Ilminster — 8 L 31
Ilsington — 4 I 32
Ilton — 8 L 31
Immingham — 45 T 23
Immingham Dock — 45 T 23
Ince Blundell — 42 K 23
Ince-in-Makerfield — 42 M 23
Inch Kenneth — 64 B 14
Inchbare — 75 M 13
Inchgrundle — 74 L 13
Inchkeith — 68 K 15
Inchlaggan — 72 E 12
Inchmarnock — 59 E 16
Inchnadamph — 84 F 9
Inchture — 68 K 14
Indaal (Loch) — 58 A 16
Inerval — 58 B 17
Ingatestone — 22 V 28
Ingbirchworth — 43 P 23
Ingham — 30 W 27
Ingleby Barwick — 50 Q 20
Ingleton *Durham* — 56 O 20
Ingleton *North Yorks.* — 49 M 21
Inglewhite — 42 L 22
Inglewood Forest — 55 L 19
Ingliston — 68 J 16
Ingoldmells — 38 V 24
Ingoldsby — 37 S 25
Ingram — 63 O 17
Ings — 48 L 20
Inkpen — 20 P 29
Innellan — 59 F 16
Inner Hebrides — 70 Y 14
Inner Sound — 77 C 11
Innerleithen — 61 K 17
Innerpeffray — 67 I 14
Innerwick — 69 M 16
Insch — 81 M 11
Insh — 73 I 12
Inshore — 84 F 8
Instow — 6 H 30
Inver *Highland* — 79 I 10
Inver *Perth and Kinross* — 68 J 14
Inver (Loch) — 84 E 9
Inver Bay — 79 I 10
Inver Mallie — 72 E 13
Inver Valley — 84 E 9
Inverallign — 78 D 11
Inverallochy — 81 O 10
Inveran — 84 G 10
Inveraray — 66 E 15
Inverarity — 69 L 14
Inverarnan — 66 F 15
Inverbeg — 66 G 15
Inverbervie — 75 N 13
Invercassley — 84 G 10
Invercauld House — 74 J 12
Inverchapel — 66 F 15
Invercreran — 72 E 14
Inverdruie — 73 I 12
Inverewe Gardens — 78 C 10
Inverey — 74 J 13
Inverfarigaig — 79 G 12

Invergarry — 72 F 12
Invergeldie — 67 H 14
Invergordon — 79 H 10
Invergowrie — 68 K 14
Inverie — 72 C 12
Inverinan — 65 E 15
Inverinate — 78 D 12
Inverkeithing — 68 J 15
Inverkeithny — 81 M 11
Inverkip — 66 F 16
Inverkirkaig — 84 E 9
Inverliever Forest — 65 D 15
Inverlochlarig — 67 G 15
Invermoriston — 73 G 12
Inverness — 79 H 11
Inversanda — 72 D 13
Inversnaid Hotel — 66 F 15
Inveruglas — 66 F 15
Inverurie — 81 M 12
Invervar — 73 H 14
Inwardleigh — 7 H 31
Iona — 64 A 15
Ipplepen — 4 J 32
Ipstones — 35 O 24
Ipswich — 31 X 27
Irby *East Lindsey* — 37 U 24
Irby *Wirral* — 42 K 23
Irchester — 29 S 27
Ireby — 54 K 19
Ireleth — 47 K 21
Irlam — 42 M 23
Iron Acton — 18 M 29
Ironbridge — 34 M 26
Irthington — 55 L 19
Irthlingborough — 29 S 27
Irvine — 60 F 17
Irwell (River) — 42 N 23
Isbyty Ystwyth — 25 I 27
Isla (Glen) — 74 K 13
Islay (Sound of) — 64 B 16
Isle of Whithorn — 53 G 19
Isleham — 30 V 26
Isleornsay — 71 C 12
Isleworth — 21 S 29
Islington *London Borough* — 21 T 29
Islip — 20 Q 28
Islivig — 82 Y 9
Itchingfield — 11 S 30
Ithon (River) — 25 K 27
Itteringham — 39 X 25
Iver — 21 S 29
Iver Heath — 21 S 29
Ivinghoe — 21 S 28
Ivybridge — 4 I 32
Ivychurch — 12 W 30
Iwade — 22 W 29
Iwerne Minster — 9 N 31
Ixworth — 30 W 27

J
Jacobstow — 6 G 31
Jacobstowe — 7 H 31
Jameston — 15 F 29
Jamestown *Dumfries and Galloway* — 61 K 18
Jamestown *West Dunbartonshire* — 66 G 16
Janetstown — 85 J 9
Jarrow — 56 P 19
Jaywick — 23 X 28
Jedburgh — 62 M 17
Jedburgh Abbey — 62 M 17
Jeffreyston — 15 F 28
Jemimaville — 79 H 11
Jersey *Channel I.* — 5
Jevington — 12 U 31
John Muir — 69 M 15
John o' Groats — 86 K 8
Johnshaven — 75 N 13
Johnston — 16 F 28
Johnstone — 60 G 16
Johnstonebridge — 54 J 18
Jura (Isle of) — 58 B 16
Jura (Sound of) — 65 C 16
Jura Forest — 65 B 16
Jura Ho — 58 B 16
Jurby West — 46 G 20

K
Kainakill — 77 C 11
Kames — 65 E 16
Katrine (Loch) — 67 G 15
Kea — 2 E 33
Keal — 37 U 24
Keal (Loch na) — 65 B 14
Kearsley — 42 M 23
Keasden — 49 M 21

Kebock Head .... 82 A 9
Kedington .... 30 V 27
Kedleston Hall .... 36 P 25
Keelby .... 45 T 23
Keevil .... 19 N 30
Kegworth .... 36 Q 25
Keig .... 75 M 12
Keighley .... 43 O 22
Keillmore .... 65 C 16
Keinton Mandeville .... 8 M 30
Keir Mill .... 53 I 18
Keiss .... 86 K 8
Keith .... 80 L 11
Keld .... 49 N 20
Kellas Angus .... 69 L 14
Kellas Moray .... 80 J 11
Kelleth .... 49 M 20
Kellie Castle .... 69 L 15
Kellington .... 44 Q 22
Kelloe .... 56 P 19
Kelly Bray .... 3 H 32
Kelmarsh .... 28 R 26
Kelsall .... 34 L 24
Kelso .... 62 M 17
Kelston .... 19 M 29
Keltneyburn .... 73 H 14
Kelty .... 68 J 15
Kelvedon .... 30 W 28
Kelvedon Hatch .... 22 U 29
Kemble .... 19 N 28
Kemnay .... 75 M 12
Kempley .... 26 M 28
Kempsey .... 27 N 27
Kempsford .... 19 O 28
Kempston .... 29 S 27
Kemsing .... 22 U 30
Kendal .... 48 L 21
Kenfig .... 17 I 29
Kenilworth .... 27 P 26
Kenknock .... 67 G 14
Kenmore Highland .... 77 C 11
Kenmore
  Perthshire and Kinross ... 67 I 14
Kenn .... 18 L 29
Kennet (River) .... 19 O 29
Kennethmont .... 80 L 11
Kenninghall .... 30 X 26
Kennington Kent .... 22 W 30
Kennington Oxon. .... 20 Q 28
Kennoway .... 68 K 15
Kenovay .... 70 Z 14
Kensaleyre .... 77 B 11
Kentallen .... 72 E 13
Kentford .... 30 V 27
Kentisbeare .... 7 K 31
Kentmere .... 48 L 20
Kenton .... 4 J 32
Kents Bank .... 48 L 21
Keoldale .... 84 F 8
Keresley .... 28 P 26
Kerrera .... 65 D 14
Kerry .... 26 K 26
Kersey .... 30 W 27
Kershader .... 82 A 9
Kershopefoot .... 55 L 18
Kesgrave .... 31 X 27
Kessingland .... 31 Z 26
Keswick .... 54 K 20
Kettering .... 28 R 26
Kettleness .... 50 R 20
Kettleshulme .... 43 N 24
Kettletoft .... 87 M 6
Kettlewell .... 49 N 21
Ketton .... 37 S 26
Kew .... 21 T 29
Kewstoke .... 18 L 29
Kexbrough .... 43 P 23
Kexby .... 44 R 23
Keyingham .... 45 T 22
Keymer .... 11 T 31
Keynsham .... 18 M 29
Keyworth .... 36 Q 25
Kibworth Harcourt .... 36 R 26
Kidderminster .... 27 N 26
Kidermorie Lodge .... 79 G 10
Kidlington .... 20 Q 28
Kidsgrove .... 35 N 24
Kidstones .... 49 N 21
Kidwelly / Cydweli .... 15 H 28
Kielder .... 55 M 18
Kielder Forest .... 55 M 18
Kielder Reservoir .... 55 M 18
Kiiphedir .... 85 I 9
Kilamarsh .... 44 Q 24
Kilbarchan .... 60 G 16
Kilbirnie .... 60 F 16
Kilbrannan Sound .... 59 D 17

Kilbride .... 65 D 14
Kilburn Amber Valley .... 36 P 24
Kilburn Hambleton .... 50 Q 21
Kilchattan .... 59 E 16
Kilchenzie .... 59 C 17
Kilcheran .... 65 D 14
Kilchiaran .... 58 A 16
Kilchoan .... 71 B 13
Kilchoman .... 58 A 16
Kilchrenan .... 65 E 14
Kilconquhar .... 69 L 15
Kilcreggan .... 66 F 16
Kildale .... 50 Q 20
Kildary .... 79 H 10
Kildavanan .... 59 E 16
Kildonan .... 59 E 17
Kildonan Lodge .... 85 I 9
Kildrummy .... 74 L 12
Kildrummy Castle .... 74 L 12
Kilfinnan .... 72 F 12
Kilgetti .... 15 F 28
Kilham
  Berwick-upon-Tweed ..... 63 N 17
Kilham
  East Riding of Yorkshire . 51 S 21
Kilkhampton .... 6 G 31
Killay .... 15 H 29
Killean .... 59 D 17
Killay .... 15 H 29
Killen .... 79 H 11
Killerton .... 7 J 31
Killiechronan .... 65 C 14
Killilan .... 78 D 12
Killin .... 67 H 14
Killinghall .... 50 P 21
Killundine .... 71 C 14
Kilmacolm .... 60 G 16
Kilmaluag .... 77 B 10
Kilmany .... 69 L 14
Kilmarie .... 71 B 12
Kilmarnock .... 60 G 17
Kilmartin .... 65 D 15
Kilmaurs .... 60 G 17
Kilmelford .... 65 D 15
Kilmersdon .... 19 M 30
Kilmington East Devon ...... 8 K 31
Kilmington Salisbury .... 9 N 30
Kilmorack .... 79 G 11
Kilmore .... 71 C 12
Kilmory Ardnamurchan .... 71 B 13
Kilmory Argyll and Bute .... 65 C 16
Kilmory I. Rhum .... 71 A 12
Kilmory North Ayrshire ..... 59 E 17
Kilmuir .... 77 A 11
Kilmun .... 66 F 16
Kilncadzow .... 61 I 16
Kilninver .... 65 D 14
Kilnsey .... 49 N 21
Kiloran .... 64 B 15
Kilpeck .... 26 L 28
Kilrenny .... 69 L 15
Kilsyth .... 67 H 16
Kilt Rock .... 77 B 11
Kiltarlity .... 79 G 11
Kilvaxter .... 77 A 11
Kilwinning .... 60 F 17
Kimberley Broxtowe .... 36 Q 25
Kimberley South Norfolk .... 38 X 26
Kimble .... 20 R 28
Kimbolton .... 29 S 27
Kimmeridge .... 9 N 32
Kimpton .... 21 T 28
Kinbrace .... 85 I 9
Kinbuck .... 67 I 15
Kincardine Fife .... 67 I 15
Kincardine Highland .... 79 G 10
Kincardine O'Neil .... 75 L 12
Kinclaven .... 68 J 14
Kincraig .... 73 I 12
Kineton .... 28 P 27
Kinfauns .... 68 J 14
Kingairloch .... 72 D 14
Kingarth .... 59 E 16
Kinghorn .... 68 K 15
Kinglassie .... 68 K 15
King's Bromley .... 35 O 25
King's Cliffe .... 37 S 26
Kings Langley .... 21 S 28
King's Lynn .... 38 V 25
King's Meaburn .... 55 M 20
King's Somborne .... 10 P 30
King's Sutton .... 28 Q 27
King's Walden .... 29 T 28
Kings Worthy .... 10 Q 30
Kingsbarns .... 69 M 15
Kingsbridge .... 4 I 33
Kingsburgh .... 77 A 11

Kingsbury Episcopi .... 8 L 31
Kingsclere .... 20 Q 30
Kingscote .... 19 N 29
Kingsdon .... 8 L 30
Kingsdown .... 23 Y 30
Kingsgate .... 23 Y 29
Kingshouse Highland .... 72 F 14
Kingshouse Stirling .... 67 H 14
Kingskerswell .... 4 J 32
Kingskettle .... 68 K 15
Kingsland .... 26 L 27
Kingsley East Hampshire .... 10 R 30
Kingsley
  Staffordshire Moorlands .. 35 O 24
Kingsmuir .... 74 L 14
Kingsnorth .... 12 W 30
Kingsteignton .... 4 J 32
Kingsthorpe .... 28 R 27
Kingston Devon .... 4 I 33
Kingston East Hampshire .... 69 L 15
Kingston Moray .... 80 K 10
Kingston
  South Cambridgeshire ... 29 T 27
Kingston Bagpuize .... 20 P 28
Kingston Deverill .... 9 N 30
Kingston Lacy .... 9 N 31
Kingston Lisle .... 20 P 29
Kingston Seymour .... 18 L 29
Kingston-St. Mary .... 8 K 30
Kingston-upon-Hull .... 45 S 22
Kingston-upon-Thames
  London Borough .... 21 T 29
Kingstone .... 26 L 27
Kingswear .... 4 J 32
Kingswinford .... 27 N 26
Kingswood .... 19 M 29
Kingswood Powys .... 34 K 26
Kingswood South Glos. ...... 18 M 29
Kington .... 26 K 27
Kington Langley .... 19 N 29
Kington-St. Michael .... 19 N 29
Kingussie .... 73 H 12
Kinkell .... 75 M 12
Kinkell Bridge .... 67 I 15
Kinknockie .... 81 O 11
Kinlet .... 27 M 26
Kinloch .... 71 B 12
Kinloch Hourn .... 72 D 12
Kinloch Lodge .... 84 G 8
Kinloch Rannoch .... 73 H 13
Kinlochard .... 67 G 15
Kinlochbervie .... 84 E 8
Kinlocheil .... 72 E 13
Kinlochewe .... 78 E 11
Kinlochleven .... 72 F 13
Kinlochmoidart .... 71 C 13
Kinloss .... 80 J 11
Kinmuck .... 75 N 12
Kinnaird .... 68 K 14
Kinneff .... 75 N 13
Kinnelhead .... 61 J 18
Kinnerley .... 34 L 25
Kinnersley .... 26 L 27
Kinnesswood .... 68 K 15
Kinninvie .... 56 O 20
Kinnoulton .... 36 R 25
Kinross .... 68 J 15
Kinrossie .... 68 K 14
Kintbury .... 20 P 29
Kintessack .... 80 I 11
Kintore .... 75 M 12
Kintra .... 58 B 17
Kintyre (Peninsula) .... 59 D 17
Kinver .... 27 N 26
Kippax .... 43 P 22
Kippen .... 67 H 15
Kippford .... 53 I 19
Kirby Bellars .... 36 R 25
Kirby Cross .... 31 X 28
Kirby Hall .... 29 S 26
Kirby Misperton .... 50 R 21
Kirby Muxloe .... 36 Q 26
Kirby Underwood .... 37 S 25
Kirkford .... 11 S 30
Kirk Ella .... 45 S 22
Kirk Ireton .... 35 P 24
Kirk Merrington .... 56 P 19
Kirk Michael .... 46 G 21
Kirk Yetholm .... 63 N 17
Kirkbampton .... 54 K 19
Kirkbean .... 53 J 19
Kirkbride .... 54 K 19
Kirkbuddo .... 74 L 14
Kirkburn .... 51 S 22
Kirkburton .... 43 O 23
Kirkby .... 42 L 23
Kirkby Fleetham .... 50 P 20

Kirkby-in-Ashfield .... 36 Q 24
Kirkby-la-Thorpe .... 37 S 25
Kirkby Lonsdale .... 48 M 21
Kirkby Malham .... 49 N 21
Kirkby Mallory .... 36 Q 26
Kirkby Malzeard .... 49 P 21
Kirkby Overblow .... 50 P 22
Kirkby Stephen .... 49 M 20
Kirkby Thore .... 55 M 20
Kirkbymoorside .... 50 R 21
Kirkcaldy .... 68 K 15
Kirkcolm .... 52 E 19
Kirkconnel .... 60 I 17
Kirkcowan .... 52 G 19
Kirkcudbright .... 53 H 19
Kirkcudbright Bay .... 53 H 19
Kirkfieldbank .... 61 I 16
Kirkgunzeon .... 53 I 19
Kirkham .... 42 L 22
Kirkheaton .... 56 O 18
Kirkhill .... 79 G 11
Kirkhope .... 61 J 18
Kirkinner .... 52 G 19
Kirkintilloch .... 67 H 16
Kirkland
  Dumfries and Galloway .. 53 I 18
Kirkland Eden .... 55 M 19
Kirklees .... 43 O 23
Kirklevington .... 50 P 20
Kirklington
  North Yorkshire .... 50 P 21
Kirklington
  Nottinghamshire .... 36 R 24
Kirkliston .... 68 J 16
Kirkmaiden .... 52 F 19
Kirkmichael
  Perthshire and Kinross . 74 J 13
Kirkmichael
  South Ayrshire .... 60 G 17
Kirkmuirhill .... 61 I 17
Kirknewton
  Berwick-upon-Tweed ..... 63 N 17
Kirknewton
  West Lothian .... 61 J 16
Kirkoswald .... 59 F 18
Kirkpatrick Durham .... 53 I 18
Kirkpatrick-Fleming .... 54 K 18
Kirkstone Pass .... 48 L 20
Kirkton
  Dumfries and Galloway .. 53 J 18
Kirkton Scottish Borders ... 62 L 17
Kirkton Manor .... 61 K 17
Kirkton of Culsalmond ...... 81 M 11
Kirkton of Durris .... 75 M 12
Kirkton of Glenisla .... 74 K 13
Kirkton of Kingoldrum ...... 74 K 13
Kirkton of Largo .... 69 L 15
Kirkton of Skene .... 75 N 12
Kirkton of Strathmartine ... 69 K 14
Kirktown of Auchterless .... 81 M 11
Kirktown of Deskford .... 80 L 11
Kirkwall .... 86 L 7
Kirkwhelpington .... 56 N 18
Kirmington .... 45 T 23
Kirn .... 66 F 16
Kirriemuir .... 74 K 13
Kirtlebridge .... 54 K 18
Kirtling .... 28 Q 28
Kirtlington .... 20 Q 28
Kirtomy .... 85 H 8
Kirton Boston .... 37 T 25
Kirton Suffolk Coastal ..... 31 X 27
Kirton End .... 37 T 25
Kirton-in-Lindsey .... 44 S 23
Kirwall .... 86 L 7
Kishorn (Loch) .... 78 D 11
Kislingbury .... 28 R 27
Kitchener Memorial .... 86 J 6
Kiveton .... 44 Q 23
Knaresborough .... 50 P 21
Knarsdale .... 55 M 19
Knebworth .... 29 T 28
Kneesall .... 36 R 24
Kneesworth .... 29 T 27
Knighton / Trefyclawdd ..... 26 K 26
Knightshayes Court .... 7 J 31
Kniveton .... 35 O 24
Knock Argyll and Bute ...... 65 C 14
Knock Moray .... 80 L 11
Knock Western Isles .... 83 B 9
Knockandhu .... 80 K 12
Knockbrex .... 53 H 19
Knockie Lodge .... 73 G 12
Knockin .... 34 L 25
Knocknaha .... 59 C 17
Knocksharry .... 46 G 21
Knockvennie Smithy .... 53 I 18
Knole .... 22 U 30
Knossington .... 36 R 25

Knottingley .... 44 Q 22
Knowe .... 52 G 18
Knowehead .... 53 H 18
Knowesgate .... 55 N 18
Knowle .... 27 O 26
Knowsley .... 42 L 23
Knoydart .... 72 D 12
Knutsford .... 42 M 24
Kyle Forest .... 60 G 17
Kyle of Durness .... 84 F 8
Kyle of Lochalsh .... 77 C 12
Kyle of Sutherland .... 79 G 10
Kyle of Tongue .... 84 G 8
Kyleakin .... 77 C 12
Kylerhea .... 72 C 12
Kyles Scalpay .... 82 Z 10
Kylestrome .... 84 E 9
Kynance Cove .... 2 E 34
Kyre park .... 26 M 27

L

La Rocque Jersey I. 5
Laceby .... 45 T 23
Lacey Green .... 20 R 28
Lache .... 34 L 24
Lacock .... 19 N 29
Ladder Hills .... 74 K 12
Ladock .... 3 F 33
Ladybank .... 68 K 15
Ladybower Reservoir .... 43 O 23
Ladyhill .... 55 N 18
Lagg .... 65 C 16
Laggan Argyll and Bute ..... 58 B 16
Laggan near Invergarry ..... 72 F 12
Laggan
  near Newtonmore .... 73 H 12
Laggan (Loch) .... 73 G 13
Laggan Point .... 58 B 16
Lagganulva .... 64 B 14
Laide .... 78 D 10
Lair .... 78 E 11
Lairg .... 84 G 9
Lake District National Park . 48 K 20
Lakenheath .... 30 V 26
Lamanva .... 2 E 33
Lamberhurst .... 12 V 30
Lambeth London Borough .... 21 T 29
Lambley Gedling .... 36 Q 24
Lambley Tynedale .... 55 M 19
Lambourn .... 20 P 29
Lamerton .... 3 H 32
Lamington .... 61 J 17
Lamlash .... 59 E 17
Lamlash Bay .... 59 E 17
Lammermuir Hills .... 62 L 16
Lampeter /
  Llanbedr Pont Steffan .. 15 H 27
Lamplugh .... 54 J 20
Lamport .... 28 R 26
Lanark .... 61 I 16
Lancaster .... 48 L 21
Lanchester .... 56 O 19
Lancing .... 11 T 31
Landmark Visitor Centre .... 79 I 12
Landrake .... 3 H 32
Land's End .... 2 C 33
Landulph .... 3 H 32
Lane End .... 20 R 29
Laneast .... 6 G 32
Lanercost .... 55 L 19
Langar .... 36 R 25
Langavat (Loch) Lewis ...... 82 Z 9
Langavat (Loch)
  South Harris .... 76 Z 10
Langbank .... 66 G 16
Langcliffe .... 49 N 21
Langdale End .... 51 S 21
Langdale Valley .... 48 K 20
Langdon Beck .... 55 N 19
Langenhoe .... 30 W 28
Langford
  Mid Bedfordshire .... 29 T 27
Langford
  West Oxfordshire .... 19 P 28
Langford Budville .... 8 K 31
Langham .... 36 R 25
Langholm .... 54 L 18
Langleeford .... 63 N 17
Langley .... 21 S 29
Langley Park .... 56 O 19
Langold .... 44 Q 23
Langport .... 8 L 30
Langrick .... 37 T 24
Langrish .... 10 Q 30
Langsett .... 43 O 23
Langshaw .... 62 L 17
Langstrothdale Chase .... 49 N 21

Langthwaite .... 49 O 20
Langtoft .... 51 S 21
Langton .... 50 R 21
Langton Matravers .... 9 O 32
Langwathby .... 55 L 19
Lanhydrock .... 3 F 32
Lanivet .... 3 F 32
Lanlivery .... 3 F 32
Lanreath .... 3 G 32
Lansallos .... 3 G 32
Lanton .... 62 M 17
Lapford .... 7 I 31
Larachbeg .... 71 C 14
Larbert .... 67 I 15
Largs .... 59 F 16
Larkhall .... 61 I 16
Larkhill .... 19 O 30
Larling .... 30 W 26
Lasswade .... 61 K 16
Lastingham .... 50 R 21
Latchingdon .... 22 W 28
Latton .... 19 O 29
Lauder .... 62 L 16
Lauderdale .... 62 L 16
Laugharne .... 15 G 28
Laughton Wealden .... 12 U 31
Laughton West Lindsey ..... 44 R 23
Launcells .... 6 G 31
Launceston .... 6 G 32
Launton .... 28 Q 28
Laurencekirk .... 75 M 13
Laurieston .... 53 H 19
Lauriston Castle .... 68 K 16
Lavendon .... 29 S 27
Lavenham .... 30 W 27
Laverstock .... 9 O 30
Laverstoke .... 20 Q 30
Lawford .... 30 X 28
Lawrenny .... 16 F 28
Lawshall .... 30 W 27
Laxay .... 82 A 9
Laxey .... 46 G 21
Laxey Bay .... 46 G 21
Laxfield .... 31 Y 27
Laxford (Loch) .... 84 E 8
Laxford Bridge .... 84 E 8
Laxo .... 87 Q 2
Laxton
  East Riding of Yorkshire . 44 R 22
Laxton
  Newark and Sherwood .... 36 R 24
Layer-de-la-Haye .... 30 W 28
Layer Marney .... 22 W 28
Laytham .... 44 R 22
Layton .... 42 K 22
Lazonby .... 55 L 19
Lea Herefordshire .... 26 M 28
Lea North Wiltshire .... 19 N 29
Lea West Lindsey .... 44 R 23
Leaden Roding .... 22 U 28
Leadenham .... 37 S 24
Leadgate Derwentside .... 56 O 19
Leadgate Eden .... 55 M 19
Leadhills .... 61 I 17
Leafield .... 20 P 28
Leagrave .... 29 S 28
Lealholm .... 50 R 20
Lealt .... 65 C 15
Leargybreck .... 65 C 16
Leasingham .... 37 S 24
Leathaid Bhuain (Loch an) . 84 F 9
Leatherhead .... 21 T 30
Leathley .... 49 P 22
Leavening .... 50 R 21
Lebberston .... 51 S 21
Lechlade .... 19 O 28
Lecht Road .... 74 K 12
Leckmelm .... 78 E 10
Leconfield .... 44 S 22
Ledbury .... 27 M 27
Ledmore .... 84 F 9
Ledsham .... 44 Q 22
Lee .... 16 H 30
Lee-on-the-Solent .... 10 Q 31
Leebotwood .... 34 L 26
Leeds Kent .... 22 V 30
Leeds West Yorks. .... 43 P 22
Leedstown .... 2 D 33
Leek .... 35 N 24
Leek Wootton .... 27 P 27
Leeming Bar .... 50 P 21
Leeswood .... 34 K 24
Legerwood .... 62 M 16
Leicester .... 36 Q 26
Leicester Forest East ...... 36 Q 26
Leigh .... 42 M 23

A B C D E F G H I J K L M N O P Q R S T U V W X Y Z

Leigh *Mole Valley* .....21 T 30
Leigh *North Wiltshire* .....19 O 29
Leigh *Sevenoaks* .....22 U 30
Leigh *West Dorset* .....8 M 31
Leigh-on-Sea .....22 V 29
Leigh Sinton .....27 N 27
Leighterton .....19 N 29
Leighton Buzzard .....29 S 28
Leim .....58 C 17
Leintwardine .....26 L 26
Leirinmore .....84 F 8
Leiston .....31 Y 27
Leith .....68 K 16
Leitholm .....62 M 16
Lemreway .....82 A 9
Lendalfoot .....52 F 18
Lenham .....22 W 30
Lennoxtown .....67 H 16
Leominster .....26 L 27
Leonard Stanley .....19 N 28
Lepe .....10 P 31
Lephinmore .....65 E 15
Lerwick .....87 Q 3
Lesbury .....63 P 17
Leslie *Aberdeenshire* .....81 L 12
Leslie *Fife* .....68 K 15
Lesmahagow .....61 I 17
Leswalt .....52 E 19
Letchworth .....29 T 28
Letham *Angus* .....75 L 14
Letham *Fife* .....68 K 15
Letheringsett .....38 X 25
Letterewe Forest .....78 D 10
Letterfearn .....78 D 12
Lettermore .....84 G 8
Letters .....78 E 10
Letterston .....24 F 28
Leuchars .....69 L 14
Leurbost .....82 A 9
Leven
  East Riding of Yorks. .....51 T 22
Leven *Fife* .....69 K 15
Leven (Loch) .....72 E 13
Leven (River) .....72 F 13
Levens .....48 L 21
Levens Hall .....48 L 21
Levenwick .....87 Q 4
Leverington .....37 U 25
Leverton
  with Habblesthorpe .....44 R 24
Levington .....31 X 27
Levisham .....50 R 21
Lewannick .....3 G 32
Lewdown .....6 H 32
Lewes .....11 U 31
Lewis (Isle of) .....82 Z 9
Lewis and Harris (Isle of) .....82 Z 8
Lewisham
  London Borough .....21 T 29
Lewknor .....20 R 28
Leyburn .....49 O 21
Leyland .....42 L 22
Leysdown-on-Sea .....22 W 29
Lezant .....3 G 32
Lhanbryde .....80 K 11
Lhen (The) .....46 G 20
Liathach .....78 D 11
Libberton .....61 J 16
Lichfield .....35 O 25
Liddesdale .....55 L 18
Lidgate .....30 V 27
Lifton .....6 H 32
Ligger or Perran Bay .....2 E 32
Lilbourne .....28 Q 26
Lilleshall .....35 M 25
Lilliesleaf .....62 L 17
Limmerhaugh .....60 H 17
Limpsfield .....21 U 30
Linchmere .....10 R 30
Lincoln .....44 S 24
Lincolnshire Wolds .....45 T 23
Lindfield .....11 T 30
Lindores .....68 K 14
Lingague .....46 F 21
Lingay *near Eriskay* .....70 X 12
Lingay *near Pabbay* .....70 X 13
Lingen .....26 L 27
Lingfield .....21 T 30
Liniclate .....76 X 11
Linlithgow .....67 J 16
Linn of Dee .....74 J 13
Linn of Tummel .....74 I 13
Linneraineach .....84 E 9
Linney Head .....14 E 29
Linnhe (Loch) .....72 D 14
Linslade .....29 R 28
Lintmill .....80 L 10

Linton *Craven* .....49 N 21
Linton *Herefordshire* .....26 M 28
Linton *Scottish Borders* .....62 M 17
Linton
  South Cambridgeshire .....30 U 27
Linton *South Derbyshire* .....35 P 25
Linton-on-Ouse .....50 Q 21
Lintrathen (Loch of) .....74 K 13
Linwood *Renfrewshire* .....60 G 16
Linwood *West Lindsey* .....45 T 23
Liphook .....10 R 30
Liskeard .....3 G 32
Lismore .....65 D 14
Liss .....10 R 30
Lisset .....51 T 21
Lisvane .....18 K 29
Litcham .....38 W 25
Litchborough .....28 Q 27
Litchfield .....20 P 30
Litherland .....42 L 23
Little-Baddow .....22 V 28
Little-Barningham .....39 X 25
Little Berkhamsted .....21 T 28
Little Brington .....28 Q 27
Little Budworth .....34 M 24
Little Bytham .....37 S 25
Little Chalfont .....21 S 28
Little Clacton .....31 X 28
Little Colonsay .....64 B 14
Little-Coxwell .....19 P 29
Little Cumbrae Island .....59 F 16
Little Dewchurch .....26 L 28
Little Galdenoch .....52 E 19
Little Glenshee .....67 J 14
Little Hadham .....29 U 28
Little Hallingbury .....22 U 28
Little Harrowden .....28 R 27
Little Houghton .....28 R 27
Little Loch Broom .....78 D 10
Little Loch Roag .....82 Z 9
Little Mill .....18 L 28
Little-Milton .....20 Q 28
Little Minch (The) .....76 Z 11
Little Moreton Hall .....35 N 24
Little Ouse (River) .....30 V 26
Little Ouseburn .....50 Q 21
Little-Raveley .....29 T 26
Little Snoring .....38 W 25
Little-Stretton .....26 L 26
Little-Stukeley .....29 T 26
Little Torrington .....6 H 31
Little Urswick .....48 K 21
Little Walsingham .....38 W 25
Little Waltham .....22 V 28
Little Wenlock .....34 M 26
Littleborough .....43 N 23
Littlebourne .....23 X 30
Littlebury .....30 U 27
Littlecote House .....20 P 29
Littleferry .....79 H 10
Littleham .....4 J 32
Littlehampton .....11 S 31
Littlemill .....79 I 11
Littleport .....30 U 26
Littlestone-on-Sea .....12 W 31
Littleton .....10 P 30
Littleworth .....20 P 28
Litton Cheney .....5 M 31
Liverton .....50 R 20
Liverpool .....42 L 23
Livet (Glen) .....80 K 12
Livingston .....61 J 16
Lizard .....2 E 34
Lizard Peninsula .....2 E 33
Llam .....35 O 24
Llan .....33 J 26
Llan-non .....15 H 28
Llan-y-Bri .....15 G 28
Llanarmon-yn-Ial .....34 K 24
Llanarthne .....24 H 28
Llanarthney .....15 H 28
Llanasa .....41 J 23
Llanbadarn Fawr .....25 H 26
Llanbedr .....33 H 25
Llanbedr Pont Steffan /
  Lampeter .....15 H 27
Llanbedrog .....32 G 25
Llanberis .....33 H 24
Llanberis (Pass of) .....33 H 24
Llanbister .....26 K 26
Llanboidy .....15 G 28
Llanbradach .....18 K 29
Llanbrynmair .....33 J 26
Llanddarog .....15 H 28
Llanddeiniol .....25 H 27
Llanddeusant .....40 G 22

Llanddewi Brefi .....25 I 27
Llanddewi Ystradenni .....26 K 27
Llanddona .....40 H 23
Llanddowror .....15 G 28
Llanddulas .....41 J 23
Llandegla .....34 K 24
Llandenny .....18 L 28
Llandinam .....25 J 26
Llandissilio .....15 F 28
Llandogo .....18 L 28
Llandovery / Llanymddyfri .....25 I 28
Llandrindod Wells .....25 J 27
Llandrinio .....34 K 25
Llandudno .....41 I 23
Llandudno Junction .....41 I 23
Llandwrog .....32 H 24
Llandybie .....15 H 28
Llandyfaelog .....15 H 28
Llandysul .....15 H 27
Llanegryn .....33 H 26
Llanelidan .....34 K 24
Llanellen .....18 K 28
Llanelli .....15 H 28
Llanelltyd .....33 I 25
Llanengan .....32 G 25
Llanerchymedd .....40 G 23
Llanerfyl .....33 J 25
Llanfachraeth .....40 G 23
Llanfaethlu .....40 G 22
Llanfair .....33 H 25
Llanfair-Caereinion .....34 K 26
Llanfair-Pwllgwyngyll .....40 H 23
Llanfair-ym-Muallt /
  Builth Wells .....25 J 27
Llanfair-yn-Neubwll .....40 G 23
Llanfairfechan .....41 I 23
Llanfairynghornwy .....40 G 22
Llanfechell .....40 G 22
Llanferres .....34 K 24
Llanfihangel-ar-arth .....15 H 27
Llanfihangel Glyn Myfyr .....33 J 24
Llanfihangel Nant Bran .....25 J 28
Llanfihangel Rhyditon .....26 K 27
Llanfihangel-y-Creuddyn .....25 I 26
Llanfilo .....26 K 28
Llanfoist .....18 K 28
Llanfrynach .....25 J 28
Llanfwrog .....40 G 23
Llanfyllin .....34 K 25
Llanfynydd *Carmarthenshire /*
  Sir Gaerfyrddin .....15 H 28
Llanfynydd *Flintshire /*
  Sir y Fflint .....34 K 24
Llanfyrnach .....15 G 28
Llangadfan .....33 J 25
Llangadog .....25 I 28
Llangain .....15 G 28
Llangammarch Wells .....25 J 27
Llangarron .....26 L 28
Llangathen .....15 H 28
Llangedwyn .....34 K 25
Llangefni .....40 H 23
Llangeinor .....17 J 29
Llangeitho .....25 H 27
Llangeler .....15 G 27
Llangenith .....15 H 29
Llangennech .....15 H 28
Llangernyw .....33 I 24
Llangoed .....40 H 23
Llangollen .....34 K 25
Llangorse .....26 K 28
Llangorwen .....25 H 26
Llangrannog .....15 G 27
Llangunllo .....26 K 27
Llangunnor .....15 H 28
Llanguig .....25 J 26
Llangwm *Monmouthshire /*
  Sir Fynwy .....18 L 28
Llangwm *Pembrokeshire /*
  Sir Benfro .....16 F 28
Llangwnnadl .....32 F 25
Llangwyryfon .....25 H 27
Llangybi .....15 H 27
Llangyndeyrn .....15 H 28
Llangynidr .....26 K 28
Llangynog *Carmarthenshire /*
  Sir Gaerfyrddin .....15 G 28
Llangynog *Powys* .....33 J 25
Llangynwyd .....17 J 29
Llangywer .....33 J 25
Llanharan .....17 J 29
Llanharry .....17 J 29
Llanhilleth .....18 K 28
Llanidloes .....25 J 26

Llanilar .....25 H 26
Llanishen .....18 L 28
Llanllwchaiarn .....26 K 26
Llanllyfni .....32 H 24
Llanmadoc .....15 H 29
Llannefydd .....41 J 23
Llanon .....25 H 27
Llanpumsaint .....15 H 28
Llanrhaeadr .....33 J 24
Llanrhaeadr-ym-
  Mochnant .....34 K 25
Llanrhidian .....15 H 29
Llanrhystud .....25 H 27
Llanrug .....33 H 24
Llanrwst .....33 I 24
Llansanffraid Glan Conwy .....41 I 23
Llansannan .....33 J 24
Llansantffraid .....25 H 27
Llansantffraid-ym-Mechain .....34 K 25
Llansawel .....15 H 27
Llansilin .....34 K 25
Llansoy .....18 L 28
Llansteffan .....15 G 28
Llanthony .....26 K 28
Llanthony Priory .....26 K 28
Llantilio Crossenny .....18 L 28
Llantrisant .....17 J 29
Llantwit Major .....17 J 29
Llanuwchllyn .....33 I 25
Llanvetherine .....18 L 28
Llanwddyn .....33 J 25
Llanwenog .....15 H 27
Llanwnda .....32 H 24
Llanwnen .....15 H 27
Llanwnog .....25 J 26
Llanwrda .....25 I 28
Llanwrin .....33 I 26
Llanwrtyd Wells .....25 J 27
Llanwyddelan .....33 J 26
Llanybydder .....15 H 27
Llanychaer .....24 F 28
Llanymawddwy .....33 J 25
Llanymddyfri / Llandovery .....25 I 28
Llanymynech .....34 K 25
Llanynghenedl .....40 G 23
Llanystumdwy .....32 H 25
Llawhaden .....15 F 28
Llechryd .....15 G 27
Lledrod .....25 I 27
Lleyn Peninsula .....32 G 25
Llithfaen .....32 G 25
Llowes .....26 K 27
Llston .....15 H 29
Llwndafydd .....24 G 27
Llwyngwril .....33 H 25
Llwynmawr .....34 K 25
Llyfnant Valley .....33 I 26
Llyn Brianne .....25 I 27
Llyn Celyn .....33 I 25
Llyn Tegid or Bala Lake .....33 J 25
Llyswen .....26 K 27
Llysworney .....17 J 29
Llywel .....25 J 28
Loanhead .....61 K 16
Lochailort .....72 D 13
Lochaline .....65 C 14
Lochans .....52 E 19
Locharbriggs .....53 J 18
Lochassynt Lodge .....84 E 9
Lochawe .....66 E 14
Lochay (Glen) .....67 G 14
Lochboisdale .....70 Y 12
Lochbuie .....65 C 14
Lochcarron .....78 D 11
Lochdonhead .....65 C 14
Lochdrum .....78 F 10
Lochearnhead .....67 H 14
Locheport .....76 Y 11
Locherben .....61 J 18
Lochfoot .....53 I 18
Lochgair .....65 D 15
Lochgarthside .....73 G 12
Lochgelly .....68 K 15
Lochgilphead .....65 D 15
Lochgoilhead .....66 F 15
Lochinver .....84 E 9
Lochluichart .....78 F 11
Lochmaben .....54 J 18
Lochmaddy .....76 Y 11
Lochore .....68 K 15
Lochportain .....76 Y 11
Lochranza .....59 E 16
Lochsie (Glen) .....74 J 13
Lochstack .....84 F 8
Lochton *Aberdeenshire* .....75 M 12
Lochton *South Ayrshire* .....52 F 18
Lochtyn / Ynys .....15 G 27

Lochuisge .....72 D 14
Lochwinnoch .....60 G 16
Lochy (Loch) .....72 F 13
Lockerbie .....54 J 18
Lockerley .....9 P 30
Locking .....18 L 30
Loddington .....28 R 26
Loddon .....39 Y 26
Lode .....30 U 27
Lodsworth .....11 R 31
Lofthouse .....49 O 21
Loftus .....50 R 20
Logan Gardens .....52 F 19
Loggerheads .....35 M 25
Logie Coldstone .....74 L 12
Logiealmond .....67 I 14
Login .....15 F 28
Lomond (Loch) .....66 G 15
Londesborough .....51 R 22
London .....21 T 29
London Colney .....21 T 28
Long (Loch) *Angus* .....68 K 14
Long (Loch)
  Argyll and Bute .....66 F 15
Long Ashton .....18 M 29
Long Bennington .....36 R 25
Long Bredy .....5 M 31
Long Buckby .....28 Q 27
Long Clawson .....36 R 25
Long Crendon .....20 R 28
Long Eaton .....36 Q 25
Long Hanborough .....20 P 28
Long Itchington .....28 P 27
Long Lawford .....28 Q 26
Long Man (The) .....12 U 31
Long Marston .....50 Q 22
Long Marton .....55 M 20
Long Melford .....30 W 27
Long Mountain .....34 K 26
Long Mynd (The) .....26 L 26
Long Preston .....49 N 21
Long Stratton .....31 X 26
Long Sutton *Lincs.* .....37 U 25
Long Sutton *Somerset* .....8 L 30
Long Wittenham .....20 Q 29
Longay .....77 C 12
Longbenton .....56 P 18
Longborough .....27 O 28
Longbridge Deverill .....9 N 30
Longburton .....8 M 31
Longcot .....19 P 29
Longdon .....35 O 25
Longfield .....22 U 29
Longford
  Derbyshire Dales .....35 O 25
Longford *Tewkesbury* .....27 N 28
Longforgan .....68 K 14
Longformacus .....62 M 16
Longframlington .....63 O 18
Longhirst .....56 P 18
Longhorsley .....56 O 18
Longhoughton .....63 P 17
Longleat House .....19 N 30
Longmanhil .....81 M 11
Longnewton .....50 P 20
Longney .....19 M 28
Longniddry .....69 L 16
Longnor .....35 O 24
Longridge *Ribble Valley* .....42 M 22
Longridge
  South Staffordshire .....35 N 25
Longridge *West Lothian* .....61 I 16
Longside .....81 O 11
Longstanton .....29 U 27
Longton *South Ribble* .....42 L 22
Longton *Stoke-on-Trent* .....35 N 25
Longtown *Carlisle* .....54 L 18
Longtown *Herefordshire* .....26 L 28
Longwick .....20 R 28
Longworth .....20 P 28
Lonmore .....77 A 11
Looe .....3 G 32
Loose .....22 V 30
Loppington .....34 L 25
Lorn .....65 E 14
Lorn (Firth of) .....65 D 14
Lossiemouth .....80 K 10
Lostwithiel .....3 G 32
Lothbeg .....85 I 9
Lothersdale .....49 N 22
Lothmore .....85 I 9
Loudwater .....21 R 29
Loughborough .....36 Q 25
Loughor (River) .....17 H 29
Loughton .....21 U 29
Louth .....45 U 23
Lovington .....8 M 30

Low Bradley .....49 O 22
Low Crosby .....55 L 19
Low Row *Carlisle* .....55 M 19
Low Row *Richmondshire* .....49 N 20
Low Street .....39 Y 25
Lowca .....53 J 20
Lowdham .....36 Q 24
Lower Beeding .....11 T 30
Lower Bentham .....49 M 21
Lower Boddington .....28 Q 27
Lower Broadheath .....27 N 27
Lower Cam .....19 M 28
Lower Diabaig .....78 C 11
Lower Dounreay .....85 I 8
Lower Dunsforth .....50 Q 21
Lower Halstow .....22 W 29
Lower Hardres .....23 X 30
Lower Heyford .....28 Q 28
Lower Killeyan .....58 B 17
Lower Largo .....69 L 15
Lower Mayland .....22 W 28
Lower Peover .....42 M 24
Lower Upham .....10 Q 31
Lower-Whitley .....42 M 24
Lowestoft .....31 Z 26
Lowgill .....49 M 21
Lowick
  Berwick-upon-Tweed .....63 O 17
Lowick
  East Northamptonshire .....29 S 26
Lowick Bridge .....48 K 21
Lowther .....55 L 20
Lowther Hills .....61 J 18
Loxwood .....11 S 30
Loyal (Loch) .....84 G 8
Loyne (Loch) .....72 E 12
Lùb Score .....77 A 10
Lubcroy .....84 F 10
Lubenham .....28 R 26
Lubnaig (Loch) .....67 H 15
Luccombe .....17 J 30
Luce Bay .....52 F 19
Lucker .....63 O 17
Luddesdown .....22 V 29
Ludford *East Lindsey* .....45 T 23
Ludford *South Shropshire* .....26 L 26
Ludgershall *Bucks.* .....20 Q 28
Ludgershall *Wilts.* .....19 P 30
Ludgvan .....2 D 33
Ludham .....39 Y 25
Ludlow .....26 L 26
Lugton .....60 G 16
Luib *Highland* .....77 B 12
Luib *Stirling* .....67 G 14
Luichart (Loch) .....78 F 11
Luing .....65 D 15
Lullington .....35 P 25
Lulsgate Bottom .....18 L 29
Lulworth Cove .....9 N 32
Lumphanan .....75 L 12
Lumsden .....80 L 12
Lunan .....75 M 14
Lunanhead .....74 L 14
Luncarty .....68 J 14
Lund .....51 S 22
Lundie .....68 K 14
Lundie (Loch) .....78 C 11
Lundin Links .....69 L 15
Lundy .....16 G 30
Lunning .....87 Q 2
Lurgainn (Loch) .....84 E 9
Lurgashall .....11 S 30
Luskentyre .....82 Z 10
Luss .....66 G 15
Lusta .....77 A 11
Lustleigh .....4 I 32
Luston .....26 L 27
Luthermuir .....75 M 13
Luthrie .....68 K 14
Luton .....29 S 28
Luton Hoo .....21 S 28
Lutterworth .....28 Q 26
Lutton .....37 U 25
Luxborough .....7 J 30
Lybster .....86 K 9
Lydbury North .....26 L 26
Lydd .....12 W 31
Lydd-on-Sea .....12 W 31
Lydden .....23 X 30
Lydeard-St. Lawrence .....8 K 30
Lydford *Mendip* .....8 M 30
Lydford *West Devon* .....4 H 32
Lydham .....26 L 26
Lydiard Millicent .....19 O 29
Lydiard Park .....19 O 29
Lydiate .....42 L 23
Lydlinch .....9 M 31

Lydney .... 18 M 28
Lydstep .... 15 F 29
Lyme Bay .... 5 L 32
Lyme Park .... 43 N 23
Lyme Regis .... 5 L 31
Lyminge .... 13 X 30
Lymington .... 10 P 31
Lymm .... 42 M 23
Lympne .... 13 X 30
Lympstone .... 4 J 32
Lyndhurst .... 10 P 31
Lyne .... 61 K 17
Lyneham *North Wiltshire* .... 19 O 29
Lyneham *West Oxfordshire* .... 27 P 28
Lynemouth .... 56 P 18
Lyness .... 86 K 7
Lynmouth .... 17 I 30
Lynton .... 17 I 30
Lyon (Glen) .... 73 H 14
Lyonshall .... 26 L 27
Lytchett Matravers .... 9 N 31
Lytchett Minster .... 9 N 31
Lytes Cary .... 8 L 30
Lyth .... 86 K 8
Lytham .... 42 L 22
Lytham St. Anne's .... 42 K 22
Lythe .... 51 R 20

M
Maaruig .... 82 Z 10
Mabie .... 53 J 18
Mablethorpe .... 45 U 23
Macaskin (Island) .... 65 D 15
Macclesfield .... 43 N 24
Macduff .... 81 M 10
Machars (The) .... 52 G 19
Machen .... 18 K 29
Machir Bay .... 58 A 16
Machrihanish .... 58 C 17
Machrihanish Bay .... 58 C 17
Machynlleth .... 33 I 26
Madderty .... 67 I 14
Maddiston .... 67 I 16
Maddy (Loch) .... 76 Y 11
Madeley *Staffs* .... 35 M 24
Madeley *Telford and Wrekin* .... 35 M 26
Madingley .... 29 U 27
Madron .... 2 D 33
Maenclochog .... 15 F 28
Maentwrog .... 33 I 25
Maerdy *Conwy* .... 33 J 25
Maerdy *Rhondda, Cynon, Taf* .... 17 J 28
Maes Howe .... 86 K 7
Maesbrook .... 34 K 25
Maesteg .... 17 J 29
Maghull .... 42 L 23
Magor .... 18 L 29
Maiden Bradley .... 9 N 30
Maiden Castle .... 8 M 31
Maiden Newton .... 8 M 31
Maidenhead .... 20 R 29
Maidens .... 59 F 17
Maidford .... 28 Q 27
Maidstone .... 22 V 30
Maidwell .... 28 R 26
Mainland *Orkney Islands* .... 86 J 6
Mainland *Shetland Islands* .... 87 R 3
Mainstone .... 26 K 26
Maisemore .... 27 N 28
Malborough .... 4 I 33
Maldon .... 22 W 28
Malham .... 49 N 21
Mallaig .... 71 C 12
Mallory Park Circuit .... 36 P 26
Mallwyd .... 33 I 25
Malmesbury .... 19 N 29
Malpas .... 34 L 24
Maltby .... 44 Q 23
Maltby-le-Marsh .... 45 U 24
Malton .... 50 R 21
Malvern Wells .... 27 N 27
Mamble .... 26 M 26
Mamore Forest .... 72 F 13
Man (Isle of) .... 46 G 21
Manaccan .... 2 E 33
Manaton .... 4 I 32
Manchester .... 43 N 23
Manderston .... 62 N 16
Manea .... 29 U 26
Mangersta .... 82 Y 9
Mangotsfield .... 18 M 29
Manish .... 76 Z 10
Manningford Bruce .... 19 O 30

Mannings Heath .... 11 T 30
Manningtree .... 31 X 28
Manorbier .... 15 F 29
Mansfield .... 36 Q 24
Mansfield Woodhouse .... 36 Q 24
Manstone .... 9 N 31
Manton .... 36 R 26
Manuden .... 30 U 28
Maplebeck .... 36 R 24
Mapledurham .... 20 Q 29
Mappleton .... 45 T 22
Mappowder .... 9 M 31
Mar (Forest of) .... 74 J 12
Marazion .... 2 D 33
March .... 37 U 26
Marcham .... 20 P 29
Marchington .... 35 O 25
Marchwood .... 10 P 31
Marden .... 22 V 30
Maree (Loch) .... 78 D 10
Mareham-le-Fen .... 37 T 24
Maresfield .... 11 U 31
Margam .... 17 I 29
Margaretting .... 22 V 28
Margate .... 23 Y 29
Margnaheglish .... 59 E 17
Marham .... 38 V 26
Marhamchurch .... 6 G 31
Marholm .... 37 T 26
Marian-Glas .... 40 H 22
Marishader .... 77 B 11
Mark *Sedgemoor* .... 18 L 30
Mark *South Ayrshire* .... 52 E 18
Market Bosworth .... 36 P 26
Market Deeping .... 37 T 25
Market Drayton .... 34 M 25
Market Harborough .... 28 R 26
Market Lavington .... 19 O 30
Market Overton .... 36 R 25
Market Rasen .... 45 T 23
Market Weighton .... 44 S 22
Markfield .... 36 Q 25
Markinch .... 68 K 15
Marks Tey .... 30 W 28
Marksbury .... 18 M 29
Markyate .... 21 S 28
Marlborough .... 19 O 29
Marldon .... 4 J 32
Marlesford .... 31 Y 27
Marloes .... 14 E 28
Marlow .... 20 R 29
Marnhull .... 9 N 31
Marple .... 43 N 23
Marros .... 15 G 28
Marsden .... 43 O 23
Marsett .... 49 N 21
Marsh Gibbon .... 28 Q 28
Marsham .... 39 X 25
Marshaw .... 48 M 22
Marshchapel .... 45 U 23
Marshfield *Casnewydd / Newport* .... 18 K 29
Marshfield *South Gloucestershire* .... 19 N 29
Marshwood .... 8 L 31
Marske .... 49 O 20
Marske-by-the-Sea .... 57 Q 20
Marstch .... 20 Q 28
Marston .... 37 R 25
Marston Magna .... 8 M 31
Marston Moretaine .... 29 S 27
Martham .... 39 Y 25
Martin *New Forest* .... 9 O 31
Martin *North Kesteven* .... 37 T 24
Martin (Isle) .... 84 E 10
Martin Mill .... 23 Y 30
Martindale .... 48 L 20
Martinstown .... 5 M 31
Martlesham .... 31 X 27
Martletwy .... 15 F 28
Martley .... 27 M 27
Martock .... 8 L 31
Marton *Harrogate* .... 50 P 21
Marton *Macclesfield* .... 35 N 24
Marvig .... 82 A 9
Marwell Zoological Park .... 10 Q 31
Mary Arden's House .... 27 O 27
Mary Tavy .... 4 H 32
Marybank .... 79 G 11
Maryburgh .... 79 G 11
Maryculter .... 75 N 12
Maryfield .... 87 Q 3
Marykirk .... 75 M 13
Marypark .... 80 J 11
Maryport *Allerdale* .... 53 J 19
Maryport *Dumfries and Galloway* .... 52 F 19

Marywell *Aberdeenshire* .... 75 L 12
Marywell *Angus* .... 69 M 14
Masham .... 49 P 21
Matching Green .... 22 U 28
Mathry .... 14 E 28
Matlock .... 36 P 24
Matlock Bath .... 35 P 24
Mattersey .... 44 R 23
Mattingley .... 20 R 30
Mattishall .... 38 X 26
Mauchline .... 60 G 17
Maud .... 81 N 11
Maughold .... 46 H 21
Maughold Head .... 46 H 21
Mawbray .... 54 J 19
Mawnan .... 2 E 33
Maxstoke .... 27 P 26
Maxton .... 62 M 17
Maybole .... 60 F 17
Mayfield *East Sussex* .... 12 U 30
Mayfield *Staffs* .... 35 O 24
Mc Arthur's Head .... 58 B 16
Meadie (Loch) .... 84 G 9
Meal Bank .... 48 L 20
Mealsgate .... 54 K 19
Meare .... 8 L 30
Measach (Falls of) .... 78 E 10
Measham .... 36 P 25
Meavaig .... 82 Z 10
Meavy .... 4 H 32
Medbourne .... 28 R 26
Medmenham .... 20 R 29
Medstead .... 10 Q 30
Medway (River) .... 22 W 29
Meidrim .... 15 G 28
Meifod .... 34 K 25
Meigle .... 68 K 14
Meikleour .... 68 J 14
Melbost .... 83 B 9
Melbourn .... 29 U 27
Melbourne *East Riding of Yorkshire* .... 44 R 22
Melbourne *South Derbyshire* .... 36 P 25
Melbury Osmond .... 8 M 31
Meldon .... 56 O 18
Melfort .... 65 D 15
Melgarve .... 73 G 12
Melksham .... 19 N 29
Melldalloch .... 65 E 16
Mellerstain .... 62 M 17
Melling .... 48 M 21
Mellon Charles .... 78 D 10
Mellon Udrigle .... 78 D 10
Mells .... 19 M 30
Melmerby *Eden* .... 55 M 19
Melmerby *Harrogate* .... 50 P 21
Melrose .... 62 L 17
Meltham .... 43 O 23
Melton .... 31 X 27
Melton Mowbray .... 36 R 25
Melvaig .... 77 C 10
Melvich .... 85 I 8
Memsie .... 81 N 11
Menai Bridge / Porthaethwy .... 40 H 23
Menai Strait .... 33 H 24
Mendip Hills .... 18 L 30
Mendlesham .... 31 X 27
Menheniot .... 3 G 32
Mennock .... 61 I 17
Menston .... 43 O 22
Menstrie .... 67 I 15
Menteith Hills .... 67 H 15
Mentmore .... 29 R 28
Meonstoke .... 10 Q 31
Meopham .... 22 V 29
Mepal .... 29 U 26
Mere *Cheshire* .... 42 M 24
Mere *Wilts* .... 9 N 30
Mereworth .... 22 V 30
Meriden .... 27 P 26
Merkland Lodge .... 84 F 9
Mermaid Inn .... 32 H 24
Merrick .... 52 G 18
Merriott .... 8 L 31
Merrylaw .... 62 K 18
Mersey (River) .... 42 M 23
Merthyr Cynog .... 25 J 27
Merthyr Tydfil .... 17 J 28
Merton *Cherwell* .... 20 Q 28
Merton *Devon* .... 7 H 31
Merton *London Borough* .... 21 T 29
Meshaw .... 7 I 31
Messing .... 30 W 28
Messingham .... 44 S 23
Metfield .... 31 Y 26

Metheringham .... 37 S 24
Methil .... 69 K 15
Methlick .... 81 N 11
Methven .... 68 J 14
Methwold .... 38 V 26
Mevagissey .... 3 F 33
Mexborough .... 44 Q 23
Mhór (Loch) .... 73 G 12
Miavaig .... 82 Z 9
Michaelchurch Escley .... 26 L 27
Michaelstow .... 3 F 32
Micheldever .... 10 Q 30
Michelham Priory .... 12 U 31
Micklefield .... 44 Q 22
Mickleover .... 36 P 25
Mickleton *Cotswold* .... 27 O 27
Mickleton *Teesdale* .... 55 N 20
Mid Ardlaw .... 81 N 10
Mid Calder .... 61 J 16
Mid Lavant .... 10 R 31
Mid Sannox .... 59 E 17
Mid Yell .... 87 Q 2
Midbea .... 86 L 6
Middle Barton .... 28 P 28
Middle Rasen .... 45 S 23
Middle Tysoe .... 28 P 27
Middle Wallop .... 9 P 30
Middle Woodford .... 9 O 30
Middlebie .... 54 K 18
Middleham .... 49 O 21
Middlesbrough .... 57 Q 20
Middlestown .... 43 P 23
Middleton *Argyll and Bute* .... 64 Z 14
Middleton *Berwick-upon-Tweed* .... 63 O 17
Middleton *Bradford* .... 49 O 22
Middleton *Gtr. Mches.* .... 43 N 23
Middleton Cheney .... 28 Q 27
Middleton-in-Teesdale .... 55 N 20
Middleton-on-Sea .... 11 S 31
Middleton on the Wolds .... 51 S 22
Middleton St. George .... 50 P 20
Middleton Tyas .... 49 P 20
Middletown *Powys* .... 34 K 25
Middlewich .... 35 M 24
Midgeholme .... 55 M 19
Midhurst .... 10 R 31
Midlem .... 62 L 17
Midsomer Norton .... 18 M 30
Midtown .... 78 C 10
Miefield .... 53 H 19
Migdale (Loch) .... 79 H 10
Milborne Port .... 8 M 31
Milborne St. Andrew .... 9 N 31
Milbourne .... 56 O 18
Milburn .... 55 M 20
Mildenhall *Forest Heath* .... 30 V 26
Mildenhall *Kennet* .... 19 O 29
Mile End .... 30 W 28
Milfield .... 63 N 17
Milford .... 11 S 30
Milford Haven / Aberdaugleddau .... 14 E 28
Milford-on-Sea .... 9 P 31
Millbrook .... 3 H 32
Millhouse .... 59 E 16
Millmeece .... 35 N 25
Millom .... 47 K 21
Millport .... 59 F 16
Milltown *Dumfries and Galloway* .... 54 K 18
Milltown *Highland* .... 78 F 11
Milltown *Moray* .... 80 L 11
Milnathort .... 68 J 15
Milngavie .... 67 H 16
Milnrow .... 43 N 23
Milnthorpe .... 48 L 21
Milovaig .... 76 Z 11
Milton .... 79 H 10
Milton *Cambs* .... 29 U 27
Milton *Carlisle* .... 55 L 19
Milton *Dumfries* .... 53 I 18
Milton *Highland* .... 79 G 11
Milton *Stranraer* .... 52 F 19
Milton Abbas .... 9 N 31
Milton Abbot .... 3 H 32
Milton Bryan .... 29 S 28
Milton Ernest .... 29 S 27
Milton Keynes .... 28 R 27
Milton Libourne .... 19 O 29
Milton of Campsie .... 67 H 16
Milton of Cushnie .... 75 L 12
Milton-on-Stour .... 9 N 30
Miltonduff .... 80 J 11
Miltown of Edinville .... 80 K 11
Milverton .... 8 K 30

Milwich .... 35 N 25
Minard .... 65 E 15
Minch (The) .... 83 C 9
Minehead .... 17 J 30
Minety .... 19 O 29
Mingary .... 76 X 12
Minginish .... 77 B 12
Mingulay .... 70 X 13
Minnigaff .... 52 G 19
Minster *near Sheerness* .... 22 W 29
Minster *near Ramsgate* .... 23 X 29
Minsterley .... 34 L 26
Minsterworth .... 19 N 28
Minterne Magna .... 8 M 31
Minting .... 45 T 24
Mintlaw .... 81 O 11
Minto .... 62 L 17
Mirfield .... 43 O 22
Miserden .... 19 N 28
Misson .... 44 R 23
Misterton *Notts* .... 44 R 23
Misterton *Somerset* .... 8 L 31
Mistley .... 31 X 28
Mitcheldean .... 26 M 28
Mitchell .... 2 E 32
Mitford .... 56 O 18
Mithcham .... 21 T 29
Mithian .... 2 E 33
Moaness .... 86 K 7
Mochdre .... 41 I 23
Mochrum .... 52 G 19
Modbury .... 4 I 32
Moelfre .... 40 H 22
Moffat .... 61 J 17
Moidart .... 72 C 13
Moira .... 36 P 25
Mol-Chlach .... 71 B 12
Mold / Yr Wyddgrug .... 34 K 24
Molland .... 7 I 30
Monach Islands .... 76 W 11
Monadhliath Mountains .... 73 H 12
Monar (Loch) .... 78 E 11
Monar Lodge .... 78 F 11
Monaughty Forest .... 80 J 11
Moneydie .... 68 J 14
Moniaive .... 53 I 18
Monifieth .... 69 L 14
Monikie .... 69 L 14
Monk Fryston .... 44 Q 22
Monkland .... 26 L 27
Monkokehampton .... 7 H 31
Monks Eleigh .... 30 W 27
Monksilver .... 7 K 30
Monkton .... 60 G 17
Monmouth / Trefynwy .... 18 L 28
Monreith .... 52 G 19
Montacute .... 8 L 31
Montgarrie .... 75 L 12
Montgomery / Trefaldwyn .... 34 K 26
Montrose .... 75 M 13
Monyash .... 35 O 24
Monymusk .... 75 M 12
Monzie .... 67 I 14
Moonen Bay .... 76 Z 11
Moor Monkton .... 50 Q 21
Moorends .... 44 R 23
Moorfoot Hills .... 61 K 16
Moors (The) .... 52 F 19
Moortown .... 45 S 23
Morar .... 71 C 13
Moray Firth .... 79 H 11
Morchard Bishop .... 7 I 31
Morcott .... 37 S 26
Morden .... 9 N 31
Mordiford .... 26 M 27
More (Glen) *near Kinloch* .... 84 F 9
More (Loch) *near Westerdale* .... 85 J 8
Morebath .... 7 J 30
Morebattle .... 62 M 17
Morecambe .... 48 L 21
Morecambe Bay .... 48 L 21
Moresby .... 53 J 20
Moreton *Epping Forest* .... 22 U 28
Moreton *Purbeck* .... 9 N 31
Moreton-in-Marsh .... 27 O 28
Moreton-on-lugg .... 26 L 27
Moreton Say .... 34 M 25
Moretonhampstead .... 4 I 32
Morfa Nefyn .... 32 G 25
Moricambe Bay .... 54 K 19
Morie (Loch) .... 79 G 10
Moriston (Glen) .... 72 F 12
Morland .... 55 M 20
Morley .... 43 P 22
Morlich (Loch) .... 74 I 12

Morpeth .... 56 O 18
Morriston .... 17 I 29
Morte Bay .... 6 H 30
Mortehoe .... 16 H 30
Mortimer .... 20 Q 29
Morton *near Bourne* .... 37 S 25
Morton *near Gainsborough* .... 44 R 23
Morton *North East Derbyshire* .... 36 P 24
Morton on Swale .... 50 P 21
Morval .... 3 G 32
Morven .... 85 I 9
Morvern .... 71 C 14
Morvich .... 72 D 12
Morville .... 34 M 26
Morwelham .... 3 H 32
Morwenstow .... 6 G 31
Mosborough .... 43 P 24
Moss Bank .... 42 L 23
Mossdale .... 53 H 18
Mossend .... 60 H 16
Mossley .... 43 N 23
Mosstodloch .... 80 K 11
Mostyn .... 41 K 23
Motherwell .... 61 I 16
Moulin .... 74 I 13
Moulton *Forest Heath* .... 30 V 27
Moulton *Lincs* .... 37 T 25
Moulton *Northants* .... 28 R 27
Moulton Chapel .... 37 T 25
Mount Pleasant .... 9 P 31
Mountain Ash / Aberpennar .... 17 J 28
Mount's Bay .... 2 D 33
Mountsorrel .... 36 Q 25
Mousa .... 87 Q 4
Mousehole .... 2 D 33
Mouswald .... 54 J 18
Mow Cop .... 35 N 24
Mowtie .... 75 N 13
Moy .... 79 H 11
Muasdale .... 59 C 17
Much Dewchurch .... 26 L 28
Much Hadham .... 29 U 28
Much Hoole .... 42 L 22
Much Marcle .... 26 M 28
Much Wenlock .... 34 M 26
Muchalls .... 75 N 12
Muchelney .... 8 L 30
Muchrachd .... 78 F 11
Muck .... 71 B 13
Muckle Roe .... 87 P 2
Mucklestone .... 35 M 25
Muddiford .... 7 H 30
Mudford .... 8 M 31
Mugeary .... 77 B 11
Muick (Loch) .... 74 K 13
Muie .... 85 H 9
Muir of Fowlis .... 75 L 12
Muir of Ord .... 79 G 11
Muirdrum .... 69 L 14
Muirhead .... 60 H 16
Muirkirk .... 60 H 17
Muirshearlich .... 72 E 13
Muker .... 49 N 20
Mulbarton .... 39 X 26
Mulben .... 80 K 11
Muldoanich .... 70 X 13
Mull (Isle of) .... 64 B 14
Mull (Sound of) .... 71 C 14
Mull of Galloway .... 52 F 20
Mull of Oa .... 58 A 17
Mullardoch (Loch) .... 78 E 12
Mullardoch House .... 78 F 11
Mullion .... 2 E 33
Mumbles (The) .... 15 H 29
Mumby .... 45 U 24
Mundesley .... 39 Y 25
Mundford .... 30 V 26
Mundham .... 10 R 31
Munlochy .... 79 H 11
Munlochy Bay .... 79 H 11
Munslow .... 26 L 26
Murlaggan .... 72 E 13
Murrayfield .... 68 K 16
Mursley .... 28 R 28
Murton *Easington* .... 57 P 19
Murton *Eden* .... 55 M 20
Musbury .... 5 K 31
Musselburgh .... 68 K 16
Muston .... 51 T 21
Muthill .... 67 I 15
Mwnt .... 15 G 27
Mybster .... 85 J 8
Myddfai .... 25 I 28
Myddle .... 34 L 25

A B C D E F G H I J K L M N O P Q R S T U V W X Y Z

A B C D E F G H I J K L M N O P Q R S T U V W X Y Z

Mydroilyn ....15 H 27
Mynach Falls ....25 I 26
Mynachlog-ddu ....15 F 28
Mynydd Eppynt ....25 J 27
Mynydd Mawr ....32 F 25
Mynydd Preseli ....15 F 28
Myrelandhorn ....86 K 8
Mytchett ....21 R 30
Mytholmroyd ....43 O 22

N
Na Cùiltean ....58 C 16
Naburn ....50 Q 22
Nacton ....31 X 27
Nafferton ....51 S 21
Nailsea ....18 L 29
Nailstone ....36 P 26
Nailsworth ....19 N 28
Nairn ....79 I 11
Nant (Loch) ....65 E 14
Nant-y-Moch Reservoir ....25 I 26
Nant-y-moel ....17 J 29
Nantgwynant Valley ....33 H 24
Nantwich ....34 M 24
Nantyglo ....18 K 28
Napton ....28 Q 27
Narberth / Arberth ....15 F 28
Narborough Blaby ....36 Q 26
Narborough Breckland ....38 V 25
Naseby ....28 R 26
Nash Point ....17 J 29
Nassington ....37 S 26
Nateby ....49 M 20
National Exhibition Centre .....27 O 26
National Motor Museum .....10 P 31
Naunton ....27 O 28
Navenby ....37 S 24
Naver (Loch) ....84 G 9
Nayland ....30 W 28
Naze (The) ....31 X 28
Neap ....87 Q 3
Neath / Castell-nedd ....17 I 29
Neath (River) ....17 I 28
Nebo ....33 I 24
Necton ....38 W 26
Needham Market ....31 X 27
Needingworth ....29 T 27
Needles (The) ....10 P 32
Nefyn ....32 G 25
Neidpath Castle ....61 K 17
Neilston ....60 G 16
Neist Point ....76 Z 11
Nelson
    Caerffili / Caerphilly ....18 K 29
Nelson Pendle ....43 N 22
Nene (River) ....37 T 26
Nenthead ....55 M 19
Nercwys ....34 K 24
Nereabolls ....58 A 16
Ness ....83 B 8
Ness (Loch) ....73 G 12
Nesscliffe ....34 L 25
Nestley Marsh ....10 P 31
Neston ....42 K 24
Nether Broughton ....36 R 25
Nether Kellet ....48 L 21
Nether Langwith ....44 Q 24
Nether Stowey ....8 K 30
Nether Wasdale ....47 J 20
Nether Whitecleuch ....61 I 17
Netheravon ....19 O 30
Netherbrae ....81 M 11
Netherbury ....8 L 31
Netherend ....18 M 28
Netherhampton ....9 O 30
Nethermill ....54 J 18
Netherthong ....43 O 23
Netherton ....63 N 17
Nethertown ....86 K 7
Netherwitton ....56 O 18
Nethy Bridge ....74 J 12
Netley ....10 P 31
Nettlebed ....20 R 29
Nettleham ....44 S 24
Nettleton ....45 T 23
Nevern ....15 F 27
Nevis (Glen) ....72 E 13
Nevis (Loch) ....72 C 12
New Abbey ....53 J 19
New Aberdour ....81 N 11
New Alresford ....10 Q 30
New Buckenham ....31 X 26
New Byth ....81 N 11
New Clipstone ....36 Q 24
New Cumnock ....60 H 17
New Deer ....81 N 11
New Edlington ....44 Q 23

New Forest National Park .....9 P 31
New Galloway ....53 H 18
New Holland ....45 S 22
New Hythe ....22 V 30
New Leeds ....81 N 11
New Luce ....52 F 19
New Marske ....57 Q 20
New Mills ....43 O 23
New Mills Powys ....33 K 26
New Milton ....9 P 31
New Pitsligo ....81 N 11
New Quay / Ceinewydd .....24 G 27
New Rackheath ....39 Y 26
New Radnor ....26 K 27
New Romney ....12 W 31
New Rossington ....44 Q 23
New Sauchie ....67 I 15
New Scone ....68 J 14
New Silksworth ....57 P 19
New Tredegar ....18 K 28
New Waltham ....45 T 23
Newark-on-Trent ....36 R 24
Newbiggin Eden ....55 L 19
Newbiggin Teesdale ....55 N 19
Newbiggin-by-the-Sea .....56 P 18
Newbigging Angus ....69 L 14
Newbigging
    South Lanarkshire .....61 J 16
Newbold Verdon ....36 P 26
Newborough
    East Staffordshire .....35 O 25
Newborough
    Isle of Anglesey .....32 G 24
Newbridge Caerffili /
    Caerphilly ....18 K 29
Newbridge Isle of Wight .....10 P 31
Newbridge-on-Wye ....25 J 27
Newbrough ....55 N 18
Newburgh Aberdeenshire .....81 N 11
Newburgh Fife ....68 K 14
Newburgh Lancashire .....42 L 23
Newburn ....56 O 19
Newbury ....20 Q 29
Newby Bridge ....48 L 21
Newby Hall ....50 P 21
Newcastle Monmouthshire /
    Sir Fynwy ....18 L 28
Newcastle
    South Shropshire .....26 K 26
Newcastle Emlyn /
    Castell Newydd Emlyn .15 G 27
Newcastle-under-Lyme ....35 N 24
Newcastle-upon-Tyne .....56 P 19
Newcastle-upon-Tyne
    Airport ....56 O 18
Newcastleton ....55 L 18
Newchapel ....15 G 27
Newchurch Carmarthenshire /
    Sir Gaerfyrddin .....15 G 28
Newchurch Isle of Wight ..10 Q 32
Newchurch Powys ....26 K 27
Newchurch Shepway .....12 W 30
Newdigate ....11 T 30
Newent ....27 M 28
Newgale ....14 E 28
Newhall ....34 M 24
Newham Isle of Wight .....63 O 17
Newham London Borough ..21 U 29
Newhaven ....11 U 31
Newick ....11 U 31
Newington ....22 V 29
Newland ....18 M 28
Newlyn ....2 D 33
Newmachar ....75 N 12
Newmains ....61 I 16
Newmarket Isle of Lewis ..82 A 9
Newmarket Suffolk ....30 V 27
Newmill Moray ....80 L 11
Newmill Scottish Borders ..62 L 17
Newmilns ....60 G 17
Newnham Daventry ....28 Q 27
Newnham Glos. ....18 M 28
Newnham Kent ....22 W 30
Newnham Bridge ....26 M 27
Newport Essex ....30 U 28
Newport I.O.W. ....10 Q 31
Newport Pembrokes. .....15 F 27
Newport Stroud ....19 M 28
Newport
    Telford and Wrekin .....35 M 25
Newport /
    Casnewydd Newport .18 L 29
Newport-on-Tay ....69 L 14
Newport Pagnell ....28 R 27
Newquay ....2 E 32
Newsham ....49 O 20
Newstead ....36 Q 24

Newstead Abbey ....36 Q 24
Newton Aberdeenshire ..81 O 11
Newton Argyll and Bute ..65 E 15
Newton Babergh ....30 W 27
Newton Moray ....80 J 11
Newton Ribble Valley .....49 M 22
Newton Rushcliffe ....36 R 25
Newton Abbot ....4 J 32
Newton-Arlosh ....54 K 19
Newton-Aycliffe ....56 P 20
Newton Ferrers ....4 H 33
Newton Flotman ....39 X 26
Newton-le-Willows ....42 M 23
Newton Longville ....28 R 28
Newton Mearns ....60 H 16
Newton-on-Rawcliffe .....50 R 21
Newton-on-Trent ....44 R 24
Newton Poppleford ....5 K 31
Newton Reigny ....55 L 19
Newton St. Cyres ....7 J 31
Newton Stewart ....52 G 19
Newton Tracey ....7 H 30
Newton Wamphray ....54 J 18
Newtongrange ....61 K 16
Newtonhill ....75 N 12
Newtonmore ....73 H 12
Newtown Cheshire ....43 N 23
Newtown Heref. ....26 M 27
Newtown Highland ....73 F 12
Newtown Isle of Man .....46 G 21
Newtown /
    Drenewydd Powys ....26 K 26
Newtown Linford ....36 Q 25
Newtown St. Boswells .....62 L 17
Newtyle ....68 K 14
Neyland ....16 F 28
Nicholaston ....15 H 29
Nigg ....79 H 10
Nigg Bay ....79 H 10
Nine Ladies ....35 P 24
Ninebanks ....55 M 19
Ninfield ....12 V 31
Nisbet ....62 M 17
Nith (River) ....53 J 19
Niths ....61 I 18
Niton ....10 Q 32
Nocton ....37 S 24
Nolton ....14 E 28
Nordelph ....38 U 26
Norfolk Broads ....39 Y 25
Norham ....63 N 16
Normanby ....50 R 21
Normandy ....21 S 30
Normanton ....43 P 22
Normanton-on-the-Wolds ..36 Q 25
North Baddesley ....10 P 31
North Ballachulish ....72 E 13
North Berwick ....69 L 15
North Bovey ....4 I 32
North Bradley ....19 N 30
North Brentor ....4 H 32
North Cadbury ....8 M 30
North Cave ....44 S 22
North-Cerney ....19 O 28
North-Charlton ....63 O 17
North Cliffe ....44 R 22
North Cowton ....50 P 20
North Crawley ....29 S 27
North Creake ....38 W 25
North Curry ....8 L 30
North Dalton ....51 S 22
North Deighton ....50 P 22
North Erradale ....77 C 10
North Esk (Riv.) ....75 L 13
North Fearns ....77 B 11
North Foreland ....23 Y 29
North Frodingham ....51 T 22
North Grimston ....51 R 21
North Harris ....82 Z 10
North Hill ....3 G 32
North Hinksey ....20 Q 28
North Holmwood ....21 T 30
North Hykeham ....37 S 24
North Kelsey ....45 S 23
North Kessock ....79 H 11
North Kyme ....37 T 24
North Leigh ....20 P 28
North-Molton ....7 I 30
North Morar ....72 C 13
North Newbald ....44 S 22
North Nibley ....19 M 29
North Otterington ....50 P 21
North Petherton ....8 K 30
North Petherwin ....6 G 31
North Rigton ....50 P 22
North Ronaldsay ....87 M 5
North-Scarle ....36 R 24

North-Shian ....65 D 14
North Shields ....56 P 18
North Shore ....42 K 22
North Somercotes ....45 U 23
North Sound (The) ....87 L 6
North Stainley ....50 P 21
North Stainmore ....49 N 20
North Sunderland ....63 P 17
North Tamerton ....6 G 31
North-Tawton ....7 I 31
North Thoresby ....45 T 23
North Tidworth ....19 P 30
North Uist ....76 X 11
North Walsham ....39 Y 25
North Warnborough ....20 R 30
North Water Bridge ....75 M 13
North Weald Bassett .....22 U 28
North Wootton ....38 V 25
North York Moors
    National Park ....50 R 20
Northallerton ....50 P 20
Northam ....6 H 30
Northampton ....28 R 27
Northaw ....21 T 28
Northchapel ....11 S 30
Northchurch ....21 S 28
Northfleet ....22 V 29
Northiam ....12 V 31
Northleach ....19 O 28
Northleigh ....5 K 31
Northlew ....7 H 31
Northop ....34 K 24
Northrepps ....39 Y 25
Northton ....76 Y 10
Northumberland
    National Park ....63 N 18
Northwich ....42 M 24
Northwold ....38 V 26
Northwood ....34 L 25
Norton Daventry ....28 Q 27
Norton Doncaster ....44 Q 23
Norton Ryedale ....50 R 21
Norton Tewkesbury ....27 N 28
Norton Disney ....36 R 24
Norton Fitzwarren ....8 K 30
Norton in Hales ....35 M 25
Norton St. Philip ....19 N 30
Norwich ....39 X 26
Norwick ....87 R 1
Noss (Isle of) ....87 Q 3
Noss Head ....86 K 8
Nottingham ....36 Q 25
Nuffield ....20 Q 29
Nunburnholme ....51 R 22
Nuneaton ....28 P 26
Nuneham Courtenay .....20 Q 28
Nunney ....19 M 30
Nunthorpe ....50 Q 20
Nunton ....76 X 11
Nutley ....11 U 30
Nympsfield ....19 N 28

O
Oa (The) ....58 B 17
Oadby ....36 Q 26
Oakamoor ....35 O 24
Oakdale ....18 K 28
Oakengates ....35 M 25
Oakford ....7 J 31
Oakham ....36 R 25
Oakhill ....18 M 30
Oakington ....29 U 27
Oakley Aylesbury Vale ..20 Q 28
Oakley Bedfordshire .....29 S 27
Oakley Fife ....68 J 15
Oaksey ....19 N 29
Oakworth ....43 O 22
Oare Kennet ....19 O 29
Oare Swale ....22 W 30
Oare West Somerset .....17 I 30
Oathlaw ....74 L 13
Oban ....65 D 14
Occold ....31 X 27
Ochil Hills ....68 I 15
Ochiltree ....60 G 17
Ockbrook ....36 P 25
Ockle ....71 C 13
Ockley ....11 S 30
Odd Down ....19 M 29
Odell ....29 S 27
Odiham ....20 R 30
Odland ....18 M 29
Odstock ....9 O 30
Offa's Dyke Path ....26 K 26
Offord Cluny ....29 T 27
Ogbourne St. Andrew ....19 O 29
Ogbourne St. George .....19 O 29
Ogil ....74 L 13
Ogle ....56 O 18

Ogmore-by-Sea ....17 J 29
Ogmore Vale ....17 J 29
Oich (Loch) ....73 F 12
Oidhche (Loch na h-) .....78 D 11
Oigh-Sgeir ....71 Z 13
Okeford Fitzpaine ....9 N 31
Okehampton ....4 H 31
Old Alresford ....10 Q 30
Old Bolingbroke ....37 U 24
Old Burghclere ....20 Q 30
Old Castleton ....55 L 18
Old Colwyn ....41 I 23
Old Dailly ....59 F 18
Old Deer ....81 N 11
Old Fletton ....37 T 26
Old Harry Rocks ....9 O 32
Old Head ....87 L 7
Old Hurst ....29 T 26
Old Hutton ....48 L 21
Old Kilpatrick ....67 G 16
Old Knebworth ....29 T 28
Old Leake ....37 U 24
Old Man of Hoy ....86 J 7
Old Man of Storr ....77 B 11
Old Radnor ....26 K 27
Old Rayne ....81 M 11
Old' Sarum ....9 O 30
Old Sodbury ....19 M 29
Old Somerby ....37 S 25
Old Warden ....29 S 27
Old Windsor ....21 S 29
Oldany Island ....84 E 9
Oldbury ....27 N 26
Oldbury on Severn ....18 M 29
Oldcotes ....44 Q 23
Oldham ....43 N 23
Oldhamstocks ....69 M 16
Oldmeldrum ....81 N 11
Oldshoremore ....84 E 8
Olgrinmore ....85 J 8
Ollaberry ....87 P 2
Ollach ....77 B 11
Ollay (Loch) ....76 X 12
Ollerton Macclesfield ....42 M 24
Ollerton
    Newark and Sherwood ..36 Q 24
Olney ....28 R 27
Olveston ....18 M 29
Ombersley ....27 N 27
Once Brewed ....55 M 19
Onchan ....46 G 21
Onecote ....35 O 24
Onich ....72 E 13
Onllwyn ....17 I 28
Opinan ....83 D 10
Orchy (Glen) ....66 F 14
Ord ....71 C 12
Ordie ....74 L 12
Orford ....31 Y 27
Orford Ness ....31 Y 27
Orkney Islands 87
Orleton ....26 L 27
Ormesby ....50 Q 20
Ormesby St. Margaret ..39 Z 25
Ormiston ....62 L 16
Ormskirk ....42 L 23
Oronsay ....64 B 15
Orosay near Fuday ....70 X 12
Orosay near Lochboisdale ..70 X 12
Orphir ....86 K 7
Orrin (Glen) ....78 F 11
Orrin Reservoir ....78 F 11
Orsay ....58 A 16
Orsett ....22 V 29
Orston ....36 R 25
Orton ....48 M 20
Orwell ....29 T 27
Orwell (River) ....31 X 28
Osborne House ....10 Q 31
Osdale ....77 A 11
Osgaig (Loch) ....83 E 9
Osgodby ....45 S 23
Oskaig ....77 B 11
Osmington ....9 M 32
Ossett ....43 P 22
Ossington ....36 R 24
Oswaldtwistle ....42 M 22
Oswestry ....34 K 25
Otford ....22 U 30
Othery ....8 L 30
Otley Suffolk ....31 X 27
Otley West Yorks. ....49 O 22
Otterbourne ....10 P 30
Otterburn ....55 N 18
Otternish ....76 Y 10
Otterswick ....87 Q 2
Otterton ....5 K 32

Ottery St. Mary ....5 K 31
Ottringham ....45 T 22
Oulton Broad ....39 Z 26
Oulton Park Circuit .....34 M 24
Oundle ....29 S 26
Ouse (River)
    English Channel ....11 T 30
Ouse (River) North Sea ..50 Q 21
Out-Rawcliffe ....42 L 22
Out Skerries ....87 R 2
Outer Hebrides ....82 Y 9
Outhgill ....49 M 20
Outwell ....38 U 26
Over ....29 U 27
Over Compton ....8 M 31
Overseal ....35 P 25
Overstrand ....39 Y 25
Overton Hants. ....20 Q 30
Overton Lancs. ....48 L 21
Overton Wrexham ....34 L 25
Overtown ....61 I 16
Ower ....10 P 31
Owermoigne ....9 N 32
Owlswick ....20 R 28
Owslebury ....10 Q 30
Owston ....36 R 26
Owston Ferry ....44 R 23
Oxburgh Hall ....38 V 26
Oxen Park ....48 K 21
Oxenhope ....43 O 22
Oxford ....20 Q 28
Oxnam ....62 M 17
Oxted ....21 T 30
Oxton
    Newark and Sherwood ..36 Q 24
Oxton Scottish Borders ..62 L 16
Oxwich ....15 H 29
Oxwich Bay ....15 H 29
Oykel (Glen) ....84 F 9
Oykel Bridge ....84 F 10
Oyne ....81 M 12

P
Pabay ....77 C 12
Pabbay near Harris .....76 Y 10
Pabbay near Mingulay ..70 X 13
Pabbay (Sound of) ....76 Y 10
Packington ....36 P 25
Padbury ....28 R 28
Paddock Wood ....22 V 30
Paddockhole ....54 K 18
Padiham ....42 N 22
Padstow ....3 F 32
Pagham ....10 R 31
Paignton ....4 J 32
Pailton ....28 Q 26
Painscastle ....26 K 27
Painswick ....19 N 28
Paisley ....60 G 16
Pakefield ....31 Z 26
Palnackie ....53 I 19
Pamber End ....20 Q 30
Pandy
    Monmouthshire / Sir Fynwy .26 L 28
Pandy Powys ....33 J 26
Pangbourne ....20 Q 29
Pant ....34 K 25
Pantymenyn ....15 F 28
Papa Stour ....87 O 3
Papa Westray ....87 L 5
Papplewick ....36 Q 24
Paps of Jura ....65 B 16
Papworth Everard ....29 T 27
Parbh (The) ....84 F 8
Parbold ....42 L 23
Parc Cefn Onn ....18 K 29
Parham House ....11 S 31
Park Gate ....10 Q 31
Park of Pairc ....82 A 9
Parkeston ....31 X 28
Parkgate ....53 J 18
Parkhurst ....10 Q 31
Parnham House ....8 L 31
Parracombe ....17 I 30
Parrett (River) ....8 K 30
Parson Drove ....37 U 26
Partney ....37 U 24
Parton Copeland ....54 J 20
Parton
    Dumfries and Galloway ....53 H 18
Partridge Green ....11 T 31
Parwich ....35 O 24
Patchway ....18 M 29
Pateley Bridge ....49 O 21
Path of Condie ....68 J 15
Pathhead ....62 L 16
Patna ....60 G 17

Patrick ....46 F 21
Patrington ....45 T 22
Patrixbourne ....23 X 30
Patterdale ....48 L 20
Pattingham ....35 N 26
Pattishall ....28 Q 27
Paulerspury ....28 R 27
Paull ....45 T 22
Paulton ....18 M 30
Paxton ....63 N 16
Peacehaven ....11 T 31
Peak District
   National Park ....43 O 23
Pearsie ....74 K 13
Peasedown St. John ....19 M 30
Peasemore ....20 P 29
Peasenhall ....31 Y 27
Peaslake ....21 S 30
Peasmarsh ....12 W 31
Peat Inn ....69 L 15
Peatknowe ....81 M 11
Pebmarsh ....30 W 28
Pebworth ....27 O 27
Peebles ....61 K 17
Peel ....46 F 21
Peel Fell ....62 M 18
Pegswood ....56 P 18
Pegwell Bay ....23 Y 30
Peinchorran ....77 B 12
Peldon ....22 W 28
Pelton ....56 P 19
Pelynt ....3 G 32
Pembrey ....15 H 28
Pembridge ....26 L 27
Pembroke / Penfro ....16 F 28
Pembroke Dock /
   Doc Penfro ....16 F 28
Pembrokeshire Coast
   National Park ....15 F 29
Pembury ....12 V 30
Pen-y-bont / Bridgend ....17 J 29
Pen-y-groes ....32 H 24
Penalun ....15 F 29
Penarth ....18 K 29
Pencader ....15 H 27
Pencaitland ....62 L 16
Pencarrow ....3 F 32
Penclawdd ....15 H 29
Pencombe ....26 M 27
Penderyn ....17 J 28
Pendine ....15 G 28
Pendine Sands ....15 G 28
Pendlebury ....42 N 23
Pendoylan ....17 J 29
Penelewey ....2 E 33
Penfro / Pembroke ....16 F 28
Pengethley ....26 M 28
Penhow ....18 L 29
Penicuik ....61 K 16
Penifiler ....77 B 11
Peninver ....59 D 17
Penistone ....43 P 23
Penketh ....42 L 23
Penkridge ....35 N 25
Penley ....34 L 25
Penmaen ....15 H 29
Penmaenmawr ....41 I 23
Penmaenpool ....33 I 25
Penmark ....17 J 29
Penmon ....40 H 23
Pennal ....33 I 26
Pennant ....33 J 26
Pennerley ....34 L 26
Pennines (The) ....49 N 20
Pennyghael ....65 B 14
Penpont ....53 I 18
Penrhiwpal ....15 G 27
Penrhyn ....40 H 23
Penrhyn Bay ....41 I 23
Penrhyndeudraeth ....33 H 25
Penrith ....55 L 19
Penruddock ....55 L 20
Penryn ....2 E 33
Pensarn ....41 I 23
Penshaw ....56 P 19
Penshurst ....22 U 30
Pensilva ....3 G 32
Pentewan ....3 F 33
Pentire Point ....3 F 32
Pentland Firth ....86 K 7
Pentland Hills ....61 J 16
Pentland Skerries ....87 L 7
Pentraeth ....40 H 23
Pentre-Berw ....40 H 23
Pentre-Celyn ....34 K 24
Pentrebeirdd ....34 K 25
Penwith ....2 D 33

Penybont ....26 K 27
Penysarn ....40 H 22
Penzance ....2 D 33
Pernrhyn-Coch ....25 I 26
Perranarworthal ....2 E 33
Perranporth ....2 E 32
Perranzabuloe ....2 E 33
Pershore ....27 N 27
Pertenhall ....29 S 27
Perth ....68 J 14
Peterborough ....37 T 26
Peterculter ....75 N 12
Peterhead ....81 O 11
Peterlee ....57 P 19
Petersfield ....10 R 30
Peterstone Wentlooge ....18 K 29
Peterstow ....26 M 28
Petham ....23 X 30
Petrockstowe ....7 H 31
Pett ....12 V 31
Pettaugh ....31 X 27
Petworth ....11 S 31
Pevensey Bay ....12 V 31
Pewsey ....19 O 29
Pickering ....50 R 21
Picklescott ....34 L 26
Picton Castle ....16 F 28
Piddlehinton ....9 M 31
Piddletrenthide ....9 M 31
Piercebridge ....49 O 20
Pierowall ....86 L 6
Pilgrims Hatch ....22 U 29
Pillerton Hersey ....28 P 27
Pillerton Priors ....27 P 27
Pilley ....43 P 23
Pilling ....48 L 22
Pilning ....18 M 29
Pilton ....8 M 30
Pinchbeck ....37 T 25
Pinchbeck-West ....37 T 25
Pinhoe ....4 J 31
Pinmore Mains ....52 F 18
Pinner ....21 S 29
Pinvin ....27 N 27
Pinxton ....36 Q 24
Pirbright ....21 S 30
Pirnmill ....59 D 17
Pirton ....29 T 28
Pishill ....20 R 29
Pitcaple ....81 M 12
Pitcombe ....8 M 30
Pitcur ....68 K 14
Pitlochry ....74 I 13
Pitmedden ....81 N 11
Pitminster ....8 K 31
Pitscottie ....69 L 15
Pitsford ....28 R 27
Pittentrail ....85 H 10
Pittenweem ....69 L 15
Pladda ....59 E 17
Plaistow ....11 S 30
Plas Newydd *Anglesey* ....33 H 24
Plas Newydd
   Denbighshire ....34 K 25
Plean ....67 I 15
Pleasington ....42 M 22
Pleasley ....36 Q 24
Plenmeller ....55 M 19
Plockton ....78 D 11
Pluckley ....22 W 30
Plumbland ....54 K 19
Plumpton ....11 T 31
Plymouth ....4 H 32
Plympton ....4 H 32
Plymstock ....4 H 32
Plymtree ....7 J 31
Plynlimon
   (Pumlumon Fawr) ....25 I 26
Pocklington ....50 R 22
Point Lynas ....40 H 22
Point of Ayr *Flintshire* ....41 K 22
Point of Ayre *Isle of Man* ....46 G 20
Polbain ....83 D 9
Pole of Itlaw (The) ....81 M 11
Polebrook ....29 S 26
Polegate ....12 U 31
Polesden Lacey ....21 S 30
Polesworth ....35 P 26
Polkerris ....3 F 32
Polloch ....72 D 13
Pollock House ....60 H 16
Polmont ....67 I 16
Polperro ....3 G 33
Polruan ....3 G 33
Polwarth ....62 M 16
Pondersbridge ....29 T 26

Pont-ar-Gothi ....15 H 28
Pontardawe ....17 I 28
Pontarddulais ....15 H 28
Pontarfynach /
   Devil's Bridge ....25 I 26
Pontargothi ....15 H 28
Pontarsais ....15 H 28
Pontefract ....44 Q 22
Ponteland ....56 O 18
Ponterwyd ....25 I 26
Pontesbury ....34 L 26
Pontllyfni ....32 G 24
Pontlottyn ....18 K 28
Pontlyfni ....32 G 24
Pontneddfechan ....17 J 28
Pontrhydfendigaid ....25 I 27
Pontrhydygroes ....25 I 26
Pontrilas ....26 L 28
Pontsticill ....17 J 28
Pontyates ....15 H 28
Pontyberem ....15 H 28
Pontyclun ....17 J 29
Pontycymer ....17 J 29
Pontypool / Pontypwl ....18 K 28
Pontypridd ....17 J 29
Pontypwl / Pontypool ....18 K 28
Poole ....9 O 31
Poole Bay ....9 O 31
Poolewe ....78 D 10
Pooley Bridge ....55 L 20
Pooltiel (Loch) ....76 Z 11
Porlock ....17 J 30
Port Appin ....65 D 14
Port Askaig ....58 B 16
Port Bannatyne ....59 E 16
Port Carlisle ....54 K 19
Port Charlotte ....58 A 16
Port Driseach ....65 E 16
Port Ellen ....58 B 17
Port Erin ....46 F 21
Port-Eynon ....15 H 29
Port-Eynon Point ....15 H 29
Port Gaverne ....3 F 32
Port Glasgow ....66 F 16
Port Henderson ....77 C 10
Port Isaac ....3 F 32
Port Lamont ....59 E 16
Port Logan ....52 F 19
Port Mòr ....71 B 13
Port of Menteith ....67 H 15
Port of Ness ....83 B 8
Port Ramsay ....65 D 14
Port St. Mary ....46 F 21
Port Talbot ....17 I 29
Port William ....52 G 19
Portavadie ....59 E 16
Portchester ....10 Q 31
Portencross ....59 F 16
Portesham ....5 M 31
Portgordon ....80 K 11
Portgower ....85 I 9
Porth ....17 J 29
Porth Neigwl
   or Hell's Mouth ....32 G 25
Porth Tywyn /Burry Port ....15 H 28
Porthaethwy /
   Menai Bridge ....40 H 23
Porthcawl ....17 I 29
Porthcothan ....2 E 32
Porthcurno ....2 D 33
Porthgwarra ....2 C 33
Porthkerry ....17 K 29
Porthleven ....2 E 33
Porthmadog ....33 H 25
Porthtowan ....2 E 33
Porthyrhyd ....15 H 28
Portinnisherrich ....65 E 15
Portishead ....18 L 29
Portknockie ....80 L 10
Portland (Isle of) ....8 M 32
Portlethen ....75 N 12
Portmahomack ....79 I 10
Portmeirion ....33 H 25
Portnacroish ....72 D 14
Portnaguran ....83 B 9
Portnahaven ....58 A 16
Portnalong ....77 A 12
Portobello ....68 K 16
Portreath ....2 E 33
Portree ....77 B 11
Portscatho ....3 F 33
Portskerra ....85 I 8
Portskewett ....18 L 29
Portslade ....11 T 31
Portslogan ....52 E 19
Portsmahomack ....2 D 33
Portsmouth ....10 Q 31
Portsoy ....81 L 10
Portuairk ....71 B 13

Postbridge ....4 I 32
Potten End ....21 S 28
Potter Heigham ....39 Y 25
Potter Street ....21 U 28
Potterhanworth ....37 S 24
Potterne ....19 N 30
Potters Bar ....21 T 28
Potton ....29 T 27
Poughill ....6 G 31
Poulshot ....19 N 29
Poulton ....19 O 28
Poulton-le-Fylde ....42 L 22
Poundstock ....6 G 31
Powburn ....63 O 17
Powerstock ....8 L 31
Powick ....27 N 27
Powis ....34 K 26
Powmill ....68 J 15
Poynings ....11 T 31
Poynton ....43 N 23
Praa Sands ....2 D 33
Prawle Point ....4 I 33
Praze-an-Beeble ....2 E 33
Prees ....34 M 25
Preesall ....48 L 22
Prendwick ....63 O 17
Prescot ....42 L 23
Prestatyn ....41 J 22
Prestbury *Cheltenham* ....27 N 28
Prestbury *Macclesfield* ....43 N 24
Presteigne ....26 K 27
Preston
   East Riding of Yorks. ....45 T 22
Preston *Kent* ....23 X 30
Preston *Lancs.* ....42 L 22
Preston *Rutland* ....36 R 26
Preston *West Sussex* ....11 S 31
Preston Candover ....10 Q 30
Preston Capes ....28 Q 27
Prestonpans ....69 L 16
Prestonpans ....69 L 16
Prestwich ....42 N 23
Prestwick ....60 G 17
Prestwood ....20 R 28
Prickwillow ....30 V 26
Priest Island ....83 D 10
Priest Weston ....34 K 26
Princes Risborough ....20 R 28
Princethorpe ....28 P 26
Princetown ....4 I 32
Priors Marston ....28 Q 27
Probus ....3 F 33
Prosen (Glen) ....74 K 13
Prudhoe ....56 O 19
Puckeridge ....29 U 28
Pucklechurch ....19 M 29
Pucks Gutter ....23 X 30
Puddletown ....9 M 31
Pudsey ....43 P 22
Pulborough ....11 S 31
Pulford ....34 L 24
Pulham ....9 M 31
Pulham Market ....31 X 26
Puncheston ....24 F 28
Puncknowle ....7 H 30
Punchardon ....7 H 30
Purbeck (Isle of) ....9 N 32
Purbrook ....10 Q 31
Puriton ....8 L 30
Purleigh ....22 V 28
Purley ....20 Q 29
Purse Caundle Manor ....9 M 31
Purston Jaglin ....43 P 22
Purton ....19 O 29
Putsborough ....6 H 30
Pwllheli ....32 G 25
Pyecombe ....11 T 31
Pyle ....17 I 29
Pylle ....8 M 30

Quainton ....28 R 28
Quantock Hills ....8 K 30
Quarff ....87 Q 3
Quarr ....10 Q 31
Quatt ....27 M 26
Quedgeley ....19 N 28
Queen Camel ....8 M 30
Queen Elizabeth
   Forest Park ....67 G 15
Queenborough ....22 W 29
Queensbury ....43 O 22
Queensferry ....34 K 24
Quendon ....30 U 28
Quenington ....19 O 28
Quina Brig ....84 E 9
Quines's Hill ....46 G 21
Quinish Point ....71 B 14
Quiraing ....77 B 11

Quoich (Loch) ....72 E 12
Quorndon ....36 Q 25
Quothquan ....61 J 17

R

Raasay (Island of) ....77 B 11
Raasay (Sound of) ....77 B 11
Raasay Ho ....77 B 11
Rachub ....33 H 24
Rackenford ....7 J 31
Rackwick ....86 J 7
Radcliffe ....42 N 23
Radcliffe-on-Trent ....36 Q 25
Radlett ....21 T 28
Radley ....20 Q 28
Radnor Forest ....26 K 27
Radstock ....18 M 30
Radyr ....18 K 29
Rafford ....80 J 11
Raglan ....18 L 28
Ragley Hall ....27 O 27
Rainford ....42 L 23
Rainham ....22 V 29
Rainworth ....42 N 23
Rait ....68 K 14
Ramasaig ....76 Z 11
Rampisham ....8 M 31
Rampside ....47 K 21
Rampton ....44 R 24
Ramsbottom ....42 N 23
Ramsbury ....19 P 29
Ramsey *Cambs.* ....29 T 26
Ramsey *Isle of Man* ....46 G 21
Ramsey Bay ....46 G 21
Ramsey Island ....14 D 28
Ramsey St. Mary's ....29 T 26
Ramsgate ....23 Y 29
Ramsgill-in-Nidderdale ....49 O 21
Ranby ....44 Q 24
Randwick ....19 N 28
Ranfurly ....60 G 16
Rangeworthy ....18 M 29
Ranish ....82 A 9
Rankinston ....60 G 17
Rannoch (Loch) ....73 H 13
Rannoch Moor ....73 F 14
Rannoch Sta ....73 G 13
Ranskill ....44 Q 23
Ranton ....35 N 25
Ranworth ....39 Y 25
Rapness ....87 L 6
Rappach ....84 F 10
Ratby ....36 Q 26
Rathen ....81 O 11
Rathmell ....49 N 21
Ratho ....68 J 16
Ratlinghope ....34 L 26
Rattlesden ....30 W 27
Rattray ....68 K 14
Rattray Head ....81 O 11
Raunds ....29 S 26
Ravenglass ....47 J 20
Ravenscar ....51 S 20
Ravensthorpe ....28 Q 27
Ravenstone ....36 P 25
Ravenstonedale ....49 M 20
Ravensworth ....49 O 20
Rawcliffe ....44 R 22
Rawmarsh ....44 P 23
Rawtenstall ....42 N 22
Rayleigh ....22 V 29
Rayne ....30 V 28
Read ....42 M 22
Reading ....20 R 29
Rearsby ....36 Q 25
Reay ....85 I 8
Reay Forest ....84 F 9
Reculver ....23 X 29
Red Wharf Bay ....40 H 23
Redbourn ....21 S 28
Redbourne ....44 S 23
Redbridge
   London Borough ....21 U 29
Redcar ....57 Q 20
Redcliff Bay ....18 L 29
Reddding ....67 I 16
Redditch ....27 O 27
Redesmouth ....55 N 18
Redford ....69 L 14
Redhill *North Somerset* ....18 L 29
Redhill
   Reigate and Banstead .....21 T 30
Redisham ....31 Y 26
Redmarley d'Abitot ....27 M 28
Redmarshall ....57 P 20
Redmire ....49 O 21
Redpoint ....77 C 11
Redruth ....2 E 33

Redwick ....18 L 29
Reedham ....39 Y 26
Reekie Linn ....74 K 13
Reepham ....45 S 24
Reeth ....49 O 20
Regarby ....46 G 20
Reiff ....83 D 9
Reigate ....21 T 30
Reighton ....51 T 21
Reiss ....86 K 8
Relubbus ....2 D 33
Rempstone ....36 Q 25
Rendcomb ....19 O 28
Rendham ....31 Y 27
Renfrew ....60 G 16
Renish Point ....76 Z 10
Renishaw ....44 P 24
Rennington ....63 O 17
Renton ....66 G 16
Renwick ....55 M 19
Repton ....36 P 25
Rescobie ....75 L 14
Resipole ....72 C 13
Resolven ....17 I 28
Resort (Loch) ....82 Z 9
Restalrig ....68 K 16
Reston ....63 N 16
Restormel Castle ....3 G 32
Retford ....44 R 24
Rettendon ....22 V 29
Reynoldston ....15 H 29
Rhaeadr / Rhayader ....25 J 27
Rhaeadr Ddu ....33 I 25
Rhandirmwyn ....25 I 27
Rhayader / Rhaeadr ....25 J 27
Rheidol (Vale of) ....25 I 26
Rhenigidale ....82 Z 10
Rhian ....84 G 9
Rhiconich ....84 F 8
Rhigos ....17 J 28
Rhilochan ....85 H 9
Rhinns of Galloway (The) ....52 E 19
Rhinns of Kells ....53 G 18
Rhondda ....17 J 29
Rhoose ....17 J 29
Rhos ....17 I 28
Rhoscolyn ....40 G 23
Rhoscrowther ....14 E 28
Rhosllanerchrugog ....34 K 24
Rhosmaen ....25 I 28
Rhosneigr ....40 G 23
Rhossili ....15 H 29
Rhostyllen ....34 K 24
Rhosybol ....40 G 22
Rhu ....66 F 15
Rhuddlan ....41 J 23
Rhum ....71 A 13
Rhuthun / Ruthin ....34 K 24
Rhyd-Ddu ....33 H 24
Rhydaman / Ammanford ....15 I 28
Rhydcymerau ....15 H 27
Rhydd ....27 N 27
Rhyddhywel ....25 J 26
Rhydowen ....15 H 27
Rhyl ....41 J 23
Rhymmi / Rhymney ....18 K 28
Rhymney / Rhymmi ....18 K 28
Rhynie ....80 L 12
Ribble (River) ....49 N 22
Ribblesdale ....49 N 21
Ribchester ....42 M 22
Riber Castle ....36 P 24
Riccall ....44 Q 22
Riccarton ....60 G 17
Richards Castle ....26 L 27
Richborough ....23 X 30
Richmond ....49 O 20
Richmond-upon-Thames
   London Borough ....21 T 29
Rickarton ....75 N 13
Rickmansworth ....21 S 29
Ridgeway Cross ....27 M 27
Ridgeway Path (The) ....20 P 29
Ridsdale ....55 N 18
Rievaulx Abbey ....50 Q 21
Rigg ....77 B 11
Rigside ....61 I 17
Rillington ....51 R 21
Rimington ....49 N 22
Rimsdale (Loch) ....85 H 9
Ringford ....53 H 19
Ringmer ....11 U 31
Ringshall ....30 W 27
Ringstead
   East Northamptonshire ....29 S 26
Ringstead *King's Lynn*
   and West Norfolk ....38 V 25

A B C D E F G H I J K L M N O **P** **Q** **R** S T U V W X Y Z

A B C D E F G H I J K L M N O P Q R S T U V W X Y Z

Ringwood ....9 O 31
Ringwould ....23 Y 30
Rinnes (Glen) ....80 K 11
Rinns of Islay ....58 A 16
Rinns Point ....58 A 16
Ripe ....12 U 31
Ripley Derbs. ....36 P 24
Ripley North Yorks. ....50 P 21
Ripley Surrey ....21 S 30
Riplingham ....44 S 22
Ripon ....50 P 21
Rippingale ....37 S 25
Ripponden ....43 O 22
Risabus ....58 B 17
Risby ....30 V 27
Risca ....18 K 29
Risegate ....37 T 25
Riseley ....29 S 27
Rishton ....42 M 22
Risplith ....50 P 21
Ristol (Isle) ....83 D 9
Roadside of Kinneff ....75 N 13
Roag (Loch) ....77 A 11
Roag (Loch) ....82 Z 9
Roan of Graigoch ....60 F 18
Roberton
  Dumfries and Galloway ....61 I 17
Roberton
  Scottish Borders ....62 L 17
Robertsbridge ....12 V 31
Robin Hood's Bay ....51 S 20
Roby ....42 L 23
Rocester ....35 O 25
Rochdale ....43 N 23
Roche ....3 F 32
Rochester ....22 V 29
Rochester
  Northumberland ....63 N 18
Rochford ....22 W 29
Rock ....3 F 32
Rockcliffe *Cumbria* ....54 K 19
Rockcliffe
  Dumfries and Galloway ....53 I 19
Rockfield ....18 L 28
Rockingham ....28 R 26
Rode ....19 N 30
Rode Heath ....35 N 24
Rodel ....76 Z 10
Rodmel ....11 U 31
Rodney Stoke ....18 L 30
Rogart ....85 H 9
Rogerstone ....18 K 29
Rogiet ....18 L 29
Rokeby Hall ....49 O 20
Rolleston *Notts.* ....36 R 24
Rolleston-on-Dove *Staffs.* ...35 P 25
Rolvenden ....12 V 30
Romannobridge ....61 J 16
Romiley ....43 N 23
Romney Marsh ....12 W 30
Romsey ....10 P 31
Romsley ....27 N 26
Rona (Island of) ....77 C 11
Ronaldsway ....46 G 21
Ronas Voe ....87 P 2
Ronay ....76 Y 11
Rookhope ....55 N 19
Roos ....45 T 22
Rootpark ....61 I 16
Ropley ....10 Q 30
Ropsley ....37 S 25
Rora ....81 O 11
Rora Head ....86 J 7
Rosedale Abbey ....50 R 20
Rosehearty ....81 N 10
Rosemarket ....16 F 28
Rosemarkie ....79 H 11
Rosewell ....61 K 16
Rosgill ....48 L 20
Roshven ....71 C 13
Rosley ....54 K 19
Roslin ....61 K 16
Rosliston ....35 P 25
Rosneath ....66 F 15
Ross
  Berwick-upon-Tweed ....63 O 17
Ross
  Dumfries and Galloway ....53 H 19
Ross of Mull ....64 B 15
Ross-on-Wye ....26 M 28
Rossall Point ....48 K 22
Rossett ....34 L 24
Rosudgeon ....2 D 33
Rosyth ....68 J 15
Rothbury ....63 O 18
Rothbury Forest ....63 O 18
Rotherfield ....12 U 30

Rotherham ....43 P 23
Rothersthorpe ....28 R 27
Rothes ....80 K 11
Rothesay ....59 E 16
Rothienorman ....81 M 11
Rothiesholm ....87 M 6
Rothwell *Leeds.* ....43 P 22
Rothwell *Northamp.* ....28 R 26
Rotterspury ....28 R 27
Rottingdean ....11 T 31
Roughburn ....73 F 13
Roughsike ....55 L 18
Roughton ....39 X 25
Rounton ....50 P 20
Rousay ....86 K 6
Routh ....45 S 22
Rowardennan Lodge ......66 G 15
Rowington ....27 O 27
Rowland's Castle ....10 R 31
Rowland's Gill ....56 O 19
Rownhams ....10 P 31
Rowsley ....35 P 24
Roxburgh ....62 M 17
Roxwell ....22 V 28
Roy (Glen) ....72 F 13
Royal Leamington Spa ...28 P 27
Royal Military Academy ...20 R 29
Royal Tunbridge Wells ...12 U 30
Roybridge ....72 F 13
Roydon *Essex* ....21 U 28
Roydon *Norfolk* ....31 X 26
Royston *Herts.* ....29 T 27
Royston *South Yorks.* ....43 P 23
Royton ....43 N 23
Ruabon ....34 K 25
Ruan High Lanes ....3 F 33
Ruan Minor ....2 E 34
Ruardean ....18 M 28
Rubbha na Faing ....58 A 16
Rubha a' Mhail ....64 B 16
Rubha Còigeach ....83 D 9
Rubha Dubh ....70 Z 14
Rubha Hunish ....77 A 10
Rubha na h-Easgainne ...71 B 12
Rubha Réidh ....77 C 10
Rubha Suisnish ....71 B 12
Rubh'an Dùnain ....71 A 12
Rudbaxton ....24 F 28
Ruddington ....36 Q 25
Rudgeway ....18 M 29
Rudgwick ....11 S 30
Rudha Ban ....70 Y 12
Rudston ....51 T 21
Rufford Old Hall ....42 L 23
Rufforth ....50 Q 22
Rugby ....28 Q 26
Rugeley ....35 O 25
Rumburgh ....31 Y 26
Rumney ....18 K 29
Runcorn ....42 L 23
Runswick Bay ....50 R 20
Runtaleave ....74 K 13
Runwell ....22 V 29
Rushall ....19 O 30
Rushden ....29 S 27
Ruskington ....37 S 24
Rusland ....48 K 21
Rusper ....11 T 30
Ruspidge ....18 M 28
Rustington ....11 S 31
Ruswarp ....51 S 20
Rutherglen ....60 H 16
Ruthin / Rhuthun ....34 K 24
Ruthven *Aberdeenshire* ...80 L 11
Ruthven *Angus* ....74 K 14
Ruthven *Highland* ....79 I 11
Ruthven (Loch) ....79 H 12
Ruthven Barracks ....73 H 12
Ruthwell ....54 J 19
Rutland Water ....37 S 26
Ruyton
  of the Eleven Towns ....34 L 25
Ryal ....56 O 18
Rycote ....20 Q 28
Rydal ....48 L 20
Ryde ....10 Q 31
Rye ....12 W 31
Ryhall ....37 S 25
Ryhill ....43 P 23
Ryhope ....57 P 19
Ryton ....56 O 19

S

Sabden ....42 M 22
Sacriston ....56 P 19

Sadberge ....50 P 20
Saddell ....59 D 17
Saddell Bay ....59 D 17
Sadgill ....48 L 20
Saffron Walden ....30 U 27
Saham Toney ....38 W 26
St. Abbs ....63 N 16
St. Abb's Head ....63 N 16
St. Agnes ....2 E 33
St. Albans ....21 T 28
St. Aldhelm's Head ....9 N 32
St. Andrews ....69 L 14
St. Ann's ....54 J 18
St. Ann's Head ....14 E 28
St. Arvans ....18 L 29
St. Asaph ....41 J 23
St. Athan ....17 J 29
St. Austell ....3 F 32
St. Bees ....47 J 20
St. Bees Head ....47 J 20
St. Blazey ....3 F 32
St. Boswells ....62 M 17
St. Breock ....3 F 32
St. Breward ....3 F 32
St. Briavels ....18 M 28
St. Brides ....14 E 28
St. Bride's Bay ....14 E 28
St. Brides Major ....17 J 29
St. Brides-Super-Ely ......17 K 29
St. Bridge-Wentlooge .....18 K 29
St. Buryan ....2 D 33
St. Catherine's Point ......10 Q 32
St. Clears / Sanclêr ....15 G 28
St. Cleer ....3 G 32
St. Columb Major ....3 F 32
St. Combs ....81 O 11
St. Cyrus ....75 M 13
St. David's / Tyddewi .....14 E 28
St. David's Head ....14 D 28
St. Day ....2 E 33
St. Dennis ....3 F 32
St. Dogmaels ....15 F 27
St. Dominick ....3 H 32
St. Donats ....17 J 29
St. Endellion ....3 F 32
St. Erth ....2 D 33
St. Ewe ....3 F 33
St. Fagans ....18 K 29
St. Fergus ....81 O 11
St. Fillans ....67 H 14
St. Florence ....15 F 28
St. Gennys ....6 G 31
St. Germans ....3 H 32
St. Giles ....7 H 31
St. Giles-on-the-Heath ....6 H 31
St. Govan's Head ....16 F 29
St. Harmon ....25 J 26
St. Helen Auckland ....56 O 20
St. Helens *I.O.W.* ....10 Q 31
St. Helens *Merseyside* ....42 L 23
St. Helier *Jersey* 5
St. Ishmael's ....14 E 28
St. Issey ....3 F 32
St. Ive ....3 G 32
St. Ives *Cambs.* ....29 T 27
St. Ives *Cornwall* ....2 D 33
St. John's ....46 G 21
St. John's Chapel ....55 N 19
St. John's Loch ....86 J 8
St. Jude ....46 G 20
St. Just ....2 C 33
St. Just in Roseland ....2 F 33
St. Keverne ....2 E 33
St. Kew ....3 F 32
St. Leonards *Dorset* ....9 O 31
St. Leonards *East Sussex* ...12 V 31
St. Mabyn ....3 F 32
St. Magnus Bay ....87 P 2
St. Margaret's at Cliffe ...23 Y 30
St. Margaret's Bay ....23 Y 30
St. Margaret's Hope ....87 L 7
St. Mark's ....46 G 21
St. Martin's ....34 K 25
St. Mary in the Marsh .....12 W 30
St. Mary's *Orkney Islands* ...86 L 7
St. Mary's
  Perth and Kinross ......73 I 14
St. Mary's-Bay ....13 W 30
St. Mary's-Hoo ....22 V 29
St. Mary's Loch ....61 K 17
St. Mawes ....2 E 33
St. Mawgan ....3 F 32
St. Mellion ....3 H 32
St. Mellons ....18 K 29
St. Merryn ....3 F 32
St. Michael Penkevil ....2 E 33
St. Michael's Mount ....2 D 33

St. Michaels-on-Wyre ....42 L 22
St. Minver ....3 F 32
St. Monans ....69 L 15
St. Neot ....3 G 32
St. Neots ....29 T 27
St. Nicholas *Pembrokes* ...14 E 28
St. Nicholas
  Vale of Glamorgan ....17 K 29
St. Nicholas-at-Wade ......23 X 29
St. Ninian's Isle ....87 P 4
St. Osyth ....23 X 28
St. Patrick's Isle ....46 F 21
St. Paul's Walden ....29 T 28
St. Peter Port *Guernsey* ...5
St. Peter's ....23 Y 29
St. Pool ....4 I 33
St. Stephen ....3 F 32
St. Teath ....3 F 32
St. Tudwal's Islands ......32 G 25
St. Tudy ....3 F 32
St. Vigeans ....69 M 14
St. Wenn ....3 F 32
St. Weonards ....26 L 28
Salcombe ....4 I 33
Salcombe Regis ....5 K 31
Sale ....42 N 23
Salehurst ....12 V 31
Salen *Argyll and Bute* .....65 C 14
Salen *Highland* ....71 C 13
Salford ....42 N 23
Salfords ....21 T 30
Salhouse ....39 Y 25
Saline ....68 J 15
Salisbury ....9 O 30
Salisbury Plain ....19 O 30
Sallachy
  Ben More Assynt ....84 G 9
Sallachy
  near Kyle of Lochalsh ....78 D 12
Scamblesby ....45 T 24
Saltash ....3 H 32
Saltburn ....79 H 10
Saltburn-by-the-Sea ......57 R 20
Saltcoats ....59 F 17
Salter ....48 M 21
Saltfleet ....45 U 23
Saltford ....18 M 29
Salthouse ....38 X 25
Saltney ....34 L 24
Salton ....50 R 21
Samala ....76 X 11
Samlesbury Old Hall .....42 M 22
Sampford Courtenay .....7 I 31
Sampford Peverell ....7 J 31
Sanaigmore ....58 A 16
Sanclêr / St. Clears ....15 G 28
Sancreed ....2 D 33
Sancton ....44 S 22
Sand Side ....47 K 21
Sanda Island ....59 D 18
Sanday *Highland* ....71 A 12
Sanday *Orkney Islands* ...87 M 6
Sandbach ....35 M 24
Sandbank ....66 F 16
Sandbanks ....9 O 31
Sandend ....80 L 10
Sandford *Eden* ....49 M 20
Sandford *Mid Devon* ......7 J 31
Sandford *North Somerset* ...18 L 30
Sandford
  South Lanarkshire ......60 H 17
Sandford Orcas ....8 M 31
Sandgate ....13 X 30
Sandgreen ....53 H 19
Sandhaven ....81 N 10
Sandhurst *Berks.* ....20 R 29
Sandhurst *Kent* ....12 V 30
Sandleigh ....20 Q 28
Sandlins ....31 Y 27
Sandness ....87 P 3
Sandon
  North Hertfordshire ......29 T 28
Sandon *Stafford* ....35 N 25
Sandown ....10 Q 32
Sandray ....70 X 13
Sandridge ....21 T 28
Sandringham House ....38 V 25
Sandsend ....51 R 20
Sandwell ....27 O 26
Sandwich ....23 Y 30
Sandwick *Eden* ....48 L 20
Sandwick *Eilean Siar* .....76 Y 11
Sandwick *Shetland Islands* ...87 Q 4
Sandwood Loch ....84 E 8
Sandy ....29 T 27
Sandygate ....46 G 20
Sandyhills ....53 I 19

Sanna ....71 B 13
Sanquhar ....61 I 17
Santon Downham ....30 W 26
Santon Head ....46 G 21
Sapperton ....19 N 28
Saracan's Head ....37 T 25
Sarclet ....86 K 8
Sarisbury ....10 Q 31
Sark *Channel I.* 5
Sarn Meyllteyrn ....32 G 25
Sarre ....23 X 29
Satley ....56 O 19
Satterthwaite ....48 K 21
Sauchen ....75 M 12
Saughall ....42 L 24
Saughtree ....62 L 18
Saundersfoot ....15 F 28
Saunderton ....20 R 28
Sawbridgeworth ....21 U 28
Sawrey ....48 L 20
Sawston ....29 U 27
Sawtry ....29 T 26
Saxby ....36 R 25
Saxilby ....44 S 24
Saxlingham Nethergate ...39 X 26
Saxmundham ....31 Y 27
Saxtead Green ....31 X 27
Scadavay (Loch) ....76 Y 11
Scaddle (Glen) ....72 D 13
Scafell Pikes ....47 K 20
Scagglethorpe ....50 R 21
Scalasaig ....64 B 15
Scalby ....51 S 21
Scaldwell ....44 Q 24
Scalford ....36 R 25
Scalloway ....87 Q 3
Scalpay *Highland* ....77 C 12
Scalpay *Western Isles* ....77 A 10
Scampton ....44 S 24
Scaniport ....79 H 11
Scapa Flow ....86 K 7
Scarba ....65 C 15
Scarborough ....51 S 21
Scarcliffe ....44 Q 24
Scardroy ....78 F 11
Scarfskerry ....86 K 8
Scarisbrick ....42 L 23
Scarista ....76 Y 10
Scarp ....82 Y 9
Scavaig (Loch) ....71 B 12
Scawby ....44 S 23
Schiehallion ....73 H 13
Scilly (Isles of) ....2 B 34
Scone Palace ....68 J 14
Scopwick ....37 S 24
Scoraig ....83 D 10
Scorton ....50 P 20
Scotby ....55 L 19
Scotch-Corner ....49 P 20
Scothern ....45 S 24
Scotlandwell ....68 K 15
Scotney ....12 V 30
Scotstown ....72 D 13
Scotter ....44 S 23
Scotton *Harrogate* ....50 P 21
Scotton *Richmondshire* ...49 O 20
Scottow ....39 Y 25
Scourie ....84 E 8
Scousburgh ....87 Q 4
Scrabster ....85 J 8
Scraptoft ....36 Q 26
Scredington ....37 S 25
Scridain (Loch) ....64 B 14
Scruton ....50 P 21
Sculthorpe ....38 W 25
Scunthorpe ....44 S 23
Sea Palling ....39 Y 25
Seaford ....12 U 31
Seaforth (Loch) ....82 Z 10
Seaforth Head ....82 A 9
Seagrave ....36 Q 25
Seaham ....57 P 19
Seale ....21 R 30
Sealga (Loch na) ....78 D 10
Seamer *Hambleton* ....50 Q 20
Seamer *Scarborough* .....51 S 21
Seamill ....59 F 16
Seasalter ....23 X 29
Seascale ....47 J 20
Seaton *Allerdale* ....53 J 20
Seaton *East Devon* ....5 K 31
Seaton Carew ....57 Q 20
Seaton Delaval ....56 P 18
Seaton Delaval Hall ....56 P 18
Seaton Ross ....44 R 22
Seaton Sluice ....56 P 18

Seave Green ....50 Q 20
Seaview ....10 Q 31
Sebergham ....54 L 19
Sedbergh ....49 M 21
Sedgebrook ....36 R 25
Sedgefield ....56 P 20
Sedgley ....27 N 26
Sedlescombe ....12 V 31
Seend ....19 N 29
Seething ....39 Y 26
Seighford ....35 N 25
Seil (Isle of) ....65 D 15
Seilich (Loch an t-) ....73 H 13
Selattyn ....34 K 25
Selborne ....10 R 30
Selby ....44 Q 22
Selker Bay ....47 J 21
Selkirk ....62 L 17
Sellafirth ....87 Q 1
Sellindge ....13 W 30
Selmeston ....12 U 31
Selsey ....10 R 31
Selston ....36 Q 24
Selworthy ....17 J 30
Semley ....9 N 30
Senghenydd ....18 K 29
Sennen ....2 C 33
Sennybridge ....25 J 28
Sessay ....50 Q 21
Settle ....49 N 21
Seven Sisters
  East Sussex ....12 U 31
Seven Sisters
  Neath and Port Talbot ...17 I 28
Sevenhampton ....27 O 28
Sevenoaks ....22 U 30
Severn (River) ....27 M 28
Severn Bridge ....18 M 29
Severn Stoke ....27 N 27
Sgibacleit (Loch) ....82 A 9
Sgiwen ....17 I 29
Sgurr Mór ....78 E 10
Shader ....82 A 8
Shaftesbury ....9 N 30
Shalbourne ....20 P 29
Shaldon ....4 J 32
Shalfleet ....10 P 31
Shalford ....21 S 30
Shandon ....66 F 15
Shanklin ....10 Q 32
Shap ....48 L 20
Shapinsay ....87 L 6
Shapwick ....8 L 30
Shardlow ....36 P 25
Shardston ....43 P 23
Sharnbrook ....29 S 27
Sharnford ....28 Q 26
Sharperton ....63 N 18
Sharpness ....18 M 28
Shavington ....34 M 24
Shaw *Gtr. Mches.* ....43 N 23
Shaw *West Berkshire* .....20 Q 29
Shaw *Wilts.* ....19 N 29
Shawbost ....82 Z 9
Shawbury ....34 M 25
Shawford ....10 Q 30
Shawhead ....53 I 18
Shebbear ....6 H 31
Shebster ....85 I 8
Sheepwash ....6 H 31
Sheepy Magna ....36 P 26
Sheering ....22 U 28
Sheerness ....22 W 29
Sheffield ....43 P 23
Sheffield Park ....11 T 31
Shefford ....29 S 27
Sheldon ....19 N 29
Sheldon Manor ....19 N 29
Sheldwich ....22 W 30
Shell or Sealg (Loch) .....82 A 9
Shelley ....43 O 23
Shellingford ....20 P 29
Shelsley Beauchamp .....27 M 27
Shelton *Rushcliffe* ....36 R 25
Shelton *South Norfolk* ...31 X 26
Shelton Lock ....36 P 25
Shelve ....34 L 26
Shenley Church End ......28 R 27
Shenstone ....27 O 26
Shenval ....80 K 11
Shepley ....43 O 23
Sheppey (Isle of) ....22 W 29
Shepreth ....29 U 27
Shepshed ....36 Q 25
Shepton Mallet ....18 M 30
Sherborne *Cotswold* ......19 O 28
Sherborne *West Dorset* ...8 M 31
Sherborne St. John ....20 Q 30
Sherburn *Durham* ....56 P 19

Sherburn Ryedale ...... 51 S 21
Sherburn-in-Elmet ...... 44 Q 22
Shere ...... 21 S 30
Sherfield English ...... 9 P 31
Sheriff Hutton ...... 50 Q 21
Sheriffhales ...... 35 M 25
Sheringham ...... 39 X 25
Sherington ...... 28 R 27
Shernborne ...... 38 V 25
Sherston ...... 19 N 29
Sherwood Forest ...... 36 Q 24
Shetland Islands 87
Shevington ...... 42 L 23
Shiant (Sound of) ...... 82 A 10
Shiant Island ...... 82 A 10
Shiel (Glen) ...... 72 D 12
Shiel (Loch) ...... 72 D 13
Shieldaig Loch Gairloch ...... 78 C 10
Shieldaig Loch Torridon ...... 78 D 11
Shieldaig (Loch) ...... 78 C 11
Shieldhill ...... 67 I 16
Shifnal ...... 35 M 25
Shilbottle ...... 63 O 17
Shildon ...... 56 P 20
Shillay ...... 76 W 11
Shillingford ...... 7 J 30
Shillingstone ...... 9 N 31
Shillington ...... 29 S 28
Shilton Rugby ...... 28 P 26
Shilton West Oxfordshire ...... 19 P 28
Shimpling ...... 31 X 26
Shin (Loch) ...... 84 G 9
Shiney Row ...... 56 P 19
Shinfield ...... 20 R 29
Shipdham ...... 38 W 26
Shiplake ...... 20 R 29
Shipley Salop ...... 35 N 26
Shipley West Yorks. ...... 43 O 22
Shipston-on-Stour ...... 27 P 27
Shipton Bridgnorth ...... 26 M 26
Shipton Cotswold ...... 27 O 28
Shipton Hambleton ...... 50 Q 21
Shipton Moyne ...... 19 N 29
Shipton-under-Wychwood ...... 19 P 28
Shiptonthorpe ...... 44 R 22
Shira (Lochan) ...... 66 F 14
Shirebrook ...... 36 Q 24
Shiremoor ...... 56 P 18
Shirenewton ...... 18 L 29
Shirley Derbyshire ...... 35 O 25
Shirley Solihull ...... 27 O 26
Shoadoxhurst ...... 12 W 30
Shobdon ...... 26 L 27
Shoeburyness ...... 22 W 29
Shoreham ...... 11 T 31
Shorne ...... 22 V 29
Shotesham ...... 39 X 26
Shotley Bridge ...... 56 O 19
Shotley Gate ...... 31 X 28
Shottenden ...... 22 W 30
Shottermill ...... 10 R 30
Shotton Colliery ...... 57 P 19
Shotts ...... 61 I 16
Shouldham ...... 38 V 26
Shrewsbury ...... 34 L 25
Shrewton ...... 19 O 30
Shrivenham ...... 19 P 29
Shuna Sound ...... 65 D 15
Shurdington ...... 27 N 28
Shurrery ...... 85 J 8
Sibbertoft ...... 28 Q 26
Sibford Ferris ...... 28 P 27
Sible Hedingham ...... 30 V 28
Sibsey ...... 37 U 24
Sidbury ...... 5 K 31
Siddington ...... 19 O 28
Siddlington ...... 43 N 24
Sidford ...... 5 K 31
Sidinish ...... 76 Y 11
Sidlaw Hills ...... 68 K 14
Sidlesham ...... 10 R 31
Sidmouth ...... 5 K 31
Sighthill ...... 68 K 16
Sileby ...... 36 Q 25
Silecroft ...... 47 K 21
Silkstone ...... 43 P 23
Silloth ...... 54 J 19
Silsden ...... 49 O 22
Silver End ...... 30 V 28
Silverdale Lancaster ...... 48 L 21
Silverdale
  Newcastle-under-Lyme ...... 35 N 24
Silverstone ...... 28 Q 27
Silverstone Circuit ...... 28 Q 27
Silverton ...... 7 J 31
Simonburn ...... 55 N 18
Simonsbath ...... 7 I 30

Sinclair's Bay ...... 86 K 8
Sinclairston ...... 60 G 17
Singleton Chichester ...... 10 R 31
Singleton Fylde ...... 42 L 22
Sionascaig (Loch) ...... 84 E 9
Sissinghurst ...... 12 V 30
Sithney ...... 2 E 33
Sittingbourne ...... 22 W 29
Sixpenny Handley ...... 9 N 31
Skara Brae ...... 86 J 6
Skares ...... 60 H 17
Skeabost ...... 77 B 11
Skegness ...... 38 V 24
Skellingthorpe ...... 44 S 24
Skelmanthorpe ...... 43 P 23
Skelmersdale ...... 42 L 23
Skelmorlie ...... 59 F 16
Skelpick ...... 85 H 8
Skelton Cleveland ...... 50 R 20
Skelton Cumbria ...... 55 L 19
Skelwith Bridge ...... 48 K 20
Skene ...... 75 M 12
Skene (Loch of) ...... 75 M 12
Skenfrith ...... 26 L 28
Skeroblingarry ...... 59 D 17
Skidby ...... 44 S 22
Skiddaw ...... 54 K 20
Skigersta ...... 83 B 8
Skilgate ...... 7 J 30
Skillington ...... 37 S 25
Skinburness ...... 54 J 19
Skipness ...... 59 D 16
Skipport (Loch) ...... 76 Y 12
Skipsea ...... 51 T 22
Skipton ...... 49 N 22
Skipton-on-Swale ...... 50 P 21
Skipwith ...... 44 R 22
Skirlaugh ...... 45 T 22
Skirling ...... 61 J 17
Skirwith ...... 55 M 19
Skirza ...... 86 K 8
Skokholm Island ...... 14 E 28
Skomer Island ...... 14 E 28
Skye (Isle of) ...... 77 B 12
Slaggyford ...... 55 M 19
Slaidburn ...... 49 M 22
Slaithwaite ...... 43 O 23
Slamannan ...... 67 I 16
Slapin (Loch) ...... 71 B 12
Slapton ...... 4 J 33
Sleaford ...... 37 S 25
Sleagill ...... 48 M 20
Sleat (Sound of) ...... 71 C 12
Sledmere ...... 51 S 21
Sleekburn ...... 56 P 18
Sleights ...... 51 S 20
Slickly ...... 86 K 8
Sligachan ...... 77 B 12
Sligachan (Loch) ...... 77 B 12
Slimbridge ...... 19 M 28
Slindon ...... 11 S 31
Slingsby ...... 50 R 21
Slochd ...... 79 I 12
Slockavullin ...... 65 D 15
Sloy (Loch) ...... 66 F 15
Slumbay ...... 78 D 11
Slyne ...... 48 L 21
Smailholm ...... 62 M 17
Smailholm Tower ...... 62 M 17
Small Dole ...... 11 T 31
Small Hythe ...... 12 W 30
Smallfield ...... 11 T 30
Smarden ...... 12 W 30
Smart'Hill ...... 12 U 30
Smedmore ...... 9 N 32
Smithfield ...... 55 L 19
Snaefell ...... 46 G 21
Snainton ...... 51 S 21
Snaith ...... 44 Q 22
Snape ...... 31 Y 27
Snetterton Circuit ...... 30 W 26
Snettisham ...... 38 V 25
Snitterfield ...... 27 O 27
Snizort (Loch) ...... 77 A 11
Snodland ...... 22 V 30
Snowdon / Yr Wyddfa ...... 33 H 24
Snowdonia National Park ...... 33 I 24
Snowshill ...... 27 O 27
Soa ...... 70 Z 14
Soa Island ...... 64 A 15
Soar (River) ...... 36 Q 25
Soay ...... 71 B 12
Soay Sound ...... 71 B 12
Soham ...... 30 V 26

Solent (The) ...... 10 Q 31
Solihull ...... 27 O 26
Sollas ...... 76 X 11
Solva ...... 14 E 28
Solway Firth ...... 53 J 19
Somerby ...... 36 R 25
Somercotes ...... 36 P 24
Somerford Keynes ...... 19 O 29
Somersham
  Huntingdonshire ...... 29 U 26
Somersham Mid Suffolk ...... 31 X 27
Somerton Norfolk ...... 39 Y 25
Somerton Oxon. ...... 28 Q 28
Somerton Somerset ...... 8 L 30
Sompting ...... 11 S 31
Sonning Common ...... 20 R 29
Sopley ...... 9 O 31
Sorbie ...... 52 G 19
Sorisdale ...... 71 A 13
Sorn ...... 60 H 17
Sortat ...... 86 K 8
Soulby ...... 49 M 20
Sound (The) ...... 4 H 32
Sourhope ...... 63 N 17
South-Alloa ...... 67 I 15
South Balloch ...... 60 G 18
South Brent ...... 4 I 32
South Cairn ...... 52 E 19
South Carrine ...... 59 C 18
South Cave ...... 44 S 22
South Cerney ...... 19 O 28
South Charlton ...... 63 O 17
South Croxton ...... 36 R 25
South Downs ...... 11 R 31
South Elmsall ...... 44 Q 23
South Esk (River) ...... 75 L 13
South Ferriby ...... 44 S 22
South Foreland ...... 23 Y 30
South Glendale ...... 70 Y 12
South Hanningfield ...... 22 V 29
South Harris ...... 76 Z 10
South Harris Forest ...... 82 Z 10
South Hayling ...... 10 R 31
South-Heighton ...... 11 U 31
South Hetton ...... 56 P 19
South Kelsey ...... 45 S 23
South Killingholme ...... 45 T 23
South Kirkby ...... 44 Q 23
South Kyme ...... 37 T 24
South Lancing ...... 11 T 31
South Leverton ...... 44 R 24
South Lopham ...... 30 X 26
South-Marston ...... 19 O 29
South Mary Bourne ...... 20 P 30
South Mimms ...... 21 T 28
South Molton ...... 7 I 30
South Morar ...... 72 C 13
South Moreton ...... 20 Q 29
South Newington ...... 28 P 28
South-Newton ...... 9 O 30
South Normanton ...... 36 P 24
South Ockendon ...... 22 U 29
South Otterington ...... 50 P 21
South Oxhey ...... 21 S 29
South Petherton ...... 8 L 31
South Petherwin ...... 3 G 32
South Queensferry ...... 68 J 16
South Rauceby ...... 37 S 25
South Raynham ...... 38 W 25
South Ronaldsay ...... 87 L 7
South Shields ...... 56 P 19
South Shore ...... 42 K 22
South Stack ...... 40 F 23
South Stainley ...... 50 P 21
South Tawton ...... 4 I 31
South Thoresby ...... 45 U 24
South Uist ...... 70 X 12
South Walls ...... 86 K 7
South Warnborough ...... 20 R 30
South Witham ...... 37 S 25
South Woodham Ferrers ...... 22 V 29
South Wootton ...... 38 V 25
South Wraxall ...... 19 N 29
South Zeal ...... 4 I 31
Southam
  Stratford-on-Avon ...... 28 P 27
Southam Tewkesbury ...... 27 N 28
Southampton ...... 10 P 31
Southborough ...... 12 U 30
Southbourne Dorset ...... 9 O 31
Southbourne West Sussex ...... 10 R 31
Southend ...... 59 D 18
Southend-on-Sea ...... 22 W 29
Southerness ...... 53 J 19
Southery ...... 38 V 26
Southill ...... 29 T 27
Southminster ...... 22 W 29

Southport ...... 42 K 23
Southrop ...... 19 O 28
Southsea ...... 10 Q 31
Southwaite ...... 55 L 19
Southwater ...... 11 S 30
Southwell ...... 36 R 24
Southwick
  East Northamptonshire ...... 29 S 26
Southwick Sunderland ...... 56 P 19
Southwick West Sussex ...... 11 T 31
Southwick Wilts. ...... 19 N 30
Southwick Widley ...... 10 Q 31
Southwold ...... 31 Z 27
Sowerby Bridge ...... 43 O 22
Spalding ...... 37 T 25
Spaldwick ...... 29 S 26
Spanish Head ...... 46 F 21
Sparkford ...... 8 M 30
Spaxton ...... 8 K 30
Spean (Glen) ...... 73 F 13
Spean Bridge ...... 72 F 13
Speeton ...... 51 T 21
Speldhurst ...... 12 U 30
Spelsbury ...... 28 P 28
Spelve (Loch) ...... 65 C 14
Spennymoor ...... 56 P 19
Spey (River) ...... 73 G 12
Spey Bay ...... 80 K 10
Speymouth Forest ...... 80 K 11
Spilsby ...... 37 U 24
Spinningdale ...... 79 H 10
Spithead ...... 10 Q 31
Spittal Dumfries
  and Galloway ...... 52 G 19
Spittal Highland ...... 85 J 8
Spittal Northumb. ...... 63 O 16
Spittal Pembrokeshire /
  Sir Benfro ...... 24 F 28
Spittal of Glenshee ...... 74 J 13
Spixworth ...... 39 X 25
Spofforth ...... 50 P 22
Spondon ...... 36 P 25
Spooner Row ...... 39 X 26
Spott ...... 69 M 16
Spreyton ...... 7 I 31
Spridlington ...... 44 S 23
Springfield ...... 68 K 15
Springholm ...... 53 I 18
Sproatley ...... 45 T 22
Sprotbrough ...... 44 Q 23
Sproughton ...... 31 X 27
Sprouston ...... 62 M 17
Sprowston ...... 39 X 26
Spurn Head ...... 45 U 23
Sronlairig Lodge ...... 73 G 12
Sronphadruig Lodge ...... 73 H 13
Stack (Loch) ...... 84 F 8
Stack Island ...... 70 Y 12
Stack Rocks ...... 16 E 29
Staffa ...... 64 A 14
Staffin Bay ...... 77 B 11
Stafford ...... 35 N 25
Stagsden ...... 29 S 27
Staincross ...... 43 P 23
Stainforth North Yorks. ...... 49 N 21
Stainforth South Yorks. ...... 44 Q 23
Stainton ...... 55 L 20
Stainton-le-Vale ...... 45 T 23
Stair Allerdale ...... 54 K 20
Stair South Ayrshire ...... 60 G 17
Staithes ...... 50 R 20
Stakeford ...... 56 P 18
Stalbridge ...... 9 M 31
Stalham ...... 39 Y 25
Stalisfield ...... 22 W 30
Stalling Busk ...... 49 N 21
Stallingborough ...... 45 T 23
Stalmine ...... 48 L 22
Stalybridge ...... 43 N 23
Stamford ...... 37 S 26
Stamford Bridge ...... 50 R 22
Stamfordham ...... 56 O 18
Stanbridge ...... 29 S 28
Standford-in-the-Vale ...... 20 P 29
Standing Stones ...... 82 Z 9
Standish ...... 42 M 23
Standon ...... 29 U 28
Stane ...... 61 I 16
Stanford ...... 13 X 30
Stanford-le-Hope ...... 22 V 29
Stanford-on-Avon ...... 28 Q 26
Stanghow ...... 50 R 20
Stanhoe ...... 38 W 25

Stanhope ...... 55 N 19
Stanion ...... 29 S 26
Stanley Durham ...... 56 O 19
Stanley
  Perthshire and Kinross ...... 68 J 14
Stanley Wakefield. ...... 43 P 22
Stanmer Park ...... 11 T 31
Stannington ...... 43 P 23
Stansted Abbotts ...... 21 U 28
Stansted Mountfitchet ...... 30 U 28
Stanton ...... 30 W 27
Stanton Harcourt ...... 20 P 28
Stanton Long ...... 26 M 26
Stanton-upon-Hine-Heath ...... 34 M 25
Stanway ...... 27 O 28
Stanwell ...... 21 S 29
Stanwick ...... 29 S 27
Staple Fitzpaine ...... 8 K 31
Stapleford Melton ...... 36 R 25
Stapleford Notts. ...... 36 Q 25
Stapleford Wilts. ...... 9 O 30
Staplehurst ...... 22 V 30
Starcross ...... 4 J 32
Start Point ...... 4 J 33
Startforth ...... 49 O 20
Stathern ...... 36 R 25
Staughton Highway ...... 29 S 27
Staunton Forest of Dean ...... 27 N 28
Staunton Monmouthshire /
  Sir Fynwy ...... 18 M 28
Staveley Cumbria ...... 48 L 20
Staveley Derbs. ...... 43 P 24
Staxigoe ...... 86 K 8
Staxton ...... 51 S 21
Staylittle ...... 25 J 26
Steart ...... 18 K 30
Stebbing ...... 30 V 28
Stedham ...... 10 R 31
Steep ...... 10 R 31
Steeple ...... 22 W 28
Steeple Ashton ...... 19 N 30
Steeple Aston ...... 28 Q 28
Steeple Barton ...... 28 P 28
Steeple Bumpstead ...... 30 V 27
Steeple Claydon ...... 28 R 28
Steeple Langford ...... 9 O 30
Steeple Morden ...... 29 T 27
Steeton ...... 49 O 22
Stelling Minnis ...... 23 X 30
Stenhousemuir ...... 67 I 15
Stenness Orkney Islands ...... 86 K 7
Stenness Shetland Islands ...... 87 P 2
Stenton ...... 69 M 16
Steppingley ...... 29 S 27
Stevenage ...... 29 T 28
Stevenston ...... 60 F 17
Steventon ...... 20 Q 29
Stewartby ...... 29 S 27
Stewarton ...... 60 G 16
Stewkley ...... 28 R 28
Steyning ...... 11 T 31
Steynton ...... 16 E 28
Stichill ...... 62 M 17
Sticker ...... 3 F 33
Sticklepath ...... 4 I 31
Stickney ...... 37 U 24
Stiffkey ...... 38 W 25
Stilligarry ...... 76 X 12
Stillingfleet ...... 44 Q 22
Stillington Hambleton ...... 50 Q 21
Stillington
  Stockton-on-Tees ...... 56 P 20
Stilton ...... 29 T 26
Stirling ...... 67 I 15
Stithians ...... 2 E 33
Stob Choire Claurigh ...... 72 F 13
Stobo ...... 61 K 17
Stobs Castle ...... 62 L 17
Stock ...... 22 V 29
Stockbridge ...... 10 P 30
Stocke Talmage ...... 20 Q 28
Stockland ...... 8 K 31
Stockland Bristol ...... 18 K 30
Stockport ...... 43 N 23
Stocksbridge ...... 43 P 23
Stocksfield ...... 56 O 19
Stockton Heath ...... 42 M 23
Stockton-on-Tees ...... 50 P 20
Stockton-on-Teme ...... 27 M 27
Stockton on the Forest ...... 50 R 22
Stoer ...... 83 D 9
Stogumber ...... 7 K 30
Stogursey ...... 18 K 30
Stoke ...... 22 V 29
Stoke Albany ...... 28 R 26
Stoke Ash ...... 31 X 27
Stoke-by-Nayland ...... 30 W 28

Stoke Climsland ...... 3 H 32
Stoke Fleming ...... 4 J 33
Stoke Gabriel ...... 4 J 32
Stoke Goldington ...... 28 R 27
Stoke Hammond ...... 28 R 28
Stoke Lacy ...... 26 M 27
Stoke Lyne ...... 28 Q 28
Stoke Mandeville ...... 20 R 28
Stoke-on-Trent ...... 35 N 24
Stoke Orchard ...... 27 N 28
Stoke Poges ...... 21 S 29
Stoke-St. Mary ...... 8 K 31
Stoke-St. Michael ...... 18 M 30
Stoke St. Milborough ...... 26 M 26
Stoke sub Hamdon ...... 8 L 31
Stokeham ...... 44 R 24
Stokenchurch ...... 20 R 29
Stokenham ...... 4 I 33
Stokesay ...... 26 L 26
Stokesley ...... 50 Q 20
Stone Bucks. ...... 20 R 28
Stone Staffs. ...... 35 N 25
Stone Edge ...... 36 P 24
Stonehaugh ...... 55 N 18
Stonehaven ...... 75 N 13
Stonehenge ...... 9 O 30
Stonehouse Glos. ...... 19 N 28
Stonehouse
  South Lanarkshire ...... 61 I 16
Stoneleigh ...... 28 P 26
Stonesfield ...... 20 P 28
Stoney Cross ...... 9 P 31
Stoney Stanton ...... 36 Q 26
Stoneybridge ...... 76 X 12
Stoneykirk ...... 52 F 19
Stoneywood ...... 75 N 12
Stony Stratford ...... 28 R 27
Stornoway ...... 82 A 9
Storr (The) ...... 77 B 11
Storrington ...... 11 S 31
Stort (River) ...... 29 U 28
Stotfold ...... 29 T 27
Stottesdon ...... 26 M 26
Stoughton ...... 10 R 31
Stoul ...... 72 C 13
Stoulton ...... 27 N 27
Stour (River)
  English Channel ...... 9 N 31
Stour (River) North Sea ...... 30 V 27
Stour (River) R. Severn ...... 27 N 26
Stourbridge ...... 27 N 26
Stourhead House ...... 9 N 30
Stourport-on-Severn ...... 27 N 26
Stourton Caundle ...... 9 M 31
Stourton ...... 27 N 27
Stow ...... 62 L 16
Stow-on-the-Wold ...... 27 O 28
Stowbridge ...... 38 V 26
Stowe-by-Chartley ...... 35 O 25
Stowe School ...... 28 Q 27
Stowmarket ...... 30 W 27
Stowupland ...... 30 X 27
Straad ...... 59 E 16
Strachan ...... 75 M 12
Strachur ...... 66 E 15
Stradbroke ...... 31 X 27
Stradishall ...... 30 V 27
Stradsett ...... 38 V 26
Straloch ...... 74 J 13
Stranraer ...... 52 E 19
Strata Florida Abbey ...... 25 I 27
Stratfield Saye ...... 20 Q 29
Stratford St. Mary ...... 30 W 28
Stratford-upon-Avon ...... 27 O 27
Strath Brora ...... 85 H 9
Strath Dearn ...... 79 I 11
Strath Halladale ...... 85 I 8
Strath Isla ...... 80 K 11
Strath More ...... 78 E 10
Strath Mulzie ...... 78 F 10
Strath of Kildonan ...... 85 I 9
Strath Oykel ...... 84 F 10
Strath Skinsdale ...... 85 H 9
Strath Tay ...... 68 J 14
Strathallan ...... 67 I 15
Strathan ...... 72 E 13
Strathardle ...... 74 J 13
Strathaven ...... 60 H 16
Strathbeg (Loch of) ...... 81 O 11
Strathblane ...... 67 H 16
Strathbogie ...... 80 L 11
Strathbraan ...... 67 I 14
Strathcanaird ...... 84 E 10
Strathcarron ...... 78 D 11
Strathcoil ...... 65 C 14
Strathconon ...... 78 F 11
Strathconon Forest ...... 78 F 11

A
B
C
D
E
F
G
H
I
J
K
L
M
N
O
P
Q
R
S
T
U
V
W
X
Y
Z

Tullibody ....67 I 15
Tullymurdoch ....74 K 14
Tumble ....15 H 28
Tummel (Loch) ....73 I 13
Tunstall
  East Riding of Yorkshire ...45 T 22
Tunstall Staffs. ....35 N 24
Tunstall Suffolk ....31 Y 27
Tur Langton ....36 R 26
Turnberry ....59 F 18
Turnditch ....35 P 24
Turret
  (Loch and Reservoir) ...67 I 14
Turriff ....81 M 11
Turvey ....29 S 27
Tusker Rock ....17 I 29
Tutbury ....35 O 25
Tuxford ....44 R 24
Twatt ....86 K 6
Tweed (River) ....61 J 17
Tweeddale ....61 J 17
Tweedmouth ....63 N 16
Tweedsmuir Hills ....61 J 17
Twemlow Green ....35 N 24
Twickenham ....21 S 29
Two Dales ....35 P 24
Twyford Berks. ....20 R 29
Twyford Hants. ....10 Q 30
Twyford Leics. ....36 R 25
Twynholm ....53 H 19
Twynllanan ....25 I 28
Tydd-St. Giles ....37 U 25
Tydd St. Mary ....37 U 25
Tyddewi / St. David's ....14 E 28
Tyldesley ....42 M 23
Tylorstown ....17 J 29
Tyne (River) ....56 P 19
Tynehead ....62 L 16
Tynemouth ....56 P 18
Tynewydd ....17 J 28
Tynron ....53 I 18
Tythegston ....17 J 29
Tytherington ....18 M 29
Tywardreath ....3 F 32
Tywi (River) ....25 I 27
Tywyn ....33 H 26

U
Ubiey ....18 L 30
Uckfield ....11 U 31
Uddingston ....60 H 16
Udimore ....12 V 31
Uffculme ....7 K 31
Uffington ....37 S 26
Ufford ....31 Y 27
Ugadale Bay ....59 D 17
Ugborough ....4 I 32
Ugbrooke House ....4 J 32
Ugthorpe ....50 R 20
Uig Highland ....77 A 11
Uig Western Isles ....82 Y 9
Uisg (Loch) ....65 C 14
Uiskevagh (Loch) ....76 Y 11
Ulbster ....86 K 8
Ulceby East Lindsey ....45 U 24
Ulceby North Lincolnshire ...45 T 23
Ulcombe ....22 V 30
Uldale ....54 K 19
Uley ....19 N 28
Ulgham ....56 P 18
Ullapool ....78 E 10
Ulleskelf ....44 Q 22
Ullesthorpe ....28 Q 26
Ullinish ....77 A 11
Ullock ....54 J 20
Ullswater ....48 L 20
Ulpha ....47 K 21
Ulsta ....87 Q 2
Ulva ....64 B 14
Ulverston ....48 K 21
Unapool ....84 E 9
Union Mills ....46 G 21
Unst ....87 R 1
Upavon ....19 O 30
Upchurch ....22 V 29
Uphall ....68 J 16
Uphill ....18 L 30
Upleadon ....27 M 28
Uplyme ....5 L 31
Upottery ....8 K 31
Upper Arley ....27 M 26
Upper Badcall ....84 E 9
Upper Beeding ....11 T 31
Upper Bighouse ....85 I 8
Upper Broughton ....36 R 25
Upper Chapel ....25 J 27
Upper Chute ....20 P 30

Upper Dicker ....12 U 31
Upper Hale ....20 R 30
Upper Heyford ....28 Q 28
Upper Hindhope ....62 M 17
Upper Knockando ....80 J 11
Upper Loch Torridon ....78 D 11
Upper Poppleton ....50 Q 22
Upper Sandaig ....72 D 12
Upper Tean ....35 O 25
Uppertown ....86 K 7
Uppingham ....36 R 26
Upton Dorset ....9 N 31
Upton Notts. ....36 R 24
Upton Vale of White Horse ...20 Q 29
Upton Wakefield ....44 Q 23
Upton West Somerset ....7 J 30
Upton Grey ....20 Q 30
Upton-in-Gordano ....18 L 29
Upton Magna ....34 M 25
Upton Noble ....9 M 30
Upton Scudamore ....19 N 30
Upton-upon-Severn ....27 N 27
Upwell ....38 U 26
Upwood ....29 T 26
Urchfont ....19 O 30
Ure (River) ....50 Q 21
Urigill (Loch) ....84 F 9
Urmston ....42 M 23
Urquhart ....80 K 11
Urquhart (Glen) ....79 G 11
Urquhart Castle ....79 G 12
Urrahag (Loch) ....82 A 8
Ushaw Moor ....56 P 19
Usk / Brynbuga ....18 L 28
Usk (River) ....18 K 28
Uttoxeter ....35 O 25
Uyea ....87 R 2
Uyeasound ....87 R 1

V
Vallay Strand ....76 X 11
Valle Crucis ....34 K 25
Valley ....40 G 23
Valtos ....82 Z 9
Vatersay ....70 X 13
Vatten ....77 A 11
Ve Skerries ....87 O 2
Venachar (Loch) ....67 H 15
Ventnor ....10 Q 32
Verham Dean ....20 P 30
Verulamium ....21 S 28
Verwood ....9 O 31
Veryan ....3 F 33
Veyatie (Loch) ....84 E 9
Vindolanda ....55 M 19
Voe ....87 Q 2
Voil (Loch) ....67 G 14
Vowchurch ....26 L 27
Vyrnwy (Lake) ....33 J 25

W
Waddesdon ....20 R 28
Waddingham ....44 S 23
Waddington Lancs. ....42 M 22
Waddington Lincs. ....37 S 24
Wadebridge ....3 F 32
Wadhurst ....12 U 30
Wag ....85 I 9
Wainfleet All Saints ....38 U 24
Wainstalls ....43 O 22
Wakefield ....43 P 22
Wakerley ....37 S 26
Wakes Colne ....30 W 28
Walberswick ....31 Y 27
Walcott ....37 T 24
Walden Head ....49 N 21
Walderslade ....22 V 29
Waldringfield ....31 X 27
Waldron ....12 U 31
Walesby ....44 R 24
Walford ....34 L 25
Walgherton ....34 M 24
Walgrave ....28 R 26
Walkden ....42 M 23
Walkeringham ....44 R 23
Walkern ....29 T 28
Wall ....35 O 26
Wallace Monument ....67 I 15
Wallasey ....42 K 23
Wallend ....22 W 29
Wallingford ....20 Q 29
Wallington House ....56 O 18
Walls ....87 P 3
Wallsend ....56 P 18
Wallyford ....69 K 16
Walney (Isle of) ....47 K 21
Walpole ....31 Y 27

Walpole St. Andrew ....38 U 25
Walpole St. Peter ....38 U 25
Walsall ....35 O 26
Walsden ....43 N 22
Walsham le Willows ....30 W 27
Walshford ....50 P 22
Walston ....61 J 16
Waltham Kent ....23 X 30
Waltham North East Lincs. ...45 T 23
Waltham Abbey ....21 U 28
Waltham Forest
  London Borough ....21 T 29
Waltham-on-the-Wolds ...36 R 25
Walton Carlisle ....55 L 19
Walton Leeds ....50 Q 22
Walton Powys ....26 K 27
Walton-East ....24 F 28
Walton-in-Gordano ....18 L 29
Walton-le-Dale ....42 M 22
Walton-on-Thames ....21 S 29
Walton-on-the-Naze ....31 X 28
Walton-Upon-Trent ....35 O 25
Walworth ....49 P 20
Wanborough ....19 O 29
Wandsworth
  London Borough ....21 T 29
Wangford ....31 Y 26
Wanlockhead ....61 I 17
Wansford
  East Riding of Yorkshire ...51 S 22
Wansford Peterborough ...37 S 26
Wanstrow ....9 M 30
Wantage ....20 P 29
Wappenham ....28 Q 27
Warboys ....29 T 26
Warbstow ....6 G 31
Warcop ....49 M 20
Wardington ....28 Q 27
Wardour Castle ....9 N 30
Ware ....21 T 28
Wareham ....9 N 31
Wargrave ....20 R 29
Wark near Coldstream ...63 N 17
Wark near Hexham ...55 N 18
Wark Forest ....55 M 18
Warkworth ....63 P 17
Warley ....27 O 26
Warlingham ....21 T 30
Warmington
  East Northamptonshire ...29 S 26
Warmington
  Stratford-on-Avon ....28 P 27
Warminster ....19 N 30
Warmsworth ....44 Q 23
Warmwell ....9 M 31
Warnborough ....20 R 30
Warnford ....10 Q 30
Warnham ....11 S 30
Warren ....43 N 24
Warren (The) ....13 X 30
Warrington ....42 M 23
Warsash ....10 Q 31
Warslow ....35 O 24
Warsop ....36 Q 24
Warter ....51 R 22
Warton Alnwick ....63 O 18
Warton near Morecambe ...48 L 21
Warton near Preston ...42 L 22
Warwick ....27 P 27
Warwick Bridge ....55 L 19
Wasbister ....86 K 6
Wasdale Head ....47 K 20
Wash (The) ....38 U 25
Washington
  Tyne and Wear ....56 P 19
Washington West Sussex ....11 S 31
Wast Water ....47 K 20
Watchet ....17 K 30
Watchfield ....19 P 29
Watchgate ....48 L 20
Water Orton ....27 O 26
Waterbeach ....30 U 27
Waterbeck ....54 K 18
Watergate Bay ....2 E 32
Waterhead ....74 L 13
Waterhouses ....35 O 24
Wateringbury ....22 V 30
Waterlooville ....10 Q 31
Waternish Point ....77 A 11
Waters Upton ....34 M 25
Waterside ....60 G 17
Waterstein ....76 Z 11
Watford Daventry ....28 Q 27
Watford Watford ....21 S 29
Wath ....50 P 21
Wath-upon-Dearne ....44 P 23
Watlington ....20 Q 29

Watten ....85 K 8
Watton Breckland ....38 W 26
Watton
  East Riding of Yorkshire ...51 S 22
Watton at Stone ....29 T 28
Waunfawr ....33 H 24
Waveney (River) ....31 Y 26
Waverton Allerdale ....54 K 19
Waverton Chester ....34 L 24
Wawne ....45 S 22
Wear (River) ....56 O 20
Weardale ....55 N 19
Weasenham St. Peter ...38 W 25
Weaver (River) ....34 M 24
Weaverthorpe ....51 S 21
Wedmore ....18 L 30
Wednesbury ....35 N 26
Wednesfield ....35 N 26
Weedon-Bec ....28 Q 27
Week St. Mary ....6 G 31
Weeley ....31 X 28
Weem ....73 I 14
Weeting ....30 V 26
Weeton ....42 L 22
Welburn ....50 R 21
Welby ....37 S 25
Welcombe ....6 G 31
Welford Daventry ....28 Q 26
Welford Stratford-on-Avon ...27 O 27
Welford West Berkshire ...20 P 29
Welham Green ....21 T 28
Well ....50 P 21
Welland ....27 N 27
Welland (River) ....37 T 25
Wellesbourne ....27 P 27
Wellingborough ....29 R 27
Wellington
  Herefordshire ....26 L 27
Wellington Salop ....34 M 25
Wellington Somerset ....8 K 31
Wellow
  Bath and North East ...19 M 30
Wellow
  Newark and Sherwood ...36 R 24
Wells ....18 M 30
Wells-next-the-Sea ....38 W 25
Wells of Ythan ....81 M 11
Welney ....38 U 26
Welsh Newton ....26 L 28
Welshampton ....34 L 25
Welshpool / Trallwng ...34 K 26
Welton Allerdale ....54 K 19
Welton Daventry ....28 Q 27
Welton West Lindsey ...44 S 24
Welton-le-Wold ....45 T 23
Welwyn ....21 T 28
Welwyn Garden City ...21 T 28
Wem ....34 L 25
Wembdon ....8 K 30
Wembley ....21 T 29
Wembury ....4 H 33
Wembworthy ....7 I 31
Wemyss Bay ....59 F 16
Wendens Ambo ....30 U 27
Wendlebury ....28 Q 28
Wendover ....20 R 28
Wendron ....2 E 33
Wenlock Edge ....26 L 26
Wennington ....48 M 21
Wensley ....49 O 21
Wensleydale ....49 O 21
Wentbridge ....44 Q 23
Wentnor ....26 L 26
Wentworth ....43 P 23
Wenvoe ....18 K 29
Weobley
  Hereford and Worcester ...26 L 27
Wereham ....38 V 26
Werrington ....6 G 32
West Alvington ....4 I 33
West Auckland ....56 O 20
West-Barns ....69 M 16
West Bay ....8 M 32
West Bergholt ....30 W 28
West-Bradenham ....38 W 26
West Bridgford ....36 Q 25
West Bromwich ....27 O 26
West-Buckland
  North Devon ....7 I 30
West-Buckland
  Taunton Deane ....8 K 31
West Butterwick ....44 R 23
West Calder ....61 J 16
West Camel ....8 M 30
West Charleton ....4 I 33
West Chevington ....63 P 18
West Chiltington ....11 S 31

West-Chinnock ....8 L 31
West Coker ....8 L 31
West Dean ....9 P 30
West-Dereham ....38 V 26
West Down ....7 H 30
West End ....10 Q 31
West Farleigh ....22 V 30
West-Felton ....34 L 25
West-Firle ....11 U 31
West Geirinish ....76 X 11
West-Grinstead ....11 T 31
West Hanningfield ....22 V 28
West Harptree ....18 M 30
West Heath ....20 R 30
West Heslerton ....51 S 21
West-Hill ....5 K 31
West Hoathly ....11 T 30
West-Huntspill ....18 L 30
West Kilbride ....59 F 16
West Kingsdown ....22 U 29
West Kirby ....41 K 22
West Langwell ....85 H 9
West Lavington ....19 O 30
West Linton ....61 J 16
West Loch Roag ....82 Z 9
West Loch Tarbert
  Argyll and Bute ....59 D 16
West Loch Tarbert
  Western Isles ....82 Z 10
West Looe ....3 G 32
West Lulworth ....9 N 32
West Lutton ....51 S 21
West Malling ....22 V 30
West Malvern ....27 M 27
West Meon ....10 Q 30
West Mersea ....22 W 28
West Moors ....9 O 31
West-Overton ....19 O 29
West Putford ....6 G 31
West-Quantoxhead ....8 K 30
West Rainton ....56 P 19
West Runton ....39 X 25
West Stafford ....9 M 31
West Strathan ....84 G 8
West Tanfield ....50 P 21
West Tarbert ....59 D 16
West Thorney ....10 R 31
West Town ....18 L 29
West-Tytherley ....9 P 30
West Walton ....37 U 25
West Wellow ....9 P 31
West Wickam ....21 T 29
West Winch ....38 V 25
West Wittering ....10 R 31
West Witton ....49 O 21
West Woodburn ....55 N 18
West Wycombe ....20 R 28
Westbourne ....10 R 31
Westbury Cheshire ....34 L 25
Westbury Wilts. ....19 N 30
Westbury-on-Severn ...19 M 28
Westcliff ....22 W 29
Westcott ....21 S 30
Westenhanger ....13 X 30
Wester Ross ....78 D 11
Westerdale Highland ...85 J 8
Westerdale Scarborough ...50 R 20
Westerham ....21 U 30
Westerleigh ....18 M 29
Western Cleddau ....24 E 28
Westfield Highland ....85 J 8
Westfield Rother ....12 V 31
Westfield West Lothian ...67 I 16
Westgate-on-Sea ....23 Y 29
Westham ....12 U 31
Westhoughton ....42 M 23
Westleton ....31 Y 27
Westmeston ....11 T 31
Westmill ....29 T 28
Westnewton ....54 J 19
Weston Devon ....8 K 31
Weston
  North Hertfordshire ...29 T 28
Weston South Holland ...37 T 25
Weston
  South Northamptonshire ...28 Q 27
Weston Staffs. ....35 N 25
Weston-by-Welland ....28 R 26
Weston Favell ....28 R 27
Weston-on-the-Green ...28 Q 28
Weston-on-Trent ....36 P 25
Weston Rhyn ....34 K 25
Weston-super-Mare ....18 L 29
Weston Turville ....20 R 28
Weston-under-Lizard ...35 N 25
Weston-under-Penyard ...26 M 28
Westonbirt ....19 N 29

Westonzoyland ....8 L 30
Westray ....86 K 6
Westruther ....62 M 16
Westward ....54 K 19
Westward Ho ....6 H 30
Westwood ....19 N 30
Wetheral ....55 L 19
Wetherby ....50 P 22
Wetheringsett ....31 X 27
Wethersfield ....30 V 28
Wetwang ....51 S 21
Wey (River) ....10 R 30
Weybourne ....39 X 25
Weybridge ....21 S 29
Weyhill ....20 P 30
Weymouth ....8 M 32
Whaddon ....28 R 28
Whaley Bridge ....43 O 24
Whalley ....42 M 22
Whalsay ....87 R 2
Whalton ....56 O 18
Whaplode ....37 T 25
Whaplode Drove ....37 T 25
Wharfe (River) ....44 Q 22
Wharfedale ....49 O 22
Whatlington ....12 V 31
Whatsandwell ....36 P 24
Whauphill ....52 G 19
Whaw ....49 N 20
Wheathampstead ....21 T 28
Wheatley Notts. ....44 R 23
Wheatley Oxon. ....20 Q 28
Wheatley Hill ....56 P 19
Wheaton Aston ....35 N 25
Wheldrake ....50 R 22
Whepstead ....30 W 27
Whernside ....48 M 21
Wherwell ....10 P 30
Whickham ....56 O 19
Whimple ....7 J 31
Whipsnade ....21 S 28
Whissendine ....36 R 25
Whissonsett ....38 W 25
Whitburn South Tyneside ...57 P 19
Whitburn West Lothian ...61 I 16
Whitby ....51 S 20
Whitchurch
  Basingstoke and Deane ...20 P 30
Whitchurch
  Bath and N.E. Somerset ..18 M 29
Whitchurch Bucks. ....28 R 28
Whitchurch
  Caerdydd / Cardiff ...18 K 29
Whitchurch Devon ....4 H 32
Whitchurch
  Heref. and Worc. ...18 M 28
Whitchurch Oxon. ....20 Q 29
Whitchurch Salop ....34 L 25
White Coomb ....61 K 17
White Horse Hill ....20 P 29
White Scarcaves ....49 M 21
White Waltham ....20 R 29
Whitebridge ....73 G 12
Whitecairns ....75 N 12
Whitchurch Canonicorum ...5 L 31
Whitefield ....42 N 23
Whitehall ....87 M 6
Whitehaven ....47 J 20
Whitehill ....10 R 30
Whitehills ....81 M 10
Whitehouse
  Aberdeenshire ....75 M 12
Whitehouse
  Argyll and Bute ....59 D 16
Whitekirk ....69 M 15
Whiten Head ....84 G 8
Whiteness Sands ....79 I 10
Whiteparish ....9 P 30
Whiterashes ....81 N 12
Whitermire ....79 I 11
Whitesand Bay Cornwall ...2 C 33
Whitesand Bay
  Pembrokes ....14 E 28
Whiteshill ....19 N 28
Whiteside ....55 M 18
Whitewell ....49 M 22
Whitewreath ....80 K 11
Whitfield Dover ....23 X 30
Whitfield
  South Northamptonshire ...28 Q 27
Whitfield Tynedale ....55 M 19
Whitgift ....44 R 22
Whithorn ....52 G 19
Whiting Bay ....59 E 17
Whitland ....15 G 28
Whitley ....20 R 29
Whitley Bay ....56 P 18

Whitley Bridge ... 44 Q 22
Whitley Chapel ... 55 N 19
Whitminster ... 19 N 28
Whitmore ... 35 N 25
Whitnash ... 28 P 27
Whitsand Bay ... 3 H 32
Whitstable ... 23 X 29
Whitstone ... 6 G 31
Whittingham ... 63 O 17
Whittington Derbs. ... 43 P 24
Whittington King's Lynn
  and West Norfolk ... 38 V 26
Whittington Lancaster ... 48 M 21
Whittington Shrops. ... 34 L 25
Whittle le Woods ... 42 M 22
Whittlebury ... 28 R 27
Whittlesey ... 37 T 26
Whittlesford ... 29 U 27
Whitton North Lincolnshire .. 44 S 22
Whitton Powys ... 26 K 27
Whitton Suffolk ... 31 X 27
Whittonstall ... 56 O 19
Whitwell Derbs. ... 44 Q 24
Whitwell I.O.W. ... 10 Q 32
Whitwell-on-the-Hill ... 50 R 21
Whitwick ... 36 P 25
Whitworth ... 43 N 23
Whixall ... 34 L 25
Whygate ... 55 M 18
Wiay Highland ... 77 A 11
Wiay Western Isles ... 76 Y 11
Wibtoft ... 28 Q 26
Wick Bro Morgannwg /
  The Vale of Glamorgan .... 17 J 29
Wick Highland ... 86 K 8
Wick South Glos. ... 19 M 29
Wicken Cambs. ... 28 R 27
Wicken Northants. ... 30 U 27
Wickenby ... 45 S 24
Wickersley ... 44 Q 23
Wickford ... 22 V 29
Wickham ... 10 Q 31
Wickham Market ... 31 Y 27
Wickhambrook ... 30 V 27
Wickwar ... 19 M 29
Widdrington ... 63 P 18
Wide Open ... 56 P 18
Widecombe-in-the-Moor ... 4 I 32
Wideford Hill Cairn ... 86 K 7
Widemouth Bay ... 6 G 31
Widford ... 21 U 28
Widnes ... 42 L 23
Wigan ... 42 M 23
Wiggenhall
  St. Mary Magdalen ... 38 V 25
Wigglesworth ... 49 N 21
Wight (Isle of) ... 10 P 32
Wighton ... 38 W 25
Wigmore Herefordshire ... 26 L 27
Wigmore Medway ... 22 V 29
Wigston ... 36 Q 26
Wigton ... 54 K 19
Wigtown ... 52 G 19

Wigtown Bay ... 53 H 19
Wilberfoss ... 50 R 22
Wilcot ... 19 O 29
Wild Animal Kingdom ... 29 S 28
Wilkhaven ... 79 I 10
Wilkieston ... 61 J 16
Willand ... 7 J 31
Willenhall Coventry ... 28 P 26
Willenhall Walsall ... 35 N 26
Willerby ... 45 S 22
Willersey ... 27 O 27
Willingdon ... 12 U 31
Willingham ... 29 U 27
Willingham Forest ... 45 T 23
Willington Beds. ... 29 S 27
Willington Derbs. ... 35 P 25
Willington Durham ... 56 O 19
Williton ... 7 K 30
Willoughby ... 28 Q 27
Wilmcote ... 27 O 27
Wilmington East Essex ... 12 U 31
Wilmington Kent ... 22 U 29
Wilmslow ... 43 N 24
Wiloughby ... 45 U 24
Wilpshire ... 42 M 22
Wilsford ... 37 S 25
Wilstead ... 29 S 27
Wilton ... 9 O 30
Wimbledon ... 21 T 29
Wimblington ... 29 U 26
Wimborne Minster ... 9 O 31
Wimborne St. Giles ... 9 O 31
Wincanton ... 9 M 30
Wincham ... 42 M 24
Winchburgh ... 68 J 16
Winchcombe ... 27 O 28
Winchelsea ... 12 W 31
Winchester ... 10 Q 30
Winchfield ... 20 R 30
Wincle ... 35 N 24
Windermere ... 48 L 20
Windhill ... 79 G 11
Windlesham ... 21 S 29
Windrush ... 19 O 28
Windrush (River) ... 19 O 28
Windsor ... 21 S 29
Windsor Great Park ... 21 S 29
Windygates ... 68 K 15
Winfarthing ... 31 X 26
Winford ... 18 M 29
Winforton ... 26 K 27
Winfrith Newburgh ... 9 N 32
Wing ... 28 R 28
Wingate ... 57 P 19
Wingerworth ... 36 P 24
Wingfield
  near Alfreton ... 36 P 24
Wingfield
  near Chesterfield ... 36 P 24
Wingham ... 23 X 30
Wingrave ... 28 R 28
Winkfield ... 21 R 29
Winkleigh ... 7 I 31

Winksley ... 50 P 21
Winmarleigh ... 48 L 22
Winnersh ... 20 R 29
Winscombe ... 18 L 30
Winsford Cheshire ... 34 M 24
Winsford Somerset ... 7 J 30
Winsham ... 8 L 31
Winshill ... 35 P 25
Winslow ... 28 R 28
Winster Derbyshire Dales .... 35 P 24
Winster South Lakeland ... 48 L 20
Winston ... 49 O 20
Winstone ... 19 N 28
Winterborne Kingston ... 9 N 31
Winterborne Stickland ... 9 N 31
Winterborne Whitechurch ... 9 N 31
Winterbourne ... 18 M 29
Winterbourne Abbas ... 5 M 31
Winterbourne Dauntsey ... 9 O 30
Winterbourne Monkton ... 19 O 29
Winterbourne Stoke ... 9 O 30
Winteringham ... 44 S 22
Winterton ... 44 S 23
Winterton-on-Sea ... 39 Z 25
Winton ... 49 N 20
Wintringham ... 51 S 21
Winwick ... 29 S 26
Wirksworth ... 35 P 24
Wirral ... 42 K 24
Wisbech ... 37 U 25
Wisbech-St. Mary ... 37 U 26
Wisborough Green ... 11 S 30
Wishaw ... 61 I 16
Wisley ... 21 S 30
Wissey (River) ... 38 V 26
Wistanstow ... 26 L 26
Wistanswick ... 34 M 25
Wistaston ... 34 M 24
Wiston
  Dumfries and Galloway .... 61 J 17
Wiston Pembrokeshire /
  Sir Benfro ... 16 F 28
Wistow ... 44 Q 22
Witchampton ... 9 N 31
Witchford ... 30 U 26
Witham ... 22 V 28
Witham (River) ... 37 T 24
Witham Friary ... 9 M 30
Witheridge ... 7 I 31
Withern ... 45 U 24
Withernsea ... 45 U 22
Withernwick ... 45 T 22
Withington Cotswold ... 19 O 28
Withington Herefordshire ... 26 M 27
Withnell ... 42 M 22
Withycombe ... 4 J 32
Withypool ... 7 J 30
Witley ... 11 S 30
Witney ... 20 P 28
Witsome ... 63 N 16
Wittering ... 37 S 26
Wittersham ... 12 W 30
Witton le Wear ... 56 O 19

Wiveliscombe ... 7 K 30
Wivelsfield ... 11 T 31
Wivenhoe ... 30 W 28
Woburn ... 29 S 28
Woburn Abbey ... 29 S 28
Woburn Sands ... 29 S 27
Woking ... 21 S 30
Wokingham ... 20 R 29
Wold Newton ... 45 T 23
Woldingham ... 21 T 30
Wollaston ... 29 S 27
Wollaton Hall ... 36 Q 25
Wolsingham ... 56 O 19
Wolston ... 28 P 26
Wolvercote ... 20 Q 28
Wolverhampton ... 35 N 26
Wolverton ... 28 R 27
Wolvey ... 28 P 26
Wolviston ... 57 Q 20
Wombleton ... 50 R 21
Wombourne ... 27 N 26
Wombwell ... 43 P 23
Womersley ... 44 Q 22
Wonersh ... 21 S 30
Wood Dalling ... 39 X 25
Woodborough ... 36 Q 24
Woodbridge ... 31 X 27
Woodbury ... 4 J 31
Woodchurch ... 12 W 30
Woodcote ... 20 Q 29
Woodford Halse ... 28 Q 27
Woodhall Spa ... 37 T 24
Woodham Ferrers ... 22 V 29
Woodhouse ... 43 P 23
Woodhouse Eaves ... 36 Q 25
Woodingdean ... 11 T 31
Woodland ... 56 O 20
Woodlands ... 9 O 31
Woodley ... 20 R 29
Woodnesborough ... 23 X 30
Woodseaves ... 35 N 25
Woodsetts ... 44 Q 23
Woodsford ... 9 M 31
Woodstock ... 20 P 28
Woodton ... 39 Y 26
Woody Bay ... 17 I 30
Wookey ... 18 L 30
Wookey Hole ... 18 L 30
Wool ... 9 N 31
Woolacombe ... 16 H 30
Wooler ... 63 N 17
Woolfardisworthy ... 6 G 31
Woolhampton ... 20 Q 29
Woolpit ... 30 W 27
Woolsthorpe ... 36 R 25
Wooperton ... 63 O 17
Woore ... 35 M 25
Wootton Bedford ... 29 S 27
Wootton Northampton ... 28 R 27
Wootton Bassett ... 19 O 29
Wootton Brige ... 10 Q 31
Wootton Courtenay ... 17 J 30
Wootton Rivers ... 19 O 29

Wootton-Wawen ... 27 O 27
Worcester ... 27 N 27
Workington ... 53 J 20
Worksop ... 44 Q 24
Worle ... 18 L 29
Wormbridge ... 26 L 28
Wormingford ... 30 W 28
Worminghall ... 20 Q 28
Wormit ... 69 L 14
Worms Head ... 15 H 29
Wormsley ... 26 L 27
Worplesdon ... 21 S 30
Worsbrough ... 43 P 23
Worsley ... 42 M 23
Worsthorne ... 43 N 22
Worth Matravers ... 9 N 32
Worthen ... 34 L 26
Worthenbury ... 34 L 24
Worthing ... 11 S 31
Wortley ... 43 P 23
Worton ... 19 N 30
Wortwell ... 31 Y 26
Wotton-under-Edge ... 19 M 29
Wrafton ... 6 H 30
Wragby East Lindsey ... 45 T 24
Wragby Wakefield ... 43 P 23
Wrangle ... 37 U 24
Wrawby ... 44 S 23
Wray ... 48 M 21
Wrea Green ... 42 L 22
Wreay ... 55 L 19
Wrecsam / Wrexham ... 34 L 24
Wrekenton ... 56 P 19
Wremtham ... 31 Z 26
Wrenbury ... 34 M 24
Wrestlingworth ... 29 T 27
Wrexham / Wrecsam ... 34 L 24
Wrington ... 18 L 29
Writtle ... 22 V 28
Wroot ... 44 R 23
Wrotham ... 22 U 30
Wroughton ... 19 O 29
Wroxall ... 10 Q 32
Wroxham ... 39 Y 25
Wroxton ... 28 P 27
Wyberton ... 37 T 25
Wyche ... 27 M 27
Wye ... 22 W 30
Wye (River) ... 26 M 28
Wykeham ... 51 S 21
Wylam ... 56 O 19
Wylye ... 9 O 30
Wymeswold ... 36 Q 25
Wymondham Leics. ... 36 R 25
Wymondham Norfolk ... 39 X 26
Wyre ... 87 L 6
Wysall ... 36 Q 25
Wyvis Lodge ... 79 G 10

Y Rhiw ... 32 G 25
Yafforth ... 50 P 20
Yalding ... 22 V 30
Yapton ... 11 S 31
Yardley Gobion ... 28 R 27
Yardley Hastings ... 28 R 27
Yare (River) ... 38 W 26
Yarm ... 50 P 20
Yarmouth ... 10 P 31
Yarnton ... 20 Q 28
Yarrow ... 62 K 17
Yate ... 19 M 29
Yateley ... 20 R 29
Yatton ... 18 L 29
Yatton Keynell ... 19 N 29
Yaxham ... 38 W 26
Yaxley ... 29 T 26
Yeadon ... 43 O 22
Yealand Conyers ... 48 L 21
Yealmpton ... 4 I 32
Yedingham ... 51 S 21
Yelden ... 29 S 27
Yell ... 87 Q 1
Yelvertoft ... 28 Q 26
Yelverton ... 4 H 32
Yeolmbridge ... 6 G 32
Yeovil ... 8 M 31
Yeovilton ... 8 M 30
Yesnaby ... 86 J 6
Yetminster ... 8 M 31
Yetts o' Muckhart ... 68 J 15
Yielden ... 29 S 27
Ynys / Lochtyn ... 15 G 27
Ynysddu ... 18 K 29
Ynyslas ... 25 H 26
Ynysybwl ... 17 J 29
Yockenthwaite ... 49 N 21
Yockleton ... 34 L 25
York ... 50 Q 22
Yorkletts ... 23 X 30
Yorkley ... 18 M 28
Yorkshire Dales
  National Park ... 49 N 21
Yorkshire Wolds ... 51 S 21
Youlgreave ... 35 O 24
Yoxall ... 35 O 25
Yoxford ... 31 Y 27
Yr Wyddfa / Snowdon ... 33 H 24
Yr Wyddgrug / Mold ... 34 K 24
Ysbyty Ifan ... 33 I 24
Ystalyfera ... 17 I 28
Ystrad-Aeron ... 25 H 27
Ystrad Mynach ... 18 K 29
Ystradfellte ... 17 I 28
Ystradgynlais ... 17 I 28
Ystradowen ... 17 J 29
Ystwyth (River) ... 25 H 26

Y

Y-Fenni / Abergavenny ... 18 L 28
Y Ffor ... 32 G 25
Y Llethr ... 33 I 25

Z

Zennor ... 2 D 33

A
B
C
D
E
F
G
H
I
J
K
L
M
N
O
P
Q
R
S
T
U
V
W
X
Y
Z

A

Aasleagh ... 105 D7
Abbert ... 106 F7
Abbey ... 100 G8
Abbeydorney ... 93 C10
Abbeyfeale ... 93 E10
Abbeylara ... 107 J6
Abbeyleix / Mainistir Laoise ... 101 J9
Abbeyshrule ... 107 J7
Abington ... 94 G10
Achill ... 104 C6
Achill Head ... 110 B6
Achill Island ... 104 B6
Achill Sound ... 104 C6
Achillbeg Island ... 104 C6
Achonry ... 112 G5
Aclare ... 112 F5
Acoose (Lough) ... 89 C11
Adamstown ... 96 L10
Adare ... 94 F10
Adrigole ... 89 C12
Aghaboe ... 101 J9
Aghabullogue ... 90 F12
Aghada ... 90 H12
Aghadiffin ... 106 F6
Aghadoe ... 89 D11
Aghadoon ... 110 B5
Aghadowey ... 118 M2
Aghagallon ... 114 N4
Aghagower ... 105 D6
Aghalane ... 113 J5
Aghalee ... 114 N4
Aghamore *Leitrim* ... 107 I6
Aghamore *Mayo* ... 105 F6
Aghamuck ... 106 H6
Aghavannagh ... 103 M9
Aghavas ... 107 I6
Aghaville ... 89 D13
Aghinlig ... 114 M4
Aghla Mountain ... 116 H3
Aghleam ... 110 B5
Aghnablaney ... 113 I4
Aghnacliff ... 107 J6
Aghnamullen ... 108 L5
Aghowle ... 96 M9
Agivey ... 118 M2
Aglish *Tipperary* ... 100 H8
Aglish *Waterford* ... 91 I11
Agnew's Hill ... 115 O3
Ahakista ... 89 D13
Ahalia (Loughs) ... 105 D7
Ahascragh ... 106 G7
Ahenny ... 95 J10
Aherla ... 90 F12
Aherlow ... 94 H10
Aherlow (Glen of) ... 95 H10
Ahoghill ... 118 M3
Aillwee Cave ... 99 E8
Ailt an Chorráin / Burtonport ... 116 G3
Aird Mhór / Ardmore ... 91 I12
Akeragh Lough ... 93 C10
Aldergrove ... 115 N4
Allaghaun ... 102 L6
Allen ... 102 L8
Allen (Bog of) ... 102 K8
Allen (Lough) ... 112 H5
Allenwood ... 102 L8
Allihies ... 88 B13
Allistragh ... 114 L4
Alloon Lower ... 106 G7
Allow ... 94 F11
Allua (Lough) ... 89 E12
Altagowlan ... 112 H5
Altan Lough ... 117 H2
Altnamackan ... 114 M5
Altnapaste ... 117 I3
An Blascaod Mór / Blasket Islands ... 92 A11
An Bun Beag / Bunbeg ... 116 H2
An Caisleán Nua / Newcastle West ... 93 E10
An Caisleán Riabhach / Castlerea ... 106 G6
An Chathair / Caher ... 95 I10
An Cheathrú Rua / Carraroe ... 98 D8
An Chloich Mhóir / Cloghmore ... 104 C6
An Clochán / Clifden ... 104 B7
An Clochán / Cloghan *Donegal* ... 117 I3
An Clochán Liath / Dungloe ... 116 G3
An Cloigeann / Cleegan ... 104 B7

An Cóbh / Cobh ... 90 H12
An Coimín / Commeen ... 117 I3
An Coireán / Waterville ... 88 B12
An Creagán / Mount Bellew ... 106 G7
An Daingean / Dingle ... 92 B11
An Dúchoraidh / Doocharry ... 116 H3
An Fál Carrach / Falcarragh ... 117 H2
An Fhairche / Clonbur ... 105 D7
An Geata Mór ... 110 B5
An Gleann Garbh / Glengarriff ... 89 D12
An Gort / Gort ... 99 F8
An Gort Mór / Gortmore ... 105 D7
An Leacht / Lahinch ... 98 D9
An Longfort / Longford ... 107 I6
An Mám / Maam Cross ... 105 D7
An Mhala Raithní / Mulrany ... 104 C6
An Móta / Moate ... 101 I7
An Muileann gCearr / Mullingar ... 107 J7
An Nás / Naas ... 102 M8
An Ráth / Charleville ... 94 F10
An Ros / Rush ... 109 N7
An Sciobairín / Skibbereen ... 89 E13
An Seanchaisleán / Oldcastle ... 108 K6
An Spidéal / Spiddal ... 99 E8
An tAonach / Nenagh ... 100 H9
An Teampall Mór / Templemore ... 101 I9
An Tearmann / Termon ... 117 I2
An tInbhear Mór / Arklow ... 97 N9
An Tulach / Tullow ... 102 L9
An Uaimh / Navan ... 108 L7
Anascaul ... 92 B11
Anayalla ... 114 L5
Anglesborough ... 94 H10
Anglesey Bridge ... 95 H9
Annacarriga ... 99 G9
Annacarty ... 95 H10
Annaclone ... 115 N5
Annacloy ... 115 O4
Annacotty ... 94 G9
Annadorn ... 115 O5
Annagary ... 116 H2
Annagassan ... 109 M6
Annageeragh (River) ... 98 D9
Annagh Head ... 110 B5
Annagh Island ... 110 C6
Annaghdown ... 105 E7
Annaghmore Lough ... 106 H6
Annahilt ... 115 N4
Annalee ... 107 J5
Annalong ... 109 O5
Annamoe ... 103 N8
Annes Grove Gardens ... 94 G11
Annestown ... 91 K11
Annfield ... 95 I9
Annie Brady Bridge ... 111 C5
Annsborough ... 115 O5
Antrim ... 115 N3
Antrim (Glens of) ... 119 N2
Antrim Coast ... 119 O2
Antrim Mountains ... 119 N2
Anure (Lough) ... 116 H3
Araglin ... 95 H11
Árainn Mhór / Aran or Aranmore Island ... 116 G2
Aran Islands / Oileáin Árainn ... 98 C8
Archdale (Castle) ... 113 I4
Archerstown ... 108 K7
Ard ... 104 C8
Ardagh *Donegal* ... 117 J3
Ardagh *Limerick* ... 93 E10
Ardan ... 101 J8
Ardanairy ... 103 N9
Ardanew ... 108 L7
Ardara ... 116 G3
Ardattin ... 96 L9
Ardboe ... 114 M4
Ardcath ... 109 M7
Ardcloon ... 105 F7
Ardcrony ... 100 H9
Ardea ... 89 C12
Arderin ... 101 J8
Ardfert ... 93 C11
Ardfield ... 89 F13
Ardfinnan ... 95 I11
Ardgehane ... 90 F13
Ardglass ... 115 P5
Ardglass ... 90 H11

Ardgroom ... 88 C12
Ardgroom Harbour ... 88 C12
Ardkeen ... 115 P4
Ardlea ... 101 J9
Ardlougher ... 107 J5
Ardmillan ... 115 O4
Ardmoney ... 113 J5
Ardmore *Derry* ... 117 K3
Ardmore *Galway* ... 104 C8
Ardmore Point *Antrim* ... 114 N4
Ardmore Point *Craigavon* ... 114 M4
Ardmore Point *Dunganstown East* ... 103 N9
Ardmorney ... 101 J7
Ardmoy ... 106 G6
Ardnagreevagh ... 104 B7
Ardnasodan ... 105 F7
Ardpatrick ... 94 G10
Ardrahan ... 99 F8
Ardreagh ... 118 M2
Ardress House ... 114 M4
Ards Forest Park ... 117 I2
Ards Peninsula ... 115 P4
Ardscull ... 102 L8
Ardshankill ... 113 I4
Ardstraw ... 113 J3
Ardgideen ... 89 F13
Argory (The) ... 114 M4
Arigna ... 112 H5
Arinagh ... 112 F5
Arless ... 102 K9
Armagh ... 114 M4
Armaghbrague ... 114 M5
Armoy ... 118 N2
Arney ... 113 I5
Arra Mountains ... 100 G9
Arrow (Lough) ... 106 H5
Arryheernabin ... 117 J2
Artane ... 103 N7
Arthurstown ... 96 L11
Articlave ... 118 L2
Artigarvan ... 117 J3
Asdee ... 93 D10
Ashbourne ... 109 M7
Ashford *Glenealy* ... 103 N8
Ashford *Limerick* ... 93 E10
Ashford Castle ... 105 E7
Ashleam Bay ... 104 B6
Ashton ... 90 F12
Askamore ... 97 M9
Askanagap ... 103 M9
Askeaton ... 94 F10
Askill ... 112 H4
Atedaun (Lough) ... 99 E9
Áth Cinn / Headford ... 105 E7
Athassel Abbey ... 95 I10
Athboy ... 108 L7
Athea ... 93 E10
Athgarvan ... 102 L8
Athlacca ... 94 G10
Athleague ... 106 H7
Athnid ... 95 I9
Athy / Baile Átha Í ... 102 L9
Atlantic Drive (The) ... 104 C6
Atorick (Lough) ... 99 G8
Attanagh ... 101 J9
Attavally ... 111 C5
Attical ... 109 N5
Attymass ... 111 E5
Attymon ... 99 G8
Aucloggen ... 105 F7
Audley's Castle ... 115 P4
Aughacasla ... 92 C11
Aughagault ... 117 I3
Aughamullan ... 114 M4
Augher ... 114 K4
Aughils ... 92 C11
Aughinish ... 99 E8
Aughinish Island ... 93 E10
Aughkeely ... 117 I3
Aughnacleagh ... 118 M3
Aughnacloy ... 114 L4
Aughnanure Castle ... 105 E7
Aughnasheelan ... 107 I5
Aughrim *Galway* ... 100 H8
Aughrim *Wicklow* ... 103 N9
Aughris ... 112 F5
Aughris Head ... 112 F5
Aughrus More ... 104 B7
Avoca ... 103 N9
Avoca (River) ... 103 N9
Avoca (Valle of) ... 103 N9
Avonbeg ... 103 N9
Avondale Forest Park ... 103 N9
Avonmore (River) ... 103 N9
Awbeg ... 94 G11

B

Baginbun Head ... 96 L11
Baile an Fheirtéaraigh / Ballyferriter ... 92 A11
Baile an Mhóta / Ballymote ... 112 G5
Baile an Róba / Ballinrobe ... 105 E7
Baile an Sceilg / Ballinskelligs ... 88 B12
Baile Átha an Rí / Athenry ... 99 F8
Baile Átha Cliath / Dublin ... 103 N8
Baile Átha Fhirdhia / Ardee ... 108 M6
Baile Átha Luain / Athlone ... 107 I7
Baile Átha Troim / Trim ... 108 L7
Baile Brigín / Balbriggan ... 109 N7
Baile Chláir / Claregalway ... 99 F7
Baile Locha Riach / Loughrea ... 99 G8
Baile Mhic Andáin / Thomastown ... 96 K10
Baile Mhistéala / Mitchelstown ... 94 H11
Baile na Finne / Fintown ... 117 H3
Baile na Lorgan / Castleblayney ... 108 L5
Baile Uí Fhiacháin / Newport ... 105 D6
Baile Uí Mhatháin / Newport ... 107 I7
Baileysmill ... 115 O4
Baldoyle ... 103 N7
Balla ... 105 E6
Ballaba ... 99 F8
Ballagan Point ... 109 N5
Ballagh *Fermanagh* ... 113 J5
Ballagh *Galway* ... 106 F7
Ballagh *Limerick* ... 93 E10
Ballagh near Curraghroe ... 106 H7
Ballagh near Nahara ... 106 H7
Ballagh *Tipperary* ... 95 I10
Ballagh (Neck of the) ... 112 G3
Ballaghaderreen / Bealach an Doirín ... 106 G6
Ballaghbeama Gap ... 89 C12
Ballaghbehy ... 93 E10
Ballaghisheen Pass ... 88 C12
Ballaghkeen ... 97 M10
Ballaghmore ... 101 I9
Ballaghnatrillick ... 112 G4
Ballard ... 97 M9
Ballardiggan ... 99 F8
Balleen ... 101 J9
Ballickmoyler ... 102 K9
Balliggan ... 115 P4
Ballina ... 99 G9
Ballina / Béal an Átha ... 111 E5
Ballinaboy ... 104 B7
Ballinabrackey ... 102 K7
Ballinabranagh ... 102 L9
Ballinaclash ... 103 N9
Ballinacor ... 103 N9
Ballinadee ... 90 G12
Ballinafad *Aghanagh* ... 106 G5
Ballinafad *Galway* ... 104 C7
Ballinagar ... 101 J8
Ballinagleragh ... 113 I5
Ballinakill ... 101 K9
Ballinalack ... 107 J7
Ballinalea ... 103 N8
Ballinalee ... 107 J6
Ballinamallard ... 113 J4
Ballinamara ... 95 J9
Ballinameen ... 106 H6
Ballinamore Bridge ... 106 G7
Ballinamuck ... 107 I6
Ballinascarty ... 90 F12
Ballinaspick ... 91 I11
Ballinclashet ... 90 G12
Ballincloher ... 93 C10
Ballincollig ... 90 G12
Ballincrea ... 96 K11
Ballincurrig ... 90 H12
Ballindaggan ... 96 L10
Ballindarragh ... 113 J5
Ballinderreen ... 99 F8
Ballinderry *Cookstown* ... 114 M4
Ballinderry *Terryglass* ... 100 H8
Ballinderry *Wicklow* ... 103 N9
Ballinderry Bridge ... 114 M4
Ballindine ... 105 F6
Ballindrait ... 117 J3
Ballineanig ... 92 A11
Ballineen ... 89 F12
Ballingarrane ... 94 F10

Ballingarry *Galway* ... 100 H8
Ballingarry *Limerick* ... 94 F10
Ballingarry *Tipperary* ... 95 J10
Ballingeary / Béal Átha an Ghaorthaidh ... 89 E12
Ballingurteen ... 89 E12
Ballinhassig ... 90 G12
Ballinkillin ... 96 L10
Ballinlea ... 118 M2
Ballinleeny ... 94 F10
Ballinloghig ... 92 B11
Ballinlough *Meath* ... 108 K6
Ballinlough *Roscommon* ... 106 G6
Ballinruan ... 99 F9
Ballinspittle ... 90 G12
Ballintogher ... 106 G6
Ballintotty ... 100 H9
Ballintra *Donegal* ... 112 H4
Ballintra near Leabgarrow ... 116 G3
Ballintubber ... 105 E6
Ballinunty ... 95 I10
Ballinure ... 95 I10
Ballinure (River) ... 100 H8
Ballinvarry ... 96 L10
Ballitore ... 102 L8
Ballivor ... 108 L7
Ballon ... 96 L9
Balloo Cross Roads ... 115 O4
Balloor ... 112 G4
Balloughter ... 97 M10
Ballure ... 112 H4
Ballvengland ... 94 F10
Ballyagran ... 94 F10
Ballyallinan ... 94 F10
Ballyalton ... 115 P5
Ballyard ... 113 J4
Ballybannon ... 102 L9
Ballybay near Carrickmacross ... 108 L5
Ballybay near Castleblayney ... 108 L5
Ballybeg ... 95 I11
Ballyboghil ... 109 N7
Ballybogy ... 118 M2
Ballyboley Forest ... 115 O3
Ballyboy ... 101 I8
Ballybrack *Dublin* ... 103 N8
Ballybrack *Kerry* ... 88 B12
Ballybrittas ... 101 K8
Ballybrommel ... 96 L9
Ballybrood ... 94 G10
Ballybrophy ... 101 J9
Ballybryan ... 101 K7
Ballybunnion ... 93 D10
Ballycahill ... 95 I10
Ballycallan ... 95 J10
Ballycanew ... 97 N10
Ballycarney ... 97 M10
Ballycarry ... 115 O3
Ballycastle *Mayo* ... 111 D5
Ballycastle *Moyle* ... 119 N2
Ballycastle Bay ... 119 N2
Ballyclare *Newtownabbey* ... 115 N3
Ballyclare *Roscommon* ... 107 I6
Ballyclerahan ... 95 I10
Ballyclery ... 99 F8
Ballyclogh ... 94 F11
Ballycolla ... 101 J9
Ballycommon ... 100 H9
Ballyconneely ... 104 B7
Ballyconneely Bay ... 104 B7
Ballyconnell *Cavan* ... 113 J5
Ballyconnell *Sligo* ... 112 G4
Ballycorick ... 99 E9
Ballycotton ... 91 H12
Ballycotton Bay ... 91 H12
Ballycrossaun ... 100 H8
Ballycroy ... 110 C5
Ballycuirke Lough ... 99 E8
Ballycullane ... 96 L11
Ballycumber ... 101 I8
Ballydangan ... 100 H7
Ballydavid *Galway* ... 100 G8
Ballydavid *Kilmalkedar* ... 92 A11
Ballydavid Head ... 92 A11
Ballydavis ... 101 K8
Ballydehob ... 89 D13
Ballydesmond ... 93 E11
Ballydonegan ... 88 B13
Ballydonegan Bay ... 88 B13
Ballyduff *Dingle* ... 92 B11

Ballyduff *Kerry* ... 93 D10
Ballyduff *Waterford* ... 91 H11
Ballyduff *Wexford* ... 97 M10
Ballyeaston ... 115 O3
Ballyeighter Loughs ... 99 F9
Ballyfad ... 97 N9
Ballyfair ... 102 L8
Ballyfarnagh ... 105 F6
Ballyfarnan ... 106 H5
Ballyfasy ... 96 K10
Ballyfeard ... 90 G12
Ballyferis Point ... 115 P4
Ballyfin ... 101 J8
Ballyfinboy ... 100 H8
Ballyforan ... 106 H7
Ballyfore ... 102 K8
Ballyfoyle ... 96 K9
Ballygalley ... 119 O3
Ballygalley Head ... 119 O3
Ballygar ... 106 H7
Ballygarrett ... 97 N10
Ballygarries ... 105 E6
Ballygarvan ... 90 G12
Ballygawley *Dungannon* ... 114 K4
Ballygawley *Sligo* ... 112 G5
Ballyglass near Cornanagh ... 105 E6
Ballyglass near Kilmovee ... 106 G6
Ballygorman ... 117 K1
Ballygowan *Ards* ... 115 O4
Ballygowan *Newry-Mourne* ... 109 N5
Ballygriffin ... 95 I10
Ballyhack ... 96 L11
Ballyhacket ... 102 L9
Ballyhaght ... 94 G10
Ballyhahill ... 93 E10
Ballyhaise ... 107 K5
Ballyhalbert ... 115 P4
Ballyhale *Galway* ... 105 E7
Ballyhale *Kilkenny* ... 96 K10
Ballyhar ... 93 D11
Ballyhaunis / Béal Átha hAmhnais ... 106 F6
Ballyhean ... 105 E6
Ballyhear ... 105 E7
Ballyheelan ... 107 J6
Ballyheerin ... 117 I2
Ballyheige ... 93 C10
Ballyheige Bay ... 93 C10
Ballyhillin ... 117 J1
Ballyhoe Bridge ... 118 N2
Ballyhoe Lough ... 108 L6
Ballyhoge ... 96 M10
Ballyhooly ... 94 G11
Ballyhornan ... 115 P5
Ballyhoura Mountains ... 94 G11
Ballyhuppahane ... 101 J8
Ballyjamesduff ... 107 K6
Ballykean ... 101 K8
Ballykeefe ... 95 J10
Ballykeel ... 115 N4
Ballykeeran ... 107 I7
Ballykelly ... 118 K2
Ballykilleen ... 102 K8
Ballykinler ... 115 O5
Ballyknockan ... 103 M8
Ballylacy ... 97 N9
Ballylaghnan ... 99 G9
Ballylanders ... 94 G10
Ballylaneen ... 91 J11
Ballylesson ... 115 O4
Ballylickey ... 89 D12
Ballyliffin ... 117 J2
Ballyline ... 95 J10
Ballylintagh ... 118 L2
Ballylongford ... 93 D10
Ballylongford Bay ... 93 D10
Ballylooby ... 95 I11
Ballyloughbeg ... 118 M2
Ballylynan ... 102 K9
Ballymacarbry ... 95 I11
Ballymacaw ... 96 K11
Ballymachugh ... 107 K6
Ballymack ... 96 K10
Ballymackilroy ... 114 K4
Ballymacoda ... 91 I12
Ballymacrevan ... 115 N4
Ballymacurly ... 106 H6
Ballymacward ... 106 G7
Ballymadog ... 91 I12
Ballymagan ... 117 J2
Ballymagaraghy ... 118 K2
Ballymagorry ... 117 J3
Ballymakeagh ... 91 I12

A
B
C
D
E
F
G
H
I
J
K
L
M
N
O
P
Q
R
S
T
U
V
W
X
Y
Z

A B C D E F G H I J K L M N O P Q R S T U V W X Y Z

Ballymakeery / Baile Mhic Íre ...89 E 12
Ballymakenny ...109 M 6
Ballymartin ...109 O 5
Ballymartle ...90 G 12
Ballymena ...119 N 3
Ballymoe ...106 G 6
Ballymoney Ballymoney ...118 M 2
Ballymoney Limavady ...118 K 3
Ballymore Donegal ...117 I 2
Ballymore Westmeath ...107 I 7
Ballymore Eustace ...103 M 8
Ballymore Lough ...111 E 5
Ballymurphy ...96 L 10
Ballymurragh ...93 E 10
Ballymurray ...106 H 7
Ballynabola ...96 L 10
Ballynacallagh ...88 B 13
Ballynacally ...99 E 9
Ballynacarrick ...116 H 3
Ballynacarriga ...89 E 12
Ballynacarrigy ...107 J 7
Ballynacarrow ...112 G 5
Ballynaclogh ...100 H 9
Ballynacorra ...90 H 12
Ballynacourty ...91 J 11
Ballynadrumny ...102 L 7
Ballynafid ...107 J 7
Ballynagaul ...91 J 11
Ballynagoraher ...105 D 6
Ballynagore ...101 J 7
Ballynagree ...90 F 12
Ballynaguilkee ...95 I 11
Ballynahinch ...115 O 4
Ballynahinch Lake ...104 C 7
Ballynahow ...88 A 12
Ballynahown Kilcummin ...98 D 8
Ballynahown Westmeath ..101 I 7
Ballynakill Carlow ...96 L 9
Ballynakill Offaly ...101 K 8
Ballynakill Westmeath ...107 I 7
Ballynakill Harbour ...104 B 7
Ballynakilla ...88 C 13
Ballynakilly Upper ...88 C 11
Ballynamallaght ...117 K 3
Ballynamona ...90 G 11
Ballynamult ...95 I 11
Ballynana ...92 A 11
Ballynare ...103 M 7
Ballynashannagh ...117 J 2
Ballynaskeagh ...114 N 5
Ballynaskreena ...93 C 10
Ballynastangford ...105 E 6
Ballynastraw ...97 M 10
Ballynchatty ...113 K 4
Ballyneaner ...118 K 3
Ballyneety ...94 G 10
Ballyneill ...95 J 10
Ballynoe Cork ...90 H 11
Ballynoe Down ...115 O 5
Ballynure ...115 O 3
Ballyorgan ...94 G 11
Ballypatrick ...95 J 10
Ballypatrick Forest ...119 N 2
Ballyporeen ...95 H 11
Ballyquin ...92 B 11
Ballyquintin Point ...115 P 5
Ballyragget ...101 J 9
Ballyrashane ...118 M 2
Ballyreagh Dungannon ...114 L 4
Ballyreagh Fermanagh ...113 J 4
Ballyroan ...101 K 9
Ballyroddy ...106 H 6
Ballyroebuck ...97 M 10
Ballyronan ...114 M 3
Ballyroney ...115 N 5
Ballyroon ...88 C 13
Ballysadare ...112 G 5
Ballysadare Bay ...112 G 5
Ballyshannon Donegal ...112 H 4
Ballyshannon Kildare ...102 L 8
Ballysloe ...95 J 10
Ballysteen ...94 F 10
Ballyteige Bay ...96 L 11
Ballytoohy ...104 C 6
Ballyvaughan ...99 E 8
Ballyvaughan Bay ...99 E 8
Ballyvester ...115 P 4
Ballyvoge / Baile Uí Bhuaigh ...89 E 12
Ballyvoneen ...106 G 7
Ballyvourney / Baile Bhuirne ...89 E 12
Ballyvoy ...119 N 2
Ballyvoyle Head ...91 J 11
Ballywalter ...115 P 4
Ballyward ...115 N 5

Ballywilliam ...96 L 10
Balnamore ...118 M 2
Balrath ...108 M 7
Balrothery ...109 N 7
Balscaddan ...109 N 7
Baltimore ...89 D 13
Baltray ...109 N 6
Banada ...106 F 5
Banagher ...101 I 8
Banagher Forest ...118 L 3
Banbridge ...114 N 4
Bandon River ...89 F 12
Bangor Mayo ...111 C 5
Bangor North-Down ...115 O 4
Bangor Trail ...111 C 5
Bann (River) Lough Neagh ...115 N 5
Bann (River) River Slaney ...97 M 10
Banna ...93 C 10
Banna Strand ...93 C 11
Bannow ...96 L 11
Bannow Bay ...96 L 11
Bansha ...95 H 10
Banteer ...94 F 11
Bantry / Beanntraí ...89 D 12
Bantry Bay ...89 C 13
Barefield ...99 F 9
Barley Cove ...88 C 13
Barna Limerick ...94 H 10
Barna Offaly ...101 I 9
Barnacahoge ...105 F 6
Barnaderg ...106 F 7
Barnesmore ...113 H 3
Barnesmore Gap ...113 I 3
Barnmeen ...115 N 5
Barnycarroll ...105 F 6
Baronscourt Forest ...113 J 3
Barr na Trá / Barnatra ...110 C 5
Barra (Lough) ...117 H 3
Barrack Village ...101 K 9
Barraduff ...89 D 11
Barrigone ...93 E 10
Barringtonsbridge ...94 G 10
Barrow (River) ...102 K 8
Barrow Harbour ...93 C 11
Barry ...107 I 7
Barry's Point ...90 F 13
Batterstown ...108 M 7
Baunskeha ...96 K 10
Bauntlieve ...99 E 9
Baurtregaum ...93 C 11
Bawn Cross Roads ...94 F 11
Bawnboy ...113 I 5
Beagh Galway ...105 F 7
Beagh Roscommon ...112 H 5
Beagh (Slieve) ...117 I 2
Beagh (Slieve) ...113 K 4
Beal ...93 D 10
Béal an Átha / Ballina ...111 E 5
Béal an Átha Mhóir / Ballinamore ...107 I 5
Béal an Mhuirthead / Belmullet ...110 C 5
Béal Átha an Ghaorthaidh / Ballingeary ...89 E 12
Béal Átha na Muice / Swinford ...105 F 6
Béal Átha na Sluaighe / Ballinasloe ...100 H 8
Béal Átha Seanaidh / Ballyshannon ...112 H 4
Béal Deirg / Belderrig ...111 D 5
Beal Point ...93 D 10
Béal Tairbirt / Belturbet ...107 J 5
Bealach Conglais / Baltinglass ...102 L 9
Bealach Féich / Ballybofey ...117 I 3
Bealaclugga / New Quay ...99 E 8
Bealad Cross Roads ...89 F 13
Bealadangan ...105 D 8
Bealaha ...98 D 9
Bealalaw Bridge ...88 C 12
Bealanabrack ...104 C 7
Bealin ...107 I 7
Bealnablath ...90 F 12
Beara ...89 C 12
Beara / Barna ...99 E 8
Beaufort ...89 D 11
Bective ...108 L 7
Beehive Huts ...92 A 11
Beenmore ...88 B 11
Beenoskee ...92 B 11
Beg (Lough) Antrim ...114 N 4
Beg (Lough) River Bann ...114 M 3
Beginish Island ...88 B 12

Behy ...88 C 11
Bekan ...105 F 6
Belcarra ...105 E 6
Belclare ...105 F 7
Belcoo ...113 I 5
Belderg Harbour ...111 D 5
Belfarsad ...104 C 6
Belfast ...115 O 4
Belfast Lough ...115 O 3
Belgooly ...90 G 12
Belhavel Lough ...112 H 5
Bellacorick ...111 D 5
Belladrihid ...112 G 5
Bellagarvaun ...110 C 6
Bellaghy ...114 M 3
Bellahy ...106 F 6
Bellameeny ...106 H 7
Bellamont Forest ...108 K 5
Bellanaboy Bridge ...111 C 5
Bellanacargy ...107 K 5
Bellanagare ...106 G 6
Bellanagraugh Bridge ...112 F 5
Bellanaleck ...113 J 5
Bellanamore ...117 H 3
Bellanamullia ...107 H 7
Bellananagh ...107 J 6
Bellanode ...114 K 5
Bellarena ...118 L 2
Bellavary ...105 E 6
Belleek ...114 M 5
Belleek ...113 H 4
Bellewstown ...109 M 7
Belmont ...101 I 8
Belmore Mountain ...113 I 5
Beltra Croaghmoyle ...105 D 6
Beltra Sligo ...112 G 5
Beltra Lough ...105 D 6
Belvelly ...90 H 12
Belview Port ...96 K 11
Belville ...111 D 5
Ben Gorm ...104 C 7
Benbane Head ...118 M 2
Benbaun ...104 C 7
Benbo ...112 H 5
Benbrack ...113 I 5
Benbreen ...104 C 7
Benbulben ...112 G 4
Benburb ...114 L 4
Bencroy or Gubnaveagh ...113 I 5
Bendooragh ...118 M 2
Benettsbridge ...96 K 10
Benmore ...111 D 5
Benmore or Fair Head ...119 N 2
Bennacunneen ...105 D 7
Benwee Head ...111 C 4
Beragh ...114 K 4
Bere Haven ...88 C 13
Bere Island ...88 C 13
Bernish Rock ...114 M 5
Berrings ...90 F 12
Bertraghboy Bay ...104 C 7
Bessbrook ...114 M 5
Bettystown ...109 N 6
Big Dog Forest ...113 I 4
Big Island ...100 H 8
Big Trosk ...119 N 2
Bilboa ...102 K 9
Bilboa (River) ...95 H 10
Billis Bridge ...108 K 6
Bills Rocks ...104 B 6
Binevenagh ...118 L 2
Binn Éadair / Howth ...103 N 7
Biorra / Birr ...101 I 8
Birdhill ...99 G 9
Birreencorragh ...105 D 6
Bishops Court ...115 P 5
Black Galway ...105 E 7
Black (River) Longford ...107 I 6
Black Ball Head ...88 B 13
Black Bull ...103 M 7
Black Gap (The) ...113 I 4
Black Head Clare ...99 E 8
Black Head Larne ...115 O 3
Black Lion ...101 J 8
Black Rock ...110 B 5
Blacklion ...113 I 5
Blackpool ...94 G 10
Blackrock Cork ...90 G 12
Blackrock Louth ...109 M 6
Blackrock Rathdown ...103 N 8
Blackskull ...114 N 4
Blacksod Bay ...110 B 5
Blacksod Point ...110 B 5
Blackstairs Mountains ...96 L 10
Blackwater ...97 M 10
Blackwater (River) Cork ...89 F 11

Blackwater (River) Lough Neagh ...114 L 4
Blackwater (River) River Boyne ...108 L 6
Blackwater Bridge Innfield ...102 L 7
Blackwater Bridge Tahilla ...88 C 12
Blackwater Harbour ...97 N 10
Blackwatertown ...114 L 4
Blanchardstown ...103 M 7
Blane Bridge ...93 E 10
Blaney ...113 I 4
Blarney ...90 G 12
Blasket Sound ...92 A 11
Bleach ...99 G 8
Bleach Lake ...94 F 10
Blennerville ...93 C 11
Blessington ...103 M 8
Bloody Foreland ...116 H 2
Blue Ball ...101 J 8
Blue Stack Mountains ...113 H 3
Blueford ...93 E 11
Boa Island ...113 I 4
Boardmills ...115 O 4
Boderg (Lough) ...107 I 6
Bodyke ...99 G 9
Bofeenaun ...105 E 6
Bofin ...104 B 7
Bofin (Lough) Galway ...105 D 7
Bofin (Lough) Roscommon ...107 I 6
Bogay ...117 J 3
Boggan Meath ...108 L 6
Boggan Tipperary ...95 J 9
Boggaun ...101 I 9
Boggeragh Mountains ...89 F 11
Bohateh ...99 G 9
Bohaun ...105 D 6
Boheeshil ...88 C 12
Boher ...94 G 10
Boheraphuca ...101 I 8
Boherbue ...93 E 11
Bohereen ...94 G 10
Boherlahan ...95 I 10
Bohermeen ...108 L 7
Boherquill ...107 J 6
Boho ...113 I 4
Bohola ...105 E 6
Bola (Lough) ...104 C 7
Bolea ...118 L 2
Boleran ...118 L 2
Boley ...102 L 8
Bolinglanna ...104 C 6
Boliska Lough ...99 E 8
Bolton's Cross Roads ...93 D 10
Bolus Head ...88 A 12
Bonet ...112 H 5
Boola ...91 I 11
Boolakennedy ...95 H 10
Boolattin ...95 J 11
Boolteens ...93 C 11
Boolyduff ...99 E 9
Boolyglass ...96 K 10
Borris ...96 L 10
Borris in Ossory ...101 J 9
Borrisoleigh ...100 I 9
Boston ...99 F 8
Bottlehill ...90 G 11
Bouladuff ...95 I 9
Boviel ...118 L 3
Bow ...99 G 9
Boyerstown ...108 L 7
Boyle (River) ...106 H 6
Boyne (River) ...102 K 7
Brackagh ...101 K 8
Brackley Lough ...113 I 5
Bracklin ...108 K 7
Brackloon Mayo ...106 F 6
Brackloon Roscommon ...106 G 6
Bracknagh Offaly ...102 K 8
Bracknagh Roscommon ...107 H 7
Brackwanshagh ...111 E 5
Brandon Bay ...92 B 11
Brandon Head ...92 B 11
Brandon Hill ...96 L 10
Brannock Islands ...98 C 8
Brannockstown ...102 L 8
Bray Head Kerry ...88 A 12
Bray Head Wicklow ...103 N 8
Bré / Bray ...103 N 8
Breaghva ...98 C 10
Breaghwy ...105 E 6
Bree ...96 M 10
Breenagh ...117 I 3
Brickeens ...105 F 6
Bricklieve Mountains ...106 G 5
Bride Cork ...89 F 12

Bride River Blackwater ...91 I 11
Bridebridge ...90 H 11
Brideswell Ballyellis ...97 M 9
Brideswell Ballynamona ...106 H 7
Bridge End ...117 J 2
Bridgeland ...103 M 9
Bridget Lough ...99 G 9
Bridgetown
    Cannock Chase ...96 M 11
Bridgetown Clare ...99 G 9
Bridgetown Donegal ...112 H 4
Briensbridge ...99 G 9
Brittas Limerick ...94 G 10
Brittas Saggart ...103 M 8
Brittas Bay ...103 N 9
Britway ...90 H 11
Broad Haven ...110 C 5
Broad Meadow ...109 N 7
Broadford Clare ...99 G 9
Broadford Limerick ...94 F 10
Broadway ...97 M 11
Brookeborough ...113 J 5
Broomfield ...108 L 5
Brosna ...93 E 11
Brosna (River) ...101 I 8
Broughal ...101 I 8
Broughane Cross Roads ...93 D 11
Brougher Mount ...113 J 4
Broughshane ...119 N 3
Brow Head ...88 C 13
Brown Flesk ...93 D 11
Brownstown ...96 K 11
Brownstown Head ...96 K 11
Bruckless ...112 G 4
Bruff ...94 G 10
Bruree ...94 G 10
Bryansford ...115 O 5
Buckna ...119 N 3
Buckode ...112 H 4
Buiríos Uí Chéin / Borrisokane ...100 H 9
Bulgaden ...94 G 10
Bull (The) ...88 B 13
Bull Point ...119 N 2
Bullaba ...117 J 3
Bullaun ...99 G 8
Bull's Head ...92 B 11
Bun Cranncha / Buncrana ...117 J 2
Bun Dobhráin / Bundoran ...112 H 4
Bun na hAbhna / Bunnahowen ...110 C 5
Bun na Leaca / Brinlack ...116 H 2
Bunaclugga Bay ...93 D 10
Bunacurry ...110 C 6
Bunatrahir Bay ...111 D 5
Bunaveela Lough ...111 D 5
Bunaw ...88 C 12
Bunbrosna ...107 J 7
Bunclody ...96 M 10
Bunlahy ...107 J 6
Bunmahon ...91 J 11
Bunnafollistran ...105 E 7
Bunnaglass ...99 F 8
Bunnahown ...104 C 7
Bunnanaddan ...112 G 5
Bunny (Lough) ...99 F 8
Bunnyconnellan ...111 E 5
Bunowen ...105 C 6
Bunratty ...99 F 9
Burncourt ...95 H 11
Burnfoot Birdstown ...117 J 2
Burnfoot Limavady ...118 L 3
Burnfort ...90 G 11
Burr Point ...115 P 4
Burren Clare ...99 E 8
Burren Cork ...90 F 12
Burren Mayo ...105 E 6
Burren (The) ...99 E 8
Burren Centre Kifenora ...99 E 8
Burrenfadda ...99 E 9
Burrishoole Abbey ...105 D 6
Burrow ...97 M 11
Burtown ...102 L 9
Bush (The) Dungannon ...114 L 4
Bush (The) Rathcor ...109 N 6
Bushfield ...100 G 9
Bushmills ...118 M 2
Butler's Bridge ...107 J 5
Butlerstown ...90 F 13
Buttevant ...94 F 11
Butts (The) ...101 K 9
Bweeng ...90 F 11

C
Cabragh ...114 L 4

Cadamstown Kildare ...102 L 7
Cadamstown Offaly ...101 J 8
Caddy ...114 N 3
Caggan ...105 D 7
Caha Mountains ...89 C 12
Caha pass ...89 D 12
Caher Clare ...99 G 9
Caher Mayo ...105 E 7
Caher Island ...104 B 6
Caher Roe's Den ...96 L 10
Caheradrine ...99 F 8
Caheragh ...89 E 13
Caherbarnagh Corcaigh / Cork ...89 E 11
Caherconlish ...94 G 10
Caherconnel ...99 E 8
Caherconree ...92 C 11
Caherdaniel ...88 B 12
Caherea ...99 E 9
Caherlistrane ...105 E 7
Cahermore Cork ...88 B 13
Cahermore Galway ...99 F 8
Cahermurphy ...98 D 9
Cahernahallia ...95 H 10
Cahore Point ...97 N 10
Caiseal / Cashel ...95 I 10
Caisleán an Bharraigh / Castlebar ...105 E 6
Caisleán an Chomair / Castlecomer ...101 K 9
Calafort Ros Láir / Rosslare Harbour ...97 M 11
Caledon ...114 L 4
Calf Islands ...89 D 13
Callaghansmills ...99 F 9
Callainn / Callan ...95 J 10
Callow Galway ...104 B 7
Callow Mayo ...105 E 6
Callow Roscommon ...106 G 6
Caltra ...106 G 7
Caltraghlea ...100 H 7
Calverstown ...102 L 8
Cam Forest ...118 L 2
Camlin (River) ...107 I 6
Camlough ...114 M 5
Camoge ...94 G 10
Camolin ...97 M 10
Camowen ...113 K 4
Camp ...92 C 11
Campile ...96 L 11
Campsey ...118 K 2
Camross ...101 J 8
Camus Bay ...105 D 8
Canglass Point ...88 B 12
Canningstown ...108 K 6
Canon Island ...99 E 9
Cappagh Dungannon ...114 L 4
Cappagh Limerick ...94 F 10
Cappagh River ...100 G 8
Cappagh White ...95 H 10
Cappaghmore ...99 F 8
Cappalinnan ...101 J 9
Cappamore ...94 G 10
Cappanacreha ...105 D 7
Cappanrush ...101 J 7
Cappataggle ...100 G 8
Cappeen ...89 F 12
Car (Slieve) ...111 D 5
Caragh (Lough) ...88 C 11
Caragh (River) ...89 C 12
Caragh Bridge ...92 C 11
Caragh Lake ...92 C 11
Carbery's Hundred Isles ...89 D 13
Carbury ...102 L 7
Cardy ...115 P 4
Cargan ...119 N 3
Carhan House ...88 B 12
Carland ...114 L 4
Carlanstown ...108 L 6
Carlingford ...109 N 5
Carlingford Lough ...109 N 5
Carn ...113 I 4
Carna ...104 C 8
Carnageer ...119 O 3
Carnagh ...117 J 2
Carnalbanagh Sheddings ...119 N 3
Carnanelly ...114 L 3
Carnanreagh ...118 K 3
Carnaross ...108 L 6
Carnaween ...112 H 3
Carncastle ...119 O 3
Carndonagh / Carn Domhnach ...118 K 2
Carnduff ...119 N 2

Carne ....97 M 11
Carneatly ....119 N 2
Carnew ....97 M 9
Carney *Sligo* ....112 H 4
Carney *Tipperary* ....100 H 9
Carnlough ....119 O 3
Carnlough Bay ....119 O 3
Carnmore ....99 F 8
Carnoneen ....105 F 7
Carnowen ....117 J 3
Carnsore Point ....97 M 11
Carnteel ....114 L 4
Carntogher ....118 L 3
Carra (Lough) ....105 E 6
Carracastle ....106 F 6
Carragh ....102 L 8
Carraholly ....105 D 6
Carraig Airt / Carrigart ..117 I 2
Carraig Mhachaire Rois /
  Carrickmacross ....108 L 6
Carraig na Siúire /
  Carrick-on-Suir ......95 J 10
Carran ....99 E 8
Carrantuohill ....89 C 11
Carrick *Wexford* .....96 L 11
Carrick / An Charraig
  Donegal ....112 G 4
Carrick-a-Rede
  Rope Bridge ....118 M 2
Carrick-on-Shannon /
  Cora Droma Rúisc ..107 H 6
Carrickaboy ....107 K 6
Carrickashedoge .....108 L 6
Carrickboy ....107 I 7
Carrickfergus ....115 O 3
Carrickhugh ....118 K 2
Carrickmore ....114 K 4
Carrickroe ....114 K 4
Carrig ....94 G 11
Carrig Island ....93 D 10
Carrigadrohid ....90 F 12
Carrigafoyle Castle ...93 D 10
Carrigagulla ....90 F 11
Carrigaholt ....93 C 10
Carrigaholt Bay ....93 C 10
Carrigahorig ....100 H 8
Carrigaline ....90 G 12
Carrigallen ....107 J 6
Carrigan ....107 J 6
Carrigan Head ....112 F 4
Carriganimmy ....89 E 12
Carrigans ....117 J 3
Carrigatogher ....100 H 9
Carrigfadda ....89 E 13
Carrigglass Manor ...107 I 6
Carriggower ....103 N 8
Carrigkerry ....93 E 10
Carrignavar ....90 G 12
Carrigrohane ....90 G 12
Carrigtohill ....90 H 12
Carrowbehy ....106 G 6
Carrowdore ....115 P 4
Carrowkeel *Donegal* ..117 J 2
Carrowkeel *Galway* ..99 G 8
Carrowkennedy .....105 D 6
Carrowmore *Galway* ..99 F 8
Carrowmore *Kilmacowen* ..112 G 5
Carrowmore
  near Cloonacool ..112 F 5
Carrowmore
  near Crossboyne ..105 E 6
Carrowmore
  near Killasser ....105 F 6
Carrowmore
  near Killogeary ..111 E 5
Carrowmore Lake ..110 C 5
Carrowmore Point ...98 D 9
Carrowmoreknock ..105 E 7
Carrownacon ....105 E 6
Carrowneden ....112 F 5
Carrownisky ....104 C 6
Carrowntanlis ....105 F 7
Carrowreagh
  Roscommon ....100 H 7
Carrowreagh *Sligo* ..112 F 5
Carrowrory ....107 I 7
Carry Bridge ....113 J 5
Carrybeg ....95 J 10
Carryduff ....115 O 4
Casheen bay ....98 C 8
Cashel *Donegal* ...117 I 2
Cashel *Mayo* ......104 C 6
Cashel
  near Glennamaddy ..106 G 7
Cashel / An Caiseal
  Galway ....104 C 7
Cashel (Rock of) ....95 I 10

Cashelgarran ....112 G 4
Cashelmore ....117 I 2
Cashen River ....93 D 10
Cashla ....99 F 8
Cashla Bay ....98 D 8
Cashleen ....104 B 7
Casla / Costelloe ....98 D 8
Casltepollard ....107 K 6
Cassagh ....96 L 10
Castle Carry ....118 K 2
Castle Coole ....113 J 4
Castle Gardens ......90 F 13
Castle Haven ....89 E 13
Castle Island ....89 D 13
Castle Point ....98 C 10
Castlebaldwin ......112 G 5
Castlebar (River) ...105 E 6
Castlebellingham ...109 M 6
Castleblakeney .....106 G 7
Castlebridge ....97 M 10
Castlecaulfield .....114 L 4
Castleconnell ....99 G 9
Castleconor ....111 E 5
Castlecove ....88 B 12
Castlecuffe ....101 J 8
Castledawson ....114 M 3
Castlederg ....113 J 3
Castledermot ....102 L 9
Castlefinn ....117 J 3
Castlefreke ....89 F 13
Castlegal ....112 G 4
Castlegar ....99 E 8
Castlegregory ....92 B 11
Castlehill *Ballycroy South* ..110 C 6
Castlehill
  near Rake Street ..111 D 5
Castlejordan ....102 K 7
Castleknock ....103 M 7
Castlellis ....97 M 10
Castlelyons ....90 H 11
Castlemaine ....93 C 11
Castlemaine Harbour ..92 C 11
Castlemartyr ....90 H 12
Castleplunket ......106 G 6
Castlequin ....88 B 12
Castlerahan ....108 K 6
Castlerock ....118 L 2
Castleroe ....118 M 2
Castleshane ....114 L 5
Castletown *Clare* ..99 E 8
Castletown *Cork* ..89 F 12
Castletown *Laois* ..101 J 9
Castletown *Limerick* ..94 F 10
Castletown *Meath* ..108 L 6
Castletown *near Finnea* ..107 K 6
Castletown *Westmeath* ..107 J 7
Castletown *Wexford* ..97 N 9
Castletown House ...103 M 7
Castletownbere ....88 C 13
Castletownroche ...94 G 11
Castletownshend ..89 E 13
Castleville ....105 E 7
Castleward House ..115 P 4
Castlewarren ....96 K 9
Castlewellan ....115 O 5
Castlewellan Forest Park ..115 O 5
Cathair na Mart /
  Westport ....105 D 6
Cathair Saidhbhín /
  Cahersiveen ......88 B 12
Cathedral Rocks ...104 B 6
Causeway ....93 C 10
Causeway Head ....118 M 2
Cavan / An Cabhán ..107 J 6
Cavanagarvan ......114 L 5
Cavangarden ....112 H 4
Cé Bhréanainn / Brandon ..92 B 11
Ceanannas / Ceanannus Mór
  (Kells) ....108 L 6
Ceann Toirc / Kanturk ..94 F 11
Ceapach Choinn /
  Cappoquin ....91 I 11
Ceatharlach / Carlow ..102 L 9
Ceathrú Thaidhg /
  Carrowteige ....111 C 5
Cecilstown ....94 F 11
Celbridge ....103 M 7
Chanonrock ....108 M 6
Chapeltown *Down* ..115 P 5
Chapeltown
  near Portmagee ..88 A 12
Chapeltown *near Tralee* ..93 C 11
Charlemont ....114 L 4
Charlestown *Craigavon* ..114 M 4
Charlestown *Mayo* ..106 F 6
Cheekpoint ....96 K 11

Cherryville ....102 L 8
Chesney's Corner ..114 M 3
Church Ballee .....115 P 5
Church Cross ....89 D 13
Church Hill *Donegal* ..117 I 3
Church Hill *Fermanagh* ..113 I 4
Church Quarter ...119 N 2
Church Town ......117 J 3
Church Village ....105 E 6
Churchstreet ......106 G 6
Churchtown *Cookstown* ..114 L 3
Churchtown *Cork* ..90 H 12
Churchtown *Down* ..115 P 4
Churchtown *Wexford* ..96 L 11
Churchtown Point ..114 M 3
Cill Airne / Killarney ..89 D 11
Cill Chainnigh / Kilkenny ..96 K 10
Cill Chaoi / Kilkee ..98 D 9
Cill Dalua / Killaloe ..99 G 9
Cill Dara / Kildare ..102 L 8
Cill Mhantáin / Wicklow ..103 N 9
Cill Mocheallóg /
  Kilmallock ....94 G 10
Cill Orglan / Killorglin ..93 C 11
Cill Rois / Kilrush ..93 D 10
Cill Rónáin / Kilronan ..98 C 8
Cionn tSáile / Kinsale ..90 G 12
City Walls ....96 K 11
Clabby ....113 J 4
Cladagh ....113 I 5
Claddagh ....106 F 7
Claddaghduff ......104 B 7
Clady *Antrim* .....115 N 4
Clady *Magherafelt* ..118 M 3
Clady *Strabane* ..117 J 3
Clady (River) ....116 H 2
Clady Milltown ....114 M 5
Claggan *Donegal* ..117 J 2
Claggan *Mayo* ...104 C 6
Clamper Cross ....93 E 11
Clanabogan ....113 J 4
Clane ....102 L 8
Clár Chlainne Mhuiris /
  Claremorris ......105 F 6
Clara ....103 N 9
Clara (Valle of) ...103 N 9
Clarahill ....101 J 8
Clare *Armagh* ...114 M 5
Clare *Craigavon* ..114 N 4
Clare (River) ....105 F 7
Clare Island ....104 B 6
Clarecastle ....99 F 9
Clareen ....101 I 8
Clarina ....94 F 10
Clarinbridge ....99 F 8
Clark's Cross Roads ..107 J 7
Clash ....100 H 9
Clash North ....93 E 10
Clashmore ....91 I 11
Claudy ....118 K 3
Clear (Cape) ....89 D 13
Cleggan / An Cloigeann ..104 B 7
Cleggan Bay ....104 B 7
Cléire (Oileán) /
  Clear Island .....89 D 13
Cleristown ....96 M 11
Clew Bay ....104 C 6
Clifden Bay ....104 B 7
Cliff ....112 H 4
Clifferna ....108 K 6
Cliffony ....112 G 4
Clogga *Kilkenny* ..96 K 11
Clogga *Wicklow* ..97 N 9
Clogh *Ballymena* ..119 N 3
Clogh *Kilkenny* ..101 K 9
Clogh *Laois* ......101 J 9
Clogh *Wexford* ..97 M 10
Cloghan *Offaly* ..101 I 8
Cloghan *Westmeath* ..107 K 7
Cloghane ....92 B 11
Cloghaneely ....117 H 2
Clogharinka ......102 K 7
Cloghaun ....105 F 7
Cloghboley ......112 G 4
Cloghbrack *Cloonbur* ..105 D 7
Cloghbrack *Meath* ..108 K 7
Clogheen ....95 I 11
Clogher *Dungannon* ..113 K 4
Clogher *Kerry* ...93 D 11
Clogher
  near Carrownacon ..105 E 6
Clogher *near Westport* ..105 D 6
Clogher *Roscommon* ..107 H 7
Clogher Head Kerry ..92 A 11
Clogher Head *Louth / Lú* ..109 N 6
Cloghera ....99 G 9
Clogherhead ......109 N 6

Cloghjordan ....100 H 9
Cloghmacoo ......108 L 6
Cloghoge ....109 M 5
Cloghroe *Cork* ...90 G 12
Cloghroe *Donegal* ..117 I 3
Cloghy ....115 P 4
Cloghy Bay ....115 P 4
Clohamon ....96 M 10
Clohernagh ......96 K 11
Cloich na Coillte /
  Clonakilty ....89 F 13
Clóirtheach / Clara ..101 J 7
Clomantagh ......95 J 9
Clonakenny ......101 I 9
Clonakilty Bay ...90 F 13
Clonalis House ..106 G 6
Clonalvy ....109 M 7
Clonard ....108 K 7
Clonaslee ....101 J 8
Clonavoe ....101 K 8
Clonbern ....106 G 7
Clonbulloge .....102 K 8
Cloncagh ....94 F 10
Clonco Bridge ...100 G 8
Cloncrave ....108 K 7
Cloncurry ....102 L 7
Clondalkin ....103 M 8
Clondaw ....97 M 10
Clonderalaw Bay ..93 E 10
Clondulane ......90 H 11
Clonea ....95 J 11
Clonea Bay ......91 J 11
Clonee ....103 M 7
Cloneen ....95 J 10
Clonegall ....96 M 9
Clonelly ....113 I 4
Clonevin ....97 N 10
Connagh ....100 G 9
Clonkeevy ......112 G 5
Clonleigh ....117 J 3
Clonlost ....107 K 7
Clonmacnoise ..101 I 8
Clonmany ......117 J 2
Clonmellon ....108 K 7
Clonmore *Carlow* ..103 M 9
Clonmore *Tipperary* ..101 I 9
Clonmult ....90 H 12
Clonony ....101 I 8
Clonoulty ....95 I 10
Clonroche ....96 L 10
Clonsilla ....103 M 7
Clontarf ....103 N 7
Clontibret ......114 L 5
Clontubbrid ....101 J 9
Clonycavan .....108 L 7
Clonygowan ....101 K 8
Cloon Lake .....88 C 12
Cloonacleigha Lake ..112 G 5
Cloonacool ......112 F 5
Cloonagh Lough ..106 F 6
Cloonaghlin Lough ..88 C 12
Cloonaghmore ...111 D 5
Cloonboo ....105 E 7
Cloondaff ....105 D 6
Cloondara ....107 I 6
Cloone ....107 I 6
Cloone Grange ..107 I 6
Cloonee Loughs ..89 C 12
Cloonfad *Kiltullagh* ..106 F 6
Cloonfad *near Old Town* ..100 H 8
Cloonfallagh ....105 F 6
Cloonfinish .....105 F 6
Cloonfree Lough ..106 H 6
Cloonkeen *Kerry* ..89 E 12
Cloonkeen *Mayo* ..105 D 6
Cloonkeen *Roscommon* ..106 G 6
Cloonlara ....99 G 9
Cloonloogh ......106 G 6
Cloonlusk ....94 H 10
Cloonmore ....106 F 6
Cloonoon ....100 H 8
Cloontia ....106 G 6
Cloonusker ......99 G 9
Cloonymorris ....100 G 8
Cloonyquin .....106 H 6
Cloran ....108 L 7
Clough ....115 O 5
Cloughmills .....118 M 3
Cloverhill *Cavan* ..107 J 5
Cloverhill *Galway* ..105 E 7
Cloyfin ....118 M 2

Cloyne ....90 H 12
Cluain Eois / Clones ..113 K 5
Cluain Meala / Clonmel ..95 I 10
Cluainín / Manorhamilton ..112 H 5
Clydagh ....105 E 6
Clynacantan ......88 A 12
Coachford ....90 F 12
Coagh ....114 M 4
Coalbrook ....95 J 10
Coalisland ....114 L 4
Coan ....101 K 9
Cod's Head ....88 B 13
Coill an Chollaigh /
  Bailieborough ..108 L 6
Colbinstown .....102 L 8
Coldwood ....99 F 8
Colebrooke ......113 J 5
Colehill ....107 I 7
Coleraine ....118 L 2
Colgagh ....112 G 5
Colgagh Lough ..112 G 5
Colligan (River) ..95 I 11
Collin Top ....119 N 3
Collinstown .....107 K 7
Collon ....109 M 6
Collooney ....112 G 5
Colly ....88 C 12
Colmanstown ...106 G 7
Comber ....115 O 4
Comeragh Mountains ..95 J 11
Commeen ....117 H 3
Commons ....95 J 10
Conay Island ....112 G 5
Cong / Conga ...105 E 7
Conlig ....115 O 4
Conn (Lough) ...111 E 5
Conna ....90 H 11
Connagh ....100 G 9
Connemara .....104 C 7
Connemara
  National Park ..104 C 7
Connolly ....99 E 9
Connonagh ......89 E 13
Connor ....115 N 3
Connor Pass .....92 B 11
Convoy ....117 I 3
Coogue ....105 F 6
Cookstown ......114 L 4
Coola ....112 G 5
Coolagarry ......106 H 7
Coolaney ....112 G 5
Coolattin ....97 M 9
Coolbaun ....101 K 9
Coolbawn ....100 H 9
Coolboy ....97 M 9
Coolcull ....96 L 11
Coolderry ....101 I 8
Coole (Castle) ...113 J 4
Coole Abbey ....90 H 11
Coolea / Cúil Aodha ..89 E 12
Coolearagh ......102 L 8
Cooley Point ....109 N 6
Coolgrange ......96 K 10
Coolgreany ....97 N 9
Coolkeeragh .....117 K 2
Coolkellure .....89 E 12
Coolmeen ....93 E 10
Coolmore ....112 H 4
Coolnareen ......101 J 9
Coolrain ....101 J 9
Coolroebeg .....96 K 10
Coolshaghtena ..107 H 6
Coolteige ....106 H 6
Coomacarrea ....88 B 12
Coomakesta Pass ..88 B 12
Coomasaharn Lake ..88 C 12
Coomhola ....89 D 12
Coomhola Bridge ..89 D 12
Coonagh ....94 F 10
Cooraclare ......98 D 9
Coorleagh ....96 K 9
Coornagillagh ...89 C 12
Cootehall ....106 H 6
Copany ....113 H 4
Copeland Island ..115 P 3
Coppanagh .....108 L 6
Cora Droma Rúisc /
  Carrick-on-Shannon ..107 H 6
Corbally
  Castleconor West ..111 E 5
Corbally *Clare* ...98 D 9
Corbally *Kildare* ..102 L 8
Corbay Upper ...107 I 6
Corbet Milltown ..115 N 4
Corcaigh / Cork ..90 G 12
Corclogh ....110 B 5
Corcomroe Abbey ..99 E 8

Cordal ....93 D 11
Cordarragh ....105 D 6
Corduff ....109 N 7
Cork Harbour ...90 H 12
Corkey ....119 N 2
Corkscrew Hill ...99 E 8
Corlea ....107 I 7
Corlee ....105 E 5
Corlis Point ......93 D 10
Corn Hill ....107 I 6
Cornafulla ....101 H 7
Cornagillagh ....117 I 3
Cornamona ......105 D 7
Cornanagh ......105 E 6
Corracloona .....113 H 4
Corrakyle ....99 G 9
Corraleehan ....113 I 5
Corran Cross Roads ..114 M 5
Corrandulla .....105 F 7
Corranny ....113 K 5
Corraree ....106 H 7
Corraun Hill ....104 C 6
Corraun Peninsula ..104 C 6
Corraun Point ...110 B 5
Corrawaleen ....107 I 5
Correllstown ....107 K 7
Corrib (Lough) ..105 E 7
Corries ....96 L 10
Corriga ....107 I 6
Corrigeenroe ...106 H 5
Corrofin ....99 E 9
Corronoher .....94 F 10
Corroy ....111 E 5
Corry ....112 H 5
Corstown ....95 J 10
Cortown ....108 L 6
Corvally ....108 L 6
Corvoley ....111 D 5
Cottoners ......89 C 11
Coulagh Bay ...88 B 12
Coumfea ....95 J 11
Courtmacsherry ..90 F 13
Courtmacsherry Bay ..90 G 13
Courtown ....97 N 10
Cousane Gap ...89 E 12
Craanford ....97 M 9
Craffield ....103 M 9
Crag Cave ....93 D 11
Craggaunowen
  Megalithic Centre ..99 F 9
Craig ....118 K 3
Craigantlet .....115 O 4
Craigavad .....115 O 4
Craigavon .....114 M 4
Craignamaddy ..114 K 3
Craigs ....118 M 3
Crana ....117 J 2
Cranagh ....114 K 3
Cranfield Point ..109 N 5
Cranford ....117 I 2
Crannogeboy ...116 G 3
Cranny ....99 E 9
Cratloe ....99 F 9
Craughwell .....99 F 8
Crawfordsburn ..115 O 4
Crazy Corner ...107 K 7
Creagh ....113 J 4
Creagh (The) ..114 M 3
Creaghanroe ...114 L 5
Crean's Cross Roads ..90 F 13
Crecora ....94 F 10
Creegh ....98 D 9
Creeslough ....117 I 2
Creevagh ......111 D 5
Creevagh Head ..111 E 5
Creeves ....93 E 10
Creevykeel .....112 G 4
Cregg *Clare* ...99 E 8
Cregg *Cork* ...89 E 13
Cregg *Galway* ..105 E 7
Cregg *Sligo* ...112 G 5
Creggan *Armagh* ..108 M 5
Creggan *Dungannon* ..114 K 4
Creggaun ......104 C 6
Creggs ....106 G 7
Crilly ....114 L 4
Crindle ....118 L 2
Crinkill ....101 I 8
Croagh *Donegal* ..112 G 3
Croagh *Limerick* ..94 F 10
Croagh Patrick ..105 C 6
Croaghaun ....110 B 6
Croaghmoyle ...105 D 6
Croaghnageer ..113 I 3
Croaghnakeela Island ..104 C 8
Croaghrimbeg ..105 D 6

A B C D E F G H I J K L M N O P Q R S T U V W X Y Z

Croan (Lough) ... 106 H7
Croangar (Lough) ... 116 H3
Crockaneel ... 119 N2
Crockets Town ... 111 E5
Crockmore ... 113 I4
Crocknasmug ... 118 L2
Croghan *Offaly* ... 101 K7
Croghan *Roscommon* ... 106 H6
Croghan Mountain ... 103 N9
Crohane ... 89 D12
Crohy Head ... 116 G3
Crois Mhaoiliona / Crossmolina ... 111 E5
Croithlí / Crolly ... 116 H2
Cromane ... 92 C11
Cromoge ... 101 J9
Croob (Slieve) ... 115 N4
Crookedwood ... 107 K7
Crookhaven ... 88 C13
Crookstown *Kildare* ... 102 L8
Crookstown *Moviddy* ... 90 F12
Croom ... 94 F10
Croos ... 106 H7
Cross *Cong* ... 105 E7
Cross *Waterford* ... 91 I11
Cross (River) ... 105 D7
Cross Barry ... 90 G12
Cross Keys *Cavan* ... 107 K6
Cross Keys *Meath* ... 108 K6
Cross Keys *Meath* ... 108 M7
Cross Roads ... 117 I3
Crossabeg ... 97 M10
Crossakeel ... 108 K6
Crossboyne ... 105 E6
Crossconnell ... 100 H8
Crossdoney ... 107 J6
Crossea ... 107 J7
Crosserlough ... 107 K6
Crossgar ... 115 O4
Crossgare ... 118 L2
Crosshaven ... 90 H12
Crossmaglen ... 108 M5
Crossna ... 106 H5
Crossooha ... 99 F8
Crosspatrick *Kilkenny* ... 101 J9
Crosspatrick *Wicklow* ... 97 M9
Crosswell ... 106 G7
Crove ... 112 G3
Crow Head ... 88 B13
Crownarad ... 112 G4
Cruit Island ... 116 G2
Crumlin *Antrim* ... 115 N4
Crumlin *Cong* ... 105 D7
Crusheen ... 99 F9
Crutt ... 101 K9
Cúil an tSúdaire / Portarlington ... 101 K8
Cuilcagh ... 113 I5
Cuilkillew ... 111 E5
Cuilmore ... 105 F6
Culdaff ... 118 K2
Culdaff Bay ... 118 K2
Culfadda ... 106 G5
Culfin ... 104 C7
Culky ... 113 I5
Cullahill ... 101 J9
Cullane ... 94 G10
Cullaun ... 94 H10
Cullaville ... 108 M5
Culleens ... 111 F5
Cullen *Cork* ... 94 H10
Cullen *Tipperary* ... 93 E11
Cullenagh (River) ... 99 E9
Cullenstown *near Duncormick* ... 96 L11
Cullenstown *near Newbawn* ... 96 L10
Cullin ... 105 E6
Cullin (Lough) ... 105 E6
Cullybackey ... 118 M3
Cullyhanna ... 108 M5
Culmore ... 117 K2
Culnady ... 118 M3
Cummeragh ... 88 B12
Cunningburn ... 115 P4
Curlew Mountains ... 106 G6
Curracloe ... 97 M10
Curragh ... 91 I12
Curragh (The) ... 102 L8
Curragh Camp ... 102 L8
Curragh West ... 106 G7
Curragha ... 109 M7
Curraghbonaun ... 106 F6
Curraghboy ... 107 I7
Curraghmore Gardens ... 95 J11
Curraghroe ... 107 H6
Curraglass ... 91 H11

Currahchase Forest Park ... 94 F10
Curran ... 114 M3
Currane (Lough) ... 88 B12
Currans ... 93 D11
Curraun ... 105 D7
Curreel (Lough) ... 104 C7
Curreeny ... 100 H9
Currow ... 93 D11
Curry ... 105 E6
Curryglass ... 88 C12
Curryskeskin ... 118 M2
Cushendall ... 119 N2
Cushendun ... 119 N2
Cusher ... 114 M5
Cushina ... 101 K8
Cut (The) ... 101 J8
Cutra (Lough) ... 99 F8

D
Dahybaun (Lough) ... 111 D5
Daingean ... 101 K8
Dalgan ... 105 F7
Dalkey ... 103 N8
Damastown ... 109 N7
Damerstown ... 101 K9
Damhead ... 118 M2
Dan (Lough) ... 103 N8
Danesfort *Kilkenny* ... 96 K10
Danesfort *Longford* ... 107 I6
Dangan *Cork* ... 91 H12
Dangan *Waterford* ... 96 K11
Darby's Gap ... 97 M10
Dargle ... 103 N8
Dark Hedges (The) ... 118 M2
Darkley ... 114 L5
Darragh ... 99 E9
Dartry Mountains ... 112 G4
Davagh Forest Park ... 114 L3
Davidstown ... 103 M9
Dawros ... 104 C7
Dawros Head ... 116 G3
Dead ... 94 H10
Dealagh ... 98 D9
Dee ... 108 L6
Deel *Limerick* ... 94 F10
Deel *Mayo* ... 111 D5
Deel *Westmeath* ... 108 K7
Deel Bridge ... 111 D5
Deele (River) ... 117 I3
Deelish ... 89 E12
Deenish Island ... 88 B12
Delamont ... 115 O4
Delany ... 103 N8
Delphi ... 104 C7
Delvin ... 108 K7
Delvin (River) ... 109 N7
Dennet (Burn) ... 117 J3
Derg ... 113 J3
Derg (Lough) *near Donegal* ... 113 I4
Derg (Lough) *near Nenagh* ... 100 H9
Dergalt ... 117 J3
Dernagree ... 93 E11
Derravaragh (Lough) ... 107 J7
Derreen *near Ballynagoraher* ... 105 D6
Derreen *near Cloghmore* ... 104 C7
Derreen *near Formoyle* ... 99 E8
Derreen *near Lahinch* ... 98 D9
Derreen Gardens ... 89 C12
Derreendarragh ... 89 C12
Derreeny ... 88 C12
Derreeny Bridge ... 89 E13
Derriana Lough ... 88 C12
Derries ... 101 J8
Derryadd ... 114 M4
Derryanvil ... 114 M4
Derrybeg ... 116 H2
Derryboye ... 115 O4
Derrybrien ... 99 G8
Derryclare Lough ... 104 C7
Derrycooly ... 101 I8
Derrycraff ... 105 D6
Derrydruel ... 116 G3
Derryerglinna ... 105 D7
Derryfadda ... 101 J8
Derrygolan ... 101 J8
Derrygonnelly ... 113 I4
Derrygoolin ... 100 G9
Derrygrogan ... 101 J8
Derrykeevan ... 114 M4
Derrykeighan ... 118 M2
Derrylea ... 104 C7
Derrylin ... 113 J5
Derrylough ... 116 G3

Derrymore ... 93 C11
Derrymore Island ... 93 C11
Derrynane ... 88 B12
Derrynane House ... 88 B12
Derrynasaggart Mountains ... 89 E11
Derrynawilt ... 113 K5
Derryneen ... 104 C7
Derrynoose ... 114 L5
Derryrush ... 104 C7
Derrytrasna ... 114 M4
Derryveagh Mountains ... 117 H3
Derryvohy ... 105 E6
Derrywode ... 106 G6
Dervock ... 118 M2
Desertmartin ... 114 L3
Devenish Island ... 113 J4
Devilsbit ... 101 I9
Devilsmother ... 105 D7
Diamond (The) *Antrim* ... 114 N4
Diamond (The) *Cookstown* ... 114 M4
Diamond (The) *Omagh* ... 113 J4
Dingle / Daingean Uí Chúis ... 92 B11
Dingle Bay ... 92 B11
Dingle Harbour ... 92 B11
Divis ... 115 N4
Doagh *Newtownabbey* ... 115 N3
Doagh *Rosguill* ... 117 I2
Doagh Beg / Dumhaigh Bhig ... 117 J2
Doagh Isle ... 117 J2
Dodder ... 103 M8
Doe Castle ... 117 I2
Dolla ... 100 H9
Dollingstown ... 114 N4
Domhnach Phádraig / Donaghpatrick ... 108 L6
Donabate ... 109 N7
Donacarney ... 109 N6
Donadea ... 102 L7
Donagh ... 113 J5
Donaghadee ... 115 P4
Donaghaguy ... 109 N5
Donaghcloney ... 114 N4
Donaghey ... 114 L4
Donaghmore ... 114 L4
Donaghmore *Meath* ... 109 M7
Donard *Wexford* ... 96 L10
Donard *Wicklow* ... 103 M8
Donard (Slieve) ... 115 O5
Donaskeagh ... 95 H10
Donegal / Dún na nGall ... 113 H4
Donegal Airport ... 116 G2
Donegal Bay ... 112 G5
Donegal Point ... 98 D9
Doneraile ... 94 G11
Donohill ... 95 H10
Donore ... 109 M6
Donoughmore ... 90 F12
Doo (Lough) ... 99 E9
Doo Lough ... 104 C7
Doo Lough Pass ... 104 C7
Dooagh ... 110 B6
Doobehy ... 111 D5
Doocastle ... 106 G5
Dooega Head ... 104 B6
Dooey Point ... 116 G3
Doogary ... 107 J5
Dooghbeg ... 104 C6
Doogort ... 110 B5
Doohooma ... 110 C5
Dooish Mount ... 117 J3
Doolough Point ... 110 C5
Doon *Galway* ... 100 G7
Doon *Limerick* ... 94 H10
Doon Lough ... 99 F9
Doona ... 110 C5
Doonaha ... 93 D10
Doonbeg ... 98 D9
Doonloughan ... 104 B7
Doonmanagh ... 92 B11
Doorin Point ... 112 H4
Dooyork ... 110 C5
Dore ... 116 H2
Dorrusawillin ... 107 H5
Dough ... 88 C13
Douglas ... 90 G12
Douglas Bridge ... 113 J3
Doulus Bay ... 88 A12
Doulus Head ... 88 A12
Dowdallshill ... 109 M5
Dowling ... 96 K10
Downhill ... 118 L2
Downpatrick ... 115 O5
Downpatrick Head ... 111 D5
Downs (The) ... 107 K7
Dowra ... 113 H5

Dowth ... 109 M6
Drains Bay ... 119 O3
Drangan ... 95 J10
Draperstown ... 114 L3
Dreen ... 118 K3
Dreenagh ... 92 C10
Drimoleague ... 89 E13
Drinagh *Cork* ... 89 E13
Drinagh *Wexford* ... 97 M11
Drinaghan ... 111 E5
Dring ... 107 J6
Dripsey ... 90 F12
Dripsey (River) ... 90 F11
Drishaghaun ... 105 D7
Drishane Bridge ... 89 D13
Droichead Átha / Drogheda ... 109 M6
Droichead na Bandan / Bandon ... 90 F12
Drom ... 101 I9
Dromahair ... 112 H5
Dromara ... 115 N4
Dromcolliher ... 94 F10
Dromin *Limerick* ... 94 G10
Dromin *Louth* ... 109 M6
Dromina ... 94 F11
Dromineer ... 100 H9
Dromiskin ... 109 M6
Dromkeen ... 94 G10
Drommahane ... 90 F11
Dromod ... 107 I6
Dromoland Castle ... 99 F9
Dromore *Banbridge* ... 115 N4
Dromore *Omagh* ... 113 J4
Dromore Lake ... 94 F10
Dromore West ... 112 F5
Dromtrasna ... 93 E10
Drones (The) ... 118 M2
Drowes ... 112 H4
Drum *Monaghan* ... 108 K5
Drum *Roscommon* ... 101 H7
Drum *Sligo* ... 112 G5
Drum Manor Forest Park ... 114 L4
Drumahoe ... 117 K3
Drumandoora ... 99 F8
Drumaness ... 115 O4
Drumano Head ... 112 G4
Drumatober ... 100 G8
Drumbane ... 95 I10
Drumbeg *Feddyglass* ... 117 J3
Drumbeg *Lisburn* ... 115 O4
Drumbo ... 115 O4
Drumbologe ... 117 I3
Drumcar ... 109 M6
Drumcard ... 113 I5
Drumcliff ... 112 G5
Drumcliff Bay ... 112 G5
Drumcondra ... 108 M6
Drumcong ... 107 I5
Drumcree ... 108 K7
Drumcullen ... 114 M3
Drumduff ... 113 J4
Drumena Cashel ... 115 O5
Drumfea ... 96 L10
Drumfin ... 112 G5
Drumfree ... 117 J2
Drumgoft ... 103 M9
Drumintee ... 109 M5
Drumkeary ... 99 G8
Drumkeen ... 117 I3
Drumkeeran ... 112 H5
Drumlaheen Lough ... 107 I5
Drumlea ... 107 I5
Drumlegagh ... 113 J4
Drumlish ... 107 I6
Drumlosh ... 101 I7
Drummannon ... 114 M4
Drummin ... 96 L10
Drummullin ... 106 H6
Drumnakilly ... 114 K4
Drumone ... 108 K6
Drumquin ... 113 J4
Drumraney ... 107 I7
Drumreagh ... 110 B5
Drumshanbo ... 107 H5
Drumsna ... 107 H6
Drumsurn ... 118 L3
Duagh ... 93 D10
Dually ... 95 I10
Dublin Bay ... 103 N7
Duff ... 112 H4
Duffy ... 102 L7
Duleek ... 109 M7
Dumha Éige / Dooega ... 104 B6
Dún Aengus ... 98 C8

Dún A'Rí Forest Park ... 108 L6
Dún Chaoin / Dunquin ... 92 A11
Dún Dealgan / Dundalk ... 109 M5
Dún Garbhán /Dungarvan ... 91 J11
Dun Laoghaire ... 103 N8
Dún Mánmhaí / Dunmanway ... 89 E12
Dún Mór / Dunmore ... 106 F7
Dún na nGall / Donegal ... 113 H4
Dunabrattin Head ... 91 K11
Dunadry ... 115 N3
Dunaff ... 117 J2
Dunaff Head ... 117 J2
Dunaghy ... 118 M2
Dunagree Point ... 118 L2
Dunamase (Rock of) ... 101 K8
Dunamon ... 106 H7
Dunany ... 109 N6
Dunany Point ... 109 N6
Dunbel ... 96 K10
Dunboyne ... 103 M7
Dunbrody Abbey ... 96 L11
Dunbulcaun Bay ... 99 F8
Duncannon ... 96 L11
Duncormick ... 96 M11
Dunderrow ... 90 G12
Dunderry ... 108 L7
Dundonald ... 115 O4
Dundrod ... 115 N4
Dundrum *Down* ... 115 O5
Dundrum *Dublin* ... 103 N8
Dundrum *Tipperary* ... 95 H10
Dundrum Bay ... 115 O5
Dunfanaghy ... 117 I2
Dungannon ... 114 L4
Dunganstown ... 96 L10
Dungarvan Harbour ... 91 J11
Dungiven ... 118 L3
Dungloe / An Clochán Liath ... 116 G3
Dungonnell Dam ... 119 N3
Dungourney ... 90 H12
Dunguaire Castle ... 99 F8
Dunhill ... 91 K11
Duniry ... 100 G8
Dunkellin ... 99 F8
Dunkerrin ... 101 I9
Dunkineely ... 112 G4
Dunkitt ... 96 K11
Dunlavin ... 102 L8
Dunleer ... 109 M6
Dunlewy ... 117 H2
Dunloe (Gap of) ... 89 D11
Dunloy ... 118 M2
Dunluce Castle ... 118 M2
Dunmanus ... 89 D13
Dunmanus Bay ... 88 C13
Dunmore ... 109 O5
Dunmore Cave ... 96 K10
Dunmore East *Tipperary* ... 96 L11
Dunmore Head *Dunquin* ... 92 A11
Dunmore Head *near Culdaff* ... 118 K2
Dunmore Head *near Portnoo* ... 116 G3
Dunmurry ... 115 N4
Dunnamaggan ... 96 K10
Dunnamanagh ... 117 K3
Dunnamore ... 114 L3
Dunnycove Bay ... 89 F13
Dunowen Head ... 89 F13
Dunree Head ... 117 J2
Dunsany ... 108 M7
Dunshaughlin ... 108 M7
Dunworly Bay ... 90 F13
Durlas / Thurles ... 95 I9
Durrow ... 101 J9
Durrus ... 89 D13
Dursey Head ... 88 B13
Dursey Island ... 88 B13
Duvillaun Beg ... 110 B5
Duvillaun More ... 110 B5
Dyan ... 114 L4
Dysart ... 107 J7
Dysert O'Dea ... 99 E9

E
Éadan Doire / Édenderry ... 102 K7
Eagle (Mount) ... 92 A11
Eagle Island ... 110 B5
Eagles Hill ... 88 B12
Eany ... 112 H3
Eanymore ... 112 H3
Easky ... 111 F5
Easky Lough ... 112 F5
East Ferry ... 90 H12

East Town ... 116 H2
Eddy Island ... 99 F8
Eden ... 115 O3
Ederny ... 113 J4
Edgeworthstown / Meathas Troim ... 107 J6
Egish (Lough) ... 108 L5
Eglinton ... 118 K2
Eglish ... 114 L4
Eighter ... 108 K6
Eleven Lane Ends ... 114 M5
Ellistrin ... 117 I3
Elly Bay ... 110 B5
Elphin ... 106 H6
Elton ... 94 G10
Elva (Slieve) ... 99 E8
Emlagh Point ... 104 C6
Emly ... 94 G10
Emmoo ... 106 H7
Emo ... 101 K8
Emo Court ... 101 K8
Emyvale ... 114 L4
Ennel (Lough) ... 107 J7
Ennis / Inis ... 99 F9
Enniscorthy / Inis Córthaidh ... 97 M10
Enniskean ... 89 F12
Enniskerry ... 103 N8
Enniskillen ... 113 J4
Ennistimon / Inis Díomáin ... 99 E9
Eochaill / Youghal ... 91 I12
Erne (Lower Lough) ... 113 I4
Erne (River) ... 107 J6
Erne (Upper Lough) ... 113 J5
Erra ... 107 I6
Errew Abbey ... 111 E5
Erriff (River) ... 105 D7
Errigal Mountain ... 117 H2
Erril ... 101 I9
Erris Head ... 110 B5
Errisbeg ... 104 C7
Errislannan ... 104 B7
Errit Lough ... 106 F6
Ervey Cross Roads ... 118 K3
Eshnadarragh ... 113 K5
Eshnadeelada ... 113 K5
Eske ... 113 H3
Eske (Lough) ... 113 H3
Esker ... 99 F8
Esker South ... 107 I6
Eskeragh ... 111 D5
Eskragh ... 113 K4
Eyeries ... 88 C12
Eyrecourt ... 100 H8

F
Faha ... 91 J11
Fahamore ... 92 B11
Fahan ... 117 J2
Fahy ... 100 H8
Fahy Lough ... 110 C5
Fair Green ... 99 F9
Fair Head ... 88 C13
Fairyhouse ... 108 M7
Fairymount ... 106 G6
Fallmore ... 110 B5
Fanad ... 117 I2
Fanad Head ... 117 J2
Fane River ... 108 M5
Fanore ... 99 E8
Farahy ... 94 G11
Fardrum ... 101 I7
Fardurris Point ... 98 D8
Farmer's Bridge ... 93 D11
Farnagh ... 101 I7
Farnaght ... 107 I6
Farnanes Cross Roads ... 90 F12
Farnoge ... 96 K10
Farran ... 90 F12
Farran Forest Park ... 90 F12
Farrancassidy Cross Roads ... 112 H4
Farranfore ... 93 D11
Fastnet Rock ... 89 D13
Faughan ... 118 K3
Fawney ... 117 K3
Fea (Lough) ... 114 L3
Feagarrid ... 95 I11
Feakle ... 99 G9
Feale (River) ... 93 D10
Fearn Hill ... 113 J3
Fedamore ... 94 G10
Fee (Lough) ... 104 C7
Feeagh (Lough) ... 105 D6
Feeard ... 93 C10
Feenagh ... 94 F10

Feeny ....118 K 3
Feevagh ....106 H 7
Fenagh ....107 I 5
Fenit ....92 C 11
Fennagh ....96 L 9
Fennor ....91 K 11
Feohanagh Kerry ....92 A 11
Feohanagh Limerick ....94 F 10
Feohanagh (River) ....92 B 11
Ferbane ....101 I 8
Fergus (River) ....99 E 9
Fern (Lough) ....117 I 2
Ferns ....97 M 10
Ferry Bridge ....94 F 10
Ferrybank ....97 N 9
Ferrycarrig ....97 M 10
Ferta ....88 B 12
Fethard ....96 L 11
Fews ....95 J 11
Feystown ....119 O 3
Fiddown ....96 K 10
Fieries ....93 D 11
Finavarra ....99 E 8
Finglas ....103 N 7
Finglass ....89 C 11
Finn (Lough) ....117 H 3
Finn (River) ....117 J 3
Finnea ....107 J 6
Finnisglin ....104 C 7
Fintona ....113 K 4
Fintragh Bay ....112 G 4
Finuge ....93 D 10
Finvoy ....118 M 2
Fiodh Ard / Fethard ....95 I 10
Fionnaithe / Finny ....105 D 7
Firkeel ....88 B 13
Fisherhill ....105 E 6
Five Corners ....115 N 3
Fivealley ....101 I 8
Fivemilebridge ....90 G 12
Fivemiletown ....113 K 4
Flagmount Corlea ....99 G 9
Flagmount Kilkenny ....96 K 10
Flat Head ....90 G 12
Flesk ....89 D 11
Florence Court ....113 I 5
Florence Court
   Forest Park ....113 I 5
Foaty Island/Fota Island ..90 H 12
Foilycleara ....95 H 10
Folk Park ....99 F 9
Fontstown ....102 L 8
Forbes (Lough) ....107 I 6
Fordstown ....108 L 6
Fore ....107 K 6
Forkill ....109 M 5
Forlorn Point ....96 M 11
Formoyle Lonford ....107 I 7
Formoyle Mayo ....104 C 6
Formoyle
   near Ballivaghan ....99 E 8
Formoyle near Inagh ....99 E 9
Formoyle (Lough) ....105 D 7
Fort Stewart ....117 J 2
Forthill ....107 I 7
Fota Island ....90 H 12
Foul Sound ....98 D 8
Foulksmills ....96 L 11
Fountain Cross ....99 E 9
Four Mile House ....106 H 7
Four Roads ....106 H 7
Fourknocks ....109 N 7
Foxford ....105 E 6
Foxhall ....105 E 7
Foyle (Lough) ....118 K 2
Foynes ....93 E 10
Foynes Island ....93 E 10
Francis' Gap ....99 G 8
Freemount ....94 F 11
Frenchpark ....106 G 6
Freshford ....95 J 9
Freynestown ....102 L 8
Frosses ....112 H 3
Frower Point ....90 G 12
Fuerty ....106 H 7
Funshin More ....99 F 8
Funshinagh (Lough) ....106 H 7
Funshion ....94 G 11
Furbogh ....99 E 8
Furnace ....105 D 7
Furnace Lough ....105 D 6
Furness ....103 M 8
Fyagh (Slieve) ....111 D 5

G

Gabriel (Mount) ....89 D 13
Gaddagh ....89 C 11

Gaillimh / Galway ....99 E 8
Gainestown ....107 K 7
Galbally Dungannon ....114 L 4
Galbally Limerick ....94 H 10
Galbally Wexford ....96 M 10
Galbolie ....108 K 6
Galey ....93 D 10
Galgorm ....118 N 3
Gallarus Oratory ....92 A 11
Galley Head ....89 F 13
Gallion (Slieve) ....114 L 3
Galmoy ....101 J 9
Galty Mountains ....95 H 10
Galtymore Mountain ....95 H 10
Galway Bay ....98 D 8
Galways Bridge ....89 D 12
Gaoth Dobhair /
   Gweedore ....116 H 2
Gaoth Sáile / Geesala ......110 C 5
Gap (The) ....95 I 11
Gara (Lough) ....106 G 6
Garadice ....102 L 7
Garadice Lough ....107 I 5
Garbally ....100 H 8
Garinish Island ....88 C 12
Garnavilla ....95 I 10
Garnish Point ....88 B 13
Garrane ....89 E 12
Garranlahan ....106 G 6
Garraun Clare ....98 D 9
Garraun Galway ....100 G 8
Garraun (Mount) ....104 C 7
Garries Bridge ....89 D 12
Garrison ....112 H 4
Garristown ....109 M 7
Garron Point ....119 O 2
Garrycloonagh ....111 E 5
Garrycullen ....96 L 11
Garryduff ....118 M 2
Garryfine ....94 F 10
Garrykennedy ....100 G 9
Garryspillane ....94 G 10
Garryvoe ....91 H 12
Gartan Lough ....117 I 3
Gartree Point ....114 N 4
Garty Lough ....107 J 6
Garvagh Coleraine ....118 L 3
Garvagh Rowan ....107 I 6
Garvaghy ....114 K 4
Garvary ....113 J 4
Gattabaun ....101 J 9
Gearagh (The) ....90 F 12
Gearha Bridge ....88 C 12
Geashill ....101 K 8
Geevagh ....112 H 5
George (Lough) ....99 F 9
Gerahies ....89 D 13
Giant's Causeway ....118 M 2
Giles Quay ....109 N 6
Gilford ....114 M 4
Gill (Lough) near Sligo ....112 G 5
Gill (Lough) nearTralee ....92 B 11
Glanaruddery Mountains ...93 D 11
Glandore ....89 E 13
Glandore Harbour ....89 E 13
Glangevlin ....113 I 5
Glanmire ....90 G 12
Glanmore Lake ....89 C 12
Glanoe ....93 D 10
Glantane ....90 F 11
Glanworth ....94 G 11
Glarryford ....118 M 3
Glasdrumman ....109 O 5
Glaslough ....114 L 5
Glasmullan ....117 J 2
Glassan ....107 I 7
Glasshouse Lake ....107 J 6
Glassillaun ....104 C 6
Glastry ....115 P 4
Gleann Cholm Cille /
   Glencolumbkille ....112 F 3
Gleann Domhain /
   Glendowan ....117 I 3
Gleann na Muaidhe /
   Glenamoy ....111 C 5
Glen ....117 I 2
Glen (River) Cork ....90 F 11
Glen (River) Donegal ......112 G 3
Glen Bay ....112 F 3
Glen Head ....112 F 3
Glen Lough Donegal ......117 I 2
Glen Lough Westmeath ...107 J 7
Glenaan ....119 N 2
Glenade ....112 H 4
Glenade Lough ....112 H 4
Glenamoy (River) ....111 D 5
Glenariff ....119 N 2

Glenariff Forest Park ......119 N 2
Glenariff or Waterfoot ....119 N 2
Glenarm ....119 O 3
Glenavy ....115 N 4
Glenballyemon ....119 N 2
Glenbeg Lough ....88 C 12
Glenbeigh ....92 C 11
Glenboy ....112 H 5
Glenbridge Lodge ....103 M 8
Glenbrohane ....94 G 10
Glenbrook ....90 G 12
Glencar ....88 C 12
Glencar Lough ....112 G 4
Glencloy ....119 O 3
Glencolmcille Folk Village ..112 F 3
Glencree ....103 N 8
Glencullen ....103 N 8
Glendalough Brockagh ....116 H 2
Glendalough Waterford ....95 J 11
Glenderry ....92 C 10
Glendorragha ....116 G 3
Glendovan Mountains ......117 H 3
Glendree ....99 F 9
Glendum ....119 N 2
Glenealy ....103 N 9
Gleneely near Ballybofey ..113 I 3
Gleneely near Cardonagh ..118 K 2
Glenelly ....114 K 3
Glenelly Valley ....114 K 3
Glenfarne ....113 I 5
Glenflesk ....89 D 11
Glengad Head ....118 K 1
Glengarriff (River) ....89 D 12
Glengarriff Harbour ....89 D 12
Glengesh Pass ....112 G 3
Glengormley ....115 O 3
Glenhead ....118 K 2
Glenhull ....114 K 3
Glenicmurrin Lough ....98 D 8
Glenmacnass ....103 M 8
Glenmalur ....103 M 9
Glenmore Clare ....99 E 9
Glenmore Kilkenny ....96 K 10
Glennagevlagh ....105 D 7
Glennamaddy ....106 G 7
Glennascaul ....99 F 8
Glenoe ....115 O 3
Glenshane Pass ....118 L 3
Glenshesk ....119 N 2
Glentaisie ....119 N 2
Glentane ....106 G 7
Glenties ....116 H 3
Glentogher ....118 K 2
Glentrasna ....105 D 7
Glenvale ....118 M 3
Glenvar / Gleann Bhairr ...117 J 2
Glenveagh National Park ..117 I 2
Glenville ....90 G 11
Glin ....93 E 10
Glin Castle ....93 E 10
Glinsce / Glinsk ....104 C 7
Glinsk Donegal ....117 I 2
Glinsk Mayo ....111 D 5
Glounthaune ....90 G 12
Glyde (River) ....108 M 6
Glynn Carlow ....96 L 10
Glynn Larne ....115 O 3
Gneevgullia ....93 E 11
Gob an Choire /
   Achill Sound ....104 C 6
Gobbins (The) ....115 O 3
Gokane Point ....89 E 13
Gola Island / Gabhla ......116 G 2
Golagh Lough ....113 H 4
Golam Head ....98 C 8
Golden ....95 I 10
Golden Vale ....95 H 10
Goleen ....88 C 13
Goold's Cross ....95 I 10
Goresbridge ....96 K 10
Gorey / Guaire ....97 N 9
Gormanston ....109 N 7
Gort an Choirce /
   Gortahork ....117 H 2
Gortaclare ....113 K 4
Gortahill ....113 I 5
Gortaleam ....106 F 7
Gortarevan ....100 H 8
Gortaroo ....91 I 12
Gortaway ....117 J 2
Gorteen ....106 G 6
Gorteen Bridge ....101 J 8
Gorteeny ....100 G 8
Gortgarriff ....88 C 12
Gortgarrigan ....112 H 5
Gortin ....113 K 3
Gortin Glen Forest Park ....113 K 3

Gortletteragh ....107 I 6
Gortmore near Ballycastle .111 D 5
Gortmore near Bangor ......111 C 5
Gortmullan ....113 J 5
Gortnadeeve ....106 G 7
Gortnahoo ....95 J 9
Gortnasillagh ....106 G 6
Gortree ....117 J 3
Gortymadden ....100 G 8
Gorumna Island ....98 C 8
Gosford Forest Park ....114 M 5
Gougane Barra
   Forest Park ....89 D 12
Gougane Barra Lake ....89 E 12
Gouladoo ....89 C 13
Gowla ....104 C 7
Gowlaun ....104 C 7
Gowlin ....96 L 10
Gowna (Lough) ....107 J 6
Gowran ....96 K 10
Gracehill ....118 N 3
Graffy ....116 H 3
Gráig na Manach /
   Graiguenamanagh ....96 L 10
Graigue ....102 L 9
Graigue Hill ....96 L 9
Graigue More ....96 M 10
Graigues ....88 B 12
Granabeg ....103 M 8
Gránard / Granard ....107 J 6
Grand Canal ....101 I 8
Graney ....102 L 9
Graney (Lough) ....99 G 9
Graney (River) ....99 G 9
Grange Kildare ....102 K 7
Grange Kilkenny ....96 K 10
Grange Louth ....109 N 5
Grange Sligo ....112 G 4
Grange Waterford ....91 I 12
Grange (River) ....106 F 7
Grange Con ....102 L 9
Grangebellew ....109 M 6
Grangeford ....102 L 9
Grangegeeth ....108 M 6
Granias Gap ....117 K 2
Grannagh ....99 F 8
Gransha ....115 O 3
Granville ....114 L 4
Greagh ....107 I 6
Great Blasket Island ....92 A 11
Great Island ....90 H 12
Great Newtown Head ......96 K 11
Great Skellig ....88 A 12
Great Sugar Loaf ....103 N 8
Greatman's Bay ....98 D 8
Greenan ....103 N 9
Greenanstown ....109 N 7
Greencastle Donegal ....118 L 2
Greencastle
   Newry-Mourne ....109 N 5
Greencastle Omagh ....114 K 3
Greenfield ....105 E 7
Greenisland ....115 O 3
Greenore ....109 N 5
Greenore Point ....97 N 11
Gregans Castle ....99 E 8
Gregory's Sound ....98 D 8
Grenagh ....90 G 11
Grey Abbey ....115 P 4
Grey Point ....115 O 3
Greysteel ....118 K 2
Greystone ....114 L 4
Grianan of Aileach ....117 J 2
Grogan ....101 I 8
Groomsport ....115 P 3
Gubaveeny ....113 I 5
Gubbaroe Point ....113 I 4
Gulladoo Lough ....107 J 6
Gulladuff ....118 M 3
Gullion (Slieve) ....109 M 5
Gur (Lough) ....94 G 10
Gurteen Cappalusk ....99 G 7
Gurteen Leitrim ....112 H 5
Gusserane ....96 L 11
Gweebarra Bridge ....116 H 3
Gweebarra ....116 H 3
Gweebarra Bay ....116 G 3
Gweedore ....116 H 2
Gweestion ....105 E 6
Gyleen ....90 H 12

H

Hacketstown ....103 M 9
Hags Head ....98 D 9
Hamiltonsbawn ....114 M 4
Hand Cross Roads (The) ...99 E 9
Hannahstown ....115 N 4

Hare Island ....89 D 13
Harristown ....96 K 10
Harrow (The) ....97 M 10
Healy Pass ....89 C 12
Helen's Bay ....115 O 3
Helvick Head ....91 J 11
Herbertstown ....94 G 10
High Island ....104 B 7
Highwood ....112 H 5
Hill Street ....107 H 6
Hillsborough ....115 N 4
Hilltown Harristown ....96 L 11
Hilltown
   Newry and Mourne ......115 N 5
Hind ....106 H 7
Hog's Head ....88 B 12
Holeopen Bay West ....90 G 13
Hollyford ....95 H 10
Hollyfort ....97 M 9
Hollymount ....105 E 7
Hollywood ....103 M 8
Holy Cross ....95 I 10
Holy Island ....99 G 9
Holycross ....94 G 10
Holywell ....113 I 5
Holywell Hill ....117 J 2
Holywood ....115 O 4
Hook Head ....96 L 11
Hore Abbey ....95 I 10
Horn Head ....117 I 2
Horse and Jockey ....95 I 10
Horse Island ....89 D 13
Horseleap ....101 J 7
Hospital ....94 G 10
Hugginstown ....96 K 10
Hungry Hill ....88 C 12
Hurlers Cross ....99 F 9
Hurley ....109 M 7
Hyne (Lough) ....89 E 13

I

Ilen ....89 E 13
Illaunstookagh ....92 C 11
Illauntannig ....92 B 11
Illies ....117 J 2
Illnacullin ....89 D 12
Inagh ....99 E 9
Inagh (Lough) ....104 C 7
Inch Donegal ....117 J 2
Inch near Whitegate ....90 H 12
Inch near Youghal ....91 I 12
Inch Tipperary ....95 H 9
Inch Wexford ....97 N 9
Inch Abbey ....115 O 4
Inch Island ....117 J 2
Inchagoill ....105 E 7
Inchamore Bridge ....108 L 7
Inchbeg ....96 J 9
Inchcleraun ....107 H 7
Inchee Bridge ....89 D 12
Inchicronan Lough ....99 F 9
Inchigeelagh ....89 E 12
Inchiquin ....105 E 7
Inchiquin Lough Clare ......99 E 9
Inchiquin Lough Kerry ......89 D 12
Inchmore ....107 I 7
Inchnamuck ....95 H 11
Inchydoney Island ....90 F 13
Indreabhán / Inveran ....98 D 8
Inis / Ennis ....99 F 9
Inis Bó Finne / Inishbofin ..117 H 2
Inis Meáin / Inishmaan ....98 D 8
Inis Mór / Inishmore ....98 C 8
Inis Oírr / Inisheer ....98 D 8
Inishannon ....90 G 12
Inishbarra ....98 C 8
Inishbiggle ....110 C 6
Inishbofin ....104 B 7
Inishcarra ....90 G 12
Inishcarra Reservoir ....90 F 12
Inishcrone ....111 E 5
Inishdoorus ....105 D 7
Inishfarnard ....88 B 12
Inishfree Bay ....116 G 2
Inishfree Upper ....116 G 2
Inishglora ....110 B 5
Inishkea North ....110 B 5
Inishkea South ....110 B 5
Inishmaine Island ....105 E 7
Inishmicatreer ....105 E 7
Inishmurray ....112 G 4
Inishnabro ....92 A 11
Inishnee ....104 C 7
Inishowen ....118 K 2
Inishowen Head ....118 L 2
Inishshark ....104 B 7

Inishtooskert ....92 A 11
Inishtrahull ....118 K 1
Inishtrahull Sound ....118 K 1
Inishturk ....104 B 6
Inishvickillane ....92 A 11
Inistioge ....96 K 10
Innfield ....102 L 7
Innisfree ....112 G 5
Inniskeen ....108 M 5
Inny (River) ....107 J 6
Inver Donegal ....112 H 4
Inver Mayo ....110 C 5
Inver Bay ....112 H 4
Ireland's Eye ....103 N 7
Irish Agricultural
   Museum ....97 M 11
Irishtown ....105 F 7
Iron (Lough) ....107 J 7
Iron Mountains ....113 I 5
Irvinestown ....113 J 4
Island Lake ....106 F 6
Island Reavy (Lough) ......115 N 5
Islandmagee ....115 O 3
Islandmore ....115 P 4
Iveragh ....88 B 12

J

J. F. Kennedy Park ....96 L 11
Jamestown Cloonteem ....107 H 6
Jamestown Laois ....101 K 8
Japanese Gardens ....102 L 8
Jerpoint Abbey ....96 K 10
Jerrettspass ....114 M 5
Johnstown Kildare ....103 M 8
Johnstown Kilkenny ....101 J 9
Johnstown Meath ....108 M 7
Johnstown near Arklow ....103 N 9
Johnstown
   near Coolgreany ....97 N 9
Johnstown Bridge ....107 I 6
Johnstownbridge ....102 L 7
Jonesborough ....109 M 5
Joyce ....105 D 7
Julianstown ....109 N 6

K

Kanturk Castle ....94 F 11
Katesbridge ....115 N 5
Keadew ....107 H 5
Keady ....114 L 5
Keady Mountain ....118 L 2
Kealduff ....89 C 12
Kealkill ....89 D 12
Kearney ....115 P 4
Kearney Point ....115 P 4
Keel ....110 B 6
Keel (Lough) ....117 I 2
Keel Lough ....110 B 6
Keeloges ....106 G 7
Keem Strand ....110 B 6
Keenagh Longford ....107 I 7
Keenagh Mayo ....111 D 5
Keeraunnagark ....98 D 8
Keereen ....91 I 11
Keimaneigh (The pass of) ..89 E 12
Kells Ballymena ....115 N 3
Kells Kerry ....88 B 12
Kells Kilkenny ....96 K 10
Kells (Ceanannus Mor) /
   Ceanannas Meath ....108 L 6
Kells Priory ....96 K 10
Kellysgrove ....100 H 8
Kenmare River ....88 B 12
Kentstown ....108 M 7
Kerry (Ring of) ....88 B 12
Kerry Head ....92 C 10
Kesh Fermanagh ....113 I 4
Kesh Toomour ....106 G 5
Keshcarrigan ....107 I 5
Key (Lough) ....106 H 5
Kid Island ....110 C 5
Kilbaha ....93 C 10
Kilbaha Bay ....93 C 10
Kilbane ....99 G 9
Kilbarry ....89 E 12
Kilbeacanty ....99 F 8
Kilbeggan ....101 J 7
Kilbeheny ....94 H 11
Kilbennan ....105 F 7
Kilberry Bert ....108 L 6
Kilberry Kildare ....102 K 8
Kilbreedy ....94 F 10
Kilbrickan ....105 D 7
Kilbricken ....101 J 9
Kilbride near Blessington ..103 M 8

A B C D E F G H I J K L M N O P Q R S T U V W X Y Z

A B C D E F G H I J K L M N O P Q R S T U V W X Y Z

Kilbride *near Ratoah* 103 M7
Kilbride *near Trim* 108 L7
Kilbride *near Wicklow* ... 103 N9
Kilbrien 95 J11
Kilbrin 94 F11
Kilbrittain 90 F12
Kilcaimin 99 F8
Kilcar 112 G4
Kilcarn 108 L7
Kilcatherine Point 88 B12
Kilcavan 101 J8
Kilchreest 99 G8
Kilclaran 99 G9
Kilclief 115 P5
Kilcloher 93 C10
Kilclonfert 101 J8
Kilclooney 116 G3
Kilcock 102 L7
Kilcogy 107 J6
Kilcolgan 99 F8
Kilcolman *Cashel* 90 F12
Kilcolman
 Dunmoylan East 93 E10
Kilcoltrim 96 L10
Kilcomin 101 I9
Kilcommon *near Caher* ...95 I10
Kilcommon *near Milestone* ..95 H9
Kilcon 111 E5
Kilconly *Galway* 105 F7
Kilconly *Kerry* 93 D10
Kilcoo 115 N5
Kilcoole 103 N8
Kilcormac 101 I8
Kilcornan 94 F10
Kilcotty 97 M10
Kilcredan 91 I12
Kilcredaun Point 93 C10
Kilcrohane 89 C13
Kilcrow 100 H8
Kilcullen 102 L8
Kilcummin *Kerry* 92 B11
Kilcummin *Mayo* 111 E5
Kilcummin Farmhill 93 D11
Kilcurly 109 M5
Kilcurry 109 M5
Kildalkey 108 L7
Kildangan 102 K8
Kildavin 96 L9
Kilderry 96 K9
Kildoney Point 112 H4
Kildorrery 94 G11
Kildress 114 L4
Kildrum 115 N3
Kilfeakle 95 H10
Kilfearagh 98 D10
Kilfenora 99 E9
Kilfinnane 94 G10
Kilfinny 94 F10
Kilflyn 93 D10
Kilgarvan 89 D12
Kilglass *Galway* 106 G7
Kilglass *Sligo* 111 E5
Kilglass Lough 107 H6
Kilgobnet *Kerry* 89 C11
Kilgobnet *Waterford* 91 J11
Kilgory Lough 99 E9
Kilgowan 102 L8
Kiljames 96 K10
Kilkea 102 L9
Kilkeary 100 H9
Kilkeasy 96 K10
Kilkeel 109 N5
Kilkeeran High Crosses ..95 J10
Kilkenny West 107 I7
Kilkerrin 106 G7
Kilkieran / Cill Chiaráin .. 104 C8
Kilkieran Bay 104 C7
Kilkiernan 96 K9
Kilkinamurry 115 N5
Kilkinlea 93 E10
Kilkishen 99 F9
Kill *Cavan* 108 K5
Kill *Waterford* 91 J11
Killabunane 89 D12
Killaclug 94 H11
Killacolla 94 F10
Killadangan 105 D6
Killadeas 113 I4
Killadoon 104 C6
Killadysert 99 E9
Killafeen 99 F8
Killag 96 M11
Killagan Bridge 118 M2
Killaghteen 93 E10
Killahy 95 J9
Killakee 103 N8
Killala 111 E5

Killala Bay 111 E5
Killallon 108 K6
Killaloo 118 K3
Killamery 95 J10
Killane 102 K8
Killanena 99 F9
Killann 96 L10
Killard 98 D9
Killard Point 115 P5
Killarga 112 H5
Killarney National Park ... 89 D11
Killarone 105 E7
Killashandra 107 J5
Killashee 107 I6
Killasser 105 F6
Killavally *Mayo* 105 D6
Killavally *Westmeath* 101 J7
Killavil 106 G5
Killavullen 94 G11
Killea *Donegal* 117 J3
Killea *Tipperary* 101 I9
Killeagh 91 H12
Killealy 115 N3
Killeany 98 D8
Killedmond 96 L10
Killeedy 93 E10
Killeen *Ardamullivan* 99 F9
Killeen *Armagh* 114 M5
Killeen *Dungannon* 114 M4
Killeenaran 99 F8
Killeeneenmore 99 F8
Killeenleagh Bridge 88 B12
Killeevan 113 K5
Killeglan 106 H7
Killeigh 101 J8
Killen 113 J3
Killenagh 97 N10
Killenaule 95 I10
Killeshil 101 K8
Killeshin 102 K9
Killeter 113 I3
Killeter Forest 113 I3
Killevy 109 M5
Killevy Churches 109 M5
Killilan Bridge 99 G8
Killimer 93 D10
Killimor 100 H8
Killinaboy 99 E9
Killinaspick 96 K10
Killinchy 115 O4
Killincooly 97 N10
Killiney *Dublin* 103 N8
Killiney *Kerry* 92 B11
Killiney Bay 103 N8
Killinick 97 M11
Killinierin 97 N9
Killinkere 108 K6
Killinny 99 F8
Killinthomas 102 K8
Killinure Lough 107 I7
Killiskey 103 N8
Killkelly 105 F6
Killmuckridge 97 N10
Killogeary 111 E5
Killogeenaghan 101 I7
Killonecaha 88 B12
Killoran 100 G8
Killoscobe 106 G7
Killough 115 P5
Killough 103 N8
Killowen 109 N5
Killucan 108 K7
Killukin 107 H6
Killoom 107 H7
Killurly 88 B12
Killusty 95 J10
Killwaughter 115 O3
Killyclogher 113 K4
Killyclug 117 I3
Killycolpy 114 M4
Killygordon 117 I3
Killykeen Forest Park 107 J5
Killylea 114 L4
Killyleagh 115 P4
Killyon 101 I8
Kilmacanoge 103 N8
Kilmacduagh Monastery ..99 F8
Kilmacoo 103 N9
Kilmacow 96 K11
Kilmacrenan 117 I2
Kilmacteige 111 F5
Kilmacthomas 95 J11
Kilmactranny 106 H5
Kilmacurragh 103 N9
Kilmaganny 96 K10

Kilmaine 105 E7
Kilmainham Wood 108 L6
Kilmakilloge Harbour 88 C12
Kilmaley 99 E9
Kilmalkedar 92 B11
Kilmanagh 95 J10
Kilmeadan 96 K11
Kilmeage 102 L8
Kilmeedy 94 F10
Kilmeelickin 105 D7
Kilmeena 105 D6
Kilmessan 108 M7
Kilmichael
 near Castletownbere ... 88 B13
Kilmichael *near Macroom* ... 89 E12
Kilmichael Point 97 N9
Kilmihil 98 E9
Kilmona 90 G12
Kilmoon 89 D13
Kilmore *Armagh* 114 M4
Kilmore *Clare* 99 G9
Kilmore *Down* 115 O4
Kilmore *Mayo* 105 E6
Kilmore *Roscommon* 107 H6
Kilmore *Wexford* 96 M11
Kilmore Quay 96 M11
Kilmorna 93 D10
Kilmorony 102 L9
Kilmovee 106 F6
Kilmurry *Cork* 90 F12
Kilmurry *Limerick* 94 G10
Kilmurry *near Kilkishen* ... 99 F9
Kilmurry *near Milltown* 98 D9
Kilmurry *Wicklow* 102 L9
Kilmurry Mac Mahon 93 E10
Kilmurvy 98 C8
Kilmyshall 96 M10
Kilnagross 107 I6
Kilnalag 106 G6
Kilnaleck 107 K6
Kilnamanagh 97 M10
Kilnamona 99 E9
Kilntown 115 N4
Kilpatrick 90 F12
Kilpeacan Cross Roads 88 B12
Kilpedder 103 N8
Kilquigguin 97 M9
Kilraghts 118 M2
Kilrane 97 M11
Kilrea 118 M3
Kilrean 116 H3
Kilreekill 100 G8
Kilroghter 99 E8
Kilross *Donegal* 117 I3
Kilross *Tipperary* 94 H10
Kilruddery 103 N8
Kilsallagh *Galway* 106 G7
Kilsallagh *Mayo* 104 C6
Kilsallaghan 103 N7
Kilsally 114 M4
Kilsaran 109 M6
Kilshanchoe 102 L7
Kilshannig 92 B11
Kilshanny 99 E9
Kilsheelan 95 J11
Kilskeer 108 L6
Kilskeery 113 J4
Kiltealy 96 L10
Kilteel 103 M8
Kilteely 94 G10
Kiltegan 103 M9
Kilternan 103 N8
Kiltimagh 105 E6
Kiltober 101 J7
Kiltoom 107 H7
Kiltormer 100 H8
Kiltullagh 99 G8
Kittyclogher 113 H4
Kilvine 105 F7
Kilworth 94 H11
Kilworth Mountains 94 H11
Kinale (Lough) 107 J6
Kinard 93 E10
Kinawley 113 J5
Kincasslagh 116 G2
Kindrohid 117 J2
Kindrum 117 I2
Kingarrow 117 H3
Kings River 95 J10
Kingscourt 108 L6
Kingsland 106 G6
Kingsmill 114 M4
Kingstown 104 B7
Kinlough 112 H4
Kinnadoohy 104 C6
Kinnagoe Bay 118 K2
Kinnegad 108 K7

Kinnitty 101 I8
Kinsale (Old Head of) 90 G13
Kinsale Harbour 90 G12
Kinsalebeg 91 I12
Kinsaley 103 N7
Kinvarra
 near Camus Bay 105 D7
Kinvarra
 near Kinvarra Bay 99 F8
Kinvarra Bay 99 F8
Kippure 103 N8
Kircubbin 115 P4
Kirkhills 118 M2
Kirkistown 115 P4
Kishkeam 93 E11
Kitconnell 100 G8
Knappagh 105 D6
Knappogue Castle 99 F9
Knight's Town 88 B12
Knock *Clare* 93 E10
Knock *Mayo* 105 F6
Knock *Tipperary* 101 I9
Knockaderry 94 F10
Knockadoon Head 91 I12
Knockainy 94 G10
Knockalla Mount 117 J2
Knockalongy 112 F5
Knockalough 99 E9
Knockanaffrin 95 J11
Knockananna 103 M9
Knockanefune 93 E11
Knockanevin 94 G11
Knockanillaun 111 E5
Knockanimpaha 93 E10
Knockanure 93 D10
Knockaunalour 90 G11
Knockaunavoher 94 G10
Knockaunnaglashy 92 C11
Knockboy *near Dungarvan* ...95 I11
Knockboy *near Waterford* ...96 K11
Knockboy (Mount) 89 D12
Knockbrack 117 I3
Knockbrandon 97 M9
Knockbride 108 L6
Knockbridge 109 M6
Knockbrit 95 I10
Knockcloghrim 114 M3
Knockcroghery 106 H7
Knockdrin 107 K7
Knockerry
 near Enniscorthy 96 M10
Knockferry 105 E7
Knocklayd 119 N2
Knocklofty 95 I10
Knocklomena 89 C12
Knocklong 94 G10
Knockmealdown 95 I11
Knockmealdown
 Mountains 95 H11
Knockmore 104 B6
Knockmore (Mount) 104 C6
Knockmourne 90 H11
Knockmoy Abbey 106 F7
Knocknaboul Cross 93 E11
Knocknacarry 119 N2
Knocknacree 102 L9
Knocknadobar 88 B12
Knocknagantee 88 C12
Knocknagashel 93 D11
Knocknagree 93 E11
Knocknahilan 90 F12
Knocknalina 110 C5
Knocknalower 110 C5
Knockowen 89 C12
Knockraha 90 G12
Knocks *Cork* 89 F12
Knocks *Fermanagh* 113 J5
Knocks *Laois* 101 J8
Knockshanahullion 95 H11
Knockskagh 89 F12
Knocktopher 96 K10
Knocktown 96 M11
Knockvicar 106 H5
Knowth 108 M6
Kylemore Abbey 104 C7
Kylemore Lough 104 C7

L

Laban 99 F8
Labasheeda 93 E10
Lack 113 J4
Lackagh 102 K8
Lackan *Carlow* 96 K9
Lackan *Wicklow* 103 M8
Lackan bay 111 E5
Lackareagh 89 F12

Laconnell 116 G3
Ladies View 89 D12
Lady's Island Lake 97 M11
Ladysbridge 90 H12
Ladywell 96 K10
Laffansbridge 95 I10
Lag 117 K2
Lagan (River) 115 N4
Lagan Valley 115 O4
Lagavara 118 M2
Lagganstown 95 I10
Laghey Corner 114 L4
Laghtnafrankee 95 J11
Laghy 113 H4
Lahardaun 111 E5
Lakyle 93 E10
Lambay Island 109 N7
Lambeg 115 N4
Lamb's Head 88 B12
Lanesborough 107 I6
Laney (River) 89 F12
Laracor 108 L7
Laragh *Kildare* 102 L7
Laragh *Monaghan* 108 L5
Laragh *Wicklow* 103 N8
Largan *Mayo* 111 D5
Largan *Sligo* 111 F5
Largy 112 G4
Largydonnell 112 H4
Larne 115 O3
Larne Lough 115 O3
Lattin 94 H10
Laune (River) 93 C11
Lauragh 88 C12
Laurelvale 114 M4
Laurencetown 100 H8
Lavagh 112 F5
Lavagh More 117 H3
Lawrencetown 114 N4
Leabgarrow 116 G3
League (Slieve) 112 F4
League Point 89 D13
Leamaneh Castle 99 E9
Leamlara 90 H12
Leamore Strand 103 N8
Leane (Lough) 89 D11
Leannan (River) 117 I2
Leap 89 E13
Leap (The)
 near Enniscorthy 96 M10
Leap (The) *near New Ross* ..96 L10
Lecale Peninsula 115 O5
Lecarrow *Leitrim* 112 H5
Lecarrow *Roscommon* 107 H7
Leckanarainey 112 H4
Leckanvy 105 C6
Leckaun 112 H5
Leckavrea Mountain 105 D7
Leckemy 118 K2
Lee 93 C11
Lee (River) 90 G12
Lee Reservoir 90 F12
Leek Point 93 C10
Leenane 104 C7
Legan or Lenamore 107 J7
Legananny Dolmen 115 N5
Leggah 107 J6
Legoniel 115 O4
Lehardan 117 J2
Leighlinbridge 96 L9
Leinster (Mount) 96 L10
Leitir Mealláin /
 Lettermullan 98 C8
Leitir Mhic an Bhaird /
 Lettermacaward 116 H3
Leitrim *Banbridge* 115 O5
Leitrim *Creegh* 98 D9
Leitrim *Leitrim* 107 H6
Leixlip 103 M7
Lemanaghan 101 I8
Lemybrien 91 J11
Lenadoon Point 111 E5
Lenan Head 117 J2
Lene (Lough) 107 K7
Lerrig 93 C10
Leslie Hill 114 L5
Letterbarra 112 H3
Letterbreen 113 I5
Lettercallow 98 C8
Lettercraffroe Lough 105 D7
Letterfinish 88 C12
Letterfrack 104 C7
Letterkelly 99 E9
Letterkenny /
 Leitir Ceanainn 117 I3
Letterleague 117 I3
Lettermore 98 D8

Lettermore Island 98 C8
Levally 106 F7
Levally Lough 105 E6
Licketstown 96 K11
Liffey (River) 102 M8
Light House Island 115 P3
Lifford 117 J3
Limavady 118 L2
Limerick / Luimneach 94 G10
Limerick Junction 95 H10
Lios Dúin Bhearna /
 Lisdoonvarna 99 E8
Lios Mór / Lismore 91 I11
Lios Póil / Lispole 92 B11
Lios Tuathail / Listowel 93 D10
Lisacul 106 G6
Lisbane 115 O4
Lisbellaw 113 J5
Lisburn 115 N4
Liscannor 98 D9
Liscannor Bay 98 D9
Liscarney 105 D6
Liscarroll 94 F11
Liscolman 118 M2
Liscoole 117 J3
Lisdoart 114 K4
Lisdowney 101 J9
Lisduff *Cavan* 108 K6
Lisduff *Leitrim* 107 I6
Lisduff *Offaly* 101 I8
Lisgarode 100 H9
Lisgoold 90 H12
Lislea *Magherafelt* 118 M3
Lislea *Newry-Mourne* 114 M5
Lismacaffry 107 J6
Lismoghry 117 J3
Lismoyle 106 H7
Lisnacree 109 N5
Lisnageer 108 K5
Lisnagleer 114 L4
Lisnagry 94 G9
Lisnagunogue 118 M2
Lisnamuck 118 L3
Lisnarrick 113 I4
Lisnaskea 113 J5
Lisnavagh 102 L9
Lispatrick 90 G13
Lisroe 99 E9
Lisronagh 95 I10
Lisryan 107 J6
Lissadell House 112 G4
Lissalway 106 G6
Lissamona 89 D13
Lissatinnig Bridge 88 C12
Lissavaird 89 F13
Lisselton 93 D10
Lissinagroagh 112 H5
Lissiniska 112 H4
Lissycasey 99 E9
Listellick 93 C11
Listerlin 96 K10
Listooder 115 O4
Lisvarrinane 94 H10
Little Bray 103 N8
Little Island 90 G12
Little Skellig 88 A12
Littleton 95 I10
Lixnaw 93 D10
Loanends 115 N4
Lobinstown 108 M6
Loch Garman / Wexford ...97 M10
Loghill 93 E10
Lombardstown 94 F11
Londonderry 117 K3
Lonehort Point 88 C13
Long Island 89 D13
Longford 101 I8
Longhill 101 K9
Longwood 108 L7
Loo Bridge 89 D12
Loobagh 94 G10
Loop Head 92 C10
Lorrha 100 H8
Loskeran 91 J11
Losset *Cavan* 107 J6
Losset *Donegal* 117 I2
Lough Bradan Forest 113 J4
Lough Gowna 107 J6
Lough Key Forest Park 106 H6
Lough Navar Forest 113 I4
Loughanavally 107 J7
Loughanillaunmore 98 D8
Loughanure 116 H2
Loughbrickland 114 N5
Lougher 92 C11
Loughermore 118 K3
Loughfad Hill 113 I4

Loughgall ....114 M 4
Loughglinn ....106 G 6
Loughguile ....119 N 2
Loughinisland ....115 O 4
Loughlinstown ....103 N 8
Loughmoe ....101 I 9
Loughmorne ....108 L 5
Loughros More Bay ....116 G 3
Loughros Point ....116 G 3
Loughsalt Mount ....117 I 2
Loughshinny ....109 N 7
Louisburgh ....104 C 6
Loup (The) ....114 M 3
Louth ....108 M 6
Lower Ballinderry ....114 N 4
Lower Lake ....103 N 8
Lowertown ....89 D 13
Lowerymore ....113 I 3
Lowtown ....115 N 5
Lucan ....103 M 7
Luggacurren ....101 K 9
Lugnaquillia Mountain ....103 M 9
Luimneach / Limerick ....94 G 10
Lukeswell ....96 K 10
Lullymore ....102 L 8
Lurgan Craigavon ....114 N 4
Lurgan Frenchpark ....106 G 6
Lurganboy Donegal ....117 J 2
Lurganboy Leitrim ....112 H 5
Lusk ....109 N 7
Lyle ....115 N 3
Lyracrumpane ....93 D 10
Lyre ....90 F 11
Lyrenaglogh ....95 H 11

M

Maas ....116 G 3
Mac Gregor's Corner ....119 N 3
Mac Laughlins Corner ....118 M 3
Mac Mahon's Town ....114 K 4
Mac Swyne's Bay ....112 G 4
Mace ....105 D 6
Mace Head ....104 C 8
Macgillycuddy's Reeks ....89 C 12
Machugh (Lough) ....116 G 3
Mackan ....113 J 5
Macnean Lower (Lough) ...113 I 5
Macnean Upper (Lough) ...113 I 5
Macosquin / ....118 L 2
Macroom /
    Maigh Chromtha ....89 F 12
Maddan ....114 L 5
Maddockstown ....96 K 10
Maganey ....102 L 9
Maghaberry ....115 N 4
Maghanlawaun ....89 C 12
Maghera Clare ....99 F 9
Maghera Donegal ....116 G 3
Maghera Down ....115 O 5
Maghera Magherafelt ....118 L 3
Magherabane ....117 J 2
Magherafelt ....114 M 3
Magheragall ....115 N 4
Magheralin ....114 N 4
Magheramason ....117 J 3
Magheramore ....115 O 3
Magheraveely ....113 K 5
Maghery near Dungannon .114 M 4
Maghery near Dunglow ...116 G 3
Magilligan ....118 L 2
Magilligan Point ....118 L 2
Magilligan Strand ....118 L 2
Maguiresbridge ....113 J 5
Mahee Island ....115 P 4
Mahon ....95 J 11
Mahon (Lough) ....90 G 12
Mahoonagh ....93 E 10
Maigh Chromtha /
    Macroom ....89 F 12
Maigh Cuilinn /
    Moycullen ....105 E 7
Maigh Nuad / Maynooth ..103 M 7
Maigue (River) ....94 F 10
Main ....118 N 3
Maine (River) ....93 C 11
Mainham ....102 L 8
Mainistir Fhear Maí /
    Fermoy ....90 H 11
Mainistir na Búille /
    Boyle ....106 H 6
Mainistir na Corann /
    Midleton ....90 H 12
Máistir Gaoithe /
    Mastergeehy ....88 B 12
Mal Bay ....98 D 9
Mala / Mallow ....94 G 11
Málainn Bhig / Malin Beg ..112 F 3

Malin ....118 K 2
Malin Bay ....112 F 3
Malin Head ....117 J 1
Malin More ....112 F 3
Mallusk ....115 N 3
Mamore (Gap of) ....117 J 2
Manger ....112 H 4
Mangerton Mountain ......89 D 12
Mannin Bay ....104 B 7
Mannin Lake ....105 F 6
Manorcunningham ....117 J 3
Manselstown ....95 I 9
Mansfieldstown ....109 M 6
Mantua ....106 H 6
Manulla ....105 E 6
Manulla (River) ....105 E 6
Maothail / Mohill ....107 I 6
Marble Arch Caves ....113 I 5
Marble Hill ....117 I 2
Mardyke ....95 J 10
Markethill ....114 M 5
Marshalstown ....96 M 10
Martin ....90 G 12
Martinstown Emlygrennan ...94 G 10
Martinstown
    Grennanstown ....108 L 7
Martinstown
    South Somerset ....119 N 3
Mask (Lough) ....105 D 7
Massford ....115 N 4
Masshill ....112 F 5
Masterstown ....95 I 10
Matehy ....90 G 12
Matrix (Castle) ....94 F 10
Mattock (River) ....108 M 6
Mauherslieve ....95 H 9
Maum ....105 D 7
Maumakeogh ....111 D 5
Maumeen Lough ....104 B 7
Maumtrasna ....105 D 7
Maumturk Mountains ....104 C 7
Mauricesmills ....99 E 9
Mayo ....105 E 6
Mayo (Plains of) ....105 E 6
Mayobridge ....114 N 5
Mazetown ....115 N 4
Mealagh ....89 D 12
Meanus ....94 G 10
Meathas Troim /
    Edgeworthstown ....107 J 6
Meela (Lough) ....116 G 3
Meelick ....100 H 8
Meelin ....93 E 11
Meenaclady ....116 H 2
Meenacross ....116 G 3
Meenanarwa ....117 H 3
Meenaneary /
    Min na Aoire ....112 G 3
Meenatotan ....116 H 3
Meenavean ....112 F 3
Meencorwick ....116 H 3
Meenglass ....113 I 3
Meenlaragh ....117 H 2
Meenreagh ....113 I 3
Meentullynagarn ....112 G 3
Meenybraddan ....112 H 3
Meeting of the Waters ......103 N 9
Mellifont Abbey ....109 M 6
Melmore Head ....117 I 2
Melvin (Lough) ....112 H 4
Menlough ....106 G 7
Mew Island ....115 P 3
Michelstown Caves ....95 H 11
Middletown ....116 H 2
Middletown Armagh ....114 L 5
Midfield ....105 F 6
Mile ....117 J 2
Milebush ....115 O 3
Milehouse ....96 M 10
Milemill ....102 L 8
Milestone ....95 H 9
Milford Armagh ....114 L 5
Milford Cork ....94 F 10
Mill Town ....114 L 5
Millbay ....115 O 3
Millbrook Derry ....118 K 3
Millbrook Larne ....115 O 3
Millbrook Oldcastle ....108 K 6
Milleen ....93 E 11
Millford ....117 I 2
Millisle ....115 P 4
Millroad ....96 M 11
Millstreet Cork ....89 E 11
Millstreet Waterford ....91 I 11
Milltown Armagh ....114 L 5
Milltown Ballymoney ....118 M 2
Milltown Banbridge ....114 N 5

Milltown Cavan ....107 J 5
Milltown Craigavon ....114 M 4
Milltown Dublin ....103 M 8
Milltown Kildare ....102 L 8
Milltown near Dingle ......92 B 11
Milltown
    near Mount Bellew ......106 G 7
Milltown near Tralee ......93 C 11
Milltown near Tuam ....105 F 7
Milltown Omagh ....114 K 4
Milltown Wexford ....97 M 10
Miltownpass ....107 K 7
Minane Bridge ....90 G 12
Minard Head ....92 B 11
Mine Head ....91 J 12
Minerstown ....115 O 5
Minterburn ....114 L 4
Mizen Head ....88 C 13
Moanmore ....98 D 9
Modelligo ....91 I 11
Modreeny ....100 H 9
Mogeely ....90 H 12
Moglass ....95 I 10
Moher (Cliffs of) ....98 D 9
Moher Lough ....105 D 6
Mohil ....96 K 9
Móinteach Milic /
    Mountmellick ....101 K 8
Moira ....115 N 4
Moll's Gap ....89 D 12
Monard ....95 H 10
Monaseed ....97 M 9
Monaster ....94 G 10
Monasteraden ....106 G 6
Monasteranenagh Abbey ...94 G 10
Monasterboice ....109 M 6
Monasterevin ....102 K 8
Monavullagh Mountains ...95 J 11
Mondello Park ....102 L 8
Monea ....113 I 4
Moneen Clare ....93 C 10
Moneen Galway ....105 F 7
Money Point ....93 D 10
Moneydig ....118 M 3
Moneygall ....101 I 9
Moneyglass ....114 M 3
Moneygold ....112 G 4
Moneylahan ....112 G 4
Moneymore ....114 L 3
Moneyneany ....118 L 3
Moneyreagh ....115 O 4
Monilea ....107 K 7
Monivea ....106 F 7
Monkstown Cork ....90 G 12
Monkstown
    Newtownabbey ....115 O 3
Monroe ....107 J 7
Montpelier ....99 G 9
Mooncoin ....96 K 11
Moone ....102 L 9
Moord ....91 I 12
Moore Bay ....98 C 9
Moorfields ....115 N 3
More (Island) ....105 D 6
Morenane ....94 F 10
Morley's Bridge ....89 D 12
Morningstar ....94 G 10
Mornington ....109 N 6
Mosney ....109 N 7
Moss-Side ....118 M 2
Mossley ....115 O 3
Mothel ....95 J 11
Motte Stone ....103 N 9
Mount Falcon ....111 E 5
Mount Garret ....96 L 10
Mount Hamilton or Sperrin 114 K 3
Mount Melleray Monastery .95 I 11
Mount Norris ....114 M 5
Mount Nugent ....107 K 6
Mount Stewart Gardens ...115 P 4
Mount Talbot ....106 H 7
Mount Temple ....107 I 7
Mount Uniacke ....91 H 12
Mount Usher Gardens ...103 N 8
Mountbolus ....101 J 8
Mountcastle ....117 J 3
Mountcharles ....112 H 4
Mountcollins ....93 E 11
Mountfield ....114 K 4
Mounthenry ....105 E 7
Mountjoy Dungannon ......114 M 4
Mountjoy Omagh ....113 J 4
Mountrath ....101 J 8
Mountrivers Bridge ....98 D 9
Mountshannon ....100 G 9
Mourne (Lough)
    near Ballybofey ....113 I 3

Mourne (Lough)
    near Carrickfergus ....115 O 3
Mourne Beg ....113 I 3
Mourne Mountains ....109 N 5
Mourne River ....113 J 3
Moveen ....98 C 10
Moville / Bun an Phobail ...118 K 2
Mowhan ....114 M 5
Moy ....114 L 4
Moy (River) ....111 E 5
Moyagh ....117 J 3
Moyallan ....114 M 4
Moyard ....104 B 7
Moyarget ....118 N 2
Moyasta ....98 D 9
Moydow ....107 I 7
Moygashel ....114 L 4
Moyglass ....99 G 8
Moylough Galway ....106 G 7
Moylough Sligo ....106 F 5
Moynalty ....108 L 6
Moynalvy ....108 L 7
Moyne Roscommon ....106 G 6
Moyne Tipperary ....107 J 6
Moyne Wicklow ....103 M 9
Moyne Abbey ....111 E 5
Moyrus ....104 C 7
Moyteoge Head ....110 B 6
Moyvally ....102 L 7
Moyvore ....107 J 7
Moyvoughly ....107 I 7
Muck (Isle of) ....115 O 3
Muckamore ....115 N 3
Muckanagh Lough ....99 F 9
Muckish Mountain ....117 H 2
Mucklon ....102 L 7
Muckno Lake ....108 L 5
Muckros Head ....112 G 4
Muckross ....89 D 11
Muff ....117 K 2
Muggort's Bay ....91 J 11
Muinchille / Cootehill ....108 K 5
Muine Bheag /
    Bagenalstown ....96 L 9
Muineachán / Monaghan ...114 L 5
Muing ....111 D 5
Muingnabo ....111 C 5
Mulhuddart ....103 M 7
Mulkear ....94 G 10
Mullach Íde / Malahide ...103 N 7
Mullagh Cavan ....108 L 6
Mullagh Galway ....100 G 8
Mullagh Mayo ....104 C 6
Mullagh Meath ....103 M 7
Mullaghanattin ....88 C 12
Mullaghanish ....89 E 12
Mullaghareirk Mountains ...93 E 10
Mullaghash ....118 K 3
Mullaghbane ....109 M 5
Mullaghboy ....115 O 3
Mullaghcarn ....113 K 3
Mullaghcleevaun ....103 M 8
Mullaghclogha ....114 K 3
Mullaghmore
    Cliffony North ....112 G 4
Mullaghmore Magherafelt ..118 L 3
Mullaghmore Head ....112 G 4
Mullaghroe ....106 G 6
Mullan Coleraine ....118 L 2
Mullan Figullar ....114 L 4
Mullany'sCross ....111 F 5
Mullartown ....109 O 5
Mullen ....106 G 6
Mullenbeg ....96 K 10
Mullet Peninsula ....110 B 5
Mullinahone ....95 J 10
Mullinasole ....112 H 4
Mullinavat ....96 K 10
Mulroy Bay ....117 I 2
Multeen ....95 H 10
Multyfarnham ....107 J 7
Mungret ....94 F 10
Muntervary
    or Sheep's Head ....88 C 13
Murley ....113 K 4
Murlough Bay ....119 N 2
Murntown ....97 M 11
Murreagh ....92 A 11
Murrisk ....105 D 6
Murroe ....94 G 10
Murroogh ....99 E 8
Musheramore ....89 F 11
Mussenden Temple ....118 L 2
Mutton Island ....98 D 9
Mweelrea Mountains ....104 C 7
Mweenish Island ....104 C 8
Myshall ....96 L 9

N

Na Cealla Beaga /
    Killybegs ....112 G 4
Na Clocha Liatha /
    Greystones ....103 N 8
Na Dúnaibh / Downies ...117 I 2
Na Sceirí / Skerries ....109 N 7
Nacorra (Lough) ....105 D 6
Nacung (Lough) ....117 H 2
Nad ....90 F 11
Nafooey (Lough) ....105 D 7
Nagles Mountains ....90 G 11
Nalughraman (Lough) ......116 G 3
Naminn (Lough) ....117 J 2
Namona (Lough) ....88 B 12
Nanny ....108 M 7
Narin ....116 G 3
Narraghmore ....102 L 8
Narrow Water Castle ....109 N 5
Naul ....109 N 7
Neagh (Lough) ....114 M 4
Neale ....105 E 7
Nealstown ....101 I 9
Neidín / Kenmare ....89 D 12
Nenagh ....100 H 9
Nephin ....111 D 5
Nephin (Glen) ....105 D 6
Nephin Beg ....111 D 5
Nephin Beg Range ....111 C 5
New Birmingham ....95 I 10
New Buildings ....117 J 3
New Inn Cavan ....108 K 6
New Inn Galway ....100 G 8
New Kildimo ....94 F 10
New Quay / Bealaclugga ...99 E 8
New Twopothouse Village ...94 G 11
Newbawn ....96 L 10
Newbliss ....113 K 5
Newbridge Fingal ....109 N 7
Newbridge Limerick ....94 F 10
Newbridge
    near Tuomard ....106 G 7
Newbridge /
    An Droichead Nua ....102 L 8
Newcastle Down ....115 O 5
Newcastle Dublin ....103 M 8
Newcastle Galway ....99 F 8
Newcastle Tipperary ....95 I 11
Newcastle Wicklow ....103 N 8
Newcestown ....90 F 12
Newchapel ....95 I 10
Newferry ....114 M 3
Newgrange ....109 M 6
Newinn ....95 I 10
Newmarket Cork ....93 F 11
Newmarket Kilkenny ....96 K 10
Newmarket on Fergus ....99 F 9
Newmills Donegal ....117 I 3
Newmills Dungannon ....114 L 4
Newport Tipperary ....100 G 9
Newport Bay ....105 C 6
Newport Trench ....114 M 4
Newry ....114 M 5
Newtown Cork ....94 G 11
Newtown Galway ....99 F 8
Newtown Kildare ....102 L 7
Newtown Laois ....101 K 9
Newtown Limerick ....94 G 10
Newtown near Knock ....101 I 9
Newtown near Nenagh ...100 H 9
Newtown Offaly ....100 H 8
Newtown Roscommon ....100 H 7
Newtown Tipperary ....95 H 10
Newtown Waterford ....95 I 11
Newtown Wexford ....96 M 11
Newtown Cashel ....107 I 7
Newtown Cloghans ....111 E 5
Newtown-Crommelin ....119 N 3
Newtown Cunningham ...117 J 3
Newtown Forbes ....107 I 6
Newtown Gore ....107 I 5
Newtown
    Mount Kennedy ....103 N 8
Newtown Sandes ....93 D 10
Newtownabbey ....115 O 4
Newtownards ....115 O 4
Newtownbreda ....115 O 4
Newtownbutler ....113 J 5
Newtownhamilton ....114 M 5
Newtownlow ....101 J 7
Newtownlynch ....99 E 8
Newtownshandrum ....94 F 10
Newtownstewart ....113 J 3
Nier ....95 J 11
Ninemilehouse ....95 J 10
Nobber ....108 L 6

Nohaval ....90 G 12
Nore ....101 J 9
Nore (River) ....96 K 10
North Channel ....119 O 2
North Ring ....90 F 13
North Sound ....98 C 8
Nose of Howth ....103 N 7
Noughaval Doora ....99 F 9
Noughaval Noughaval ....99 E 8
Nowen Hill ....89 E 12
Nuns Quarter ....115 O 4
Nurney Carlow ....96 L 9
Nurney Kildare ....102 L 8
Nutt's Corner ....115 N 4

O

Oaghley ....93 D 10
Oatfield ....99 F 9
Oatquarter ....98 C 8
O'Brien's Tower ....98 D 9
O'Flynn (Lough) ....106 G 6
Oghil Clare ....100 H 8
Oghil Galway ....98 C 8
Ogonnelloe ....99 G 9
O'Grady (Lough) ....99 G 9
Oileán Ciarraí /
    Castleisland ....93 D 11
Oilgate ....97 M 10
Oily ....112 G 4
Old Court ....89 E 13
Old Head Ballymackean ...90 G 13
Old Head Louisburgh ....104 C 6
Old Kilcullen ....102 L 8
Old Kildimo ....94 F 10
Old Ross ....96 L 10
Old Town Donegal ....117 I 3
Old Town Laois ....101 J 9
Old Town Roscommon ...100 H 8
Old Town Wexford ....96 L 10
Old Twopothouse ....94 G 11
Oldleighlin ....96 K 9
Oldmill Bridge ....93 E 10
Oldtown Dublin ....109 N 7
Oldtown Roscommon ....101 I 7
Omagh ....113 K 4
Omeath ....109 N 5
Omey Island ....104 B 7
Onaght ....98 C 8
Oola ....94 H 10
Oorid Lough ....105 D 7
Oranmore ....99 F 8
Oriel (Mount) ....108 M 6
Oristown ....108 L 6
Oritor ....114 L 4
Ossian's Grave ....119 N 2
Oughter (Lough) ....107 J 6
Oulart ....97 M 10
Ovens ....90 G 12
Owel (Lough) ....107 J 7
Owenascaul ....92 B 11
Owenator ....116 H 3
Owenavorragh ....97 M 10
Owenbeagh ....117 H 3
Owenbeg ....111 F 5
Owenbeg (River) ....112 G 5
Owenboliska ....99 F 8
Owenboy ....90 G 12
Owenbristy ....99 F 8
Owencarrow ....117 I 2
Owendalulleegh ....99 G 8
Owenea ....116 G 3
Owengarve Clew Bay ....105 D 6
Owengarve River Moy ....106 F 5
Owenglin ....104 C 7
Owenmore ....111 D 5
Owenkillew Glenelly ....114 K 3
Owenkillew Lough Swilly ...117 J 2
Owenmore Bridge ....105 D 6
Owennacurra ....90 H 12
Owenreagh Hill ....117 J 3
Owenriff ....105 D 7
Owentaraglin ....93 E 11
Owentocker ....116 H 3
Owenur (River) ....106 H 6
Ower ....105 E 7
Owning ....95 J 10
Owroe Bridge ....88 B 12
Owvane ....89 D 12
Oysterhaven ....90 G 12

P

Palace ....96 L 10
Palatine ....102 L 9
Pallas ....101 J 8
Pallas Cross ....100 I 9
Pallas Green ....94 G 10
Pallaskenry ....94 F 10

A B C D E F G H I J K L M N O P Q R S T U V W X Y Z

Paps (The) ....89 E 11
Park *Bellavary* ....105 E 6
Park *Derry* ....118 K 3
Parke's Castle ....112 H 5
Parkgate ....115 N 3
Parkmore ....99 F 8
Parkmore Point ....92 A 11
Parknasilla ....88 C 12
Parteen ....99 G 9
Partry ....105 E 6
Partry Mountains ....105 D 7
Passage ....106 H 7
Passage East ....96 L 11
Passage West ....90 G 12
Patrickswell ....94 F 10
Patterson's Spade Mill ....115 N 3
Paulstown ....96 K 9
Peake ....90 F 12
Peatlands ....114 M 4
Peterswell ....99 F 8
Pettigoe ....113 I 4
Phoenix Park ....103 M 7
Piercetown ....97 M 11
Pigeons (The) ....107 I 7
Pike ....100 H 8
Pike (The) *near Boola* ....91 I 11
Pike (The) *near Lamybrien* ....91 J 11
Pike (The) *Tipperary* ....100 H 8
Pike Corner ....108 L 7
Pike of Rush Hall ....101 J 9
Piltown ....95 K 10
Pluck ....117 J 3
Plumbridge ....113 K 3
Pollagh ....101 I 8
Pollan Bay ....117 J 2
Pollatomish ....111 C 5
Pollnalaght ....113 J 4
Pollshask ....106 G 7
Pomeroy ....114 L 4
Pontoon ....105 E 6
Port ....116 F 3
Port Ballintrae ....118 M 2
Port Durlainne / Porturlin ....111 C 5
Port Láirge / Waterford ....96 K 11
Port Laoise / Portlaoise ....101 K 8
Port Omna / Portumna ....100 H 8
Portacloy ....111 C 5
Portadown ....114 M 4
Portaferry ....115 P 4
Portaleen ....118 K 2
Portavogie ....115 P 4
Portbradden ....118 M 2
Portglenone ....118 M 3
Portland ....100 H 8
Portlaw ....96 K 11
Portmagee ....88 A 12
Portmagee Channel ....88 A 12
Portmarnock ....103 N 7
Portmuck ....115 O 3
Portnablagh ....117 I 2
Portnoo ....116 G 3
Portrane ....109 N 7
Portroe ....100 G 9
Portrush ....118 M 2
Portsalon ....117 J 2
Portstewart ....118 L 2
Poulaphouca Reservoir ....103 M 8
Poulnamucky ....95 I 10
Poulnasherry Bay ....98 D 10
Power Head ....90 H 12
Power's Cross ....100 H 8
Powerscourt Demesne ....103 N 8
Powerstown ....96 K 10
Poyntz Pass ....114 M 5
Priesthaggard ....96 L 11
Prosperous ....102 L 8
Puckaun ....100 H 9
Puffin Island ....88 A 12
Punchestown ....103 M 8

Q
Quarrytown ....119 N 3
Querrin ....93 D 10
Quigley's Point ....118 K 2
Quilty ....98 D 9
Quin ....99 F 9
Quoile ....115 O 4

R
Rabbit Islands ....89 E 13
Race End ....117 I 2
Raffrey ....115 O 4
Raghly ....112 G 5
Raghtin More ....117 J 2
Rahan ....101 J 8
Rahanagh ....93 E 10
Rahara ....106 H 7

Raharney ....108 K 7
Raheen ....96 L 10
Raigh ....105 D 7
Railyard ....101 K 9
Rake Street ....111 D 5
Ram Head ....91 I 12
Ramor (Lough) ....108 K 6
Ramore Head ....118 M 2
Rams Island ....114 N 4
Ramsgrange ....96 L 11
Randalstown ....114 N 3
Rapemills ....101 I 8
Raphoe ....117 J 3
Rasharkin ....118 M 3
Rashedoge ....117 I 3
Rath ....101 I 8
Ráth Caola / Rathkeale ....94 F 10
Ráth Droma / Rathdrum ....103 N 9
Rathangan ....102 L 8
Rathaspick ....107 J 7
Rathbrit ....95 I 10
Rathcabban ....100 H 8
Rathconrath ....107 J 7
Rathcool ....89 F 11
Rathcoole ....103 M 8
Rathcor ....109 N 6
Rathcore ....102 L 7
Rathcormack *near Fermoy* ....90 H 11
Rathcormack *near Sligo* ....112 G 5
Rathcroghan ....106 H 6
Rathdangan ....103 M 9
Rathdowney ....101 J 9
Rathduff ....90 G 11
Rathedan ....96 L 9
Rathfeigh ....108 M 7
Rathfriland ....115 N 5
Rathfylane ....96 L 10
Rathgarogue ....96 L 10
Rathgormuck ....95 J 11
Rathkeevin ....95 I 10
Rathkenny ....108 M 6
Rathlackan ....111 E 5
Rathlee ....111 E 5
Rathlin Island ....119 N 2
Rathlin O'Birne Island ....112 F 4
Rathlin Sound ....119 N 2
Rathmelton ....117 J 2
Rathmines ....103 N 8
Rathmolyon ....108 L 7
Rathmore ....89 E 11
Rathnew ....103 N 9
Rathnure ....96 L 10
Rathoma ....111 E 5
Rathowen ....107 J 7
Rathvilla ....101 K 8
Rathvilly ....102 L 9
Ratoath ....108 M 7
Raven Point (The) ....97 M 10
Ravensdale ....109 M 5
Ray *near Dunfanaghy* ....117 H 2
Ray *near Rathmillan* ....117 J 2
Ray (River) ....117 H 2
Rea (Lough) ....99 G 8
Reaghstown ....108 M 6
Reananeree / Rae na nDoiri ....89 E 12
Reanascreena ....89 E 13
Rear Cross ....95 H 9
Red Bay ....119 N 2
Redcastle ....118 K 2
Redcross ....103 N 9
Redgate ....97 M 10
Redhills ....107 K 5
Ree (Lough) ....107 I 7
Reelan ....117 H 3
Reen ....89 D 12
Reens ....94 F 10
Reevanagh ....96 K 9
Relaghbeg ....108 L 6
Rerrin ....88 C 13
Rhode ....101 K 7
Richhill ....114 M 4
Ridge ....96 K 9
Ridge Point ....110 C 5
Rine (River) ....99 F 9
Rineanna Point ....99 F 9
Ringabella Bay ....90 H 12
Ringarogy Island ....89 D 13
Ringaskiddy ....90 H 12
Ringboy ....115 P 4
Ringfad Point ....115 P 5
Ringsend ....118 L 2
Ringstown ....101 J 8
Ringville / An Rinn ....91 J 11
Rinmore Point ....117 I 2

Rinn (River) ....107 I 6
Rinn Lough ....107 I 6
Rinneen *Clare* ....98 D 9
Rinneen *Cork* ....89 E 13
Rinroe Point ....110 C 5
Rinville ....99 F 8
Rinvyle ....104 C 7
Rinvyle Castle ....104 B 7
Rinvyle Point ....104 B 7
River ....110 B 6
Riverchapel ....97 N 10
Riverstick ....90 G 12
Riverstown *Cork* ....90 G 12
Riverstown *Sligo* ....112 G 5
Riverstown *Tipperary* ....101 I 8
Riverville ....93 D 11
Roadford ....98 D 8
Roaninish ....116 G 3
Roaringwater Bay ....89 D 13
Robe ....105 E 6
Robert's Head ....90 H 12
Robertstown ....102 L 8
Robinstown ....108 L 7
Roche's Point ....90 H 12
Rochestown ....96 K 11
Rochfortbridge ....101 K 7
Rock (The) ....114 L 4
Rock Island ....98 C 8
Rockabill ....109 N 7
Rockchapel ....93 E 11
Rockcorry ....108 K 5
Rockhill ....94 F 10
Rockmills ....94 G 11
Rodeen ....107 H 6
Roe ....118 L 3
Roe Valley ....118 L 2
Roney Point ....97 N 10
Rooaun ....100 H 8
Roonagh Quay ....104 C 6
Roonah Lough ....104 C 6
Roosky *Leitrim* ....112 H 4
Roosky *Mayo* ....106 F 6
Roosky *Roscommon* ....107 I 6
Ropefield ....112 G 5
Ros an Mhil / Rossaveel ....98 D 8
Ros Comáin / Roscommon ....106 H 7
Ros Cré / Roscrea ....101 I 9
Ros Láir / Rosslare ....97 M 11
Ros Mhic Thriúin / New Ross ....96 L 10
Rosapenna ....117 I 2
Rosbercon ....96 L 10
Rosegreen ....95 I 10
Rosenallis ....101 J 8
Rosguill ....117 I 2
Roskeeragh Point ....112 F 4
Rosmuck ....105 D 7
Rosmult ....95 I 9
Rosnakill ....117 I 2
Ross *Lough Leane* ....89 D 11
Ross *Lough Sheelin* ....107 K 6
Ross Abbey ....105 E 7
Ross Lake ....105 E 7
Ross Port ....111 C 5
Ross West ....105 E 6
Rossan Point ....112 F 3
Rossbeg ....116 G 3
Rossbeigh Creek ....92 C 11
Rossbrin ....89 D 13
Rosscahill ....105 E 7
Rosscarbery ....89 E 13
Rosscarbery Bay ....89 E 13
Rosscor ....113 H 4
Rossdohan Island ....88 C 12
Rosserk Abbey ....111 E 5
Rosses (The) ....116 G 2
Rosses Bay ....116 G 2
Rosses Point ....112 G 5
Rossgeir ....117 J 3
Rossglass ....115 O 5
Rossinver ....112 H 4
Rosslare Bay ....97 M 11
Rosslare Point ....97 M 11
Rosslea ....113 K 5
Rossmore *Cork* ....89 F 12
Rossmore *Laois* ....102 K 9
Rossmore Forest Park ....114 L 5
Rossmore Island ....88 C 12
Rossnowlagh ....112 H 4
Rostellan ....90 H 12
Rostrevor ....109 N 5
Rosturk ....105 C 6
Rough Point ....92 B 11
Roughty ....89 D 12
Roundfort ....105 E 7
Roundstone ....104 C 7

Roundwood ....103 N 8
Roury ....89 E 13
Rousky ....114 K 3
Rowallane Gardens ....115 O 4
Rower (The) ....96 L 10
Royal Canal ....107 I 7
Royaloak ....96 L 9
Ruan ....99 F 9
Rubane ....115 P 4
Rue Point ....119 N 2
Runabay Head ....119 N 2
Runnabackan ....106 H 6
Rushen (Slieve) ....113 J 5
Russborough House ....103 M 8
Rutland Island ....116 G 3
Ryefield ....108 K 6
Ryehill ....106 F 7
Rylane Cross ....90 F 12

S
Saddle Head ....110 B 5
Saggart ....103 M 8
St. Finan's Bay ....88 A 12
St. John's Lough ....107 I 5
St. John's Point ....115 P 5
St. John's Point ....112 G 4
St. Macdara's Island ....104 C 8
St. Margaret's ....103 N 7
St. Mochta's House ....108 M 6
St. Mullin's ....96 L 10
Saintfield ....115 O 4
Saleen *Cork* ....90 H 12
Saleen *Kerry* ....93 D 10
Salia ....104 C 6
Sallahig ....88 B 12
Sallins ....102 M 8
Sally Gap ....103 N 8
Sallybrook ....90 G 12
Sallypark ....100 H 9
Salrock ....104 C 7
Saltee Islands ....96 M 11
Salthill ....99 E 8
Sandholes ....114 L 4
Sandyford ....103 N 8
Santry ....103 N 7
Saul ....115 O 4
Sawel Mountain ....118 K 3
Scalp Mountain ....117 J 2
Scardaun *Mayo* ....105 E 7
Scardaun *Roscommon* ....106 H 7
Scarnagh ....97 N 9
Scarriff / An Scairbh ....99 G 9
Scarriff Island ....88 B 12
Scartaglin ....93 D 11
Scarva ....114 M 5
Scattery Island ....93 D 10
Schull / Skull ....89 D 13
Scolban (Lough) ....113 H 4
Scotch Town ....114 K 3
Scotshouse ....113 K 5
Scotstown ....114 K 5
Scrabo Hill ....115 O 4
Scramoge ....107 H 6
Screeb Cross ....105 D 7
Screen ....97 M 10
Screggan ....101 J 8
Scribbagh ....113 H 4
Scullogue Gap ....96 L 10
Scur (Lough) ....107 I 5
Seaforde ....115 O 5
Seapatrick ....114 N 4
Seefin ....95 J 11
Seskinore ....113 K 4
Seskinryan ....96 L 9
Seven Heads ....90 F 13
Seven Hogs or Magharee Islands (The) ....92 B 11
Shalwy ....112 G 4
Shanacashel ....88 C 11
Shanagarry ....90 H 12
Shanaglish ....99 F 8
Shanagolden ....93 E 10
Shanahoe ....101 J 9
Shanballard ....99 G 7
Shanbally *Cork* ....90 G 12
Shanbally *Galway* ....106 G 7
Shanballymore ....94 G 11
Shanco ....114 L 4
Shanes Castle ....114 N 3
Shankill ....103 N 8
Shanlaragh ....89 E 12
Shanlis ....108 M 6
Shannagh (Lough) ....115 N 5
Shannakea ....93 E 10
Shannawona ....105 D 7
Shannon ....99 F 9

Shannon (River) ....100 H 8
Shannon Airport ....99 F 9
Shannon Harbour ....101 I 8
Shannonbridge ....100 H 8
Shanragh ....101 K 9
Shantonagh ....108 L 5
Sharavogue ....101 I 8
Sheddings (The) ....119 N 3
Sheeanamore ....103 M 9
Sheeaun ....99 G 9
Sheeffry Hills ....105 C 6
Sheehan's Point ....88 B 12
Sheelin (Lough) ....107 K 6
Sheep Haven ....117 I 2
Sheever (Lough) ....107 K 7
Shehy Mountains ....89 D 12
Shercock ....108 L 6
Sherkin Island ....89 D 13
Sherky Island ....88 C 12
Sheskin ....111 D 5
Sheskinapoll ....117 J 3
Shillelagh ....97 M 9
Shinrone ....101 I 9
Shiven ....106 G 7
Shoptown ....115 N 3
Shot Head ....89 C 13
Shranamanragh Bridge ....110 C 5
Shrule ....105 E 7
Silent Valley ....109 O 5
Sillan (Lough) ....108 L 5
Silver Bridge ....108 M 5
Silver Strand ....104 C 6
Silvermine Mountains ....100 H 9
Silvermines ....100 H 9
Sinking ....106 F 7
Sion Mills ....113 J 3
Six Crosses ....93 D 10
Six Road Ends ....115 P 4
Six Towns (The) ....114 L 3
Sixmilebridge ....99 F 9
Sixmilecross ....114 K 4
Skannive (Lough) ....104 C 8
Skeagh ....107 J 7
Skehana ....101 K 9
Skehanagh ....106 G 7
Skerries (The) ....118 M 2
Skerries ....109 N 7
Skreen *Meath* ....108 M 7
Skreen *Sligo* ....112 F 5
Sky Road ....104 B 7
Slade ....96 L 11
Slane ....108 M 6
Slane (Hill of) ....108 M 6
Slaney (River) ....97 M 10
Slat (Lough) ....92 B 11
Slate (River) ....102 L 8
Slea Head ....92 A 11
Slemish Mountain ....119 N 3
Sliabh na Caillighe ....108 K 6
Slieve Anierin ....113 I 5
Slieve Aught Mountains ....99 G 8
Slieve Bernagh ....99 G 9
Slieve Bloom Mountains ....101 J 8
Slieve Gamph or the Ox Mountains ....111 F 5
Slieve Mish Mountains ....93 C 11
Slieve Miskish Mountains ....88 C 13
Slieveanorra ....119 N 2
Slievecallan ....99 E 9
Slievefelim Mountains ....94 H 9
Slievekimalta ....100 H 9
Slievekirk ....117 K 3
Slievemore *Dungannon* ....114 K 4
Slievemore *Mayo* ....110 B 5
Slievemurry ....106 G 7
Slievenamon ....95 J 10
Slieveroe ....96 K 11
Slievetooey ....116 G 3
Sligeach / Sligo ....112 G 5
Sligo Bay ....112 F 5
Sliveardagh Hills ....95 J 10
Slyne Head ....104 B 7
Smerwick ....92 A 11
Smerwick Harbour ....92 A 11
Smithborough ....114 K 5
Smithstown ....101 K 9
Snaght (Slieve) *Derryveagh Mts.* ....117 H 3
Snaght (Slieve) *Inishowen* ....117 J 2
Snave ....89 D 12
Sneem ....88 C 12
Sord / Swords ....103 N 7
South Sound ....98 D 8
Spa ....93 C 11
Spa (The) ....115 O 4
Spanish Point *Locality* ....98 D 9
Spanish Point *Mal Bay* ....98 D 9

Speenoge ....117 J 2
Spelga Dam ....115 N 5
Sperrin Mountains ....118 K 3
Spink ....101 K 9
Spittaltown ....101 J 7
Springfield ....113 I 4
Springhill ....114 M 3
Springwell Forest ....118 L 2
Squires Hill ....115 O 4
Sraghmore ....103 N 8
Srah / An tSraith ....105 E 6
Srahduggaun ....111 C 5
Srahmore *near Bangor* ....111 C 5
Srahmore *near Newport* ....105 D 6
Srahmore *River* ....105 D 6
Sráid na Cathrach / Milltown Malbay ....98 D 9
Stabannan ....109 M 6
Stackallan ....108 M 6
Stack's Mountains ....93 D 11
Staffordstown ....114 M 3
Stags (The) ....89 E 13
Stags of Broad Haven ....111 C 4
Staigue Stone Fort ....88 B 12
Stamullin ....109 N 7
Staplestown ....102 L 8
Stepaside ....103 N 8
Stewartstown ....114 L 4
Stickstown ....90 F 12
Stillorgan ....103 N 8
Stone Bridge ....113 K 5
Stonyford *Kilkenny* ....96 K 10
Stonyford *Lisburn* ....115 N 4
Stormont ....115 O 4
Strabane ....117 J 3
Stracashel ....117 H 3
Stradbally *Kerry* ....92 B 11
Stradbally *Laois* ....101 K 8
Stradbally *Waterford* ....91 J 11
Strade ....105 E 6
Stradone ....107 K 6
Stradreagh ....118 L 2
Straffan ....103 M 8
Stragar ....112 G 3
Strahart ....96 M 10
Straid *Donegal* ....117 J 2
Straid *Larne* ....115 O 3
Straid *Moyle* ....118 M 2
Straith Salach / Recess ....104 C 7
Strand ....93 E 10
Strandhill ....112 G 5
Strangford ....115 P 4
Strangford Lough ....115 P 4
Stranocum ....118 M 2
Stranorlar ....117 I 3
Stratford ....102 L 9
Stravally ....112 G 3
Streamstown ....104 B 7
Streedagh Point ....112 G 4
Streek Head ....89 C 13
Street ....107 J 6
Strokestown ....106 H 6
Stroove ....118 L 2
Struell Wells ....115 O 5
Strule ....113 J 3
Sturrakeen ....95 H 10
Suck (River) ....106 G 6
Suir (River) ....101 I 9
Summercove ....90 G 12
Summerhill ....108 L 7
Suncroft ....102 L 8
Sunderlin (Lough) ....107 I 7
Swan ....101 K 9
Swanlinbar ....113 I 5
Swan's Cross Roads ....114 K 5
Swatragh ....118 L 3
Sweep (The) ....95 J 10
Swilly (Lough) ....117 J 2
Swilly (River) ....117 J 2
Sybil Head ....92 A 11

T
Table Mountain ....103 M 8
Tacumshane ....97 M 11
Tacumshin Lake ....97 M 11
Taghmon ....96 M 11
Taghshinny ....107 I 7
Tagoat ....97 M 11
Tahilla ....88 C 12
Talbot Island ....104 B 7
Talbotstown ....102 M 9
Tallaght ....103 M 8
Tallanstown ....108 M 6
Tallow ....91 H 11
Tallowbridge ....91 H 11
Talt (Lough) ....111 F 5
Tamlaght *Fermanagh* ....113 J 5

Tamlaght *Magherafelt* ....118 M 3
Tamnamore ....114 M 4
Tandragee ....114 M 4
Tang ....107 I 7
Tangaveane ....116 H 3
Tappaghan Mount ....113 J 4
Tara (Hill of) ....108 M 7
Tarbert ....93 D 10
Tardree Forest ....115 N 3
Tarker (Lough) ....108 L 5
Tarmon ....112 H 5
Tarsaghaunmore ....111 C 5
Tassagh ....114 L 5
Taughblane ....115 N 4
Taur ....93 E 11
Tawin ....99 E 8
Tawin Island ....99 E 8
Tawny ....117 I 2
Tawnyinah ....106 F 6
Tawnylea ....112 H 5
Tay ....95 J 11
Tay (Lough) ....103 N 8
Taylor's Cross ....101 I 8
Tearaght Island ....92 A 11
Tedavnet ....114 K 5
Teelin ....112 G 4
Teemore ....113 J 5
Teeranea ....98 D 8
Teeranearagh ....88 B 12
Teerelton ....89 F 12
Teermaclane ....99 E 9
Teernakill ....105 D 7
Teeromoyle ....88 B 12
Teevurcher ....108 L 6
Temple ....115 O 4
Temple of the Winds .....115 P 4
Templeboy ....112 F 5
Templederry ....100 H 9
Templeglentan ....93 E 10
Templehouse Lake ....112 G 5
Templemartin ....90 F 12
Templenoe ....89 C 12
Templeoran ....101 J 7
Templepatrick ....115 N 3
Templeshanbo ....96 L 10
Templetouhy ....101 I 9
Templetown ....96 L 11
Tempo ....113 J 4
Terenure ....103 N 8
Termon ....98 D 10
Termonbarry ....107 I 6
Termonfeckin ....109 N 6

Terryglass ....100 H 8
Tevrin ....107 K 7
Thomas Street ....106 H 7
Thomastown *Meath* ...108 L 6
Thomastown *Tipperrary* ....95 H 10
Thoor Ballylee ....99 F 8
Three Castle Head ....88 C 13
Three Castles ....96 J 9
Three Rock ....103 N 8
Tiduff ....92 B 11
Tievealehid ....116 H 2
Tievemore ....113 I 4
Tillyvoos ....112 H 4
Tiltinbane ....113 I 5
Timahoe ....102 L 8
Timoleague ....90 F 13
Timolin ....102 L 9
Tinahely ....103 M 9
Tinnahinch ....96 L 10
Tinriland ....102 L 9
Tiobraid Árann /
   Tipperary ....95 H 10
Tirnaneill ....114 L 5
Tirneevin ....99 F 8
Toames ....89 F 12
Tobar an Choire /
   Tubbercurry ....112 F 5
Tober ....101 J 7
Toberbeg ....102 M 8
Toberdoney ....118 M 2
Tobermore ....114 L 3
Tobernadarry ....105 E 7
Toberscanavan ....112 G 5
Toe Head ....89 E 13
Toem ....95 H 10
Togher *Cork* ....89 E 12
Togher *Louth* ....109 N 6
Togher *Offaly* ....101 K 8
Tolka ....103 M 7
Tollymore Forest Park ...115 O 5
Tombrack ....97 M 10
Tomdarragh ....103 N 8
Tomhaggard ....97 M 11
Tonabrocky ....99 E 8
Tonakeera Point ....104 C 7
Tonyduff ....108 K 6
Toomaghera ....99 E 8
Toomard ....106 G 7
Toombeola ....104 C 7
Toome ....114 M 3
Toomyvara ....100 H 9
Toor ....100 H 9

Tooraree ....93 E 10
Tooreencahill ....93 E 11
Toorlestraun ....112 F 5
Toormore ....89 D 13
Toormore Bay ....89 D 13
Toornafulla ....93 E 10
Toraigh /
   Tory Island ....116 H 2
Torc Waterfall ....89 D 11
Torneady Point ....116 G 2
Torr Head ....119 N 2
Tory Sound ....117 H 2
Tourig (River) ....91 I 11
Tower ....90 G 12
Trá Lí / Tralee ....93 C 11
Trá Mhór /
   Tramore ....96 K 11
Trabane Strand ....112 F 4
Tracton ....90 G 12
Trafrask ....89 D 12
Tragumna ....89 E 13
Tralee Bay ....92 C 11
Tramore Bay ....96 K 11
Tranarossan Bay ....117 I 2
Travara Bridge ....88 C 12
Trawbreaga Bay ....117 K 2
Trawenagh Bay ....116 G 3
Trawmore Bay ....110 C 5
Trean ....105 D 7
Treantagh ....117 I 2
Treehoo ....107 K 5
Trien ....106 G 6
Trillick ....113 J 4
Tristia ....110 C 5
Trory ....113 J 4
Trostan ....119 N 2
Truskmore ....112 G 4
Trust ....100 H 9
Tuaim / Tuam ....105 F 7
Tuamgraney ....99 G 9
Tuar Mhic Éadaigh /
   Tourmakeady ....105 D 7
Tubber ....99 F 8
Tubbrid *Kilkenny* ....95 J 9
Tubbrid *Tipperary* ....95 I 11
Tulach Mhór /
   Tullamore ....101 J 8
Tulla *near Ennis* ....99 F 9
Tulla *near Gort* ....99 F 8
Tullagh Point ....117 J 2
Tullaghan ....112 G 4
Tullaghan Bay ....110 C 5

Tullaghanstown ....108 L 7
Tullagher ....96 K 10
Tullaghobegly ....117 H 2
Tullaherin ....96 K 10
Tullahought ....95 J 10
Tullakeel ....88 C 12
Tullamore ....93 D 10
Tullaroan ....95 J 10
Tullig ....92 C 11
Tullig Point ....93 C 10
Tullokyne ....105 E 7
Tully
   Lower Lough Erne ..113 I 4
Tully *near Ballyshannon* ....113 H 4
Tully *Upper Lough Erne* ...113 J 5
Tully Cross ....104 C 7
Tully National Stud ....102 L 8
Tullyallen ....109 M 6
Tullyamalra ....108 L 5
Tullycanna ....96 L 11
Tullydush ....117 J 2
Tullyhogue ....114 L 4
Tullylease ....94 F 11
Tullymacreeve ....109 M 5
Tullynaha ....112 H 3
Tullynally Castle ....107 J 6
Tullyroan ....114 M 4
Tullyvin ....108 K 5
Tulrohaun ....105 F 6
Tulsk ....106 H 6
Turlough ....105 E 6
Turloughmore ....105 F 7
Turner's Rock Tunnel .....89 D 12
Turreen ....107 I 7
Tuskar Rock ....97 N 11
Twelve Pins (The) ....104 C 7
Twomileborris ....95 I 9
Tylas ....108 M 7
Tynagh ....100 G 8
Tynan ....114 L 5
Tyrella ....115 O 5
Tyrellspass ....101 J 7

Uachtar Ard /
   Oughterard ....105 E 7
Uaigh / Owey Island .....116 G 2
Ugga Beg (Lough) ....98 D 8
Ulster American
   Folk Park ....113 J 4
Ulster Folk
   Museum (The) ....115 O 4

Union Hall ....89 E 13
Unshin ....112 G 5
Upper Ballinderry ....115 N 4
Upper Lake ....103 M 8
Upperchurch ....95 H 9
Upperlands ....118 M 3
Urbalreagh ....117 K 1
Urglin Glebe ....102 L 9
Urlaur ....106 F 6
Urlaur Lough ....106 F 6
Urlingford ....95 J 9

V

Valencia Island ....88 A 12
Valley ....110 C 5
Valleymount ....103 M 8
Vartry Reservoir ....103 N 8
Ventry ....92 A 11
Ventry Harbour ....92 A 11
Vicarstown ....102 K 8
Victoria Bridge ....113 J 3
Villierstown ....91 I 11
Virginia ....108 K 6
Virginia Road ....108 K 6
Vow ....118 M 3

W

Waddingtown ....96 M 11
Walshestown ....97 M 11
Walshtown ....90 H 12
Ward ....103 N 7
Ward (River) ....103 N 7
Waringsford ....115 N 4
Waringstown ....114 N 4
Warrenpoint ....109 N 5
Washing Bay ....114 M 4
Watch Ho.-Village ....96 M 9
Waterfall ....90 G 12
Waterfoot or Glenariff ...119 N 2
Waterford Harbour ....96 L 11
Watergrasshill ....90 G 11
Waterworks ....114 L 3
Wattle Bridge ....113 J 5
Welchtown ....117 I 3
Wellington Bridge ....96 L 11
Wells Cross ....114 M 4
Wesport Bay ....105 C 6
West Town ....116 H 2
Westcove ....88 B 12
Westport House ....105 D 6
Westport Quay ....105 D 6
Wexford Bay ....97 N 10

Wexford Harbour ....97 M 10
Whale Head ....117 J 2
Wheathill ....113 I 5
Whiddy Island ....89 D 12
White *Limerick* ....93 E 10
White *Louth* ....109 M 6
White Castle ....118 K 2
White Hall ....89 D 13
White Island ....113 I 4
White Park Bay ....118 M 2
White Strand ....98 D 9
Whiteabbey ....115 O 3
Whitechurch *Cork* ....90 G 12
Whitechurch *Waterford* .....91 I 11
Whitecross ....114 M 5
Whitegate ....90 H 12
Whitehall *Roscommon* .107 I 6
Whitehall *Westmeath* ..107 K 7
Whitehead ....115 O 3
Whites Town ....109 N 6
White'sCross ....90 G 12
Whitesides Corner ....114 M 3
Wicklow Gap ....103 M 8
Wicklow Mountains ......103 N 8
Wicklow Way ....103 N 8
Wildfowl
   and Wetlands Trust ...115 O 4
Wilkinstown ....108 L 6
Willbrook ....99 E 9
Williamstown *Galway* ..106 G 6
Williamstown
   Westmeath ....107 I 7
Windgap ....95 J 10
Windmill ....102 L 7
Windy Gap *Kerry* ....89 D 12
Windy Gap *Louth* ......109 N 5
Windy Gap *Mayo* ......105 E 6
Wolfhill ....101 K 9
Womanagh ....91 I 12
Woodburn ....115 O 3
Woodcock Hill ....99 F 9
Woodenbridge ....103 N 9
Woodford (River) ....99 G 8
Woodstown ....96 L 11

Y

Yellow Furze ....108 M 6
Yganavan (Lough) ....92 C 11
Youghal ....100 H 9
Youghal Bay ....91 I 12

A B C D E F G H I J K L M N O P Q R S T U V W X Y Z

Town plans

Sights
Place of interest - Tower
Interesting place of worship

Roads
Motorway - Dual carriageway
Numbered junctions: complete, limited
Major thoroughfare
Unsuitable for traffic or street subject to restrictions
Pedestrian street - Tramway
Car park - Park and Ride
Tunnel
Station and railway
Funicular
Cable-car

Various signs
Place of worship
Mosque - Synagogue
Tower - Ruins
Windmill
Garden, park, wood - Cemetery
Stadium - Golf course - Racecourse
Outdoor or indoor swimming pool
View - Panorama
Monument - Fountain
Pleasure boat harbour - Lighthouse
Tourist Information Centre
Airport - Underground station
Coach station
Ferry services:
passengers and cars - passengers only
Main post office with poste restante - Hospital
Covered market
Gendarmerie - Police
Town Hall
University, College
Public buildings located by letter:
Museum - Theatre

Plans

Curiosités
Bâtiment intéressant - Tour
Édifice religieux intéressant

Voirie
Autoroute - Double chaussée de type autoroutier
Échangeurs numérotés : complet - partiels
Grande voie de circulation
Rue réglementée ou impraticable
Rue piétonne - Tramway
Parking - Parking Relais
Tunnel
Gare et voie ferrée
Funiculaire, voie à crémaillère
Téléphérique, télécabine

Signes divers
Édifice religieux
Mosquée - Synagogue
Tour - Ruines
Moulin à vent
Jardin, parc, bois - Cimetière
Stade - Golf - Hippodrome
Piscine de plein air, couverte
Vue - Panorama
Monument - Fontaine
Port de plaisance - Phare
Information touristique
Aéroport - Station de métro
Gare routière
Transport par bateau :
passagers et voitures, passagers seulement
Bureau principal de poste restante - Hôpital
Marché couvert
Gendarmerie - Police
Hôtel de ville
Université, grande école
Bâtiment public repéré par une lettre :
Musée - Théâtre

Stadtpläne

Sehenswürdigkeiten
Sehenswertes Gebäude - Turm
Sehenswerter Sakralbau

Straßen
Autobahn - Schnellstraße
Nummerierte Voll- bzw. Teilanschlussstellen
Hauptverkehrsstraße
Gesperrte Straße oder mit Verkehrsbeschränkungen
Fußgängerzone - Straßenbahn
Parkplatz - Park-and-Ride-Plätze
Tunnel
Bahnhof und Bahnlinie
Standseilbahn
Seilschwebebahn

Sonstige Zeichen
Sakralbau
Moschee - Synagoge
Turm - Ruine
Windmühle
Garten, Park, Wäldchen - Friedhof
Stadion - Golfplatz - Pferderennbahn
Freibad - Hallenbad
Aussicht - Rundblick
Denkmal - Brunnen
Yachthafen- Leuchtturm
Informationsstelle
Flughafen - U-Bahnstation
Autobusbahnhof
Schiffsverbindungen:
Autofähre, Personenfähre
Hauptpostamt (postlagernde Sendungen) - Krankenhaus
Markthalle
Gendarmerie - Polizei
Rathaus
Universität, Hochschule
Öffentliches Gebäude, durch einen Buchstaben gekennzeichnet:
Museum - Theater

Plattegronden

Bezienswaardigheden
Interessant gebouw - Toren
Interessant kerkelijk gebouw

Wegen
Autosnelweg - Weg met gescheiden rijbanen
Knooppunt / aansluiting: volledig, gedeeltelijk
Hoofdverkeersweg
Onbegaanbare straat, beperkt toegankelijk
Voetgangersgebied - Tramlijn
Parkeerplaats - P & R
Tunnel
Station, spoorweg
Kabelspoor
Tandradbaan

Overige tekens
Kerkelijk gebouw
Moskee - Synagoge
Toren - Ruïne
Windmolen
Tuin, park, bos - Begraafplaats
Stadion - Golfterrein - Renbaan
Zwembad: openlucht, overdekt
Uitzicht - Panorama
Gedenkteken, standbeeld - Fontein
Jachthaven - Vuurtoren
Informatie voor toeristen
Luchthaven - Metrostation
Busstation
Vervoer per boot:
Passagiers en auto's - uitsluitend passagiers
Hoofdkantoor voor poste-restante - Ziekenhuis
Overdekte markt
Marechaussee / rijkswacht - Politie
Stadhuis
Universiteit, hogeschool
Openbaar gebouw, aangegeven met een letter:
Museum - Schouwburg

Piante

Curiosità
Edificio interessante - Torre
Costruzione religiosa interessante

Viabilità
Autostrada - Doppia carreggiata tipo autostrada
Svincoli numerati: completo, parziale
Grande via di circolazione
Via regolamentata o impraticabile
Via pedonale - Tranvia
Parcheggio - Parcheggio Ristoro
Galleria
Stazione e ferrovia
Funicolare
Funivia, cabinovia

Simboli vari
Costruzione religiosa
Moschea - Sinagoga
Torre - Ruderi
Mulino a vento
Giardino, parco, bosco - Cimitero
Stadio - Golf - Ippodromo
Piscina: all'aperto, coperta
Vista - Panorama
Monumento - Fontana
Porto turistico - Faro
Ufficio informazioni turistiche
Aeroporto - Stazione della metropolitana
Autostazione
Trasporto con traghetto:
passeggeri ed autovetture - solo passeggeri
Ufficio centrale di fermo posta - Ospedale
Mercato coperto
Carabinieri - Polizia
Municipio
Università, scuola superiore
Edificio pubblico indicato con lettera:
Museo - Teatro

Planos

Curiosidades
Edificio interessante - Torre
Edificio religioso interessante

Vías de circulación
Autopista - Autovía
Enlaces numerados: completo, parciales
Via importante de circulacíon
Calle reglamentada o impracticable
Calle peatonal - Tranvía
Aparcamiento - Aparcamientos «P+R»
Túnel
Estación y línea férrea
Funicular, línea de cremallera
Teleférico, telecabina

Signos diversos
Edificio religioso
Mezquita - Sinagoga
Torre - Ruinas
Molino de viento
Jardín, parque, madera - Cementerio
Estadio - Golf - Hipódromo
Piscina al aire libre, cubierta
Vista parcial - Vista panorámica
Monumento - Fuente
Puerto deportivo - Faro
Oficina de Información de Turismo
Aeropuerto - Estación de metro
Estación de autobuses
Transporte por barco:
pasajeros y vehículos, pasajeros solamente
Oficina de correos - Hospital
Mercado cubierto
Policía National - Policía
Ayuntamiento
Universidad, escuela superior
Edificio público localizado con letra :
Museo - Teatro

Plans de ville
Town plans / Stadtpläne / Stadsplattegronden
Piante di città / Planos de ciudades

GREAT BRITAIN
- Aberdeen 150
- Bath 150
- Birmingham. 151
- Bournemouth 152
- Brighton and Hove 153
- Bristol 154
- Cambridge. 155
- Canterbury. 156
- Cardiff 157
- Chester 158
- Coventry. 159
- Dundee. 159
- Durham. 160
- Edinburgh 161
- Exeter. 162
- Glasgow 163
- Leeds 164
- Leicester 165
- Lincoln. 165
- Liverpool 166-167
- Greater London 168-169
- London 170-171
- Manchester 172
- Newcastle-upon-Tyne . . . 173
- Norwich 174
- Nottingham. 174
- Oxford 175
- Perth 176
- Plymouth 177
- Portsmouth
  and Southsea 178
- Southampton 179
- Stirling. 180
- Stratford-upon-Avon 181
- Winchester. 182
- Windsor. 183
- York 184

IRELAND
- Belfast 185
- Cork 186
- Galway. 187
- Dublin 188-189
- Killarney 190
- Limerick 191

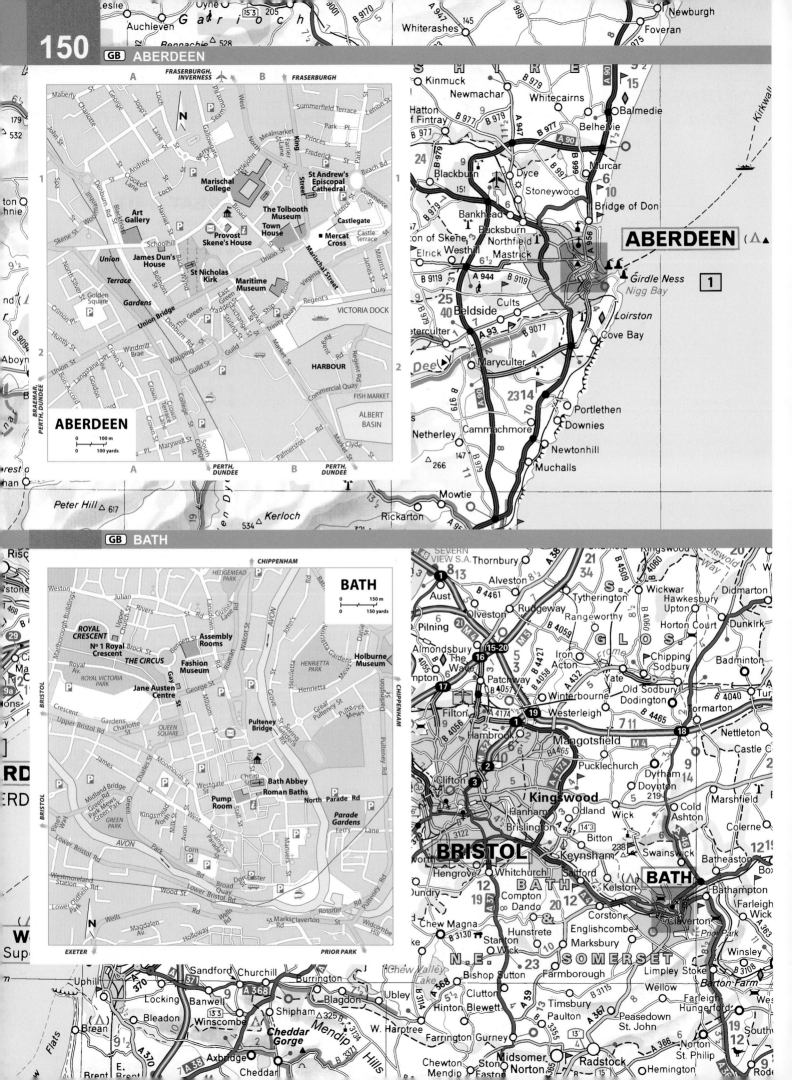

Bournemouth (city map)

FERNDOWN
SOUTHAMPTON
DORCHESTER
LYMINGTON

MEYRICK PARK

Braidley Rd
Braidley Rd
Central Drive
Bodorgan Rd
Wimborne Rd
Dean Park Rd
Cavendish Rd
ST. PAUL
BOURNEMOUTH
St. Pauls Rd
Northcote Rd
Southcote Rd
Holdenhurst Rd
Lansdowne
St. Swithuns Rd South
Frances Rd
Knyveton Rd
Cotlands Rd

RICHMOND HILL
Richmond Gardens
Wessex Way
Dean Park Crescent
Madeira Rd
Lorne Park Rd
Old Christchurch Rd
Stafford Rd
POL
Christchurch Rd
Manor Rd

BOURNEMOUTH WEST
Wessex Way
Bourne
Bradburne
Stephen's Way
Richmond Hill
B'r Yelverton Rd
Albert Rd
Hinton Rd
Old
Glen Fern Rd
St. Peter's Rd
Bath Rd
Gervis Rd
Gervis Rd
Grove Rd
Grove Rd
East Overcliff Drive

Suffolk Rd
Cambridge Rd
Norwich Av West
Norwich Av
Upper Norwich Rd
The Triangle
Commercial Rd
Poole Hill
Post Office
Gervis Place
Old Christchurch Rd
Exeter Rd
Upper Hinton Rd
Parsonage Rd
Russell-Cotes Art Gallery and Museum
Undercliff Drive

UPPER CENTRAL GARDENS
Somerville Rd
West Cliff Rd
Durley Chine Rd South
Chine Crescent
Terrace
Exeter Rd
LOWER CENTRAL GARDENS
Westover Rd
Bath Rd
Undercliff Drive

West Overcliff Drive
Durley Chine Rd
Michael's Rd
Priory Rd
West Hill Rd
West Cliff Rd
Beacon Rd
WATERFRONT COMPLEX
Pier Approach
Undercliff Prom
West Undercliff Prom

INTERNATIONAL CENTRE

BOURNEMOUTH
N
0   200 m
0   200 yards

Regional map

Salisbury Plain
Upton Scudamore
Warminster
Corsley
Chapmanslade
Frome
Shrewton
Larkhill
Durrington
Amesbury
Cholderton
Allington
Idmiston
Winterbourne Dauntsey
Winterslow
Laverstock
SALISBURY
Farley
Alderbury
Downton
Redlynch
Landford
Nomansland
Fordingbridge
Alderholt
Ibsley
Ringwood
Burley
St. Leonards
Bransgore
Sopley
Hurn
Burton
Highcliffe
Christchurch
Mudeford

Lydlinch
Child Okeford
Tarrant Gunville
Tarrant Hinton
Gussage All Saints
Wimborne St. Giles
Cranborne
Woodlands
Verwood
Horton
Okeford Fitzpaine
Shillingstone
Pimperne
Signals Museum
Tarrant Monkton
Witchampton
Holt
W. Moors
Wimborne Minster
Ferndown
Durweston
Blandford Forum
Hazelbury Bryan
Pulham
Mappowder
Buckland Newton
Winterborne Stickland
Hilton
Milton Abbas
Charlton Marshall
Tarrant Keyneston
Spetisbury
Kingston Lacy
Hampreston
Minterne Magna
Alton Pancras
Plush
Cheselbourne
Winterborne Whitechurch
Sturminster Marshall
Corfe Mullen
Broadstone
Piddletrenthide
Piddlehinton
Milborne St. Andrew
Winterborne Kingston
Morden
Lytchett Matravers
Upton
Poole
Boscombe
Southbourne
Tolpuddle
Bere Regis
Lytchett Minster
BOURNEMOUTH
Hengistbury Head
Charminster
Puddletown
Athelhampton
Hardy's Cottage
Affpuddle
Clouds Hill
Holton Heath
Hamworthy
Sandbanks
Dorchester
Woodsford
Moreton
Tank Museum
Arne
Brownsea Island
Poole Harbour
Poole Bay
W. Stafford
Crossways
Frome
Wareham
Broadmayne
Warmwell
Wool
Studland
White Horse
Winfrith Newburgh
Blue Pool
Old Harry Rocks
Osmington
Owermoigne
E. Lulworth
Church Knowle
Corfe Castle
Lodmoor
W. Lulworth
Kimmeridge
Smedmore
Langton Matravers
Swanage
Weymouth
Weymouth Bay
Durdle Door
Lulworth Cove
Dorset Coast Path
Worth Matravers
Durlston Head
Portland Harbour
Fortuneswell
Easton
St. Aldhelm's Head
Cherbourg-en-Cotentin
Jersey
Guernsey

CRAWLEY · LEWES

PRESTON PARK

PORTSMOUTH · WORTHING

St. Bartholomews

DYKE ROAD PARK

HOVE · WILBURY

LONDON ROAD

PARK CRESCENT

ST. ANN'S WELL GARDENS

FURZE HILL

BRIGHTON

QUEEN'S PARK

THE LANES

Brighton Museum and Art Gallery

ROYAL PAVILION

NEWHAVEN

BRIGHTON AND HOVE

0 — 300 m
0 — 300 yards

N

ENGLISH CHANNEL

Marine · Madeira Drive

Parade · Madeira Drive

WEST SUSSEX

Bucks Green
Loxwood
Plaistow
chapel
Kirdford
Wisborough Green
Petworth
Pulborough
Littleworth
Hardham
Bury
Amberley
Parham House
Storrington
Washington
Steyning
Findon
Arundel
Angmering
Sompting
Lancing
Shoreham
Portslade
WORTHING (▲)
Ford
Preston
Rustington
Climping
Littlehampton (▲)
Middleton-on-Sea
...r Regis (▲)

Broadbridge Heath
Horsham
Itchingfield
Billingshurst (▲)
Southwater
Coolham
Cowfold
Bolney
W. Grinstead
Hickstead
Dial Post
Partridge Green
Thakeham
Ashington
Henfield
Small Dole
Upr. Beeding
Fulking
Southwick
Hove
BRIGHTON

St. Leonard's Forest
Mannings Heath
Lr. Beeding
Cuckfield
Albourne
Hassocks
Clayton
Pyecombe
Poynings
Falmer
Woodingdean
Rottingdean
Peacehaven

Wakehurst Place
Balcombe
Handcross
Ardingly
Nymans
Ouse
Burgess Hill
Hurstpierpoint
Keymer
Ditchling
Westmeston
Ditchling Common
Wivelsfield
Chailey
Newick
Ditchling Beacon
Stanmer Park
Lewes
Castle
Beddingham
Rodmell
W. Firle
Newhaven
Seaford

Wych Cross
Chelwood Gate
Horsted Keynes
Danehill
Nutley
Fletching
Maresfield
Sheffield Park
Haywards Heath
Uckfield
Framfield
Waldron
Halland
E. Hoathly
Chiddin...
Ringmer
Laughton
Glyndebourne
Glynde
Ripe
Upr. Dicker
Selmeston
Alfriston
Heighton
Wilmington
Jevington
Charles... Manor
Eastdean
Seven Sisters

Ashdown Forest
Crowbo...
Buxted
Blackb...

SOUTH DOWNS

South Downs Way

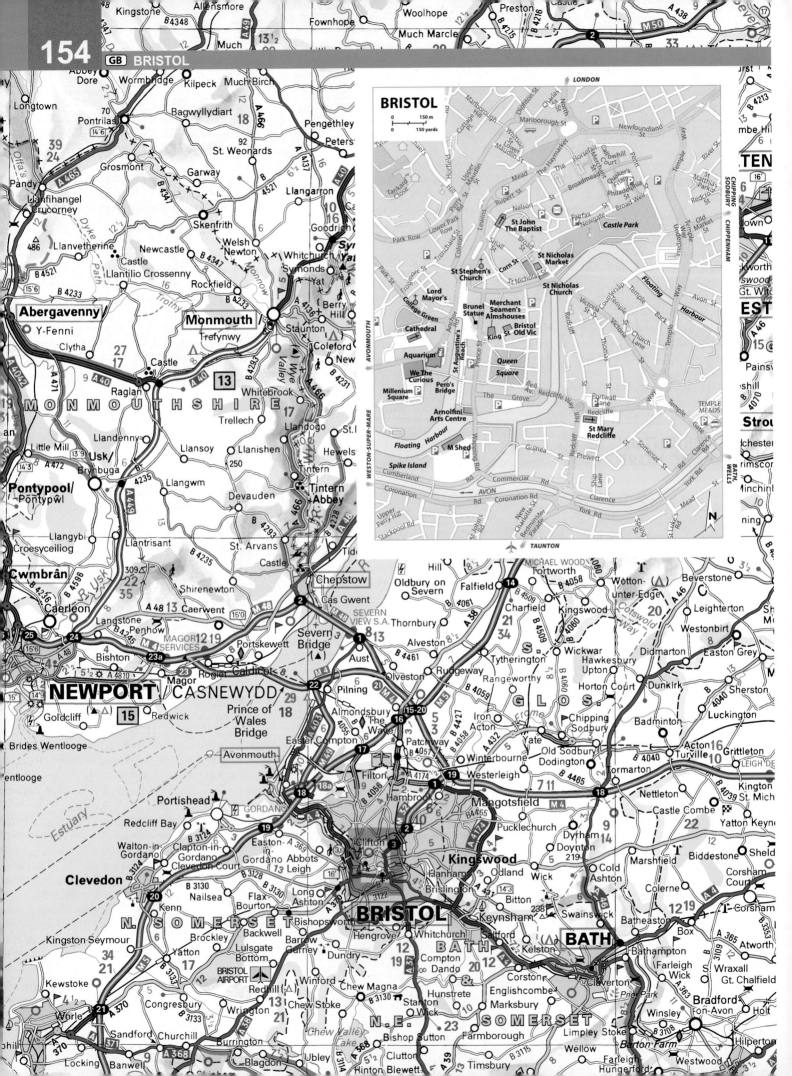

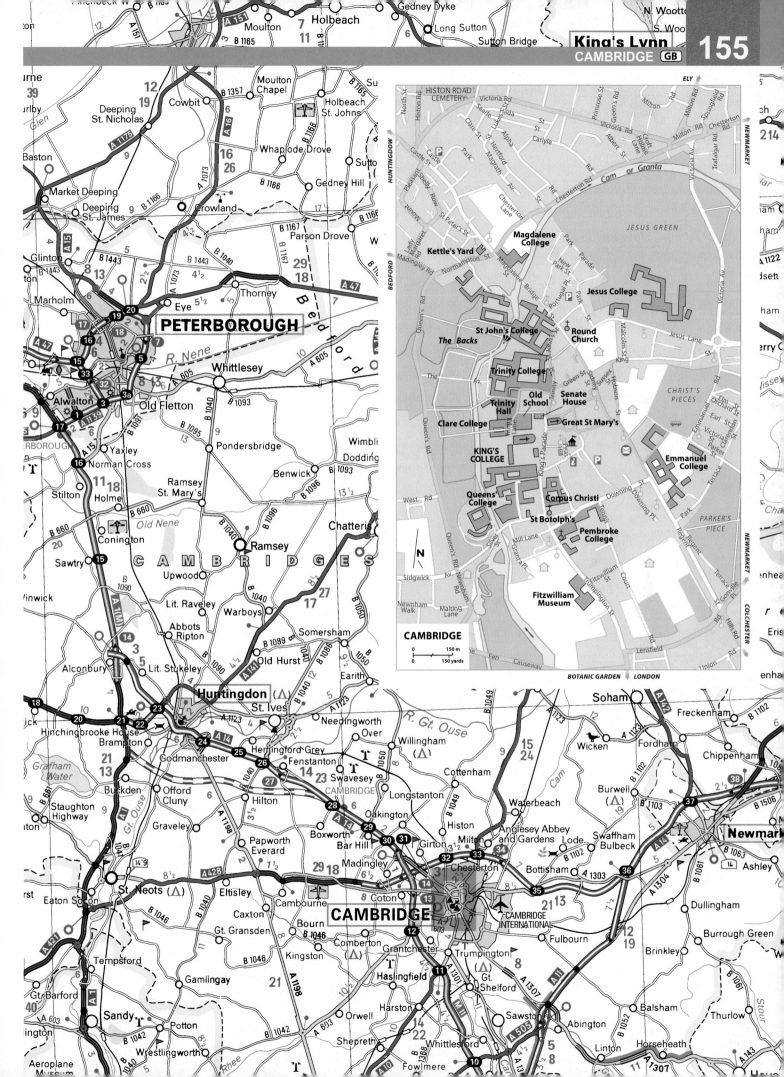

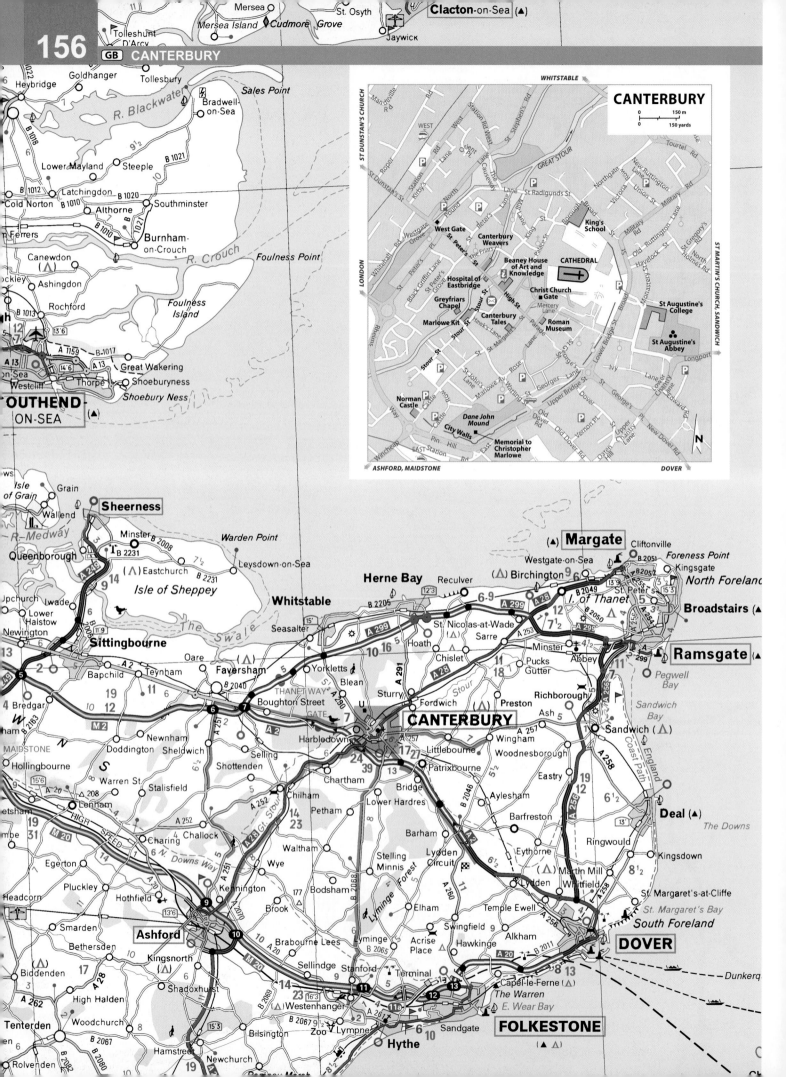

CANTERBURY

0 150 m
0 150 yards

WHITSTABLE

ST DUNSTAN'S CHURCH

WEST

LONDON

West Gate
Canterbury Weavers
St Radigunds St
King's School
Beaney House of Art and Knowledge
CATHEDRAL
Christ Church Gate
Hospital of Eastbridge
Greyfriars Chapel
Mercery Lane
Canterbury Tales
Roman Museum
Marlowe Kit
Norman Castle
St Augustine's College
St Augustine's Abbey
Dane John Mound
City Walls
Memorial to Christopher Marlowe

ST MARTIN'S CHURCH, SANDWICH

N

ASHFORD, MAIDSTONE   DOVER

Southend / Blackwater area

Mersea
Mersea Island
Cudmore Grove
St. Osyth
Clacton-on-Sea (▲)
Jaywick

Tollesbury
Tollesbury D'Arcy
Heybridge
Goldhanger
Sales Point
Bradwell-on-Sea
R. Blackwater
B 1018
Lower Mayland
Steeple
B 1021
Latchingdon
B 1020
Cold Norton
Althorne
Southminster
B 1010
Ferrers
Burnham-on-Crouch
Canewdon (Λ)
R. Crouch
Foulness Point
Ashingdon
Rochford
Foulness Island
B 1013
A 1159
A 13
Great Wakering
Shoeburyness
Westcliff
Thorpe
Shoebury Ness
SOUTHEND-ON-SEA (▲)

Isle of Grain
Grain
Wallend
Sheerness
R. Medway
Queenborough
Minster
B 2008
Warden Point
B 2231
Eastchurch
Leysdown-on-Sea
Isle of Sheppey
Jpchurch
Iwade
Lower Halstow
Newington
The Swale
Sittingbourne
Herne Bay
Reculver
Whitstable
Seasalter
Margate (▲)
Cliftonville
Westgate-on-Sea
Foreness Point
Birchington
B 2051
Kingsgate
North Foreland
I. of Thanet
St Peter's
Broadstairs (▲
A 299
A 28
St. Nicolas-at-Wade
Sarre
Minster
Ramsgate (▲
Oare
Faversham
Yorkletts
Blean
Sturry
Hoath
Chislet
Pucks Gutter
Abbey
Pegwell Bay
A 2
Teynham
B 2040
THANET WAY
Boughton Street
GATE
Harbledown
CANTERBURY
Fordwich
Preston
Richborough
Sandwich Bay
Bapchild
Bredgar
Newnham
Doddington
Sheldwich
Selling
Shottenden
Chartham
Harbledown
Littlebourne
Patrixbourne
Wingham
Woodnesborough
Sandwich (Λ)
England Coast Path
MAIDSTONE
Hollingbourne
Warren St
Stalisfield
Chilham
Petham
Bridge
Eastry
Aylesham
Deal (▲)
The Downs
Lenham
Charing
Challock
Waltham
Wye
Stelling Minnis
Barham
Barfreston
Ringwould
Kingsdown
Egerton
Pluckley
Hothfield
Brook
Bodsham
Elham
Lydden Circuit
Eythorne
Martin Mill
St Margaret's-at-Cliffe
Smarden
Bethersden
Ashford
Kingsnorth
Brabourne Lees
Lyminge Forest
Swingfield
Temple Ewell
Whitfield
St Margaret's Bay
South Foreland
Biddenden
High Halden
Woodchurch
Kennington
Stanford
Acrise Place
Hawkinge
Alkham
DOVER
Tenterden
Headcorn
Shadoxhurst
Westenhanger
Sellindge
Terminal
Capel-le-Ferne (Λ)
The Warren
E. Wear Bay
Dunkerq
Hamstreet
Bilsington
Zoo
Lympne
Sandgate
FOLKESTONE
Rolvenden
Newchurch
Hythe
(▲ ▲Λ)

M2
M20
A 20
A 28
A 2070
A 252
A 251
A 28
A 291
A 290
A 257
A 256
A 258
A 260
A 2
A 253
A 299

CARDIFF

0   200 m
0   200 yards

N

SWANSEA — MERTHYR TYDFIL · CAERPHILLY — BRISTOL

WELSH OFFICE · UNIVERSITY COLLEGE · CATHAYS
TEMPLE OF PEACE · ALEXANDRA GARDENS
National Museum Cardiff
OLD COUNTY HALL · City Hall · Gorsedd Gardens
Bute Park · Law Courts
Cardiff Castle · Military Museums
St John's Church · ST DAVID'S SHOPPING CENTRE
QUEEN ST · CAPITOL CENTRE
Cardiff Arms Park · Central Market · The Old Library
Millennium Stadium
CARDIFF CENTRAL · CALLAGHAN SQUARE
SWAMINARAYANA TEMPLE
Pendyris St · Pentre Gardens
SEVENOAKS PARK
Bute East Dock
GRANGETOWN MUSLIM CULTURAL CENTRE
THE SALVATION ARMY
BUTETOWN · Coal Exchange
THE RED DRAGON CENTRE
CARDIFF BAY
ST CUTHBERT'S
Techniquest · Pierhead Building · Y Senedd
Wales Millennium Centre
MERMAID QUAY
Norwegian Church
HAMADRYAD PARK
CARDIFF BAY YACHT CLUB
CARDIFF BAY WETLANDS RESERVE
QUEEN ALEXANDRA DOCK
LECKWITH WOODS
THOMPSON'S PARK

PENARTH — BRIGEND

CAERPHILLY
Cymmer · Tonyrefail · Pontypridd · Beddau
Senghenydd · Llanbradach · Machen · Risca
Bedwas · Rogerstone · Caerleon · Caerwent
Langstone · Penhow · Portskewett
Caerphilly / Caerffili · Parc Cefn Onn
Thornhill · Castleton · Marshfield
NEWPORT / CASNEWYDD · Magor · Rogiet · Caldicot
MAGOR SERVICES
SEVERN VIEW S.A. · Severn Bridge · Aust · Pilning
Tongwynlais · Lisvane · Llanishen
Goldcliff · Redwick · Prince of Wales Bridge
Almondsbury · Easter Compton · Filton
Pentyrch · Whitchurch · St Mellons · Rumney
Peterstone Wentlooge · St Brides Wentlooge
Avonmouth · Portishead · GORDANO
Radyr · CARDIFF WEST S.A.
St Brides-Super-Ely · Ely · St Fagans
Redcliff Bay · Walton-in-Gordano · Clapton-in-Gordano
Clevedon Court · Abbots Leigh · Clifton
CARDIFF / CAERDYDD
Pendoylan · St Nicholas · Dinas Powys · Penarth
Clevedon · Kenn · Nailsea · Flax Bourton · Long Ashton
BRISTOL
Beaupre Castle · Bonvilston · Wenvoe · Penmark
N. SOMERSET · Bishopsworth
Eglwys Brewis · Penmark
St Athan · Sully · Swanbridge
Kingston Seymour · Brockley · Backwell · Barrow Gurney · Dundry
East Aberthaw · Rhoose · Porthkerry
CARDIFF AIRPORT
Barry / Barri
Flat Holm · Kewstoke · Congresbury · Winford · Chew Magna
BRISTOL AIRPORT · Redhill · Yatton · Lulsgate Bottom
Weston-Super-Mare · Wrington · Chew Stoke

Chester city inset

HOYLAKE · ELLESMERE PORT MANCHESTER, LIVERPOOL
MANCHESTER, NANTWICH, WHITCHURCH

Northgate
The Walls
King Charles' Tower
Kaleyard's Gate
Chester Cathedral
Town Hall
Eastgate
THE ROWS
Grosvenor Shopping Centre
Dewa Roman Experience
Stanley Palace
Three Old Arches
Newgate
St John's
Grosvenor Park
Grosvenor Museum
Bridgegate
QUEEN'S PARK
Roodee

N

CHESTER
0   150 m
0   150 yards

QUEENSFERRY
WREXHAM · CONWY

Regional map

SOUTHPORT
Hesketh Bank
Much Hoole
Ley
Croston
Rufford Old Hall
Mawdesley
Birkdale
Mere Brow
Rufford
Wildfowl Trust
Ainsdale
Scarisbrick
Burscough Bridge
Parbold
Newburgh
Halsall
Burscough
Formby
Gt. Altcar
Ormskirk
Skelmersdale
Ince Blundell
Aughton
Up Holland
Lydiate
Maghull
Hightown
Blundellsands
Litherland
Aintree
Kirkby
Crosby
ST. HELENS
Bootle
Knowsley
New Brighton
LIVERPOOL
Wallasey
Roby
Huyton
BIRKENHEAD
Woolton
Farnworth
Hough Green
Ditton
West Kirby
Irby
Port Sunlight
Widnes
Thurstaston
Pensby
Bebington
Speke
Hale
Bromborough
LIVERPOOL JOHN LENNON AIRPORT
Heswall
Eastham
River Mersey
Runcorn
Thornton Hough
Parkgate
Neston
Willaston
Ellesmere Port
Frodsham
Whitby
Backford Cross
Elton
Helsby
Stoak
Bridge Trafford
Little Barrow
Saughall
Sealand
Upton
Great Barrow
Ash
Rhyl
Prestatyn
Talacre
Point of Ayr
Welsh Channel
River Dee / Afon Dyfrdwy
CHESTER
Kinmel Bay
Llanasa
Trelawnyd
Mostyn
Holywell / Treffynnon
Greenfield
Flint / Fflint
Christleton
Waverton
Rhuddlan
Dyserth
Babell
Bagillt
Connah's Quay
Queensferry
Lache
Saltney
Tattenhall
Pensarn
Castle
Rhuallt
Caerwys
Halkyn
Northop
Ewloe
Hawarden
CHESHIRE WEST AND CHESTER
Abergele
Bodelwyddan
St. Asaph
Tremeirchion
Afon-wen
Northop Hall
Buckley / Bwcle
Broughton
Handbridge
Huxley
Llannefydd
Trefnant
Bodfari
Nannerch
Mold / Yr Wyddgrug
Hope
Pulford
Aldford
Handley
Burwardsley
Henllan
Cilcain
Loggerheads
Nercwys
Penyffordd
Burton
Higher Kinnerton
Denbigh / Dinbych
Llandyrnog
Moel Fammau
Waun y llyn
Rossett
FLINTSHIRE
Llanrhaeadr
Leeswood
Treuddyn
Caergwrle
Llay
Bylchau
Llanferres
Llanfynydd
Gresford
Farndon
Broxton
Ruthin / Rhuthun
Llanarmon yn-lal
Bwlchgwyn
Holt
Malpas
DENBIGHSHIRE
Cyffylliog
Clocaenog
Pentre Celyn
Llandegla
Brymbo
Coedpoeth
Rhostyllen
Tilston
Clawdd newydd
Bettws Gwerfil Goch
Bryneglwys
WREXHAM / WRECSAM
Erddig
Llanfihangel Glyn Myfyr
Llanelidan
Rhoslannerchrugog
Marchwiel
Worthenbury
Clocaenog Forest
Brenig Resr.
Offa's Dyke
Cynwyd
Worthenbury

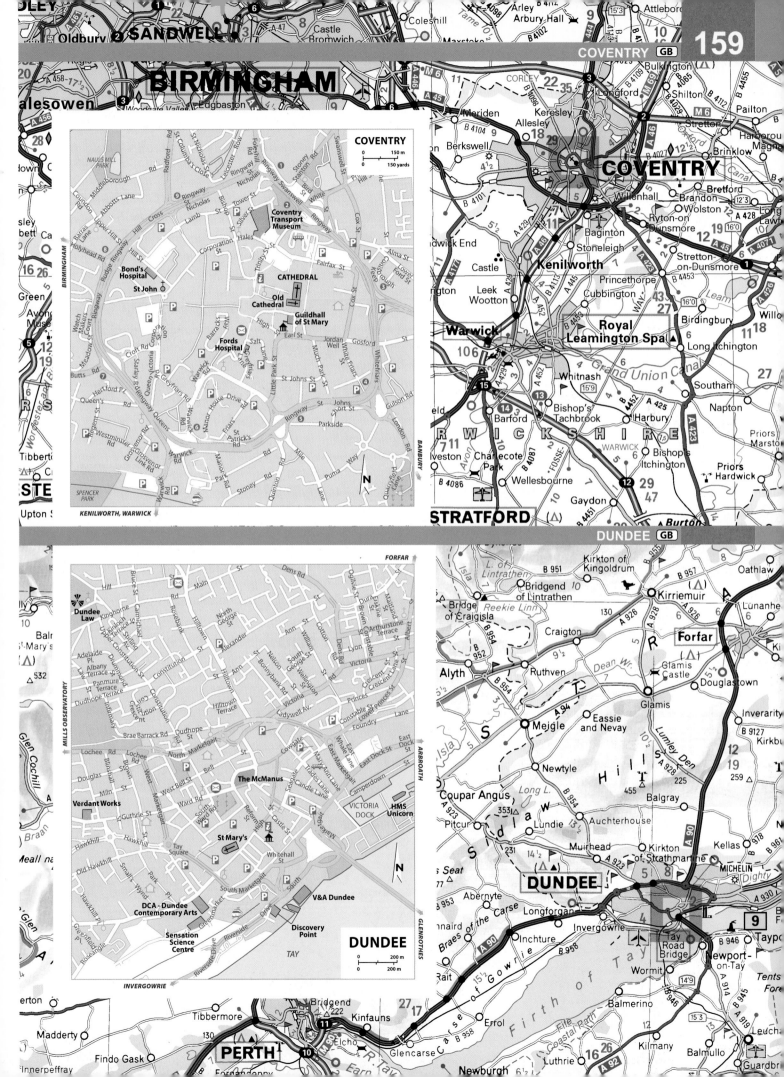

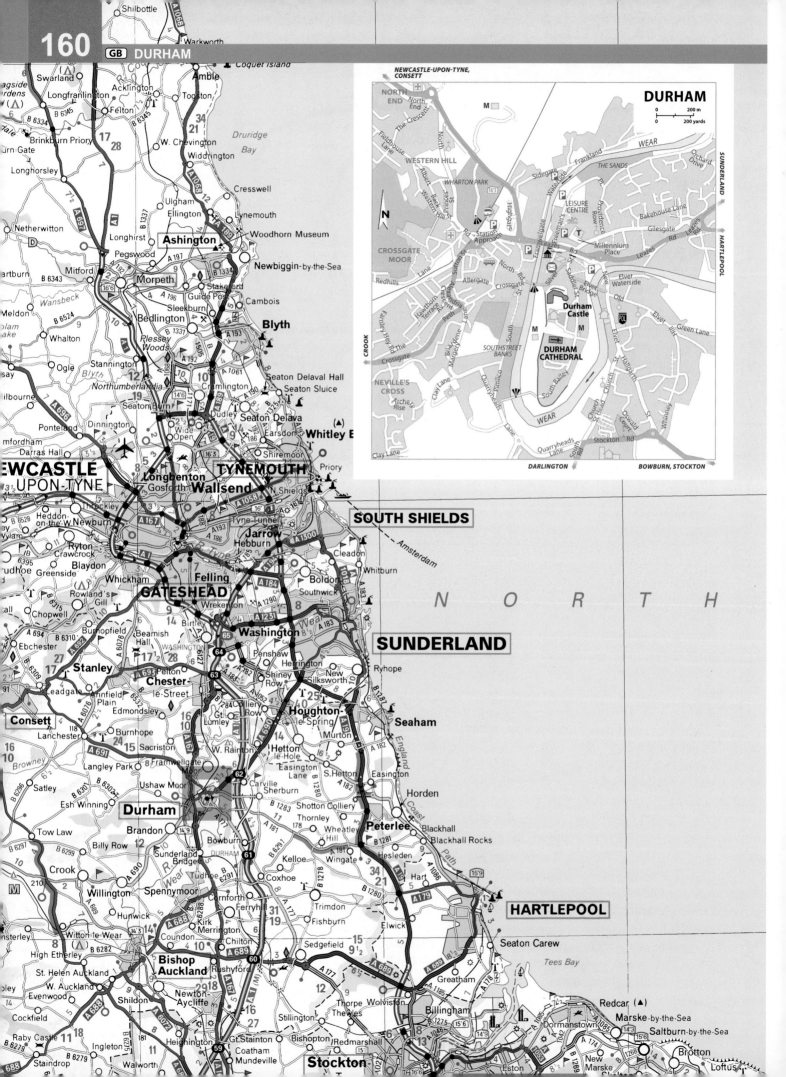

DURHAM (inset map)

NEWCASTLE-UPON-TYNE, CONSETT

NORTH END

WESTERN HILL

WHARTON PARK

CROSSGATE MOOR

NEVILLE'S CROSS

THE CRESCENT

Fieldhouse Lane

Hawthorn Terrace

Redhills

Allergate

Crossgate

The Sands

LEISURE CENTRE

Millennium Place

Durham Castle

SOUTHSTREET BANKS

DURHAM CATHEDRAL

WEAR

SUNDERLAND

HARTLEPOOL

0   200 m
0   200 yards

DARLINGTON   BOWBURN, STOCKTON

Main map

Shilbottle

Warkworth

Coquet Island

Swarland

Longframlington

Acklington

Amble

Togston

Felton

B 6345

B 6345

34

21

Brinkburn Priory

17

28

W. Chevington

Druridge Bay

Widdrington

Longhorsley

Ulgham

Ellington

Cresswell

Netherwitton

Longhirst

Pegswood

Lynemouth

Woodhorn Museum

Ashington

Newbiggin-by-the-Sea

Mitford

Morpeth

Stakeford

Guide Post

Sleekburn

Cambois

Meldon

Bedlington

Blyth

Whalton

Plessey Woods

Ogle

Stannington

Northumberlandia

Seaton Delaval Hall

Seaton Sluice

Ponteland

Dinnington

Seaton Burn

Dudley

Seaton Delaval

Darras Hall

Wide Open

Earsdon

NEWCASTLE UPON-TYNE

TYNEMOUTH

Shiremoor

Whitley B

Heddon-on-the-W

Newburn

Longbenton

Gosforth

Wallsend

N. Shields

Priory

SOUTH SHIELDS

Ryton

Crawcrock

Blaydon

Jarrow

Hebburn

Cleadon

Whitburn

Amsterdam

Greenside

Whickham

Felling

GATESHEAD

Boldon

Southwick

NORTH

Chopwell

Rowland's Gill

Birtle

Washington

Wrekenton

Ebchester

Burnopfield

Beamish Hall

WASHINGTON

Penshaw

Herrington

Ryhope

SUNDERLAND

Stanley

Pelton

Shiney Row

New Silksworth

Chester-le-Street

Colliery Row

Consett

Annfield Plain

Edmondsley

Gt. Lumley

Houghton-le-Spring

Murton

Seaham

Lanchester

Burnhope

Sacriston

Hetton le-Hole

Easington Lane

S.Hetton

Easington

Langley Park

Framwellgate

W. Rainton

Horden

Ushaw Moor

Carville

Sherburn

Durham

Brandon

Shotton Colliery

Thornley

Wheatley Hill

Peterlee

Blackhall

Tow Law

Billy Row

Bowburn

DURHAM

Kelloe

Wingate

Blackhall Rocks

Crook

Sunderland Bridge

Tudhoe

Coxhoe

Hesleden

Hart

Willington

Spennymoor

Cornforth

Ferryhill

Trimdon

Fishburn

Elwick

Seaton Carew

Hunwick

Kirk Merrington

Chilton

Sedgefield

HARTLEPOOL

Witton-le-Wear

Coundon

Tees Bay

High Etherley

St. Helen Auckland

Bishop Auckland

Rushyford

Greatham

W. Auckland

Shildon

Newton Aycliffe

Cockfield

Raby Castle

Ingleton

Staindrop

Gt. Stainton

Bishopton

Redmarshall

Thorpe Thewles

Wolviston

Billingham

Redcar

Marske-by-the-Sea

Saltburn-by-the-Sea

Brotton

Walworth

Coatham Mundeville

Stockton

Eston

Dormanstown

New Marske

Loftus

EDINBURGH (city map)

398
Craigvinean Forest
Butterstone
Blairgowrie
A 926
Rattray
A 94
Meigle
Eassie and Neva
A 923
111
12
A 92
L. of Lowes

MASNFIELD TRAQUAIR CENTRE, ROYAL BOTANIC GARDEN
LEITH

Leopold Pl. London Rd. Brunton Pl.
Royal Terrace
Calton Hill
REGENT GARDENS

Statue Sherlock Holmes
Picardy Place
York Place
St James
James Craig Observatory
Collective Gallery
National Monument
Nelson's Monument

Scottish National Portrait Gallery
N° 26
Dundas House
New Register House
Circular Greek Temple

Regent Terrace
Regent Road
Royal High School
Greek Temple
Palace of Holyroodhouse

The Scotch Malt Whisky Society
Buchan House
St Andrew and St George
St Andrew Square
Café Royal
West Register St
General Register House
Old Post Office
Old Calton Cemetery
St Andrew's House
Abbeyhill Crescent

Georgian House
Assembly Rooms
George Street
Rose St South Lane
Princes Street
Edinburgh Waverley

CHARLOTTE SQUARE
Floral Clock
East Princes Street Gardens
Canongate
Canongate Church
Scottish Parliament
Our Dynamic Earth

West Register House
West Princes Street Gardens
Jeffrey Street
Holyrood Rd

Castle
Lawmarket
St Giles' Cathedral
Mercat Cross
Parliament House
High Street
Cowgate
Infirmary

WEST END
Usher Hall
Esplanade
Cowgate
Candlemaker Row
Chambers Street
NATIONAL MUSEUM OF SCOTLAND

HOLYROOD PARK

Grassmarket
Greyfriars Church and Churchyard
Flodden Wall
George Heriot's School
Bristo Square
Student Centre
McEwan Hall
Medical School
Appleton Tower

QUARTER MILE
Dugald Stewart Building
George Square
David Hume Tower
Library

West Meadow Park
East Meadow Park
Meadow

Melville Drive

Outlook Tower and Camera Obscura .... D

EDINBURGH
0 — 250 m
0 — 250 yards

N

PEEBLES, BIGGAR
GALASHIELS
GALASHIELS, JEDBURGH

(regional map — Firth of Forth area)

Alloa
Clackmannan
Cowdenbeath
Auchtertool
Kirkcaldy (△ ▲)
18

Dunfermline
Crossgates
Kinghorn (△)

Culross
Carnock
Crossford
Rosyth
Aberdour
Burntisland

Grangemouth
Charlestown
Dalgety Bay
Inchkeith
Inchcolm
Oxcars

Falkirk
Bo' Ness
Blackness Castle
Inverkeithing
N. Queensferry
Forth Bridge
Cramond
EDINBURGH (△)

Linlithgow
Winchburgh
South Queensferry
Dalmeny
Cramond
Leith 6
Cockenzie and Port Seton

Bathgate
Broxburn
Uphall
Kirkliston
Ingliston
Murrayfield
Portobello
Prestonpans
Musselburgh

Livingston
Mid Calder
Ratho
Sighthill
Currie A720
Lasswade

Whitburn
Blackburn
Kirknewton
Balerno
Loanhead
Dalkeith (△)
Bonnyrigg
Roslin

GLASGOW

DUMBARTON   STIRLING   KIRKINTILLOCH

0   450 m
0   450 yards

N

Points of interest and streets (city centre map):

Botanic Gardens, Observatory, Hunterian Art Gallery, MACKINTOSH HOUSE, MAIN BUILDING, Hunterian Museum, University-Gilmorehill Building, WESTERN INFIRMARY, KELVIN HALL, Kelvingrove Park, Park Circus, KELVINGROVE ART GALLERY AND MUSEUM, Scottish Exhibition and Conference Center, Clyde Auditorium – The "Armadillo", Glasgow Tower, Science Centre, Imax, BBC Building, La grue Finnieston, Queen's Cross Church, Tenement House, The National Piping Centre, Beresford, Glasgow School of Art, CCA, Willow Tearoom, The Mitchell Library, Sauchiehall Street, Buchanan Street Bus Station, Buchanan Galleries, Merchants' House, Willow Tea Rooms, The Lighthouse, City Chambers, George Street, Gallery of Modern Art, Princes Square, Trades Hall, CENTRAL STATION, ST ENOCH SHOPPING CENTRE, Glasgow Cross, Tolbooth Steeple, Bridgegate Steeple, Saltmarket, The Barras, Glasgow Green, People's Palace, Doulton Fountain, Templeton Business Centre, Martyr's School, CATHEDRAL, Necropolis, St Mungo Museum of Religious Life and Art, Provand's Lordship, Royal Infirmary, Scotland Street School Museum

Kelvingrove, Charing Cross, Clydeside Expressway, Clyde Arc, Millennium Bridge, Bells Bridge, Kingston Bridge, Clyde River, Glasgow Bridge, Albert Bridge, Victoria Bridge, King George V Bridge

KILMARNOCK   MOTHERWELL   HAMILTON   KILMARNOCK   EAST KILBRIDE

Regional map (lower):

Greenock, Port Glasgow, Dumbarton, Kilpatrick Hills, Erskine Bridge, Duntocher, Milngavie, Torrance, Lennoxtown, Kirkintilloch, Condorrat, Cumbernauld, Slamannan, Langbank, Old Kilpatrick, Bearsden, Kelvin, Lenzie, Muirhead, Stepps, Riggend, Longriggend, Caldercruix, Bishopton, Clydebank, Renfrew, Coatbridge, Stand, Kilmacolm, Houston, Linwood, GLASGOW, Rutherglen, Airdrie, Chapelhall, Holytown, Salsburgh, Bridge of Weir, Ranfurly, Kilbarchan, Johnstone, PAISLEY, Barrhead, Cambuslang, Uddingston, Bothwell, Blantyre, Mossend, Bellshill, Newarthill, Carfin, Cleland, Neilston, Busby, Carmunnock, Hamilton, Motherwell, Wishaw, Newton Mearns, East Kilbride, Eaglesham, Ballageich Hill, Larkhall, Overtown, Uplawmoor, Lugton, Long Loch, Auldhouse, Kilbirnie, Beith, Barrmill, Dunlop

Loch Thom, Creuch Hill, Strathgryfe, Garvock, Muirshiel, Stake, Heathfield, Lochwinnoch, Barcraigs Resr., Balgray Resr., Barrhead

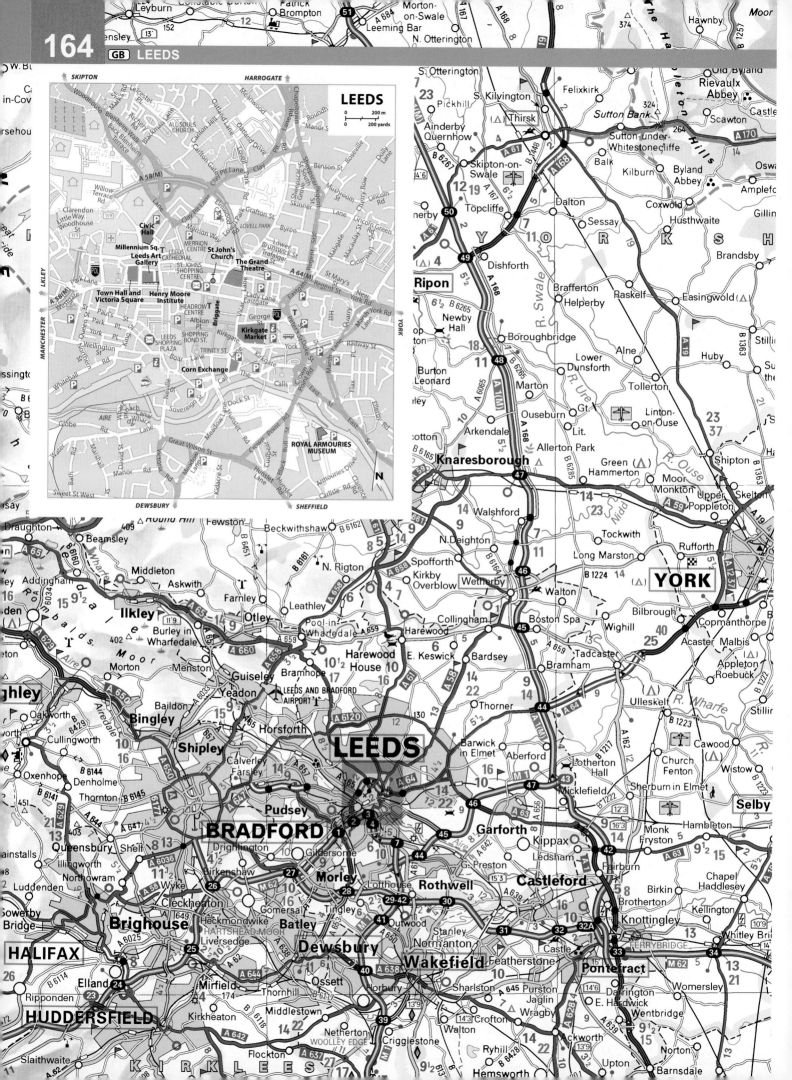

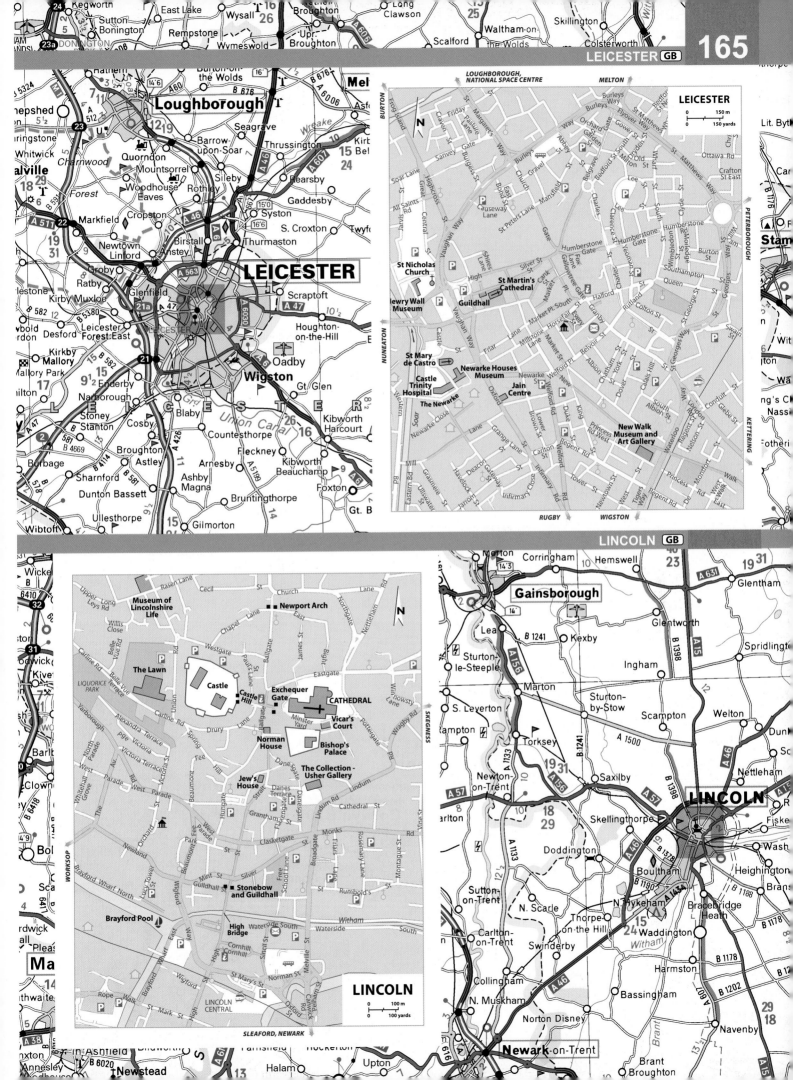

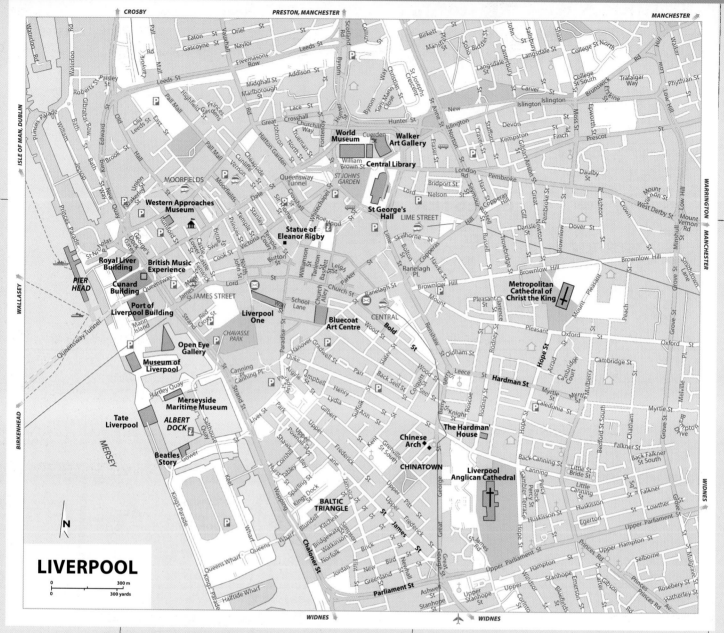

CROSBY PRESTON, MANCHESTER MANCHESTER

World Museum
Walker Art Gallery
Central Library
St John's Garden
MOORFIELDS
Western Approaches Museum
St George's Hall
LIME STREET
Statue of Eleanor Rigby
Royal Liver Building
British Music Experience
Cunard Building
Port of Liverpool Building
Metropolitan Cathedral of Christ the King
PIER HEAD
St James Street
Liverpool One
CENTRAL
Bluecoat Art Centre
Bold St
Hope St
Hardman St
Open Eye Gallery
CHAVASSE PARK
Museum of Liverpool
The Hardman' House
Merseyside Maritime Museum
Chinese Arch
CHINATOWN
Liverpool Anglican Cathedral
Tate Liverpool
ALBERT DOCK
Beatles Story
MERSEY
BALTIC TRIANGLE
Parliament St
WALLASEY
BIRKENHEAD
ISLE OF MAN, DUBLIN
WARRINGTON, MANCHESTER
WIDNES

N

LIVERPOOL
0 — 300 m
0 — 300 yards

WIDNES WIDNES

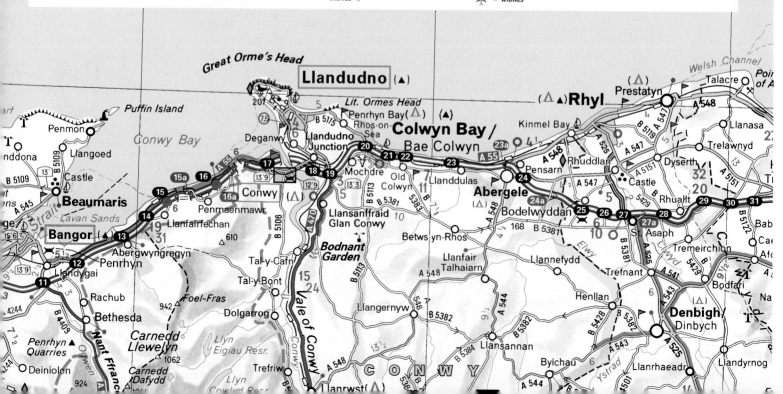

Great Orme's Head
Welsh Channel
Llandudno (▲)
Talacre
Point of A
Lit. Ormes Head
Penrhyn Bay (△)
Prestatyn
(△) ▲ Rhyl
A 548
207
Puffin Island
5
Rhos-on-Sea
Kinmel Bay
Conwy Bay
7.5
Deganwy
Llandudno Junction
Colwyn Bay / Bae Colwyn
Penmon
B 515
20
23a
Llanasa
Penmon
6
21 22
23
A 55
Trelawnyd
Pensarn
A 547
Dyserth
Rhuddlan
nddona
Llangoed
B 5109
17
13'9
18 19
Mochdre
Old Colwyn
24
A 547
Castle
32
Castle
15a 16
12'9
Llanddulas
20
A 5151
B 5109
15
16a
Conwy (△)
13'3
Llandrillo
Abergele
25 26
27
29 30 31
ens
A 545
6
Penmaenmawr
B 5106
Llansanffraid Glan Conwy
Bodelwyddan
24a
27a
B 5122
14 19
Llanfairfechan
10
A 548
St Asaph
Cae
Bangor (▲) 13
31
610
Bodnant Garden
Betws-yn-Rhos
168
6
10
Tremeirchion
13'9
12
Abergwyngregyn
Penrhyn
A 470
Llanfair Talhaiarn
Llannefydd
Trefnant
A 541
Bodfari
11
Llandygai
Rachub
Tal-y-Cafn
15
Llangernyw
A 543
Henllan
A 525
Bethesda
Tal-y-Bont
24
A 548
Denbigh / Dinbych
Foel-Fras
942
Bodnant
B 5428
B 5382
A 525
B 4409
Penrhyn Quarries
Dolgatrog
Llansannan
Bylchau
Llanrhaeadr
924
Carnedd Llewelyn
Llyn Eigiau Resr.
1062
Carnedd Dafydd
Trefriw
C O N W Y
A 544
Ystrad
Llandyrnog
Deiniolen
Llanrwst (△)
B 5381

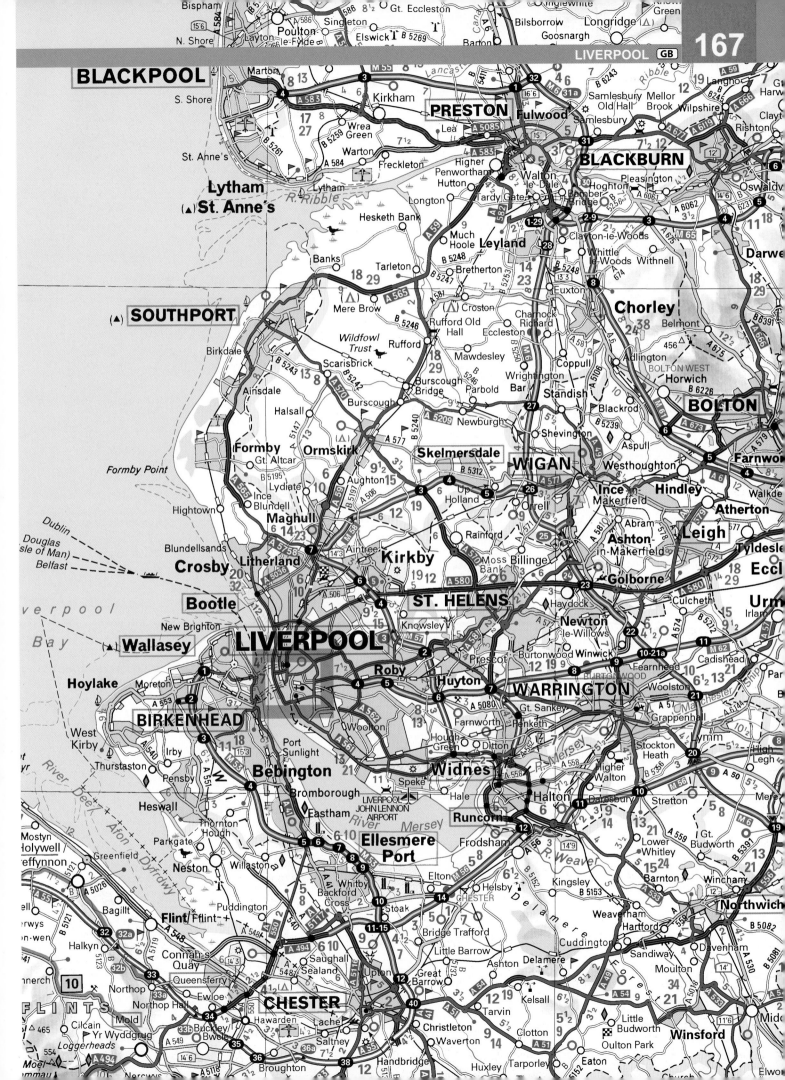

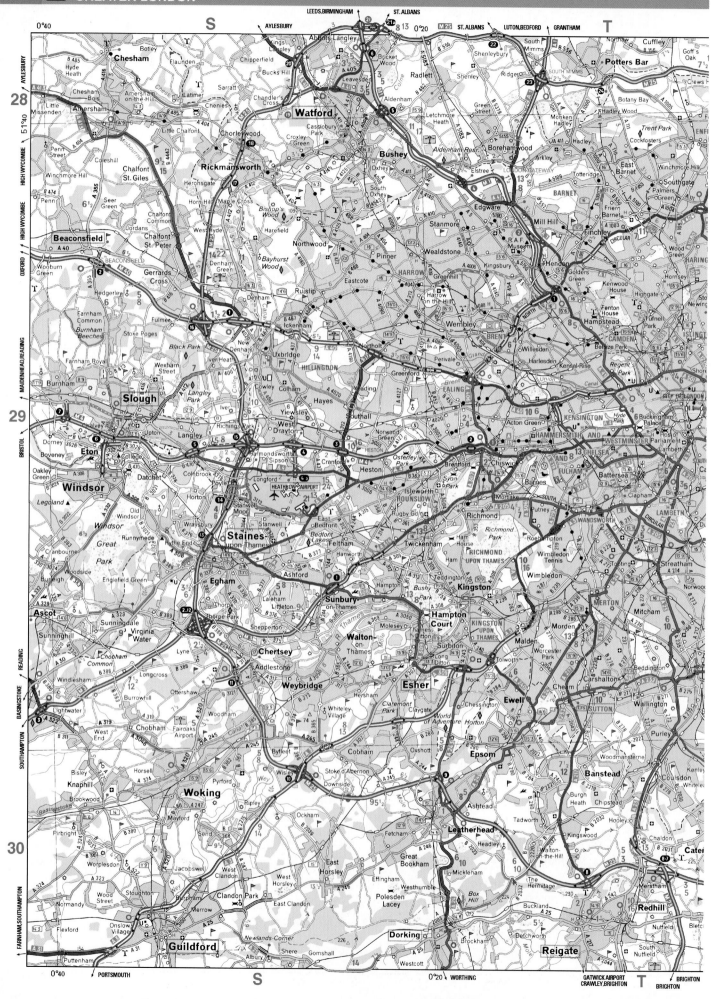

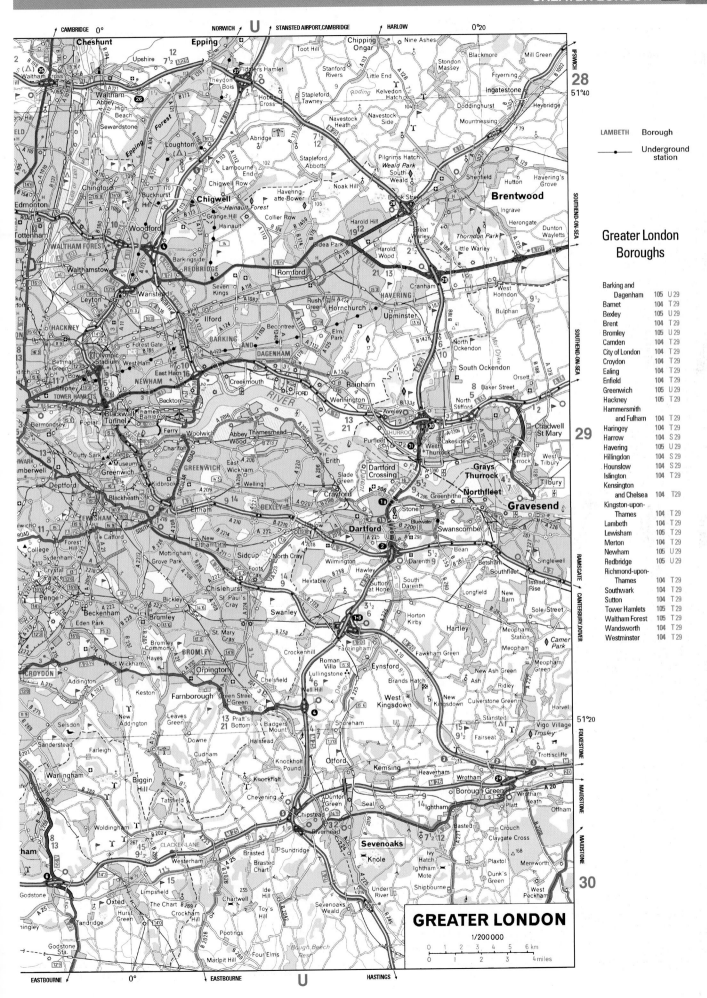

Greater London Boroughs

Borough			
Barking and Dagenham	105	U	29
Barnet	104	T	29
Bexley	105	U	29
Brent	104	T	29
Bromley	105	U	29
Camden	104	T	29
City of London	104	T	29
Croydon	104	T	29
Ealing	104	T	29
Enfield	104	T	29
Greenwich	105	U	29
Hackney	105	T	29
Hammersmith and Fulham	104	T	29
Haringey	104	T	29
Harrow	104	S	29
Havering	105	U	29
Hillingdon	104	S	29
Hounslow	104	S	29
Islington	104	T	29
Kensington and Chelsea	104	T	29
Kingston-upon-Thames	104	T	29
Lambeth	104	T	29
Lewisham	105	T	29
Merton	104	T	29
Newham	105	U	29
Redbridge	105	U	29
Richmond-upon-Thames	104	T	29
Southwark	104	T	29
Sutton	104	T	29
Tower Hamlets	105	T	29
Waltham Forest	105	T	29
Wandsworth	104	T	29
Westminster	104	T	29

LAMBETH Borough

●— Underground station

GREATER LONDON

1/200 000

0 1 2 3 4 5 6 km

0 1 2 3 4 miles

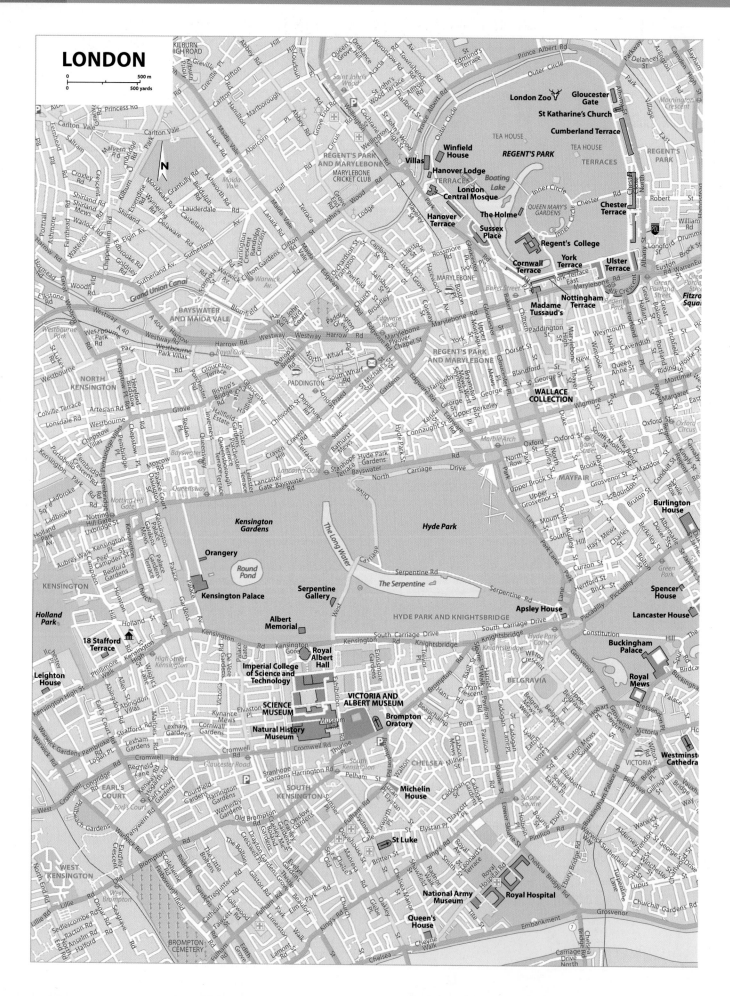

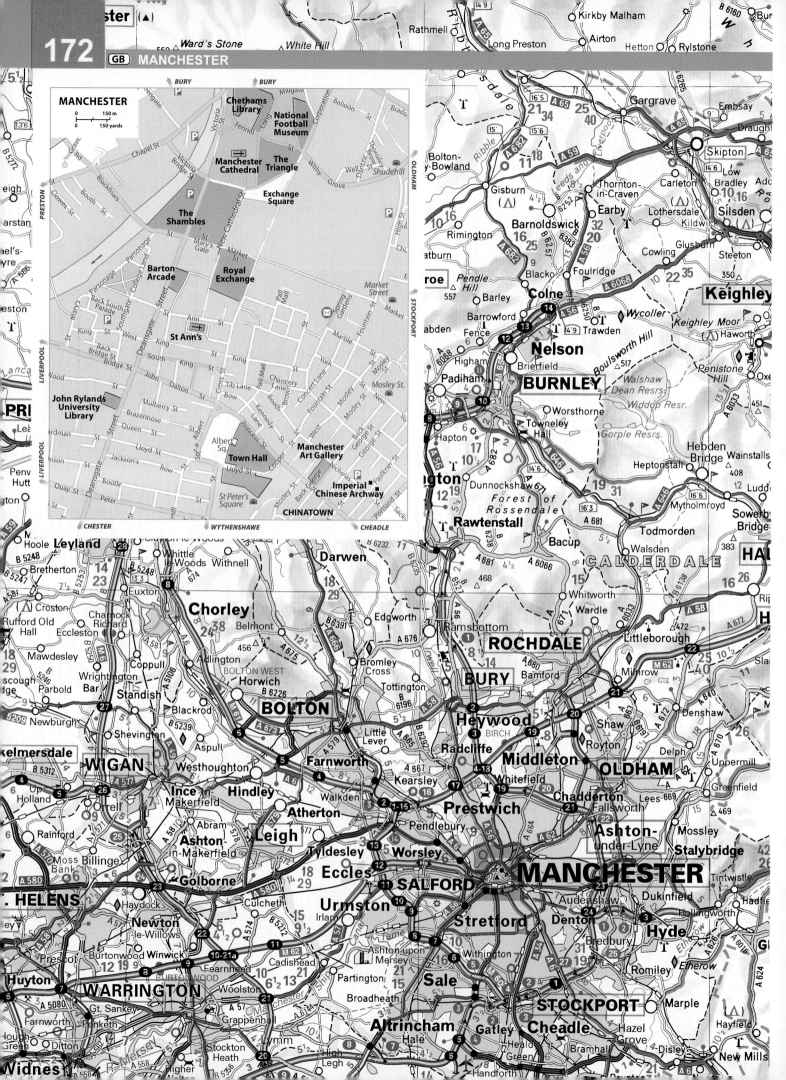

MANCHESTER

0 — 150 m
0 — 150 yards

Chethams Library
National Football Museum
Manchester Cathedral
The Triangle
Exchange Square
The Shambles
Barton Arcade
Royal Exchange
St Ann's
John Rylands University Library
Town Hall
Manchester Art Gallery
St Peter's Square
Imperial Chinese Archway
CHINATOWN

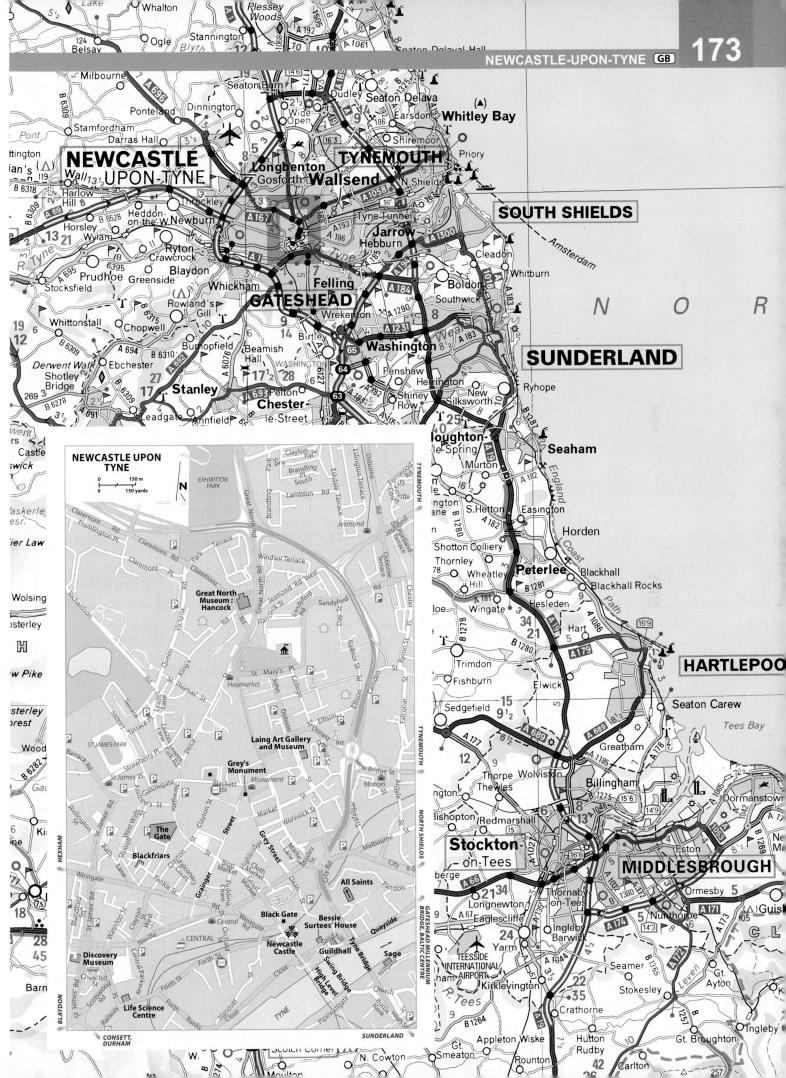

NORWICH (city map)

CROMER · WROXHAM

NORWICH
0 — 200 m
0 — 200 yards

SWAFFHAM · THETFORD · IPSWICH

St Crispins Rd · Chatham St · Barker St · Oak St · Upper Green Lane · Cowgate · Charton Rd · Barrack St · Magdalen St · Pitt St · Calvert St · Colegate · St Simon and St Jude · Bishopgate · Cotman Fields · Quay Side · Whitefriars · Bishop Bridge Rd

St Andrew's and Blackfriars Hall · Norwich Cathedral · Pull's Ferry · Ferry Lane
St Peter Hungate · Erpingham Gate · St Ethelbert's Gate · Elm Hill
St Michael at Plea · Prince of Wales Rd
Guildhall · Bedford St · Recorder Rd
City Hall · Market Place · Castle · Norwich Castle Museum · Riverside Rd
Royal Arcade · Farmers Av. · Rouen · King St · Mountergate · Thorpe Rd
CHAPEL FIELD GARDENS · St Peter Mancroft · RIVERSIDE · Lower Clarence Rd · Koblenz
Theatre St · Chantry Rd · Malthouse Rd · Surrey St · Thorn Lane · Wensum · Riverside Rd
Coburg St · St Stephens Rd · Queens Rd · Horns Lane · Carrow Rd
Cleveland Rd · Bethel St · Union St · All Saints Green · Ber St
Walls · Newmarket Rd · Grove · Trafford Rd · Ashby St · King's Lane · Carrow Bridge
Ipswich Grove · Queens Rd · Southwell Rd · Trafalgar St · Hall Rd · City Rd · Walls · Carrow Hill · Ice House Lane · Bracondale

IPSWICH · LOWESTOFT · GREAT YARMOUTH · N

SAINSBURY CENTER FOR VISUAL ARTS

NORWICH (regional map)

Bodham Street · Holt · Baconsthorpe · Aylmerton · Northrepps · Mundesley (△) · Bacton
Edgefield · Little Barningham · Itteringham · Erpingham · Roughton · Thorpe Market · Trunch · Knapton · Happisburgh
Corpusty · Blickling Hall · Felmingham · North Walsham (△) · Honing · Stalham
Blickling · Aylsham · Swanton Abbott · Worstead · Low Street
Reepham · Marsham · Scottow · Neatishead · Catfield
Cawston (△) · Hevingham · Buxton · Coltishall · Norfolk Broads · Ludham
Norfolk Wildlife Park · Lenwade · Felthorpe · Horstead · Hoveton · Horning · Ranworth · S. Walsham
Attlebridge · Hainford · Horsford · Wroxham · Salhouse
Hockering · Taverham · Horsham St. Faith · Spixworth · New Rackheath
Costessey · Drayton · Sprowston · Catton · Thorpe St. Andrew · Acle
Easton · Bawburgh · **NORWICH** · Blofield · Brundall
Barford · Hethersett · Cringleford · Surlingham · R. Yare · Cantley
Caistor St. Edmund · East Poringland · Claxton
Mulbarton · Stoke Holy Cross · Thurton · Loddon
Ashwellthorpe · Newton Flotman · Brooke · Shotesham

NOTTINGHAM (regional map)

Pleasley · Cipstone · Eakring
Mansfield · Huthwaite · Bilsthorpe · Maplebeck
Sutton-in-Ashfield · Rainworth · Kirklington · Hockerton
Kirkby-in-Ashfield · Blidworth · Farnsfield · Halam
Pinxton · Annesley Woodhouse · Newstead Abbey · Halloughton · Oxton · Thurgarton
Selston · Newstead · Papplewick · Calverton · Lowdham
Eastwood · **Hucknall** · Woodborough · Lambley · Gunthorpe
Kimberley · Bulwell · **Arnold** · Burton Joyce · Newton
NOTTINGHAM · **Carlton** · Radcliffe-on-Trent · Aslockton · Orston · Barkston
Stapleford · Wollaton Hall · **West Bridgford** · Bingham · Bottesford · Sedgebrook · Gt Gonerby · Belton
Beeston · Toton · Cotgrave · Cropwell Bishop · Granby · Redmile · Barrowby · **Grantham**
Long Eaton · Clifton · Edwalton · Langar · Harby · Belvoir · Woolsthorpe · Welby
Ruddington · Normanton-on-the-Wolds · Colston Bassett · Stathern · Denton · Harlaxton · Old Somerby
Gotham · Keyworth · Kinoulton · Hickling · Croxton Kerrial · Gt. Ponton
Bunny · East Leake · Wysall · Nether Broughton · Long Clawson · Ingoldsby
Kegworth · Sutton Bonington · Wymeswold · Skillington

NOTTINGHAM (city map)

MANSFIELD · MANCHESTER · DERBY · BEESTON · BIRMINGHAM · LEICESTER

NOTTINGHAM
0 — 200 m
0 — 200 yards

VICTORIA CENTRE · Castle · Nottingham Canal · MIDLAND · The Park · POL

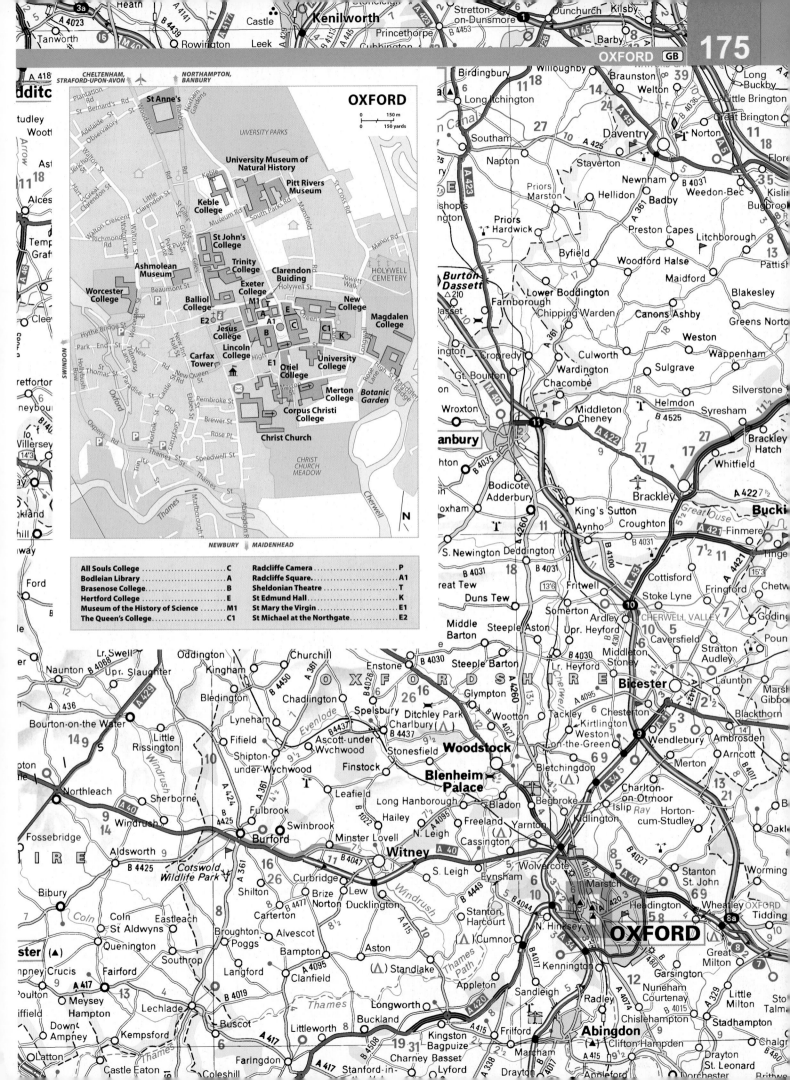

PERTH (inset map)

BRAEMAR, SCONE PALACE — COUPAR ANGUS

Scale: 0 — 100 m / 0 — 100 yards

The Black Watch Castle & Museum
BELL'S SPORTS CENTRE
North
Inch
Georgian Terraces
Atholl Crescent
Barossa Place
N°10
Rose Terrace
Old Perth Academy
Charlotte St
Melville St
Union Lane
Black Watch Gardens
Methven St
Foundry Lane
Murray St
Carpenter St
Charlotte Square
Fair Maids House
Lower City Mills
Perth Concert Hall
Perth Museum and Art Gallery
Skinnergate
High St
Scott St
New Row
Milne St
St John's St
St John's
City Hall
Maison des Évêques de Dunkeld
King James VI Hospital
County Pl.
Canal Crescent
Salutation Hotel
Sheriff Court
Kinnoull Causeway
Caledonian Rd
Alexandra St
Exchange Lane
Andrew St
Pomarium St
Victoria St
Victoria St
South William St
Canal St
Leonard St
King James Pl.
South Inch
Water Works et Fergusson Gallery
MONCREIFFE ISLAND
FORTH ROAD BRIDGE

RIVERSIDE PARK
River Tay
Perth Bridge
Gowrie Commercial St
Queen's Bridge
KINNOULL HILL
BRANKLYN GARDEN, FRIARTON BRIDGE

INVERNESS, CAITHNESS GLASS
CRIANLARICH, CRIEFF
STIRLING CHERRYBANK

Main map

Loch Muick
Glas-allt
Socach
Callater
920
998
Loch Lee
Inchgrundle
Glen
Braedownie
Glen Clova
928
896
741
Ben Tirran 778
West Knock 691
Clova
White Hill
Waterhead
726
Runtaleave
Glenprosen Village
481
246
B 955
3
Ogil
Fern
Glenisla Forest
Cat Law 678
Backwater Resr.
Dykehead
Tannadice
Balintore
Pearsie
B 955
Dykends
L. of Lintrathen
Kirkton of Kingoldrum
B 957
Oathlaw
A 90
Bridgend of Lintrathen
Kirriemuir
A 926
A 928
Lunanhead
Reekie Linn
Craigisla
Craigton
A 926
Forfar
Kingsmuir
B 951
130
Ruthven
B 954
Dean Wr.
Glamis Castle
Douglastown
B 9128
Craigie
B 952
A 94
Glamis
Inverarity
Meigle
Eassie and Nevay
B 9127
Kirkbuddo
B 978
12 19
259
Dunkeld
Clunie
B 947
R. Isla
Newtyle
Sidlaw Hills
Balgray
Inver
Birnam
A 984
Meikleour
A 984
Coupar Angus
A 923
Long L.
Lundie
Auchterhouse
Trochry
Strathbraan
R. Tay
Caputh
Kinclaven
353
Pitcur
B 954
Muirhead
Kirkton of Strathmartine
Kellas
B 978 B 961
MICHELIN A 92
28 45
B 867
101
Cargill
Burrelton
A 94
31
King's Seat 377
231
A 923
Dighty
Bankfoot
B 9099
Stanley
132
Guildtown
Kinrossie
B 953
Abernyte
Longforgan
DUNDEE
9
Broughty Ferry
Little Glenshee
A 9
Moneydie
Kinnaird
Braes of the Carse
Invergowrie
Tayport
Harrietfield
B 8063
Balbeggie
Inchture
A 90
Tay Road Bridge
B 946
Newport-on-Tay
Logiealmond
Almond
Luncarty
Scone Palace
New Scone
Rait
Carse of Gowrie
Wormit
A 914 A 945
Tentsmuir Forest
Buchanty
A 93
Huntingtower Castle
A 85
Methven
Bridgend
Kinfauns
Errol
Firth of Tay
Balmerino
Fife Coastal Path
A 914
Leuchars
Fowlis Wester
29 18
Tibbermore
222
27 17
Elcho
Glencarse
B 958
16 26 A 92
Balmullo
Guardbridge
Findo Gask
PERTH
10
R. Earn
11
Newburgh
Luthrie
Kilmany
A 91
Forgandenny
A 9
B 934
Bridge of Earn
9
A 913
Lindores
Dairsie
Strathkinness
Aberuthven
Forteviot
B 935
Abernethy
A 912
B 936
Cupar
B 940
Craigtoun
A 915
Dunning
B 9141
B 8062
229
Pitmedden Forest
Letham
Springfield
Hill of Tarvit
Pitscottie
Ceres
Peat Inn
Auchterarder
B 8062
Path of Condie
18 11
Auchtermuchty
A 91
Ladybank
Scotstarvit Tower
Craigrothie
31 50
Steele's Knowe
Glenfarg
Gateside
M 90
Strathmiglo
A 91
Howe of Fife
Kingskettle
Backmuir of New Gilston
Common of Dunning
485
316
Water of May
B 996
365
Lomond Hills
522
497
Falkland
15
Largoward

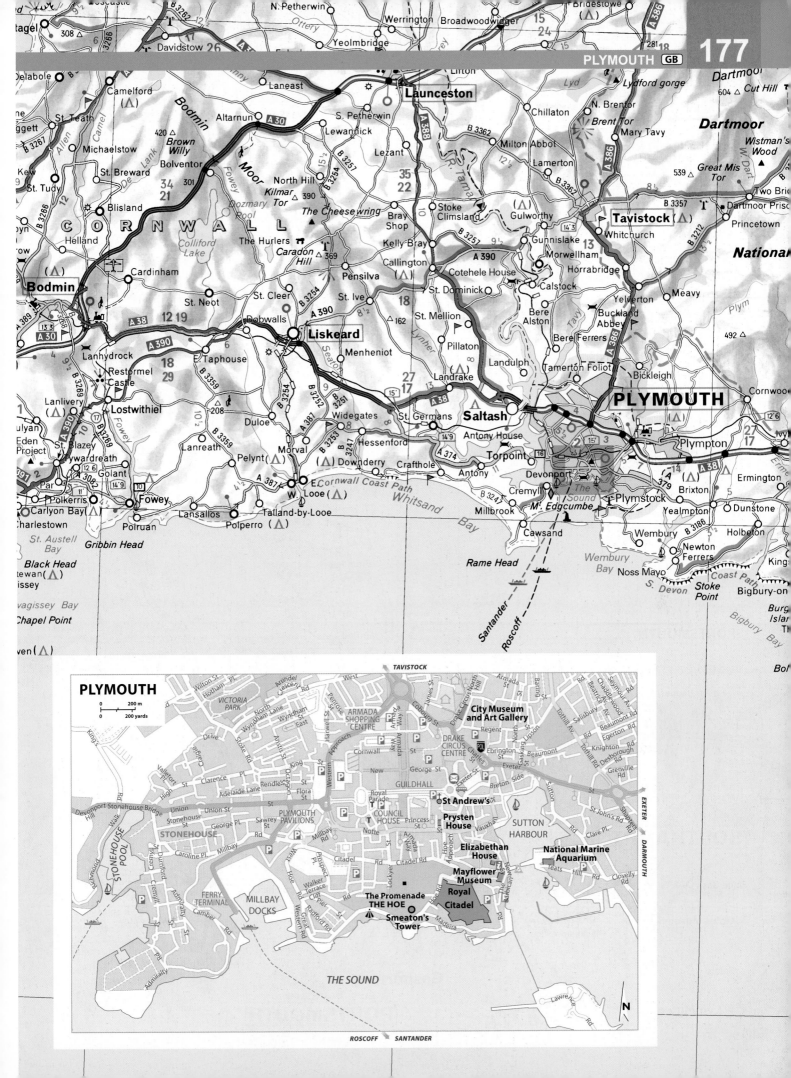

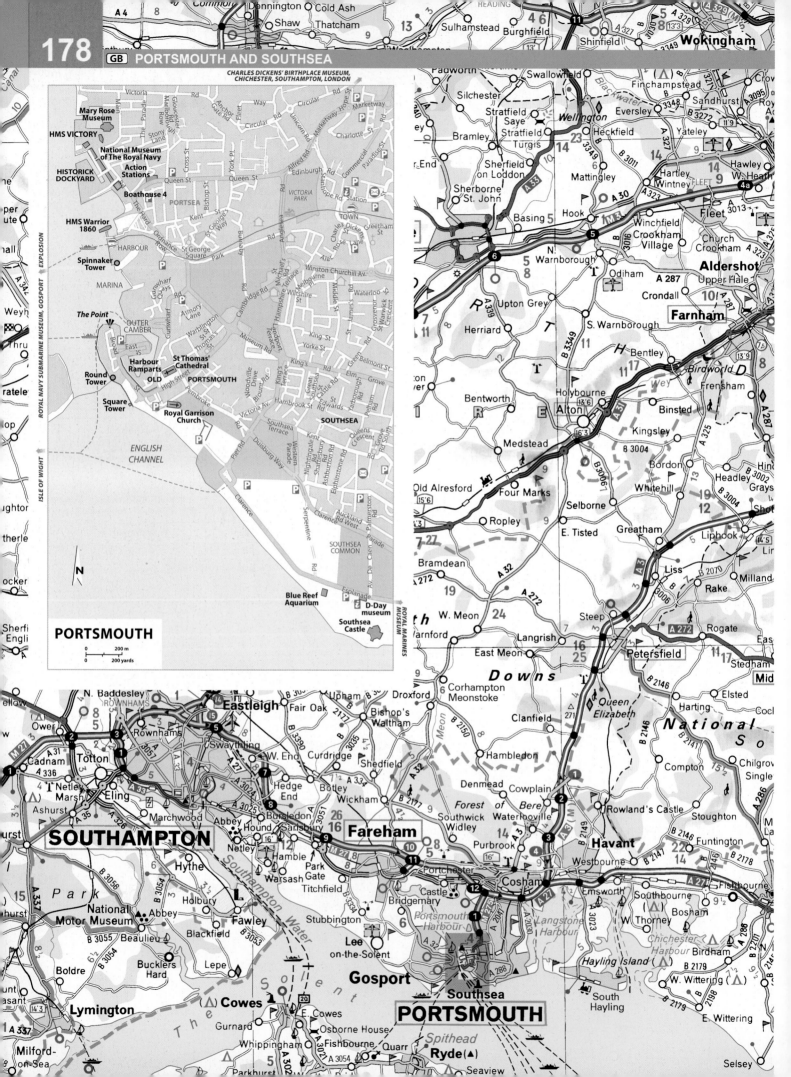

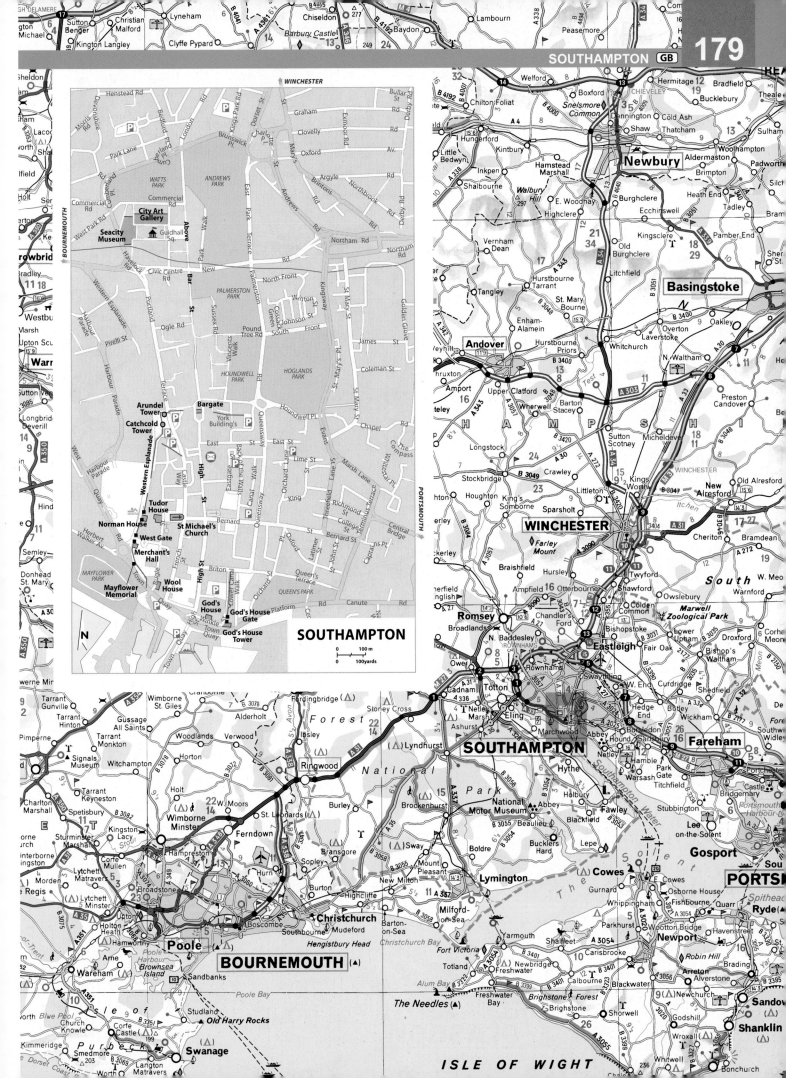

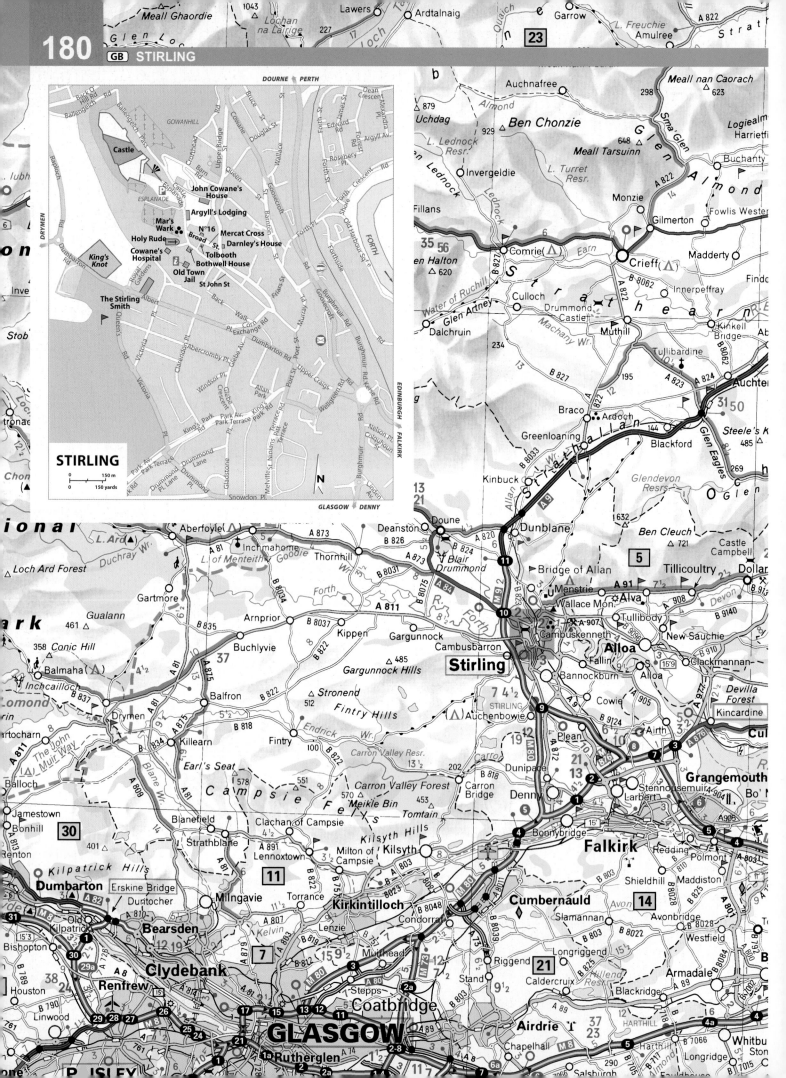

STIRLING (inset map)

Castle

GOWANHILL

Back O'Hill Rd
Ballengeich Rd
Ballengeich Pass

DOURNE • PERTH

Bruce St
Cowane St
Douglas St
Queen St
Upper Bridge St
Wallace St

Dean Crescent
Alexandra Pl
Argyll Av

Barn Rd
Crofthead
Castle Wynd

Esplanade

John Cowane's House

Argyll's Lodging

Mar's Wark

Holy Rude

N°16

Broad St

Mercat Cross

Darnley's House

Cowane's Hospital

Tolbooth

Bothwell House

King's Knot

Old Town Jail

St John St

Royal Gardens

The Stirling Smith

Albert

Victoria Rd

Queen's Rd

Clarendon Pl

Abercromby Pl

Glebe Av

Dumbarton Rd

Port St

Upper Craigs

Windsor Pl

Glebe Crescent

Allan Park

Wellgreen Rd

Kerse Rd

Colquhoun St

Nelson Pl

King's Park

Park Av

Park Terrace

Snowdon Pl

Drummond Pl Lane

Melville St

Ninians

Burghmuir Rd

EDINBURGH • FALKIRK

GLASGOW • DENNY

N

Scale: 0 — 150 m / 0 — 150 yards

Main map

Meall Ghaordie 1043

Lawers

Ardtalnaig

Garrow

L. Freuchie

Amulree

A 822

Strath

Glen Lochay

Lochan na Lairige 227

Loch Tay

23

Quaich

Auchnafree

Meall nan Caorach 623

Almond 298

879 Uchdag

929 Ben Chonzie

648 Meall Tarsuinn

Logiealmond

Harrietfield

Buchanty

L. Lednock Resr.

Invergeldie

L. Turret Resr.

Monzie

A 822 14

Fowlis Wester

Fillans

Gilmerton

35 56

Comrie

Earn

Crieff

Madderty

Innerpeffray

Findo

Glen Halton

620

Culloch

Drummond Castle

A 822

Muthill

Kinkell Bridge

B 8062

Dalchruin

234

Machany Wr.

Tullibardine

A 823 A 824

Auchter

Glen Artney

Water of Ruchill

13

B 827

195

Braco

Ardoch

144

31 50

Greenloaning

Blackford

Steele's

485

Kinbuck

Glen Eagles

269

Doune

Dunblane

Glendevon Resrs.

Glen

Deanston

Ben Cleuch 721

Castle Campbell

Aberfoyle

L. Ard

Inchmahome

Thornhill

Blair Drummond

11

5

Dollar

Duchray Wr.

L. of Menteith

Goodie

B 826

A 873

Bridge of Allan

Tillicoultry

Loch Ard Forest

Gartmore

Forth

A 811

Menstrie

Wallace Mon.

Alva

A 91

Devon

B 9140

Gualann 461

Arnprior

Kippen

Gargunnock

Cambuskenneth

Tullibody

New Sauchie

358 Conic Hill

Buchlyvie

Gargunnock

Cambusbarron

Stirling

Alloa

Clackmannan

Balmaha

37

485

Gargunnock Hills

Fallin

Alloa

Devilla Forest

Inchcailloch

Balfron

Stronend 512

Fintry Hills

Bannockburn

Kincardine

Lomond

Killearn

Fintry

Auchenbowie

Cowie

Airth

Drymen

Endrick Wr.

100

Carron Valley Resr.

Plean

Cul

Earl's Seat 578

551

Carron Valley Forest

202

Dunipace

Grangemouth

Balloch

Meikle Bin 570

453

Carron Bridge

Denny

Stenhousemuir

Larbert

Bo'

Jamestown

Bonhill

Blanefield

Clachan of Campsie

Tomtain

30

Strathblane

Kilsyth Hills

Bonnybridge

Falkirk

Redding

Polmont

401

Milton of Campsie

Kilsyth

Dumbarton

Erskine Bridge

Duntocher

Milngavie

Torrance

Kirkintilloch

Cumbernauld

14

Avonbridge

Westfield

Bearsden

Lenzie

Condorrat

Slamannan

Longriggend

Maddiston

Clydebank

7

Muirhead

21

Caldercruix

Blackridge

Renfrew

Stepps

Coatbridge

Airdrie

Harthill

GLASGOW

Rutherglen

Chapelhall

Harthill

Armadale

PAISLEY

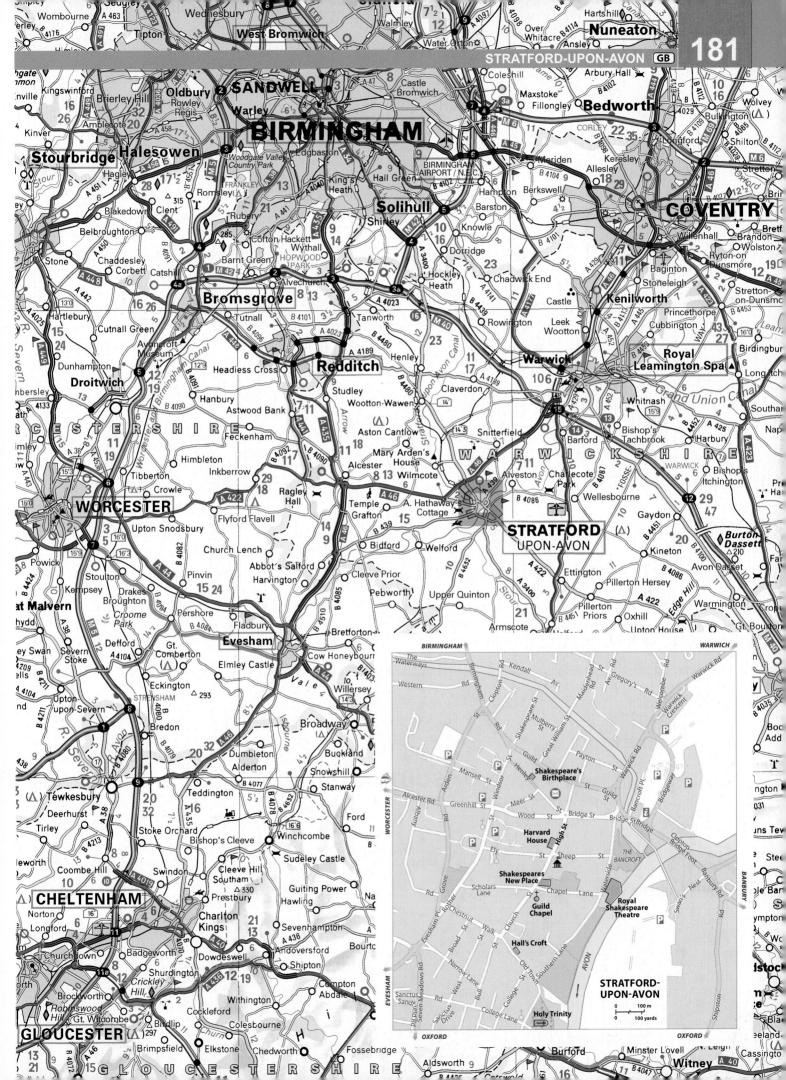

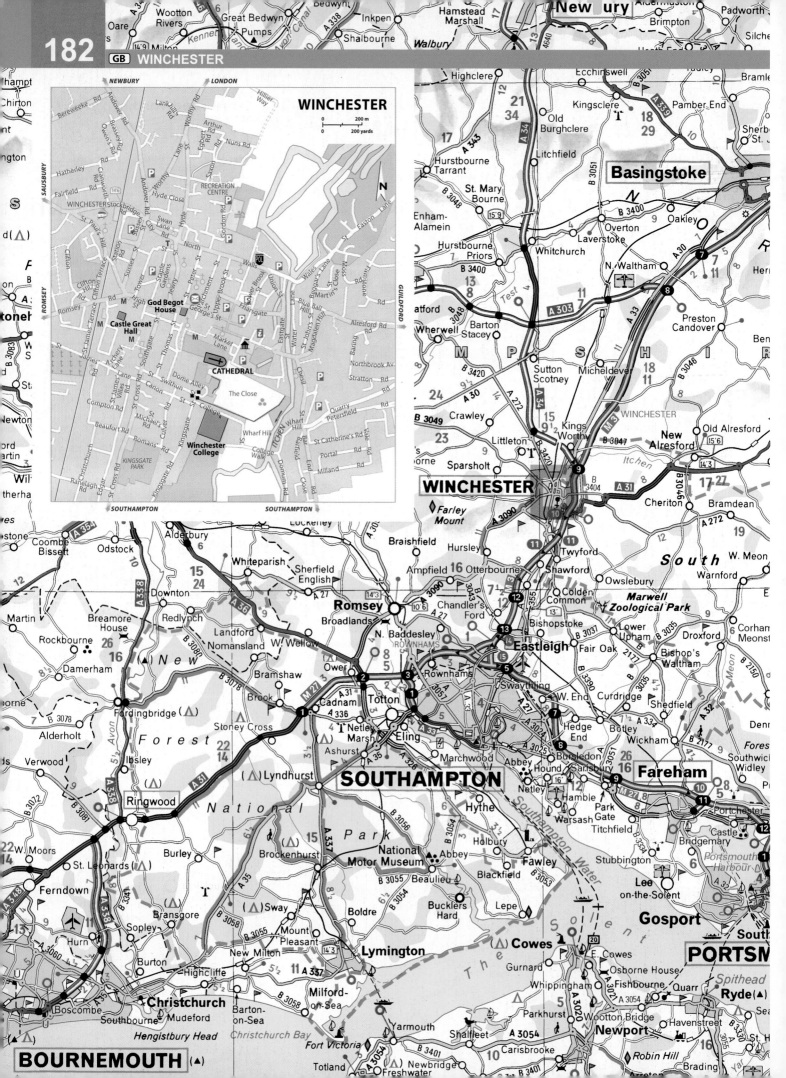

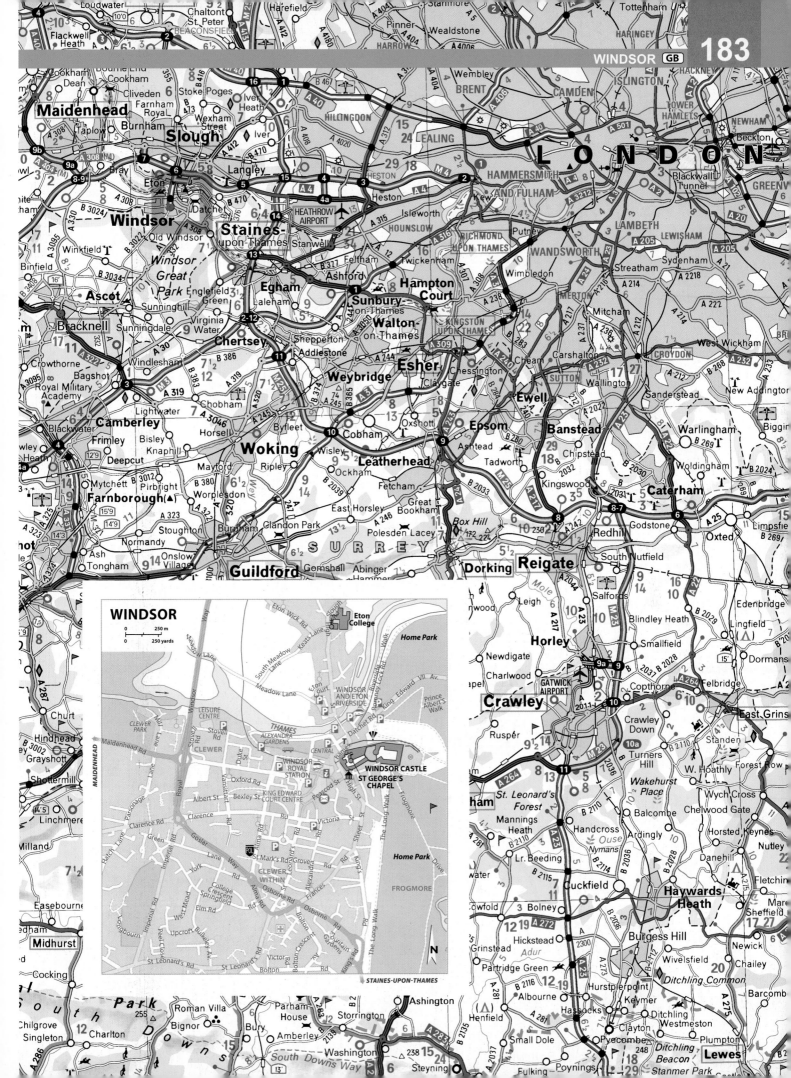

WINDSOR

0   250 m
0   250 yards

LONDON

Maidenhead
Slough
Windsor
Staines-upon-Thames
HEATHROW AIRPORT
HOUNSLOW
RICHMOND UPON THAMES
Ascot
Bracknell
Egham
Sunbury-on-Thames
Hampton Court
WANDSWORTH
LAMBETH
LEWISHAM
Camberley
Woking
Chertsey
Addlestone
Weybridge
Esher
KINGSTON UPON THAMES
CROYDON
Ewell
Epsom
Banstead
Caterham
Guildford
Leatherhead
Dorking
Reigate
Horley
GATWICK AIRPORT
Crawley
Haywards Heath
Midhurst
Lewes

STAINES-UPON-THAMES

N

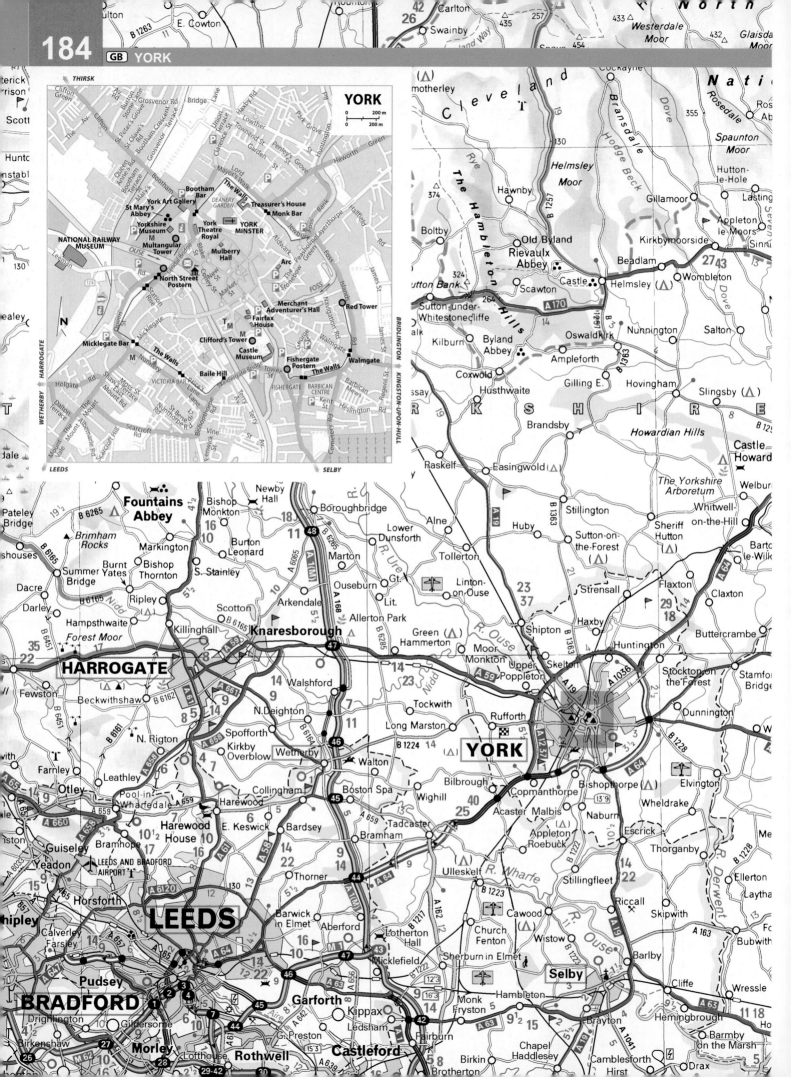

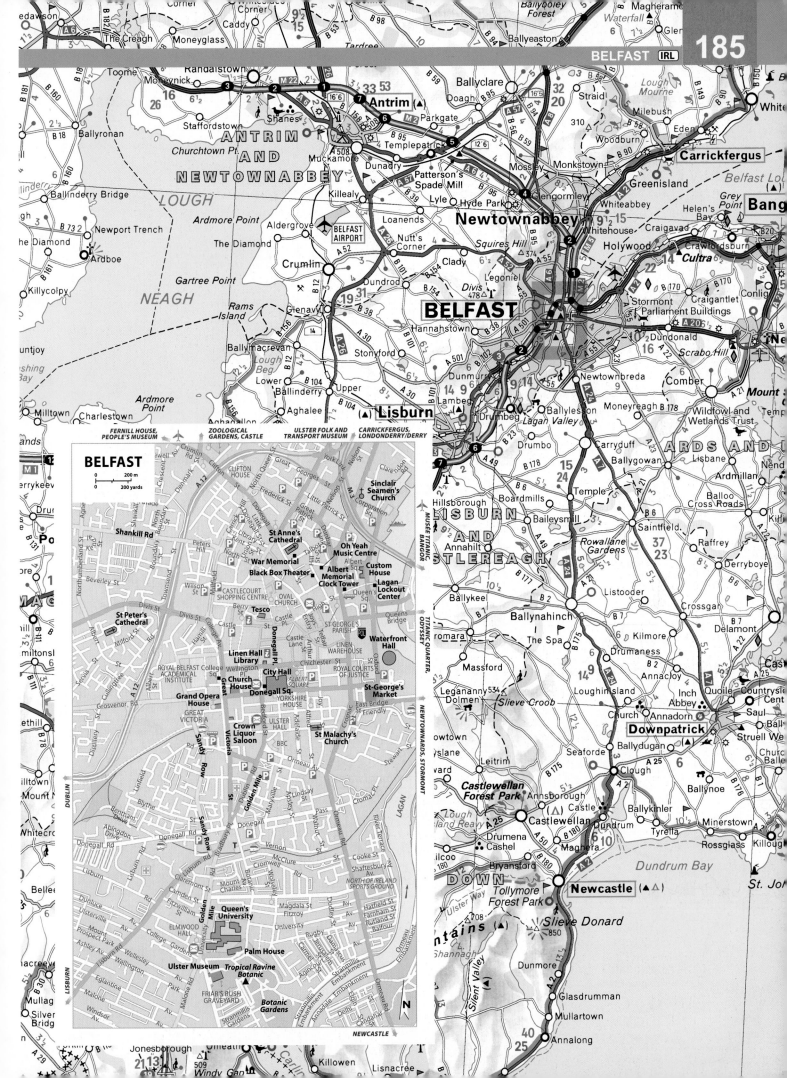

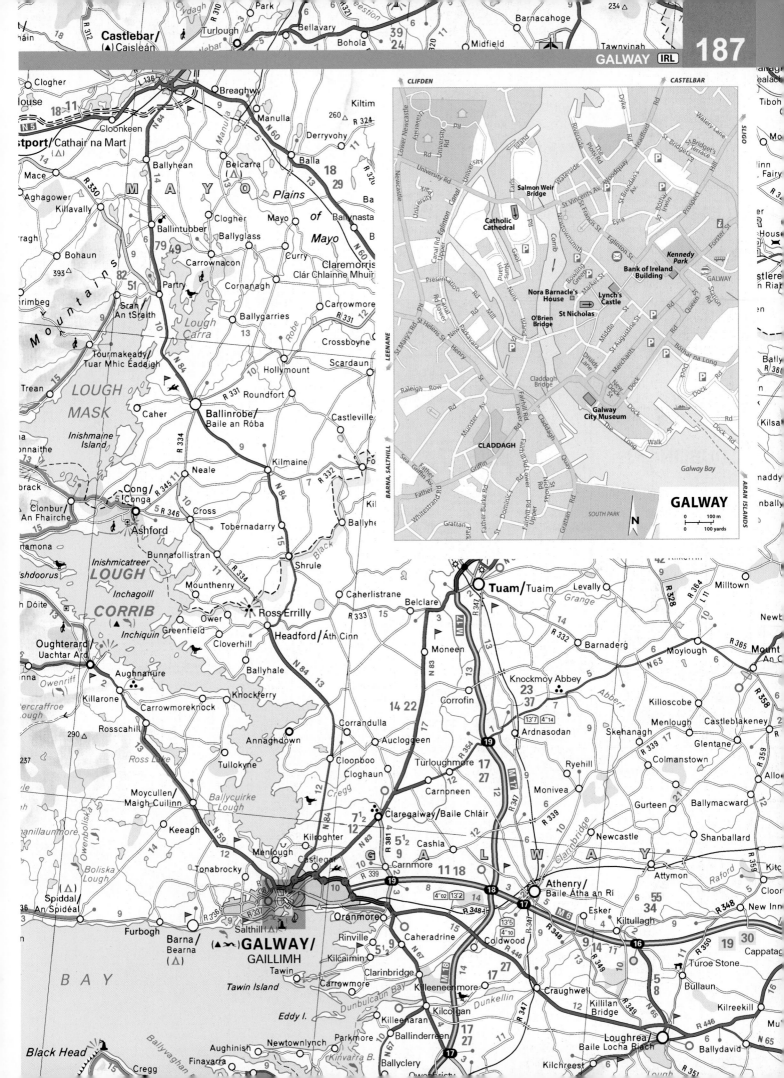

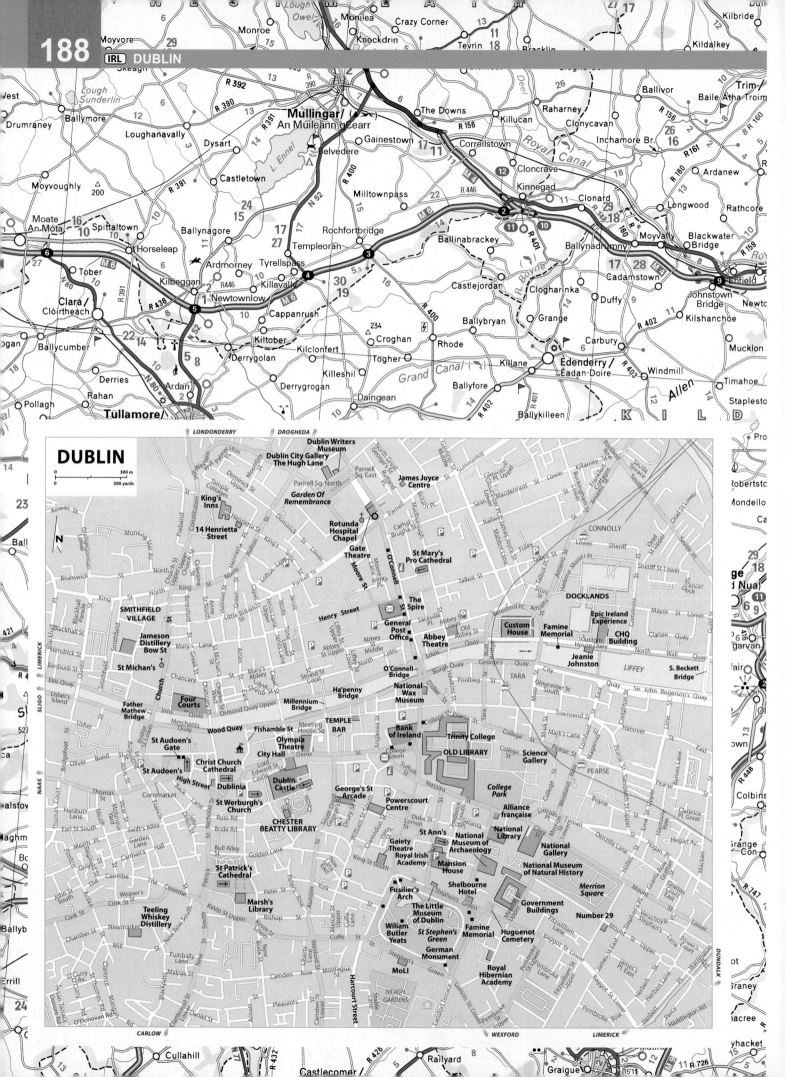

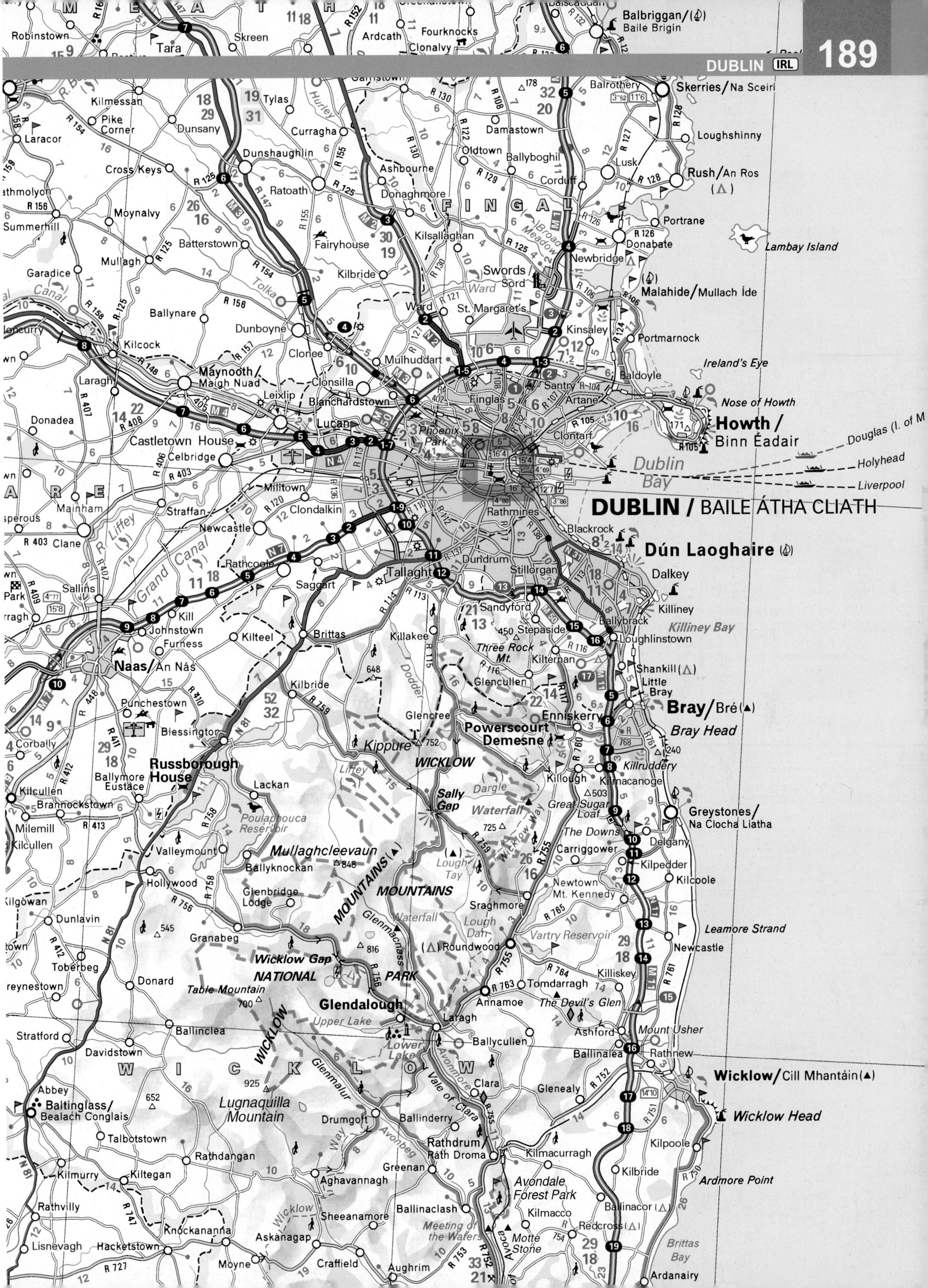

DUBLIN / BAILE ÁTHA CLIATH

Dún Laoghaire

Howth / Binn Éadair

Bray / Bré

Greystones / Na Clocha Liatha

Wicklow / Cill Mhantáin

Skerries / Na Sceirí

Rush / An Ros

Malahide / Mullach Íde

Naas / An Nás

Balbriggan / Baile Brigín

Maynooth / Maigh Nuad

FINGAL

WICKLOW

WICKLOW MOUNTAINS NATIONAL PARK

Dublin Bay

Killiney Bay

Brittas Bay

Lambay Island

Ireland's Eye

Nose of Howth

Phoenix Park

Grand Canal

Royal Canal

Douglas (I. of M)
Holyhead
Liverpool

Russborough House

Castletown House

Powerscourt Demesne

Glendalough

Lugnaquilla Mountain

Mullaghcleevaun

Kippure

Sally Gap

Wicklow Gap

Poulaphouca Reservoir

Vartry Reservoir

Lough Tay

Lough Dan

Avondale Forest Park

Mount Usher

Meeting of the Waters

Vale of Clara

Bray Head

Wicklow Head

Great Sugar Loaf

Three Rock Mt.

Table Mountain

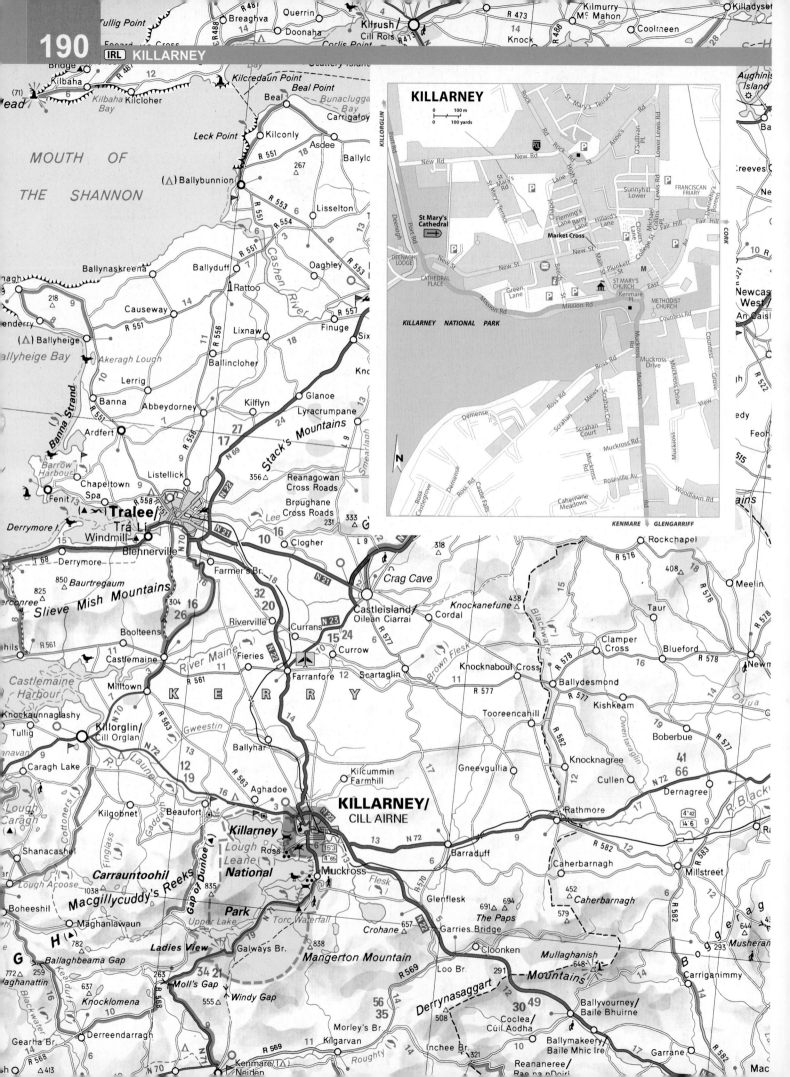

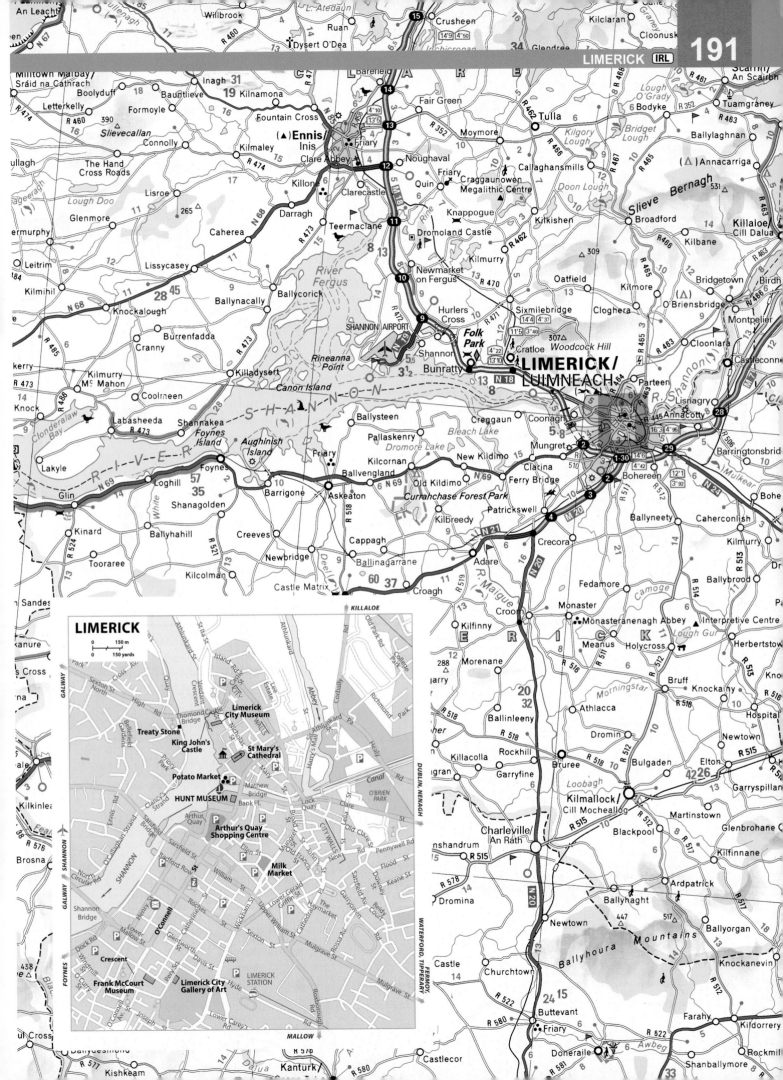

Eochair

Bóithre
Mótarbhealach - Limistéar seirbhíse
Carrbhealach dúbailte le saintréithe mótarbhealaigh
Acomhail mótarbhealaigh: iomlán - teoranta
Vimhreacha ceangail
Líonra idirnáisiúnta agus náisiúnta bóithre
Bóthar idir-réigiúnach nach bhfuil chomh plódaithe
Bóthar nuadheisithe - gan réitiú
Cosán - Conair mharcáilte / Cosán marcaíochta
Mótarbhealach, bóthar á dhéanamh
(an dáta oscailte sceidealta, mas eol)

Leithead bóithre
Carrshlí dhéach
4 lána - 2 leathanlána
2 lána - 2 chunglána

Fad bóthar
(iomlán agus meánfhad)
Bhóithre dola ar an mótarbhealach
Saor ó dhola ar an mótarbhealach
i mílte - i gciliméadair
ar an mbóthar

Aicmiú oifigiúil bóthair
Mótarshl - GB: Priomhbhealach
(Primary route)
IRL: Bóithre eile ,
(National primary and secondary route)
Priomhbóithre agus fobhóithre náisiúnta
Ceann scríbe ar ghréasán bóithre priomha

Constaicí
Timpeall - Bearnas agus a airde os cionn leibhéal na mara (i méadair)
Fána ghéar
(suas treo an gha)
IRL: Bealach deacair nó baolach
Bóthar cúng le hionaid phasála
(in Albain)
Crosaire comhréidh: iarnród ag dul, faoi bhóthar, os cionn bóthair
Bóthar toirmeasctha - Bóthar faoi theorannú
Bacainn dola - Bóthar aonsli
Teorainneacha airde
(faoi 15'6" IRL, faoi 16'6" GB)
Teorann Mheáchain
(faoi 16t)

Iompar
Leithead caighdeánach - Staisiún paisinéirí
Aerfort - Aerpháirc
Longsheirbhísí :
(Seirbhísí séasúracha: dearg)
Bád
Fartha (uas - ulach : tonnaí méadracha)
Coisithe agus lucht rothar

Lóistín - Riarachán
Teorainneacha riaracháin
Teorainn na hAlban agus teorainn na Breataine Bige

Teorainn idirnáisiúnta - Custam

Áiseanna Spóirt agus Súgartha
Machaire Gailf - Ráschúrsa
Timpeall rásaíochta - Cuan bád aeraíochta
Láthair champa , láthair charbhán
Conair mharcáilte - Páirc thuaithe
Zú - Tearmannéan mara
IRL: Lascaireacht - Ráschúrsa con Larnród thraein ghaile
Traein cábla
Carr cábla , cathaoir cábla

Amhairc
Príomhradharcanna:
féach AN EOLAÍ UAINE
Bailte nó áiteanna inspéise, baill lóistín
Foirgneamh Eaglasta - Caisleán
Fothrach - Leacht meigiliteach - Pluais
Páirc, Gáirdíní - Ionaid eile spéisiúla
IRL: Dunfort - Cros Cheilteach - Cloigtheach
Lánléargas - Cothrom Radhairc
Bealach Aoibhinn

Comharthaí Eile
Cáblashlí thionsclaíoch
Crann teileachumarsáide - Teach solais
Stáisiún Giniúna - Cairéal
Mianach - Tionsclaíocht
Scaglann - Aill
Páirc Fhoraoise Naisiúnta - Páirc Naisiúnta

Allwedd

Ffyrdd
Trafford - Mannau gwasanaeth
Ffordd ddeuol â nodweddion traffordd
Cyfnewidfeyd: wedi'i chwblhau - cyfyngedig
Rhifau'r cyffyrdd
Ffordd ar rwydwaith rhyngwladol a chenedlaethol
Ffordd rhyngranbarthol a llai prysur
Ffordd ac wyneb iddi - heb wyneb
Llwybr troed - Llwybr troed ag arwyddion / Llwybr ceffyl
Trafford - ffordd yn cael ei hadeiladu
(Os cyfyd yr achos: dyddiad agor disgwyliedig)

Ffyrdd
ffordd ddeuol
4 lôn - 2 lôn lydan
2 lôn - 2 lôn gul

Pellter
(cyfanswm a'r rhyng-bellter)
Tollffyrdd ar y drafford
Rhan di-doll ar y drafford
mewn miltiroedd - mewn kilometrau
ar y ffordd

Dosbarthiad ffyrdd swyddogol
Trafford - GB : Prif ffordd
(Primary route)
IRL: Prif ffordd genedlaethol a ffordd eilradd
(National primary and secondary route)
Ffyrdd eraill
Cylchfan ar rwydwaith y prif ffrydd

Rhwystrau
Cylchfan - Bwlch a'i uchder uwchlaw lefel y môr
(mewn metrau)
Rhiw serth
(esgyn gyda'r saeth)
IRL: Darn anodd neu beryglus o ffordd
Yn yr Alban :
ffordd gul â mannau pasio
Croesfan rheilffordd: croesfan rheilffordd, o dan y ffordd, dros y ffordd
Ffordd waharddedig - Ffordd a chyfyngiadau arni
Rhwystr Toll - Unffordd
Terfyn uchder
(llai na 15'6" IRL, 16'6" GB)
Terfyn pwysau
(llai na 16t)

Cludiant
Lled safonol - Gorsaf deithwyr
Maes awyr - Maes glanio
Llongau ceir:
(Gwasanaethau tymhorol: mewn coch)
llong
Fferi (llwyth uchaf: mewn tunelli metrig)
Teithwyr ar droed neu feic yn unig

Llety - Gweinyddiaeth
Ffiniau gweinyddol
Ffin Cymru, ffin yr Alban

Ffin ryngwladol - Tollau

Cyfleusterau Chwaraeon a Hamdden
Cwrs golf - Rasio Ceffylau
Rasio Cerbydau - Harbwr cychod pleser
Leoedd i wersylla
Llwybr troed ag arwyddion - Parc gwlad
Parc saffari, sw - Gwarchodfa natur
IRL: Pysgota - Maes rasio milgwn
Trên twristiaid
Rhaffordd, car cêbl, cadair esgyn

Golygfeydd
Gweler Llyfr Michelin

Trefi new fannau o ddiddordeb, mannau i aros
Adeilag eglwysig - Castell
Adfeilion - Heneb fegalithig - Ogof
Gerddi, parc - Mannau eraill o ddiddordeb
IRL: Caer - Croes Geltaidd - twr crwn
Panorama - Golygfan
Ffordd dygfeydd

Symbolau eraill
Lein gêbl ddiwydiannol
Mast telathrebu - Goleudy
Gorsaf bwer - Chwarel
Mwyngloddio - Gweithgarwch diwydiannol
Purfa - Clogwyn
Parc Coedwig Cenedlaethol - Parc Cenedlaethol

Comnarthaí ar phleanna bailte

Ionaid inspéise
Ionad inspéise agus
Ionad inspéise adhartha

Bóithre
Mótarbhealach, carrbhealach dúbailte le saintréithe mótar
Acomhail mótarbhealaigh : iomlán - teoranta
Priomh-thrébhealach
Sráid: neamhoiriúnach do thrácht, ach í stáit speisialta
Sráid: coisithe
Carrchlós

Comharthaí Éagsúla
Aerfort
Leithead caighdeánach - Staisiún paisinéirí
Ionad eolais turasóireachta - Ospidéal
Gairdín, páirc, coill - Reilig
Staidiam
Galfchúrsa
Stáisiún traenach faoi thalamh
Príomhoifi g phoist le poste restante
Foirgneamh poiblí curtha in iúl le litir thagartha:
Músaem
Amharclann
Póitíní (ceanncheathrú)

Symbolau ar gynlluniau'r trefi

Golygfeydd
Man diddorol
Lle diddorol o addoliad

Ffyrdd
Trafford, ffordd ddeuol
Cyfnewidfeyd : wedi'i chwblhau - cyfyngedig
Prif ffordd drwodd
Stryd : Anaddas i draffi g, cyfyngedig
Stryd: Cerddwr
Parc ceir

Arwyddion amrywiol
Maes awyr
Lled safonol - Gorsaf deithwyr
Canolfan croeso - Ysbyty
Gardd, parc, coedwig - Mynwent
Stadiwm
Cwrs golff
Gorsaf danddaearol
Prif swyddfa bost gyda poste restante
Adeilad cyhoeddus a ddynodir gan lythyren:
Amgueddfa
Theatr
Yr Heddlu (pencadlys)